W9-DHM-357

American Literary Scholarship

1975

American Literary Scholarship

An Annual / 1975

Edited by James Woodress

Essays by Lawrence Buell, J. Donald Crowley, Donald B. Stauffer, Hershel Parker, Marvin Fisher and Willis J. Buckingham, Hamlin Hill, William T. Stafford, Stuart Y. McDougal, Karl F. Zender, Jackson R. Bryer, Robert D. Arner, Warren French, David Stouck, Margaret Anne O'Connor, James H. Justus, Richard Crowder, Linda Welshimer Wagner, Jordan Y. Miller, Charles Nilon, Michael J. Hoffman, Jean Rivière, Hans Galinsky, Rolando Anzilotti, Keiko Beppu, Rolf Lundén

Duke University Press, Durham, North Carolina, 1977

 Library of Congress Catalogue Card number 65–19450. I.S.B.N. 0–8223–0384–1. Printed in the United States of America by Heritage Printers, Inc.

Foreword

This is the 13th volume of *American Literary Scholarship* to appear since the series was begun in 1965. After expanding steadily from a 224-page volume in its first year of publication to 490 pages in 1975, it marked time last year at 492 pages. This year, however, it has expanded again by about 10 percent, and it will be necessary in the future to impose space limitations on the contributors. One might hope that economic conditions in higher education and publishing would level out the rising curve of scholarly activity. I think that students and teachers alike would breathe a sigh of relief if we could contract somewhat the publication rate. The level of scholarly productivity is still too high, and there still is too much redundant and inferior scholarship.

This year, however, a new note sounds in at least two of the essays. Warren French, writer of the chapter on 19th-century literature, who is himself a veteran editor of scholarly collections, says at the conclusion of his essay: "After reading the material discussed in this review, I feel more confidence about the future of American literary scholarship than at any time during the decade that I have worked on this project. . . . Almost nothing that I perused this year has proved to be the waste of time or space that so many academic exercises have been in the recent past." Michael Hoffman, who reads scores of books each year in order to write chapter 20 ("Themes, Topics, Criticism"), reports that "so many stimulating and exciting books were published in 1975" that he cannot do justice to them all in his essay. And he concludes: ". . . one may fondly hope we are in a major period of literary study."

The large amount of excellent scholarship noted by French and Hoffman carried over in 1975 into the creation of scholarly tools. Because these items do not usually get reviewed in this volume unless they deal with specific authors or areas covered in the individual chapters of *ALS*, I'd like to mention a few here. Joseph Katz's *Proof: The Yearbook of American Bibliographical and Textual Studies* appeared in 1975 after missing 1974. Its "Register of Current Publications" continues to be an invaluable source of bibliographical and reference material. Also in 1975 Vincent Tollers (SUNY College, Brockport) and associates planned the *Literary Research Newsletter*, the first issue of which appeared in January 1976. It will contain pertinent articles and reviews, such as Robert C. Schweik's "English and American Literature: Some Recent Developments in Enumerative Bibliography and Indexing" (1:88–110). Another very useful item was the fifth edition of Richard D. Altick and Andrew Wright's *Selective Bibliography for the Study of English and American Literature* (New York: Macmillan).

As of this writing, 1976 so far has produced two bibliographies of great utility. The first is a revised fourth edition of Clarence Gohdes's *Bibliographical Guide to the Study of the Literature of the U.S.A.* (Durham, N.C.: Duke Univ. Press), and the second is a new compilation, Harold H. Kolb, Jr.'s *A Field Guide to the Study of American Literature* (Charlottesville: Univ. Press of Va.). The Gohdes bibliography is broader in its coverage, listing tools for the study of history, biography, art, religion, and philosophy as well as those for American literature, and includes more than 400 new items added since the third edition was published in 1970. The format is the same as before.

The Kolb bibliography focuses more intensively on American literature. It is organized into sections on bibliographies, literary history and criticism, reference works, editions and series, anthologies, and journals and contains excellent annotations. Both volumes are reliable, up to date, and equipped with good indexes. I recommend them highly. The final item I want to note here is *American Literature: A Study and Research Guide* (New York: St. Martin's Press) brought out by Lewis Leary with the collaboration of John Auchard. This is a well-organized handbook that should be of great use to beginning graduate students and English majors.

Among the 26 contributors to the 21 chapters of *ALS 1975* are 20 who appeared in the 1974 volume. To them go my deep appreciation for their essays and their help in providing continuity of authorship in this project. New contributors are Donald Stauffer (Poe), Marvin Fisher and Willis Buckingham (Whitman and Dickinson), Stuart McDougal (Pound and Eliot), and Charles Nilon (black literature). The chapter on black literature is new this year and replaces the folklore chapter that has been a feature of *ALS* since the second year of publication. Once again I am grateful to the Research Committee of the University of California at Davis for funds to support the editing of this volume, and my thanks go to the secretariate of the English Department for many services and to my bibliographical assistant, Gene Crumley.

James Woodress
Sept. 30, 1976

University of California, Davis

Table of Contents

Key to Abbreviations

Festschrifts, Essay Collections, and Books Discussed in More than One Chapter

The American Soldier in Fiction / Peter Aichinger, *The American Soldier in Fiction, 1880–1963: A History of Attitudes toward Warfare and the Military Establishment* (Ames, Iowa: Iowa State Univ. Press)

Artful Thunder / *Artful Thunder: Versions of the Romantic Tradition in American Literature in Honor of Howard P. Vincent*, ed. Robert J. DeMott and Sanford E. Marovitz (Kent, Ohio: Kent State Univ. Press)

The Confidence Game / Warwick Wadlington, *The Confidence Game in American Literature* (Princeton, N.J.: Princeton Univ. Press)

The Dispossessed Garden / Lewis Simpson, *The Dispossessed Garden: Pastoral and History in Southern Literature*, Mercer Univ. Lamar Memorial Lectures, 16 (Athens: Univ. of Ga. Press)

The Great War and Modern Memory / Paul Fussell, *The Great War and Modern Memory* (New York and London: Oxford Univ. Press)

A Homemade World / Hugh Kenner, *A Homemade World: The American Modernist Writers* (New York: Alfred A. Knopf)

Individual and Community / *Individual and Community: Variations on a Theme in American Fiction*, ed. Kenneth H. Baldwin and David K. Kirby (Durham, N.C.: Duke Univ. Press)

The Lay of the Land / Annette Kolodny, *The Lay of the Land: Metaphor as Experience and History in American Life and Letters* (Chapel Hill: Univ. of N.C. Press)

Literature and Ideas / *Literature and Ideas in America: Essays in Memory of Harry Hayden Clark*, ed. Robert Falk (Athens: Ohio Univ. Press)

Published in Paris / Hugh Ford, *Published in Paris: American and British Writers, Printers, and Publishers in Paris, 1920–1939* (New York: Macmillan)

The Puritan Origins of the American Self / Sacvan Bercovitch, *The Puritan Origins of the American Self* (New Haven, Conn.: Yale Univ. Press)

Symbolism: The Manichean Vision / Daniel Schneider, *Symbolism: The Manichean Vision—A Study in the Art of James, Conrad, Woolf, and Stevens* (Lincoln: Univ. of Nebr. Press)

The Tenth Muse / Albert Gelpi, *The Tenth Muse: The Psyche of the American Poet* (Cambridge: Harvard Univ. Press)

Three on the Tower / Louis Simpson, *Three on the Tower: The Lives and Works of Ezra Pound, T. S. Eliot, and William Carlos Williams* (New York: William Morrow)

The Twenties / *The Twenties: Fiction, Poetry, Drama*, ed. Warren French (Deland, Fla.: Everett/Edwards)

Periodicals, Annuals, Series

AH / American Heritage
AIULM / Annali Istituto Universitario di Lingue Moderne (Feltre)
AL / American Literature
ALR / American Literary Realism
ALS / American Literary Scholarship
AmerR / American Review
AmerS / American Studies
AmS / Amerikastudien
AN&Q / American Notes and Queries
APR / American Poetry Review
AQ / American Quarterly
AR / Antioch Review
Ariel / Ariel: A Quarterly Review of the Arts and Sciences in Israel
ArielE / Ariel: A Review of International English Literature
ArmD / Armchair Detective (White Bear Lake, Minn.)
ArQ / Arizona Quarterly
ASch / American Scholar
ASoc / Arts in Society
ASS / American Studies in Scandinavia
AtM / Atlantic Monthly
ATQ / American Transcendental Quarterly
BB / Bulletin of Bibliography
BlackI / Black Images: A Critical Quarterly on Black Arts and Culture
BlackIC / black i: A Canadian Journal of Black Expression
BlackS / Black Scholar
BlackW / Black World
BMWMLA / Bulletin of the Mid-West Modern Language Association
BNYPL / Bulletin of the New York Public Library
Boundary 2 / Boundary 2: A Journal of Postmodern Literature
BRMMLA / Bulletin of the Rocky Mountain Modern Language Association
BSUF / Ball State Univ. Forum
BUJ / Boston Univ. Journal
BYUS / Brigham Young Univ. Studies
C&L / Christianity and Literature
CE / College English
CEAA / Center for Editions of American Authors
CentR / The Centennial Review
ChR / Chicago Review
CimR / Cimarron Review
CL / Comparative Literature
CLAJ / College Language Association Journal
CLQ / Colby Library Quarterly
CM / Carlton Miscellany
CollL / College Literature (Westchester State College)
ColQ / Colorado Quarterly
ConL / Contemporary Literature
ConnR / Connecticut Review
ContempR / Contemporary Review (London)
ContP / Contemporary Poetry
Costerus / Costerus: Essays in English and American Language and Literature
CP / Concerning Poetry
CRCL / Canadian Review of Comparative Literature
CRevAS / Canadian Review of American Studies
Crit / Critique: Studies in Modern Fiction
CritI / Critical Inquiry
Criticism / Criticism (Wayne State)
Critique / Critique (Paris)
CSR / Christian Scholar's Review
DAI / Dissertation Abstracts International
DN / Dreiser Newsletter
DR / Dalhousie Review
EA / Etudes Anglaises
EAL / Early American Literature
ECS / Eighteenth-Century Studies
EDB / Emily Dickinson Bulletin
EIC / Essays in Criticism
EIE / English Institute Essays: 1975 vol., *Emerson—Prophecy, Metamorphosis, and Influence*, ed. David Levin (New York: Columbia Univ. Press)
EIHC / Essex Institute Historical Collections
EIL / Essays in Literature (Western Ill. Univ.)

ELH / English Literary History
ELN / English Language Notes
ELUD / Essays in Literature (Univ. of Denver)
EngR / English Record
EngRev / English Review
ES / English Studies
ESA / English Studies in Africa (Johannesburg)
ESQ / Emerson Society Quarterly
ETC. / ETC.: A Review of General Semantics
ETJ / Educational Theatre Journal
Expl / Explicator
FHA / Fitzgerald-Hemingway Annual
FOB / Flannery O'Connor Bulletin
ForumH / Forum (Houston)
GaR / Georgia Review
GyS / Gypsy Scholar
HAB / Humanities Association Bulletin (Canada)
HC / Hollins Critic
HJP / Higginson Journal of Poetry
HLB / Harvard Library Bulletin
HLQ / Huntington Library Quarterly
HMPEC / Historical Magazine of the Protestant Episcopal Church
HN / Hemingway Notes
HTR / Harvard Theological Review
HudR / Hudson Review
IFR / International Fiction Review
IllQ / Illinois Quarterly
IowaR / Iowa Review
IR / Iliff Review
ISSQ / Indiana Social Studies Quarterly
ItalAm / Italian Americana
JAAS / Journal of Afro-American Studies
JAmS / Journal of American Studies
JBlS / Journal of Black Studies
JBS / John Berryman Studies
JHI / Journal of the History of Ideas
JLN / Jack London Newsletter
JML / Journal of Modern Literature
JNH / Journal of Negro History
JNT / Journal of Narrative Technique
JPC / Journal of Popular Culture
KanQ / Kansas Quarterly
KN / Kwartalnik Neofilologiczny (Warsaw)
L&I / Literature and Ideology
L&P / Literature and Psychology
LaS / Louisiana Studies
LFQ / Literature/Film Quarterly
LGJ / Lost Generation Journal
LHY / Literary Half-Yearly
LWU / Literatur in Wissenschaft und Unterricht (Kiel)
MarkhamR / Markham Review
MD / Modern Drama
MFS / Modern Fiction Studies
MHRev / Malahat Review
MichA / Michigan Academician (replaces *PMASAL*)
MinnR / Minnesota Review
MissQ / Mississippi Quarterly
MLN / Modern Language Notes
MLQ / Modern Language Quarterly
MLS / Modern Language Studies
ModR / Modern Review
Mosaic / Mosaic: A Journal for the Comparative Study of Literature and Ideas
MPS / Modern Poetry Studies
MQ / Midwest Quarterly
MQR / Michigan Quarterly Review
MR / Massachusetts Review
MSLC / Modernist Studies: Literature and Culture, 1920–1940
MTJ / Mark Twain Journal
NA / Nuova Antologia
NALF / Negro American Literature Forum
N&Q / Notes and Queries
NAR / North American Review
NCarF / North Carolina Folklore
NCF / Nineteenth-Century Fiction
NConL / Notes on Contemporary Literature
NEQ / New England Quarterly
New / New: American and Canadian Poetry
NewRep / New Republic
NewRev / The New Review (London)
NHJ / Nathaniel Hawthorne Journal
NLauR / New Laurel Review
NMW / Notes on Mississippi Writers
NN / Northwestern Univ. Press—Newberry Library
NS / Die Neueren Sprachen
NWR / Northwest Review
NYFQ / New York Folklore Quarterly
NYH / New York History

NYHSQ / New York Historical Society Quarterly
NYT / New York Times
NYTBR / New York Times Book Review
OR / Occasional Review
PAAS / Papers of the American Antiquarian Society
Paideuma / Paideuma: A Journal Devoted to Ezra Pound Scholarship
PanA / Pan African Journal
PAPA / Publications of the Arkansas Philological Association
ParisR / Paris Review
PBSA / Papers of the Bibliographical Society of America
Person / The Personalist
PLL / Papers on Language and Literature
PMLA / Publications of the Modern Language Association
PN / Poetry Now
PoeS / Poe Studies
PQ / Philological Quarterly
PR / Partisan Review
Proof / Proof: Yearbook of American Bibliographical and Textual Studies, ed. Joseph Katz (Columbia, S.C.: J. Faust)
Prospects / Prospects: An Annual Journal of American Cultural Studies (New York: Burt Franklin)
PrS / Prairie Schooner
PsyR / Psychoanalytic Review
QJS / Quarterly Journal of Speech
RALS / Resources for American Literary Study
RE / La Revue d'Esthétique
ReAL / Re: Arts and Letters
REH / Revista de Estudios Hispánicos
Rendezvous / Rendezvous: A Journal of Arts and Letters (Idaho State)
RES / Review of English Studies
RJN / Robinson Jeffers Newsletter
RLC / Revue de Littérature Comparée
RLMC / Revista di Letterature Moderne e Comparate (Firenze)
RS / Research Studies (Wash. State Univ.)
SA / Studi Americani
SAB / South Atlantic Bulletin
SAF / Studies in American Fiction
SAmH / Studies in American Humor
SAmL / Studies in American Literature
SAQ / South Atlantic Quarterly
SBL / Studies in Black Literature
Scan / Scandinavica
SCR / South Carolina Review
SDR / South Dakota Review
SELit / Studies in English Literature (Japan)
SFQ / Southern Folklore Quarterly
SFS / Science Fiction Studies
SHR / Southern Humanities Review
SIR / Studies in Romanticism
SLitI / Studies in the Literary Imagination
SLJ / Southern Literary Journal
SLRJ / St. Louis Univ. Research Journal of the Graduate School of Arts and Sciences
SNNTS / Studies in the Novel (North Tex. State Univ.)
SoR / Southern Review
SR / Sewanee Review
SSF / Studies in Short Fiction
STC / Studies in the Twentieth Century
StQ / Steinbeck Quarterly
SwR / Southwest Review
TCL / Twentieth-Century Literature
TDR / Drama Review (formerly *Tulane Drama Review*)
ThS / Theatre Survey
TJQ / Thoreau Journal Quarterly
TriQ / Tri-Quarterly
TSB / Thorean Society Bulletin
TSE / Tulane Studies in English
TSER / T. S. Eliot Review
TSL / Tennessee Studies in Literature
TSLL / Texas Studies in Literature and Language
TUSAS / Twayne United States Authors Series
UDQ / Univ. of Denver Quarterly
UTQ / Univ. of Toronto Quarterly
UWR / Univ. of Windsor Review
VMHB / Virginia Magazine of History and Biography
VQR / Virginia Quarterly Review
VWQ / Virginia Woolf Quarterly
WAL / Western American Literature

WHR / *Western Humanities Review*
WWR / *Walt Whitman Review*
WWS / Western Writers Series
YR / *Yale Review*
YULG / *Yale Univ. Library Gazette*
ZRL / *Zagadnienia Rodzajów Literakich* (Lodz, Poland)

Part I

1. Emerson, Thoreau, and Transcendentalism

Lawrence Buell

i. General Studies

Donald Koster's *Transcendentalism in America* (Boston: Twayne) is a 97-page introductory survey. Broader in scope than Paul Boller's *American Transcendentalism* (*ALS 1974*, p. 3) it attempts to outline the main events of the movement, its leading ideas, literary aspects, reception, and legacy, devoting additional chapters to profiles of Emerson, Thoreau, Whitman, and minor figures. Although this scheme is good, the presentation is skimpy and too often based on secondary material no longer recognized as authoritative. In short, we still lack a good basic guidebook to Transcendentalism.

Among topical studies, of special interest is the final chapter of Sacvan Bercovich's *The Puritan Origins of the American Self* (New Haven, Conn.: Yale Univ. Press), especially pp. 163–86, an earlier version of which appears in *EIE*, pp. 1–27. This is a learned, brilliant, difficult, contentious book, required reading for students of Transcendentalism. Bercovich's thesis is that Puritan ideology reacted to the conditions of exodus to the new world by creating a particular conception of the relation of self to society which lasted at least through the mid-19th century. Cotton Mather and Emerson are his chief exhibits. Both Puritan and post-Puritan, Bercovich argues, share a prophetic tradition which celebrates, defines, and justifies the self in terms of the fulfillment of larger patterns of national destiny. Altogether this is the most ambitious attempt yet made to view American literary history as an emanation from Puritanism, and though objections can be raised to it (e.g., how central is Bercovich's nationalist theme in Transcendentalist writing?), even unbelievers should find much to admire.

Abraham Blinderman, in *American Writers on Education before*

1865 (Boston: Twayne), pp. 133–51, 166–67, briskly summarizes the educational ideas of Emerson, Thoreau, Alcott, Fuller, Brownson, Ripley, and Peabody. Though necessarily superficial, his account is the best available. Edward Foster's *The Civilized Wilderness* (New York and London: Macmillan) has much to say on Emerson and Thoreau vis-à-vis contemporary fashions in travel, domestic architecture, and landscape gardening. Though quite impressionistic, Foster is illuminating in patches, especially in his treatment of *Walden* as an instance of the popular genre of the "country book" (pp. 100–18). J. P. Rao Rayapati, in *Early American Interest in Vedanta* (New York: Asia Publishing House [1973]), surveys "Early Vedic Readings by American Transcendentalists" (pp. 93–106), concluding that neither Emerson nor Thoreau became seriously interested in Vedic thought until after 1840. Unfortunately Rayapati does not try to show how their interest later developed, and so his discussion seems unduly abrupt and negative in tone.

Two articles which analyze significant Transcendentalist ideas both as concepts and as principles of style are Elizabeth Meese's "Transcendentalism: The Metaphysics of the Theme," *AL* 47:1–20 and Catherine Albanese's "The Kinetic Revolution: Transformation in the Language of the Transcendentalists," *NEQ* 48:319–40. Meese deals with correspondential vision, Albanese with images of flux and dynamism. Neither has anything really new to say about these much-discussed topics.

Quite the opposite is true of Elizabeth McKinsey's *The Western Experiment: New England Transcendentalism in the Ohio Valley* (Cambridge, Mass.: Harvard Univ. Press [1973]), an exceptionally fine undergraduate honors thesis, which reviews the western adventures of Clarke, Cranch, and W. H. Channing and explains why they returned east disillusioned. McKinsey portrays them as genteel idealists unable to cope with rough western ways and occasional hostility. In this respect, she argues, their short-lived missions prefigured the failure of Transcendentalism as a whole to come to fruition as a social movement. At times McKinsey becomes overly judgmental and condescending, but her thesis is convincing and well presented.

Three recollections of Transcendentalist utopianism are edited by Joel Myerson in "An Ungathered Sanborn Lecture on Brook Farm" (*ATQ* 26:1–11), and "Two Unpublished Reminiscences of Brook Farm" (NEQ 48:253–60). These pieces reflect and should give further encouragement to the recent upsurge of serious interest in Brook Farm and Fruitlands. "Eight Lowell Letters from Concord in 1838," also edited by Myerson (*IllQ* 38:20–42), includes much satirical commentary on Emerson, Thoreau, and the local scene. Two other sketches of 19th-century Concord, both by Concordians, are "Reminiscences of Augusta Bowers French" (*TSB* 130:5–7) and "Concord by [Alfred?] Monroe" (*TSB* 133:1–3), ed. Walter Harding.

Finally, Kenneth Cameron reprints George Willis Cooke's *Historical and Biographical Introduction* to *The Dial* (*ATQ* 27:1–122) and provides another of his useful compendia of newspaper clippings on Emerson, Thoreau, Alcott, and others in "Transcendental Log" (*ATQ* 28:1–345).

ii. Emerson

***a.* Edition.** The year 1975 saw the publication of volume 11 of Emerson's *Journals and Miscellaneous Notebooks* (Cambridge, Mass.: Harvard Univ. Press), ably edited by A. W. Plumstead, William Gilman, and Ruth Bennett. This volume is remarkable chiefly for Emerson's unexpurgated outrage at the Compromise of 1850 and for previously unpublished notebooks on his midwestern lecture tours in the early 1850s and on Margaret Fuller Ossoli. This new material is helpful more for the sake of completing the record than for new disclosures, though there are some of the latter. We note, for instance, that in 1851 Emerson incorrectly remembered the year of his son's death (p. 506).

***b.* Life and Nonliterary Ideas.** Phyllis Cole's "Emerson, England, and Fate," *EIE*, pp. 83–105, is a meticulous account of how Emerson's impressions of industrialized England and his reaction to the Fugitive Slave controversy helped to crystallize his notion of fate and make his later writing more socially conscious. William Clebsch's *American Religious Thought: A History* (Chicago: Univ. of Chicago Press [1973]) is actually a book about Jonathan Edwards, Emerson (pp. 69–111), and William James. The middle section gives a lucid, concise outline of Emerson on religious institutions, spiritual experience, and the doctrines of Oversoul, compensation, and self-reliance. Peter Obuchowski, in "Emerson's Science: An Analysis" (*PQ* 54:624–32), contends that Emerson's interest in science went farther beyond the poetic-mythological level than is commonly supposed, but he qualifies this claim to the point that it loses all its force. Gay Wilson Allen, in "A New Look at Emerson and Science" (*Literature and Ideas*, pp. 58–78), reviews Emerson's early lectures on science, finding as we would expect that the chief long-range importance of Emerson's researches was to encourage him in a quest for a science of spiritual laws informing both nature and mind.

c. Literary Criticism. Emerson was the subject of the 1975 *English Institute Essays*, consisting of eight essays delivered at the 1973 and 1974 sessions. Though somewhat uneven, the collection as a whole is a significant one. Most contributions deal in part or whole with Emerson's place in American literary history.

The papers of Bercovich and Cole have already been mentioned. Like the former, Daniel Shea's "Emerson and the American Metamorphosis" (pp. 29–56) is a panoramic survey, which astutely traces the theme of metamorphosis in Emerson's life, thought, and literary method and places him as "the central figure" in an American tradition of metamorphosis extending from the Puritan view of conversion to Saul Bellow's fictional protagonists. Emerson, Shea observes, proved on both the biographical and the stylistic levels that " 'men are convertible,' " that life and art proceed by transformation. James M. Cox, on the other hand, stresses the constant elements in Emerson in "The Circles of the Eye" (pp. 57–81), an essay which rings familiar changes on the title image—the importance to Emerson of the power of perception; its fitfulness and his ensuing alternations of hope and despair; his willingness to turn those around him into material for his visions. Maurice Gonnaud's "Emerson and the Imperial Self" (pp. 107–28) is a labored critique of Quentin Anderson's interpretation of Emerson, which Gonnaud understandably finds provocative but simplistic.

The two remaining essays deal more directly with Emersonian aesthetics. Albert Gelpi's "Emerson: The Paradox of Organic Form" (pp. 149–70) is incorporated into his longer chapter on Emerson in *The Tenth Muse* (pp. 57–111). The *EIE* contribution reviews the main features of Emerson's poetic theory and reaffirms his position as the somewhat hesitant originator of the "Dionysian" strain of American poetry. *The Tenth Muse* also includes a brief review of Emerson in light of the Puritans and Swedenborg, analyses of some

Emerson poems, a shrewd comparison of Bryant to Emerson, and some thoughtful reflections about sexual metaphor in Emerson's writings about nature and poetic creation. Gelpi's discussions are rarely novel, but they are interesting for their obiter dicta.

Somewhat the same can be said of Harold Bloom's "The Freshness of Transformation: Emerson's Dialectics of Influence" (pp. 129–48), which was previously published in *ATQ* 21:57–63 (*ALS 1974*, p. 9), except for a final section dissociating Emerson from deconstructionist aesthetics. In Bloom's case the orthodoxy is of course of his own devising, but now that his theories of influence are well known, the reader can anticipate his conclusions. In *A Map of Misreading* (New York: Oxford Univ. Press, pp. 160–92) and *Kabbalah and Criticism* (New York: Seabury) Bloom also deals with Emerson's role as the father of American poetry in what is by now a familiar way.

The year 1975 was especially memorable for the quantity of scholarship on Emerson as poet, which was the subject of a book by Hyatt Waggoner, *Emerson as Poet* (Princeton, N.J.: Princeton Univ. Press), and an *ATQ* symposium, as well as essays by Bloom, Gelpi, and others.

Emerson as Poet is excellent in some respects but must finally be regarded as an unsuccessful attempt to justify the respect for Emerson's poetry which one intuitively feels it deserves. The Introduction, comprising fully one-fourth of the volume, is a most able and authoritative summary of the vicissitudes of Emerson's poetic reputation. Waggoner also shows resourcefulness and tact in exposing, on the one hand, the inappropriateness of judging Emerson's poems by formalistic standards and conceding, on the other, that their positive achievement is limited. But when Waggoner tries to pinpoint that achievement on the level of technique as opposed to prophetic content, he becomes rather insecure and vague. His unifying thesis, that Emerson is a poet in the "tradition of paradoxy," is convincing as far as it goes, but it commits him too closely to the New Critical virtues he would question and prevents him from dealing with Emerson's prosody.

The symposium in *ATQ* 25:1–65, edited by Carl Strauch, includes seven articles on Emerson's verse. Four are readings of individual poems. Strauch himself gives an erudite and painstaking analysis of "Emerson's Adaptation of Myth in 'The Initial Love'" (pp. 51–65). His evaluation of the poem is too generous, but his account of Emerson's transformation of source material is first-rate, as is his discussion of Cupid's metamorphoses during the poem. Charles W. Mignon's "Starsdown Poet, Abstemious Muse" (pp. 33–41) is the first full-scale interpretation of Emerson's unfinished poem "The Poet." Richard Tuerk's "Emerson's Darker Vision: 'Hamatreya' and 'Days'" (pp. 28–33) is solid but less original. In "Emerson's 'Days': A Psychoanalytic Study" (pp. 6–11), John Clendenning locates the ultimate sources of the poem in the poet's earlier traumas. The elusive women, for instance, are figures of maternal abandonment. The essay is ingenious but facile, based on insufficient biographical data.

One of the symposium's best pieces is Michael Cowan's "The Loving Proteus: Metamorphosis in Emerson's Poetry" (pp. 11–22), which traces both the origins of the concept (in classical mythology, oriental religion, 19th-century science, etc.) and its operation as an informing principle in several poems, "Threnody" in particular. Cowan's essay, like Strauch's, is valuable in suggesting that Emerson used metamorphosis as an aesthetic principle with almost as much dexterity in his poems as in his prose. Carl Dennis provides a helpful overview of "Emerson's Poetics of Inspiration" (pp. 22–28), distinguishing three primary traits of bardic style: roughness, paradoxy, and impersonality of tone. John Q. Anderson, in "Emerson's 'Eternal Pan'—The Re-Creation of Myth" (pp. 2–6), briefly recites Emerson's sources.

Other articles on Emerson's poems include Robert Hodges's "Public Sentiment and Poetic Diction" (*Vis-à-Vis* 3,i:15–19), an attentive, occasionally overingenious reading of the "Concord Hymn"; and two notes on allusions in *Expl* 33: "Emerson's 'The Poet, I,' 1–6," by the University of Nebraska's 17th-Century Poetry Group (item 54), and "Emerson's Days,'" by Frances Hernández (item 44).

The year's one analysis of an individual essay, Merton Sealts's "Emerson on the Scholar, 1838: A Study of 'Literary Ethics' (*Literature and Ideas*, pp. 40–57), calls attention to a neglected work—its structure, its relation to "The American Scholar" and the Divinity School Address, and in particular its qualified success in balancing the two antithetical elements in Emerson's prescription for the scholar's life: inspiration and discipline. The one interpretation of a single book, Jay Hoar's "A Study of Emerson's *English Traits*" (*Northern New England Review*, 1,i[1973]:48–57), is a sketchy overview of two contradictions in Emerson's critique: the generosity of his praise of England vs. the strength of his reservations, and his confidence in America's future vs. his excessive deprecation of its intellectual achievements thus far.

A number of miscellaneous articles compare Emerson to other figures and/or trace his impact and influence. Sam Girgus, in "The Scholar as Prophet: Brownson vs. Emerson and the Modern Need for Moral Humanism" (*MQ* 17:88–99), finds in the contrast between individualistic and collective emphases in their definitions of the scholar's responsibility an analogue and prefigurement of the split in contemporary academic progressive thought between philosophies stressing personal growth and those stressing group consciousness and action. David Robinson, in "The Romantic Quest in Poe and Emerson: 'Ulalume' and 'The Sphinx'" (*ATQ* 26:26–30), notes that the two works represent in different ways the romantic pursuit of a transpersonal ideal in order to escape the confines of the self. Donald Ross's "Emerson's Stylistic Influence on Whitman" (*ATQ* 25:41–51) is a computer-assisted study comparing "Song of Myself" with the essay on "The Poet," demonstrating in the process the statistical significance of a number of stylistic resemblances between the two writers. In "Emerson Giving Joy: Summer of 1855" (*WWR* 21:162–63) Florence Freedman notes for the nth time that Whitman was not the only writer towards whom Emerson displayed the syndrome of initial enthusiasm giving way to critical wariness. Victor J. Vitanza, in "Melville's *Redburn* and Emerson's 'General Education of the Eye'" (*ESQ* 21:40–45), sees affinities in the use of the eye motif to show intellectual/spiritual growth. Luther S. Luedtke, in "First Notices of Emerson in England and Germany" (*N&Q* 220:106–08), shows that Emerson was reviewed in England as early as 1835 and that early German notices relied on British reviews. Gloria Young, in "'The Fountainhead of All Forms'" (*Artful Thunder*, pp. 241–67), explores "Poetry and the Unconscious in Emerson and Howard Nemerov," finding that Emerson anticipates the theories of Nemerov and Jung: e.g., water and light as images of the unconscious, the role of the unconscious in creation, the unification of psyche and spirit through creative language. Dolores Brien understandably finds "Robert Duncan: A Poet in the Emerson-Whitman Tradition" (*CentR* 19:308–16).

iii. Thoreau

***a.* Edition.** The fourth volume of the CEAA edition of Thoreau's works was published in 1975: *Early Essays and Miscellanies* (Princeton, N.J.: Princeton Univ. Press), carefully edited by Joseph Moldenhauer, Edwin Moser, and Alexander Kern. Fifty-three pieces dating from *ca.* 1828–52 are printed here, including all of Thoreau's extant college themes, seven items from *The Dial*, the essays on Sir Walter Raleigh and Thomas Carlyle, and the two manifestoes on love and sex sent to H. G. O. Blake. Though most of this material has been published before, these earlier versions are scattered, mostly corrupt, and out of print. Thus the new volume is valuable not only for its correct text but also as a convenient index to Thoreau's growth as a writer during his apprenticeship period. One pattern immediately obvious, for example, is the increasing independence and aggressiveness of Thoreau's Harvard compositions. The book's one serious defect is the virtual absence of explanatory footnotes. As a piece of textual scholarship it is scrupulous; but unlike the Harvard Emerson it makes no real attempt to identify allusions and quotations, supply cross-references, or even to translate Thoreau's Greek and Latin. Yet most readers would rather have this information than a complete list of emendations.

Two discussions of Thoreau texts, both by Joseph McElrath, Jr., are "Practical Editions: Henry D. Thoreau's *Walden*" (*Proof* 4:175–82) and "The First Two Volumes of the Writings of Henry D. Thoreau: A Review Article" (ibid., pp. 215–35). The former closely evaluates ten textbook editions of *Walden*. The latter compliments the Princeton edition of *The Maine Woods* and excoriates the Princeton *Walden*. The criticisms seem warranted, but the tone is too harsh.

***b.* Life and Nonliterary Ideas.** Factual and speculative biography are the subject of several articles. A notable piece of detective work, Walter Harding's "Was It Legal? Thoreau in Jail" (*AH* 26,v:36–37) shows that Sam Staples broke the law when he jailed Henry. Thomas Woodson meticulously reconstructs "Thoreau's Excursion to the Berkshires and Catskills" in 1844 (*ESQ* 21:82–92). Leon Edel, in "Walden: The Myth and the Mystery" (*ASch* 44:272–81), conjectures that Thoreau's accidental burning of the Concord woods was decisive in prompting his retreat to Walden, which Edel interprets both as a semi-withdrawal from a hostile community and as a personal quest intermixing nostalgia for lost things with a search for "the mature experiences of this world." David Lyttle's "Thoreau's 'Diamond Body,'" (*TJQ* 7,ii:18–29) examines Thoreau's writing of the early 1850s in light of the discrepancy between *Walden's* optimism and the *Journal's* recurring despondency and finds Thoreau seeking with partial success to recover from a personal nadir in 1851.

Turning to studies of Thoreau's ideas, Alexander Kern, in "Church, Scripture, Nature and Ethics in Henry Thoreau's Religious Thought" (*Literature and Ideas*, pp. 79–95), shows why Thoreau is justly regarded as a "significant if unorthodox" outgrowth of American protestantism. William Herr, in "A More Perfect State: Thoreau's Concept of Civil Government" (*MR* 16:470–87), argues that Thoreau's respect for the proper role of the state has been underestimated. Thoreau, says Herr, believed the state should serve the ends of promoting individual freedom and a level of self-development sufficient to render government unnecessary, and he countenanced civil disobedience only when the state betrays those purposes. In "Thoreau on Violence" (*TSB* 131:2–3) Herr reminds us that Thoreau never categorically rejected war and violence.

c. Literary Criticism: General. Richard Turek's *Central Still: Circle and Sphere in Thoreau's Prose* (The Hague: Mouton) is a monograph on a motif whose ramifications have been pursued extensively by other critics, such as Tuerk's mentor Charles Anderson. Yet this unpretentious study commands respect for competence and thoughtfulness if not for originality. Tuerk carefully traces the rise and decline (after *Walden*) of the circle/sphere figure as a way of adumbrating structured images of reality and human possibility without falsifying natural fact. At times Tuerk's Thoreau seems too much like a mere connoisseur of configurations, a 19th-century Wallace Stevens, but this may be an inevitable defect of the motif study as a genre.

A number of shorter studies deal with other thematic-stylistic aspects of Thoreau's writing. The two which most impressed me were Annette Woodlief's "The Influence of Theories of Rhetoric on Thoreau" (*TJQ* 7,i:13–22) and Lewis Miller, Jr.'s "The Artist as Surveyor in *Walden* and *The Maine Woods*" (*ESQ* 21:76–81). Woodlief shows that Thoreau's college texts, particularly Whately's *Elements of Rhetoric*, could have encouraged him to develop such characteristic techniques as paradoxy, exaggeration, irony, antithesis, and compression, a suggestion the newly published *Early Essays and Miscellanies* will support. Miller points out that Thoreau's notion of extravagance presupposes fixed boundaries, the lack of which baffled him in Maine.

Another Miller article, "Thoreau's Telegraphy" (*ATQ* 26:14–18), describes Thoreau's attempt to convert a fact of industrialization into metaphor. Two other studies of Thoreauvian metaphor explore his literary uses of the Indian: D. M. Murray's "Thoreau's Indians and His Developing Art of Characterization" (*ESQ* 21:222–29), which identifies a progress toward understanding the Indian as an organizing principle in *The Maine Woods*, and Lauriat Lane, Jr.'s "Thoreau's Autumnal Indian" (*CRevAS* 6:228–36), which finds an association between Indians and fall in *A Week* and several essays. Lane also argues, less convincingly, that Thoreau regarded John Brown's death as a ritual autumn sacrifice, in "Thoreau's Autumnal, Archetypal Hero" (*Ariel* 6:41–49). Three articles by Richard Fleck discuss Thoreau's interest in myth in more general terms: "Thoreau as Mythologist" (*RS* 40[1972]:195–206); "Thoreau as Mythmaker and Fabulist" (*Rendezvous* 9:23–32); and "Thoreau's Mythological Humor" (*Concord Saunterer*, 10,ii:1–7). Each does little more, however, than merely call attention to Thoreau's wide-ranging interest in myth and fable.

Richard Schneider, in "Reflections in Walden Pond: Thoreau's Optics" (*ESQ* 21:65–75), finds that Thoreau studied the physics of light and reflection as part of his general concern with the interplay of mind and nature in the act of poetic creation. Gordon Boudreau, in "Seeds" (*Concord Saunterer*, 10,i:9–11), notes Thoreau's interest in images of germination. Ralph LaRosa, in "David Henry Thoreau: His American Humor" (*SR* 83:602–22), identifies a variety of characteristically American comic devices in Thoreau, including shape-changing—hence the essay's title. LaRosa has most to say about personae in *Walden*, on which subject he largely echoes Anderson and Moldenhauer. John Seelye's "Some Green Thoughts on a Green Theme," in *Literature in Revolution* (Chicago: Northwestern, 1972, pp. 576–638), a collection of essays by various hands, deals extensively with Thoreau as an instance of two antithetical traditions of pastoral that Seelye finds in American literature: "reactionary" pastoral, which is Virgilian and Jeffersonian, based on nostalgia, the agrarian ethos, and ties with the establishment; and "revolutionary" pastoral, identified with the frontier, the idea of wildness and the Christian tradition of the sanctity of the individual as opposed to authority. The essay is glib yet provocative, an ambitious and significant attempt to reexamine a thesis which has hardened into orthodoxy since Henry Nash Smith and Leo Marx.

***d.* Literary Criticism: Individual Works.** Articles on *Walden* again predominated, although not as much as usual. James Tillman's "The Transcendental Georgic in *Walden*" (*ESQ* 21:137–41) is an excellent short discussion of the extent to which the book fits the genre. Tillman's precision on the distinction between georgic and pastoral makes his article a good counterbalance to an essay like Seelye's. David Hoch, in "*Walden*: Yoga and Creation" (*Artful Thunder*, pp. 85–102), traces Indian influence on the shaping of some of Thoreau's key images (house, seat, the ponds) and his conception of spiritual awakening. Even those who believe that Thoreau's orientalism was more superficial than Hoch concedes will profit from this well-researched article. Annette Woodlief's "*Walden*: A Checklist of Literary Criticism through 1973" (*RALS* 5:15–58) is a helpful comprehensive critical bibliography. Minor explications include Rupin Desai's, "Biblical Light on Thoreau's Axe" (*TSB* 134:3–4) and Thomas Woodson's two pieces, "Notes for the Annotation of *Walden*" (*AL* 46:550–55) and "Thoreau's *Walden*, I, Paragraph 63" (*Expl* 33:item 56). In "Early Reviews of *Walden* by the *Alta California* and Its 'Lady Correspondent'" (*TSB* 131:1–2), James Matlack prints two favorable 1854 notices by Elizabeth Stoddard, whose critical orientation is further described in "The *Alta California's* Lady Correspondent" (*NYHSQ* 58[1974]:280–303).

Turning to other works, Carol Krob, in "Columbus of Concord: *A Week* as a Voyage of Discovery" (*ESQ* 21:215–21), makes too much of Thoreau's passing reference to a historical account of the explorer; Katherine Brogan, in "Thoreau's First Experience with Myth in *A Week*" (*TJQ* 7,i:3–9), simply calls attention to the book's mythic elements; Gail Baker, in "Friendship in Thoreau's *A Week*" (*TJQ* 7,ii:3–15), provides a commentary on that essay and argues tenuously for the thematic importance of the first person plural mood throughout the book; Walter Harding, ed., in "An Early Review of Thoreau's *Week*" (*TSB* 130:8), reprints a favorable notice from an unidentified newspaper.

G. Thomas Couser's "Thoreau's Cape Cod Pilgrimage" (*ATQ* 26:31–36), is a provocative albeit somewhat facile reading of Thoreau's literary excursion as a symbolic pilgrimage showing his "lifelong search for self-fulfillment through exploration of the American landscape" as ending at its easternmost point. Koh Kasegawa's "Color in Nature: A View of 'Autumnal Tints'" (*TJQ* 7,iii:20–24) is a miscellaneous commentary. A. G. Ullyat's "'Wait Not Till Slaves Pronounce the Word'" (*TSB* 132:1–2) is a brief appreciation of Thoreau's antislavery poem.

***e.* Reputation, Legacy, Relationships.** Philip Gura, in "Thoreau and John Josselyn" (*NEQ* 48:505–18), notes a literary/spiritual kinship between the two and argues persuasively that links between Thoreau and other early American descriptive writers should be further explored. Thomas Ford, in "Thoreau's Cosmic Mosquito and Dickinson's Terrestrial Fly" (ibid., pp. 487–504), fails to make his case for the influence of Thoreau on Dickinson. G. Thomas Couser, in "'The Old Manse,' *Walden*, and the Hawthorne-Thoreau Relationship" (*ESQ* 21:11–20), overstates the resemblance between the two works but finds a number of arresting parallels in theme, organization, and technique, which one hopes will receive further study. Raymond Borst's "Footnotes on Thoreau Taken from *The Critic*" (*TSB* 133:3–7), documents the growth of Thoreau's reputation during the 1890s. C. D. Narasimhaiah's "Where Thoreau and Gandhi Differed" (*TJQ* 7,iii:11–20) predictably concludes that the divergence was in their degree of commitment to social action.

iv. Individual Minor Transcendentalists

Studies of the "other" Transcendentalists were few but generally of good quality. In addition to McKinsey (see sec. i above), the following should be noted.

Joel Myerson, in "Frederick Henry Hedge and the Failure of Transcendentalism" (*HLB* 23:396–410), ably reconstructs from scattered sources Hedge's record of initial participation in the movement followed by strategic retreat. Myerson establishes, inter alia, that Hedge took the initiative in organizing the Transcendental Club. Myerson's "'A True & High Minded Person': Transcendentalist Sarah Clarke" (*SwR* 59[1974]:163–72), is a helpful profile of an obscure figure. Peter Carafoil, in "James Marsh: Transcendental Puritan" (*ESQ* 21:127–36), correctly defines Marsh's ideological stance as transitional between orthodoxy and Transcendentalism, though his generalizations about orthodoxy are not entirely reliable. David Robinson has two significant articles on Very. "Jones Very: An Essay in Bibliography" (*RALS* 5:131–46), is a comprehensive critical survey of scholarship to date. "Jones Very, the Transcendentalists, and the Unitarian Tradition" (*HTR* 68:103–24), shows that Very's mysticism should be regarded as an outgrowth of Unitarian piety.

Finally, two articles which deal with minor Transcendentalists in part are James Barcus's "Structuring the Rage Within: the Spiritual Autobiographies of Newman and Orestes Brownson" (*Cithara* 15:45–57), which contrasts Brownson's emphasis on reason and logic with Newman's emphasis on feeling and the mystery of grace; and Bertram Wyatt-Brown's "Three Generations of Yankee Parenthood: The Tappan Family" (*IllQ* 38:12–28), which makes passing reference to the husband of Caroline Sturgis.

Oberlin College

2. Hawthorne

J. Donald Crowley

Quantitatively considered, Hawthorne criticism in 1975 yielded the same relatively light harvest as in 1974. For the third straight year, in fact, there were no book-length studies; nor were there, in 1975, additional Centenary volumes to whet the textual-bibliographical palate. *Nineteenth-Century Fiction*, an index to earlier golden days of burgeoning essays on Hawthorne, printed only one brief note during the year. And the number of completed dissertations devoted exclusively or centrally to Hawthorne dropped by almost half, from 16 in 1974 (and 19 in 1973) to just 9 in 1975. But beneath the smaller numbers is another perceptible trend towards generally higher quality. Hawthorne criticism continues to show signs of emerging, reinvigorated, from the dilemmas of the late 1960s and early 1970s: emerging on the one hand from the implied condescension epitomized by Lionel Trilling's "our" Hawthorne and, on the other, from the initially nervous and ineffectual responses to Frederick Crews's *The Sins of the Fathers*, a Freudian complaint which, by insisting that Hawthorne was an id-driven writer, eroded many of our formalist presuppositions about the relation between Hawthorne's life and Hawthorne's art. One meets with fewer purely formalist analyses of this and that work nowadays; and if recent criticism has not yet developed a full, fresh holistic approach to Hawthorne's corpus, it does tend to be more deeply contextual—and more positively speculative—about the terms of Hawthorne's creative psychology. The best of that criticism seems to me to reflect a new vitality along the lines suggested by Roy R. Male (*ALS 1969*). Its interests often involve a reexamination of the nature, function, and

Editor's note: Nina Baym points out that the words in *ALS 1974*, p. 16, purportedly quoted from Hershel Parker's article, "Regularizing Accidentals," *Proof* 3:1–20, were in fact her words representing an interpretation of that article.

value of daydream, fantasy, and fiction by way of post-behaviorist insights. This new direction or recovery is sounded in Roy Harvey Pearce's reference to "ego psychology," in James M. Cox's masterful elaboration of "his" Hawthorne, and in the various ways in which other critics pursue the influence of Hawthorne's art upon his life. Meanwhile, too, the traditional modes of historical and bibliographical scholarship continue to shed their lights on Hawthorne's times, career, and text.

i. Manuscripts, Texts, Life, Reputation, Bibliography

Though no further volumes of the Centenary Edition were published in 1975, controversy about various editorial practices in establishing a definitive Hawthorne text remained lively. "Textual Studies in the Novel," a special fall issue of *Studies in the Novel* (vol. 7) containing a forum on CEAA projects, includes several essays which address these vexing questions. G. Thomas Tanselle provides an analytical and ranging survey of the problematic nature of many editorial decisions in "Problems and Accomplishments in Editing the Novel," pp. 323–60. Whatever one's doubts or certitudes about Fredson Bowers's principles and practices of emendation, it is extremely useful to see them put in the broad context of other editors' determinations of the texts of British and American fiction in the last fifteen years. In "Greg's Theory of Copy-Text and the Textual Criticism in the CEAA Editions," pp. 375–88, John Freehafer argues that only the textual collations and the historical commentaries deserve to be called definitive. Objecting to the paucity of textual notes and numerous inadequacies of CEAA "Textual Introductions," Freehafer is another critic who censures Bowers for his treatment of accidental variants and for his restoration, not only of three manuscript passages Hawthorne deleted from *The Blithedale Romance*, but also—in spite of what Freehafer calls the conflicting "abundant external evidence" presented in Claude M. Simpson's historical introduction—various readings in *The Marble Faun*. Bruce Bebb and Hershel Parker, in "Freehafer on Greg and the CEAA: Secure Footing and 'Substantial Shortfalls,'" pp. 391–94, dispute several of Freehafer's conclusions, but they do not quarrel with these. The one other noteworthy feature in this issue is "Textual Studies in the Novel: A Selected Checklist, 1950–74," pp. 445–71, by James T. Cox, Margaret Putnam, and

Marvin Williams, a compilation which includes numerous essays on Hawthorne together with a large, convenient grouping of theoretical statements and applied studies on other individual novelists.

Many if not most of the troubles surrounding the Hawthorne text arise naturally out of the fact that so few of his manuscripts have survived in any state. Thus the discovery of even the smallest fragment is good news. Claude M. Simpson, in "A Manuscript Mystery: Hawthorne's 1839 Scrap-Book," *NHJ* 5:28–33, traces the fascinating and curious history of a single leaf of a pocket notebook Hawthorne kept during two weeks of February. This leaf, discovered by C. E. Frazer Clark, Jr., in a special set of the Autograph Edition he acquired in a small Illinois town, is apparently one of ten such pages. Its location in that special set not only illustrates some of the vagaries of American publishing but offers hope that the other pages may still turn up. Simpson cites several readings at variance with the corresponding passages in the Centenary text of *The American Notebooks.* Two other essays bear directly or tangentially on the Hawthorne text. In "Evidence of Editorial Additions to Hawthorne's 'Fragments from the Journal of a Solitary Man,'" *NHJ* 5:210–26, David W. Pancost suggests that five framework passages voiced by the deceased Oberon's literary executor are not Hawthorne's but Park Benjamin's, made by him after plans to serialize "The Story Teller" had failed. Pancost cites several inconsistencies between the narrator's and Oberon's versions of events and points to external evidence that makes the question of authorship at least problematic. His argument that the style of these passages is inconsistent with Hawthorne's is much less convincing if one recalls the similarly sentimental framework Hawthorne wrote and then deleted from "The Vision of the Fountain." The internal inconsistencies, moreover, are hardly more glaring than those Hawthorne let stand in "The Custom-House" after the change in the makeup of *The Scarlet Letter* volume. But Pancost's argument, if by no means conclusive, is a worthwhile and worrisome complication of the text of this fragment. Though not explicitly textual in nature, Lee H. Warner's "With Pierce, and Hawthorne, in Mexico," *EIHC* 3:213–20, shows Hawthorne "revising" the materials of Pierce's military-campaign diary both in ways that evince his practical political savvy and in others similar to those by which he polished his major fiction. Warner concisely compares Pierce's diary and Hawthorne's campaign biography with Roy Frank Nichols's standard biography and shows that, when necessary, Hawthorne too could tell the truth mainly. Of note is that Hawthorne saw fit to delete from Pierce's description of sickness in the ranks every use of "vomito" and "diarrhea"—word changes of the sort that have too often been misunderstood as forced upon Hawthorne by a skittish Sophia.

Another aspect of Hawthorne's public role is clarified in Mark Francis Sweeney's dissertation, "An Annotated Edition of Nathaniel Hawthorne's Official Dispatches to the State Department, 1853–57," *DAI* 36:2209A (Bowling Green), which records Hawthorne's attitudes and concerns as United States consul in Liverpool. Sweeney proposes that the grimness of some of his duties may have had an adverse effect on Hawthorne's later ability to write fiction. Wayne Allen Jones writes two essays which deal with Hawthorne's early difficulties in establishing himself as a writer expecting decent pay: "Sometimes Things Just Don't Work Out: Hawthorne's Income from *Twice-Told Tales* (1837), and Another 'Good Thing' for Hawthorne," *NHJ* 5:11–26, and "The Hawthorne-Goodrich Relationship and a New Estimate of Hawthorne's Income from *The Token*," *NHJ* 5:91–140. Its title notwithstanding, the real subject of the first of these is the widespread erroneous attribution to Mary T. Peabody of a letter to Horace Mann, dated March 3, 1838. The true author of most of its contents, we find, is sister Elizabeth. Her sketchy remarks can hardly be said, at this late date, to reveal "important information by providing a contemporary portrait of Hawthorne's personality and attitudes," nor do they offer an airtight proof that Hawthorne was never paid any sum for his first published collection. The second essay, likewise carefully researched, is equally diffuse: centrifugal in its multiple subjects and 202 footnotes and, in most of its information, a thrice-told tale. The few new facts about Hawthorne's *Token* pay which Jones has painstakingly unearthed would have been far more impressive isolated in a concise, coherent note.

Other scholarly diggings relating to Hawthorne's life, letters, and reputation tend to be slight. C. E. Frazer Clark, Jr., describes and reproduces another unpublished letter, this one from Hawthorne to an admiring autograph seeker, in "*The Scarlet Letter*—A 'Fourteen-Mile-Long Story,'" *NHJ* 5:[2]–4, and Roger Howell, Jr., in "Hawthorne at Bowdoin: A Letter Concerning His Arrival," *NHJ* 5:5–9, reproduces in full a letter of Robert Manning's, Hawthorne's uncle-benefactor, detailing events of the author's first day at the college. Artem Lozynsky, citing a brief, casual contrast made by Dr. Richard Maurice Bucke in a letter to Harry Buxton Forman, dignifies the point with a title that promises more than the page delivers: "Whitman the Man and Hawthorne the Artist: An English Evaluation," *NHJ* 5:270–71. Such items take their place as useful keepsakes among *NHJ*'s often handsome illustrations. Recent interest in Hawthorne abroad is the subject of David Timms's "Hawthorne Studies in Britain," *NHJ* 5:259–63, and Fumio Ano's "Hawthorne Studies in Japan," *NHJ* 5:264–69. Whereas little Hawthorne criticism has been done recently by British critics in British journals, since 1964 Hawthorne has shared with Henry James the largest attention Japanese writers have paid any American writer. One other bibliographical study deserves mention here: Wayne Allen Jones's checklist, "Recent Hawthorne Scholarship, 1973–74, with Supplementary Entries from Other Years Added," *NHJ* 5:281–316. The items include editions and translations of Hawthorne's works, book-length studies, essays, and dissertations, and they appear comprehensive for two years. The rationale for the supplementary entries, however, is nebulous.

ii. General Studies

The most compelling essays of those concerned with topics of a general nature take up the old but still unanswered question of the stresses Hawthorne perceived and felt existing between the Actual and the Imaginary. Like so much of Hawthorne's own work, the essays themselves tend to have a greater force collectively than separately. Darrel Abel's "Hawthorne, Ghostland, and the Jurisdiction of Reality," *ATQ* 24:30–38, is essentially a prolegomenon, a tentative, eclectic discussion of the various ways in which epistemological skepticism and its effects influence the development of Hawthorne's fiction. Alluding to Nietzsche, Coleridge, Bergson, William James, and Santayana, among others, Abel traces Hawthorne's preoccupation with the absence of "objective evidence and certitude" and his response to the modern philosophical shift away from ideal absolutes to an orientation in the collective unconscious. The early tales and sketches, Abel says, "are in effect thinly objectified analyses of the working of his imagination, suggesting that the writer is simply a kind of amanuensis for some ghostly prompter who supplies him with 'truth,'" and "treat history as enacted dream which can be redeemed by sympathetic imagination." If Hawthorne's artist is a Proteus as subject, he is also, in making a subject an art object, a Prospero, endowed with an active strength that selects and controls the insights of the passive sensibility. Abel's Hawthorne promises a view of "the 'real' human world [as] a world of fictions dreamed into reality from the 'panpsychic universe.'"

Abel's suggestive essay has obvious implications for Hawthorne's use of literary sources and, especially, of what had already become the archaisms of allegory. Two essays, both skillfully conceived and persuasively presented, treat the matter in dramatically different ways. Buford Jones, in "Hawthorne and Spenser: From Allusion to Allegory," *NHJ* 5:71–90, argues that Hawthorne, far from seeking to conceal his borrowings, reworked various Spenserian materials throughout his career until what had often been contrived and undeveloped allusions in the tales became elaborate, extended transformations in the romances. Jones concentrates on Hawthorne's references to Mammon and Talus in his portrayals of Judge Pyncheon and Hollingsworth; he concludes that Spenserian sources allowed Hawthorne to discard inappropriate "allegorical machinery" but to retain what he wished of *The Faerie Queene*'s "moral framework." What Jones leaves indeterminate is the extent to which Hawthorne can be thought of as positively "adding a dimension of moral allegory to his non-allegoric" materials. In "Hawthorne's Concept of Allegory: A Reconsideration," *PQ* 54:494–510, John O. Rees, Jr., following Northrop Frye's distinction between Spenser's "continuous allegory" and Hawthorne's "freistimmig style in which allegory may be picked up and dropped again at pleasure," sees Hawthorne's allegorical effects as revolutionary and prophetic in that they typically measure the limits of perception and constitute in fact a criticism of the allegorical impulse not as a literary mode per se but as a reality of psychology. Rees suggests, with force and lucidity, that Hawthorne's characters, unlike Eliot's Henry James, are often victims of the tyranny of their own "allegorical" interpretations of their experiences and that his fiction repeatedly dramatizes those very moments when such interpretations fail to verify allegory's traditional certitudes. It is an eloquent statement.

Several other essays examine the related question of the tenuous, oftentimes mutually oppressive, relationship between the ideality of art and the actuality of the real world. Leo B. Levy's "'Lifelikeness' in Hawthorne's Fiction," *NHJ* 5:141–45, proceeds from the insight that "Hawthorne celebrates art in the light of his disappointment with it" since for him an art object's "lifelikeness" is simultaneously a triumph and a liability. The Actual at once threatens both artist and artifact and is a necessary corrective to the life-denying effects of the aesthetic consciousness. Levy comments succinctly on several of the tales and two of the romances and concludes that in Hawthorne's fiction artifacts "are cherished and despised, alternately removed from the hostility of the real world or cast down before it to be annihilated." In "Cherubs and Humblebees: Nathaniel Hawthorne and the Visual Arts," *Criticism* 17:168–81, Judith Kaufman Budz writes informatively about the outlines of Hawthorne's tastes in the visual arts and his use of pictorialist techniques for moral-aesthetic purposes in his fiction. Sharing his age's predisposition, Hawthorne was appreciative of the high idealization of classical art and the exacting realism of 17th-century Dutch genre painting—and, as Budz points out, deeply ambivalent about both. Budz traces Hawthorne's literary transformations of various aspects of the landscapes of Claude and Salvator and numerous details of Gothic architecture; she suggests that he found them fit analogues by which to account for the complexities of human behavior. Not so convincing is her conclusion that in *The Marble Faun* Hilda's assessments become not only dominant but indistinguishable from Hawthorne's own. Also touching on the art-reality dichotomy is Jerry Herndon's "Hawthorne's Dream Imagery," *AL* 46:538–45, an essay far too cursory to comprehend its title. Claiming mistakenly that critics have not yet asserted a "consistent pattern" in the dream imagery, Herndon finds that pattern to be in Hawthorne's persistent suggestion that "mortal life [is] a 'dim sphere of half development' in which good and evil blend ambiguously." Which is not really startlingly new. Herndon's generalizations lead to several contrived and simplistic judgments: critics have distorted "The May-Pole of Merry Mount," for example, "because of their unwillingness to accept its resolution in favor of the Puritans," a resolution decisively favoring life over dream.

Beyond mere contrivance is the meretricious and Samuel I. Bellman's "'The Joke's on *You*!: Sudden Revelation in Hawthorne," *NHJ* 5:192–99, which gives us Hawthorne decked out as his own Mother Rigby and striving after the condition of Sut Lovingood.

"No mere sermonizer on Original Sin and man's fallen nature, on the devil and his wiles, Hawthorne loved to see his characters squirm; he had a penchant for the *come on*, the *put on*, and the *put down*." And for not nearly so many pieces of italicized jargon. As Howells noted long ago, "we are always perceiving new Hawthornes." And some of them aren't even there.

iii. Long Romances

Robert Sattelmeyer advances the previous insights of Carl Bode, Robert E. Gross, and Terence Martin in his compactly argued essay, "The Aesthetic Background of Hawthorne's *Fanshawe*," *NHJ* 5:200–209. He demonstrates the large degree to which the immature Hawthorne relied on the postulates of Scottish Common-Sense philosophy—particularly its theory of moral sentiments and its concrete guidelines for intensifying the imaginative effects of his materials—in constructing his scenes and defining his characters' fields of motivation. In "*Fanshawe* and Hawthorne's Developing Comic Sense," *ESQ* 22:24–27, James G. Janssen takes note of Hawthorne's early verbal cleverness—his use of deliberate circumlocution, rhetorical excess, ironic understatement—his depiction of comic characters, and his creation of a tone combining grief and gaiety.

In "Hawthorne's 'The Custom-House' and the Problem of Point of View in Historical Fiction," *Anglica* 93:391–412, Ursula Brumm attempts to add to recent symbolist, structuralist, and contextual commentaries on the nature of Hawthorne's preface, calling her own method, somewhat inaccurately, a historicist approach. Hawthorne's essay drew upon four models—a widespread tradition of autobiographical sketches, the framing devices of Scott's historical novels, the essays of Lamb, and something that Brumm vaguely mentions as an "acute and troubled sense of American history." She finds not an organic unity residing in the preface and the romance but "a calculated disparity" expressive of the narrator's disjunctive roles as historian on the one hand and romancer on the other. But Brumm asks questions which demand attention to evidence she seems to ignore: evidence from the analyses in the critical essays she only cites and evidence from the fiction itself. Haven't narrative tones, history and romance, author, persona, reader, and character come together in that magnificently "historicist" metaphor in "The Prison-Door" and the remark about the rose-bush that "Finding it so directly on the threshold of our narrative, which is now about to issue from that inauspicious portal, we could hardly do otherwise than pluck one of its flowers and present it to the reader"?

One of the year's finest essays is James M. Cox's "*The Scarlet Letter*: Through the Old Manse and the Custom House," *VQR* 51:431–47, which responds ever so perceptively to Crews's interpretation by seeing Hawthorne as "a man whose art caused his life—whose art, in other words, was the primary cause of the world he invented." Cox comments brilliantly indeed on the dynamic oppositions within Hawthorne's creative psychology and their manifestations in the polarities of the tale and sketch forms, and these he relates astutely to those biographical "mysteries" of Hawthorne's "dismal chamber." In Cox's fable "The Minister's Black Veil" serves as "a perfect emblem of Hawthorne's art of the tale" since the veil, preceding and causing experience, literally "causes the story, almost as if it were itself the author." Just so, it is Hawthorne's sustained commitment to such acts of invention that "cause" him, in 1837, in giving his name for the first time to his fiction, to create an identity as artist by publicly recovering "the old spelling of his name which the American experience had deleted." Cox traces, intricately and lucidly, the growing interpenetration of Hawthorne's art and life and of tale and sketch through "The Old Manse" to their coalescence in the charged vision which makes "The Custom-House" and *The Scarlet Letter* a powerfully continuous form in which the very process of Hawthorne's conception of Hester constitutes his own "original sin: the sin of art itself." In the process Cox defines what strikes me as the essential historicist truth that in Hawthorne's view the burden of fiction is to recover "the experience suppressed by history."

Other essays on *The Scarlet Letter* itself tend to have a more limited value. Reed Sanderlin, in "Hawthorne's *Scarlet Letter*: A Study of the Meaning of Meaning," *SHR* 9:145–57, adds less substantially than he should to the work of Feidelson and others in seeing the romance's subject as psychological and epistemological rather than singularly moral. James G. Janssen, in "Pride and Prophecy: The Final Irony of *The Scarlet Letter*," *NHJ* 5:241–47, contends that by the end of the story Hester has in fact already become the prophetess endowed with the power to "establish the whole relation between man and woman on a surer ground of human happiness."

The theory is dubious at best and is hardly consonant with the somber tone of the book's "Conclusion." Two other essays suggest additional sources for Chillingworth. Max L. Autrey, in "A Source for Roger Chillingworth," *ATQ* 26:24–26, notes several parallels between Hawthorne's character and one by the same name in James Malcolm Rymer's "penny-dreadful," *Varney the Vampire: or, The Feast of Blood.*" And Mona Scheuermann, in "Outside the Human Circle: Views from Hawthorne and Godwin," *NHJ* 5:182–91, argues that Hawthorne's treatment of the Dimmesdale-Chillingworth mésalliance "owes so much" to *Caleb Williams.* The essay pays the price of that distortion and overstatement characterizing so many source studies: the critic, engaged in creating an amalgam of heightened similarities and parallels, neglects other sources and is forced into articulating generalized patterns which drain the individual fictions of their unique shapes. In the urge to prove samenesses, the critic's interest in differences diminishes.

In "Hawthorne's House of Pyncheon: A Theory of American Drama" (*Artful Thunder*, pp. 69–84) Edward Stone celebrates *The House of the Seven Gables* as "the first American Domestic Tragedy." Hawthorne having allied his art with the cause of liberal political nationalism, his House is a modern "House of Atreus," Hepzibah the fifth-act heroine of his "American Oresteia." If it is true that "for the first time in American literature a heroine had appeared in the costume of her own times and from the ranks of the common man to be beset with the struggles heretofore allotted only to the princely ranks in situations of the remote past," Stone's brush strokes painting the ideological content of the romance seem overdrawn. He leaves nagging generic questions unanswered and does not account for Hawthorne's authorial happiness in being able to view the work as characteristic of his mind because of its "sunshine." But the essay is in parts more tightly reasoned and thought-provoking. Joel R. Kehler, in "*The House of the Seven Gables*: House, Home, and Hawthorne's Psychology of Habitation," *ESQ* 21:142–53, makes an important comment on one of Hawthorne's most persistent themes. He defines the romance as Hawthorne's fullest elaboration of "the role of habitation in the shaping of human destiny" and analyzes "the home-seeking activity" as Hawthorne's leading metaphor for the individual's urge to reconcile the contradictory impulses toward nature on the one hand and human community on the other. His categorization of the various habitations is cogent and penetrating.

James H. Justus, in "Hawthorne's Coverdale: Character and Art in *The Blithedale Romance*," *AL* 47:21–36, follows a recent critical pattern in seeing Hawthorne's supreme achievement in his third romance as Coverdale's failure as poet and person: "The character of this narrator finally cannot be abstracted from the form which he encloses (the story he tells), but, more crucially, he cannot be abstracted from the form which encloses him (the story which Hawthorne tells)." Hawthorne has dramatized the human costs of weakness "without diminishment of his own tough-minded standards for the conduct of life" and has created in Coverdale an emotional cripple who anticipates James's Winterbourne and Marcher as well as central figures in Fitzgerald, Hemingway, and Eliot. In "Coverdale's Confession, a Key to Meaning in *The Blithedale Romance*" (*Literature and Ideas*, pp. 96–110) Richard Dilworth Rust describes the romance as a compelling failure because Hawthorne was experimenting with unfamiliar materials and was overly intricate in his treatment of them. Fiction and exorcised autobiography interesect in Hawthorne's writing of the book, Coverdale's Prufrockian bachelorhood having become sterile, Rust says, just as Hawthorne, through his marriage to Sophia, had begun to live. More illuminating still is Roy Harvey Pearce's "Day-Dream and Fact: The Import of *The Blithedale Romance*" (*Individual and Community*, pp. 49–63), which reexamines the romance as an anti-utopian satiric fiction that fails to conform to its novelistic requirements. One of the reasons, Pearce speculates, is that "in creating Coverdale Hawthorne is trying to exorcise out of himself a fundamental drive in his own character, as in creating Blithedale and its special society, he is trying to come to see as 'fact' a long-gone 'day-dream,' and so come to grips with a vital portion of his own history." Pearce's critique of the Arcadian motif and the characters' regressive urges toward the childlike, and his relating these themes to Hawthorne's recent writing of *A Wonder-Book*, are suggestive and compelling. In Pearce's fable of the "inside story" of *The Blithedale Romance* Eustace Bright, the narrator of Hawthorne's Greek myths for children, having gone to Brook Farm with Hawthorne and never recovered from it, is metamorphosed as Coverdale. It is he who stands Prufrockian behind Coverdale, allow-ing the story to be told, as it were, only because he will not be heard. Pearce's strategies are much like Cox's, and the essays, taken together, are fresh clarifications of the intersecting points of Hawthorne's life and art. One other essay, much less probing, is Nancy Joyner's note on "Bondage in Blithedale," *NHJ* 5:227–31, which asserts that Coverdale ironically enjoys no happiness even though he is the only character not literally enslaved by conditions of his own making.

The Marble Faun prompted two studies: Rita K. Gollin's "Painting and Character in *The Marble Faun*," *ESQ* 21:1–10, and Edgar A. Dryden's "The Limits of Romance: A Reading of *The Marble Faun*," in *Individual and Community*, pp. 17–48. Gollin, trying to counter the recent views of Paul Brodtkorb, Jr., and Nina Baym, contends somewhat mechanically that Hawthorne's last complete romance is not an "elegy for art" but his "carefully qualified brief for it." Her analysis insists too strongly on a firm reconciliation between life and art and seems to slight the implications of Kenyon and Hilda's return home to America. Dryden's essay is different: allusively ranging, grounded in theoretical considerations, closely analytic—and not to be neatly summarized. Dryden finds the book's fictive world permeated with a quiet, chilling despair deriving from Hawthorne's perception that "sympathetic communication" is ultimately impossible. The literary enterprise "is derivative, the product of a probing interpretive act which focuses on something which is already an interpretation, and it generates in the reader not a gentle and sympathetic interest but a desire to question and probe—that is to say interpret." For Dryden Hawthorne's preface and romance share an integral unity, the death of Hawthorne's "Gentle Reader" being the equivalent of the loss of sympathy which Donatello and Hilda suffer. The achievement of Dryden's essay is that the critic shares so fully the burdens weighing down Hawthorne, his persona, his characters.

In "Flower Imagery in Hawthorne's Posthumous Narratives," *SNNTS* 7:215–26, Max L. Autrey draws some questionable conclusions about Hawthorne's often conflicting uses of plant analogues in *Dr. Grimshawe's Secret*, *Septimius Felton*, and *The Dolliver Romance*. Not the least of these is that the flower's organic life offers proof of Hawthorne's active belief in the Puritan work ethic. Hawthorne seems saddled here with a commitment to a "value system" of "growth and productivity patterns" superimposed on him from a technological age.

iv. Short Works

Prabhat K. Pandeya looks at "The Drama of Evil in 'The Hollow of the Three Hills,'" *NHJ* 5:177–81, but says very little not made abundantly clear within the tale itself. Daniel G. Coffey, on the other hand, presents a perceptive argument, in "Hawthorne's 'Alice Doane's Appeal': The Artist Absolved," *ESQ* 21:230–40, that Hawthorne's reworked remnant of "Alice Doane" evinces tightly knit causalities in its apparent disjunctions between interior narrative and framework materials. Coffey's analysis of what he calls Hawthorne's "dissolving forms" may seem ingenious at points but no less so, it might be argued, than Hawthorne's own obviously convoluted strategies. Coffey elucidates well the intensely reflexive nature of this story of storytelling, and his close examination of various crucial passages justifies his claim that Hawthorne's imperceptible shifts of narrative tones, settings (historical, natural, fictional), and characters (interior narrative and framework) fuse them in an artifice that embraces all these permutations. The kinds of interrelationships he discloses are not unlike those existing between Hawthorne's later prefaces and romances. A question not attended to, however, is why Hawthorne was so willing to forget the tale and never acknowledged or collected it. If Coffey's thesis has validity, the puzzle is the greater.

Subtleties of narrative technique are the subject of other essays on individual tales, among them Roger P. Wallins's "Robin and the Narrator in 'My Kinsman, Major Molineux,'" *SSF* 12:173–79. Wallins begins by charging virtually all previous critics with neglecting the "very significant relationship" of his title and thus overlooking it as the key to Robin's steady, gradual growth. This is measured by the modulations of the narrative voice, particularly its varying tones in references to Robin's "shrewdness." Robin does become "shrewd," Wallins insists; but Wallins's unexamined assumption—that, because Robin's early sense of his own shrewdness is unreliable and treated ironically, shrewdness itself is the tale's *summum bonum*—seems wrong-headed. Given the subject, Wallins might have done well to examine the narrator's relationship to Robin as it is unobtrusively registered in that possessive pronoun of the tale's title. If Wallins makes shrewdness a bit too virtuous, Sheldon Liebman, in "'Roger Malvin's Burial': Hawthorne's Allegory of the Heart," *SSF* 12:253–60, burdens Reuben Bourne with the willful obduracy of a Richard

Digby or a Roderick Elliston and sees him on a quest which, like Ethan Brand's, leads him ultimately "to suicide." There is, in this reading of the tale, the suggestion as well that Reuben has before him, if he would only see them, easily available possibilities for a village-uncle felicity. I sense an occupational hazard for Hawthorne criticism here when the game becomes one of outwitting duped protagonists with post-Boothian rhetorical weaponry. In Liebman's "The Reader in 'Young Goodman Brown,'" *NHJ* 5:156–69, the successful reader redeems himself by astutely separating his own responses from those of the misguided Goodman Brown. By withdrawing from the solipsistic blindness of Hawthorne's protagonist, who is himself guilty of withdrawal, such a reader, becoming the story's chief protagonist, emerges from it with the solid assurance of having made a redemptive moral choice.

This difficult tale is discussed much more successfully in two other essays. In "The Concluding Paragraph of 'Young Goodman Brown,'" *SSF* 12:29–30, Edward J. Gallagher answers the objection of those readers who find Hawthorne's conclusion a digressive anticlimax which subverts the artful circularity of his plot. He points out, in an old-fashioned but crisp New Critical way, numerous verbal echoes, ironic restatements, and images that fulfill rather than ruin Hawthorne's total design. Few essays so brief manage to say so much. A still more striking achievement is James W. Clark, Jr.'s "Hawthorne's Use of Evidence in 'Young Goodman Brown,'" *EIHC* 111:12–34, perhaps the year's finest piece of historical scholarship on Hawthorne. Clark sorts his way through New England witchcraft sources to elucidate very well indeed Hawthorne's studiously controlled and imaginative revisioning of those materials—episodes, personalities, facts. He deals perceptively with Hawthorne's creative response to his own ancestral involvement in the Salem trials. Because he manages to simultaneously assert specific prototypes and sustain a well-tempered interpretive vision of the tale itself as transmuted data become art, his essay transcends the bounds of the conventional source study.

"The Minister's Black Veil" receives deserving treatment in James B. Reece's "Mr. Hooper's Vow," *ESQ* 21:93–102. It is a sensitive, thoughtful analysis which gathers impressive evidence, internal and external alike, that the clergyman's mysterious conduct springs not from psychological weakness or from secret sin but from his steadfast and tormented loyalty to a sacred vow made so that he could fulfill his priestly task of moving his fallen congregation to salvation. Reece's reading gives full play to the story's poignant ironies and ambiguous symbols and, at the same time, attends to Hawthorne's clear-sighted criticism of the rigidities of Calvinist doctrines. He succeeds in delineating Hawthorne's profound ambivalences about the psychological effects of Puritan beliefs without denuding those ambivalences of their intense passion and coherence. Helpful too, if less complex, is a brief note by Joseph J. Feeney, S.J., "The Structure of Ambiguity in Hawthorne's 'The Maypole of Merry Mount,'" *SAF* 3:[211]–16. Feeney finds Hawthorne's delicate balancing of eight abstracted levels of ambiguity interrelated in what, following Daniel Hoffman, he names a unified "equivocality of vision." Plot and allegory "favor" the Puritans; imagery and sound, the Anglicans; characterization, diction, symbolism, and theme, neither of the parties. The scheme is perhaps too tidy, too well wrought, too artificial in that it is only in the critic's act, not in the continuity of the tale itself, that these "discrete" aspects are isolated so as to be put back together again. Reading the essay in the company of Reece's, I find Feeney's exclusively structural and formal focus stopping short, unnecessarily, of the point where structure meets, informs, becomes value.

Jackson Campbell Boswell's "Bosom Serpents Before Hawthorne: Origin of a Symbol," *ELN* 112:279–87, surveys succinctly the appearances of "enbosomed serpents" from Aesop through Eastern "mystery religions" and the Hebraic tradition to its permeation of English Renaissance literature and the writings of Puritan divines. Boswell does not attempt to comment on Hawthorne's immediate sources or on his transmutations of them in "Egotism" and elsewhere; but he leaves no question that Hawthorne inherited a lengthy and ambiguous literary tradition which contained ample precedent for literal as well as figurative bosom snakes and embraced a spectrum of symbolic portent ranging all the way from perfidiousness to suggestions of redemption, grace, and salvation. In "'The Birthmark' in Perspective," *NHJ* 5:232–40, David J. Baxter argues that Aylmer is not to be grouped, as recent critics have suggested, with Ethan Brand, Rappaccini, and Chillingworth as one of Hawthorne's cold scientists become fiends but with Owen Warland as a scientist-artist who wants only to make a very good thing still better. Viewing the work as a love story, Baxter finds Hawthorne's vision essentially tragic, a rueful comment on the limits of Transcendentalism rather than a rejection of it. In "The Sources for Hawthorne's 'The Artist of the Beautiful,'" *NCF* 30:105–11, Harry C. West sees Hawthorne as neither lamenting Warland's fate nor hailing his persistent courage. This balanced vision stems, West hypothesizes, from Hawthorne's familiarity with Isaac D'Israeli's *Curiosities of Literature*, which contains two differing accounts of an interesting anecdote concerning Thomas Aquinas's destruction of a fragile mechanism constructed by Albertus Magnus. The plight of the artist persecuted by an unsympathetic society is answered to only by a satisfaction essentially private and incommunicable. In a slighter and less convincing note, "'Earth's Holocaust': Hawthorne's Parable of the Imaginative Process," *KanQ* 7:85–89, Norman H. Hostetler argues that the naïveté and unreliability of the narrator comprise the very substance of the sketch by forcing the reader into the role of protagonist.

v. Hawthorne and Others

No fewer than five essays are devoted to Hawthorne's relationship with and influence on Melville. Allen F. Stein, in "Hawthorne's Zenobia and Melville's Urania," *ATQ* 26:11–14, objects to the earlier view that the sexually anguished astronomer of Melville's "After the Pleasure Party" is a scarcely disguised autobiographical rendering and claims, instead, that Melville drew most heavily on Zenobia. Numerous parallels are pointed to, from the plight of the two women in a male-dominated world to the weed imagery they are "linked" with. The similarities are inconclusive but at times suggestive. Whereas Stein finds a positive genetic strain, Rita K. Gollin, in "The Intelligence Offices of Hawthorne and Melville," *ATQ* 26:44–47, sees Chapter 22 of *The Confidence-Man* as "a nihilistic comment on Hawthorne's tale." Admitting that no explicit proof exists for conjoining the two pieces, Gollin uses the comparison to restate the notion that finally the greater skepticism belongs to Melville. A genuinely satisfying model for this kind of investigation, on the other hand, is Richard H. Gamble's "Reflections of the Hawthorne-Melville Relationship in *Pierre*," *AL* 47:629–32. Previous critics have suggested that Melville portrayed Hawthorne as Plotinus Plinlimmon, as Isabel, or as Pierre himself. Gamble, however, suggests instead that Melville drew upon the contours of his Berkshire friendship with Hawthorne in describing, in book 15, "The Cousins," the decline of Pierre's ardent relationship with his cousin Glen Stanley. Gamble deftly juxtaposes Melville's letters to Hawthorne and Pierre's to Glen to show that both correspondences reflect a similar fear of rejection and the same hopeful, cajoling air. Concise and carefully argued, Gamble's essay makes a significant biographical probe: "If Melville did use his own experience with Hawthorne as a basis for 'The Cousins,' then the estrangement which occurred resulted not from a later misunderstanding but from strains within the relationship which were becoming clear to Melville by early 1852."

The most sweeping claims for Hawthorne's influence on Melville are made by Marvin Fisher, in "Portrait of the Artist in America: 'Hawthorne and His Mosses,'" *SR* 11:156–66, and by Edward Stone, in "More on Hawthorne and Melville," *NHJ* 5:59–70. Both critics feel that Melville would have been more accurate if he had dated his life, not from his 25th year, but from his meeting with Hawthorne on August 5, 1850. Fisher speaks more generally, seeing Hawthorne as having genuinely inspired Melville and Melville, in his long review-essay, creating out of that inspiration not so much a comment on *Mosses* as a projected and idealized self-portrait. Melville's shock of recognition, Fisher says, was such as to lead him, as if for the first time, into the bold techniques of his later tales: "extravagant and audacious symbolism, a deceptively indirect narrative style, and a highly innovative use of allusion." The fact of his meeting Hawthorne Melville turns into a rich fiction which has the two writers participating in "a sacramental conception of literary creativity . . . a dramatic vision of cultural mythology." Fisher captures the tone of Melville's deeply private urge toward literary nationalism. His claims of the crucial importance Hawthorne had for Melville have at times the same extravagance that typifies Melville's celebration of *Mosses*. But they also have a Melvillian ring of truth and are especially welcome in the light of such recent pronouncements as Alfred Kazin's that "To those who value past writers because they influence our living and thinking now, Hawthorne is unreal." Stone risks the specific and contends that even as early as *Moby-Dick* Melville borrowed not only from *Mosses* but from *The Scarlet Letter* and *The House of the Seven Gables*, various specific aspects of Ahab's characterization being drawn from Chillingworth and Melville's sense of the nature of "democratic" tragedy stemming, not from Shakespeare, but from Hawthorne's portrayal of Hepzibah. Stone's readings are sufficiently substantial to suggest strongly that, his fictionalized account in the *Literary World* review notwithstanding, Melville had a broader acquaintance with Hawthorne's fiction than he revealed.

J. Lasley Dameron's "Hawthorne and the *Edinburgh Review* on the Prose Romance," *NHJ* 5:170–76, demonstrates that an anonymous 1837 review of "Recent English Romances" might well be added to that long list of theoretical statements that helped shape Hawthorne's ideas in the preface to *The House of the Seven Gables*. Other essays show that if Hawthorne could bask for a while in Melville's sublime conception of his genius he also had to contend with the plague of popular fiction. In "Hawthorne's 'Scribbling Women,'" *NEQ* 48:231–40, John T. Frederick finds Hawthorne's complaint that "America is wholly given over to a damned mob of scribbling women" to be a dismayingly accurate assessment of public taste. Between 1850 and 1855, he reminds us, only five pieces of American fiction—all written by women and all, except for *Uncle Tom's Cabin*, forgettable—sold in the hundreds of thousands immediately upon publication. (Sales of American copies of *The Scarlet Letter* during Hawthorne's lifetime, meanwhile, fell short of 14,000.) Hawthorne's problems in publishing fiction in book form were matched, Frederick contends, by women's increasingly dominant roles as contributors to and editors of magazines and annuals. An ampler analysis of these issues is Raymona E. Hull's "'Scribbling' Females and Serious Males: Hawthorne's Comments from Abroad on Some American Authors," *NHJ* 5:35–58, which complements Frederick's essay by demonstrating that, while Hawthorne was understandably frustrated by the economic success accruing to the "shoddy sentimentality, superficial optimism, and bad taste" of various women writers, he and Sophia shared the deeper "Victorian" objection that writing for a public audience inevitably violated feminine, domestic delicacy. These abiding motives, Hull concludes fairly, led Hawthorne to be instinctively more generous in his judgments of the works of male writers.

University of Missouri, Columbia

3. Poe

Donald B. Stauffer

No books were published on Poe in 1975, if we except the reprinting of Richard Benton's *Eureka* symposium. In surveying some 50 articles and chapters of books I find that a few rereadings of some tales, some important spadework in sources and circumstances of composition, some new speculations and discoveries about *Eureka*, and two French structuralist readings of *Pym* published in 1974 are among the highlights of a rather humdrum year. The shift in interest in recent years away from the poetry continues to be felt: the emphasis is more and more on the fiction, particularly *Pym*, the humorous tales and landscape sketches, and *Eureka*. Not one essay was specifically about Poe as a critic, although several made connections between his criticism and his writing. Nine new dissertations are listed in *DAI*, and articles from at least two of them are already in print.

i. Bibliography, Sources, Texts

The best kind of source study makes us take a fresh look at the text itself, and this is the case with George Soule, Jr., in "Another Source for Poe: Trelawney's *The Adventures of a Younger Son*," *PoeS* 8:35–37. Future studies of "Ms. Found in a Bottle" will need to take this article into account. Soule has found a number of parallel passages in Poe's tale and Trelawney's book, a popular tale of life as a corsair in Malaysian waters, published in 1831. Poe also used passages from the same book in *Pym*, "William Wilson," and possibly elsewhere, but in every case he altered the style.

Burton P. Pollin's researches into Poe's sources continue to be fruitful, and he has turned up three items of interest. The most fascinating of these is a long-overdue study, "*Undine* in the Works of Poe," *SIR* 14:59–74. Every reader of Poe has noticed the frequency with which he refers to this romance by de la Motte Fouqué; Pollin gathers up these scattered references and shows why the book appealed to Poe, how he used it in his criticism, and, finally, how he used its themes in three tales: "Usher," "Island of the Fay," and "Elenora." In "Poe's Use of the Name De Vere in 'Lenore,'" *Names* 23:1–5, Pollin argues that Poe uses not only Tennyson's poem, "Lady Clara Vere de Vere," and Robert Plumber Ward's 1827 novel *De Vere; or, the Man of Independence*, but also the character of Lord de Vere in Hawthorne's "The Great Carbuncle." He also sees what he calls "a slight influence" of Dickens on Poe, in the form of one of the interpolated tales of *Nicholas Nickleby*, in which some of the comic touches seem to have been adapted by Poe for "The Devil in the Belfry" ("*Nicholas Nickleby* in 'The Devil in the Belfry,'" *PoeS* 8:23).

Three other sources or parallels have been suggested, two of them from folklore. Benjamin Franklin Fisher, in "Poe, *Blackwood's* and 'The Murders in the Rue Morgue,'" *AN&Q* 12 (1974):109–10, points out that a model for Poe's orangutan can be found in a *Blackwood's* article entitled "A Chapter on Goblins," 16 (December 1823). Charles C. Doyle, in "The Imitating Monkey: A Folktale Motif in Poe (*NCarF* 23:89–91), makes no claim for a specific source, but describes a frequently recurring folktale motif which parallels the incident of the orangutan's murder of Madame L'Espanaye by imitating its master's shaving habits and slitting her throat. In the 16th-century versions he cites, however, the monkeys always used the razors on themselves, with suicidal results.

Elmer R. Pry finds "A Folklore Source for 'The Man That Was Used Up'" (*PoeS* 8:46) in a widely retold frontier anecdote. W. T. Bandy has found a possible source for a remark attributed to Victor Hugo calling Poe "the prince of American literature" ("Hugo's View of Poe," *RLC* 49:480–83).

New light has been cast upon the "Autography" series in the *Southern Literary Messenger*: Dwight Thomas has found the probable source of as many as a dozen writers in a previously unnoticed letter in the Griswold Collection of the Boston Public Library ("James F. Otis and 'Autography': A New Poe Correspondent," *PoeS* 8:12–15). The letter refers to a number of autographs of Maine writers and others which Otis, a writer for Washington's *Daily National Intelligencer*, furnished to Poe.

Joel R. Kehler has found himself on a kind of miniature road to

Xanadu in his efforts to trace the sources of Poe's landscape sketches in "New Light on the Genesis and Progress of Poe's Landscape Fiction" (*AL* 47:173–83). He begins by questioning the point made by a number of scholars that Poe had read Andrew Jackson Downing's *A Treatise on the Theory and Practice of Landscape Gardening* before writing "The Landscape Garden." He finds parallel passages in a *review* of that book published in Duyckinck and Mathews's magazine *Arcturus* which lead him to think Poe possibly had read only the review. Later in 1845, however, when Poe was editor of the *Broadway Journal*, an anonymous review article of Downing's other book, *Cottage Residences*, appeared, which may or may not have been his but which contains some striking parallels to his descriptions in "Landor's Cottage." Kehler shifts his ground disconcertingly here in his statement that while there is not conclusive evidence that Poe had read Downing directly there is the possibility that he had read Downing prior to writing both pieces but chose to use him directly only in "Landor's Cottage."

In addition, he finds evidence that Poe had run across Marvell's "The Garden" and had read Peacock's *Headlong Hall*, both of which shaped his treatment of Ellison in "The Domain of Arnheim." Ellison's views on landscape art are like those of Mr. Foster, the perfectibilitarian, who believes that the physical state of the planet can be ameliorated. "*Headlong Hall*, therefore, played a major part in the coalescence of Poe's thematic intention in 'The Domain of Arnheim.' " This is an important essay, which contains a number of other minor discoveries and provocative suggestions.

Penguin Books has issued an attractive edition of *The Narrative of Arthur Gordon Pym*, ed. Harold Beaver, with a long introduction synthesizing recent scholarship and criticism, and Jules Verne's *Le Sphinx des Glaces* included in an appendix.

It is a pleasure to welcome the return of "Fugitive Poe References: A Bibliography" (*PoeS* 8:21–22). This compilation by Judy Osowski has been helpful in the past with its items which focus on Poe in a larger context or with a special angle of vision, often turning up in very unexpected places.

ii. General Studies and Miscellaneous

The general studies range widely over a variety of topics and approaches. The Folio Club tales receive particular attention, there are interesting studies of Poe's aesthetics as revealed in the fiction, and there is a new look at him as a science fiction writer.

It is interesting to compare the methods of Kehler in his source approach to the landscape trilogy with those of E. W. Pitcher, since the two approaches epitomize the extremes in Poe studies today: the reliance on sources vs. the kind of wide-ranging speculation in terms of the Poe "myth." The landscape pieces have attracted increasing attention in the past few years, not merely as documents of a 19th-century interest in landscape art but also as they reveal some of the allegorical undercurrents of Poe's work. Richard Wilbur has written at length about "The Domain of Arnheim," and his approach is used by Pitcher in "The Arnheim Trilogy: Cosmic Landscapes in the Shadow of Poe's *Eureka*" (*CRevAmS* 6:27–35), where he links "The Landscape Garden," "The Domain of Arnheim," and "Landor's Cottage" to Poe's conversation and colloquies leading to *Eureka* as explorations of the ordering principles of the universe. The first of these sketches is concerned mainly with art, Pitcher notes, while in "Arnheim" Poe adds a four-stage journey toward the after-life, or Paradise." "Landor's Cottage" is much less obviously allegorical, but more complex both for its cryptic suggestiveness and its double point of view, in which the successive stages of the journey are seen both from the human and the divine point of view, the latter revealing the divine pattern or plan which only can be partially perceived by the voyager himself.

Alexander Hammond's challenging project of reconstructing the 11-story version of the 1833 Folio Club collection continues in a new essay which raises many vital issues and suggests new directions for research in Poe's early fiction. In "Further Notes on Poe's Folio Club Tales" (*PoeS* 8:38–42) Hammond modifies some of the arguments he set forth in two earlier essays (see *ALS 1972*, p. 224) and suggests perspectives for future critical studies of the Folio Club stories as a group. He reexamines the question of why Poe did not publish "Raising the Wind" until 1843, but still maintains that internal evidence argues for its being considered the tale told by Mr. Snap and written prior to 1833. He now believes that all of "Loss of Breath," rather than merely the "The Quick Among the Dead" episode, was told by Mr. Blackwood Blackwood, and was revised by Poe to emphasize the elements of parody of *Blackwood's*.

Some ingenious speculation and scholarship further lead Hammond to believe that the "very little man in a black coat" possibly is Poe himself, and that the "stout gentleman who admired Sir Walter Scott" alludes not to the "Palace of Wines" episode in Disraeli's *Vivian Grey*, but to an exchange between Scott and Irving concerning the latter's 1822 story, "The Stout Gentleman."

In the most important and stimulating section of this article Hammond contends that much critical work on these tales needs to be done in the context of the Folio Club framework, which is far more complex than many readers recognize. "Studies of particular tales should analyze them first," he writes, "as the expressions of individualized characters within a larger story, second as literary imitations with comic and satiric implications." One particularly fruitful direction for these studies is to consider them as being concerned with the creation and interpretation of fiction, a concern which Hammond sees in most of the stories, particularly "Siope—A Fable," perhaps told by Poe himself, in which the Demon's manipulation of a landscape "read" by the man on the rock leads to questions about the relationship of author, reader, and text. It is interesting to note that this type of question is also being asked in quite different contexts by French structuralist critics, such as Ricardou, Mourier, Lévy, and others (see below). In the present instance the studies have their origins in detailed and painstaking scholarship; the structuralists, on the other hand, are working strictly with the text, but there seems to be a coming together on the focusing of attention on the relationship of Poe to his text and his reader. Hammond's scholarly attention to some of the critical problems concerning these tales is long overdue, and such speculations should direct new interest and attention to these early tales and to their centrality to the rest of Poe's work.

Other questions concerning the Folio Club tales are raised in a study of an important influence on Poe in "History, Myth, Fable, and Satire: Poe's Use of Jacob Bryant" (*ESQ* 21:197–214). Here Stuart and Susan Levine show that Poe had a long acquaintance with Bryant's *Mythology*, first published in 1774–76 and republished in 1807. Bryant was a learned antiquarian who used his learning to put together, Casaubon-like, his own key to all mythologies: in his view all ancient mythology was a retelling of the primordial story of the Flood. Poe both admired and laughed at Bryant's pedantry, and the Levines offer some convincing examples of Poe's allusions to his work in several tales.

The parody seems most pervasive in "Four Beasts in One," in which Poe pokes fun at Bryant's fussy pedantry, his antiquarianism, and his use of etymology in the study of history. The Levines also speculate on the member of the Folio Club who is telling the tale, and although they accept the idea that the narrator is Chronologos Chronology, they do not agree with Hammond (see *ALS 1972*, p. 224) that he is modeled on Mordecai Noah. Instead they see a multiple object of the satire: Andrew Jackson, Bulwer-Lytton (whom Poe associated with displays of antiquarian lore), Bryant, and other mythologists in general.

They also find Bryant's influence throughout "Shadow" and "Silence." The word "Charonian," for example, called a coinage by Burton Pollin (see *ALS 1974*, p. 32), is found in Bryant's phrase, "foul Charonian canal," which Poe uses verbatim in "Shadow." Other details of setting and language convince the Levines that Bryant is one, if not the only, object of satire in these tales. Still another interesting discovery in Bryant is the source of Poe's frequent allusions to the "Nubian geographer's" account of the "Mare Tenebrarum," which he mentions in "A Descent Into the Maelstrom," "Eleonora," "Mellonta Tauta," and *Eureka*.

Poe and science fiction? Not a new approach certainly, but David Ketterer goes beyond mere cataloguing of devices and effects to arrive at some new ways of seeing the connections in a thoughtful chapter of his book-length study ("Edgar Allan Poe and the Visionary Tradition of Science Fiction," *New Worlds for Old: The Apocalyptic Imagination, Science Fiction, and American Literature*, New York/Bloomington: Anchor/Indiana Univ. Press[1974], pp. 50–75). He finds that the surface use of scientific knowledge and of pseudoscience are science-fictional *elements* only, and the way Poe uses these is always for different purposes than those of science-fiction writers. The discussion is too wordy and discursive but is nevertheless interesting in showing how Poe's preference for other worlds outside his own (a "visionary reality"), sometimes supported by science-fiction devices, as in "Mesmeric Revelation," inaugurated a visionary tradition of science fiction. One might be inclined to quarrel with Ketterer's equating Poe's devices for escaping a conventional reality with science-fiction space-time warps, but in context it is plausible since this is a sophisticated attempt to see Poe as a precursor of science fiction in other than conventional terms, and the chapter is designed partly as a theoretical underpinning to the book as a whole. Ketterer concludes that none of Poe's tales are truly science fiction: he is primarily a visionary apocalyptic in whose case the science-fiction writer "is subservient to the transcendental visionary."

A study of Poe's aesthetics that should be read in conjunction with Richard Benton's symposium on *Eureka* (see below) is Kent Ljungquist's "Poe and the Sublime: His Two Short Sea Tales in the Context of an Aesthetic Tradition" (*Criticism* 17:131–51). Ljungquist approaches Poe from the point of view of 18th-century aesthetics and wrestles with some of Poe's slippery critical terminology in examining what he sees as a shift in his conception of and attitude toward the sublime and its relation to beauty that took place during his career. In his early criticism Poe made a firm distinction between the sublime and the beautiful, associating, as did Burke, the sublime as residing in a realm of Ideality that transcends the sensuous world. On "MS. Found in a Bottle," Ljungquist takes the position that the narrator's voyage toward the unknown should be read seriously as a process of discovery of a transcendental, sublime experience which lies beyond material knowledge (rather than as a satire, as recent critics tend to do). Ljungquist takes issue with attempts to read "A Descent Into the Maelstrom" either as a tale of ratiocination or as an attack on rationality and attempts to reconcile these opposing views through the sublime aesthetic found in Schiller and Kant. But when he says that "Descent" is "a fictive representation of man's enlarged and strained faculties coming to grips with nature's grandeur and horror and finally achieving a conception of the ideal and supersensible sublime," he does not differ from critics such as Gerard Sweeney (see *ALS 1973*, pp. 48–49) as much as he thinks he does.

J. Gerald Kennedy, in "The Limits of Reason: Poe's Deluded Detectives" (*AL* 47:184–96), makes a case for the idea that the period of the ratiocinative tales was an attempt by Poe to discover a sense of order as a distraction from his vision of a nightmarish universe. Kennedy's original contributions to this familiar argument are his readings of "The Man of the Crowd," which he sees as an effort on the part of the narrator to satisfy a rage for order and clarity by penetrating the mystery of the man he pursues; and of "The Oblong Box," in which the narrator's perverse blindness to obvious appearances is a reductio ad absurdum of rational analysis and in effect

Poe's farewell to reason as a means to understanding the universe.

"The Man of the Crowd" is seen as revealing alternating psychological patterns in a structuralist study of the psychogeography of several tales by Bernard Marcade, "Pour une Psychogéographie de l'Espace Fantastique: les Architectures Arabesques et Grotesques chez E. A. Poe" (*RE* 27[1974]:41–56). Marcade maintains that there is a constant interplay between the surface aspects of Poe's interiors and exteriors and their psychological undertones. Using the term *psychogeography* to mean the study of the precise effects of a geographical setting, consciously arranged or not, directly affecting the behavior of individuals, he applies it to several tales to reveal patterns of alternation between realism and deception. The narrator of "The Man of the Crowd" wandering through the labyrinth of London streets illustrates the play of alternation between shadow/light, populous/deserted, wide/narrow, and his corresponding states of euphoria/depression, satisfaction/anguish. But he wanders with no apparent purpose, and is therefore guided by the "logic of the terrain and by the psychological resonances which it implies."

Similarly, there is a system of alternation in "The Masque of the Red Death," between exterior/interior—revealing an uneasy state between wanting to escape and wanting to remain. This sense of the "odd," or the uncanny, is what is so disquieting to the narrator at the outset of "The Fall of the House of Usher," where the aspect of the house presents a combination of the familiar and the uncanny, as Freud uses the term (*unheimlich*). In "The Domain of Arnheim" and "The Landscape Garden" Marcade sees Poe attempting to order and conceal every flaw in nature, and then to conceal the concealments themselves. Thus, "the text of Poe is to be understood as an incessant oscillation between the burying of the real and its unburying."

The importance of reading Poe in his geographical (in the more conventional sense) and historical contexts is given additional support by a gracefully written if not very penetrating essay by Thomas Hubert, "The Southern Element in Poe's Fiction" (*GaR* 18[1974]: 200–211). The most notable qualities that Poe shares with other southern writers from Simms to the Agrarians are, he writes, an antidemocratic bias, a lack of sympathy with the doctrines of progress and perfectibility, and a skepticism about technology and its effects. Julia Wolf Mazow finds that the theme of survival in Poe's fiction "attests to the positive values to be found throughout the works, underscoring explicitly an affirmative view of humankind" ("The Survival Theme in Selected Tales of Edgar Allan Poe," *SAF* 3:216–23).

Poe's revelations and conjectures about Maelzel's chess player are examined and found wanting in Charles M. Carroll's informative book about the famous automaton, *The Great Chess Automaton* (New York: Dover). Poe did add a few original thoughts to the contemporary literature about the chess player, including the fact that the Turk played whenever the opponent had moved, a trait uncharacteristic of machinery, and that when William Schlumberger, an expert chess player touring with Maelzel, was taken ill in Richmond, the exhibitions stopped until he recovered. But Poe was in error in believing that the human operator was concealed inside the figure of the Turk, when actually he was in the cabinet, working with an elaborate system of magnetized chessmen, each of which moved a pointer on the underside of the cabinet. Poe thought the candles were present to dazzle the spectators, when actually they were used to conceal the odor of the burning candle the operator needed inside the cabinet to see what he was doing. And Poe's inaccurate use of dubious background sources leads Carroll to conclude that "far from being the work of an 'unerring, abstract reasoner' [Hervey Allen], Poe's article stands as a remarkable piece of hack work, competently expressed, but netting miserable results all the time."

iii. Poetry

With the exception of Albert Gelpi's ambitious overview in *The Tenth Muse* the interest in Poe as a poet remains minimal: a few short pieces, mostly explication. Most critics today apparently have rejected the 19th-century emphasis on the poet rather than the writer of tales. Gelpi's detailed study, Armistead's brief article on "For Annie," and a handful of explicatory pieces are all that break the complete silence that surrounded the poems in 1975.

The most important treatment of Poe's poetry to appear since Floyd Stovall's book (see *ALS 1969*, pp. 193–94) is in Albert Gelpi's book-length study of five American poets before 1900 (Taylor, Emerson, Poe, Whitman, and Dickinson), the first of a projected two-part study. It is a broadly psychological approach to their work, making the poet's psyche an inclusive term applicable not only to the promptings of the unconscious but to the social and cultural aspects of his conscious "mind." The chapter on Poe, "Edgar Allan Poe: The Hand of the Maker" (pp. 115–51), is an effort to show how Poe's role as poet is a result of his lifelong sense of being at odds with his culture, his society, his environment, and finally, his universe. Against Poe, Gelpi places Emerson, intuitively perceiving the organic wholeness of the universe, whose poems were an outgrowth of the integrative process of Transcendentalism. Poe, at the mercy of his vision of a chaotic universe over which he desperately strove to gain control, used artificial and literary symbols in his effort to use language to impose form upon a chaotic world. In this respect he is like Stevens: creating works of art which are self-fulfilling worlds, denying the idea of "inspiration" and embracing the idea of artist as craftsman; creating a world which approaches the ideal—"supernal beauty" or the "Supreme Fiction." But in Poe's case Gelpi feels the poems are "failing attempts to soar: overwrought technically as well as emotionally."

Gelpi's essay covers much ground that is familiar to Poe scholars, and overemphasizes the idea of the *poète maudit*, but he is particularly good at showing how Poe's conception of himself as a "genius," standing apart from the world in his ability to soar above the world and abandon mortal affairs, yet paradoxically cursed and condemned to imprisonment in his "sense of self," is the source of a poetry that treats of an existence at odds with itself—of an unintegrated personality. Read in this context, for example, "Sonnet—Silence" reveals a basic psychological conflict between the poet's earthly identity and his immortal soul.

In Poe, who is at the mercy of his own imaginings, Gelpi finds that his own psyche is his muse, more than for most American poets, and this leads to claustrophobic writing. Throughout his career, Poe was concerned with bringing control and mastery over his material—a tendency which reaches its apotheosis in *Eureka*, which, Gelpi says, "declares the triumph of Spirit over corruptible Matter and the triumph of the poet's mind over the vast riddle of its existence." Poe therefore represents one of the two strains of American Romanticism: Emerson's poet was ideally a Dionysian God, while Poe's was Apollonian, "extending his masterful hand over the confusion of things in the shaping act of language."

The remaining articles deal with individual poems. In an effort to go beyond both explication and biographical reference, J. M. Armistead places "For Annie" in the context of literary history in "Poe and Lyric Conventions: The Example of 'For Annie'" (*PoeS* 8:1–5). He finds Poe's love letter to "Annie" Richmond to be full of attitudes found in European love conventions dating back to Petrarch, Dante, and Ronsard. The poem which grew out of these feelings "weaves these traditional threads into an integral piece of work . . . by subordinating them to another conventional theme—entrancement by love"—and by controlling them through a "unique" dramatic technique. Poe's originality in this poem therefore lies in his use of a dramatic setting, which links him with Browning, rather than with the earlier Romantic lyricists. Thus, "instead of marking Poe as a decayed Romantic, 'For Annie' designates him as the American precursor of Robinson, Masters, Frost, and Eliot, insofar as they used dramatic monologue to evoke sympathy with the mental and behavioral aberrations of neurotic misfits." Armistead sides with those who see the speaker as dying rather than dead.

"Dream-Land" is the subject of two short pieces. In one, "Poe's 'Dream-Land': Nightmare or Sublime Vision?" (*PoeS* 8:5–8), Dennis W. Eddings argues unconvincingly that the dreamer is moving *out* of an "Ideal" Dream-Land into a nightmarish "material" world. He reasons by analogy from Poe's description of a dualistic cosmology in *Eureka*, in which the physical world is seen to be at war with itself. Eddings's explication and his argument on formal grounds—that the "ultimate dim Thule" of the first six lines and that of the last line are not the same—suffer considerably if we recall that Poe used these lines in two other parts of the poem as a refrain when he first published it in *Graham's*. The quality of the dream imagery in the poem is seen by James B. Reece to be characteristic of opium visions, as described by DeQuincey, Crabbe, Walter Colton, and Coleridge ("Poe's 'Dream-Land' and the Imagery of Opium Dreams," *PoeS* 8:24).

Finally, two other writers take a look at that much-studied poem, "Ulalume." David Robinson's interesting reexamination of the role of the ghouls in the last stanza raises the possibility of seeing them as "supreme ironists," who promise the narrator blissful release from the painful memory of Ulalume, but give him instead the knowledge of death ("'Ulalume'—The Ghouls and the Critics," *PoeS* 8:8–10). He argues that the ghouls are "merciful" because they have revealed not the peace of fulfillment but, ironically, the peace of spiritual death. This is a reply to critics (Basler, Carlson), who see the ghouls as well-intentioned beings who attempt to prevent the narrator from discovering the tomb. Robinson reiterates this argument in "The Romantic Quest in Poe and Emerson: 'Ulalume' and 'The Sphinx' (*ATQ* 26, suppl.:26–30). Both poems, he says, are comments on human psychology: Poe's narrator realizes peace and death are the same, while Emerson "seeks peace through process." David Strickland, on the other hand, believes the ghouls are merciful because they have conspired with Astarte to prevent the narrator from confronting Ulalume, who has risen from the tomb ("Poe's 'Ulalume,' Stanza 10," *Expl* 34, Item 19).

iv. Fiction

"Morella," a tale not much discussed in recent years, comes under examination from two different points of view, both of them yielding excellent and not contradictory results. James Gargano gives it a stimulating rereading in his modestly titled "Poe's 'Morella': A Note on her Name" (*AL* 47:259–64). When the name is seen as a diminutive of *mors* it is suggestive of mortality, an association reinforced by reference to "morel," with its meaning from the Italian "morella," black nightshade. Poe's use of the name is central to the effect of the tale, evoking the narrator's fears of mortality, and his intellectual resistance to her is seen as a failure on his part to recognize the limits of human life and the all-pervasiveness of death. Gargano sensitively analyzes the relationship between the narrator and the wife-as-death in three stages: at her death the narrator seems to triumph by extricating himself from her authority; in the naming and death of the second Morella, "he becomes totally subject to the tyranny he has helped to perpetrate by his arrogant intellectualism. Third, in her final phase, Morella refines herself into a spirit or disembodied name eternally and pervasively existing . . . in the mind of man."

There is a growing interest in examining Poe's tales in terms of Jungian psychology, as evidenced by such studies as Robert Reeder's of "The Black Cat" (see *ALS 1974*, p. 38) and Colin Martindale's of "Usher" (see *ALS 1972*, p. 219). Martin Bickman's "Animatopoeia: Morella as Siren of the Self" (*PoeS* 8:29–32) combines Jungian psychology with the philosophical framework of Romantic thought to cast light on the symbolic suggestiveness of Morella's reemergence and death. Jung's theory of individuation describes the ego emerging out of primordial wholeness and fragmenting the self, but later often rejoining the rest of the self in a fuller integration of personality. Bickman shows that this process may be compared with the pattern of unity-division-reintegration found in Romantic thought by both Frye and Abrams, a version of which also appears in *Eureka*, with its patterns of diffusion and reintegration.

In this context Morella may be seen as an anima figure who tries to interest the rationalistic narrator (ego) in a transcendental view of "identity," but is destroyed. This destruction-repression causes a greater disruption of his psyche, resulting in her reappearance in the second Morella. The narrator's ultimate failure to control the anima's drive toward individuation is seen at the end when the anima, Morella, becomes coterminous with the all, "taking the ego with it, into the unconscious realm from which it emerged." Although this may seem at first to be a different reading than Gargano's, they may profitably be read together, since they are complementary. Both readers associate Morella with death, but while Bickman is concerned with the death of the ego as it is engulfed by the collapsing anima, Gargano, reading more literally, is concerned with the narrator's psychological disintegration through his obsession with death.

Two studies of "The Fall of the House of Usher" add little to our knowledge or understanding. The connections between the painting of Roderick Usher and that of modern abstract and surrealist art have often been observed. Nathalia Wright, in "Poe's Turn-of-the-Century Artist" (*Artful Thunder*, pp. 55–67), has extended that idea in attempting to demonstrate that Usher was a precursor of modern artists in a number of media: "The Haunted Palace" is a Symbolist poem; Usher's painting looks forward to Kandinsky, the Abstractionists, and the Surrealists; Poe's description of Usher's musical compositions suggests Debussy. His practice of the three arts of poetry, painting, and music links him with those turn-of-the-century artists who combined two or more art forms, such as Wagner, but "above all" Usher seems "a potential creator of ballets," such as Nijinsky. Wright intends to suggest links between the artistic sensibility of Poe's mad artist and that of the artists of the early modernist years by suggesting a number of influences and collaborations. But unfortunately she does not cast much light on questions of the nature of art that are inevitably raised by these comparisons. These questions have been briefly but perceptively treated, however, by H. Wells Phillips in "Poe's Usher: Precursor of Abstract Art," (*PoeS* 5[1972]:14–16), and there is still room for study here. Wright is also led astray by her attempts to identify "the last waltz of Von Weber," an issue presumably laid to rest by Burton Pollin in *Discoveries in Poe.* The title of Peter Obuchowski's "Unity of Effect in Poe's 'The Fall of the House of Usher'" (*SSF* 12:407–12) fairly sums up its thesis, its lack of originality, and its ignorance of a century of criticism.

Feelings of *déjà vu* are aroused again by Robert Coskren in "'William Wilson' and the Disintegration of Self" (*SSF* 12:155–62), which uses the techniques of explication and the language of developmental psychology to restate the familiar idea that the tale centers on a conflict of wills, between the internal and the external self. Coskren seems to have written the article in a vacuum, paying no attention to the writings of Davidson, Quinn, Wilbur, etc., etc.

A number of close studies of Poe's revisions by Benjamin Franklin Fisher have provided interesting critical insights. The most recent of these, coauthored with David E. E. Sloane, is "Poe's Revisions in 'Berenice': Beyond the Gothic" (*ATQ* 24, suppl. 2[1974]:19–23). The authors show that between the first (1835) and the last (1845) versions Poe softened many of the more repulsive physical details, and suppressed altogether the passage describing Egaeus's visit to Berenice's death chamber. The result is a shift of emphasis from the externals of Gothic horror to the internal psychological aberrations of Egaeus himself. This conclusion confirms a point made in more general terms by Clark Griffith some years ago (see *ALS 1972*, p. 216).

Two readings of "The Cask of Amontillado" make use of the Catholic elements in the tale. Philip M. Pittman, in "Motive and Method in 'The Cask of Amontillado'" (*MHRev* no. 34:87–100), reads it as a drama between Christ and Satan, reversing the roles assigned to the two characters by Donald Pearce (*N&Q* 199[1954]: 448–49) and instead seeing Fortunato as a Mephistophelean figure and Montresor as "playing out a role in which he extracts a fully Christian resolution." Montresor's listener at the opening of the tale is not a priest at a confessional, but the reader himself, drawn into the tale in such a way as to render Montresor a universal alter ego. This is emphasized by the spiritual associations of the narrator's name, "my treasure," and the story may be read as a working out of the two related themes of ritual and revenge, in which Montresor attempts to recover his lost spiritual treasure. Pittman uses many of the religious details and overtones in the tale, such as Fortunato's Masonic associations and Montresor's Catholicism (a conflict earlier but less fully explored by Kathryn M. Harris [see *ALS 1969*, p. 191]), to arrive at his view that the tale is universalized to become a ritual reenactment of mankind's victory over Satan: "a retelling of the resolution of the conflict between man and devil, replete with all of the appropriate biblical echoes." The Catholic-Masonic conflict has been frequently noticed and commented upon, most recently by James Rocks (*PoeS* 5[1972]:50–51), but whereas Rocks places it in its historical and political context, with Montresor seen as a defender of the faith, here Pittman emphasizes the allegorical qualities which turn it into a kind of morality play of God against Satan.

Charles A. Sweet, Jr., also sees ritual elements in the tale, but for him it is a ritual of scapegoating ("Retapping Poe's 'Cask of Amontillado'" [*PoeS* 8:10–12]). He suggests that Montresor's actions on the conscious level are not the important ones; that on the unconscious level he is burying and repressing his unconscious, dilettantish self. This is a view similar to that of Daniel Hoffman in *Poe Poe Poe Poe Poe Poe Poe*, whose Freudian emphasis, however, turns the conflict into one between spirit (Montresor) and body (Fortunato). Sweet, on the other hand, argues that Montresor's attempted repression has failed. His argument turns on an unconvincing distinction between suicide (killing of the despised self) and incarceration (repression). In his view, Montresor's confession is "a recognition of the guilt stemming from his act of incarceration, not from his sense of a self-suicide," and it fails because "it is relief from guilt, not forgiveness for a crime, he ultimately desires." Sweet tries to have it both ways, reading the tale simultaneously on the conscious and unconscious levels, but in his analysis the two tend to fuse and the distinctions between them lose force.

An extraordinary piece of linguistic and structuralist legerdemain is W. Bronzwaer's "Deixis As a Structuring Device in Narrative Discourse: An Analysis of Poe's 'The Murders in Rue Morgue'" (*ES* 56:345–59). Bronzwaer closely analyzes the function of *this* and *these* as modifiers in the tale and arrives at a "deep structure" which separates the opening "example story" from the main part of the tale. Further linguistic analysis reveals parallels between the deep structures of the example story and the Dupin story itself. The effect, as Bronzwaer sees it, is to take the horror story of the murder and reduce it to an inferior level of significance. "This must have been precisely the intended effect: to take a story sufficiently interesting and horrifying in its own right, and present it in such a way that the real interest of the reader comes to center not on the story itself but on the way it is detected." [!] Exactly—but what is remarkable is the way in which this conventional conclusion is arrived at (or confirmed?) by means of a technically dazzling analysis of deictic time-adverbs.

The Narrative of Arthur Gordon Pym continues to absorb the attention of critics, who are unflagging in their attempts to unlock its mysteries, sometimes made even more mysterious by their efforts. In addition to the sociocultural approach of Eric Mottram, two 1974 French essays pick up on Jean Ricardou's structuralist reading, and there are some interesting shorter notices, including two of somewhat peripheral interest.

In his wide-ranging essay, "Poe's Pym, and the American Social Imagination" (*Artful Thunder*, pp. 25–53), Eric Mottram sees *Pym* as a *Gestalt* of Poe's sensibility and argues that it reflects a basic American theme: "isolated men discovering the nature of dominance and submission in societies divided along the color line." Perfection as white and the alternation of white and black—"the pattern of moral and racial color theory in the Christian West"—are themes that *Pym* shares with other central 19th-century American works, *Moby-Dick*, *Uncle Tom's Cabin*, and *Pudd'nhead Wilson*. This ingenious and subtle argument is developed from Mottram's view of *Eureka*, the Dupin detections, and the escape tales as dramatizations of tension between order and chaos, "the myth of the free individual and the fact of social enclosure, in which Poe works for the stability of reason against uncontrollable psychic, elemental, sexual and social forces." Mottram sees Pym's personality as that of a "philobat," a person whose pleasure lies in arousing and bearing anxiety, and is therefore compelled to live dangerously. The book contains the recurring pattern of deliverance from the overpowering, the division of appearance and reality, and the experience of power in recovery. It is this exercise of power, of resolving antithetical opposites, of surviving the threats to his superiority—seen particularly in the struggle and triumph of white over black—that leaves Pym (and, by extension, Poe) in a position of having made the complex simple and established a hierarchy of values where white is supreme. This is far from a rehash of Sidney Kaplan's introduction to *Pym*; it ranges much wider in its social speculations and its drawing of inferences. A concluding, and provocative, remark is that "the goal of human experience—the South [in *Pym*]—is to experience and to feel the energic connections between natural self and natural environment, human body and the body of the world. That this may be either a mania for hierarchy or a madness for the unchanging absolute is the core of Poe's vision. How near to the center of the American Dream that vision remains, has become increasingly obvious." This stimulating essay should add to the growing literature, starting with D. H. Lawrence and William Carlos Williams, concerning Poe as a writer central to the American experience.

In 1967 the nouveau-romaniste Jean Ricardou gave us his startling structuralist reading of *Pym* (see *ALS 1968*, p. 171, and *ALS 1973*, p. 440), suggesting, among other things, that the strange properties of the Tsalalian water become an analogy for the text itself; and that one must look at the text as nothing more than the black letters on the white page. Described in these stark terms, the argument seems like a dead end, yet two French critics, Maurice Mourier and Maurice Lévy, explore some of the implications of this approach in essays which see the text of *Pym* as an effort to deny the Void. Ricardou had stated that, like the water, the text if read slowly presents opacities which eventually open out into multiple meanings. Starting with this water-text analogy, but offering a meaning of his own for the strangely limpid waters, Mourier pursues additional meanings which he finds in the closing chapters ("Le Tombeau d'Edgar Poe," *Esprit* 42[1974]:902–26).

Mourier's main argument is that both Pym the character and Poe the author are faced with glimpses of their eventual annihilation, and his evidence rests on an ingenious exegesis of the cryptographic chasms and the inscriptions they contain. By inverting and transcribing the mysterious legend in the postscript, Mourier gets the symbols to resemble characters in the Roman alphabet, and finds both "E. A. P." and "A. G. Pym" hidden in them. He explains Pym's own refusal to decipher the characters that spell his name as analogous to the experience of finding one's own name carved on a tombstone. Pym, then, by refusing to "read" the inscription, which he insists is there from natural causes, does not have to acknowledge death and nothingness. Mourier then takes the design of the caverns themselves, in Chapter 23, and turns them into Roman characters spelling "E. A. POE." These abysses therefore both hide and reveal the author's own name and at the same time symbolize annihilation. So Poe-Pym find their own death in the landscape and on the page.

The note at the end (Mourier calls it Chapter 26) indicates for him four separate levels on which the fiction may be read. The first, superficial one is that of the phantom editor who edits "Chapter 26" after the death of Pym; the second is the Mr. Poe whose name is associated with Pym and who seems reluctant to unravel the mystery; the third is the fiction itself, told by Pym; the fourth is the strange biblical statement at the chapter's close, the deepest level of all. "Across its four levels of reading, and the sinuous arrangement of the cryptogram, the text of *Pym* mimics/denies/exorcises the death of the narrator (of all narrators), the death of the *I* and of his text, the narrator-character concealing in it the benumbed writer who disappears and childishly throws back upon his character all the responsibility of his fictional mise-en-scène." In this view the text works as a deadly machine, an apparatus for self-annihilation.

Lévy takes off from both Ricardou and Tzetan Todorov's generic study of the fantastic (see *ALS 1973*, p. 418) in an attempt to arrive at a useful definition of the fantastic tale through a study of *Pym* ("*Pym*, Conte Fantastique?" *EA* 27[1974]:38–44). Noting its combination of verisimilitude and dream, and Poe's efforts to offer commonplace explanations of fantastic events, he suggests that the fantastic is that gap in the text between the familiar (*das Heimliche*) and the uncanny (*das Unheimliche*) that Freud describes in his essay on the uncanny. Or it could be defined as a lower level of discourse beneath the text—a way of looking at what some theoreticians of the fantastic genre call the "brutal eruption of mystery into the framework of real life."

But two "lower levels" he cannot accept are Bonaparte's reductive Freudianism and Bachelard's psychology of dreams. He prefers to start with Ricardou's assertion that one must begin with nothing more than the black letters on the white page, and to see that at the end Pym is engulfed, not by a natural cataract or a maternal figure, but by "the bottomless abyss of a virgin page." What Lévy suggests is the possibility that the text contains no hidden meaning, Oedipal or other, but merely masks the Void, and in his compulsive efforts to supply realistic details Pym is therefore trying to mask the abyss that lies beyond the printed text. The voyage becomes a voyage to the end of the page, ending in Mallarmé's "vide papier que la blancheur défend." In the context of genre study this is an engaging hypothesis, even though it does not necessarily add to the "meaning" of the tale.

Of interest to students of *Pym* is Hans-Joachim Lang's and Benjamin Lease's "The Authorship of Symzonia: The Case for Nathaniel Ames" (*NEQ* 48:241–52). Lang and Lease base their case on parallels of style and content between this work and Ames's *A Mariner's Sketches* (1830) and *Nautical Reminiscences* (1832), the former praised by Dana and used as a source by Melville. The argument is persuasive, even though no direct evidence exists that Ames was the author; and Ames emerges incidentally as an interesting early American writer. Charles N. Watson finds parallels between *Pym* and *Israel Potter* that add weight to the argument that Melville had read *Pym* closely, as previously argued by parallels with *Moby-Dick* ("Premature Burial in *Arthur Gordon Pym* and *Israel Potter*," *AL* 47:105–07). And in "Three More Early Notices of *Pym* and the Snowden Collection" (*PoeS* 8:32–35), Burton R. Pollin adds further support to his case (see *ALS 1974*, p. 30) that the book was not ignored by contemporary reviewers with his discovery of reviews which appeared in the summer of 1838: in *Alexander's Weekly Messenger*, the New York *Sunday Morning News*, and *Snowden's Ladies' Companion*.

v. Eureka

The only book to appear this year may not be recognized as such by some since it originally appeared in two different issues of *ATQ*, and the second half, a "new edition" of *Eureka* by Richard P. Benton (*ATQ* 22[1974]:1–77), also appeared in book form (see *ALS 1973*, p. 34). In 1975 Benton assembled an interesting but uneven symposium by ten scholars: "Poe as Literary Cosmologer: Studies in *Eureka*" (*ATQ* 26:1–68). The two sections have been republished as a book: *Poe as Literary Cosmologer in "Eureka"* (Hartford, Conn.: Transcendental Books), and librarians, perhaps understandably exasperated by the duplicative and confusing publishing practices of *ATQ* and Transcendental Books, should be encouraged to order either of these versions, preferably the single-bound volume.

The papers on *Eureka* present on the whole a heady and stimulating view of some of the issues raised by the poem and its critics today, although the weaker ones retrace familiar ground or are of peripheral interest. Implicit in most of them is acknowledgment of the important early work of Auden, Davidson, Quinn, Moldenhauer, Thompson, and others in raising fundamental questions about *Eureka*'s purpose, philosophy, and tone. The best of the essays go far to advance our understanding of the prose poem, although I would agree with the editor's comment, that "notwithstanding their rich insights, I believe we are still only part way through the labyrinth." I shall discuss the individual essays in the collection in some detail, since taken as a whole it helps establish where we are today in our understanding of *Eureka* and points in some new directions. Most important among these are a view of its intellectual roots in 18th-century philosophy, its connections with the Romantic movement, and its rhetorical strategies.

Burton R. Pollin's "Contemporary Reviews of *Eureka*: A Checklist" (pp. 26–30) takes us far beyond our ordinary expectations of a checklist with his discussion of the chronology of events leading up to Poe's lecture, "The Cosmogony of the Universe," and the publication of *Eureka*. Pollin's annotations of the roughly 30 items he has assembled fill us in on the circumstances surrounding the lecture and the book. It is surprising to learn how many responses to Poe's two-hour-long lecture were favorable; the book was also favorably reviewed by some, including the New York Evening *Express*, which said, "[We] cannot do justice to this extraordinary essay, which consummately expands the lecture into an elegant volume. With its reasoning power and depth, this new theory of the universe, unequaled since Newton's day, is highly recommended."

The critical essays, as I have said, are concerned with such questions as the work's relation to Romantic thought and 18th-century philosophy and rhetoric, its use of irony, its rhetorical strategies, its relation to Poe's other work, and the overriding question of what it reveals about Poe's world-view. Three of them, including Barton Levi St. Armand's outstanding opening essay, concern themselves directly with this question, and all conclude that *Eureka* contains a positive vision and is not a glimpse into the Void.

St. Armand works closely with sources to argue persuasively against seeing the work as nihilistic and blasphemous or impious

("'Seemingly Intuitive Leaps': Belief and Unbelief in Eureka," pp. 4–15). He places the work in the tradition of Natural Theology and Apologetics, particularly the writings of William Paley, whose *Natural Theology* (1802) bears the subtitle, *Evidences of the Existence and attributes of the Deity collected from the Appearances of Nature.* Poe, according to St. Armand, came increasingly to reject the Romantic doctrine of inspiration as the source of art and to adopt a philosophy of intuition and insight, in which creativity consisted of sublime insights into God's creations. Seen in the light of this critical theory, "*Eureka* is a criticism, in the widest possible sense, of the universe itself," and should also be seen as a late contribution to the Natural Theology movement in its efforts to illuminate the general and continuing revelation of nature through a pious accumulation of scientific knowledge. St. Armand is effective in countering the arguments of those who would see *Eureka* as an outgrowth of Coleridgean Romanticism and those who would see it as a denial of a benign Christian God. "Poe in fact rejected the prime Romantic theory of the imagination for a conception of 'Fancy' that Coleridge had tried to relegate to a philosophical dustbin. In thus refurbishing 'Fancy' to stand for a unitary, non-discriminatory, non-mystical concept of imagination, Poe also avoided that aesthetic schizophrenia which has continued to characterize Romantic applications of 'creativity' and 'inspiration' to individual works of art."

David Ketterer opens with a statement with which few would disagree, to the effect that *Eureka* is less important as science than as a cosmological structure based on aesthetic principles, but many of his points are controversial ("Protective Irony and 'The Full Design' of *Eureka*," pp. 46–55). He is at odds, for example, with St. Armand, who sees Poe using "fancy" to stand for his own brand of imagination; Ketterer instead believes Poe "slides over the distinction between reason and imagination by using the concept of 'intuition'." He finds the work studded with ironic contradictions, particularly Poe's definitions of intuition, which reveal Poe "torn between the desire to throw out reason entirely in favour of imagination or to accommodate reason, in disguise, by an ambiguous conception of intuition." But since Poe views the universe as full of ironic contraries, such confusions and contradictions are "ironically defensible." In this position Ketterer is taking issue with G. R. Thompson's view that Poe's irony mocks a transcendent belief in unity and is the underpinning of a nihilistic vision. Ketterer sees the irony not as revealing absurd and therefore nihilistic contradictions, but rather as "the verbal equivalent of that 'perfect consistency'" which Poe hoped characterizes the true nature of the universe. This position also enables Ketterer to argue that the satiric elements are not central to the work. This is an important essay, complementing St. Armand's essay and the earlier work of Joseph Moldenhauer (see *ALS 1968*, pp. 159–60). He makes some interesting and challenging asides as well, including the speculation that Melville had read *Eureka* before writing *Moby-Dick*, and the idea that *Eureka* may be read as a political or historical "allegory" of the "many into one" of the United States.

Poe's Lucretian vision of matter and motion did not allow him to reject science in favor of poetry, but instead led him to try to reconcile his mechanistic universe (matter) with his poetry (spirit). This thesis is elaborately developed by Curtis M. Brooks, in "The Cosmic God: Science and the Creative Imagination in *Eureka*" (pp. 60–68), starting with studies of "The Island of the Fay" and "Mesmeric Revelation." In *Eureka* Brooks finds "Poe's last and best answer to the question which had so haunted him: How is it possible that atoms should dream and think, and what, ultimately, do these dreams and thoughts come to?" The argument is buttressed by many interesting references to contemporary scientific and philosophical thinkers, and the footnotes are as interesting to read as the essay itself, which adds still another dimension to the essays of St. Armand and Ketterer, all three of whom are in broad agreement, although they differ on a number of details.

Kevin M. McCarthy, in "Unity and Personal Identity in *Eureka*" (pp. 22–26), makes some connections between Locke's theories relating to the idea that the identity of a person is spiritual rather than material and Poe's stories in which more than one body seems to share the same soul: "Ligeia," "Morella," "Eleonora," "William Wilson," "The Fall of the House of Usher." He argues, not very clearly or convincingly, that *Eureka* is a compendium of these ideas which Poe borrowed from Locke, ending with the final union of Man with God.

Two essays focus on the rhetorical strategies in what many have seen as a chaotic and inconsistent work. John P. Hussey disagrees, offering a lucid argument for seeing it as following the formulae in Blair's *Lectures on Rhetoric and Belles-Lettres* ("Narrative Voice and Classical Rhetoric in Eureka," pp. 37–42). He reminds us that Poe's view of the artist requires him to create narrators who either succeed or fail to persuade their audience. The narrator of *Eureka* successfully adopts a series of masks (humble seeker of truth, satirist, master scholar, and man of transcendent vision) to accomplish the rhetorician's purpose of effectively swaying his audience through the use of a variety of appropriate masks or poses. In addition, after plausibly arguing that the structure of *Eureka* follows Blair's recommended pattern for an epideictic oration on the Sublime, Hussey concludes that Poe "must have referred to Blair (or some other expositor of the rhetorical tradition)" while composing *Eureka.* This is a helpful piece of rhetorical analysis for dealing with the vexed question of the shifting tones and masks that Poe adopts in the work.

Julia W. Mazow also focuses on the narrator, but she is more concerned with the correspondence between the cyclical rhythms of the narrator's rhetorical progress and the cyclical aspect of the cosmology he describes. Using Wayne Booth's concept of the narrator-guide, she finds Poe's narrator "reliable," a dramatized spokesman for the implied author. "Exemplifying the ability to perceive and to understand truth without any external aids, the narrator contains within himself the audience necessary for survival," and he leads the reader through this process in the course of the essay ("The Undivided Consciousness of the Narrator in *Eureka*, pp. 55–59).

William Drake, in "The Logic of Survival: *Eureka* in Relation to Poe's Other Works," (pp. 15–22), takes a different approach, choosing to see the work primarily as a poem, naturally evolving out of some of the themes and concerns found in earlier poems, particularly "Al Aaraaf," "The Raven," and "Ulalume." The plight of the "passionate idealist in the hostile real world" is the subject of these poems. The conflicts in life that Poe earlier perceived and was unable to reconcile are resolved, Drake says, in *Eureka*, where the use of pure logic instead of empirical science treated an ideal and perfect system, based on an intuitive glimpse of a unifying vision of life. The argument is acceptable as far as it goes, but is wordy and prolix, does not take into account the intellectual backgrounds and milieu, and makes very little reference to current scholarship. It also depends rather heavily on some questionable readings of too few poems, and makes no mention of the important late colloquies as steps in Poe's intellectual development.

In "Poe's *Eureka*: The Triumph of the Word" (pp. 42–46), Dawson Gaillard ruminates in a muddled way on the connections between the revelation of the Word of God in language and Poe's use of language as a vehicle of revelation of Divine Creation in *Eureka*. He is in fundamental agreement with St. Armand, Ketterer, and others that Poe moved away from the scientific, rational, and logical toward the intuitive mode of thinking and expression.

Finally, Perry F. Hoberg reveals the shortcomings of anthropological and Jungian criticism in an interesting but somewhat self-defeating essay ("Poe: Trickster-Cosmologist," pp. 30–37). He is interested in defining Poe's social and psychological roles as revealed in *Eureka* by viewing him in the satiric opening section as a "shaman-trickster" of neolithic tradition and in the remainder as a "cosmological speculator," using the principle of negation as a force for metamorphosis. The downward journeys of Poe's narrators into darkness and the abyss reenact a process of reconstruction and transcendent renewal, a pattern Poe also describes in *Eureka*. This is an idea already developed in different terms by Richard Wilbur, Harry Levin, and others, as Hoberg points out. What he adds is an overlay of analogues from Mircea Eliade, Jung, Kabbalism, Hinduism, and Dante, which obscure and distract rather than clarify.

Roland W. Nelson's dissertation, "The Definitive Edition of Edgar Allan Poe's *Eureka: A Prose Poem*" (*DAI* 35:4445A Bowling Green), is a "critical reconstruction," using the 1848 Putnam first edition as copy-text and corrections made by Poe in four copies of that edition: the one he presented to Mary Osborne, one he presented to Sarah Helen Whitman, the "Nelson-Mabbott" copy, and the "Hurst-Wakeman" copy. It has a textual introduction, a general introduction, and full textual apparatus and notes.

State University of New York at Albany

4. Melville

Hershel Parker

My first consolation from a new volume of *ALS* comes from those passages which prove that fellow contributors have been suffering the same torments I have as they confront a scholarship and criticism without minimum yearly requirements for originality and good sense. James H. Justus (author of Chapter 15) seems to have bled through the writing on Melville when he appeals for "a criticism of larger perspectives and what Maurice Beebe calls 'hard-core scholarship'" (*ALS 1973*, p. 258). The grandest attempt at hard-core scholarship, the CEAA, was weakened, as Justus says, because "textual technocrats" ensnared their authors by "pious and rigid orthodoxies"; and he might have added that some of the most touted CEAA work has proved error-ridden. Now the CEAA is dead, but one legacy may redeem the whole enterprise—the accumulated evidence that it is folly to attempt to write criticism on a literary work without knowing all that can be learned (not merely all that others have written) about how it came to be composed and published. Yet most writers on Melville, judging from 1975, still assume there is a wall (steel-reinforced concrete, not pasteboard) between scholarship and criticism. Melville critics go their innocent ways, the best of them fascinated by the process of reading a book but unconcerned with the process by which it reached the form they hold in hand. Lesser critics merely base their studies on earlier criticism rather than freshly confronting the literary works. Scholarship is different, we pretend—sometimes dull but always substantial. Not so: this year several "scholars" have found a fine new way of writing biography—by running a topic through the indexes to the *Log*, the *Letters*, and perhaps another source or two, then stringing quotations together into a brand new survey of "Melville and Something" or "Melville and Somebody," thereby producing a publishable product without the nuisance of original research. Even editors have begun to "edit" Melville not from manuscript or from original editions but from modern scholarly editions!

We *can* have a drastic reform. Biographical and textual evidence is available as never before, and models exist for gathering further evidence. Especially among the phenomenological and reader-response crowds, criticism is undergoing the most intelligent ferment in many years. Wonder of wonders, a few scholar-critics are beginning to use biographical and textual evidence in critical arguments. The time is ripe for a New Scholarship, one encompassing the best of scholarly and critical approaches. Only when the voice of the true scholar-critic is heard in the land can a writer of the Melville chapter approach the task with gusto and conclude it with the gratification of having learned richly.

i. Textual Studies

New letters rarely turn up, but Hennig Cohen in "Melville to Mrs. Gifford, 1888" (*CollL* 2:229) prints one Melville wrote to his wife's cousin, Ellen Marrett Gifford, on November 6, 1888: "My Dear Mrs Gifford: / By mail I send you a small volume, some portions of which, I hope, may prove more or less interesting to you.—Lizzie tells me she is about writing you, so I leave her to tell you whatever news there may be. / Your Friend / H. Melville." The volume was the privately printed *John Marr and Other Sailors*. Richard S. Moore thinks Melville reviewed *Southey's Commonplace Book* in the *Literary World* for August 4, 1849, but his various arguments are all so dubious that "A New Review by Melville" (*AL* 47:265–70) ought to have been followed by a question mark, if printed at all. Now, with *American Literature* tacitly vouching for the attribution, we can expect sheep-like acceptance of it, just as all dubiety seems to have vanished about Melville's authorship of "The Death Craft," even though conclusive evidence has never been presented. In his remarkably comprehensive (and genuinely pioneering) "Problems and Accomplishments in the Editing of the Novel" (*SNNTS* 7:323–60) G. Thomas Tanselle makes scattered reference to Melville's texts. In the same special number James T. Cox, Margaret Putnam, and Marvin Williams include 20 entries on Melville in their "Textual Studies in the Novel: A Selected Checklist, 1950–74" (*SNNTS* 7:445–71). The list is narrowly defined (excluding editions of Melville) but useful, and the checklist as a whole is an admirable contribution to textual studies and to critical work based on textual investigations.

An oddity is a new "edition" of *Billy Budd, Sailor* (Indianapolis: Bobbs-Merrill) based not upon a fresh analysis and transcription of the manuscript but upon the Hayford-Sealts Genetic Text. The editor gleaning after the editors is Milton R. Stern, who reasonably suggests that Hayford and Sealts copy-edited rather more than necessary after they had established the text but who blunders badly in his inclusion of material Melville rejected from the manuscript. Hayford and Sealts probably made a tactical blunder themselves by not including the rejected material (most conspicuously, the so-called "Preface") somewhere in the notes to the paperback edition, for teachers have found it hard to stop talking about familiar passages, even though Melville had finally discarded them. The real interest of Stern's "edition" is his long introduction, discussed in section xiii. Marjorie Dew had privately corrected the Norton editors of *Moby-Dick*, but now T. Walter Herbert, Jr. (see section viii) points out that the echo of Job 4:13 makes it clear Hayford and Parker should not have emended "In thoughts of the visions of the night" (p. 349). (At this point and elsewhere the Norton text will be brought into agreement with the Northwestern-Newberry; there will be many *more* emendations, mainly because further study has shown that Melville's handwriting was often misread in the "Extracts," but the general policy will be slightly more conservative. A couple of spellings, for instance, ought never to have been emended—most conspicuously, "Heidelburgh." One major lesson of the CEAA is that 19th-century disregard for consistency in spelling and punctuation requires editors to be extremely wary about emending. Partly because of this increasing editorial conservatism but also because of a differently defined audience, the NN *Billy Budd* will be slightly more ragged than the 1962 Chicago edition.)

ii. Biographical Studies

"Biographical" is used loosely here except for Yannella's study. In "Herman Melville and Atlantic Relations" (*History Today* 25:663–70) Charlotte Lindgren cursorily reviews some of Melville's opinions about England. Donald Kay hotly pursued page references in the index to the *Log* and a few other books before publishing "Herman

Melville's Literary Relationship with Evert Duyckinck (*CLAJ* 18:393–403)—a pathetic, demeaning essay. Donald J. Yannella's "'Seeing the Elephant' in *Mardi*" (*Artful Thunder*, pp. 105–17) may strain in suggesting that the elephant canoes of *Mardi* allude to a contemporary expression, but the essay shows that a genuine researcher can still find much valuable information about Melville's literary relationship with Evert Duyckinck. Rather than depending on published accounts, Yannella works from the original Duyckinck diaries and other sources. A typical discovery is that Leyda had mistaken "we" for "he" in a significant entry on October 23, 1847. The passage implicates Melville in Duyckinck's activities more than we had realized: "With Mathews and Melville, in the evening discussed a possible weekly newspaper which should combine the various projects of the kind which we had entertained for the last few years." Yannella is also the first to point out a Melvillean allusion in Mathews's shortlived *The Elephant*, successor to the shortlived *Yankee Doodle*. Daniel A. Wells, in "'Bartleby the Scrivener,' Poe, and the Duyckinck Circle" (*ESQ* 21:35–39), reduces "Bartleby" to a skirmish in Perry Miller's partly factitious war of words and wits in the era of Poe and Melville. (Won't *someone* give us a model demonstration that a Melville story allegorizes some real event in his life? Or is there no such story?) Wayne R. Kime, in "'The Bell-Tower': Melville's Reply to a Review" (*ESQ* 22:28–38), argues implausibly that this Poesque and Hawthornesque story is Melville's "covert fictional reply" to the Fitz-James O'Brien essay on his writings in *Putnam's Magazine*, February, 1853. For Edwin Haviland Miller's *Melville: A Biography*, see section iv.

iii. Reputation and Influence

Knowledge of Melville's critical reception has been clouded by erratic review-hunting and an imperfect sense of contemporary critical theory and practice. Effort has been duplicated because scholars have had no ready way of knowing whether or not reviews they came across were already known. Now the Melville Society has published a 100-page booklet by Steven Mailloux and Hershel Parker, *Checklist of Melville Reviews*, distributed free to members of the Melville Society and purchasable by nonmembers from Donald Yannella of Glassboro State College, Glassboro, N.J. 08028. The chronological *Checklist* identifies, barring oversights, "every review listed in every published study of Melville's contemporary reception, every new review Parker has found, and various items supplied privately by recent harvesters." Part guide and part challenge, as the foreword says, the *Checklist* is "offered to review-hunter and review-analyst alike." With a little pluck and luck, users will rapidly supplement it.

Meanwhile, scouting without a reliable checklist, Burton R. Pollin rounded up a double handful of "Additional Unrecorded Reviews of Melville's Books" (*JAmS* 9:55–68) and also published in the Melville Society newsletter "An Unnoticed Contemporary Review of *Moby-Dick*" (*Extracts* 22:3–4). Nelson Smith found "Eight British Reviews and Notices of Melville, 1846–1891" (*Extracts* 23:6–7). (These Pollin and Smith discoveries are included in the *Checklist.*) Stanton Garner had sent the NN editors a number of significant Melville items from the New York *Times* in the 1890s and 1900s, but now George Monteiro lays out the whole episode in "'Far and Away the Most Original Genius That America Has Produced': Notations on the New York *Times* and Melville's Literary Reputation at the Turn of the Century" (*RALS* 5:69–80). Monteiro also reminds us that Chapter 61 of *Moby-Dick* was reprinted in Lippincott's *Half-Hours with the Best American Authors*; see "A Half Hour with Melville, 1887" (*PBSA* 69:406–07). In "The Buried Book: *Moby-Dick* a Century Ago" (*SNNTS* 7:552–62) Edward Stone adduces parallels designed to show that William M. Davis secretly derived certain passages from Melville in *Nimrod of the Sea*, trusting that no reader would recognize his source. The parallels strike me as accidental similarities. Perhaps *Moby-Dick* was more buried than Stone supposes—so buried that Davis could remain ignorant of its existence. References to Melville occur in articles on Hart Crane and Richard Brautigan, Gregory R. Zeck's "The Logic of Metaphor: 'At Melville's Tomb'" (*TSLL* 17:673–86) and David L. Vanderwerken's "*Trout Fishing in America* and the American Tradition" (*Critique* 16[1974]: 32–40). In "The Variations on a Masked Leader: A Study on the Literary Relationship of Ralph Ellison and Herman Melville" (*SAB* 40:15–23), Stuart E. Omans redeems a hackneyed topic by his subtle attentiveness. Even if you think you know all about Ellison's debt to Melville in *Invisible Man*, read this little essay and learn more.

A major document in Melville's European reputation appeared last year in the "Wege der Forschung" series, *Herman Melville*

(Darmstadt: Wissenschaftliche Buchgesellschaft, 1974), compiled by Paul Gerhard Buchloh and Hartmut Krüger. The book contains a very well-informed introductory essay (in German) on the state of scholarship and criticism on Melville, especially on *Moby-Dick*, and a 17-page bibliography. Some 470 pages are devoted to essays on Melville, all but one in English; *Moby-Dick* comprises over 300 of these pages, the rest being restricted to "Bartleby," "Benito Cereno," and *Billy Budd.* Some selections are outdated and others seem eccentric (as anyone else's choices always do), but this is a useful compendium of essays on *Moby-Dick*, nicely supplementing (rarely repeating) *"Moby-Dick" as Doubloon* and other collections. However, the title promises more than it gives, and there is a curious discrepancy between the editors' alertness to modern American scholarship and their neglect of the bulk of Melville's achievement. A useful book, even though mislabeled.

iv. Melville and Hawthorne

Advertised on the dust jacket as "the first new biography of America's great storyteller in twenty-five years," Edwin Haviland Miller's *Melville: A Biography* (New York: George Braziller) is hardly a biography and certainly not "a major achievement." The biographical materials are old (from researches by Anderson, Davis, Gilman, Hayford, Leyda, and others) and often recklessly used, while much research (including Hayford's dissertation on Hawthorne and Melville) is ignored altogether. Miller's psychocritical approach drearily echoes Weaver, Mumford, Murray, and Arvin, although the particular stress on Melville's brother Gansevoort derives from Howard. The book begins with the often-told story of the day Hawthorne and Melville met, then slides into a biographical-critical account in which everything before the meeting is prelude and everything following Hawthorne's departure from Lenox is aftermath. The treatment of Melville and Hawthorne is so lurid that the book ought to have been called *Herman Melville: His Masquerade; Or, Cruising on Sea and Land.* Miller fabricates, as it were, a wonderful "Spanish costume" for the passionate Melville to wear the day he "decided to visit Hawthorne as a cavalier, a lover"; no doubt, Miller blithely explains, Melville had come across it by chance "somewhere in the attic, perhaps one of the garments worn by Thomas Melvill in his prosperous and romantic days abroad before he became an unsuccessful farmer at Pittsfield." What attic, pray? Sarah Morewood's? And we had thought it was Melville's religious views which made Mr. Morewood so uneasy! Totally ignoring Randall Stewart's detailed account of why Hawthorne left Lenox, Miller whispers the secret: Melville "must have introduced the subject of male friendship, not once but many times," so often that Hawthorne fled the Berkshires precipitously. (Stewart is not even listed in the bibliography, pp. 371–75.) A whole series of maniacal (the word is Miller's) "capers" and "orgies" are distorted from actual events. Some others are simply invented, as when Miller says Melville "found release" in 1856 with "what Duyckinck termed 'an orgie of indecency and blasphemy.'" Duyckinck did no such terming, for Melville was involved in no such orgy, although he did *tell* of an orgiastic female prayer meeting in the prison at Sing Sing. So the book goes, grotesque distortion upon grotesque distortion, almost equally contemptuous of the facts of Melville's life and of his works, and the worst is that distortions and errors are not always obvious: people are going to be misled. Lamenting that "no psychological critic of Melville has yet combined wide, accurate knowledge of Melville's life with perceptive analyses of his books," I once concluded (*MLQ* 33:54–66) that there "is simply nothing on Melville comparable in accuracy and perception to a book on one of his contemporaries, Edwin H. Miller's *Walt Whitman's Poetry: A Psychological Journey*." There still isn't.

Sidney Moss, who has done such good basic research on Poe's literary milieu, now writes on "Hawthorne and Melville: An Inquiry into Their Art and the Mystery of Their Friendship," in *Literary Monographs*, Vol. 7, ed. Eric Rothstein and Joseph Anthony Wittreich, Jr. (Madison: Univ. of Wisc. Press), pp. 45–84. Here Moss is on ground already trodden mushy, and he adds nothing to factual knowledge. He is unusually sensitive to the temperamental and moral differences between the two writers, although he probably exaggerates Hawthorne's response to Melville (greater familiarity with the Hawthorne notebooks would have helped him get perspective), uncritically accepts the notion that Melville "rewrote" *Moby-Dick* after it was nearly finished, and is somewhat shaky on other factual matters.

John A. Phillips's undocumented "Melville Meets Hawthorne: How a Champagne Picnic on Monument Mountain Led to a Profound Revision of *Moby Dick*—and Disenchantment" (*AH* 27:16–21, 87–90) merely recapitulates earlier accounts. His chic audience will not be perturbed by the caption to the illustration on p. 20: "Melville's wife, Elizabeth, by Ezra Ames, about 1820." (The portrait is of Melville's mother.) I thought about ignoring this popularization, but it's not any worse than what Miller does with the researches of Mansfield and others. Is there *nothing* new to be found about that Berkshire outing, gang? Marvin Fisher's "Portrait of the Artist in America: 'Hawthorne and His Mosses'" (*SoR* 11:156–66) adds little to previous studies.

v. Melville's Racial Attitudes

Several articles and a section of a book deal with Melville's racial attitudes. The most startling is Carolyn L. Karcher's "Melville's 'The 'Gees': A Forgotten Satire on Scientific Racism" (*AQ* 27:421–42). Melville's little sketch, as Karcher reads it, is a formidable attack on the pseudo-science of ethnology, which was used in the 1850s to justify Negro slavery in the United States. Karcher's lengthy punmongering sections are much less interesting than what she reminds us about ethnology, and at last her often eloquent paper testifies most strongly to our wistful desire to make Melville's racial views just as enlightened (not more enlightened) than our own. I'd like to believe she's right: "The 'Gees" would certainly be more interesting. But Edward Stone has the more balanced historical perspective toward Melville's racial attitudes. In "The Whiteness of *The Whale*" (*CLAJ* 18:348–63), Stone argues that *Moby-Dick* reveals many "gradations of racism": "A democrat both in lower and upper case, a lover of mankind of whatever color,—Herman Melville was all of these, and a racist as well. In that inconsistency more than in any other way does he come into view in the telescope of time as the thinking, feeling citizen of his day." Edward Margolies in "Melville and Blacks" (*CLAJ* 18:364–73) argues similarly that "in all probability" Melville was, "in his American fashion, unsure about what he really did feel" toward Negroes; Stone's piece is the solider of the two.

Jack Matlack's "Attica and Melville's 'Benito Cereno'" (*ATQ* 26:18–23) is a thoughtful, responsible attempt to understand the "major social tragedy" of the 1971 Attica Prison uprising and suppression in the light of "a literary text which tells a remarkably similar story and raises many of the same issues." Here is an attempt at "relevance" which does not minimize the work of art. Glenn C. Altschuler's "Whose Foot on Whose Throat? A Re-examination of Melville's *Benito Cereno*" (*CLAJ* 18:383–92) adds nothing to the best earlier criticism, most of which goes uncited. In "The Politics of Race in 'Benito Cereno'" (*AL* 46:556–66) Howard Welsh implausibly argues that Don Benito is a portrayal of a "slaveholding planter in the Southern part of the United States." Paul David Johnson's "American Innocence and Guilt: Black-White Destiny in 'Benito Cereno'" (*Phylon* 36:426–34) retraces familiar ground, then concludes that when "Delano asks Don Benito what has cast such a shadow upon him and he replies, 'The Negro,' the black transcends the symbol of evil to become a symbol of the shame and the guilt which Benito Cereno must carry within him." In *Ignoble Savage: American Literary Racism, 1790–1890* (Westport, Conn.: Greenwood) Louise K. Barnett's comments run to the overobvious (Melville sometimes links American Indians, Polynesians, and Negroes "as common victims of white oppression and exploitation"). What she says on *The Confidence-Man* is reductive and plodding, warmed-over Pearce; because the Indian-hater tale was a real American genre, Melville's use of it must be within the limits of that genre. All this year's stewing about racial attitudes broke very little new ground, despite Stone's cool good sense and Karcher's curiously appealing intermixture of solid information and flimsy wordplaying.

vi. General

Melville's Use of Classical Mythology (Amsterdam: Rodopi N.V.) by Gerard M. Sweeney is a revision of a 1971 University of Wisconsin dissertation. Traces of amateurish stoginess survive, but every Melvillean will have to read Sweeney's demonstration that "most of the critics who refer to Melville's allusive use of classical mythic heroes are really not focusing on the heroes Melville had in mind." Correcting Richard Chase, in particular, Sweeney insists that it is "really impossible for a scholar to speak accurately of Prometheus in Melville's work without first identifying the source of the specific Prometheus, without describing *what* Prometheus is being cited." In order to show the "number of complementary mythic patterns" employed in creating Ahab, Sweeney focuses on the "specific sources that Melville is known to have read." Especially useful is the preliminary survey of Melville's "random knowledge of the ancient fables" before 1849, when he bought the 37-volume set of Harper's Classical Library. Perhaps the strongest chapter is "Ahab and the Renaissance Prometheus," on the ways in which Melville's knowledge of the Prometheus myth was indebted to Bacon and Burton, both of whom "interiorized the vulture of Prometheus," Bacon seeing it as Prometheus's deep thinking and Burton seeing it as his secret grief. Anticlimactic chapters chart Melville's dwindling interest in Prometheus.

Hershel Parker's "Evidences for 'Late Insertions' in Melville's Works" (*SNNTS* 7:407–24) examines various uses and abuses of physical and critical evidence; see sections vii and viii. Undeterred by Paul McCarthy (*RS* 38[1970]:214–29; *ALS 1971*, pp. 56–57) and James Polk (*UTQ* 41:277–92; *ALS 1972*, p. 43), and not bothering to cite either of them, Janis P. Stout published "The Encroaching Sodom: Melville's Urban Fiction" (*TSLL* 17:157–73). A thin treatment of a major subject is Allison Ensor's "The Downfall of Poor Richard: Benjamin Franklin as Seen by Hawthorne, Melville, and Mark Twain" (*MTJ* 17,iii:14–18).

Marjorie Dew's "Black-Hearted Melville: 'Geniality' Reconsidered" (*Artful Thunder*, pp. 177–94) is a tough reply to Merton M. Sealts, Jr.'s "Melville's 'Geniality'" (*ALS 1968*, p. 47). In prose and poetry, early works and later ones, Dew says, "Melville lacerates his persistently genial men"; Melville was not "willing to pay the price for geniality, and especially not for the spurious sort, as Merton M. Sealts concludes he *was*." Dew is right about Melville's scorn toward many of his 'genial' characters, but Sealts himself had said plainly enough that in *The Confidence-Man* geniality is "actually Melville's rhetorical stalking-horse for an exposure of the pretentions of humanitarianism and religion." I wish Dew had cast this as a genial supplement rather than a retort, but over "a fat black bottle or two" of "Mountain-Dew" the true Melvillean "genial Friendship" may yet prevail.

vii. Typee, Omoo, Mardi, and *Redburn*

One of the best critics writing on Melville today is Warwick Wadlington, whose essay on *Moby-Dick* (*ELH* 39:309–31) won the

Samuel Willis Medal for the best Melville criticism of 1972; now he has reprinted that essay and added other chapters on Melville in *The Confidence Game*, pp. 37–178. Wadlington is a disciple of Kenneth Burke, out "to catch literature in the act, as it words itself out," employing "a processual critical method, one alert to drives and counter-resistances, the moment-by-moment activity that betrays the processual force as contrails do an aircraft at high altitude." Rightly he insists that "criticism in practice has tended too much to look at the fixed design of the artistic contrails, or recently, against Formalism and New Criticism, insisted on how that breathless coherence fades under scrutiny. In both cases, it has typically ignored the moving craft itself and the wonder that it moves at all, and continues to do so despite fixity or fading." Wadlington often lives up to this idealistic sense of criticism, but despite himself he is a product of the New Critical generation and does not act as if a finer criticism than his own might sometimes catch literature also in prepublication movement—that what scholarship can bring to bear on the creation of a work often has the most profound critical implications. Always cautioning that some of his conclusions ought to be modified by awareness of the process of composition, I recommend Wadlington's treatment of *Typee* and *Omoo* as the year's most sensitive commentary, charmingly, wittily alert to narrative postures and posturings.

In that non-Temperance Heaven where he and Hawthorne are striking glasses and heads together when they are not trying on Spanish costumes in the tiring room, Melville may laugh most uproariously at the sobersided studies of *Typee* and *Omoo* which threaten to overwhelm us. David Williams's "Peeping Tommo: *Typee* as Satire" (*CRevAS* 6:36–49) seeks "to re-examine the finished consistency of *Typee*'s art, to redefine in generic terms the distance between Melville and his narrator, and to identify the unrecognized objects and functions of satire in Melville's 'autobiographical' work." Williams so relentlessly moralizes against the selfish and egocentric Tommo that one cries out, "It's tongue-in-cheek, man, it's *funny*!" High seriousness continues in Thomas P. Joswick's "*Typee*: The Quest for Origin" (*Criticism* 17:335–54), which draws upon Lévi-Strauss to argue that "Tommo fails to find a basis for either the communal harmony he desires or the art which would become a 'new sacrament' in the community." The implications are fancy indeed, as when Tommo's sore leg "manages to mediate the antithesis of autochthony and genealogy, of the severance of familial ties and their persistence, of the denial of history and its ineluctable destiny, precisely by functioning as an arbitrary middle ground between nature and culture." Aw, shucks. In a slighter essay, "The Forbidden Fruit of *Typee*" (*MLS* 5:31–34), Rita K. Gollin says that Tommo's quest is complex: from the start, he "not only wants sensual pleasures; he perversely desires to encounter horrors"; the book's unifying structural pattern is "the perverse desire for what is forbidden." Robert E. Abrams takes on not one but two formidable books in "*Typee* and *Omoo*: Herman Melville and the Ungraspable Phantom of Identity" (*ArQ* 31:33–50). From the standpoint of artistic development, Abrams says, the importance of these two books is that they record Melville's "growing awareness of the fundamental elasticity and mutability of his so-called 'identity.'"

All of these writers operate with near-total disregard of biograpical and textual evidence, even when their topics cry out for it, as in Williams's championing of the expurgated American "Revised Edition" as Melville's artful if belated aesthetic impulse. The way Williams puts it is demonstrably false, but the topic is worth exploring more than Parker does in a footnote to his "Late Insertions" article (*SNNTS* 7:407–24): "Melville might have been somewhat reconciled to the expurgation because some of the omitted material had not formed part of his original plan. He had at least some salving basis for rationalization if he could tell himself that the whole process of expurgation was moving the book back toward the simpler story he had first written, before he began expanding it with sourcebooks." Parker's discussion deals mainly with Leon Howard's belief that John Murray had insisted that Melville make additions and changes in the manuscript of *Typee* so as to make it more documentary. Laying out the evidence chronologically, Parker concludes that probably "Melville's last-minute cobbling was not inspired by his publisher but by his own desire to eke out his brief impressions from his four weeks among the Typeeans."

Defining "grotesque" loosely, Richard M. Cook in "The Grotesque and Melville's *Mardi*" (*ESQ* 21:103–10) looks for instances where Melville "began to exploit in a comprehensive and relatively uninhibited manner the outrageous, impossible incongruities traditionally associated with grotesque art." According to the dust jacket, *That Lonely Game: Melville, "Mardi," and the Almanac* by

Maxine Moore (Columbia: Univ. of Mo. Press) explores Melville's "knowledge of astronomy, nautical navigation, astrology, and game theories" in order to unravel for the first time the puzzle he "designed to dupe his elitist British readers." In a quaint publishing gesture, a foreword by Hennig Cohen says, politely, that he doesn't believe a word of it. The lonely game is Moore's, not Melville's, but the illustrations are gorgeous—the greater trumps of the tarot, the dial of Ahaz, the constellation Argo Navis! What a handsome nonbook!

In "Opposites Meet: Melville, Hemingway, and Heroes" (*KanQ* 7:40–54) Paul McCarthy suggests some points of resemblance between *Redburn* and the Nick Adams stories: "The most significant ones lie in three vital areas of literary study: themes, techniques, and structure." In "Melville's *Redburn* and Emerson's 'General Education of the Eye' " (*ESQ* 21:40–45), Victor J. Vitanza holds that critics have neglected an important structural device, "a recurring eye motif," used to "accentuate and support the journey-maturation theme."

viii. Moby-Dick

A special issue on *Moby-Dick* was edited by Bernard Oldsey for *College Literature*, a new journal which asks the question, "*How can we directly use the special insights and information of bona fide experts in the actual teaching of classes?*" Satanic Melvillean implications of "bona fide" notwithstanding, Oldsey rounded up a respectable group of articles; but the only classic piece of criticism was Hayford's belatedly published essay on "Loomings" in *Artful Thunder*.

A by-product of writing "Historical Notes" and this chapter in *ALS*, Hershel Parker's "Being Professional in Working on *Moby-Dick*" (*CollL* 2:192–97) tries to describe the minimal requirements for writing about the book responsibly. Claude Hunsberger's "Bibliographical Compendium: Vectors in Recent *Moby-Dick* Criticism" (*CollL* 2:230–45) attempts to bring Nathalia Wright's chapter in the revised (1971) edition of *Eight American Authors* up to date.

Little progress was made in understanding the composition of the book. Several critics repeated the "two *Moby-Dicks*" theory without the slightest suspicion that it is merely a theory. On this topic Jerome M. Loving's "Melville's Pardonable Sin" (*NEQ* 47[1974]:

262–78) needs to be consulted; it seems to have appeared too late for James Barbour to use it in two articles, both elaborations of the Howard-Vincent-Stewart speculations about the composition of *Moby-Dick*. In "The *Town-Ho*'s Story: Melville's Original Whale" (*ESQ* 21:111–15) "Whale" should probably be italicized, since Barbour is arguing that chapter 54 "is a condensed version of the first whaling narrative," a huddled-up conclusion that draws together otherwise dangling ends of narrative lines. Guesswork, based upon more or less genuine narrative discontinuities. (An unintended corrective is Hayford's essay, discussed below, which demonstrates ways the first chapter foreshadows later thematic developments.) Barbour's "The Composition of *Moby-Dick*" (*AL* 47:343–60) proposes three compositional stages, not just two. He uncritically accepts much earlier theorizing and quotes without analysis the crucial letter Melville wrote Dana on May 1, 1850, which shows that from the outset the problem was getting poetry out of blubber—hardly the greatest aesthetic challenge of a supposedly straightforward whaling story. He repeatedly claims that Evert Duyckinck read the manuscript during the Berkshire vacation in August, 1850. When, given the social schedule of those days? A major weakness is Barbour's handling of more or less datable evidence, for he locks himself into the "logical" but not necessarily true position that chapters which must have been written after a given date probably were written almost *immediately* after that date; and he slights the possibility that sometimes parts of these chapters could have been added after other parts. Regularly talking about Melville's "rewriting" and "revising," Barbour almost forgets the fact that a great deal of the book was initially composed during 1851. As Hershel Parker shows in "Evidences for 'Late Insertions' in Melville's Works" (*SNNTS* 7:407–24), when Melville had time for his manuscript after April 1851, he was mainly composing the ending, although he also inserted chapters or parts of chapters into other parts of the second half of the book. Barbour has some good observations but he badly remuddies the waters that Loving tried to purify last year.

The year's only solid contribution to scholarship was Wilson L. Heflin's "Sources from the Whale-Fishery and 'The Town-Ho's Story' " (*Artful Thunder*, pp. 163–76), which presents some fascinating contemporary analogues to the events on the *Town-Ho*, in each case establishing a high degree of likelihood for Melville's acquaintance with the real occurrences.

In "*Moby-Dick*: Epic Romance" (*CollL* 2:155–70) Edward Rosenberry offers a sensitive, sophisticated excerpt from his forthcoming *Melville: An Author Guide*. As he explains, the purpose of the book "is to introduce Melville and his work to the common reader, and in keeping with this aim the present essay attempts to describe *Moby-Dick* comprehensively and systematically rather than to present a specific or original critical case." Explicitly pedagogical, Charles B. Hands's "The Comic Entrance to *Moby-Dick*" (*CollL* 2:182–91) suggests that "we get our [undergraduate] students to approach the novel through its humor, letting the humor carry them onward to their first perception of theme and their initial stirring of interest." James W. Nechas's "Ambiguity of Word and Whale: The Negative Affix in *Moby-Dick*" (*CollL* 2:198–225) employs a rather simple variety of linguistic and reader response criticism to argue that the "vocabulary of negative affix constructions" is "a paradigm of the things that the Whale is not; it is a catalogue of Ishmael's unsuccessful attempts to solve its riddle"; the "negative affix words" force the reader to undergo an experience with the "Unknown" which parallels Ishmael's own "voyage in search of the Whale."

Two articles deal with major structural elements, the so-called "gams" and whale killings. (Is it hopeless to keep pointing out that there was only *one* true gam on the last voyage of the *Pequod*?) Edward Stone's "The Functions of the Gams in *Moby-Dick*" (*CollL* 2:171–81) sensibly shows that aside from creating foreshadowing and suspense the meetings "create and sustain" the illusion of a real-life voyage without Melville's having to put the *Pequod* into port. Stone also stresses the value of the meetings in creating comic relief. (Stone is perplexed that "no news of Moby Dick reaches Ahab" from the gam with the *Town-Ho*. That is a misreading: Ahab learns well enough that Moby Dick killed Radney, but does not learn the "secret part," that the intervention of the whale kept Steelkilt from becoming Radney's murderer.) Barbara Meldrum's "Structure in *Moby-Dick*: The Whale Killings and Ishmael's Quest" (*ESQ* 21: 162–68) explores the relation of the whale killings to the ship meetings and the cetological chapters. The series, she concludes, "contrasts Ishmael's evolving concept of the whale with Ahab's avowed purpose." Looking at a single encounter at sea, Joan P. Samson in "The Ambiguity of Ambergris in *Moby-Dick*" (*CollL* 2:226–28) briefly argues that the ambiguity referred to (sweetness inside foulness) "is a type of the spiritual ambiguity of good and evil and an emblem of the deceptive quality of appearances."

T. Walter Herbert, Jr.'s "Homosexuality and Spiritual Aspiration in *Moby-Dick*" (CRevAS 6:50–58), which does not belabor its catastrophic Shakespearean and Melvillean pun, holds that Ishmael's friendship with Queequeg is a repudiation of the orthodox Calvinist attitude toward homosexuality. I would have thought Melville's comedy was less doctrinal, and I can't figure out just what Herbert means by homosexuality (does he mean men liking each other?). Maybe someone should begin assembling the dozens of accounts of enforced roomsharing and bedsharing by 19th-century travelers, including Emerson and much later the young Garland. Sanford E. Marovitz's "Old Man Ahab" (*Artful Thunder*, pp. 139–61) adopts "a confessedly limited perspective" for examining Ahab as "a mere man resenting and defying his morality." In this view Ahab's character and the book as a whole are "an exploration into the limitations of mortality through the extensive implications of the acceptance or denial and defiance of them." In "Ishmael's Voyage: The Cycle of Everyman's Faith" (*ArQ* 31:57–68) James E. Mulqueen simplistically says the "theme of *Moby-Dick* is the difficulty of achieving and maintaining religious faith, specifically faith in the Christian doctrine of death and resurrection." Robert F. Bergstrom in "The Topmost Grief: Rejection of Ahab's Faith" (*EIL* 2:171–80) treats Mapple as a false prophet and Ahab as representing "everyone"; the "characteristic which Mapple and Ahab share and which Melville repudiates in *Moby-Dick* is moral or religious certainty." Bergstrom reduces the theme to "the failure of religion in man's life." In "Melville's Apocalypse: American Millennialism and *Moby-Dick*" (*ESQ* 21:154–61) Michael T. Gilmore claims that "Melville's objective in *Moby-Dick* is nothing less than to rewrite the covenant that God was presumed to have made with the American people as the heirs of the biblical Hebrews." In "The Whale and the Machine: An Approach to *Moby-Dick*" (*AL* 47:197–211) Stephen C. Ausband takes on an old topic, mechanistic imagery, which has been well treated by Leo Marx and others. Richard D. Rust's "'Dollars damn me': Money in *Moby-Dick*," *Geschichte und Gesellschaft in der ameri-*

kanischen Literatur, ed. Karl Schubert and Ursula Müller-Richter (Heidelberg: Quelle and Meyer), glances at attitudes toward money manifested by Melville and the characters in his whaling book. Presumably this essay was submitted before Scott Donaldson's similar note appeared (*NEQ* 46:279–83).[1]

"Romantic Paradoxes of *Moby-Dick*" by Eugene L. Stelzig (*ATQ* 26:41–44) attempts to show that the book is "carefully organized according to a set of Romantic paradoxes and polarities," particularly "the opposition between reality and language, mind and matter, joy and truth," the "self-destructive nature of Ahab's quest," and "the polarity of isolation/singularity and connection/communion." Edward Stone's "Ahab Gets Girl, or Herman Melville Goes to the Movies" (*LFQ* 3:172–81), an amusing reminder "of the chasm between intellectual and popular art," is concerned mainly with the two John Barrymore vehicles, 1925's silent *Sea Beast* and 1930's talky *Moby Dick*. Especially interesting are the quotations from S. R. Buchman's apologia for the first of these versions, as printed in a 1925 reissue of *Moby-Dick* by Grosset and Dunlap.

Harrison Hayford's early reputation as a Melvillean was based not only on substantial biographical and critical publications but also on his generous private sharing of his documentary discoveries and his remarkably influential talk on Melville's prisoner imagery at Pittsfield in 1951, a talk which contained the core of other talks at various universities over the next decades. In recent years, while Hayford's reputation has been consolidated as an editor, writers have paid tribute one way or another to his study of this image cluster, but now it is good to have in print part of "the long-in-process *Melville's Prisoners*," as transcribed from the tape of a talk given at Kent State University in 1969. This section is "'Loomings': Yarns and Figures in the Fabric" (*Artful Thunder*, pp. 119–37). My own complicity with some of Hayford's other long-in-process enterprises must not deter me from calling this a classic piece of criticism. I had

1. I had intended to mention Donaldson's note this year anyhow, to clarify what I said earlier (*ALS 1973*, p. 76). Donaldson had written: "The captain [Gardiner] hopes to find his young son, lost with the boat, but Stubb attributes the search to other motives." From this reversal of chronology I concluded that Donaldson was claiming Stubb knew the son was aboard the whaleboat *before* he offered to wager that someone in the boat had worn off the captain's best coat or his watch. Donaldson did not say this in so many words, but he is gracious enough to understand why I thought he did.

all but forgotten that image study could be a breathtaking act of apprehension, not a mechanical means to publication.

ix. Pierre

No one else should bother to hunt up Richard F. Fleck's "Stone Imagery in Melville's *Pierre*" (*RS* 42[1974]:127–30). R. Scott Kellner's "Sex, Toads, and Scorpions: A Study of the Psychological Themes in Melville's *Pierre*" (*ArQ* 31:5–20) is silly in its deductions about Melville's own fear and abhorrence of sex, but sensible about Pierre's sexual sublimation. Edwin H. Miller antics his way onto some of the same ambiguous terrain, announcing that "Pierre is paranoid and so is the book," but acknowledging that "in a crazy kind of way the book is a virtuoso performance." In *Confidence Game* Wadlington's scattered comments, such as "Melville in *Pierre* tried to be directly (and scornfully) profound," are undercut by his failure to recognize that there was no single pervading purpose that impelled the book. My "Why *Pierre* Went Wrong" (*SNNTS* 8[1976]: 7–23) needs to be mentioned early because it provides new documentary evidence that Melville began the book under one impulse and finished it under another. Learning more about the circumstances of composition should encourage critics like Wadlington to reread *Pierre*.

x. "Bartleby"

Hans Bergmann and I, among others, have been turning up evidence that sentimental accounts of the Dead Letter Office were something of a journalistic fad in the years just before Melville wrote "Bartleby." Now Bergmann has published a fascinating little note, " 'Bartleby' and *The Lawyer's Story*" (*AL* 47:432–36). On February 18, 1853, two New York papers, the *Tribune* and the *Times*, published anonymously the first chapter of *The Lawyer's Story* as an advertisement for the complete serialization in the *Sunday Dispatch* and book publication by H. Long and Brother. This is the first sentence: "In the summer of 1843, having an extraordinary quantity of deeds to copy, I engaged, temporarily, an extra copying clerk, who interested me considerably, in consequence of his modest, quiet, gentlemanly demeanor, and his intense application to his duties." What Bergmann goes on to make of his remarkable find is itself remarkable for judicious restraint, a model for how to get the best out of a probable source without overinflating its importance.

Warwick Wadlington (*Confidence Game*) may not demonstrate that Bartleby is one of the Divine Inert (a term from *Moby-Dick*) "whose inertia makes them easily mistakable for the simply unaspiring," but he eloquently traces the "disturbing impact" of the story, the "ethical frustration" which "retrospectively does not allow us to feel very superior, if superior at all, to our narrator." The pages on "Bartleby" are weakened, however, by Wadlington's strategy of using it as a bludgeon against *Pierre*. Pearl Chesler Solomon's *Dickens and Melville in Their Time* (New York: Columbia Univ. Press) is not the fine comparative study that has seemed necessary ever since Leonard Woolf complained about Dickens's malign influence on Melville's style. The Melville part—mainly discrete from the Dickens part—is a dreary, unoriginal, and inexact survey of career and summary of works. Solomon has the materials for a good article-length comparative study of *A Christmas Carol* and "Bartleby" in terms of the contemporary notions of the master-employee relationship, and some passages on this topic do gain a limited but genuine interest by linking the speech of Melville's lawyer to that of real-life employers. The level of scholarly and critical sophistication, however, is absymal. I find it astounding that dissertation committees and university presses will allow such patent evasions as her string of "Quoted in . . ." footnotes. Did it occur to no one to require a little original research?

Two essays examine motifs. Allen F. Stein's "The Motif of Voracity in 'Bartleby' " (*ESQ* 21:29–34) argues, with abundant examples, that "Melville is using physical hunger as a manifestation of the consuming need for personal aggrandizement." Sanford Pinsker in " 'Bartleby the Scrivener': Language as Wall" (*CollL* 2:17–27) says the narrator "discovers that language only makes the haunting Bartleby more perplexing and less definable"; the central motif is not voracity but walls, "extending from the Wall Street locale" through "a maze of physical walls which separate one man from another" and on to "those walls of language which make human understanding impossible."

Marvin Singleton, in "Melville's 'Bartleby': Over the Republic, a Ciceronian Shadow" (*CRevAS* 6:165–73), magisterially and implausibly magnifies the references to the lawyer's bust of Cicero into a theory that the story extensively parodies Ciceronian rhetoric and "echoes jurisprudential and philosophical elements of Cicero." Bartleby is "the shade of Cicero," exemplifying "the highest reach of ideal kin/friendship commitment within the aspiration of the stoic tradition." Other pieces are even slighter. John H. Randall, III, in "Bartleby *vs.* Wall Street: New York in the 1850s" (*BNYPL* 78: 138–44), briefly argues that the image of New York City in this story is "a starkly negative one, in which the city stands for a callously self-interested mercantile society in which any deviance from its norms, if at all insisted upon, leads to punishment by imprisonment and even death." Ted Billy's "Eros and Thanatos in 'Bartleby' " (*ArQ* 31:21–32) wearily argues that the narrator and Bartleby "are fictional projections of the eros and thanatos principles in Melville's divided self." Milton Kornfeld's "Bartleby and the Presentation of Self in Everyday Life" (*ArQ* 31:51–56) attempts to read the story in the light of sociologist Erving Goffman's "theory of social interaction based on impression management" in which performers in social situations play different roles according to the contexts; Bartleby is "*the* man to whom no role was to accrue." For an article on "Bartleby" by Daniel A. Wells, see section ii.

xi. Fiction 1854–57

See section ii for Wayne R. Kime's article about "The Bell-Tower" and section iii for Stuart Oman's article on "Benito Cereno." Most discussions of "Benito Cereno" and an essay on "The 'Gees" are treated in section v. A book, *The Method of Melville's Short Fiction*, by R. Bruce Bickley, Jr. (Durham, N.C.: Duke Univ. Press), unimaginatively brings to bear the dullest clichés of the New Criticism and ends up offering commonplaces with the air of producing insights. I don't see any reason to read any of it except the pages which elaborate what William L. Hedges had said about Melville's debts to the work of Washington Irving. In the short, sensible "Reflections: The Uses of Place: Darwin and Melville on the Galapagos" (*BioScience* 25:172–75) L. D. Gottlieb disregards two longer articles,

Bruce Franklin's (*CentR* 11[1967]:353–70) and Benjamin Lease's (*Person* 49[1968]:531–39); Charles Roberts Anderson, of course, is far too antedeluvian to be consulted by one of the "golden boys, the moderns." Charles N. Watson, Jr., has two notes. The first, "Premature Burial in *Arthur Gordon Pym* and *Israel Potter*" (*AL* 47:105–07), argues that Melville drew on Poe "for the essentials of the entombment episode." Somebody ought to seek out other Gothic analogues; narrow passageways, mattresses, jugs of water, bottles of wine, and cold roasts (in pre-Sterno days) sound to me like staple hideout fare. In "Melville's *Israel Potter*: Fathers and Sons" (*SNNTS* 7:563–68) Watson says that the "central psychological theme of the novel is the association of the authority of the father with the sovereignty of the state."

Warwick Wadlington (*Confidence Game*) has the only critical rather than sociological comments on "Benito Cereno." I boggle at some passages (when he refers to the narrator's "trivial goodheartedness" is he thinking of Amasa Delano?), but he is better on the narrative purpose of the deposition than anyone else has been, as in defining the effect of coming upon "the foursquare, formally punctilious language of the deposition" after "the elusive devices of prose style and point of view in the story's opening section." Wadlington argues that as we reread the deposition "the flat, postulatory language" with "its impersonal efficiency and neatness in detailing phenomena simultaneously fumbles at painful emotional reality and—systematically refusing to impute motives—gives an enormous sense of motivational implacability." Last year I concluded that the "classic essay on the deposition remains to be written," although John McElroy's discussion was useful (*EIL* 1:206–18; *ALS 1974*, p. 54); together McElroy and Wadlington may hasten that classic essay. David K. Jeffrey's "Unreliable Narration in Melville's 'Jimmy Rose'" (*ArQ* 31:69–72) condemns the narrator for his failure to help the title character. If this portrayal of crassness makes you miserable, you can heal yourself by reading "Jimmy Rose" again.

In "The Intelligence Offices of Hawthorne and Melville" (*ATQ* 26:44–47) Rita K. Gollin makes routine comparisons between "The Intelligence Office" and chapter 22 of *The Confidence-Man.* Dennis Taylor's "The Confidence Man from *The Pardoner's Tale* to *The Fall*" (*ArQ* 31:73–85) is a trivial survey with nothing of value to say on Melville. Of much interest is "*The Confidence-Man* and Satan's Disguises in *Paradise Lost*" (*NCF* 30:200–206), Thomas L. McHaney's use of a passage in Book III of the Milton epic as evidence that the deaf-mute is one disguise of the Confidence Man, the Devil. I am most charmed by the section on guardian angels, where McHaney makes some neat connections I failed to make in the Norton Critical Edition, despite my footnote on "Committee of Safety" in the last chapter. Wadlington's critical powers do not show to best advantage in his section on *The Confidence-Man.* He seems so wary of swallowing "a reductive critical bolus" (such as that mixed by Foster and sugar-coated by Shroeder and Parker) that he avoids engagement with the book (symptomatically, misquotations abound) as well as with the scholarship on it. The basic Foster interpretation, however much it requires qualification, is anything but reductive in its informed sense of Melville's satiric targets. Melville's book is not to be read out of space, out of time, and Wadlington becomes reductive as well as evasive. I wish he would try again.

xii. Poetry

Not a vintage year. Kenneth A. Requa superficially talks about "The Pilgrim's Problems: Melville's *Clarel*" (*BSUF* 16,ii:16–20). Perhaps Patricia Chaffee exaggerates the importance of "The Kedron in Melville's *Clarel*" (*CLAJ* 18:374–82), arguing that Melville "intends that the brook with its dry bed function as a dominant, unifying image of the arid spiritual wanderings he creates in the poem"; still, she works responsibly through the many Kedron allusions. In "Hawthorne's Zenobia and Melville's Urania" (*ATQ* 26:11–14) Allen F. Stein implausibly suggests a major influence upon "After the Pleasure Party." Agnes D. Cannon in "Melville's Concepts of the Poet and Poetry" (*ArQ* 31:315–39) attempts to deduce Melville's ideas upon her subject from his marginalia. Her definition of Melville's aesthetic stance is simplistic ("poetry does not depend upon meter but upon nobility of thought and beauty of language") but her article is valuable for the reproduction (albeit nonphotographic) of several examples of Melville's markings in books of or about poetry. Cannon tantalizes us, for while we remain ignorant of the marginalia, except for samples in the *Log* and a few other sources, Walker Cowen's 1965 Harvard dissertation, *Melville's Marginalia,* seems apt to remain in its unpublished 11-volume state. Cowen would perform a splendid service by distilling his study, this time using photographic reproductions of the marked passages. Meanwhile, any serious student of Melville's ideas about almost anything has to hassle the 11 volumes through interlibrary loan.

xiii. Billy Budd, Sailor

Two pieces are slight. Julian C. Rice in "Claggart and the Satanic Type" (*ATQ* 26:37–40) says that between *Moby-Dick* and *Billy Budd* "Melville must have modified his conception of evil, or at least markedly changed his conception of the Satanic type," since "Claggart's malignity expresses a new, grimmer picture of the whale hunt which accords with an old, less Romantic archetype of Satanic folly." Robert K. Wallace fails to show that there is any connection between the two parts of his title, "*Billy Budd* and the Haymarket Hangings" (*AL* 47:108–13), much less that the story reflects Melville's "imaginative response to the Haymarket affair." Also in the same periodical "Vere's Use of the 'Forms': Means and Ends in *Billy Budd*" by Christopher W. Sten (*AL* 47:37–51) rigorously defends Vere's behavior: "Rather than an autocratically held end in itself, every one of Vere's applications of the 'forms,' like each of his deviations from them, was a deliberately chosen means to the end of insuring the security of England and thence the salvation of 'the Old World.'" Sten does not avail himself of evidence about the development of Vere during successive stages of composition, and he neglects some important criticism, particularly Berthoff's defense of Vere on rather similar grounds in *The Example of Melville*. A great deal of the prefatory material and the appendices in Milton R. Stern's Bobbs-Merrill *Billy Budd* (see section i) merely summarizes the discoveries of Hayford and Sealts, but the introduction contains vigorous sections on "The Politics of Melville's Poetry" and "Melville's Politics and the Reader." Stern argues with considerable justice that the "essentially conservative nature of Melville's poetry generally has been ignored," and that the same conservatism or "classicism" is embodied in *Billy Budd*. I wish he had followed the clues of *Billy Budd* itself into a fruitful examination of the Burke-Paine polarity which Melville was brooding over during his last years.

xiv. Postscript

I have ignored dissertations and most foreign-language publications, but otherwise I have mentioned everything I know of except a couple of filler items in *ATQ*, some routine reviews, and most items in *Extracts*. It is impossible to review *Extracts* in this chapter, except in unusual circumstances, but everyone writing on Melville owes it to himself and everyone else to subscribe by sending five dollars for membership in the Melville Society to Donald Yannella, Department of English, Glassboro State College, Glassboro, N.J. 08028.

University of Southern California

5. Whitman and Dickinson

Marvin Fisher and Willis J. Buckingham[1]

Whitman studies continue to exhibit the expected range of tone, mood, and method—from cautious and careful textual scholarship, to highly conjectural interpretations of Whitman's motives and his meanings, to even farther out assertions that stretch his mysticism into mystery and magic. More dissertations on Whitman were completed in 1975 than in 1974, according to *DAI*, but it would be interesting to know whether fewer were actually begun in 1975. Of those recorded, 17 deal in whole or in part with Walt Whitman; twelve focus directly on his poetry, his philosophy, his language, his letters sent and received, and his relation to sectionalist controversy; four consider him in relation to his contemporaries or ours; and one examines the reception of Whitman in translation in German.

Much of the scholarship in Dickinson studies has sought to survey the poet's interior world, to map the contours of her consciousness. There seems to be a growing general conviction that Dickinson's poems in some sense explicate each other. Despite fine discussions of individual works, therefore, it appears that the major hope this year has been to find new reverberations among the many notes that her poems strike.

i. Whitman

***a.* Bibliography, Collections, Editing.** Several items by William White indicate his continuing industry in the area of Whitman bibliography and documents. He corrects his previous year's citation of the earliest publication of "Beat! Beat! Drums!," having found a version that appeared four days earlier. He also provides a detailed list of Whitman's revisions between the first and second versions ("'Beat!

1. Marvin Fisher has written the Whitman section and Willis Buckingham the Dickinson.

Beat! Drums!': The First Version," *WWR* 21:43–44). White also adds to his earlier account of Whitman's short-story publication the information that "The Death of Wind-Foot" appeared in at least two more periodicals than originally noted and that "A Child Ghost: A Story of the Last Loyalist" appeared at least once more than earlier indicated ("Whitman's Short Stories: More Addenda," *PBSA* 69:402–03).

White also reprints two previously unpublished letters, one to sculptor John Quincy Adams Ward regarding five sets of Whitman's books ("A New Whitman Letter to J. Q. A. Ward," *WWR* 21:131–32) and the other to John Aldington Symonds, informing him of the newest edition (1881) of *Leaves of Grass* and the English publishing house holding the copyright, Trubner and Co. ("Whitman to J. A. Symonds: Unpublished," *WWR* 21:168). Artem Lozynsky presents two documents pertaining to Whitman and Richard M. Bucke. Both the letter and the manuscript revision show that Whitman objected to Dr. Bucke's including *Man's Moral Nature* in his *Walt Whitman* as "an intrusion and superfluity" despite its "magnificent theories" ("Whitman and *Man's Moral Nature*," *WWR* 21:36–37). In another reprinted letter Lozynsky suggests some harsh feelings between Whitman and S. Weir Mitchell ("S. Weir Mitchell on Whitman: An Unpublished Letter," *AN&Q* 13:120–21). Dated December 4, 1911, the letter contains Mitchell's expression of "not altogether agreeable reflections . . . nor perfectly pleasant memories" of Whitman and a refusal to contribute to Charles N. Elliot's *Walt Whitman as Man, Poet and Friend* (1915).

Francis Murphy has assembled a new collection of Whitman's poetry and prose, *Walt Whitman: The Complete Poems* (Harmondsworth, Middlesex, England: Penguin). It is basically the 1891–92 edition, bolstered by five appendices, among them the excluded poems, early poems, the text of the first "Song of Myself," and four prefaces. Murphy also includes a useful set of historical and textual notes in this edition, which is well worth considering for teaching purposes.

***b.* Biography.** The most substantial contribution to Whitman biography is only incidentally about the poet. In fact there is more in Jerome M. Loving's well-edited volume of *Civil War Letters of George Washington Whitman* (Durham, N.C.: Duke Univ. Press) to interest students of the Civil War than students of American poetry. On the other hand, the admirably complete introduction, intelligent editing, and useful annotation and documentation make this one of the best sources of information on the Whitman family that exists—especially on the relationship of Louisa Van Velsor Whitman to her eight children, and their relationship to her as well as to each other. Loving's book adds up to more than the sum of his recently published articles on Walt Whitman's younger brother. George Washington Whitman had enlisted in the Union forces as a private shortly after the firing on Fort Sumter in 1861 and emerged in 1865 as a brevet lieutenant colonel, a veteran of many battles and of six months in Confederate prisons. There is no doubt that Walt Whitman's response to the War drew heavily upon his relationship to and concern for his brother. Readers interested in Whitman and the war will want to look at Matthew F. Ignoffo's *What the War Did to Whitman: A Brief Study of the Effects of the Civil War on the Mind of Walt Whitman* (New York: Vantage), and also at the items by Samuel Coale, Linck C. Johnson, and R. Scott Kellner which are subsequently discussed.

There is a bit more sensation than substance in the "Walt Whitman Annual Supplement: Women in the Life of Walt Whitman," ed. William White (*The Long Islander*, 29 May:16–17, 22). White presents two of the four articles; Gay Wilson Allen and C. Carroll Hollis the other two. In his first piece White reprints in entirety Anne Gilchrist's long, impassioned announcement of her love for the man she had not yet met, except through his poems. In his second White reprints a letter of indisputable affection and attachment from Mrs. Ellen ("Nelly") O'Connor, wife of William Douglas O'Connor, who authored *The Good Gray Poet* in 1866. Allen reprints a mysterious and rather daring letter signed "Ellen Eyre," and Hollis backs the supposition that Ellen Eyre might be Ellen Grey, an actress whom Whitman might have known as early as 1856 or 1857. Several photographs reinforce the idea of the women in Whitman's life: (1) Louisa Velsor Whitman, (2) Anne Gilchrist, (3) Nelly O'Connor, and (4) Mary Oakes Davis, his housekeeper from 1885–92.

A note by Artem Lozynsky, "Walt Whitman on Marriage" (*N&Q* 22:120–21), offers related information to conjure with but not quite strong enough to base a conclusion on. Citing the assumption of many that Whitman never married because he was homosexual, Lozynsky draws contrary evidence from an unpublished letter from Dr. Richard

M. Bucke to his wife on August 2, 1880. According to Bucke, Whitman had confided that "the chief reason he never married was that he had an instinct against forming ties that would bind him to anything—an instinct to freedom and absolute unconstraint."

In another note Lozynsky offers two letters that remind us of some unfortunate aspects of Whitman's mortality ("Whitman's Death Bed: Two Nurses' Reports" *AL* 47:270–73). Mrs. Elizabeth Leavitt Keller complains in one letter to Dr. Bucke about the appalling condition of her patient's bedroom and of his house in general. In the second letter Whitman's male nurse, Warren Fritzinger, writes to Dr. John Johnston detailing either the last or the next to the last night of Whitman's life.

***c.* Criticism: General.** Gay Wilson Allen has produced a thorough, more readable revision of a familiar critical-reference work—*The New Walt Whitman Handbook* (New York: New York Univ. Press). Although the changes wrought in this book are somewhat less dramatic than the changes in *Leaves of Grass* from first to last edition, Allen has enlarged every section, tried to incorporate the shifts in Whitman biography and criticism during the past 30 years, and inevitably revealed some changes in his outlook as well. Unlike the previous editions, the new one has illustrations, suggesting a range of iconographic resources from woodcut, daguerrotype, ink drawing, comic-book page, to a photograph supplied by the Russian Embassy; but these alone do not account for the quintupling in price in less than 15 years.

Albert Gelpi has promised more than he has delivered in the Whitman chapter of *The Tenth Muse* (pp. 153–216). He announces his intention to explore "the separation of American poetry from its British parent" and to distinguish those special "qualities of imagination, voice, form, and technique which could be called American." In the chapter on Whitman, however, he treats only "Song of Myself" in any detailed way and places heavy emphasis on Freudian concepts in approaching Whitman's art and life.

Stephen A. Black delivers more than he promises in *Whitman's Journeys into Chaos: A Psychoanalytic Study of the Poetic Process* (Princeton, N.J.: Princeton Univ. Press); but the problem is whether we want to buy what he offers. He is interested in the poems as revelatory of Whitman's psychological and emotional conflicts—a concern that is only partially redeemed by assurances that it helps us to understand the creative process of Walt Whitman. For Black the poems published between 1855 and 1865 are characterized by irresolution and conflict and gain coherence only when subjected to psychoanalytical examination. A book can be used, of course, to support a critic's psychoanalytical hunches, but unlike a patient it can never protest the analyst's line of argument, nor can it be invited to support or refute the analyst's assertions. Psychological criticism is usually a highly conjectural and deeply subjective mode of argument. Assertions inevitably attain degrees of uncertainty bound to challenge or offend critics less committed to such an approach. What is most troubling about Black's analysis is that if his assertions about Whitman's state of mind and about the poetry itself were true, they would threaten many teachers of American literature and discourage students of American poetry. Readers might be made more uncomfortable with Black's image of Whitman as person and much more uncertain about the value and meaning of the poetry or the nature of the creative process.

The psychology of homosexuality, according to Robert K. Martin, is also central to Whitman's poetry ("Whitman's 'Song of Myself': Homosexual Dream and Vision," *PR* 42:80–96). He argues against those who view Whitman's sexuality—whether homo-, hetero-, or bisexuality—as "beside the point." For Martin it is the point, and contemporary liberal acceptance of Whitman's sexual emphases muddies the meaning of the poetry by equating all experience and denying the distinctiveness of the homosexual perspective. Martin analyzes "The Sleepers" and "Song of Myself" to argue that homosexuality explains these as well as the "Calamus" poems, and to assert that homosexuality gave Whitman a more complete view of women, enabling him to see them as human beings rather than mere sex objects.

Questions of sexuality give way to more general problems of humanity in John Snyder's *The Dear Love of Man: Tragic and Lyrical Communion in Walt Whitman* (The Hague: Mouton and Co.) and Linda L. Andrews's " 'I Am the Poet of the Woman the Same as the Man': Whitman's View of Women as Depicted in 'Song of Myself' " (*BSUF* 16,iv:68–76). Snyder finds that Whitman employed "two radically different modes . . . to establish communion between the one and the many." In the lyric mode the speaker exulted in shared identity with others; in the tragic mode there is only the possibility of communion and not its realization, shared experience and not shared identity, analogies and similitudes but not equivalents. He examines the poetry and prose to trace Whitman's growth into tragic awareness in several stages from 1855 to 1892, showing concern for political implications as well as literary expression and expressing regret that American self-awareness did not keep pace with the development of Whitman's tragic sense. With implications that extend beyond "Song of Myself," Andrews argues that Whitman's interest in and sympathy with the feminist movement is consistent with his general egalitarianism and his open acknowledgment of sexuality.

Several studies are devoted to the conventional topics of Whitman's place in literary history and in American culture, to explications of symbolism and elucidation of themes, and to his handling of philosophical issues. Dwight Kalita in "Walt Whitman: Ecstatic Sea Voyager" (*WWR* 21:14–22) identifies the Western Hemisphere with the Body, the Eastern Hemisphere with the Soul, and the Ocean as the means of marrying the continents into the unity graphically represented by the circling globe in *Leaves of Grass*. In a somewhat murky and pretentious essay entitled "A Whitman Primer: Solipsism and Identity" (*AQ* 27:443–60), Rohn S. Friedman argues that Whitman's use of language enables him to mediate between the me and the not me and to escape the romantic susceptibility to solipsism. Jorge Luis Borges introduces several topics in a printed version of a talk delivered several years earlier. Entitled "Walt Whitman: Man and Myth" (*CritI* 1:707–18), the essay discusses the relationship of hero, persona, and reader in *Leaves of Grass*, and then proceeds to matters such as psalmic qualities and the innocence of Whitman's eroticism, and to Whitman's image of America and the Americans. The latter topic also occupies Donald D. Kummings in "A Note on the Americanness of Walt Whitman" (*Calamus* 10:18–27). Citing earlier observations by John Kouwenhoven and Perry Miller about America as flow and process rather than product, Kummings finds that process is central to Whitman's major poems, e.g., in "Song of Myself" the act of asserting the self dominates the content of the assertion, and in other poems crossing, rocking, blooming, etc. are fundamental. Another article by Kummings, "The Poetry of Democracies: Tocqueville's Aristocratic View" (*CL* 11[1974]:306–19), argues convincingly that American critics have given de Tocqueville's celebrated remarks in *Democracy in America* more credit than they deserve for predicting the sort of poetry Whitman would write. Despite the views of Matthiessen, Pearce, and Lewis, Kummings believes that de Tocqueville anticipates Whitman's poetry only insofar as he defines some of the broader characteristics of romanticism, which Whitman to a greater or lesser degree shares with other poets, not only in America but in Europe. Whitman's hopes for American democracy and individualism are the subject of A. Helen Smith's article "Walt Whitman's 'Personality' Figure" (*BSUF* 16,ii:23–28). Smith's title refers to the sort of personality that would evolve from adherence to the political philosophy that Whitman called "Personalism," essentially a democracy of "superior equals." Intending to create a volume that would conspiciously celebrate the emergence and proliferation of the "New World Personality," Whitman ultimately came to believe that later editions of *Leaves of Grass* had incorporated this function.

Of the less conventional studies, that of Aloysus Ivanetich is most unusual: "Gentlemen, Your Facts Are Useful" (*Calamus* 10:2–17). His purpose is to show a correspondence between Whitman's intuitive grasp of the nature of the human psyche and modern brain research, and to argue furthermore that the formal and rhythmic aspects of "Song of Myself," "Starting from Paumanok," and "Song of the Open Road" reflect this correspondence.

Transcendentalism also lives in the realm of Whitman's changing punctuation practices, as interpreted by David J. Johnson in "The Effect of Suspension Dots, Parentheses, and Italics on Lyricism of 'Song of Myself'" (*WWR* 21:47–58). Noting that the most obvious changes between the 1855 and 1891–92 editions are those dealing with mechanics, Johnson argues that if "the philosophy is any more obvious in the death-bed edition . . . it is because the rhythms of Whitman's song became so elemental to the fundamental existence of man that the archetypal act or state which gave birth to the word is made real, keeping abstraction in abeyance." In his view Whitman's later use of italics fostered greater intimacy between narrator and listener, and his use of parentheses enhanced the relationship of the lyrical and the lexical. The transcendental hypothesis also underlies Estelle W. Taylor's "Moments of Silence in *Leaves of Grass*" (*WWR* 21:145–50), but Taylor seems to stop short of fully recognizing it. Citing the reference to "inaudible words" and "unspoken meanings of the earth" in "A Song of the Rolling Earth," she reasons that through these silent means Whitman implies "the necessary link between the use of . . . reflection and introspection in connection with the silent wonders of nature and . . . the true meaning of them all in relation to man and man's existence." More tough-minded is the treatment of Whitman and Transcendentalism in David Bromwich's "Suburbs and Extremities" (*Prose* 8[1974]:25–38). Bromwich argues that "As I Ebb'd with the Ocean of Life" marks the end of the American Renaissance "as surely as Emerson's *Nature* inaugurated it," and that Whitman was able to see beyond the pastoral dream to the dangers ahead, as could only a few of his contemporaries.

Somewhat querulous is Kermit Vanderbilt's expression of irritation at the bland mindlessness and pretentiousness of a specific television show which concluded with a reading of "I Hear America Singing" and his dissatisfaction with the artistic and intellectual laziness inherent in Whitman's poem. Both the poem and the television program as expressions of popular culture emphasize the need for guidance out of "the absurdity and confused evasions of reigning middle-class values" ("'I Hear America Singing': Whitman and Democratic Culture," *WWR* 21:22–28).

d. **Criticism: Individual Works.** Several items previously discussed —particularly studies by Black, Martin, Gelpi, and Andrews—discuss "Song of Myself" in some detail. The remaining articles discuss aspects or segments of the poem. Emilio De Grazia studies point of view in section 11 of "Song of Myself" in "More on Whitman's Twenty-eight Young Men" (*WWR* 21:158–60). And Bernard Goldberg discusses "Patriotic Allusions in Section 15 and 33 of 'Song of Myself' " (*WWR* 21:58–66).

Three articles focus closely on "The Sleepers." Robert E. Abrams examines Whitman's concern with the "dark, hallucinatory world of sleep" and "oneiric fantasy" in "The Function of Dreams and Dream-Logic in Whitman's Poetry" (*TSLL* 17:599–616). He finds Whitman to have been a daring explorer of the unconscious mind. Mutlu Blasing sees the poem as the poet's dramatization of personal transcendence by means of a metaphorical journey through night, darkness, and sleep—a journey that takes him through the experience of sex and beyond the limits of death (" 'The Sleepers': The Problem of the Self in Whitman," *WWR* 21:111–19). In "The Individualization of a Poet: the Process of Becoming in Whitman's 'The

Sleepers'" (*WWR* 21:101–10), Harry James Cook supports Jungian concepts and terminology as the best analytical approach to Whitman's poetry in general and "The Sleepers" in particular.

In marked contrast to the studies of Stephen A. Black and Robert K. Martin cited earlier, Russell A. Hunt, in "Whitman's Poetics and the Unity of 'Calamus'" (*AL* 46:482–94), argues that readings emphasizing homoeroticism are "superficial and isolated." He views the "Calamus" cycle as an *ars poetica*, illustrating organically "the origin and nature of Whitman's own poetry—how it should be read and by whom, and what effects its reading is likely to have." Focusing on only one of the "Calamus" poems, R. Galen Hanson, in "Anxiety as Human Predicament: Whitman's 'Calamus' No. 9" (*WWR* 21:73–75), reads "Hours Continuing Long, Sore, and Heavy Hearted" as a treatise on anxiety expressing tension and disequilibrium and leading to a "heightened awareness of one's own finitude."

David M. Stuehler treats "Significant Form in Whitman's 'Out of the Cradle Endlessly Rocking'" (*Calamus* 10:28–39), offering not only a conventional summary of the poem's meaning but also a discussion of its structure and strategy. Charles Stubblefield examines the historical context and the cultural rather than the formal strategy of another major poem in "The Great Circle: Whitman's 'Passage to India'" (*PrS* 49:19–30). He sees the technological achievements of the late 1860s as the conclusion of the epoch which began with Columbus's quest and the poem as Whitman's announcement of a new epoch in which the visionary poet launches a new quest.

Several articles deal with some lesser poems. J. T. Ledbetter, in "Whitman's Power in the Short Poem: A Discussion of 'Whispers of Heavenly Death'" (*WWR* 21:155–58), offers a close analysis of the poem, with attention to tone and imagery. John R. Stillgoe, in "Possible Lockean Influence in 'The World Below the Brine'" (*WWR* 21:150–55), considers the possibility not only of Lockean influence but also of pre-Darwinian evolutionary thought. James C. McCullagh, in "'Proud Music of the Storm': A Study in Dynamics" (*WWR* 21:66–73), traces the stanza-by-stanza progression by means of which the sounds of the storm provoke and inspire new poems, which in turn mediate between life and death, body and soul, nature and art. Joseph F. Doherty contributes a more intensive and extensive reading of "There Was a Child Went Forth" in "Whitman's 'Poem of the Mind'" (*Semiotica* 14:345–63). Using the concepts, methods, and terminology of structural linguistics and depth psychology, he has written a complex, demanding, and, for some readers, rewarding essay.

Drum-Taps and *Specimen Days* are the subjects of two studies. Samuel Coale sets out to examine the actual effect of the Civil War on Whitman's art in "Whitman's War: The March of a Poet" (*WWR* 21:85–101). Among his conclusions are that Whitman's assistance to the wounded was reinforced by homosexual impulses, that he deepened his conceptual acceptance of death, that *Drum-Taps* exhibits stages of emotional response from blatant patriotism to melancholy calm, that he gained a larger sense of purpose and his poetry gained greater formal assurance. Linck C. Johnson argues against those who have described *Specimen Days* as essentially formless and untidy in "The Design of Walt Whitman's *Specimen Days*" (*WWR* 21:3–14). According to Johnson, Whitman "carefully selected and reworked his jottings, arranging them in a design which would reveal the bond between his experience and the communal experience of his country-men during a crucial period in this nation's history." The conversational style and the vernacular immediacy cloak the unity attained by emphasis on time, death, and resurrection.

Discussion of later works is provided by Harold W. Blodgett in "*Democratic Vistas*—100 Years After," in *Geschichte und Gesellschaft in der amerikanischen Literatur*, ed. Karl Schubert and Ursula Müller-Ricter (Heidelberg: Quelle and Meyer, pp. 114–31), by Dwight Kalita in "Whitman and the Correspondent Breeze" (*WWR* 21:125–30), and by Rose Cherie Reissman in "Recurrent Motifs in *Good-Bye My Fancy*" (*WWR* 21:28–35). Blodgett deals with themes and style in the *Vistas* (blaming the excesses on Carlyle), places the work in a literary and historical context, and discusses its reception and neglect. Kalita's discussion of "To the Sunset Breeze" from *Good-Bye, My Fancy* identifies in Whitman's poem the five basic characteristics of Romantic nature poetry, and Reissman argues that the recurrent motifs of these old-age poems—journey, soul, water, conclusion-farewell, death-old age, and war—illuminate Whitman's emotions and rationalizations as he nears death.

***e.* Relationships, Influences, Derivations, and Inspirations.** The easiest way to discuss relationships and influences this year is roughly chronological, beginning with Whitman's relationships to his contemporaries and working toward his influence on ours. Examining "Emerson's Stylistic Influence on Whitman" (*ATQ* 25:41–51), Donald Ross assembles much evidence, including computer-aided comparisons, to prove that the exuberance of Emerson's essays affected Whitman's poetic style much more than Emerson's poetry did. Florence B. Freedman in a note that summarizes the career of Delia Bacon, who tried to gain for Francis Bacon the credit that history attributed to Shakespeare, also quotes from an Emerson letter in 1857 that brackets Ms. Bacon with Whitman as geniuses, either wild or mad. Entitled "Emerson Giving Joy: Summer of 1855" (*WWR* 21:162–63), this note covers ground that was noted years ago by Rusk in his biography of Emerson. In "Whitman, Melville and the Civil War: A Sharing of Mood and Metaphor" (*AN&Q* 13:102–05), R. Scott Kellner calls attention to a number of parallels in the two writers' responses to the War, but the circumstance is one where the points of contrast are at least as important as the points of comparison.

Two later contemporaries of Whitman draw the attention of Ernest J. Moyne and R. T. Blackwood. Moyne, in "Folger McKinsey and Walt Whitman" (*WWR* 21:135–44), summarizes the career of this Elkton, Maryland, journalist, who died in 1950, and reprints his column of December 19, 1885, which recounts a visit to Whitman's home and defends *Leaves of Grass.* Blackwood calls attention to a misquotation of a line from Whitman's "To You" in William James's essay "Pragmatism and Religion" (1907). Either James or the printer rendered it as "I have loved many men and women and men . . ." ("William James and Walt Whitman," *WWR* 21:78–79). George A. Knox and Harry Lawton have assembled and edited a volume on Whitman and Sadakitchi Hartmann, *The Whitman-Hartmann Controversy, Including "Conversations with Walt Whitman" and Other Essays* (Bern: Herbert Lang; Frankfurt/M and München: Peter Lang).

Whitman's influence in the 20th century seems to cover a broad spectrum culturally and geographically. In "A Note on Whitman in Ireland" (*WWR* 21:160–62) Richard F. Fleck cites the influence of Whitman on such Irish writers as Sean O'Casey, Patrick Kavanagh, and Frank O'Connor and such figures in labor and politics as James Connally and James Larkin. Robert P. Weeks adds to our knowledge of "Dos Passos' Debt to Whitman" in *Americana-Austriaca*, vol. 3, ed. Klaus Lanzinger (Stuttgart: Wilhelm Braumüller [1974], pp. 121–38). A similarity of attitude toward God, man, and the world underlies Arnold Mersch's comparison in "Whitman and Buber: In the Presence of Greatness" (*WWR* 21:120–25).

A number of studies attempt to relate Whitman in theory and in practice to later American poets. One such broad and informative attempt is an essay-review by David H. Hirsch of eight recent books on American poetry—"American Dionysian Poetry and Modern Poetics" (*SR* 83:334–47). Of more limited scope are Dolores E. Brien's study of "Robert Duncan: A Poet in the Emerson-Whitman Tradition (*CentR* 19:308–16), and Sy M. Kahn's account of "Two Poetic Perspectives on the Deaths of Presidents: Whitman and Ferlinghetti" (*Americana-Austriaca* 3:59–66). A study by Cary Nelson, bearing the somewhat misleading title "Whitman in Vietnam: Poetry and History in Contemporary America" (*MR* 16:55–71), examines numerous works by established poets affected by the Vietnam war. Most deal less effectively with the "interplay between poetry and history in America" than Whitman did. Only a poem by Adrienne Rich seems to Nelson "genuinely Whitmanesque" in its openness to past and future, its open form, and its "vision of bountiful death."

Several items warrant mention even though they lie outside what some consider the province of scholarship. Cumulatively they offer evidence of the way Whitman attracted creative individuals then and now and of the way his work has served as a source of inspiration in American cultural life. William White has reprinted some sketches in crayon, dated April 17, 1881, under the collective title "Whitman in 1881: Five Frank Hill Smith Sketches" (*WWR* 21:81–82). Successive issues of *Calamus*, beginning with no. 4 (1970), have contained the text of one act of the eight-act television drama by William Luther Moore, *Haughty this Song* (Act V, *Calamus* 10:40–58). The play premiered on Czechoslovakian television in 1969. Richard O'Connell has written a short poem, "Whitman's Tomb" (*ETC.* 32:276), expressing disappointment that "Whitman chose cave burial" rather than dispersal "under boot-soles." And David Hamilton in the "Music" section of *The Nation* (220:478) writes that *Lilacs*, a cantata by Roger Sessions, is the best musical treatment of a Whitman text, superior to Delius's *Sea-Drift* and Hindemuth's *A Requiem for Those We Love.*

ii. Dickinson

***a.* Bibliography, Editing.** Recent Dickinson scholarship is again surveyed reliably by Sheila Taylor in her yearly checklist ("Annual Bibliography—1974," *EDB* 28:107–11) while George Monteiro adds to the record 27 widely diverse items from 1891 to the present ("More on Dickinson," *HJP* 12:45–46). In regard to Dickinson studies abroad, the scope of the poet's reception in Japan is much clearer for Western readers since Tsuyoshi Omoto published, in roman letters and with Japanese titles translated into English, a 255-item compilation, "Emily Dickinson; A Bibliography; Writings in Japan" (*Jinbunkagaku-Nenpo* 3[1973]:113–43). Some of the results of this work are summarized by Willis J. Buckingham in "A New Bibliography of Dickinson Studies in Japan" (*EDB* 28:104–05) while Omoto himself has already carried his listing through 1974 in "Emily Dickinson . . . Writings in Japan, Supplement I" (*Senshu Univ. Jinbungaku Kenkyusho Geppo* 40–41:1–6). Scholarship and translations in Finland have been thoughtfully appraised by Sirkka Heiskanen-Makela, herself a Dickinson specialist ("Emily Dickinson in Finland," *HJP* 8[1974]:18–19).

Though there was little interest in problems of editing this year, one of the most intriguing questions in Dickinson studies, the significance of the poet's manuscript fascicles, was taken up in some detail by Arlo Duane Sletto ("Emily Dickinson's Poetry: The Fascicles," *DAI* 36:3719–20A). After examining five of the booklets, Sletto concludes that each grouping seems to constitute an aesthetically pleasing whole, unified by deliberate narrative and thematic structure. The only other item in this category is R. W. Franklin's description of two published but previously unlocated Dickinson manuscripts which are at Middlebury College ("Two Emily Dickinson Manuscripts," *PBSA* 69:114–15). One is a fair copy of 'Pink—small—and punctual," the other a birthday greeting. The texts of both are identical with published versions, except in the case of the poem, where there are differences in stanza arrangement anl punctuation.

***b.* Biography.** With Richard B. Sewall's recent biography (see *ALS 1974*, p. 70) as his point of departure, Richard Todd engages in a kind of perplexed, speculative meditation on Emily Dickinson's life ("'Are You Too Occupied to Say If My Verse Is Alive?'" *AtM*

235,i:74–81). After noting such problems for the biographer as the poet's attitude toward publication and the object of the "Master" letters (he favors Bowles), Todd concludes that Dickinson's relationship with the world was fundamentally out of balance: "Her life was a whipsaw of reckless vulnerability and excessive self-defense." In another review article, this one dealing with John Cody's psychoanalytic study of Dickinson (see *ALS 1971*, p. 71), James Hijiya also sees the poet's life as beset by contradiction ("New England Women and Madness: An Essay Review," *EIHC* 111:228–39). Hijiya suggests that Dickinson's maladjustment derives not from her mother's failure to provide an adequate model of womanhood, as Cody maintains, but rather that her culture did not supply the means by which a woman night express a masculine component in her nature. She could not be both a woman and a poet-intellectual. According to Hijiya, "her life, then, was a set of contradictions: outward submissiveness and inward assertiveness, apparent contentment and covert resentment," resulting in her becoming "neurotic as hell."

Virginia Terris finds Dickinson's habit of wearing white a sign of her assent to the 19th century's image of the genteel female as virginal, dependent, and childlike ("ED's White Frock: A Further Suggestion," *EDB* 28:127–28). Being the unmarried daughter of a respectable family allowed her to play the role of her parents' "good little girl" well into her mature years. On a similar note Cynthia Chaliff: argues that Dickinson's poems, particularly those involving bees (men) and flowers (women), reveal a set of typical Victorian attitudes toward sexuality ("The Bees, the Flowers, and Emily Dickinson," *RS* 42[1974]:93–103). What Dickinson seems to have feared in particular were the social and psychological aftereffects of sexual love, for in her poetic world dreams of intimacy and marriage often turn into an abhorrent reality. To compensate, Dickinson created a religion of idealized love in which she at times seems to enjoy taking on the role of suffering victim.

c. Criticism: General. In 1961 Theodora Ward's study of Dickinson's inner world received little attention; today there is no more current subject of research than the landscape of the poet's consciousness. Benefiting particularly from the work of existentialist critics, recent interpreters seek to define more or less coherent acts of mind implicit within Dickinson's poems. In his chapter on Dickinson in

The Tenth Muse (pp. 219–99) Albert Gelpi understands her poems as the record of events transpiring, for both reader and writer, in a kind of psychic time-space. Finding no fixed center in herself or in nature, Emily Dickinson sought self-definition through acts of consciousness in which she could, for example, come to terms with the masculine principle in her character. The lover projected in many poems is therefore not so much an actual person as the personification of the poet's emotional needs. For Gelpi all of the poems are in a sense "battles" of consciousness in which the poet occasionally wins through to sudden accessions of power and self-integration. At other moments the defensiveness and assertiveness of which Todd and Hijiya complain (see above) are what Gelpi sees as the oscillating rhythms of the poet's being as it gropes for poise in an inconstant and bewildering world. In this attempt to understand the sources of Dickinson's creativity the poems themselves remain at the center of attention. Gelpi's often original and illuminating readings make this study a model of psychological criticism, superior to the Whitman chapter in the same book. Taking what appears to be a strikingly similar approach, Martin Elliott Bickman describes Dickinson's mind in terms of the Jungian "animus," the male soulmate of a woman's imagination, and in terms of the mythological story of Persephone ("Voyages in the Mind's Return: A Jungian Study of Poe, Emerson, Whitman and Dickinson," *DAI* 36:266–A). In three interrelated articles which together comprise a single number of the *Emily Dickinson Bulletin*, Frederick L. Morey employs a Jungian framework to classify Dickinson's best poems according to whether their themes reflect "ascension," "descension," or "stasis" ("Jungian Dickinson," *EDB* 27:4–72).

The most sustained phenomenological study of the year is Jean McClure Mudge's *Emily Dickinson and the Image of Home* (Amherst: Univ. of Mass. Press). In this work Mudge argues that Emily Dickinson's spatial consciousness was informed by a variety of physical, psychic, cultural, and literary images. These figures of enclosure evoked both positive and negative responses, fear of loneliness and imprisonment alternating with dreams of security and contentment. More important, Dickinson equated home with "consciousness," a place she tirelessly explored and defended, coming to understand that her "creative inner space" was her only true home, a locus of power, "the place where poetry is conceived" (p. 111). Spatial imagery is also taken up by Heather McClave in her dissertation, "Situations of the Mind: Studies of Center and Periphery in Dickinson, Stevens, Ammons and Plath" (*DAI* 36:3715A). Conceiving otherness as an abyss, Dickinson imagines both "a protective Circuit that consolidates the self and an expansive Circumference that threatens to overwhelm it."

Robert Weisbuch avoids psychological concerns altogether in his discerning study, *Emily Dickinson's Poetry* (Chicago: Univ. of Chicago Press). If he does not explore the mind of the poet, it is because he understands the poetry to have a mind of its own, a network of underlying "silent assumptions" which can be reached through exclusive attention to style and theme. Weisbuch argues that rather than using particulars in her poems to refer to actual life experiences, Dickinson preferred "sceneless" analogies, "archtypal" situations with multiple meanings. Further, she explored conflicting possibilities of the self by assuming bardic and confessional tones of voice and by generating ecstatic and painful states of consciousness out of internalized patterns of thought, especially the Christian typology of death. There have been critical studies written with greater ease and charm, but Weisbuch's volume has the advantage of keeping the poetry steadily in view and of doing a large measure of justice to the peculiarly dialectical nature of Dickinson's thought.

In "Emily Dickinson's 'woe of ecstasy'" (*ColQ* 23:505–17) David A. Roberts apparently agrees with Weisbuch on the importance of polarities in the Dickinson canon. He explicates several poems which deal with a sense of diminution and the need for reassessment after ecstatic moments of knowledge have passed, but his discussion is not finally as useful as David Porter's study of "aftermath" in "The Crucial Experience in Emily Dickinson's Poetry" (see *ALS 1974*, p. 72). On a similar theme, but without going beyond existing studies, Jule S. Kaufmann discusses ways in which "enhancement by deprivation" becomes a "major principle" for the poet ("Emily Dickinson and the Involvement of Retreat," *TSE* 21[1974]: 77–90). Weisbuch's point about the "sceneless" quality of Dickinson's analogies is elaborated somewhat differently by David Porter in "Emily Dickinson's 'Strangely Abstracted' Images: What the Worksheets Reveal" (*BUJ* 23:22–31). Attention to manuscript variants allows Porter to catch Dickinson in the act of turning to increasingly abstract images as a way of realizing and identifying impalpable subjective experience. Such a seemingly impenetrable expression as "Dome of Abyss," for example, conveys the deeply interior and nonsensory feeling of "darkness being formed inside of night."

While a number of critics speak readily of connections in Dickinson's mind, most are wary of postulating a linear progression of thought. Joseph M. Garrison, Jr., however, hazards one. In "Emily Dickinson: From Ballerina to Gymnast" (*ELH* 42:107–24), he takes up Weisbuch's and Roberts's interest in the theme of quest and limitation, arguing that until roughly 1870 Dickinson sought an enduring certitude which always eluded her. She thereafter "seems to have recognized that the absolutizing intellect violates the essence of external things and destroys the sacredness of the world . . . ." She gradually began to advocate experience, with all its teasing contradictions, over a tyrannizing mind. Analyzing the various contexts of Dickinson's characteristic words for immortality and infinity, Robert W. Peckham also engages in a developmental study ("This Colossal Substance," *EDB* 28:112–23). He finds that while meanings of transcendence and permanence adhere consistently to these words throughout her work, they most frequently refer to love during the troubled years of 1862–65 and they are not used to denote an everlasting blank until 1863.

In " 'The Souls That Snow': Winter in the Poetry of Emily Dickinson" (*AL* 47:361–76) L. Edwin Folsom provides another context for the dichotomy in Dickinson's thought between expansive transcendental hope and the skepticism borne of experience. Folsom argues that Dickinson uses boreal imagery to warn that man must keep in touch with the inevitability of pain, hardship, and death; winter, he concludes is a "primary source of her realism." Intriguing new evidence for that realism is brought forward by Thomas W. Ford in "Thoreau's Cosmic Mosquito and Dickinson's Terrestial Fly" (*NEQ* 48:487–504). Ford believes that the source for Dickinson's "I heard a Fly buzz—when I died" is a passage from *Walden* in which Thoreau seems to hear celestial harmonies in the hum of a mosquito. Dickinson, he says, drew ironically on the language and situation of that passage, intending to untune such transcendental melodies with the dissonant buzz of her Amherst fly. Defining Dickinson's understanding of nature more philosophically, Thomas M. Davis finds that while she did not share her forebears' Calvinist beliefs in regard to natural revelation, she does come close to their "sensibility," especially to their awed attachment to the beauty of creation ("Emily Dickinson and the Right of Way to Tripoli" in *Artful Thunder*, pp. 209–19). That Dickinson occasionally rejected even Christian monotheism is the conclusion of Amy Horiuchi in her study of ten poems which refer to "gods" ("Emily Dickinson's 'Gods' In the Plurality," *HJP* 8[1974]:13–16).

One of the most suggestive articles of recent years, with radical implications for the future editing of Dickinson, is Richard Howard's "A Consideration of the Writings of Emily Dickinson" (*Prose* 6[1973]:67–97). Howard makes the point that just as Dickinson adhered to no fixed center of belief or perception, she intended her poems, with their untamed grammar and punctuation, and with their profusion of variants, to dramatize her horror of stasis. Because her poems celebrate transience, it is essential that they seem, in the very way they appear on the page, improvisational: "Hence her dashes, her lurches into enjambment, her variants, her inclusive indicatives: there was no received standard version. . . ." To alter Dickinson's manuscripts by editing them in any way is thus to arrest and obscure the central "process" phenomenology of her work. The respected British scholar, John Wain, takes up Dickinson for the first time in a wide-ranging critical appreciation which was originally delivered as a lecture at Cambridge University ("Homage to Emily Dickinson," *CM* 15:2–17). Dickinson, he believes, embodies the characteristic American habit, formed on the frontier, of "thinking *ab ovo*." Like Gelpi, Wain sees her chief subject as her own consciousness, the locus of her heroic struggles: "Poetry, for her, was something that involved the whole being—there was nothing 'literary' in her approach."

***d*. Criticism: Individual Works.** There are more than the usual number of separately published explications this year. Brenda Ann Catto reads the last line of "As Watchers hang upon the East" (*Expl* 33:item 55) to suggest Dickinson's faith in, rather than doubt of, heavenly reward. According to Hennig Cohen, the "tankards" referred to in "I taste a liquor never brewed" are suggested by actual drinking cups made of the pearly nautilus shell (*Expl* 33:item 41). Connie Doyle helpfully provides a historical context for Dickinson's use of "Austrian" to describe ominous weather in "The wind drew off" (*ELN* 12:182–84). Austria's military adventures of the 1860s, unpopular in America, had made that country's name synonymous with treachery. Allen D. Lackey insists that the seemingly irreverent line, "Burglar! Banker—Father!" in "I never lost as much but twice" actually conveys "complete trust and obedience" in the heavenly Father of orthodox Christianity (*Expl* 34:item 18). Another poem not heretofore recognized as a statement of traditional belief is analyzed by George Monteiro in "Dickinson's 'On this wondrous sea'" (*Expl* 33:item 74). Read as a two-part, question-and-answer dialogue, the "second speaker is not an earthly lover but the Pilot-God who guides the ship of the world."

Taking up one of the most enigmatic of Dickinson's riddle poems, "It's like the Light," James Ashbrook Perkins suggests that the unnamed antecedent of the title may be the spring ("What Is It That Is Like the Light: A Consideration of J.297," *EDB* 28:129–31). He admits, however, that the poem finally seems to resist even this interpretation. In "Dickinson's 'As by the dead we love to sit'" (*Expl* 33:item 49) Laurence Perrine argues that the theme of the poem "is the illogic of the emotions which magnifies the worth of a recently dead friend until it exceeds that of all the friends left living." An explication likely to be challenged is Dwight H. Purdy's interpretation of "What Soft—Cherubic Creatures" (*Expl* 33:item 67). He takes the view that since "Brittle Lady" (at the end of the poem) is singular, not plural, Dickinson must be condemning herself rather than the "Gentlewomen" who are elsewhere the subject of the poem's ironies. John Timmerman argues that the door too fearful to open in "I Years had been from Home" is the gate of heaven ("God and Image of God in J.609: A Brief Analysis," *EDB* 28:124–26). Dickinson fled from the threshold because she could not bear to have her various images of God confounded by the actual deity within the house. In regard to another poem on heaven, Thomas Werge brings the dictionary to bear on a troublesome word ("'Checks' in 'I Never Saw a Moor,'" *AN&Q* 12[1974]:101–02). According to a description of colloquial American usage in the *OED*, "checks" are counters used in card games; thus, to hand in one's checks is to die. Poems on death are also brought forward for brief discussion by D. M. Thomas in *Poetry and Crosslight* (London: Longmans), pp. 75–78. He reprints three versions of "Safe in their Alabaster Chambers" and compares "I see thee better—in the Dark" with "I see thee clearer for the Grave."

e. **Relationships.** In addition to Thomas Ford's article comparing Dickinson and Thoreau, already mentioned, two Ph.D. dissertations investigate the poet's relation to other writers. Ursula Elisabeth Howard finds Emily Dickinson and Annette von Droste-Hülshoff most alike in their search for union with God ("The Mystical Trends in the Poetry of Emily Dickinson and Annette von Droste-Hülshoff," *DAI* 35:4525A). Both poets imagine their relation to deity in terms of two central analogies: child to parent and bride to bridegroom. For both writers, also, doubt intrudes to trouble these relationships. Some of Dickinson's poems on nature are compared with those of a noted 20th century Korean folk poet by M. Claudia Lee, O.S.B., in "A Comparative Analysis of Selected Nature Poetry of Emily Dickinson and So Wol Kim" (*SLRJ* 6:333–73).

Joanne Feit, in "'Another Way to See': Dickinson and Her English Romantic Precursors" (*DAI* 35:4514A) apparently draws on the work of Jung and Harold Bloom to argue that the mysterious giant, the masculine "other" who is constantly addressed in the poems, is the "Composite Precursor." Dickinson must wrestle with this threatening figure and through strategies of subversion find her own voice. Despite her affinities with the major Romantic poets, she transformed their vision "into a darker statement—a post-Romantic perspective emphasizing alienation and anxiety." The example of Dickinson herself as a figure suggesting alienation to a later writer is treated by Hikaru Sasahara in "Tennessee Williams to Emily Dickinson—*The Glass Menagerie* wo Chushin ni" (*Eigo Seinen* 120[1974]:270–72).

Arizona State University

6. Mark Twain

Hamlin Hill

In 1975 almost half of the work done on Mark Twain concentrated on later works, from *A Connecticut Yankee* on. And a healthy portion of that half centered on the newly available fragments and symbolic writings that are so urgently in need of examination and explication. Volumes 1 and 2 of the *Notebooks & Journals* finally appeared, fulfilling expectations beyond anyone's wildest hopes. Unfortunately, George C. Carrington's *The Dramatic Unity of Huckleberry Finn*, a brilliant analysis of the novel, was delayed until 1976 by publication problems. In general 1975 was a fairly decent year for Mark Twain, though how he might have responded to the five CBS Radio Mystery Theater scripts based on his works is fascinating to contemplate.

i. Textual and Bibliographical

Mark Twain's Notebooks and Journals, Volume I (1855–1873), ed. Frederick Anderson, Michael B. Frank, and Kenneth M. Sanderson; and *Volume II (1877–1883)*, ed. Frederick Anderson, Lin Salamo, and Bernard L. Stein (Berkeley: Univ. of Calif. Press) are a monumental transcription of the first 21 of the 49 notebooks Mark Twain kept during his lifetime. When the editors have been puzzled over handwriting, or have encountered bars of music, illustrations, or undecipherable shorthand (and even a sneeze or two, I think) on the original pages, they have reproduced them photographically. They have identified every obscure name, all arcane allusions, and each possible reference, with a set of explanatory notes that ought to qualify as a certified miracle of scholarship. They have described each physical notebook—size, shape, number of leaves (both loose and still stitched to bindings), type of cover—with a precision and and exhaustiveness that approaches idolatry. One thing they decided not to do, which seems a serious fault to me, was to transcribe completely Notebook 2, the one that Clemens used when he was learning the river in 1857. Their argument is that "the abbreviated words, the frequent illegibility of penciled entries, the difficulty of identifying many of the now-vanished river points, but above all . . . the technical subject matter," persuaded them to print only "representative selections" from this journal. Somehow, though, the 5 pages of samples from a notebook that contains over 70 inscribed pages—and a notebook so germinal to his literary career and psychological makeup—are disappointingly few.

The literary overtones and values of these first two volumes are enormous—the *Quaker City* notes, the European trip of 1877–78 that produced *A Tramp Abroad*, entries for the *Library of Humor*, and the journals of the 1882 trip back to the Mississippi—all are here. Even more important, though, are those pages that record nonliterary aspects of Samuel Clemens: for instance, the repeated "didn't" and "didn't try" in Notebook 3, recording the pilot's cowardice before challenging or dangerous river passages; his hysterical vengeance plotted against Whitelaw Reid; and the constantly spectacular proofs of Clemens's total recall. As Lewis Leary has noted in a delightful review of these volumes ("Mark Twain Himself," *SR* 83:708–13), here is the essential man, unvarnished, defenses as close to down as they could probably ever get. If the paradoxes that constitute Mark Twain are ever to be comprehended or reconciled, these two volumes and their projected companions will indisputably provide the key. They are blessed, too, with what is, for notebooks, the astonishing ability to make interesting browsing.

William E. Martin, Jr., in "Letters and Remarks by Mark Twain from the Boston *Daily Journal*" (*MTJ* 18,i:1–5), reprints five items, dating from 1873 to 1886: "A Rescue at Sea," "The Jubilee Singers," "Twain as a Confederate Recruit," "Money for Battle-Flags," and "Introducing an African Explorer." Alan Gribben's fascinating but depressing account of "The Dispersal of Samuel L. Clemens' Library Books" (*RALS* 5:147–65) records the loss, sometimes irretrievably, of Clemens's personal library. Gribben catalogs as completely as possible the 1911 auction, gifts to the Mark Twain Library in Redding, the surreal 1951 Hollywood sale (organized by Clara Clemens in what was distinctly not one of her few moments of adult lucidity), dispersals to the Estelle Doheny Collection of St. John's Seminary, the Mark Twain Memorial in Hartford, the keepers of the flame in Perry (Missouri), and the Antenne-Dorrance Collection. Seven hundred volumes are known to be extant, and some of those that have disappeared, with extensive marginal annotations, constitute a tragic loss.

Guy A. Cardwell's "The Bowdlerizing of Mark Twain" (*ESQ* 21: 179–93) is a feisty but challenging survey of the "censorship" question. Starting with Brooks and DeVoto, Cardwell describes the gyrations of Twainians who argue whether or not the humorist was in fact bowdlerized, and whether such external tamperings were beneficial or harmful. As Cardwell notes, "the commentators operate within a closed universe of means and materials. They use the same makeshift tools to rearrange and reinterpret the same limited data. They cobble up explanations to satisfy their purposes." Cardwell also surveys the "limited amounts of reasonably hard evidence" regarding the censorship imputed to E. C. Stedman, James R. Osgood, Howells, Mary Mason Fairbanks, and Olivia Clemens. Without taking sides or reaching conclusions of his own, Cardwell merely insists that machinery now exists "to make detailed and rigorous examinations of the censored manuscripts and texts beyond anything we know." The problem that Cardwell ignores is that—in the absence of a manuscript with revisions in a hand other than Clemens's—there is no "hard" evidence to convert speculation to concrete fact. Until, for instance, someone finds the manuscript of *Innocents Abroad*, what Mark Twain meant when he said that Bret Harte helped him revise it must necessarily depend only on "soft" evidence.

ii. Biographical

"Mark Twain" the pen name is the subject of Guy A. Cardwell's "Samuel Clemens' Magical Pseudonym" (*NEQ* 48:175–93); Cardwell details meticulously the folklore surrounding the two versions of the origin of the name (the New Orleans–Isaiah Sellers story, and the western barroom, two-drinks-on-the-cuff alternative). He finds the New Orleans variant more plausible, even though he points out the many flaws and errors which Clemens himself voiced and which Paine accepted as gospel. David B. Kesterson's "The Mark

Twain–Josh Billings Friendship" (*MTJ* 18,i:5–9) is a quick sketch of the acquaintance, begun in 1869, together with some sample exchanges of comic letters between the two humorists.

In "Mark Twain's English Lectures and George Routledge & Sons" (*MTJ* 17,iv:1–4) M. E. Grenander reprints from the Routledge Agreement Book, 1850–76, three letters (two dated July 10, 1872, and the other from November 10, 1875) regarding English editions of *Innocents Abroad* and *The Gilded Age*. The first two provide details about the English preface and the Routledge publication; the last acknowledges a royalty check for $355.86.

Louis D. Rubin, Jr., tackles the issue of Twain's southern heritage in " 'The Begum of Bengal': Mark Twain and the South" (*Individual and Community*, pp. 64–93). Looking at the southernness of Clemens's imagination—"the forms that the imagination took, and how the imagination was formed"—Rubin suggests that the elusive figure of John Marshall Clemens is central. In his father's situation, Mark Twain found "the hallmark of his humor: the awareness of status and the effort to maintain it. Here is the southern family of good standing, minor aristocracy fallen upon evil days, seeking to hold to status and *noblesse oblige* in a more crass and democratic society where aristocratic pose comes close to being quixotic gesture and high-minded scruples of honor the vulnerability whereby the vernacular land speculator with no such scruples could bring the man of honor down to poverty and ruin." For Mark Twain, "the essence of the art" is his attempt to break away from the tension "between the pull of the old community and that of the forces separating the individual from it."

Ronald B. Jager's "Mark Twain and the Robber Barons: A View of the Gilded Age Businessman" (*MTJ* 17,iii:8–12) is a provocative study of another imaginative resource of Mark Twain's—the tycoon as a kind of creative artist whose temperament was distinct from Twain's own even though he attempted to emulate it. Twain's impetuousness, his fear of debt, and his dependence on "luck" made him envious of an art "for which he had little understanding or talent." Jager's interesting thesis is marred by its use of documentation older than *Mark Twain's Correspondence with Henry Huddleston Rogers*.

Allison Ensor's "The House United: Mark Twain and Henry Watterson Celebrate Lincoln's Birthday, 1901" (*SAQ* 74:259–68) provides a detailed account of the February 11, 1901, celebration in Carnegie Hall, a benefit for Lincoln Memorial University. Twain, whose function was to introduce Watterson, delivered a brief speech reflecting a complex and paradoxical attitude toward the South. And James H. Hyde, in "Mark Twain and Colonel George Harvey" (*MTJ* 17,iii:21), merely repeats a brief and trivial anecdote about a dinner for Lord Charles Beresford, which Harvey hosted and Clemens attended. Beresford passed out under the table; Mark Twain didn't.

iii. General Criticism

Helen L. Harris believes that, in spite of Mark Twain's tolerance for other minorities, "when he wrote of the Native American he was unfailingly hostile." "Mark Twain's Response to the Native American" (*AL* 46:495–505) cataloges the appearances of Indians in *Roughing It*, *Tom Sawyer*, and lesser works through *Letters from the Earth*, and suggests that the humorist's chauvinism about white settlers and his attempts to justify the usurpation of Indian land require him to give silent consent to injustice. (Unconfronted here is the possibility that maybe he just didn't like Indians.) Allison Ensor's "The Downfall of Poor Richard: Benjamin Franklin as seen by Hawthorne, Melville, and Mark Twain" (*MTJ* 17,iii:14–18) notes the mockery of Franklin's Poor Richard pose, even though that image of Franklin was a distorted one.

The monograph-length section on Mark Twain in Warwick Wadlington's *The Confidence Game* (pp. 181–284) was the only substantial critical overview in 1975. "The Trickster," Wadlington explains,

> embodies two antithetical, nonrational experiences of man with the natural world, his society, and his own psyche: on the one hand, a force of treacherous disorder that outrages and disrupts, and on the other hand, an unanticipated, usually unintentional benevolence in which trickery is at the expense of inimical forces and for the benefit of mankind. . . . Whether he is seen, according to social and historical circumstances, as demiurge, culture hero, savior-god, devil, shaman, or comic rogue, the Trickster has a profound fascination, abrogating

> as he does in his tricks and self-deceptions all restrictions, rules, and taboos, manipulating the untouchable, and freely tapping the unchecked powers of the subconscious or the afterworld by means of illusion and metamorphosis.

In Twain's literature (to oversimplify a complex interpretation), the author himself is the trickster of *Innocents Abroad* and *Roughing It*, who transmutes "a world into his performance of temperamental responses to it." One of the aims of *Innocents* "is to cultivate in the reader, not skepticism, but comfortable confidence. Confidence of what? Confidence of entertainment by a virtuoso whose bag of tricks, though they are recurrently humorous in tendency, really consists of a telescoping set of humours in the old sense. . . . We are invited to pleasurable anticipation about what Mark Twain will do next, how he will take advantage of the disparate opportunities for 'effect' to put everything in its place and us in ours." By the time of the writing of "Old Times on the Mississippi," we see "the protagonist's persistent naive confidence that style is substance, that entertaining impressiveness is knowledgable skill." The culmination of such strategies of role-playing is *Huckleberry Finn*, in which "each social class is carefully identified with the style in which it understands its own persuasive authority, properly circumscribed in relation to that of classes above and below." Tom, Huck, and Jim form "a social triad of high, middle, and low," and "as the mediate, marginal figure . . . Huck must somehow supply the insufficiency when Tom is missing, in order to be Huck Finn." As a result, Huck is able to "connive against Jim in the manner of a benign hierarchical superior and in a way that Jim does not object to in principle"; so that "the attempts at making new by renaming are pretenses that are consequential in refining hierarchical perceptions, and in causing peace or discomfort for a time but leave things unchanged in *essentials*." As Huck once said of another book, "interesting, but tough."

iv. Earlier Works

Edgar M. Branch traces, in "Samuel Clemens: Learning to Venture a Miracle" (*ALR* 8:91–99), Mark Twain's early ridicule (through burlesque, mostly) of the excesses of romanticism—sentimentality, gothicism, stereotypy, and idealization. All the same, Clemens's own temperament was congenial to the fabulous, the bizarre, and the mythical elements of romanticism; and the earliest uses of the Mark Twain persona distilled these qualities in almost Emersonian dimensions. Richard H. Cracroft's "Distorting Polygamy for Fun and Profit: Artemus Ward and Mark Twain Among the Mormons (*BYUS* 14[1974]:272–88) compares the two humorists' uses of Mormon materials for comic purposes. Ward "realized and utilized the Mormon material to greater advantage" for comic purposes than Mark Twain did with the "strained" comedy about Brigham Young in *Roughing It*.

Howard G. Baetzhold's "Mark Twain on Scientific Investigation: Contemporary Allusions in 'Some Learned Fables for Good Old Boys and Girls'" (*Literature and Ideas*, pp. 128–54) enumerates the extensive scientific allusion in the 1874 burlesque: specific expeditions, parallels to Sir John Franklin, Dr. David Livingstone, and Henry M. Stanley, Barnum's museum, the discovery of the Moabite Stone in 1868—all are used or exaggerated in the story so that Twain could burlesque "human presumption and gullibility." Walter Blair's comprehensive study of "Mark Twain's Other Masterpiece: 'Jim Baker's Blue-Jay Yarn'" (*SAmH* 1:132–47) details the biographical background, the specific source, the literary influences, oral techniques, comic devices, the style, and the complex framework in the "Blue-Jay Yarn" from *A Tramp Abroad*, all of which combine to make it "the greatest of the shorter" works.

v. Huckleberry Finn

Concerned predominantly with *The Sun Also Rises*, Martin Light's "Sweeping Out Chivalric Silliness: The Example of Huck Finn and The Sun Also Rises" (*MTJ* 17,iii:18–21) nevertheless traces three elements of quixotic literature (the use of literary models, adventures, and enchantment) in the characterization of Tom and Robert Cohn as opposed to the realistic depiction of Huck and Jake. Robert P. Weeks sees significant parallels between the Dolphin and George J. Adams, the drunken prophet mentioned as the leader of the Jaffa Colony Christians in chapter 57 of *Innocents Abroad*. "The Captain, the Prophet, and the King: A Possible Source for Twain's Dauphin"

(*MTJ* 18,i:9–12) suggests that the theatricality, a wide repertory of con-games, and an unquenchable alcoholic thirst are convincing similarities.

James F. Hoy is overweeningly proud of "an as yet unnoted significance" in *Huck*, the implications of grangers and shepherds in "The Grangerford-Shepherdson Feud in *Huckleberry Finn*" (*MTJ* 18,i:19–20). Although the implications of "wandering herders versus settled gardeners" have been discussed before (most recently by Robert E. Lowery in 1970), Hoy does add the insight that the Grangerfords are symbolic of "sivilization," so that the death of practically all that clan "foreshadows Huck's final rejection of civilization in favor of a wandering existence in the territories."

Along toward the end of "Humor and America: The Southwestern Bear Hunt, Mrs. Stowe, and Mark Twain" (*SR* 83:573–601), James M. Cox suggests, with that brilliantly improvisational flair of his, that *Huck* is an amalgam of the qualities of Old Southwest humor and *Uncle Tom's Cabin.* It "combines the mirth of southwest humor with the moral sense" of Mrs. Stowe's novel, but its meaning constantly contradicts itself: "In historical terms we invalidated the slavery of the past to become a truly free Republic. In psychological terms we leave the old free world of childhood to enter the slavery of adult society." And Cox yearns for an awareness of the antimeaning of *Huck*—"the book is a lie, a tall tale, a stretcher, and does not, like a serious novel, represent or even reflect the truth. . . . What we have to know—but cannot face—is that our seriousness, or conscience, our life with meaning sustains a civilization as cruel as anything all those low mean characters Huck had to dodge ever thought of." (Earlier in his article and unrelated to his commentary on *Huck*, Cox explains The Fart Theory of Laughter; it's a delight, and I will be there, lined up with all the rest, to see him on visiting day.)

vi. Later Works

Clark Griffith, in "Merlin's Grin: From 'Tom' to 'Huck' in *A Connecticut Yankee*" (*NEQ* 48:28–46), studies the two basic situations in Mark Twain's earlier fiction—"the will to play games for the sake of gamesmanship, as opposed to a capacity for entertaining moral issues and executing moral choices"—as they coalesce in Hank's character and in the structure of the novel. In the first, "Tomlike," role Hank is a tall-tale teller, a showman, a violator of all the probabilities and plausibilities. But Hank also begins to develop a Huck-like conscience and to want "to change the moral structure of his world." His attempts to reform his world, like Huck's, are doomed, for "the morally committed hero will have to lose his soul in the pursuit of some great and noble enterprise—and so end up no differently from the tall-tale fantisizer, who never had a soul to lose." In the end, Merlin, whose spells and incantations make him "the Devil's spokesman," grins the last, nihilistic grin over the darkness of Mark Twain's world-view.

Beverly R. David's "The Unexpurgated *A Connecticut Yankee*: Mark Twain and His Illustrator, Daniel Carter Beard" (*Prospects* 1:99–117) summarizes the history of the illustrating of the first edition of the novel (including Beard's conviction that he was boycotted for his radical pictures), and speculates on the provocative but unanswered question of whether Twain or Beard chose Jay Gould as the model for the portrait of the slave driver. Ann Douglas, in "Art and Advertising in *A Connecticut Yankee*: The Robber Baron Revisited" (*CRevAS* 6:182–95), makes a long analysis of the cultural and mercantile aspects of the Robber Barons, symbolized by a conflict between art and advertising. Specifically in *A Connecticut Yankee* Hank's competitive ethic, his advertising gimmicks, his irritation with Arthurian inefficiency are indications of both his entrepreneur spirit and his "unconscious yet profound need of culture and the leisure which makes it possible."

In "The Other Half of Pudd'nhead's Dog" (*MTJ* 17,iv:10–11) Harold Aspiz finds an analogue in P. T. Barnum's story of Hack Bailey, who proposed to shoot his half of an exhibition elephant in order to coerce his partner to divide the profits. John Rachal suggests that Pudd'nhead and his creator share dual identities; in "David Wilson and Sam Clemens: The Public Image vs. The Private Man" (*AN&Q* 13:6–8) he notes that each has a public ("quiet, inoffensive, accommodating") side and a private (cynical, pessimistic, iconoclastic) aspect—the latter expressed in *Pudd'nhead Wilson* only in the Calendar.

James W. Gargano argues that the recent interpretations of *Pudd'nhead Wilson* as corrosive satire misinterpret the tone of the novel. In "*Pudd'nhead Wilson*: Mark Twain as Genial Satan" (*SAQ* 74:365–75), the narrator's "voice is not overly didactic, is often genial, and rarely explores the frightening depths of human nature." By undercutting potentially tragic scenes with comic conclusions, Mark Twain avoids "writing tragedy or a polemic against society." Roxy's scene changing the babies and Pudd'nhead's courtroom melodramatics affirm the calm comic detachment which the narrator preserves. And John Gerber, in "*Pudd'nhead Wilson* as Fabulation" (*SAmH* 2:21–31), summarizes the conflicting opinions of the book and suggests that the essential question is, "Is it a novel at all?" Using Robert Scholes's term *fabulation*, Gerber argues that neither objectivity nor realism is a valid concern of the form. In a tradition of fabulations from *Tom Jones* and *Humphrey Clinker* to *Catch 22* and *Cat's Cradle*, *Pudd'nhead Wilson* is "not so sweeping and imaginative as the great fabulations before it, nor so witty and wildly absurd as those of our own time," but it "nevertheless shares characteristics of both groups and occupies a midpoint in their tradition." Twain's constant intrusion as narrator, the emphasis on external action rather than character development, and an unblushing delight in outlandish coincidences and improbabilities are the marks of *Pudd'nhead Wilson* as fabulation, which too much dependence on Victorian melodrama weakens slightly.

Three articles look at facets of *The Mysterious Stranger*. Buford Scrivner, Jr., in "*The Mysterious Stranger*: Mark Twain's New Myth of the Fall" (*MTJ* 17,iv:20–21), argues that the novel reverses the traditional Christian myth with an "anti-fall," so that at the conclusion, "Theodor, the new Adam, [is] poised between annihilation and re-creation." "Philosophically," Scrivner says, "Twain's stance is a variety of absolute idealism in which Theodor becomes not an individual but a representative of universal Mind." Bertram Mott's "The Turn-of-the-Century Mark Twain, A Revisit" (*MTJ* 18,i:13–16) suggests that Mark Twain's philosophical tenor in the later 1890s, when he wrote the Eseldorf version of the novel, was much less pessimistic than in 1904, when he wrote the conclusion. The ending is, therefore, inappropriate both structurally and historically. More complex in its analysis is Vivienne E. Perkins's "The Trouble with Satan: Structural and Semantic Problems in the *Mysterious Stranger*" (*GyS* 3:37–43). The novel contains "a kernel and a shell," or two distinct lines of action: the former is "the loose plot relating to village life in Eseldorf"; the "shell" involves the Theodor-Satan relationship. The inconsistencies in Satan's character (convincingly catalogued here) make him "reliable . . . when his purpose is satiric (for instance, when he comments on the behavior of the Eseldorfers). He is not reliable when his aim is to convince Theodor philosophically that life is (a) miserable, (b) unreal, or (c) both, and that human beings are intrinsically worthless." Since both Satan's abstract pronouncements and his language are irrational and sometimes unreliable, the reader is left with "a literary work that is only partially valid or coherent."

Thomas Werge notes two specific parallels between "The Sin of Hypocrisy in 'The Man That Corrupted Hadleyburg' and 'Inferno' XXIII" (*MTJ* 18,i:17–18): "the use of gilded lead as an image of hypocrisy, and the use of a pervasive tone and imagery of weight, weariness, and oppressiveness." Kenneth A. Requa's "Counterfeit Currency and Character in Mark Twain's 'Which Was It?'" (*MTJ* 17,iii:1–6) looks provocatively at a major motif in that fragment. "At the center of these interweaving swindles is the image of the counterfeit, but forged letters and false bills are images of the characters who in reality are the chief counterfeits," he notes. George Harrison, Squire Fairfax, and Jasper are all varieties of doubles, "but this time each pair is within a single character: each has two sides, one real but hidden from the public eye and one counterfeit but in currency."

William L. Andrews nominates the anecdote about Henry Clay Dean from chapter 57 of *Life on the Mississippi* as "The Source of Mark Twain's 'The War Prayer'" (*MTJ* 17,iv:8–9). Dean, a last-minute addition to a Civil War rally in Keokuk in 1861, had stunned his audience with his oratory. Additions to the later story—its formal language, the reversal of lunatic-archangel imagery, and the stranger's inability to influence his audience—indicate Mark Twain's pessimism in "The War Prayer." John M. Ditsky's "Mark Twain and 'The Great Dark': Religion in *Letters from the Earth*" (*MTJ* 17,iv:12–19) is a strained attempt to work the miscellaneous pieces DeVoto collected into a coherent theological system. The analysis of the title article focuses on problems in narrative technique and the dichotomy between man's God and the actual God of Automatic Law.

Eberhard Alsen proposes that Sherwood Anderson adapted from the conclusion of *What Is Man?* the notion of "partial truths" which deflect one from ultimate truth. "The Futile Pursuit of Truth in Twain's 'What Is Man?' and Anderson's 'The Book of the Grotesque'" (*MTJ* 17,iii:12–14) suggests that the "old man" of Anderson's introduction appears based on Twain's "old man" with convincing argument. Jeanne M. Schinto is less persuasive in "The Autobiographies of Mark Twain and Henry Adams: Life Studies in Despair" (*MTJ* 17,iv:5–7), a slight notice of parallels in condemnation of adult values, exemption of women from that condemnation, and fears of Gilded Age materialism. Finally, Gilbert Prince's far-fetched "Mark Twain's 'A Fable': The Teacher as Jackass" (*MTJ* 17,iii:7–8) says that in the guise of this exemplum Mark Twain favors that brand of learning which is not the teacher's own interpretation of the materials; a Montesorry reading of "A Fable," I'd say.

When God decided to bestow The Itch on mankind, He was benevolent enough to decree only a seven-year tenure. It was one of His wiser decisions, and I have written the "Mark Twain" chapters for *American Literary Scholarship* just that long. Next year, with your offprints and your prayers, Louis J. Budd crawls into the Iron Maiden to survey Mark Twain scholarship.

University of New Mexico

7. Henry James

William T. Stafford

For reasons I haven't the foggiest rationale for explaining, the year 1975 witnessed an *amount* of scholarly activity unprecedented in the history of Jamesian criticism. The *variety* of that activity I tried half-facetiously to explain last December in a little talk before an American Literature Group at MLA as resulting from the simple assertion that "no critical, scholarly, historical, biographical, bibliographical, exegetical, stylistic, or statistical method yet invented or discovered by man or by computer has failed to find in one aspect or another of the Jamesian world appropriate fodder off which to feed." And half-facetious though that explanation is, I frankly know of no other way to account for the indisputable fact that during the year *12* books (not 10, as I originally thought) were published on Henry James, no two of them, moreover, serving the same supposed need or employing the same critical approach. To be sure, some of them, in my view, are much better than others; and some of the essays of the year, better than some of the books. But here at the beginning, which, of course, I wrote after I wrote what follows, let me simply express this year my wondrous stupefaction at the critical (or is it publishing or academic or economic?) phenomenon itself, an explanation for which, *any* explanation for which, I earnestly solicit any interested party to supply.

i. Letters, Travel Sketches, Bibliographies, Indexes

Leon Edel's second volume of the selected correspondence, *Henry James Letters 1875–1883* (Cambridge, Mass.: Belknap/Harvard Univ. Press), reveals a much more self-assured, expansive, even at times a cockier[1] Henry James than the one we left at the end of

1. James writes to Thomas Sergeant Perry on May 2, 1876, that "I heard Émile Zola characterize his manner sometime since as *merde à lâ vanille*. I send you by post Zola's own last—*merde au naturel.* Simply hideous."

volume 1 on his way to Paris and in effect to expatriation. The years here covered include the exciting year in Paris (1875–76) and James's meetings with and descriptions of such writers as Turgenev, Flaubert, and Zola; his return to England and subsequent "show of fame" with *The American*, "Daisy Miller," and others prior to and throughout the composition of *The Portrait of a Lady* (1876–81); and his two melancholy returns to America at the time of the death of his parents (1882). We leave him returning to Europe in 1883 where he will remain for the next 20 years. The editorial apparatus here is much the same as in the previous volume, with a brief introduction to the whole and with factual accounts of the life as headnotes to the four sections within which the letters are grouped. We are provided a chronology, six handsomely reproduced illustrations, and an index. The footnotes are mostly for identification or explanation, although nowhere are we given an explanation of some of the cryptic references to James's two younger brothers or of whether, with one minor exception, the general absence of any letters to the two are for reasons of taste or unavailability. The James here revealed is almost as keenly observant, as eloquent, as pithy as ever, although he is almost nowhere a James with whom most scholars of the novelist are unfamiliar. High points for me include Henry's defiant intransigence in defense of his younger brother Garth over William's apparent disagreement with the novelist's execution of their father's will, a provocative and previously unknown (to me) letter to one George Pellew on Jane Austen, and Henry's reactions to Howells over public charges of critical back-scratching between the two. The famous letter to Grace Norton on the "illimitable power" of "consciousness" is a dramatically effective note on which to end, especially followed as it is by a graceful bit of twaddle to an American hostess just before James is to return to Europe.

James the travel writer is the subject of both Thomas H. Pauley's "Henry James and the Travel Sketch: The Artistry of *Italian Hours*" (*CentR* 19:108–20) and Otto Friedrich's "A Little Tour with Henry James" (*ASch* 44:643–52). Pauley's is the more useful study in its attempt to distinguish the " 'pictorial' quality" of the early written portions of the volume from the more creative parts of the later-written sections. Friedrich's is another account of a current tour of southern France with James's *A Little Tour* as modern guide and foil.

Beatrice Ricks's *Henry James: A Bibliography of Secondary Works*, No. 24 in the Scarecrow Author Bibliographies Series (Metuchen, N.J.: Scarecrow Press), although ambitious, is not always accomplished and although useful, not totally to be trusted. The number of entries, "over 4,600 items," is impressive, although some items are listed more than once. Ricks attempts four groupings—biographies, individual works, general criticism, and bibliographies—with, however, such bizarre subgroups as the "Last Dictation" or "Reviews" under Works but with no subgroups at all under General Criticism. The Topical Index is equally eccentric, with two items, for example, listed on the subject Abandonment, and four under Allusion, Literary. The second appendix, a List of Critics, is more useful. The occasional annotations are uneven. The "Also See" cross-index to studies of individual works, in the single example I checked, refers the reader to another listing of the same item it annotates! In short, use with care, grateful though we all should be for having this staggering complex of material assembled, however badly. For additional bibliographies, see section vi.

My own *A Name, Title, and Place Index to the Critical Writings of Henry James* (Englewood, Col.: Microcard Editions Books) purports to list the name, title, and those places that are described *as places* in all of James's published nonfictional work except his letters. All items are listed alphabetically by author or location, and the whole is keyed to books, chapters, and periodicals as listed in the Edel and Laurence *Bibliography*. For two reviews of the volume, I refer readers to James J. Kirschke, *ALR* 9[1976]:83–85, and to Robert Gale, *MFS* 21[1975–76]:658–59.[1]

ii. Sources, Influences, Parallels

Dale Peterson's *The Clement Vision: Poetic Realism in Turgenev and James* (Port Washington, N.Y.: Kennikat Press) is an impressive monograph, as impressive for its review of the contemporary impact Turgenev made upon the American literary scene and for his sub-

1. Kirschke calls Stafford's work "a unique and indispensable tool . . . [it] is not the kind of reference tool that is done in a single year, nor even in several years. . . . No scholar on Henry James will want to be without this *Index*."—Ed.

sequent contribution to modern fiction as for its demonstration of the variety of things Turgenev's practice contributed to James's early fiction. Six brief chapters follow an introductory definition of terms and statement of purpose: how, for example, "the *organic* conjunction of aesthetic, cultural, and temperamental leanings that made Turgenev's example, as man and artist, permanently alluring to the creative imagination of the much younger Henry James." The parallel "provincialism," temperament, and background of Turgenev and James are said to have led them to share "a clement vision of experience by grounding the possibility for redemptive aesthetic appreciations of life in a realism that insists upon the priority of perception over circumstance . . . [thus presenting] experience itself as an ongoing, integrative, aesthetic process." Of the many affinities established between the two, let me stress what Peterson does with Turgenev's "Three Meetings" (of 1852) and James's "Four Meetings" (of 1877) and, more surprisingly, his persuasive account of what the much-annotated "Daisy Miller" may well owe to the Russian's *Asya* (of 1858). How Turgenev "condensed domestic dramas that were simultaneously dramatic analogues of larger-scale cultural confrontations" is seen at work both in *Roderick Hudson* and *The American* (not to mention *The Portrait*). But his final and in some ways most adventuresome chapter is of a late, revealed affinity between Turgenev's *First Love* and *What Maisie Knew*. Peterson is perhaps overall a bit too denigratory about other influences on James, and what he sees James's fiction as "saying" is in no ways startlingly original. Even so, he does present probably the most thorough and responsible record we have of how central "the aesthetic and cultural impact of Turgenev's precedent" was "upon the evolving craft of Henry James."

Important influences (if of a totally different kind) from other acquaintances of James are the subject both of Adeline R. Tintner's "The Metamorphoses of Edith Wharton in Henry James's *The Finer Grain*" (*TCL* 21:355–79) and of Joseph Hynes's "The Transparent Shroud: Henry James and William Story" (*AL* 46:506–27). The peculiar strength of Ms. Tintner's article is not so much her central thesis that the five women of the five stories of James's volume "are all transformations or transpositions of James's relation to Mrs. Wharton" ("her problems, her decor, her fiction, and her idiosyncrasies"). It is instead in the refracted rubric she thereby supplies for still another way of demonstrating the volume's overall unity. Concomitantly, Joseph Hynes's account of James's relation to Story, although as "definitive" as any we are ever likely to have (on the facts of their relationship, the novelist's reasons for writing the biography, its strengths and weaknesses), is more centrally concerned with how the "example" of Story can affect our understanding of some of James's own work ("The Lesson of the Master," "The Death of the Lion," *Roderick Hudson*), the problem of the artistic need to know or to do everything with the simultaneous need to be " 'all there' in a given artistic instance."

Somewhat less important, it seems to me, are Ms. Tintner's other two source studies of this year, her "Henry James's Salomé and the Arts of the *Fin de Siècle*" (*MarkhamR* 5,fall:5–10) and her "Sargent in the Fiction of Henry James" (*Apollo* Aug.:128–32), buttressed though both studies are with fine illustrations of her subjects. Nothing less than "all the traditional ways of handling" the period's various "kinds" of Salomé are said to be encompassed by James in a revision of *Roderick Hudson* and in the late story "A Round of Visits." And all that James "had learned from Sargent's talent" is said to be everywhere apparent in his work, from specific allusions and treatments to fictional manifestations of "Sargent types" and particular Sargent paintings.

Of least importance in this grouping this year are two brief comparative studies. Anna S. Parrill's "Portraits of Ladies" (*TSL* 20: 92–98) poses James's Isabel Archer and George Meredith's Clara Middleton (from *The Egoist*) as two Victorian heroines who best represent "how the intelligent woman had to struggle to retain her independence and self-respect in the face of repressive conventions." Joan Zlotnick, in "Influence or Coincidence: A Comparative Study of 'The Beast in the Jungle' and 'A Painful Case' " (*CLQ* 11:132–35), points to many parallels in the two tales (of characterization, plotting, theme, technique) to speculate that Joyce "may indeed have known James's story."

Finally worthy of mention here is Hans-Joachim Lang's "The Making of Henry James's *The American*: The Contribution of Four Literatures" (*AmS* 20:55–71)—for its voluminous survey of the criticism of the novel (in some 80 often lengthy footnotes) if not for the addition of Hawthorne's *The House of the Seven Gables* as the "American" contribution to those Russian, French, and English sources already established.

iii. Criticism: General, Books

Of the six book-length studies I have gathered into this particular grouping, Kenneth Graham's *The Drama of Fulfilment, An Approach to the Novels* (New York: Oxford Univ. Press) is for me the most satisfying overall. Because I have reviewed it elsewhere, however, (see *AL* 48[1976]:88–89), I will do no more here than describe it as a scrupulously fine reading of seven representative works—*Madame de Mauves, Daisy Miller, Roderick Hudson, The Aspern Papers, The Tragic Muse, The Spoils of Poynton,* and *The Wings of the Dove.*

Also significant is Ronald Wallace's *Henry James and the Comic Form* (Ann Arbor: Univ. of Mich. Press), a book that is better than its opening pages suggest, if somewhat lesser than it generally purports to be. No one, I suppose, would question James's affinities with the traditions of high comedy, or the ways in which "an archetypal analysis of plot and character in James reveals generic, recurring, conventional aspects of comedy." Nor would one quarrel with a definition of comedy that "affirms man's ability to maintain an ideal while adjusting his vision to permit a continued social existence and a knowledge of inherent human limitation at the same time," or even a contention that the "spirit" and "tone" of comedy in James is best seen through the "touchstone" of Gabriel Nash (of *The Tragic Muse*). But when such assertions are said indiscriminately to apply to *all* of James, when a chapter entitled "The Major Phase" does not even mention *The Wings of the Dove,* and when a treatment of James's work ignores such disparate examples as *Daisy Miller, The Turn of the Screw, The Princess Casamassima,* or "The Birthplace" with no stated rationale for having done so, one begins to question the critic's perspective. Yet there are some fine things in this book—the long middle chapter on the Jamesian plot; a reading of *The Spoils of Poynton* as an example of "parodicomedy" ("a parody of romantic comedy enhanced by mock epic allusions"); the social satire in *Maisie* and *The Awkward Age*; and, most importantly, James's demonstrated ties with other comic writers (*The Spoils,* with Cervantes and Fielding; *The Sacred Fount,* with Hawthorne and Swift; *The Portrait,* with Molière, Jane Austen, and George Eliot; *Maisie,* with Dickens; and *The Ambassadors* and *The Golden Bowl,* with Shakespearean comedy). Such fresh perspectives on James are undeniably welcome, even if they are not quite "a turning point in Jamesian criticism," as the dust jacket maintains. An assumption that those who do not view James as comic inevitably view him as tragic will not quite do. I suspect that most Jamesians view his works as uniquely his own, somewhere between or beyond tragedy *or* comedy, as in Ellen Leyburn's *The Relation of Comedy to Tragedy in the Fiction of Henry James*, a book Wallace lists in his bibliography but one whose issues he nowhere directly confronts.

Equally fresh in approach—and indeed a nice complement to Wallace's book—is William Veeder's *Henry James—The Lessons of the Master: Popular Fiction and Personal Style in the Nineteenth Century* (Chicago: Univ. of Chicago Press), which curiously joins the discipline of stylistics to that of cultural history. And although for me the history is more significant than the stylistics, this close focus on an early decade, from 1871 to 1881 (from *Watch and Ward* through *The Portrait*), is generally persuasive enough in seeing in this early fiction of James "transforming conventions" of popular fiction, conventions of style (extravagance and equipoise), conventions of character (gesture and type), and conventions of social concern (for example, the Woman Question) as an apprenticeship of sorts *and* as a kind of rubric to the achievement of *The Portrait*. The argument suffers somewhat from overkill, giving much more evidence than is needed to support conclusions I, at any rate, am perfectly willing to accept without such multiple, sometimes tedious, even somewhat questionable (as in word-count tables) bolstering. James *did* know the popular fiction of his day here and abroad, and the conventions of that fiction are undeniably at work in his own, even as they are eventually transformed, even as *his* transformations are eventually to transform modern fiction itself. We are thus said to see in some new ways, for example, in *The Portrait*, the "permanent ambivalence" in the "sexual and material aspects of Isabel's return to Osmond and Pansy . . . , both the self-serving aspects of her flight from sex . . . *and* the immense social pressures for that flight." Especially fine here are some new insights into the puns in *The Portrait* and how "like a pun, our response to Isabel must sustain multiple and at times conflicting elements" or how "Isabel is finally serious in the most admirably comic of ways." Also good is Veeder's revelation of transformed sexual images, from *Watch and Ward* to *The Por-*

trait. I was least convinced by his treatment of *Washington Square* and all that he attempts to discern from James's use therein of the genteel epigram "as it were." But overall Veeder's is an original and compelling book. The inclusion of seven reproductions of previously unpublished photographs of and for James by Alvan Langdon Coburn is an unexpected bonus, totally unrelated though they are, as far as I can see, to the central concerns of the book.

The three remaining book-length studies in this grouping are of less importance. Louis Auchincloss's *Reading Henry James* (Minneapolis: Univ. of Minn. Press) is indeed a "reading," graceful, lucid, highly selective, and, of course, impressionistic. That it ultimately tells us more about Auchincloss than James is neither unexpected nor necessarily denigratory, for the appeal of James to another writer is of importance in itself. Nothing in it is particularly surprising or new to the student of James, even central assessments such as James's reputed concern with "trying to create the drama of perfect intelligence, the finest sensibility when confronted . . . with lesser intelligences and cruder sensibilities." Very brief chapters give us a little about the life; a little about the *Notebooks* (whose entries are said themselves to reveal "the ultimate quality of the tale which they engender"); a little about James the critic, the memoirist, the dramatist; and a little about the major fiction, from the earliest American-set tales in contrast to those set in Europe (and a consequent view of the "paleness" of the tragedy in *Washington Square*, as if America were incapable of reflecting any but the palest emotions); the superficiality of the so-called international conflict when taken simply as a conflict between cultures; a discussion of *The Tragic Muse* which does not mention Gabriel Nash (or one of *Maisie* which views Mrs. Wix as a kind of heroine); and a conjunction of Amerigo, Charlotte, Kate, and Densher with evil *because* of their poverty, one of Maggie and Milly with virtue *because* of their wealth. Still, Auchincloss is an engaging, readable "companion" who, however self-consciously he stresses his perspective here as that of simple reader, nevertheless comes through as himself, another novelist.

Granville H. Jones's *Henry James's Psychology of Experience* (The Hague: Mouton) is an exasperating book, alternately muddled and provocative, complicated without being complex, sweepingly ambitious and curiously limited, arbitrary on the one hand, and extraordinarily tolerant and perceptive on the other. Although a book with a simple single thesis, it nevertheless attempts some sort of attention (or so it seems to me) to every piece of fiction James wrote, in addition to the autobiography and at least one of the plays, *Guy Domville*. The book's central concept is *innocence*, one or another elastic definition of which Jones sees at the core of every Jamesian work—so elastic, in fact, that it is perhaps best summarized as almost everything in opposition to *responsibility*, a concept itself so variously defined ("experience, initiation, involvement)" that we are best off viewing it simply as "antithesis." The "synthesis" resolving this perpetual conflict is said to be *renunciation* (itself of course a new antithesis), as marked by "negation and limitation, vacancy or absence or denial." Some such sweeping dialectic seems to be at the center of the book's conception. Its "method" can be put more directly: "first, to describe the innocence on which he concentrates; second, to delineate the responsibilities in the relationships between the characters; and third, to interpret the situations culminating in renunciation." Its "arrangement" is one that moves from James's fictional children and adolescents through young adulthood to middle and old age, from an analysis of the child of "The Author of Beltraffio" as his first "subject" to a defense of John Marcher, of "The Beast in the Jungle," as his last, a form and method truly, as Jones claims, "unique among studies of Henry James." In the many, many turgid pages in between are fine insights (such as his views on Kate Croy and Maggie Verver) in frustrating alternation with the banal (a very sentimental view of Maisie, for example, or an alleged parallel between Roderick Hudson and Dostoevsky's Raskolnikov). Many passages of the book were both difficult and painful (for me) to read.

Finally, Gordon Pirie's lucid little *Henry James* in the Literature in Perspective Series (Totowa, N.J.: Rowman and Littlefield) is admittedly "a critical introduction for those coming new to James" and hence not meant for the scholar. It is nevertheless a good introduction, limited though its coverage is to a brief account of the life, chapters on *The Europeans*, *Washington Square*, *The Portrait*, *The Bostonians*, *Maisie*, and two tales, "The Aspern Papers" and "The Jolly Corner." One should thus not hesitate to recommend it to the uninitiated, especially for its opening chapter, its general sense of the comic in James, its treatment of *The Bostonians* and of *Maisie*.

iv. Criticism: General, Essays

Three or four essays within this category of general criticism are as fine as anything written on James during the year. And first among them are two pieces by Daniel J. Schneider. His long chapter, "'A Terrible Mixture in Things,' The Symbolism of Henry James" in his *Symbolism: The Manichean Vision*, pp. 62–117, is one of the best recent articles done on the novelist, carefully tracing, as it does, the symbolic antinomies, mostly as revealed in the images, in a significant early, middle, and late example, *The American*, *The Portrait*, and *The Ambassadors*. A resultant reading of the last is as good as any reading I know of. Equally good is his "The Divided Self in the Fiction of Henry James" (*PMLA* 90:447–60), a companion psychobiographical study wherein knowledge of James the man is always at the service of the fiction. "The divided self" provides Schneider with a beguiling rubric with which to read the fiction and ultimately to read James himself as one whose "liberty to be an artist employing the freest and largest of forms, the novel, was also his enslavement," condemned as James was (and as James described Maggie Verver as being) to "'the responsibility of freedom.'"

Also first-rate is J. A. Ward's "The Ambiguities of Henry James" (*SR* 83:39–60), an eloquent defense of the role of the artist "to see multiplicity, not to impose unity," for the experience of life is to be described, not prescribed. "The unity of Henry James's fiction resides in its architectural coherence, not in the unambiguous comprehensibility of the characters who inhabit it." Also good enough are Harold T. McCarthy's two chapters on James in *The Expatriate Perspective* (Cranbury, N.J.: Farleigh Dickinson Univ. Press). His "Henry James and the American Aristocracy" (pp. 81–93), which focuses on the international fiction up through *The Portrait*, stresses James's sense of "the way in which America's traditional idealism and generosity of mind were being taken over by a new economic aristocracy that was avid for all the perquisites of the old aristocracy of blood." The more important "Henry James: Love in the Anglo-Saxon World" (pp. 108–19), on the major phase, sees the novelist as now possessed of a much more inclusive sense of how the "evil" mind of the modern world "has become alienated from sensuous experience." Strether, Densher, Maggie, he contends, are all "transformed by a discovery of love, of the nature and strength of love, and of his [or her] own capacity for love."

The descriptive phrase in the title of Howard Pearce's "Henry James's Pastoral Fallacy" (*PMLA* 90:834–47) is in fact used to name the way in which James's sense of place is said to encompass both "a romantic falsification and an imaginative creation of values" throughout the canon, rather directly in such tales as *The Europeans*, "An International Episode," and, extensively, in "Brooksmith," but ambiguously in such fictions as *The Turn of the Screw* and *The Golden Bowl*. L. C. Knights's "Henry James and Human Liberty" (*SR* 83:1–18) is a reminder that the moral value of James's imagination is inescapably tied to his method. And Ross Labrie, in "The Good and the Beautiful in Henry James" (*Greyfriar: Siena* [College, N.Y.] *Studies in Literature* 16:3–15), stresses the recurrent frequency with which ethically "fine" characters such as Maggie Verver or Tina (of "The Aspern Papers") foil seemingly fine characters who are nevertheless marred by a devotion to ethical or esthetic absolutes.

Three remaining general studies deserve only the briefest mention. Sara S. Chapman's "Stalking the Beast: Egomania and Redemptive Suffering in James's 'Major Phase' " (*CLQ* 11:50–66) all too mechanically finds a kind of "spiritual salvation" at the center of three late stories. H. G. Ruthrof's "A Note on Henry James's Psychological Realism and the Concept of Brevity" (*SSF* 12:369–73) briefly recapitulates some formulations from the Prefaces and *Notebooks* as "structure-carrying elements" important to the transition from 19th- to 20th-century concepts of short fiction. And Frances E. Crowley's "Henry James's 'The Beast in the Jungle' and *The Ambassadors*" (*PsyR* 62:153–63) begins as if its thesis were that the tale "is an ironic version" of the novel, only to give its major attention to psychoanalyzing Marcher with side trips along the way into the tale's structural parallels with fairy tales and myths.

v. Criticism: Individual Tales

Any attention paid to studies of James's tales during 1975 would have to begin with E. A. Sheppard's *Henry James and "The Turn of the Screw"* (Auckland and New York: Auckland and Oxford Univ. Press), surely the most curious response yet in that curious interpretive history provoked by James's curious tale. Sheppard's is a long, careful, documented study of the context in which the tale is said to have been conceived, written, and produced. And for what? To read *The Turn of the Screw* as a "moral mystery" of a good woman with "a fatal 'psychic' faculty whose operation she completely misunderstands, and [who consequently?] with her goodness and her intelligence she acts to destroy." The long, long journey to this conclusion is much more provocative than the conclusion itself. Attention to James's life, his family, his brother William's interest in the occult, the traditional influences of Hawthorne, of Swedenborg, of English gothicism, the structure of the tale (its name and place symbolism), the revisions, even briefly, other interpretations—all are pretty much what one might have expected. Less expected, I must say, are his chapters on Jane Eyre, who is said to serve "as the model for his youthful . . . and scrupulously honest narrator," his chapter on George Bernard Shaw as "The Real Peter Quint" (because of his devilish looks, his reputation for corrupting the young, his "womanizing"), and his chapter on "The Influence of Ibsen" (to demonstrate that he had no influence). But the major attention of the book, almost its last half, after a brief chapter on the parallels in the tale to a French scandal of the time, is a history of the Society for Psychical Research, William's association with it, accounts of its subject in the popular press, and all that Henry can be demonstrated to have, or perhaps have, known of its proceedings and findings. He is, of course, said to have known quite a bit—and to have shaped his tale accordingly. It is indeed a curious book, finally much more valuable for its biographical material, its indefatigable researches into the most remote areas of James's life, his readings, his exposures, especially his relations to Shaw, than for its thesis. Valerie Purton's brief "James' 'The Turn of the Screw,' Chapter 9" (*Expl* Item 24) is thus a nice, ironic counterpart as a note quoting several passages from Fielding's *Amelia* for the "hints" *they* give to the "nature of the governess' imaginings."

Two studies of the tales tie them to national myths. Charles N. Watson, Jr.'s "The Comedy of Provincialism: James's 'The Point of View,'" (*SHR* 9:173–83) sees this tale as much pro- as anti-American, especially as revealed in Aurora's trip West at the end in terms of its Huck Finn proclivities. Adeline R. Tintner's "Iconic Analogy in 'The Lesson of the Master': Henry James's Legend of St. George and the Dragon" (*JNT* 5:116–27) describes the tale as a witty "rereading" of the legend that makes of it a veritable "Victorian saint's legend, fraught with mild profanity and impertinence."

The remaining studies of individual tales all deal with late works. Gerald Hoag's "The Death of the Paper Lion" (*SSF* 12:163–72) is a conventional upside-down explication of Neal Parraday as not so much a put-upon writer as a "venial . . . , shocking fraud." Mildred E. Hartsock's "Dizzying Summit: James's 'The Altar of the Dead' " (*SSF* 11[1974]:371–78) extensively analyzes its checkered critical history while developing an interpretation that sees it reflecting a thesis of "memory and sensibility to the past" as an "affirmative 'act of life.' " Robert N. Hudspeth's "A Hard, Shining Sonnet: The Art of Short Fiction in James's 'Europe' " (*SSF* 12:387–89) is a finely honed analysis of the tale's form, which James himself compared to that of a sonnet, wherein action is muted, time foreshortened, and a subtle but explosive contrast thereby set up between "the surface view of his character's lives and . . . extensive realities of their existence." And Adela Stycsyńska's " 'The Papers': James' Satire on the Modern Publicity System" (*KN* 22:419–36) poses James the media critic as forerunner to such modern examples as Graham Greene's *A Burnt-Out Case* and Ionesco's *Le Maître*.

Two views of "The Jolly Corner" are concerned with allusions and sources. M. E. Grenander's "Benjamin Franklin's Glass Armonica and Henry James's 'Jolly Corner' " (*PLL* 11:415–17) points to the powers of the alluded-to musical instrument to induce trancelike states to support a reading of the story in which ghosts, following Ambrose Bierce's definition, are said to be "outward and visible signs of an inward fear." And Ernest Tuveson's " 'The Jolly Corner': A Fable of Redemption" (*SSF* 12:271–80) finds in the *Proceedings* of The Society for Psychical Research a reflected view of F. W. H. Myers on "reciprocal hallucination" which James might have seen and thus might have used in his conception of the tale.

vi. Criticism: Individual Novels

Two studies of *The American* are unconsciously linked in their mutual views of Newman's failures and in their relative indifference to the novel's comedy. James D. Wilson's "The Gospel According to Christopher Newman" (*SAF* 3:83–88) makes much of the religious imagery in the book in viewing Newman's failures "to save the soul of the

Europeans" as a failure in "proselytizing for the American ideal in a world where it has no place." Susan P. Ward's "Painting and Europe in *The American*" (*AL* 46:566–74) sees Newman's failure with Claire clearly foreshadowed by his failure to understand the two paintings he views at the Louvre early in the novel. This esthetic failure, however, is said to be transformed at the novel's end.

Much more important than either of these are two studies of early transitional works. Martha Collins's "The Center of Consciousness on Stage: Henry James's *Confidence*" (*SAF* 3:39–50) finds in this novel "an incomplete synthesis" of previously tried techniques—"the center of consciousness" in *Daisy Miller* and "the dramatic method" in *The Europeans*—as meaningful apprenticeship toward later, more important fiction. But it is Millicent Bell's "Style as Subject: *Washington Square*" (*SR* 83:19–38) that is for me the best study of a single novel to have appeared during the year; it is certainly the best reading I know of this novel. Its real subject, she maintains, is "style" and the way "literary styles and their analogous life attitudes[,] as those of the realist-historian, the ironist, the melodramatist, and the romantic fabulist," are all foiled by the authenticity of James's heroine, who is described as possessed of "a style so mute and motionless as to be almost the surrender of style," freed as it is from "any social or literary convention." Thus is born, says Bell, a "new language of authenticity" which will serve James well in his first masterpiece, the shortly following *Portrait.* A truly exciting reading.

It is still, however, *The Portrait of a Lady* that attracts the most critical attention, this year: a book, three new essays, and a checklist. Robert D. Bamberg's *Henry James's "The Portrait of a Lady": An Authoritative Text, Henry James and the Novel, Reviews and Criticism* (New York: W. W. Norton) is primarily distinguished for its textual appendix of substantial variants between the first book edition (of 1881) and the New York Edition (of 1908), which is the text reprinted here. That appendix, however, includes neither accidentals nor the variants between the periodical versions and the first book version. With the exception of a single previously unpublished essay, the other apparatus of the edition is readily available in any number of places—the Preface, James from the *Notebooks* and elsewhere, some early reviews, several often reprinted essays, and a very selected bibliography. Anthony J. Mazella's "The New Isabel" (pp. 597–619) is a study of the revisions to support the thesis that the later Isabel, unlike the earlier, "embraces multiple levels of existence" and is thereby one with a "heightened consciousness," now much more aware of its preciousness and of the multiplicity of threats to it. Annette Niemtzow's "Marriage and the New Woman in *The Portrait of a Lady*" (*AL* 47:377–95) is also good, not simply for seeing the ties between Isabel's dilemma and the ideas of the elder Henry James on the subject, but also for seeing how the fictional convention of "marriage as an apocalypse" is here challenged by James, maintaining that what Isabel finally accedes to is not necessarily what James himself thinks should be acceded to. Joseph B. McCullough's "Madame Merle: Henry James's 'White Blackbird'" (*PLL* 11:312–16) is a note finding keys to Serena Merle's true character via her name and consequent allusions to Alfred de Musset, to Ovid, and to the two classical figures she is specifically associated with, Juno and Niobe. Finally, Linda J. Taylor's "*The Portrait of a Lady* and the Anglo-American Press: An Annotated Checklist, 1880–1886" (*RALS* 5:166–98) provides a useful listing in addition to a commonsensical introductory account of the varied misinformation now in print about the then-contemporary views of the novel.

The two remaining studies of single novels, outside those listed previously, are rather slight. William L. Nance's "Eden, Oedipus, and Rebirth in American Fiction" (*ArQ* 31:353–65) is a generic study of the American experience which gives central attention to Strether in the famous Lambinet scene of *The Ambassadors* as a quintessential "voyage of quest and defeat" that nonetheless involves a "rebirth." Jeffrey Meyers's "Bronzino, Veronese, and *The Wings of the Dove*," in his *Painting and the Novel* (New York: Barnes and Noble), pp. 19–30, reproduces the much-discussed Bronzino *Lucrezia* and the Veronese *The Marriage Feast at Cana* while elucidating the roles they play in the novel of enriching character, providing a "visual focus and structure for two crucial scenes," and rendering "in pictorial art the dominant themes of the book."

viii. Postscript

Perhaps it is not inappropriate to conclude this year's survey with a reference to William E. Farrell's "Henry James Is Honored, in a

Way" (*NYT* 24 May:56,1), an amusing account of a dinner held on May 23 at Chicago's Bakery in specious honor of the Master by graduate students and faculty of the University of Chicago.

Purdue University

8. Pound and Eliot

Stuart Y. McDougal

i. Pound

***a.* Textual and Bibliographical.** The state of Pound's texts remains deplorable, but no work was done in this area.

***b.* Biographical.** Louis Simpson considers the lives and works of Ezra Pound, T. S. Eliot, and William Carlos Williams with varying success in *Three on the Tower.* Contending that the three poets "had significant, I would say symbolic, lives," Simpson classifies them as "Ezra Pound, or Art," "T. S. Eliot, or Religion," and "William Carlos Williams, or Experience." Although the scholar cannot expect to find any surprises in this work, it is a brief, lively introduction. The volume has been issued in paperback, and should prove useful for undergraduates and general readers.

Additional biographical information appeared in *Paideuma.* Perdita Schaffner, the daughter of H. D., reminisces about her correspondence with Mary de Rachewiltz, and her subsequent meeting at Brunnenburg with Mary de Rachewiltz and her father ("Merano, 1962" [4:513–18]). Richard Taylor's "Ezra Pound: Editor of NŌ" (4:345–47), presents additional background material on the state of the Fenollosa materials when Pound acquired them. Taylor appends the unedited text of the Nō Drama *Yoro,* which was Yeats's model for *At the Hawk's Well* (4:349–53). Stephen J. Adams has contributed a very interesting piece on "Pound, Olga Rudge, and the 'Risveglio Vivaldiano'" (4:111–18), in which he discusses at length the contributions of Pound and Olga Rudge to the revival of Vivaldi in this century. Jerome Kavka, one of the psychiatrists who knew Pound at St. Elizabeths, contributes a short note on the issue of confidentiality, concluding that "the increasing passage of time militates toward exposure" ("Ezra Pound's Sanity: The Agony of Public Disclosure" [4:527–29]).

Charles Olson & Ezra Pound: An Encounter at Saint Elizabeths (New York: Grossman/Viking) is a collection of poems, "prose cantos," and essays ably edited by Catherine Seelye which chronicles Olson's encounters with Pound in the 1940s. Olson struggles to understand the central "contradiction" which Pound presents: "Whenever Pound remained on the level of intellect and the creative he was dead right . . . but wrong with a stink of death on all to do with politics and society." Olson's musings, at a time when he was struggling to find his own voice as a writer, are of considerable interest to all students of modern poetry. Selections from this collection were published earlier this year in Charles Olson's "Encounter with Ezra Pound" (*Antaeus* 17:73–92).

c. Criticism: Books. Louis Simpson's book, mentioned above, looks at Pound's poetry in its totality. A more specialized work is Eugene Paul Nassar's *The Cantos of Ezra Pound: The Lyric Mode* (Baltimore and London: The Johns Hopkins Univ. Press). We badly need studies of *The Cantos* and this is a modest addition. Part of the problem with the book lies in Nassar's description of a proper approach to *The Cantos*: ". . . the primary interpretive data ought to be the radiant lyric nodes of *The Cantos* themselves; secondary, and in descending order, ought to be the nonlyrical portions of *The Cantos*, Pound's other poetry, his prose, and, finally, his sources." Nassar's discussions of these passages are often quite illuminating, but they exist in a vacuum and one ends up with a very fragmentary view of Pound's poem. Another weakness of the book is Nassar's refusal to make qualitative distinctions among the cantos, other than those implied by his general approach. Nassar's contribution to Pound studies is to be welcomed, but one wishes that he had set more ambitious goals for his work.

d. Criticism: Articles. *Paideuma* continues to be the principal source of Pound criticism. Let me begin with short notes, all from the pages of this journal.

A number of these are identifications of figures in *The Cantos*. In "Pound's 'Henriot'" (4:99–100), Francis J. Bosha convincingly demonstrates that the "Henriot" mentioned in Canto 84 is not the French novelist and poet Emile Henriot (1889–1961), as was commonly supposed, but rather Philippe Henriot (?–1944), the Minister of Propaganda for Marshal Petain's Vichy Government and "a leading collaborationist radio commentator."

Fred Mormarco, following a lead provided by Guy Davenport, establishes that Schiavoni (Canto 5) was an eyewitness to the murder of Giovanni Borgia. Mormarco locates Pound's source in the diary of the Alsatian priest Johannis Burchardus ("Schiavoni: 'That Chap on the Wood Barge,'" [4:101–04]). In a supplementary note ("'Schiavoni,' or: When St. Hieronymus Turned His Back" [4:105–10]), Eva Hesse shows that Pound used the Rev. Arnold Harris Mathew's translation of Burchardus, published in London in 1910. She includes a long extract from the work to substantiate her claim.

R. Sieburth identifies François Bernouard as the friend of Remy de Gourmont who founded La Belle Edition, a French press of limited editions which went bankrupt in 1929 with the publication of the *oeuvres complètes* of Zola ("Canto 119: François Bernouard" [4:329–32]).

In "Henri Gaudier's 'Three Ninas'" (4:323–24), Timothy Materer explains Pound's reference in Canto 107 ("Gaudier has left us three Ninas"): "The 'three Ninas' are works Gaudier carved or modeled from sketches of [his model] Nina Hamnett."

Hugh Witemeyer identifies Wang (Canto 96) as David Hsin-fu Wand, the contemporary Chinese-American poet, translator, and scholar who had corresponded with Pound at St. Elizabeths ("The Flame-style King" [4:333–35]).

The other notes from *Paideuma* deal largely with Pound's sources. Bradford Morrow demonstrates that Pound's treatment of Sordello in Canto 36 was shaped by his reading of Cesare de Lollis's *Vita e Poesie di Sordello di Goito* (1896): "Indeed the entire passage [in Canto 36] . . . is either paraphrased, translated, or directly quoted out of de Lollis's *Sordello*" ("De Lollis' *Sordello* and Sordello: Canto 36" [4:93–98]).

Wendy Stallard Flory, in "Alexander Del Mar: Some Additional Sources" (4:325–27) identifies the sources of two passages in Canto 97 which are taken from Del Mar, and which had eluded Daniel Pearlman in his earlier article on the subject ("Alexander Del Mar in *The Cantos* [1:161–80]).

Stuart Y. McDougal discusses Pound's indebtedness to Walter Pater in "The Presence of Pater in '"Blandula, Tenella, Vagula"'" (4:317–21). McDougal argues that not only the title comes from

Pater (through *Marius the Epicurean*), but that the poem also reflects Pound's reading of *Aucassin and Nicolette* and the discussion of that work in Pater's *The Renaissance.*

In "Ezra Among the Old Bones" (4:355–59) David M. Gordon discusses Pound's recognition of the importance of the tortoise shell and bone inscriptions of ancient Chinese script. Gordon expands what should be a one-page note with editorializing of the following nature: "At this moment we are counting down the limited number of years left to us on the planet in order to find the answer to man. Upon these oracle-bones we may be able to decipher our future."

The only discussion of *Hugh Selwyn Mauberley* is in a note by Laurence W. Mazzeno, who explicates the meaning of "after Samothrace" in part 3 ("A Note on 'Hugh Selwyn Mauberley' " [4:89–91]). Following a suggestion by Richard Ellmann and Robert O'Clair in *The Norton Anthology of Modern Poetry*, Mazzeno cogently argues that "The Christian beauty . . . defected as the missionaries [Paul, in particular] spread the gospel westward."

In "Ruskin and the Signed Capital in Canto 45" (4:85–88) Hugh Witemeyer demonstrates that the signed capital "was a well known cultural landmark to which [Pound] was making one of his characteristic pilgrimages in 1911," and he includes illustrations of it from Ruskin's *The Stones of Venice* (1851) and George Edmund Street's *Brick and Marble in the Middle Ages: Notes of a Tour in the North of Italy* (1855). Witemeyer concludes that "Ruskin established the signed capital as a symbol of civilized craftsmanship in the 1850s. When Pound evokes the signature of Adaminus *contra usura* eighty-five years later (1936), he is working in a venerable Victorian tradition."

Turning to articles of a longer and more general nature, we can begin with Joseph N. Riddel's study of "Pound and the Decentered Image" (*GaR* 29:565–91). Riddel shows how Pound "decenters the classical sense of the term [the image]" by emphasizing the moving rather than the stationary qualities of the image. He analyzes the origin of the image for Pound, and considers its significance for Pound's short imagist poetry and for *The Cantos.* The Poundian values of clarity and concision could be employed here to advantage, for the discussion is marred by the use of jargon and the excessive length. The increasingly fashionable tendency to write without footnotes makes it difficult to examine any of the sources, and this is a problem here where errors abound in what can easily be checked. For example, Riddel prints only one poem in its entirety ("In a Station of the Metro"): the title is misquoted and there is an error in the punctuation of the second line. Such carelessness reflects badly on the method being employed.

Marjorie G. Perloff discusses Pound's debt to Rimbaud in "Pound and Rimbaud: The Retreat from Symbolism" (*IowaR* 6:91–117). Perloff states that "however much Pound may have thought he was influenced by Homer and Dante, his structures of decomposition and fragmentation have, formally speaking, almost nothing to do with the architectural design of the *Odyssey* or the "Acquinas map" of the *Commedia.* Structurally, the Malatesta or Pisan Cantos may be said to fulfill Pound's aim: to forge a conscious aesthetic out of Rimbaud's random intuitions." Although Perloff overstates her case, the influence is an important one which has not been sufficiently discussed.

Another study of influence is Thomas Rees's "Ezra Pound and the Modernization of Yeats" (*JML* 4:574–92). Rees chronicles the developing personal relationship of the two poets and their mutual interest in the Noh drama, and shows how Pound's conceptions of diction and meter influenced Yeats. Rees adds little to the earlier discussion of K. L. Goodwin in *The Influence of Ezra Pound* (New York and London: Oxford Univ. Press, 1966).

Two of Pound's translation/imitations have received extended studies, and both of these are important additions to Pound scholarship. Vincent E. Miller has examined the *Homage to Sextus Propertius* in "The Serious Wit of Pound's *Homage to Sextus Propertius.*" (*ConL* 16:452–62). Miller develops in detail two themes noted by Christine Brooke-Rose: the treatment of love as "a generous, joyous, heedless thing" and "the underworld Persephone theme." He also discovers in "Pound's description of de Gourmont's 'Sequaire' the ground plan of the *Homage of Sextus Propertius.*" He concludes by noting that "here Pound achieved for the first time what he had sought for a decade, a way to write what he considered 'poetry *of our time*': i.e., poetry that would relate the most serious and abiding of human feelings, and the trivialities and pressures of everyday life in the contemporary world." In "A Case for Pound's 'Seafarer'" (*Mosaic* 9,ii:127–45), S. J. Adams attempts to show "how truly faithful Pound is, both in letter and spirit" to the original work. Adams gives an excellent line-by-line commentary, comparing the original with Pound's version.

Most of the scholarship on *The Cantos* this year has focused on the later cantos, principally *The Pisan Cantos* and *Section: Rock-Drill de los Cantares.* Some of this material is in the form of glosses, which will no doubt be incorporated in the revised and enlarged *Annotated Index to the Cantos*, under the supervision of Carroll F. Terrell, but this work will not be available until at least 1978.

An introduction to *The Pisan Cantos* for the general reader is Donald Monk's "Intelligibility in *The Pisan Cantos*" (*JAmS* 9:213–27). Monk insists on the importance of the ideogrammic method in *The Pisan Cantos*: "Presentation of opposites is the method: accumulation of linked analogies provides the substitute for narrative progression: transcendence—the subsuming of the drab realities of the camp into the dream of the eternal city, Dioce—proves the task." In "Pound's Progress: *The Pisan Cantos*" (*Paideuma* 4:71–81), Michael Schuldiner addresses himself to a more specific problem: If, he asks, one can "accept the occurrence of a 'revelation' or illumination in Canto 81, and suggest that the sought-for 'astasal' with the 'process' finally does occur in Canto 83 . . . how does one account for the apparent reversion in Canto 84 to . . . fascism?" Schuldiner analyses the virtues of "sinceritas," "caritas," "humanitas," and "hilaritas" which are named in Canto 83, but, he asserts, not finally affirmed until Canto 84. These virtues are "the breadth, length, depth, and height of Pound's cross, which allow him to shed the burden of that world which he carries, his past." And, in an article which is informative but poorly written and far too long, A. D. Moody discusses "Pound's Allen Upward" (*Paideuma* 4:55–70), with emphasis on the "Upward ideogram" and its function in *The Pisan Cantos.*

In "Apollonius of Tyana: the Odyssean Hero of *Rock-Drill* as a Doer of Holiness" (*Paideuma* 4:3–36), D. James Neault contributes a biographical sketch of Apollonius and a thorough consideration of his role in the *Rock-Drill* cantos. A discussion of the Chinese in these cantos is provided by Thomas Grieve in "Annotations to the Chinese in *Section: Rock-Drill*" (*Paideuma* 4:362–508). Jacob Korg presents an illuminating examination of Jacob Epstein's sculpture *Rock Drill* (with photographs of the version Pound would have seen and two later versions) in "Jacob Epstein's Rock Drill and the *Cantos*" (*Paideuma* 4:301–13). Korg analyzes Pound's interest in Epstein, and suggests that these cantos are an "homage to Vorticism." A rather superficial treatment of these cantos, focusing primarily on Pound's "methods of raising the cultural consciousness of the reader" and the issue of usury, is Carol Davidsen's "*The Cantos* and Culture" (*ConnR* 8,ii:55–62).

A more detailed consideration of the meaning of usury in *The Cantos* is William Tay's "Between Kung and Eleusis: *Li Chi*, The Eleusinian Rites, Erigena and Ezra Pound" (*Paideuma* 4:37–54). Tay examines the "trinity" of Confucius, Eleusis and Erigena, which, he feels, constitute "an effective counteraction to the preposterous Geryon."

David M. Gordon presents a useful survey of the role of Edward Coke (1552–1634), the distinguished English jurist, in *The Cantos*, and gives a detailed reading of Cantos 107 and 108 ("The Azalea Is Grown" [*Paideuma* 4:223–99]). And, in "Pound's Use of the Sacred Edict in Canto 98" (*Paideuma* 4:121–68), Gordon continues the work of explication he began in "Thought Built on Sagetrieb" (*Paideuma* 3:169–90).

ii. Eliot

***a.* Textual and Bibliographical.** With the appearance of the *Selected Prose of T. S. Eliot*, edited with an introduction by Frank Kermode (New York: Harcourt Brace Jovanovich/Farrar, Straus and Giroux), a reasonably priced, representative selection of Eliot's essays is at last available. While I wish that Kermode had included more material not published elsewhere (two thirds of the selections are from *Selected Essays* and *On Poetry and Poets*), he has chosen well from among those essays which are already in print.

***b.* Criticism: Books.** Only two book-length studies of Eliot appeared this year: Louis Simpson's *Three on The Tower* (reviewed above) and Elisabeth W. Schneider's *T. S. Eliot: The Pattern in the Carpet* (Berkeley: Univ. of Calif. Press). Schneider states her objectives in her opening paragraph: "To look back and forth from the single poem . . . to the artist's entire work, aware of both simultaneously; to be aware of the signature of the artist written all over each work . . . and to perceive something of the continuity persisting beneath development and change." This is a laudable aim, but Schneider's vision appears fixated on the prayer rug in the vestibule, ignoring the larger carpet in the adjacent room, for she excludes Eliot's drama and most of his critical essays and focuses on the poetry from *Prufrock and other Observations* through *The Four Quartets.* One can learn a good deal about these poems from her discussions. But if a pattern is to be discerned in a writer's work, his total *oeuvre* should be examined. I also find unconvincing Schneider's insistence that Eliot "ironed the pattern into the carpet" (to paraphrase the title of one of her chapters), that is, that Eliot deliberately forged a consisent poetic personality for himself and a consistent pattern for his work.

***c.* Criticism: Articles.** Short articles on Eliot proliferated in 1975, due in part to the continued publication of the *T. S. Eliot Review.* Let me begin with a summary of those notes which deal with Eliot's sources.

In "A Possible Source for Prufrock" (*TSER* 2,i:4) W. B. Ahearn observes that the same issue of *Harper's* which published Henry James's "Crapy Cornelia" (suggested by Hugh Kenner as a source for "Prufrock") had a story on Edinburgh that might have provided a "cityscape" for Eliot. Elsie Leach sees Marvell's "The Garden" as a "point of departure" for "Gerontion" in " 'Gerontion' and Marvell's 'The Garden' " (*ELN* 13:45–48).

In "A Note on *The Waste Land,* l. 426" (*TSER* 2,ii:9), Robert E. Jungman proposes that Eliot may not only have had Isaiah 38:1 in mind, but also a line from Sophocles' *Antigone,* "Set your own life in order." Billie McClanahan offers "A Surprising Source for Belladonna" (*TSER* 2,i:2), the Lady of Rocks in the Whiterocks soda advertisements. Bruce Bailey discusses Joyce's possible influence on *The Waste Land* in "A Note on *The Waste Land* and Joyce's *Ulysses*" (*TSER* 2,ii:10). Dean Schnetzer associates the "man with Three Staves" with a card in the Tarot deck designed by Arthur Edward Waite, which Eliot had seen ("The Man with Three Staves in *The Waste Land*" [*BNYPL* 78:347–50]). Schnetzer convincingly demonstrates the "parallels between the picture on this card [which is reproduced in the essay] and the image of the Fisher King which appears at the end of *The Waste Land.*"

Grover Smith, in "Lamb and *Lear* in 'Little Gidding' " (*TSER* 2,i:2), suggests that the phrase "impotence of rage" echoes a remark of Charles Lamb on *King Lear*. Christopher Ricks discusses two little-known essays of Eliot's in "A Note on 'Little Gidding'" (*EIC* 25:145–53). "Notes sur Mallarmé et Poe" and "Charybde et Scylla" demonstrate "Eliot's own aftersight and foresight about 'Little Gidding.'" Both essays were originally written in English, and deserve to be reprinted.

James S. Whitlark, in "More Borrowings by T. S. Eliot from 'The Light of Asia'" (*N&Q* 220:206–07) discusses the image of the wheel, which Eliot may have taken from Sir Edwin Arnold's work. Glen W. Singer explicates two references to Nausicaa and Polypheme in "Eliot's 'Sweeney Erect'" (*Expl* 34:item 7). He notes that Polypheme is probably taken from *Idyll* XI of Theocritus rather than *Odyssey* IX, and hence Doris is a "modern but necessarily debased counterpart of Galatea."

In "A Source for 'Tradition and the Individual Talent'" (*TSER* 2,ii:11), Jan Pinkerton conjectures that Eliot may have taken the title from Stuart P. Sherman's book, *Matthew Arnold: How to Know Him* (1917). V. J. E. Cowley locates "A Source for T. S. Eliot's 'Objective Correlative'" (*RES* 26:320–21) in the phrase "the object correlative" from Newman's Sermon XLI, "Love the Safeguard of Faith against Superstition."

William Harmon contends in "Braybrooke Refuted" (*TSER* 2,i:3) that Eliot used the word "parallelopipedon" seriously, and cites a letter of 1855 from Thomas Carlyle to Edward FitzGerald where this word is used. In "A Note on T. S. Eliot's 'A Cooking Egg'" (*TSER* 2,i:3), Timothy Materer proposes that the title is used ironically to acknowledge its unwholesome quality. William Empson suggests that Eliot was without politics in "Eliot and Politics" (*TSER* 2,ii:3–4). In "Eliot's English 26, Harvard U., Spring Term, 1933" (*TSER* 2,ii:5–7), A. Stuart Daley gives Eliot's reading list and final examination. William Harmon discusses the connection of Eliot with the *Hibbert Journal*, founded in 1902 "to promote Christianity and private judgment in religion" in "Eliot, Russell, and the *Hibbert Journal*" (*TSER* 2,ii:8–9). And, in "Louis Unmasked: T. S. Eliot in *The Waves*" (*VWQ* 2:13–27), Doris L. Eder argues at length that Louis in "worldview, character and appearance" suggests T. S. Eliot.

Three detailed studies of influence appeared this year. In "Clough's *Amours de Voyage*: A Possible Source for 'The Love Song of J. Alfred Prufrock'" (*WHR* 29:55–66), James R. Locke proposes that "if we may be allowed to conjecture, we might say that Eliot saw in the drawing room setting of James's story ["Crapy Cornelia"] a means of transforming Clough's rather long and tedious poem into a more immediate and intense statement." Although there are parallels between Clough's poem and Eliot's, the question of direct influence is not convincingly demonstrated. Richard Abel presents a detailed examination of Eliot's influence on Saint-John Perse in "Saint-John Perse Encounters T. S. Eliot" (*RLC* 49:423–37). Abel compares Perse's version of "The Hollow Men, I" which appeared in *Commerce*, and suggests that this version influenced Perse's later poetry, particularly *Vents*. In addition, Abel argues that by working with Eliot on the translation of *Anabase*, Perse altered his notions of "Anglo-Saxon poetry." Clare Huffman examines Eugenio Montale's "highly eclectic" view of Eliot in "T. S. Eliot, Eugenio Montale, and the Vagaries of Influence" (*CL* 27:193–207). Huffman questions the earlier formulations of direct influence of Eliot on Montale, and emphasizes Montale's selective reading of Eliot, "which excludes the major part of his critical essays and therefore the development and expression of his overriding idealism." Finally, Huffman declares, "Montale's view of Eliot's participation and place in history tells us more about Montale than about Eliot and leads us back to Montale's own poetry."

Two articles appeared on Eliot's prose. In "T. S. Eliot and the *Egoist*: The Critical Preparation" (*DR* 55:140–54), Louis R. MacKendrick surveys Eliot's contributions to the *Egoist*, and concludes that "three motifs persist in Eliot's reviews for the *Egoist*: the nature and function of the critic, the role of tradition, and literature's needs for cross-cultural fertilization." Robert Weisberg discusses the significance of *After Strange Gods* in Eliot's career ("T. S. Eliot: The Totemic-Mosaic Dream," *BMWMLA* 2:24–44). Weisberg argues that *After Strange Gods* "stands as a central document in the dualism of the great modernists in general—that they desperately resisted the spiritual individualism, aesthetic experimentation, and philosophical relativism their own literature fostered." Weisberg notes that "myth and archtype unite the forms of modern literature with the forms of tradition. But criticism has rarely shown how the writers may well have absorbed equally the social and moral content of these mythic discoveries," which he proceeds to examine.

He concludes that "Eliot's true position in *After Strange Gods* and, more diplomatically, in the later essays, is of the Mosaic upholder of totemic principles."

In "T. S. Eliot's 'Companion' Poems: Eternal Question, Temporal Response" (*ContempR* 227:73–79), Joyce Rochat analyzes "The Love Song of J. Alfred Prufrock" and "Gerontion" as "counterpart poems" presenting "the same character at different stages of development." The comparisons are forced and do little to clarify the meaning of either poem.

In a delightful study of "T. S. Eliot's Book of Practical Cats" (*SAmH* 2:167–71), Molly Best Tinsley examines the book as an example of satire "conveying through the manipulation of perspectives an oblique commentary on human society and its conventions." In arguing against an earlier interpretation of the book, she concludes: "Indeed it is tempting to find his *Book* the receptacle not for all the 'love and charity' excised from his serious work, but rather for all the mischief and muddle that could find no place in the ordered universe of a classicist, royalist, and Anglo-Catholic."

The only extended study of *The Waste Land* is Bernard F. Dick's "*The Waste Land* and the *Descensus ad Infernos*" (*CRCL* 2:35–46). Dick examines the common pattern of the *descensus ad infernos* in *Odyssey* XI and *Aeneid* VI and rather ingeniously applies this to *The Waste Land.* The pattern certainly functions in parts of the poem (where the Dantean inferno is also a model), but Dick attempts to apply it more comprehensively than one could ever hope to do. He is not unaware of the difficulties of doing this, for he comments parenthetically that "there is not, nor will there be, any one approach to Eliot's poem that is completely satisfying, and only the most humanistic scholars have studied it without growing to hate it."

Two articles on *The Four Quartets* approach the work from a religious standpoint. F. Peter Dzwonkoski, Jr., in "Time and the River, Time and the Sea: A Study of T. S. Eliot's 'Dry Salvages' " (*CimR* 30:48–57) examines "The Dry Salvages" as though it were a theological document. He asserts that "The poem is one of Eliot's most heart felt expressions of compassion for a weakwilled and fallen humanity which simply will not see God at the heart of time, redeeming it and saving man from the waste land." Dzwonkoski's insights are marred by an evangelical tone. "Burnt Norton" is the subject of David Robinson's "Eliot's Rose Garden: Illumination or Illusion?" (*CSR* 4,iii:201–07). Robinson argues for a new interpretation of the opening of this poem: "Although the poem ultimately affirms a transcendent order beyond time, it affirms such an order through an act of faith, not through the kind of mystical insight which is generally attributed to the first section of the poem."

In "Traditional Meters in *Four Quartets*" (*ES* 66:409–20) Julia Reibetanz discusses Eliot's development of a "poetic line that enunciates major stresses but leaves unstressed syllables to cluster in irregular ways, following natural speech rhythms rather than molding to a metrical pattern." Reibetanz demonstrates how Eliot establishes a rhythmic pattern of accentual meter in *The Four Quartets*, which makes deviations to traditional meter very significant. She examines "East Coker IV" where "the verse is shaped through an iambic stanza form to create the body (as well as the soul) of a metaphysical lyric" and "The Dry Salvages I," where "Eliot builds his impressions of the powerful rhythms of river and sea on the wave-like repetition of the dactyl." Her argument is detailed and convincing.

University of Michigan

9. Faulkner

Karl F. Zender

Somewhere in my research for this essay I read that only Shakespeare, Milton, and the Bible now command more critical and scholarly attention than Faulkner. If this isn't true, it ought to be, because well over 90 books, articles, and notes that are wholly or partly concerned with his work appeared during 1975. (This figure does not include any of the 27 dissertations which have either the words "Faulkner" or "Yoknapatawpha" in their titles.) I have been selective in my treatment of this mass of material in order to comment adequately on the goodly amount of important work that it contains.

i. Bibliography, Editions, and Manuscripts

Carl Petersen's *Each in Its Ordered Place: A Faulkner Collector's Notebook* (Ann Arbor, Mich.: Ardis) records a collection of Faulkner editions, published and unpublished letters, and other materials made over the past 25 years. It is handsomely bound, scrupulously edited, and carefully indexed, and deserves a place next to Linton Massey's "*Man Working*" and James Meriwether's *The Literary Career of William Faulkner*. It should, of course, be used with caution. Like the two books mentioned above, it is the record of a collection, not a comprehensive bibliography, and hence neither pretends to nor achieves completeness. With the exception of some unpublished letters, for example, Petersen's collection, unlike Massey's, contains little or nothing in the way of manuscript or holograph materials. On the other hand, his listing seems generally more complete than Massey's in the area of editions and translations of Faulkner's work. But here too there are occasional omissions. Neither Petersen nor Massey lists the corrected Vintage paperback edition of *The Hamlet*—now the standard textbook edition—which was first published in conjunction with the boxed hardbound edition of the

Snopes trilogy. At times, too, Petersen's book seems more a tribute to his zeal than to his discrimination, as in his inclusion of a 45-rpm recording of the theme from *The Long, Hot Summer* under "Adaptations of Faulkner," and a "brick from the post office where Faulkner was postmaster" under "Secondary Material: Background and Critical." But in general the book will prove valuable to scholars as well as bibliophiles.

As more and more critical attention begins to be paid to the genesis of Faulkner's themes and techniques, access to his early unpublished work becomes increasingly important. Of this work, the single most valuable item is *The Marionettes*, six copies of which Faulkner hand-lettered in 1920. The Bibliographical Society of the University of Virginia has issued a facsimile reproduction of this play as a memorial to Linton Massey (Charlottesville: Univ. Press of Virginia). Unfortunately, it's an expensive ($100) limited edition (100 numbered copies, plus 26 lettered copies *hors commerce*).

The annual Faulkner number of *MissQ* (28) continued its custom of recent years by reprinting two previously unpublished items. In "A Fourth Book Review by Faulkner" (pp. 339–42), Carvel Collins discusses Faulkner's review of John Cowper Powys's *Ducdame*; the review is reprinted by the editor on pp. 343–46. Collins is rightly tentative in his speculations as to the possible influence of Powys's novel on "The Bear" and on the short story "Carcassonne." The review itself reveals Faulkner's concern with literary form, and displays some of his characteristic phrasing, but is otherwise of little interest. "Mac Grider's Son," the second *MissQ* reprint (pp. 347–51), is a first person account by Faulkner of his meeting with the son of John McGavock Grider, a Mississippi aviator who was slain in combat during World War I. The piece appeared in the Memphis *Commercial Appeal* in 1934. The editor's headnote clarifies the relationship of Faulkner's piece to *War Birds*, a semifictional diary by Elliott White Springs.

Two letters complete this listing of previously unpublished material. Richard Lyons's *Faulkner on Love: A Letter to Marjorie Lyons* (Fargo, N.D.: Merrykit [1974]) consists of an offset reproduction and a typeset copy of a reply Faulkner made in 1950 to a query about the anonymity of the reporter in *Pylon*. Aside from Faulkner's assertion that the reporter represents Everyman-in-love, the letter contains nothing of interest. *Steinbeck: A Life in Letters*, ed. Elaine

Steinbeck and Robert Wallsten (New York: Viking), contains an excerpt from a letter Faulkner wrote Steinbeck in response to Steinbeck's query as to how he should comport himself in Japan (pp. 564–65). The book also contains a wonderfully acerbic comment by Steinbeck on the Olympian character of Faulkner's self-presentation in one of his published interviews (apparently the one with Jean Stein).

Because of the controversy over the editing of both the hardbound and paperbound editions of *Flags in the Dust* (see *ALS 1973* and *1974*), mention should be made here of George F. Hayhoe's "William Faulkner's *Flags in the Dust*" (*MissQ* 28:370–86). This long review-essay details the case against the textual reliability of these editions.

ii. Biography

Most of the year's energy devoted to biographical matters was taken up with the assimilation and assessment of Joseph Blotner's monumental *Faulkner: A Biography* (see *ALS 1974*). Of the many reviews and review-essays occasioned by this biography during 1975, two particularly deserve mention here. James Meriwether's "Blotner's *Faulkner*" (*MissQ* 28:353–69), which I discussed in *ALS 1974*, is a judicious, balanced appraisal. It remains the single best introduction to the strengths and weaknesses of Blotner's work.

Lewis P. Simpson's "The Loneliness of William Faulkner" (*SLJ* 8,i:126–43) is rather a different kind of essay. It is not so much a review as an exemplary first instance of the kind of biographical speculation which the existence of Blotner's book now makes possible. Taking Faulkner's own distinction between a "writer" and a "literary man" as the basis for his discussion, Simpson engages in a sensitive demonstration of Faulkner's slow, reluctant, and self-denied movement from the one term to the other. The "loneliness" of Simpson's title is the condition of Faulkner in his later years, "a literary man playing an intricate confidence game with the artist; wearing the mask of the artist, fooling himself and yet not fooling himself behind the too transparent mask." This loneliness is contrasted with the attitude of Faulkner in the 1930s, when he affirmed in his then unpublished introduction for a new edition of *The Sound and the Fury* "a personal intimacy with the process of art," and thus completely violated any "decorous regard for the masking of the person of the creator."

As Simpson implies, the greatness of the works between *The Sound and the Fury* and *Absalom, Absalom!* partly lies in Faulkner's willingness to engage in "the deepest scrutiny of the self in its opposition to society and history." The slow waning of this willingness is the main burden of Simpson's argument, and one comes away from his essay with the sense that we have been far too uncritical of the comparatively tame version of his early relation to his art which Faulkner fostered—perhaps inadvertently—in his latter days. I would like to cite one minor additional piece of evidence in support of Simpson's case. The frontispiece of Petersen's *Each in Its Ordered Place* (see section i) is a photograph of the title page of a copy of *The Sound and the Fury* that Faulkner inscribed on May 26, 1932. The inscription reads, "I put my living guts into this." So he did, and the process involved merits Simpson's sensitive attention.

The last item in this section, Guido Lopez's "Faulkner and the Horses" (*YR* 64:468–76), is a translation by Ruth Feldman of a pleasant reminiscence of a visit by Faulkner to the Tesio horse farm during his 1955 trip to Italy. Like most such occasional reminiscences, it contributes as much to Faulkner's mythical biography as it does to his real one. For example, Lopez repeats Faulkner's anecdote about his arrest in Genoa in 1925. He is evidently not aware that Blotner says that it was Spratling, Faulkner's traveling companion, who actually was arrested, or that Faulkner used this incident in his story "Divorce in Naples."

iii. Criticism: General

a. **Books.** John T. Irwin's *Doubling and Incest/Repetition and Revenge: A Speculative Reading of Faulkner* (Baltimore: The Johns Hopkins Univ. Press) is the most exciting book of criticism on Faulkner to appear in many years. As its title implies, it is concerned with certain recurrent motifs. Part of the value of the book lies in the care with which Irwin examines the occurrences of these motifs in individual novels—mainly *The Sound and the Fury* and *Absalom, Absalom!*, but also *Mosquitoes*, *Sartoris*, *As I Lay Dying*, and *A Fable*. But its fullest strength lies in its demonstration of the ways in which these motifs are structurally interdependent at a deep psychological level. Irwin displays a subtler and more comprehensive understanding of the Oedipal pattern than is to be found in any previous psychoanalytic criticism of Faulkner's fiction. He demonstrates the ways in which this pattern displaces itself into a three-generation pattern of repetition, and into brother-brother and sister-brother relationships, and thus illuminates, among other things, the central dilemmas faced by Quentin in *The Sound and the Fury* and *Absalom, Absalom!*

Although I have more to say with regard to Irwin's book, I will not go further than this in elucidating his argument. It operates, as he says, by a process of "multiple counterpointing," which is similar to Faulkner's treatment of the motifs themselves, and hence needs to be read to be fully understood. Irwin says that he derived his expository method from Lévi-Strauss's *The Raw and the Cooked*; this is only one of the many ways in which he has been profoundly influenced by French structuralist and psycholinguistic criticism. Because the stagnation of much recent Faulkner criticism results from allegiance to exhausted and inadequate critical theories, Irwin's openness to this influence is one of the more considerable merits of his book.

Irwin's emancipation, though, is incomplete, for he generally confines his psycholinguistic insights within a rather traditional formalist literary aesthetic. In Jacques Derrida's term, he does not "deconstruct" the text. Even when he is concerned with the relationship between his central motifs and the need to make fictions, it is Quentin's need rather than Faulkner's that mainly commands his attention. Irwin is obviously aware that the main structure he elucidates has significant bearing on the process of literary creation: he hints at the connection repeatedly, as when he says that "Quentin evokes that father-son struggle that a man inevitably has with his own literary progenitors when he attempts to become an 'author.'" But his consideration of Faulkner's own creative struggle is brief and elliptical. Had he taken his argument one crucial step further, he would have produced a doubly seminal book, helpful to our understanding both of the Faulkner canon and of the process by which it came to be.

While in this vein I should also say that not all the details of Irwin's readings are beyond dispute. His reading of *Absalom, Absalom!*, for example, undervalues the importance of Sutpen's "innocence." And there are grounds for dispute as well with his tendency to treat masculine patterns of development as if they were the only important human ones. But these criticisms do not seriously qualify my admiration for this provocative and powerful book. By elucidating a central structure in the canon, Irwin has demonstrated the relationship between Faulkner's fiction and some of the most significant ideas of our century. His work should have profound influence on Faulkner studies in the years to come.

I now turn to a work with a markedly different purpose: John Bassett's *William Faulkner: The Critical Heritage* (London: Routledge and Kegan Paul), the first Critical Heritage Series title to deal with an American writer more recent than Henry James, and, as Bassett acknowledges, the near-contemporaneity of his subject creates a problem in determining which items should be included.

Bassett does a generally admirable job of separating the wheat from the chaff. But he does not seem to have decided whether his book should reprint documents in the history of criticism or in the history of taste. Neither does he seem to have decided whether his main purpose should be to make widely available otherwise inaccessible materials, or to reprint seminal essays regardless of their availability. Thus, an excerpt from O'Donnell's essay from the *Kenyon Review* and all of Aiken's from *Atlantic Monthly* are reprinted because of their importance, even though they have been widely reprinted elsewhere. But other important essays—ones by Vickery, Brooks, and Howe, to cite Bassett's own examples—are excluded because they have been reprinted in books by these authors. These problems sometimes inhibit the book's ability to demonstrate the development of Faulkner's critical reputation.

The chapters on Faulkner in Linda Welshimer Wagner's *Hemingway and Faulkner: Inventors/Masters* (Metuchen, N.J.: Scarecrow) comprise approximately half of the book. They are devoted to an overview of Faulkner's career, to occasional comparisons with Hemingway, and to brief discussions of techniques, influences, and themes. This study, some parts of which have been published before, should be used with caution. Wagner is generally uncritical in her use of Faulkner scholarship and criticism, and she does not draw very frequently on the most recent work. Her discussion of Faulkner's allegiance to imagist doctrines of concreteness of language, for example, should be compared with Panthea Broughton's rather more convincing consideration (in *William Faulkner: The Abstract and the Actual* [*ALS 1974*]) of Faulkner's use of abstraction. Wagner's readings of individual works are sometimes eccentric, as in her defense of Jason Compson, and her enthusiastic endorsement of the now outmoded view of *Absalom, Absalom!* as a "damnation of the South." In general her book would have merited from further revision, for it is presently loosely organized and ambiguous.

The remaining items in this section consist of one reissue of an earlier work and four books in which Faulkner receives from one to three chapters of attention. Irving Howe's *William Faulkner: A Critical Study* (3rd ed., Chicago: Univ. of Chicago Press) has stood the test of time remarkably well; after 25 years it remains one of the central statements of the strengths and weaknesses of Faulkner's fiction. Though the cover describes this edition as "revised and expanded," the revision consists only of the correction of "some factual errors" in the second edition, and the expansion contains only two elements: a brief appendix, hardly more than a page, on *Flags in the Dust*, and an encomiastic chapter on *The Reivers*, in which Howe wrongly claims that Lucius receives an "educational hiding" at the end of his adventures.

The Twenties, edited by Warren French, is the fourth volume in a series of collections of essays on different decades of 20th-century American literature. Although this book is an expansion of an earlier collection, the three essays on Faulkner are all new contributions. One of them, Gene Ruoff's "Faulkner: The Way Out of the Waste Land" (pp. 235–48), is an engagingly written but oversimplified inspection of the ways in which Faulkner's presentation of humanly understandable evil in *The Sound and the Fury* indicates a break with the "glorification of failure" in the early war stories, *Soldiers' Pay*, *Sartoris*, and *Sanctuary*. Ruoff acknowledges but does not resolve the chronological difficulty occasioned by his treatment of *Sanctuary* as typical of the fiction written prior to *The Sound and the Fury*. He also makes the inexplicable error of calling the idiot Tommy a Negro. Because the other two essays in this volume deal exclusively with *The Sound and the Fury* on the one hand and *Sanctuary* on the other, they will be considered in sections v and vi below.

John McCormick describes his *Fiction as Knowledge: The Modern Post-Romantic Novel* (New Brunswick, N.J.: Rutgers Univ. Press) as a "counterattack" on "the antihistorical bias so prevalent in the United States and in Europe over the past twenty years." But had McCormick engaged in a fuller study of the history of Faulkner criticism, he might have written a more original chapter than "William Faulkner, the Past, and History" (pp. 88–108). His discussion of *The Sound and the Fury* adds nothing to what we already know, and his treatment of *Light in August* is marred with errors, as when he asserts that "Christmas' historical character resides in his conscious choice to live his life as a black." Finally, I mention the Faulkner material in Mary Doyle Springer's *Forms of the Modern Novella* (Chicago: Univ. of Chicago Press) only to warn against its use. Springer discusses "Old Man" and "Spotted Horses," but she is evidently unaware that "Old Man" was written as a contrapuntal accompaniment to "Wild Palms," and hence hardly qualifies as an apt subject for a study which attempts to determine the distinctive characteristics of the novella form.

***b*. Articles.** Cleanth Brooks's "Faulkner and the Muse of History" (*MissQ* 28:265–79) and his "Faulkner's Criticism of Modern America" (*VQR* 51:294–308) are both quasi-popular essays. The one is a reprint of a talk and the other was evidently written for the occasion of the 50th anniversary of *VQR*. These circumstances may help to explain why both essays tend to enumerate and simplify old themes. "Modern America" has as its ostensible subject a comparison of Faulkner's "On Privacy" and Richard Goodwin's "Reflections: The American Condition," but it mainly repeats in a less convincing form the argument concerning the relation of the individual and the community which received its classic expression in Brooks's chapter on *Light in August* in *William Faulkner: The Yoknapatawpha Country*. "The Muse of History" is a generalized reflection on Faulkner's attitudes toward the history of the South and the American myth of progress, with the thesis that he transcends the one and rejects the other. This too Brooks has said before and said better.

A number of other essays of varying merit deal with general themes. Despite an irritating number of typographical errors, Roxandra Antoniadis's "The Dream as Design in Balzac and Faulkner" (*ZRL* 17,ii[1974]:45–57) deserves attention for its intelligent comparison of the place of creative inspiration and rational planning in the aesthetic doctrines of the two writers. Antoniadis's comments on the moral purposes of Faulkner's art, though, are not convincing, because she draws her evidence almost entirely from Faulkner's late public statements rather than from the works themselves. Also of value is James Watson's " 'If *Was* Existed': Faulkner's Prophets and the Patterns of History" (*MFS* 21:499–507). Watson's notion that Faulkner's characters discover the shape of the future by inspecting the past is not new, but he applies it insightfully to *Absalom, Absalom!*, *The Sound and the Fury*, and *As I Lay Dying*. Richard M. Cook's "Popeye, Flem, and Sutpen: The Faulknerian Villain as Grotesque" (*SAF* 3:3–14) is less convincing than Watson's essay, but still of some merit. It is a rather schematized attempt to apply Wolfgang Kayser's analysis of the grotesque to the characters named in its title. The essay is most convincing in its treatment of the ways in which Sutpen's grotesquerie resides in the various narrators' impressions of him. Cook's analysis of Quentin's "rescue" of Sutpen from the category of the grotesque would have been improved by attention to Shreve's role in this process.

The last item in this category is of little value. Victor Strandberg, in "Between Truth and Fact: Faulkner's Symbols of Identity" (*MFS* 21:445–57), uses Faulkner's often repeated distinction between truth and fact as a basis for an unremarkable analysis of the relationship between private vision and objective reality in some of Faulkner's characters.

iv. Criticism: Special Studies

***a.* Ideas, Influences, Intellectual Background.** The treatment of Faulkner in Lewis P. Simpson's *The Dispossessed Garden: Pastoral and History in Southern Literature* (Athens, Ga.: Univ. of Ga. Press) is limited to a brief discussion of a single speech from *Intruder in the Dust*. Fortunately, Simpson corrects this deficiency in "Faulkner and the Southern Symbolism of Pastoral" (*MissQ* 28:401–15). Like his "The Loneliness of William Faulkner" (see section ii), this essay is judicious, sensitive, and informed. The terms with which he works —"pastoral" and "history"—have enjoyed wide currency in Faulkner criticism, but they have seldom been yoked together in such a convincing and productive fashion. In both his book and his essay, Simpson argues that the presence of slavery meant that the pastoral myth of America as the new Eden was ultimately less attractive—or less workable—for southern writers than for northern ones. He argues as well that after unsuccessful 19th-century attempts to incorporate the fact of slavery into the pastoral ideal, "the pastoral resistance to history is found to be overcome by a resistance of history to pastoral." These exciting ideas deserve even more application to Faulkner than Simpson's essay provides.

Annette Kolodny's *The Lay of the Land* also places some of Faulkner's work—specifically "The Bear" and "Delta Autumn"—in the context of the history of American pastoral myth. Kolodny's comments on Ike's use of the metaphor of the land-as-woman constitute a sensitive inspection of an important but neglected element of his language. She takes a part for the whole, though, when she says that "Faulkner has attempted to introduce in *Go Down, Moses*, through the voice of Ike McCaslin . . . a vocabulary that will at once do away with the notion of the land as something to be either exclusively possessed or preyed on." If Faulkner does so, it is in an ironic context which severely limits our positive response to the attempt.

Faulkner's influence on Juan Carlos Onetti is discussed in Luis Vargas Saavedra's "La afinidad de Onetti a Faulkner" (*Cuadernos Hispanoamericanos* 292–94[1974]:257–65). Although this essay is disorganized and fanciful in its language, it will be of interest to critics concerned with Faulkner's Latin American reception. Faulkner's influence on Onetti is given some slight additional attention in Estelle Irizarry's "Procedimientos estilísticos de J. C. Onetti" (ibid., 669–95).

Surprisingly, Faulkner is not a particularly prominent figure in *Southern Literary Study: Problems and Possibilities*, ed. C. Hugh Holman and Louis D. Rubin, Jr. (Chapel Hill: The Univ. of N.C. Press), though he is mentioned in the sections on "Twentieth-Century Southern Literature" and "Thematic Problems in Southern Literature." In the first he is treated mainly as the "Dixie Special" whose presence on the track has inhibited both the work and the reception of later southern writers. In the second he is discussed at greater length in relation to the idea of community. Of more moment is James H. Justus's "On the Restlessness of Southerners" (*SoR* 11:65–83). This essay has the interesting purpose of attempting to determine the ways in which the South is like, rather than unlike, the rest of the nation. In pursuit of this objective Justus examines a number of southern writers, including Faulkner, in terms of their use of metaphors of movement and of containment. The one metaphor he identifies as a national archetype, the other as a regional one. But this is too loosely woven a net to catch so subtle a writer as Faulkner in. While it is true, as Justus says, that metaphors of movement—and representations of movement—are frequent in Faulkner's fiction, the important matter is not the quantity of movement but the kinds of it. In this regard, as well as in his narrative judgments of movement and stasis, Faulkner seems a distinctively southern writer.

D. M. Murray's "Faulkner, the Silent Comedies, and the Animated Cartoon" (*SHR* 9:241–57) scarcely deserves mention. It is coy in its tone and reductive in its readings. Murray disavows any attempt to trace indebtednesses, but does not substitute any other worthwhile purpose in its stead. Joel Grossman's "The Source of Faulkner's 'Less Oft Is Peace'" (*AL* 47:436–38), by contrast, is economical and convincing proof that Faulkner derived the phrase in the title of the note from Shelley's "To Jane: The Recollection." *The Frontier Humorists: Critical Views*, ed. M. Thomas Inge (Hamden, Conn.: Archon), also deserves notice here. It reprints Carvel Collins's "Faulkner and Certain Earlier Southern Fiction," together with Inge's own "William Faulkner and George Washington Harris: In the Tradition of Southwestern Humor." An editor's note says that Collins has revised his essay for republication in this volume.

***b.* Language and Style.** A previously neglected essay heads the brief list of items primarily concerned with Faulkner's language and style. Paul R. Lilly, Jr.'s "Caddy and Addie: Speakers of Faulkner's Impeccable Language" (*JNT* 3[1973]:170–82) presents an intelligent and well-documented demonstration of Faulkner's paradoxical bias toward silence as the purest form of language. The essay also includes an intriguing examination of the relationship between images of contained forces in *As I Lay Dying* and Addie Bundren's theories about words. It is not so successful, though, in its treatment of Caddie Compson and Addie as the narrative centers of their respective novels.

Using Lukács's criticism of modernist experimentation in style as a point of departure, Brent Harold, in "The Value and Limitations of Faulkner's Fictional Method" (*AL* 47:212–29), examines Faulkner's style and attempts to show how it constitutes "a determined struggle against dehumanization in his social milieu . . . and . . . in the literary milieu itself." This is a consistently stimulating essay, especially to be admired for its demonstration of the ways in which Faulkner rejected primitivism, positivism, and art for art's sake and for its analysis of the relationship between his style and his "defective" "sense of the dialectic of social change."

Another previously neglected item completes the material in this section. William R. Brown's "Mr. Stark on Mr. Strawson on Referring" (*Language and Style* 7[1974]:219–24) uses the occasion of a response to an essay by John Stark (*ALS 1973*) to discuss Faulkner's use of false presupposition, as in his use of the definite article in contexts where the reader can have no knowledge of what is being referred to. To someone innocent in the ways of linguistic philosophers, as I am, there seems to be an air of forced naïveté about Brown's argument. He never suggests that Faulkner may simply have used false presupposition for the old-fashioned purpose of creating suspense. Finally, mention should also be made here of Stephen Ross's "The 'Loud World' of Quentin Compson" (see section v), which contains a good examination of the language in the second section of *The Sound and the Fury*.

***c.* Race.** George E. Kent's two-part essay, "The Black Woman in Faulkner's Works, with the Exclusion of Dilsey" (*Phylon* 35[1974]: 430–41 and 36:55–67), is an unevenly written examination of Faulkner's treatment of "the three sides of the black woman which made such lasting impact upon the white consciousness: sexuality, the faithful servant, and the Mammy." It contains an interesting comparison of Faulkner's renditions of black females with those of his brother John in *Dollar Cotton*. Kent's speculations about the reasons for Faulkner's "failure" to represent triangular sexual relationships involving a black and a white female and a white male also deserve some attention.

v. Individual Works to 1929

Except for a single essay on *Mosquitoes*, all of the work for this period deals with *The Sound and the Fury*. Edwin Arnold's "Freedom and Stasis in Faulkner's *Mosquitoes*" (*MissQ* 28:281–97) is representative of a growing tendency in Faulkner studies toward an emphasis on critical dispute rather than critical insight. Arnold provides a competent examination of images of freedom and bondage in the novel, but he is mainly concerned with reevaluating the characters in moral terms. Gordon, formerly up in the eyes of the critics, is now down; David, formerly down, is now up.

With one or two exceptions, the work on *The Sound and the Fury* is of low quality. Stephen Ross's "The 'Loud World' of Quentin Compson" (*SNNTS* 7:245–57) is one of the exceptions. The opposition he uses between experience and language is rather too simple to be credited, but his essay is nonetheless a competent examination of the theme of language in the second section of the novel. It also contains a brief but intriguing examination of some of the revisions Faulkner made in the drafts of this section. I doubt, though, that the furniture dealer in *Light in August* tells his wife the story of Lena and Byron in order to "put her in the mood for lovemaking," as Ross claims.

Beyond Ross's essay, there is little to recommend in this section. Michael Groden's "Criticism in New Composition: *Ulysses* and *The Sound and the Fury*" (*TCL* 21:265–77) is a straightforward study of Joyce's influence on *The Sound and the Fury*, with occasional references to *Mosquitoes* and *Soldiers' Pay*. Groden makes some valid distinctions in the kinds of uses Faulkner makes of Joycean technique, especially in his comparison of the first and second sections of the novel. By contrast, Arthur Geffen's "Profane Time, Sacred Time, and Confederate Time in *The Sound and the Fury*" (*SAF* 2[1974]:175–97) is forced and unconvincing. Geffen argues that the Compson family is denied access to both the sacred time of Dilsey and Benjy and the progressive (northern) form of profane time. They are imprisoned, therefore, in Confederate time. In pursuit of this argument Geffen attempts to associate the dates in the novel with significant dates in southern history. This attempt has been made before, but Geffen varies it by using a "day before" pattern of association: Quentin's suicide takes place on the day before the date when Confederate Memorial Day is celebrated in several southern states, and so forth. This labored ingenuity is not convincing, especially when Geffen temporarily abandons the "day before" pattern in favor of a direct association between the April 6th and 7th of the novel and the dates of the battle of Shiloh.

Wolfgang Iser's *The Implied Reader: Patterns of Communication in Prose Fiction from Bunyan to Beckett* (Baltimore: The Johns Hopkins Univ. Press [1974]) is the author's own translation of *Der im-*

plizite Leser (Munich: Wilhelm Fink [1972]). It contains a subchapter (pp. 136–52) entitled "Perception, Temporality, and Action as Modes of Subjectivity. W. Faulkner: *The Sound and the Fury.*" Iser provides an intelligent view of the effect on the reader of the movement from one section to another of the novel, but his essay suffers from a lack of familiarity with recent American work done on the novel. Some of his readings of individual passages are suspect, as when he assumes that Quentin enters the jeweller's shop in order to have his watch fixed, or when he attributes to Quentin as a reflection what is actually his memory of something his father said.

Despite its title, Lois Gordon's "Meaning and Myth in *The Sound and the Fury* and *The Waste Land*" (*The Twenties*, pp. 269–302) is not much concerned with a comparison of Faulkner's novel and Eliot's poem. The bulk of Gordon's essay is instead devoted to an analysis of "the destruction that ungiving parents visit upon their children." While this destruction undoubtedly occurs in life, very nearly exclusive focus on it in *The Sound and the Fury* seriously distorts the nature of the novel's concerns. Gordon makes a number of odd mistakes, such as her assertion that the Compson Mile dates back to the battle of Culloden. She provides no citations for her quotations and evidence.

The remaining items in this section may be briefly treated. Michael Auer's "Caddy, Benjy, and the Acts of the Apostles: A Note on *The Sound and the Fury*" (*SNNTS* 6[1974]:475–76) attempts to associate Caddy with Candace, queen of Ethiopia, and Benjy with her eunuch. The association of Caddy and the queen is made independently and more convincingly in John T. Irwin's book (see section iii a), where the matter is placed in a wider intellectual and critical context. Mary Jane Dickerson's "'The Magician's Wand': Faulkner's Compson Appendix" (*MissQ* 28:317–37) attempts to study the appendix as a separate work of art. This is a worthwhile topic, but it is not adequately handled here. Dickerson's essay is tedious and ill-organized, and labors over insights which would occur to most critics on a first reading of the appendix. Gladys Milliner's "The Third Eve: Caddy Compson" (*MQ* 16:268–75) is also of little use. Caddy is a likely beneficiary of the kinds of critical insights afforded by a feminist perspective, but she is not well treated here. For the sake of the biblical analogies Milliner examines, it would be convenient if the tree Caddy climbs were, as she says, an apple tree. But as far as we can tell, it is a pear tree.

vi. Individual Works, 1930–39

An amazing number of studies—two books and 24 notes and essays—await discussion in this section. Only one of these items deals with *Sanctuary*. James E. Miller, Jr.'s "*Sanctuary*: Yoknapatawpha's Waste Land" (in *Individual and Community*, pp. 137–59) is disappointing. Miller needlessly reviews the harsh initial judgments of the novel and reasserts its artistic integrity. His attempt to view the novel in the context of Eliot's *The Waste Land* contains occasional apt observations, but some of the particular parallels he draws—as between the old woman Ruby stays with in Jefferson and Madame Sosostris—fail to carry conviction. (A slightly shortened version of this essay also appears in Warren French's *The Twenties*, pp. 249–67.)

Five items appeared in 1975 on *As I Lay Dying*. Stephen M. Ross's "Shapes of Time and Consciousness in *As I Lay Dying*" (*TSLL* 16:723–37) is a promising study of the way in which Faulkner uses verb tense to indicate the varying degrees of engagement of the narrators with the material they narrate. The subject, however, deserves further study. Leon Seltzer's "Narrative Function vs. Psychopathology: The Problem of Darl in *As I Lay Dying*" (*L&P* 25: 49–64) is a frustrating essay because Seltzer assumes that a literary work should be held to account for its failure to describe pathological experience accurately. As a result of this assumption, he wastes much of his essay badgering previous critics of the novel for the looseness of their use of psychological terminology and proving that Darl displays the characteristics of no single psychopathological type. Many of the points he makes, however, about the possible incompatibility of Darl's functions in the novel deserve treatment from a literary orientation.

The remaining three items on *As I Lay Dying* merit only brief mention. Matthew Little, in "*As I Lay Dying* and 'Dementia Praecox' Humor" (*SAmH* 2:61–70), attempts to detect a sophisticated humor of the *New Yorker* type in the novel. But he is unable at times to decide whether a passage is or is not humorous. In "Another *Othello* Echo in *As I Lay Dying*" (*NMW* 8:19–21), John B. Rosenman attempts unsuccessfully to connect Darl's "Jewel's mother is a horse" to the animal imagery Iago uses in describing Othello's marriage to Desdemona. Ruth H. Brady's "Faulkner's *As I Lay Dying*" (*Expl* 33:item 60) is a negligible description of the process by which Vardaman confuses his mother with a fish, and of how he gets over it.

There are eleven items on *Light in August*, three of them neglected ones from 1974. By far the most important is Regina K. Fadiman's *Faulkner's "Light in August": A Description and Interpretation of the Revisions* (Charlottesville: The Univ. Press of Virginia). This is a careful, fully detailed, study whose purpose is sufficiently described in its subtitle. The subject, as Fadiman frequently admits, is full of difficulties. Normally, a genetic study would seem to require a sequence of manuscripts or typescripts through which the process of revision might be traced. In the case of *Light in August*, we have a manuscript and a typescript, but the revisions between the two are minor in comparison to the ones that presumably occurred between a lost earlier draft and the existent one. And otherwise, we have only a relatively inconsequential four-page manuscript of an early rejected version of an opening for the novel.

In these circumstances a genetic critic must become something of a detective. Fortunately, Fadiman is a good one. On the basis of such evidence as paper thickness, ink color, and the sequences of crossed-out page numbers on the manuscript, she constructs a hypothesis as to the genesis of *Light in August*. She argues that Faulkner first wrote a present-tense narrative involving Byron Bunch, Lena Grove, and Gail Hightower. Joe Christmas figured in this narrative only in peripheral ways. But when Faulkner saw his importance, he wrote the long flashback sequence detailing his youth, and then adjusted the present-tense narrative in order to give him more importance in it. This is a speculative hypothesis, and the ambiguity of much of the evidence with which Fadiman deals is such that her argument may never compel more than qualified assent. But the care and judiciousness of her study lead me to feel that we will not soon see a more convincing account of the genesis of the novel.

Walter E. Johnston's "The Shepherdess In the City" (*CL* 26 [1974]:124–41) displays the benefits of bringing a broad knowledge of prior literature to bear on Faulkner's fiction. His study of *Light in August*, Musil's "Tonka," and *Ulysses* in the context of Virgilian and

Wordsworthian pastoralism is acute and perceptive. He is especially convincing in his analysis of the tonal complexity of Faulkner's opening presentation of Lena. In his view the combination of narratorial sophistication and simplicity of subject matter results in an ironic pastoralism which casts "a wistful glance at the possibility of an unwilled natural order." This essay is a substantial addition to Cleanth Brooks's seminal analysis of Faulkner's pastoralism in *William Faulkner: The Yoknapatawpha Country,* and could well be read in conjunction with Simpson's essay (see section iv, a). William Palmer, in "Abelard's Fate: Sexual Politics in Stendhal, Faulkner and Camus" (*Mosaic* 7,ii[1974]:29–41), also attempts to place *Light in August* in a cross-cultural context, but with much less success. Palmer draws some interesting comparisons between Faulkner's novel and *The Red and the Black* in terms of castration motifs and phallic, natural, and mechanical imagery, but his treatment of the opposition between individual and society is more singleminded than Faulkner's.

Three studies continue the examination of *Light in August* in relation to Christian and classical analogies and influences. Ilse Dusoir Lind's "Apocalyptic Vision as Key to *Light in August*" (*SAF* 3:133–41) suggests that the novel was influenced by Jewish and Christian apocalyptic writings. The resemblances are so general as not to convince me that they are anything other than accidental. Lind says with assurance that when Faulkner "began the writing of *Light in August,* his wife was expecting their first child." This may be so. But as Fadiman and others have said, all we know with certainty is that the first page of the manuscript is dated August 17, 1931—some seven months after the birth of Alabama Faulkner. Julian C. Rice's "Orpheus and the Hellish Unity in *Light in August*" (*CentR* 19:380–96) totally fails to convince me that Faulkner used the Orpheus myth in any significant way in his novel. This essay is badly written. In a single paragraph Rice asserts that Joe Christmas in his role as scapegoat "redeems the community's ability to pursue such animal necessities as procreation and eating without identity confusion or guilt," and that the community "'celebrates,' in his lynching and emasculation . . . the necessary revival of its exclusively human, non-animal identity." Peter L. Hays's "More Light on *Light in August*" (*PLL* 11:417–19), by contrast, is a brief, commonsensical inspection of the motif of transfiguration in the novel. He suggests that the presence in *August* of the Feast of the Transfiguration may be pertinent to the novel's meaning, but he wisely does not suggest any specific reference to the Feast on Faulkner's part.

Faulkner criticism abounds in various critical strategies. One of the more popular but less legitimate of these goes as follows: the critic asserts (but does not prove) the influence of some work of literature on an aspect of Faulkner's fiction. He then addresses himself to the evident discrepancies between the putative source and Faulkner's presumed use of it, and comes forth with "irony," or "ironic divergence," or "ironic inversion" as an explanation. Mario D'Avanzo's "Bobbie Allen and the Ballad Tradition in *Light in August*" (*SCR* 8,i:22–29) and his "Allusion in the Percy Grimm Episode of *Light in August*" (*NMW* 8:63–68) are no better or no worse than the majority of notes and essays that follow this paradigm. But the duplication in last names remains the only convincing correspondence between Barbara Allen of the ballad and the waitress in *Light in August*. David L. James's "Hightower's Name: A Possible Source" (*AN&Q* 13[1974]:4–5) refers us to Psalm 18:2, where the phrase "high tower" is used. The connection, we may note, is ironic.

The remaining two items on *Light in August* may be briefly treated. Glenn Young's "Struggle and Triumph in *Light in August*" (*STC* 15:33–50) is a disorganized consideration of the symbolic significance of the fire in the novel, of the question as to who sets it (no one, he says), and of the connections Faulkner draws between sex and food. Young says, mistakenly, that "Joe does not kill Joanna Burden with his open razor, but with her Civil War pistol appointed to kill him." Finally, James E. Mulqueen's "*Light in August*: Motion, Eros, and Death" (*NMW* 8:91–98) is a simplistic application of the Freudian concepts of life and death instincts to the novel.

Pylon received no attention during the year, but *Absalom, Absalom!* continued to be intensively if not always successfully studied. Cleanth Brooks, in "The Narrative Structure of *Absalom, Absalom!*" (*GaR* 29:366–94) investigates once again the question of what Quentin knows and how he knows it. His arrangement of the sources of Quentin's knowledge into "stratas" does not seem to be an improvement over his note in *William Faulkner: The Yoknapatawpha Country*, where the matter of what we know (and hence, by implication, of what Quentin knows) is succinctly and successfully handled.

It may be well, though, to have Brooks remind us again of the need for careful attention to what happens in the novel, because its dense texture produced misreadings by a number of critics during the past year. George S. Lensing, in "The Metaphor of Family in *Absalom, Absalom!*" (*SoR* 11:99–117), incorrectly identifies the two debaters on p. 234 of the novel as Sutpen and General Compson, when in fact they are two aspects of Sutpen as an adolescent. David Lenson's chapter on Faulkner in his *Achilles' Choice: Examples of Modern Tragedy* (Princeton, N.J.: Princeton Univ. Press) treats a statement about Sutpen as if it were a report of a statement by him. Elizabeth Sabiston, in "Women, Blacks, and Thomas Sutpen's Mythopoeic Drive in *Absalom, Absalom!*" (*MSLC* 1,iii:15–26), is misled by one of Rosa Coldfield's highly figurative passages into asserting that she was born by Caesarian section. Except for these errors all three of these studies are competent pieces of work. Lenson makes an intriguing attempt to apply Nietzsche's ideas about the relationship between the chorus and the actors in Greek tragedy to the relationship between the narrators and Sutpen. The idea, though, exists in embryo. Lensing's essay analyzes an important motif in the novel, but he is not convincing in his attempt to attribute the status of an "ideal family" to the Henry-Bon-Judith triangle. Despite her tendency toward an overly schematic (and anachronistic) view of the novel's themes, Sabiston provides a useful and generally well-informed treatment of Sutpen's attitudes toward blacks and women.

When viewed in the context of recent reexaminations of the concept of influence, Stephen M. Ross's "Conrad's Influence on Faulkner's *Absalom, Absalom!*" (*SAF* 2[1974]:199–209) has something of an old-fashioned air about it. Ross provides a straightforward account of the influence of *Lord Jim* and *Heart of Darkness* on the novel, but beyond a few observations on technique, he does not focus on the "swerve," to use Bloom's term, that Faulkner makes away from his master. Terrence Doody, in "Shreve McCannon and the Confessions of *Absalom, Absalom!*" (*SNNTS* 6[1974]:454–69) has a promising idea when he looks at the novel as a series of confessions. But he bends his rather restrictive definition of "confession" to the breaking point: neither Rosa nor Sutpen seems to be seeking a "community the speaker needs to confirm his identity."

The remaining two studies of *Absalom, Absalom!* are of little consequence. In her "Patterns of Reversal in *Absalom, Absalom!*" (*DR* 54:648–66), Bernice Schrank offers to resolve the conflict between the "subjectivist" and "sociological" schools of interpretation of the novel. But her resolution consists of rejecting the subjectivist school almost entirely, and of finding in the events of Sutpen's career a simple call for individual moral responsibility in the face of an indeterminate future. Sr. Cleopatra's "*Absalom, Absalom!* The Failure of the Sutpen Design" (*LHY* 16,i:74–93) is a sadly outdated study of Sutpen's moral failure.

The last item in this section, and the only work done during the year on *The Wild Palms*, is Thomas L. McHaney's *William Faulkner's "The Wild Palms": A Study* (Jackson: Univ. Press of Miss.). This book, which derives from McHaney's University of South Carolina dissertation, contains an excellent appendix detailing the chronologies of the two interlocked stories and the finances of the Wilbourne-Rittenmeyer relationship. It contains as well a convincing chapter on the interrelationship between Faulkner's novel, Anderson's *Dark Laughter*, and Hemingway's fiction, especially *A Farewell to Arms*. And it also traces in more detail than has hitherto been done the thematic, symbolic, and imagistic parallels between the alternating stories.

So much to the good. But the book is unsatisfactory as a work of criticism because of the narrow moralism of its interpretation of "Wild Palms." McHaney is puritanical in his insistence on the fatuity of Charlotte's quest for romantic fulfillment. Charlotte becomes his enemy, and his treatment of her sounds more like a courtroom prosecution than a literary analysis. His lack of sympathetic understanding of her character and role has many ill effects, but two are particularly prominent. It reduces a story which in the common view aspires to the condition of a tragedy to the condition of a tract, and it makes Wilbourne's final discovery of the value of memory seem like a non-sequitur, since the affair as McHaney describes it scarcely deserves to be endured, much less remembered. All this is a shame, because when McHaney is not dealing with Charlotte he frequently displays critical insight.

vii. Individual Works, 1940–49

Even more than is usually the case, sloppiness, repetition, and parochial critical attitudes characterize the work on *Go Down, Moses*. By far the best of the lot occurs in two studies not even primarily concerned with Faulkner. One of these, Annette Kolodny's *The Lay of the Land,* has already been discussed (see section iv. a). The other—Louis D. Rubin, Jr.'s *William Elliott Shoots a Bear: Essays on the Southern Literary Imagination* (Baton Rouge: La. State Univ. Press)—displays a mature, critical sensibility and a command of southern history in its comparison of "The Bear" with one of William Elliott's hunting sketches. Despite some eccentric readings, Weldon Thornton's "Structure and Theme in Faulkner's *Go Down, Moses*" (*Costerus* 3:73–112) contains occasional valuable insights into the unifying elements of the novel. But beyond here lies the wasteland. Annette Benert's "The Four Fathers of Isaac McCaslin" (*SHR* 9:423–33) is a casually written, derivative essay. Benert says that "neither the causes nor the extent of [Ike's] failure to live out his ideals has been very clearly established," when in fact both of these matters have been quite competently handled by earlier critics. She calls Gail Hightower "Gabriel," and mistakenly says that Uncle Buck and Uncle Buddy free their slaves on the day of their father's death. Karl F. Knight's "'Spintrius' in Faulkner's 'The Bear'" (*SSF* 12:31–32) argues that we should see in Uncle Buck's and Uncle Buddy's treatment of Percival Brownlee a statement in miniature of "the central theme of the relation between the races." Knight's argument requires that we accept the authenticity of Brownlee's spiritual vocation; it also blackens the characters of the McCaslin brothers, and violates the comic tone of the episode. In *The Sporting Myth and the American Experience: Studies in Contemporary Fiction* (Lewisburg, Pa.: Bucknell Univ. Press), Wiley Lee Umphlett presents a one-sided reading of "The Bear," in which he revives yet once again the old interpretation of Ike's repudiation of his inheritance as a morally unambiguous act of personal salvation.

Leonard A. Blanchard's "The Failure of the Natural Man: Faulkner's 'Pantaloon in Black'" (*NMW* 8:28–32) attempts unsuccessfully to magnify Rider's battle with his grief into a war with "the alien and unfriendly universe which he cannot decipher or control." Blanchard erroneously says that Rider receives his name "after he sees Mannie for the first time and abandons his old ways." An awareness of the sexual suggestiveness of the name would perhaps have prevented this error. H. R. Stoneback, in "Faulkner's Blues: 'Pantaloon in Black'" (*MFS* 21:241–45) displays such an awareness, but his attempt to draw parallels between the story and two Negro blues songs is unconvincing. No work of any consequence whatsoever was done on the other fiction of this period.

viii. Individual Works, 1950–62

Other than Irwin's brief but illuminating discussion of *A Fable* (see section iii. a), Noel Polk's "The Textual History of Faulkner's *Requiem for a Nun*" (*Proof* 4:109–28) is the only item worthy of comment on the fiction of Faulkner's last phase. Polk provides a careful and stimulating inspection of the major changes that Faulkner made in *Requiem* after it had been set in galleys. He argues that these changes substantially decrease sympathy for Gavin and Nancy, and increase it for Temple. Something of this sort seems to have taken place, but whether it occurred to the degree that Polk claims it did remains in doubt. It is hard to see how a genetic study of the work can convince us that other critics are as wrong about the meaning of the finished version as Polk claims they are. And even if Polk's reading of the finished novel is the correct one, we may still disagree with his claim that it deserves the status of a major work. The *Requiem* he describes is certainly different in meaning from the one we have grown accustomed to, but it is not necessarily better.

ix. The Stories

The comment that I made last year with regard to the work on Faulkner's short stories still holds true: much of it is characterized by inattention to the rest of the canon and to previous scholarship and criticism. Work of this sort will receive no discussion here. In one instance, though, the inattention to the rest of the canon is deliberate. Phillip Momberger's "Faulkner's 'Country' as Ideal Community" (in *Individual and Community*, pp. 112–36) clearly indicates that he has read *The Hamlet*, along with the other novels that deal with white country characters. But he here chooses to restrict his attention to the stories that make up the section subtitled "The Country" in the *Collected Stories*. This unfortunate choice entails treating as a single unit a group of stories written over a considerable period of time and for widely differing purposes. It also induces Momberger into doubtful generalizations about Faulkner's treatment of country characters. Thus, because there is no racial violence in the stories he treats, he says that "the races live in harmony in the country."

Two essays in the annual Faulkner number of *MissQ* deal with stories, neither of them with much success. Giliane Morell's "Prisoners of the Inner World: Mother and Daughter in *Miss Zilphia Gant*" (28:299–305) is a wandering consideration of this neglected story, which was first published by the Book Club of Texas in 1932. Morell's study drifts among attempts to relate the themes of the story to *Sanctuary*, "A Rose for Emily," and *Absalom, Absalom!*, critical judgments on its merits, and scattered analyses of its techniques. The other essay from *MissQ*, Phillip Castille's "'There Was a Queen' and Faulkner's Narcissa Sartoris" (28:307–15) argues unsuccessfully for a positive moral evaluation of Narcissa in the story, and in *Sanctuary* as well. Edmond Volpe's "Faulkner's 'Red Leaves': The Deciduation of Nature" (*SAF* 3:121–31) is the final item that is worthy of mention here. It provides an adequate reading of the story, together with a worthwhile analysis of its "life symbols and death symbols."

In the last essay mentioned in the section above, Edmond Volpe at one point calls the ship captain in "Red Leaves" a "Unitarian minister," even though Faulkner calls him "a deacon in the Unitarian church." Because, as it happens, there are no deacons in the Unitarian church, Volpe is in the odd position of being right by being wrong. As I reflect on what I have read for this study, I realize that many critics of Faulkner cannot count on even this degree of good fortune. Yet despite the frequent appearances of error's endless train, it has been a fairly good year, and it promises a better future. To cite only two instances, Irwin's *Doubling and Incest/Repetition and Revenge* has opened the door to recent revolutionary developments in critical theory, and Simpson's "The Loneliness of William Faulkner" has shown us what we may expect when sensitive critics fully assimilate Blotner's biography. And so the enterprise, at times wasteful, at times ludicrous, still continues to provide us with work of substance, beauty, and worth.[1]

University of California, Davis

1. I wish to thank Margaret Levin for her assistance with the Spanish essays discussed in section iv. a.

10. Fitzgerald and Hemingway

Jackson R. Bryer

The appearance in 1975 of two issues of the *Fitzgerald/Hemingway Annual* has substantially increased the length of this year's survey. Not only is there a body of extra material from the tardy 1974 *FHA*, but the enumerative checklists in both volumes have turned up a number of significant items overlooked previously.

Qualitatively this year's essay is noteworthy in that Fitzgerald studies seem to have turned a corner and are now concentrating more than ever before on the texts of the fiction. This is true with *Tender Is the Night* as well as with *Gatsby*. We should now be ready for full-length studies of the intricate patterns which critics have begun to trace in Fitzgerald's works. Hemingway's style continues to receive attention as it always has; and it is very encouraging this year to find commentators turning away from the glamorous details of his life and Fitzgerald's to focus primary attention on the fiction itself.

i. Bibliographical Work and Texts

As in past years, a substantial percentage of the best work done on Fitzgerald and Hemingway in 1975 falls into this category. Two invaluable full-length volumes head the list. Andrew T. Crosland's *A Concordance to F. Scott Fitzgerald's "The Great Gatsby"* (Detroit: Bruccoli Clark/Gale Research) is the first concordance of an American novel. Sensibly basing his work on the 1925 first-printing text as emended by Matthew J. Bruccoli in his *Apparatus* (see *ALS 1974*, pp. 139–40), Crosland helpfully provides a table keying page references in the popular Scribner Library Edition to those in the much rarer first printing. Throughout, a premium is placed on clarity of presentation and accuracy. Key words are arranged alphabetically and their appearances in the novel are presented within a maximum surrounding context of 120 words. Two frequency tables are appended, one arranged alphabetically, the other by the number of occurrences of words in the text—with the most frequently used words leading the list. In his brief but very useful Introduction, Crosland explains how the entries in the *Concordance* were checked for accuracy some ten times. The result is a model for future books of this kind; and it appears at just the right moment. Finally, as will be seen below, scholars and critics are beginning to turn their attention to the style of Fitzgerald's masterpiece. Crosland's research will help immeasurably in correcting some of the sloppy work done in the past; and it surely will encourage and assist future close attention to the text.

Audre Hanneman's *Supplement to "Ernest Hemingway: A Comprehensive Bibliography"* (Princeton, N.J.: Princeton Univ. Press) is a worthy successor to her earlier seminal work (1967). Essentially, Hanneman includes in the *Supplement* all material by and about Hemingway which appeared between 1966 and 1973; but she also provides quite a few omissions from her original volume, most notably *Fact* for July 1938, which contains Hemingway's Spanish Civil War dispatches entitled "The Spanish War." Aside from the astonishing thoroughness of Hanneman's research, the most noticeable characteristic of the *Supplement* is its size (393 pages). This book documents more graphically than any other the incredible industry which has grown up around the life and work of Ernest Hemingway. In her Preface, Hanneman notes that between 1931 and 1966 there were 21 books entirely or primarily about Hemingway, while between 1966 and 1974 there were 25. This circumstance is further reflected in some statistics which can be drawn from the *Supplement.* Part One, works by Hemingway (divided into Books and Pamphlets; Contributions and First Appearances in Books and Pamphlets; Contributions to Newspapers and Periodicals; Translations; Anthologies; and Library Holdings, Published Letters, and Ephemera), lists over 600 items, less than 50 of which predate 1966. Part Two, work about Hemingway (divided into Books on or Significantly Mentioning; and Newspaper and Periodical Material), includes more than 1,500 entries, with less than 200 predating 1966.

Hanneman's work here deserves the same sort of extravagant praise which her original volume received. With her assistance and that of the Princeton University Press, Hemingway scholars continue to have available to them perhaps the most complete and certainly the most beautifully designed and printed reference materials on any modern American author. Nevertheless, one can offer two suggestions for future editions: the material in Part Two should all be annotated or, failing that, reasons should be given for annotating some items and not others; and thought should be given to separating reviews of books by and about Hemingway from the chronological arrangement of the section on Newspaper and Periodical Material. The separate grouping of this type of item would enable the user of the volume to determine the reception of these books more easily.

While none of the other bibliographical pieces published this year approaches Crosland's and Hanneman's in lasting usefulness, there are several worthwhile items. Two of these are lengthy and polemical in tone. In "Sober Second Thoughts: The 'Author's Final Version' of Fitzgerald's *Tender Is the Night*" (*Proof* 4:111–34), Brian Higgins and Hershel Parker argue persuasively for the superiority of the original 1934 text of *Tender* as opposed to Cowley's revised 1951 edition. This matter has been debated before (Higgins and Parker review much of this earlier material), but never has it been done in such detail and with such careful attention to the text of the novel. The authors base their conclusions almost entirely on a meticulous study of the thematic and verbal patterns in the 1934 edition and the distortions in these created by the revised version. In discounting Fitzgerald's expressed wish to reorder the action of the novel, Higgins and Parker suggest that this "must be seen in the context of his frustrating sense that such reputation as he still had was needlessly dwindling further and as part of a general effort to salvage what he could of both reputation and career as a serious writer." They accuse Cowley of overlooking this explanation and of callously destroying "the effects Fitzgerald elaborately calculated." This essay is not only an excellent piece of bibliographical scholarship, but also, in its impressive marshaling of evidence from the text, a valuable close reading of the novel.

Less securely based on textual material and therefore more tenuous is Darrel Mansell's answer to the question "When Did Hemingway Write *The Old Man and the Sea*?" (*FHA* 1975:311–24). Asserting that the novel was written in 1935 or early 1936, Mansell bases his contention both on such external evidence as the differences between *The Old Man and the Sea*, the shortest novel of its author's career, and the other much longer and verbally much more expansive books he wrote before and after 1951, and the "extraordinary speed" with which Hemingway claims to have written it, and also on internal evidence. Principal among the latter are striking similarities between phrases and details in *The Old Man* and pieces Hemingway wrote in 1935 and 1936 and differences between the style of *The Old Man* and *Islands in the Stream*, a novel on which Hemingway claims he was working in 1951 and of which he says he originally planned to make the story of the old fisherman a part. In the end, however, Mansell's essay is suggestive and tentative rather than conclusive.

Four briefer textual studies are divided equally between Fitzgerald and Hemingway. In "The Discarded Ending of 'The Offshore Pirate'" (*FHA 1974*:47–49), Jennifer McCabe Atkinson sees Fitzgerald's deletion of his original ending—probably at the suggestion of agents Paul Reynolds or Harold Ober—as improving the story. Linda Berry, in "The Text of *Bits of Paradise*" (*FHA 1975*:141–45), helpfully provides a list of the variants between the original magazine texts of the stories and their reprinting in the British and American book versions, both of which were set from the same plates. Phillip R. Yannella's "Notes on the Manuscript, Date, and Sources of Hemingway's 'Banal Story'" (*FHA 1974*:175–79) is valuable chiefly for its observations on the original manuscript of the story from which the editors of the *Little Review* (where it was first published) deleted several phrases in fear of being censored by the Post Office authorities—as they already had been for publishing certain chapters of *Ulysses.* These deletions, Yannella shows, weaken Hemingway's story; but they were never restored in subsequent reprintings. Yannella also dates the story on the basis of a cover letter sent to the *Little Review* editors. His brief discussion of the story's sources is not nearly so complete as Wayne Kvam's (see below). Richard Winslow's "A Bibliographical Correction" (*FHA 1975*:307) simply redates Hemingway's unsigned Toronto *Daily Star* article, "Buying Commission Would Cut Out Waste," from April 20, 1920, to April 26, 1920.

Four recent essays concern themselves briefly with different aspects of Fitzgerald's reputation. Andrew Crosland, in "Sleeping and Waking: The Literary Reputation of *The Great Gatsby*, 1927–1944" (*FHA 1974*:15–24), provides a brief survey and unannotated listing of critical materials. Both, unfortunately, are marred by inaccuracy; and the judgments made are often superficial. Malcolm Cowley's account of "The Fitzgerald Revival, 1941–1953" (*FHA 1974*:11–13) rehashes familiar material for the most part but does include a few new tidbits: Scribner's turned down both *The Crack-Up* and Mizener's biography, and the early sales of the Viking *Portable F. Scott Fitzgerald* (1945) were less than the *Portable Hemingway* but more than the *Portable Faulkner*. In "*The F. Scott Fitzgerald and His Contemporaries* Correspondence" (*FHA 1974*:89–93), William Goldhurst summarizes and quotes briefly from letters he received from critics and Fitzgerald's contemporaries while preparing his book; none is particularly enlightening or significant. Fitzgerald's "phenomenal resurgence in popularity" on college campuses early in the 1970s is the subject of Alan S. Wheelock's "Paradise Regained: Fitzgerald on Campus" (*GyS* 1,i[1973]:60–63). Wheelock sees three basic reasons for Fitzgerald's popularity: sympathy with his theme of "the good times that were but are no more"; the fact that "a significant number of undergraduates have begun to search through Fitzgerald for images of form, grace, and beauty—images which they cannot find in this time and this place"; and Fitzgerald's "pervading sense of disillusionment," which makes a success out of failure. Wheelock's approach of not simply documenting the response to Fitzgerald but trying as well to explain it in terms of the literary and sociological currents of the day is one which we badly need, not only for the 1950s, 1960s, and 1970s, but also for the 1920s, 1930s, and 1940s.

Among the shorter bibliographical items on Hemingway, two center on his reading habits. Hans-Joachim Kann's "Ernest Hemingway and the Arts: A Necessary Addendum" (*FHA 1974*:145–54) surveys the art books in Hemingway's private library in Cuba in an attempt to add to the conclusions reached in Watts's 1971 study; the results are neither noteworthy nor surprising. Similar adjectives can be used to describe Richard Layman's listing of "Hemingway's Library Cards at Shakespeare and Company" (*FHA 1975*:191–206), although Layman simply provides an enumeration without making any of the claims that Kann does. In "The Man Behind the Masks: Hemingway as a Fictional Character" (*FHA 1974*:207–13), William F. Nolan provides an interesting footnote to Hemingway studies by describing seven novels in which Hemingway appears as a thinly disguised fictional character.

Interestingly enough, we have three studies of Hemingway's reputation abroad. The best of these is David J. Wells's "Hemingway in

French" (*FHA 1974*:235–38), which provides a brief but fascinating close examination of the problems of translating Hemingway into French. Wells points out that the translator often must violate the strict sense of Hemingway's prose in order to make it understandable to a French audience. His conclusion, that "some of Hemingway's most distinctive prose loses its character, hence much of its significance, in translation," is both disturbing and also certainly applicable to languages other than French. Less concerned with the specific problems of translation is Ernest S. Falbo in "Carlo Linati: Hemingway's First Italian Critic and Translator" (*FHA 1975*:293–306). Falbo shows that Linati, not Mario Praz as previously thought, was the first Italian to write about Hemingway (in a March 4, 1926, issue of the influential newspaper *Corriere della Sera*) and to translate his work (in a 1925 version of "Soldier's Home"). As his title, "Hemingway in the Soviet Union" (*HN* 4,i[1974]:17–19), suggests, Boris Gilenson presents an even broader perspective, glancing briefly at the career and writings of Russian Hemingway critic and translator Ivan Kashkeen, and then running quickly through major Russian works by and about Hemingway.

As usual, the enumerative listings about both Fitzgerald and Hemingway are numerous and valuable. The best is Jackson J. Benson's "A Comprehensive Checklist of Hemingway Short Fiction Criticism, Explication and Commentary," which is included in Benson's collection, *The Short Stories of Ernest Hemingway: Critical Essays* (Durham, N.C.: Duke Univ. Press), pp. 312–75. Arranged in the form of the *Modern Fiction Studies* checklists, Benson's compilation begins with "general" works (books entirely on Hemingway, dissertations on Hemingway, general books with material on Hemingway's stories, general articles with discussions of Hemingway's stories, and reviews of the short-story collections). The second half, "Criticism, Explication, and Commentary on Individual Stories," lists each story alphabetically, with the material under it including essays entirely about that story as well as sections of general works keyed back to the first half of the checklist. In addition, Benson lists all of Hemingway's short fiction, published and unpublished, regardless of whether it has received any critical comment; he also includes, where applicable, original publication data and the Hemingway collections in which each story is reprinted. Although unannotated, this is a marvelously rich reference tool.

The other enumerative items are continuing lists, most of which appear in the *FHA*. Matthew J. Bruccoli provides two more lists of Addenda to his Fitzgerald bibliography (*FHA 1974*:275–83; *FHA 1975*:337–39); Margaret M. Duggan has compiled a much-needed listing of "Reprintings of Fitzgerald" (*FHA 1974*:285–311); Linda Berry continues her work, begun in 1972, on "Fitzgerald in Translation" (*FHA 1974*:313–15); and Margaret M. Duggan contributes a "Fitzgerald Checklist" to each *FHA* volume (*1974*:317–22; *1975*:341–50). Duggan is also responsible for the "Hemingway Checklist" in the 1974 *FHA* (pp. 323–29); but William White's "Hemingway: A Current Bibliography" (*HN* 4,i[1974]:20–24) seems more comprehensive, perhaps because White has long been a Hemingway collector and critic. Significantly, the "Hemingway Checklist" in the 1975 *FHA* (pp. 351–68) is compiled by White.

Only two new texts, both related to Fitzgerald, appeared in 1975. Neither is very significant; but one, a hitherto unpublished obituary tribute to her husband by Zelda Fitzgerald (*FHA 1974*:3–7), is curiously fascinating. Written—or rather, overwritten—probably shortly after his death, it is filled with elaborate and confusing passages which nevertheless somehow convey a strangely poignant message. A sample: Fitzgerald's "tragedies were hearts at bay to the inexorable exigence of a day whose formulas no longer worked and whose ritual had dwindled to less of drama than its guignol." Next to this haunting and disquieting bit of Zelda's prose, Matthew J. Bruccoli's reprinting of five unsigned limericks from the St. Paul Academy *Now & Then*, which he attributes to Fitzgerald (*FHA 1975*:147–48), seems very insignificant.

ii. Letters and Biography

Coincidentally, the one significant new letter is also by Zelda Fitzgerald (*FHA 1975*:3–6). Far more lucidly written than the piece noted above, this was written, either in 1944 or 1945, to a childhood friend. It is mostly an extravagant but beautifully worded hymn of praise to her husband, faults and all. Scott, she notes, "liked women, who usually lionized him, unless he was intolerably scandalous: which was rare; then they usually forgave him because he kept all the rites and sent flowers and wrote notes world without end and was most ingratiating when contrite." We shall probably never have a better brief summary of Fitzgerald's personality than that contained in this unpretentious and charming letter.

Two new Fitzgerald letters and one new Hemingway letter also appeared in print; none of them is even marginally significant. Fitzgerald's "Letter to Brooks Bowman" (*FHA 1974*:9–10) suggests to the composer of the 1934–35 Princeton Triangle Club show that one of the songs be converted into a school song. A 1934 letter from Fitzgerald to James Aswell (*LaS* 12[1974]:552) and a 1929 Hemingway letter to Aswell (*LaS* 12[1974]:532) are both worthless.

Three persons who were friendly with both Hemingway and Fitzgerald have commented on these associations, two in full-length autobiographical volumes, one in an interview. Edmund Wilson, in *The Twenties: From Notebooks and Diaries of the Period*, ed. Leon Edel (New York: Farrar, Straus and Giroux), and Donald Ogden Stewart, in *By a Stroke of Luck! An Autobiography* (New York: Paddington Press), provide brief but often fascinating glimpses of times spent with Fitzgerald or Hemingway. Surprisingly, Stewart's memories are the more complete and interesting; Wilson, who certainly knew Fitzgerald better and longer than almost anyone, provides very little insight. His remarks on Hemingway are really better than those on Fitzgerald; but there too Stewart, with his vignettes of visits to Pamplona with Hemingway (including the events and persons which form the basis of *The Sun Also Rises*), is more worthwhile, although most of this material has appeared in print previously. On the other hand, Matthew J. Bruccoli's "Interview With Allen Tate" (*FHA 1974*:101–13) is specifically focused on Tate's friendships with Fitzgerald and Hemingway. Tate recalls Fitzgerald's first remark to him, "Do you like sleeping with your wife?" Tate replied, "That's none of your damn business," but he later became good friends with Fitzgerald, whom he says he came to like much better than Hemingway. Fitzgerald, Tate observes, was "a curious combination of naivety and cunning." This interview, in which Tate also comments briefly on such other twenties figures as Ford, Pound, McAlmon, and Harry and Caresse Crosby, provides one of our last opportunities to hear first-hand from someone who knew Fitzgerald and Hemingway.

Aside from Tate's interview, the most important new biographical item is Madelaine Hemingway Miller's memoir, *Ernie: Hemingway's Sister "Sunny" Remembers* (New York: Crown). The third of Hemingway's four sisters and five years his junior, Sunny obviously worshipped her older brother. Her book is most valuable for the well over 100 family photographs, many drawn from the album her mother kept for her and captioned in her mother's handwriting, which it reproduces. The narrative which accompanies them is best in its memories of the early years, especially the summers spent in Michigan. As an adult, Sunny's life apparently touched Ernest's infrequently, so that she is reduced in the last half of her book to summarizing or printing letters which recount his exploits and to intermittent glimpses on the few occasions when they were together, including an entertaining account of a visit to Key West in 1928. But Sunny's intentions here are modest and her book makes extremely easy and pleasant reading.

The biographical pieces on Fitzgerald divide, as usual, into first-hand reminiscences and those based on research. There are two of the former and five of the latter. William Katterjohn gives us "An Interview With Theodora Gager, Fitzgerald's Private Nurse" (*FHA 1974*:75–85). Miss Gager attended Fitzgerald for about a month in 1932 at La Paix. Her principal function, she recalls, was to keep him away from gin and cigarettes, a task at which she did not succeed very well. Her portrait is of a depressed alcoholic—"a brilliant young man drinking and going to the dogs"—with a mentally ill wife who "was like a ball and chain around his neck." J. T. Fain first met Fitzgerald about three years later in Hendersonville, North Carolina, and his "Recollections of F. Scott Fitzgerald" (*FHA 1975*:133–39) are not so focused on Fitzgerald's drinking, although Fain mentions that his friend was "fighting alcohol" when he knew him. Fain's emphasis is on Fitzgerald's physical and verbal charm; he remembers "a handsome, young man with his best years ahead, and I remember most the wistful curve of the left corner of his mouth when he smiled." Fain also recalls Fitzgerald's Marxism and his frequent mention of a Catholic church with which he had broken—"Just as I believed that his best work was yet to come, I believed he would have returned to the faith in some form."

The lasting effect of the Catholic church is also the subject of one of the researched biographical essays. In "The Better Fathers: The Priests in Fitzgerald's Life" (*FHA 1974*:29–39), Joan M. Allen gives brief biographical sketches of four priests (not including Father Fay) who "significantly touched" Fitzgerald's life. Her concern is with his "periodic attraction, probably in reaction to his father's inadequate example, to dynamic male models among the priests he met in the course of his life." One of these priests was Thomas Delihant, the brother of Fitzgerald's favorite cousin Ceci. Fitzgerald's friendship with and visits to Ceci in Norfolk, Virginia, is the subject of another biographical piece, William W. Seward, Jr.'s "F. Scott Fitzgerald's Associations with Norfolk and Virginia Beach" (*FHA 1974*:41–46). Seward bases his essay on interviews with Ceci's daughters, who remember Fitzgerald's visits well; and this gives his work a good deal of authenticity.

Fitzgerald's residencies in two other cities provide the subject matter for two additional biographical essays. Frederic Kelley's "F. Scott Fitzgerald: His Baltimore Years" (Baltimore *Sun*, 14 July and 21 July 1974) basically recounts the familiar story of Fitzgerald's sojourns at La Paix and in Baltimore, adding only the reminiscences of Mrs. Gaylord Estabrook, who was resident manager of the Cambridge Arms Apartments when Fitzgerald lived there. In "The Geography of Fitzgerald's Saint Paul" (*CM* 13,ii[1973]:3–30), Erling Larsen combines a view of the city as it was when Fitzgerald lived there with glimpses of how it is portrayed in his fiction. This is a very detailed piece of work, but Larsen's research does not overwhelm the reader.

Two brief notes concern Fitzgerald's associations with fellow writers. The editors of the *FHA* (*1974*:25–27) reprint from the May 18, 1958, New York *Herald Tribune* John O'Hara's account of his unsuccessful attempts in 1936 to buy the movie rights to *Gatsby* in order to do a talking-picture version. And Richard Layman, in "Fitzgerald and Horace McCoy" (*FHA 1974*:99–100), suggests a possible friendship between Fitzgerald and the author of *They Shoot Horses, Don't They?*

The Hemingway biographical essays are also divided between personal reminiscences and researched articles. Of the former type, the best is Eduardo Zayas-Bazán's "Hemingway: His Cuban Friends Remember" (*FHA 1975*:153–90), which consists of interviews with Elicio Argüelles, Mario Menocal, and Thórbald Sánchez. All three have marvelous anecdotes to tell; all make corrections in some of the previous stories about Hemingway—Menocal notes that "He never fished. Just guided the boat along. He liked to stand up on the bridge and steer the boat and have a bottle of tequila or vodka or whatever." Edward Fisher's free-form memoir, "What Papa Said" (*ConnR*

8,ii:16–20), deals with the Labor Day Hurricane of 1935 on Matecumbe Key in which many members of the Bonus Army who had been driven out of Washington drowned, along with Rosalind Groomes, "the prettiest girl in Key West." What Hemingway said to Fisher after viewing the storm damage was, "No man alone now has got a bloody [obscenity] chance," a remark which he later gave to Harry Morgan in *To Have and Have Not.*

In two briefer pieces, Joan Wheeler Redington (*FHA 1975*:309–10) tells of a passing encounter with Hemingway in a hotel lobby in Nîmes, in 1959, before a bull-fight; and Bertram D. Sarason continues his searches for real-life bases of Hemingway's fiction by reporting an interview with Krebs Friend, an acquaintance of Hemingway's in Chicago and Paris (*FHA 1975*:209–15).

Three places where Hemingway spent varying amounts of time are the subjects of other notes. In "Piggott Pandemonium: Hemingway Wasn't a Hit in This Town" (*LGJ* 3,ii:3–6), Dave Sanders presents the recollections of three Piggott, Arkansas, residents who remember Hemingway's visits to Pauline Pfeiffer Hemingway's hometown. One of the most memorable images recalled is of the world-famous author jogging through rural, conservative Piggott clad in a dirty T-shirt, dirty shorts, and tennis shoes. Jim Brasher's account of Hemingway's life in Key West, "Hemingway's Florida" (*LGJ* 1,ii[1973]:4–8), is primarily based on previously published materials but is enhanced by several photos of the interior and exterior of Hemingway's house. In "'A Good Country': Hemingway at the L Bar T Ranch, Wyoming" (*FHA 1975*:259–72), Richard Winslow presents an extremely impressionistic piece about his visit to the ranch where Hemingway spent the summers and falls of 1930, 1932, 1936, and 1939. Winslow includes the text of a conversation with Mrs. Olive Nordquist, who ran the ranch with her husband when Hemingway stayed there; but most of his rambling account concerns his own feelings as he walked the paths that Hemingway had trod before him.

Hemingway's relationships with three of his contemporaries concern Paul Somers, Jr., Herman Prescott, and Dan Agent. Somers, in "Sherwood Anderson Introduces His Friend Ernest Hemingway" (*LGJ* 3,iii:24–26), summarizes the key events of the Hemingway-Anderson friendship, presents excerpts from the letters of introduction which Anderson wrote for Hemingway to Stein, Pound, Joyce, and Beach, and then briefly traces the courses of the literary acquaintanceships Hemingway formed with these four people. In "Hemingway vs. Faulkner: An Intriguing Feud" (*LGJ* 3,iii:18–19), Prescott outlines the contacts between the two men—they never met; but they commented on one another's work on several occasions, usually in very derogatory terms. Prescott attributes this to "artistic competitiveness" and excessive "personal pride." The oft-recounted confrontation between Hemingway and Max Eastman in Maxwell Perkins's office is the center of Agent's "The Hair on Hemingway's Chest" (*LGJ* l,i[1973]:12–15), which also details other more literary aspects of their feud.

Frank M. Laurence's "5000 Grand: The Plagiarism Suit Against Hemingway" (*FHA 1974*:193–99) tells of the frivolous 1941 suit filed by Mexican-American John Igual De Montijo in which De Montijo claimed that in *For Whom the Bell Tolls* Hemingway had plagiarized from his play "The Rebel" and from the screenplay he had adapted from it, *Viva Madero!* Laurence summarizes the plots of De Montijo's works and quotes from his deposition in order to show how absurd his claims were. His essay is an entertaining account of an admittedly minor episode. A much more consequential episode in Hemingway's life was his wounding in 1918 on the Italian front; and in "American Red Cross Reports on the Wounding of Lieutenant Ernest M. Hemingway" (*FHA 1974*:131–36), C. E. Frazer Clark, Jr., reprints two accounts, one from the *Report of the Department of Military Affairs* and the other from the December 7, 1918, issue of *The American Red Cross Central Division Bulletin.*

iii. Criticism

***a.* Collections.** There is only one new collection, Jackson J. Benson's excellent volume, *The Short Stories of Ernest Hemingway: Critical Essays* (Durham, N.C.: Duke Univ. Press). In his Introduction, Benson offers convincing evidence of the popularity of Hemingway's stories, noting that, through 1968, they had been anthologized 410 times. But he also points out that while "many of Hemingway's best stories were written nearly a half-century ago, it is only within the last few years that we have begun to reach out to comprehend the full breadth and depth of Hemingway's remarkable achievements within the short story form." For this reason, he says, he has assembled this collection "to bring together out of this welter of material many of the best essays on the stories, while trying to maintain the widest possible range of commentary" and to "encourage a wider reading within the stories that have too often been overlooked." Accordingly, Benson has arranged his material into three sections: the first includes essays "with a broad focus, emphasizing qualities, themes, and connections within the stories as considered in various groupings"; the second is "totally devoted to one aspect or another of technique in the stories"; and the third is comprised "of essays that for the most part are focused on a single story." Benson's selections are judicious: most are reprinted for the first time; he emphasizes recent commentary; he uses relevant sections of books on Hemingway as well as articles; and all the important Hemingway critics—Young, Baker, Fenton, Hovey, Rovit, Lewis, DeFalco—are included. Besides the extremely useful "Comprehensive Checklist" of criticism of the stories (discussed above), Benson also contributes to the volume an extensive and sensible "Overview of the Stories" (see below).

***b.* Full-Length Studies.** If we exclude William A. Fahey's *F. Scott Fitzgerald and the American Dream* (New York: Thomas Y. Crowell, 1973), a part of Crowell's Twentieth-Century American Writers series intended for "young people in high school or junior college," we have had no full-length critical study of Fitzgerald since 1972. The situation with Hemingway studies is almost the same, with Pearsall's 1973 book the last one (see *ALS 1974*, p. 147). Linda Welshimer Wagner's *Hemingway and Faulkner: Inventors/Masters* (Metuchen, N.J.: Scarecrow) is only half on Hemingway and almost all of that material has previously been published in periodical essays already surveyed. Although Wagner's emphasis, on Hemingway's style and on how his fiction works rather than on what it says, is yet another indication of the praiseworthy direction of recent Fitzgerald and Hemingway criticism, her book succeeds best as a series of essays rather than as a tightly organized critical volume. Thus an excellent chapter on *The Sun Also Rises* as the "most sustained" example of Hemingway's Imagist prose is inexplicably followed by a chapter in which Wagner goes back to Hemingway's earliest work to see how his craft developed. Then, after a chapter on *To Have and Have Not, For Whom the Bell Tolls*, and *A Farewell to Arms*, Wagner returns, in chapter 5, to *Sun.* Many of Wagner's insights are valuable and her overall approach to the fiction is the one we need, but readers should not expect a comprehensive well-organized critical study.

***c.* General Essays.** Continuing the trend noted last year, we again have an abundance of good general essays, especially on Hemingway. We have one article, Robert F. Lucid's "Three Public Performances: Fitzgerald, Hemingway, Mailer" (*ASch* 43[1974]:447–66), which deals with both in a fascinating piece. Lucid sketches how each of his three subjects "was given public existence by the cultural imagination" and finds that the work of each, in a different way, gives off a "crucial quality," an "element of personal presence" that the reader can feel. With Fitzgerald, "our need to wonder has terribly to do with our need to be strong enough to survive the experience of failure.... The fiction hinted that Fitzgerald could claim the strength that came with such experience." In contrast, Hemingway was attractive because he implied in his work that he had learned "the secret of how to win." Lucid's argument, while certainly open to dispute, is provocative.

Unlike most of the more specific essays on Fitzgerald to be discussed below, the two general essays on him view the writer and his works at a distance, through historical, sociological, and literary perspectives. Edward Lueders's autobiographical "Revisiting Babylon: Fitzgerald and the 1920's" (*WHR* 29:285–91) is more an entertaining recollection of the ambience of the period than it is a consideration of Fitzgerald. On the other hand, C. W. E. Bigsby's "The Two Identities of F. Scott Fitzgerald" (in *The American Novel and the Nineteen Twenties*, ed. Malcolm Bradbury and David Palmer, Stratford-upon Avon studies, 13; London: Edward Arnold [1971]) is focused more narrowly. Bigsby sees Fitzgerald as one of the artists who is defined by Lionel Trilling as containing "a large part of the dialectic within themselves ... the yes and no of their culture." In his early work, Bigsby notes, Fitzgerald "could never quite bring himself to face his essential pessimism.... Despite his Catholicism and his naïve conception of Socialism he could find no faith to redeem the emptiness of society as he saw it." Only in *Tender Is the Night* does he "face the full implications of his vision and ... establish the irrevocable connection between personal tragedy and cultural decline which formed the basis of his dialectic." This is a thorough and intelligent essay.

Most of the general essays on Hemingway trace a pattern through his writings or look at his work from a particular point of view. Carlos Baker, in "Hemingway's Empirical Imagination" (in *Individual and Community*), chooses two passages, one from "The Snows of Kilimanjaro" and the other from *For Whom the Bell Tolls*, and, in a fascinating study, shows how Hemingway took these from actual events he had heard about, fictionalized them slightly, but still had them retain the ring of authenticity. In the later fiction, though, Baker sees Hemingway as preaching about experience rather than dramatizing it, as "exploiting his personal idiosyncrasies, as if he hoped to persuade readers to accept these in lieu of that powerful union of objective discernment and subjective response which he had once been able to achieve." This is an extremely suggestive thesis which Baker documents much more fully on the early Hemingway than on the later. It would be an excellent starting point for a full-length study or a dissertation.

Fredrik C. Brøgger also sees a division between two stages of Hemingway's career. In "Love and Fellowship in Ernest Hemingway's Fiction" (in *Americana-Norvegica: Norwegian Contributions to American Studies*, 4; ed. Brita Seyersted, Olso: Universitetsforlaget [1973]), Brøgger finds that, in the early novels, "because of the aimlessness, indifference, and despair of the war or the post-war world, love and fellowship revealed themselves indirectly." In the later novels, however, "there is a greater breadth of involvement . . . the commitment is part of the purposes and aims of a larger social group . . . . From the solitary fight in Hemingway's novels rises the need for love and fellowship which bring meaning to what otherwise would be an empty and meaningless universe." While this is not an overly original approach, Brøgger works it out thoroughly and convincingly.

Two essays deal with Hemingway's characters as, in different ways, isolated from the life around them. In "Hemingway: Ultimate Exile" (*Mosaic* 8,iii:77–87) John V. Hagopian deals with Hemingway's fiction as describing a life "*outside* the arena of normal human behavior," one in which his characters do not get involved with everyday activities such as washing dishes, taking care of children, or working at a normal job. Hagopian extends Hemingway's own exile to include exclusion from "his homeland, from society, from family, . . . from love" and from the Catholic Church, concluding that this all had a crucial effect on the quality of Hemingway's art. His style,

Hagopian points out, is "one of exclusion—the exclusion of complexity, of emotion, of abstraction, of thought." This is a concise and interesting piece. C. W. E. Bigsby's "Hemingway: The Recoil From History," in *The Twenties*, ed. Warren French, pp. 203–13, could well take as its premise a sentence from Hagopian's essay: "Hemingway and his heroes do not think or function in terms of history." Thus Bigsby sees the Hemingway hero as "unable to contemplate a past which seems to have lost all meaning or to be the source of unbearable pain, and yet unwilling to concede a future in which he might be required to accept responsibility for the present." Unlike Fitzgerald, whose characters "collaborate in the general disorder which is the antithesis of their search for pattern," and unlike Eliot, who "looked to the past for evidence of organic integrity," Hemingway's response was "dissociation," a "sceptical detachment" which he saw as "the only safe method of picking one's way through the ashes of a dying civilization." There are no startling insights here, but Bigsby organizes his evidence effectively and makes his points well.

Robert D. Crozier, S.J., Stephen L. Tanner, and Roy Rogers trace three other motifs through Hemingway's work. Crozier's essay, "Home James: Hemingway's Jacob" (*PLL* 11:293–301), is the most valuable. His concern is with what he calls the Jacob motif in Hemingway—basically, a wound of some sort, symbolic of the search for spiritual fulfillment. Crozier finds the origins of this motif in two already well-surveyed sources—Hemingway's wounding on the Italian front and the literary work of St. John of the Cross—and two more original ones—the rue Jacob in Paris (remembered by Hemingway for "those years of poverty, hunger, luck, love, and happiness") and the Genesis story of Jacob wrestling with the angel. Crozier overworks his discoveries of religious motifs in Hemingway's fiction; but his article is provocative and, if treated sceptically, worthwhile. Tanner is on less controversial ground in "Hemingway: The Function of Nostalgia" (*FHA 1974*:163–74) when he asserts that nostalgia functioned importantly in Hemingway's writings, both as a thematic and stylistic device. Thematically, part of the value of present experience for Hemingway "lies in what kind of memory it will make," and a man is often for Hemingway what he has experienced and how well he can order and recall that experience. Stylistically, nostalgia functions to compress a man's entire life into a brief two- or three-day period and also to help vary the tempo of the fiction by interpolating flashbacks—which are usually calm—into passages of narrative—which often deal with the chaotic rush of present events. Again, Tanner's thesis here suggests the possibility of further exploration of this topic. The same can also be said for Rogers's much briefer "Hemingway and the Tragic Curve" (*HN* 4,i[1974]:12–16). Rogers takes his basic term from Norman Mailer: the tragic curve is the progression in a character whose growth takes longer than his inevitable disaster. Hemingway's characters display this curve consistently, according to Rogers, with Santiago especially achieving "a type of immortality" through a "continuous revolt against the tyranny of the tragic curve." Because his essay is short, Rogers has little opportunity to do more than state this idea; his evidence is fragmentary.

"Why has it taken so long . . . for readers to begin writing about Hemingway and sport?" asks Robert W. Lewis in "Hemingway Ludens" (*LGJ* 3,ii:7–8, 30). Joseph DeFalco ("Hemingway, Sport, and the Larger Metaphor," *LGJ* 3,ii:18–20) offers a plausible answer: we have been so obsessed with the larger-than-life figure of Hemingway as sportsman that we've not bothered to look at sport in his work and how it functions. This explanation, of course, could be used to account for the neglect of many other important areas of both Fitzgerald's and Hemingway's artistic achievements. This year has seen reversals of this trend in several directions; and considerations of the function of sport in Hemingway is one of them. An entire number of the *Lost Generation Journal* (Spring-Summer 1975) is devoted to the subject; but the best material is Leverett T. Smith, Jr.'s detailed treatment in his *The American Dream and the National Game* (Bowling Green, Ohio: Bowling Green Univ. Popular Press). Smith traces sports through Hemingway's canon, beginning with the early stories about fishing, horse racing, boxing, and skiing, through *Sun* (a novel in which the world of sport functions "as a symbolic center for the values by which a man can establish himself apart from society"), *Death in the Afternoon* ("an important book because it presents a vision of a temporary social order which is created in the course of the bullfight and which Hemingway seems to suggest would be an ideal order for the whole human race"), and *Green Hills of Africa* (where "the world of sport is suggested as a meaningful alternative to commercial civilization"), down to "The Short Happy Life" and *Old Man*, works in which Hemingway moves from spectator sports to participatory ones. Throughout Smith bases his concepts of sport and play on those in Johan Huizinga's *Homo Ludens* (1938), and his readings of Hemingway are sensible and helpful.

Next to Smith's work the several other essays on Hemingway and sport seem little more than interesting footnotes. DeFalco (see above) stresses *Old Man* as the work in which Hemingway's use of sports as a metaphoric base reaches its full glory. Lewis's title (see above) indicates that his essay, like Smith's, is a reading of Hemingway through Huizinga. Of the three other pieces in the special issue of *LGJ*, Michael Helfand's "A Champ Can't Retire Like Anyone Else" (*LGJ* 3,ii:9–10, 35) emphasizes *Death in the Afternoon* and "Big Two-Hearted River" in its differentiation of sports competition and play, the latter being "even more crucial" than the former in Hemingway's art. Christian Messenger, in "Hemingway and the School Athletic Hero" (*LGJ* 3,ii:21–23), shows that Hemingway did not romanticize sports and that in the figure of Robert Cohn, an "unhappy Ivy League warrior," he demonstrated his disdain for "an American culture that lionizes sports heroes." And Gregory Sojka, in "A Portrait of Hemingway as Angler-Artist" (*LGJ* 3,ii:12–13), examines Hemingway's four articles on fishing written for the Toronto *Star Weekly* in 1920 as "evidence of Hemingway's talent for imaginative story-telling" and glimpses of his "ability to narrate stories from personal experience that engage the reader's imagination."

In "Ernest Hemingway's Genteel Bullfight" (in *The American Novel and the Nineteen Twenties* [see above]), Brom Weber also centers his discussion on Hemingway's view of a sport; but his observations are much more negative in tone than those of any of the above-mentioned critics. Weber starts from the debatable premise that *Sun* and *Farewell to Arms*, which established Hemingway's reputation, now "seem unable to evoke the same awesome sense of a tottering world" and "no longer seem to penetrate too deeply and steadily below the surface of existence." In asserting that the import of Hemingway's work has diminished, Weber focuses particularly on the writings on bullfighting, concluding that "it would not have been necessary for Hemingway to have written *Death in the Afternoon* as he did, and for us to read it in order to understand *The Sun Also Rises*, if he had not distorted his understanding of the bullfight and so, in effect, throttled the imaginative reach that from the outset was necessary to produce a long-enduring book." Weber's conclusion is as open to challenge as his original premise.

A frequent subject of argument has always been Hemingway's portraits of women; and two recent notes, while not adding anything startlingly original, draw the battle lines quite distinctly. Hemingway's women, Janet Lynne Pearson states, in "Hemingway's Women" (*LGJ* 1,i[1973]:16–19), are "nothing more than a bunch of naive, foolish, immature, selfish neurotics who cannot shoot lions or fight bulls." The lone exception is Pilar and she is explicitly described by Hemingway as more like a man than a woman. This rather hysterical approach is balanced by Deborah Fisher's "Genuine Heroines Hemingway Style" (*LGJ* 2,ii[1974]:35–36). Examining Maria, Pilar, Renata, and Catherine, Fisher sees them as "more believable female characters than has been noticed." She feels that Hemingway establishes the validity of his women characters through "a natural metaphor," "a varying closeness to elemental things, used to describe and develop each woman"; and that Hemingway women sometimes "seem to draw strength as well as a kind of independence" from their relationships with men. Some of his women, Fisher points out, are "a good deal smarter and more practical" than their male counterparts.

Finally, we have three essays which compare Hemingway with other writers in general terms. Two of these stress similarities; but the best, Clinton S. Burhans, Jr.'s "Hemingway and Vonnegut: Diminishing Vision in a Dying Age" (*MFS* 21:173–91), sees significant differences. Although both writers "share basically similar views of society and the human condition," Hemingway's characters "can and do transcend the conditions which hurt and destroy them: in an empty and indifferently maleficent universe, they confront the human condition directly and by living fully within it find or create meaning, order, and beauty." To Vonnegut, "the human condition has become absurd and terrifying beyond anything in Hemingway; for man himself has become the most absurd and terrifying thing in it." The only approach left then is a comic and ironic one. Burhans's essay not only sketches a clear and legitimate distinction; it also suggests that these differences have great implications for further study of the ambience in which these two writers produced their work.

Lynette Hubbard Seator's "The Antisocial Humanism of Cela and Hemingway" (*REH* 9:425–39) convincingly establishes that a comparison of the two "intensifies what is perceived as Hemingway's *Weltanschauung*." The essay is well organized, with the points of similarity clearly articulated. In "Anatomy of Fear in Tolstoy and Hemingway" (*LGJ* 3,ii:15–17), Philip Bordinat's intentions are much less ambitious, but he does make a useful distinction between two kinds of battle descriptions in Hemingway's fiction. One, "the *actual* truth," in which fear, loneliness, and helplessness are explicitly expressed, is also found in *War and Peace*; the other, "the *acceptable* truth," is seen in passages where a Hemingway character presents "the external facts in a tone out of keeping with the tragedy he is describing." As with so many of the general essays described above, this point could well be examined in other Hemingway works.

***d.* Essays on Specific Works: Fitzgerald.** Of the 30 items surveyed in this category, 21 deal with *Gatsby*. But this not unusual imbalance is rendered less regrettable because, as noted earlier, a refreshing number of these essays focus on the long-neglected subject of Fitzgerald's style, auguring well for future critical emphasis.

Ironically, the year's best essay on *Gatsby* represents an expressed desire to deal with its "meaning, its themes, its moral implications." In "Fitzgerald's *Gatsby*: The World as Ash Heap," in *The Twenties*, ed. Warren French, pp. 181–202, James E. Miller, Jr., who for many years has been one of the very few critics to concern himself with Fitzgerald as a craftsman, uses as his starting point and framework T. S. Eliot's praise of Henry James. He speculates plausibly that Eliot's praise of *Gatsby* is based on the same criteria: it " 'gets' America and the modern age, not through direct proclamation of a set of ideas . . . but through dramatization of Gatsby's pursuit of Daisy, through dramatic presentation of a number of other intricately related characters . . . and through a sequence of powerful, pervasive, and devastating images that force the reader to 'think with his feelings.' " Thereafter Miller carefully and gracefully examines such aspects of Fitzgerald's artistry as juxtaposed scenes, pervasive image patterns, the use of details of the 1920s to provide what James calls "solidity of specification," and the novel's broader meaning—it "embodies and expresses the simple, basic human desire and yearning . . . to snatch something precious from the ceaseless flux and flow of days and years and preserve it outside the ravages of time." Never very far from the text, Miller brilliantly explicates the novel, drawing upon years of reading in Fitzgerald criticism and in primary materials. This is not only the best essay on Fitzgerald published in 1975, it is one of the best we ever had. If one were asked to suggest a single essay on *Gatsby* to someone who had never read any previous critiques of it, he would do well to recommend this one.

Among the other close studies of *Gatsby*, the best and most basic is Bruce R. Stark's "The Intricate Pattern in *The Great Gatsby*" (*FHA 1974*:51–61). Drawing on an assortment of seemingly minor details—the color of Myrtle's dresses, the sounds and colors of Daisy's name, the necklace Tom buys at the end of the novel, the expensive leash Tom buys for Myrtle's dog, the rain at Gatsby's funeral—Stark skillfully demonstrates that "the words in *The Great Gatsby* participate in a multitude of complex patterns that link images, anomalous minor scenes, and even rather large units to one another in a variety of complex and subtle ways." Ruth Betsy Tenenbaum's "'The Gray-Turning, Gold-Turning Consciousness' of Nick Carraway" (*FHA 1975*:37–55), B. W. Wilson's "The Theatrical Motif in *The Great Gatsby*" (*FHA 1975*:107–13), and Joan S. Korenman's "A View From the (Queensboro) Bridge" (*FHA 1975*:93–96) all serve as further elaborations of Stark's contentions. Tenenbaum's focus is on Nick's "double vision or double consciousness": his "everyday consciousness"—"rigid, even absolutist, conventional and other-directed, opinionated and prosaic, and, not least, highly literate"; and his "poetic consciousness"—"his highly sensitized awareness to nuances and movement, his whimsical free associations (or so they seem), his wit, his acute perceptions and imaginative configurations of the grotesque, the comic, the surreal, and the absurd." Tenenbaum carefully examines the images manifested through each of these two approaches and shows how they are patterned and linked. Wilson is concerned with Gatsby's "dual role as performer and impresario and the significance such a role has for our understanding of the novel." Although he sometimes seems to be imposing a pattern on the novel, his essay stays close to the text and does prove that Fitzgerald often uses theatrical terms and metaphors. This is true of his work as a whole as well as of *Gatsby*, and a worthwhile study could be done on the topic. Korenman's note on Nick's and Gatsby's trip across the Queensboro Bridge chooses details from that passage to show "Fitzgerald's mastery of patterning and his use of irony."

Korenman also has an interesting essay on Fitzgerald's depiction of Daisy Buchanan. In "'Only Her Hairdresser . . .': Another Look at Daisy Buchanan" (*AL* 46:574–78), she notes that Daisy has many traits of the fair-haired Romantic heroine—passivity, pragmatism, a desire for security; but she also possesses "spiritual affinities with the knowledgeable, experienced dark women" of the Romantic tradition—for example, her "low, thrilling voice" has a "powerful sexual appeal." Part of Daisy's "enigmatic charm," then, is a result of this combination. William L. Nance, in "Eden, Oedipus, and Rebirth in American Fiction" (*ArQ* 31:353–65), sees an affinity between *Gatsby* and another tradition, the Classical. His parallels between Fitzgerald's novel and the Oedipus story—with Tom as the father and Gatsby as the adolescent—are far-fetched and hastily stated. G. I. Hughes is on solider if not very original ground in "Sub Specie Doctor T. J. Eckleburg: Man and God in 'The Great Gatsby'" (*ESA* 15,ii[1972]:81–92), where he contrasts Gatsby and Wilson, the only two characters in the novel who believe in anything, with all the others, who are characterized "either by irresponsible self-gratification . . . or by violent criminal acquisition . . . or by parasitic idleness." Hughes points to a "central moral irony of the book": because Gatsby and Wilson are "committed idealists in a world which admits only cynical alienation," they appear madmen.

J. S. Lawry's "Green Light or Square of Light in *The Great Gatsby*" (*DR* 55:114–32) is a bridge between the close readings and a consideration of *Gatsby* in the mythic terms in which it has all too often been studied. Lawry notes that Fitzgerald "came very close to writing either a philosophical novel about American history or an historical work upon the springs of North American psychology and philosophy"; but "fortunately for literature, he instead wrote a novel of lyrical discovery, conveyed for the most part in affective images." Two of the latter, which "in their way comment profoundly upon the North American encounter with space, time, and being, are those of a line leading to a green light, and a flat white light fixed and bounded in a square." Lawry's study of these "images" is unlike the close studies of the text mentioned above in that he merely uses them as a point of departure for his remarks on the greater meanings of *Gatsby*. Further, the two "images" which he chooses are not, strictly speaking, Fitzgerald's, but rather Lawry's rewording of Fitzgerald's prose; Miller, Stark and the others noted above stay much closer to the text of *Gatsby* in their analyses. But Lawry's work is still sounder than that of G. F. Hartford in "Reflections and Affinities: Aspects of the American Past, the American Dream, and

'The Great Gatsby'" (*ESA* 16,i[1973]:23–36). Hartford merely repeats a number of clichés about the novel's relation to the American dream and the destruction of that dream by "business materialism," an emphasis which keeps him from all but very general remarks on *Gatsby* itself. Similarly removed from the text but more interesting and original, Barry E. Gross's "Fitzgerald in the Fifties" (*SNNTS* 5[1973]:324–35) contains thoughtful speculations on the reasons for the Fitzgerald Revival. Gross sees the generation of the fifties identifying with Nick, a "little solemn," slightly complacent, avoiding entanglements but also restless for involvement, excitement, and romance. Then, at the end of the decade, that generation found its Gatsby in John F. Kennedy—he "provided an outlet for our untapped and, by 1960, nearly dead enthusiasm." Again, such investigations of the causes of Fitzgerald's uneven critical fortunes over the past six decades are very welcome.

Relationships between *Gatsby* and the work of other writers is, as usual, a popular topic this year. The best of these comparative studies is Lawrence Thornton's "Ford Madox Ford and *The Great Gatsby*" (*FHA* 1975:57–74). Asserting that the Fitzgerald-Conrad relationship has been overemphasized, Thornton suggests that a close reading of *Gatsby* and *The Good Soldier* "reveals similarities in narrative techniques, impressionistic form and romantic theme which are more instructive in terms of Fitzgerald's achievement in modern fiction than the connections made between him and Conrad would suggest." Drawing his material from biographical details which show Fitzgerald's knowledge and appreciation of Ford, as well as, most effectively, from a close reading of the two texts, Thornton makes his point forcefully and skillfully. He is particularly convincing in citing parallels between Nick and John Dowell, the narrator of Ford's novel, and in showing how they share more characteristics than Nick and Marlow do. In the end, though, Thornton is more successful in making us see the connections with Ford than he is in making us reject the ones with Conrad. That the latter still exist is reinforced by Andrew Crosland's "*The Great Gatsby* and *The Secret Agent*" (*FHA* 1975:75–81). Crosland points to characters with the same name in both novels and to parallel characters; most of his evidence is admittedly slight but there is enough of it to lend credence to his notion that Fitzgerald may have used Conrad's novel in writing his.

In "*Citizen Kane, The Great Gatsby*, and Some Conventions of

American Narrative" (*CritI* 2:307–25), Robert L. Carringer goes far beyond Roslyn Mass's brief essay (see *ALS 1974*, p. 156). Carringer begins with parallels between Gatsby and Kane, between Nick and Thompson, and between the green light and the glass globe as significant images in both works; but he is best in the last two sections of his article. These sections deal with the relationship between *Gatsby* and *American*, the first-draft screenplay of *Citizen Kane*, which contained material later deleted from the movie, and with Kane as the "representative American as an entrepreneur, magnate, or tycoon." *American* was primarily the work of John Houseman and Herman Mankiewicz; and Carringer's suggestion that Mankiewicz's friendship with Fitzgerald might account for some of the echoes seems reasonable. The last section is more helpful for students of the movie; but its linking of Kane with Franklin, Sutpen, Christopher Newman, Frank Cowperwood, and Gatsby is skillfully done.

F. A. Rodewald, in "Faulkner's Possible Use of *The Great Gatsby*" (*FHA 1975*:97–101), contends that the Sutpen-Gatsby parallels are the result of Faulkner's reading of Fitzgerald's novel. This is a tenuous assertion; and Rodewald seems unaware that the similarities have been noted several times previously. Taylor Alderman's brief remarks on "*The Great Gatsby* and *Hopalong Cassidy*" (*FHA 1975*:83–87) stress the appropriateness of Fitzgerald's placing Gatsby's resolves on the flyleaf of that particular book: Cassidy "ironically parallels Gatsby by succeeding where Gatsby fails—in love, and in his career"; and it is a novel "which portrays the violent and morally ambiguous American society similar in many ways to the America which ultimately destroys Jay Gatsby."

Of the brief notes on Gatsby, the two most worthwhile ones are by John Ower and Matthew J. Bruccoli. Ower, in "A Thematic Reference to *The Rubaiyat of Omar Khayyam* in *The Great Gatsby*" (*FHA 1975*:103–05), notes that Nick's use of the word "caravansary" is an allusion to stanza 17 of *The Rubaiyat* and proposes a number of similarities, ironic and otherwise, between the themes and images of the two works. Bruccoli's " 'How Are You and the Family, Old Sport?': Gerlach and Gatsby" (*FHA 1975*:33–36) cites a clipping in one of Fitzgerald's scrapbooks with an inscription on it which uses the phrase "old sport" as fuel for speculation about a Long Island bootlegger named Gerlach as a model for Gatsby. The other notes on *Gatsby* range from Paul A. Makurath, Jr.'s wildly speculative

"Another Source for 'Gatsby'" (*FHA 1975*:115–16), which points to a character in *The Mill on the Floss* named Gadsby, through Dorothy M. Webb's far-fetched "Fitzgerald on El Greco: A View of *The Great Gatsby*" (*FHA 1975*:89–91), with its citation of parallels between El Greco's "View of Toledo" and the novel, down to Sterling K. Eisiminger's trivial and ridiculous "Gatsby's Bluff and Fitzgerald's Blunder" (*FHA 1974*:95–98), in which factual errors in *Gatsby* are pointed out, with utter disregard for the possibility that Fitzgerald was writing fiction.

Two of this year's four essays on *Tender Is the Night* take opposite positions regarding the novel's Emersonian qualities. In an extremely well organized and clearly presented piece, "Perfect Marriage in *Tender Is the Night*: A Study in the Progress of a Symbol" (*FHA 1974*:63–73), Louis K. Greiff views Dick and Nicole as standing for "Fitzgerald's effort as a writer to reconcile the ideal with the real, to merge them through his central characters in the expectation that contrary elements will yield a new and perfected whole." Grieff relates this to passages in Emerson on the union of spirit and matter engendering "a heightened reality." Thus the novel celebrates this union in book 1 and traces its destruction in books 2 and 3, providing Fitzgerald's ultimate rejection of the workability of such a union, as well as his "terminal comment on the entire transcendental question." But in an equally useful and judicious essay, "Time's Exile: Dick Diver and the Heroic Idea" (*Mosaic* 8,iii:89–108), Richard Foster comes to somewhat different conclusions, seeing *Tender* as ending in a "late Emersonian" "note of affirmation." Foster's close reading of the novel stresses its epic qualities and includes a provocative comparison of Dick and Hamlet. Both of these contexts lead Foster to the belief that, ultimately, Dick is a "tragic hero because he found himself cut off, finally, from both his duty and his fulfillment in it."

The characterization of Dick Diver, which has both frustrated and impressed commentators since 1934, is the subject of the two other essays on *Tender*. Both go directly to the text to show that Dick's disintegration is carefully foreshadowed and plausibly motivated. In "Alienation and Disintegration in 'Tender Is the Night'" (*HAB* 22,iv[1971]:3–8), Hallvard Dahlie traces a "pattern of isolation and alienation" which illuminates Dick's downfall, showing how, even at the beginning of the book, he cannot "give of himself honestly and unselfishly" and is unable to "identify himself honestly with the characters and forces of his world." While Dahlie's evidence seems too narrowly based to support the broad conclusions he draws, his essay is useful. Juanita Williams Dudley, in "Dr. Diver, Vivisectionist" (*CollL* 2:128–34), uses as her touchstone Dick's remark early in *Tender* that he wants to give a "bad party," seeing this wish as "an architectonic device for ordering the novel and insuring unity between the parts." Viewed from this vantage, the novel "is an integrated whole with few details irrelevant to the chronicle of a brilliant and promising young man who connived at his own destruction by forces representing wealth and power." Again, this summary rests rather shakily on the slim amount of textual support offered; but, as with the other three essays on *Tender*, at least the support that is offered comes from the text.

Of the other essays on Fitzgerald's full-length works, the most substantial is Janet Lewis's "Fitzgerald's 'Philippe, Count of Darkness'" (*FHA 1975*:7–32). An excellent complementary piece to Kermit W. Moyer's 1974 article (see *ALS 1974*, p. 157), Lewis's study ranges widely over a variety of topics relating to Fitzgerald's unfinished novel—the details of its composition, summaries of the episodes, Fitzgerald's reworking of the original manuscripts, his plans for its completion, inconsistencies between the various installments, and, most interestingly, a close study of the text. Lewis sees Fitzgerald as, anachronistically, employing the style of the "tough guy" fiction of the '30's in the series and views Philippe as a fictional rendering of Hemingway and "an incongruous composite of Errol Flynn and Humphrey Bogart." This is a full and conclusive treatment.

In "*This Side of Paradise*: The Ghost of Rupert Brooke" (*FHA 1975*:117–30), Robert Roulston uses Fitzgerald's fascination with Brooke and his references to him in the text of the novel to illuminate its defects and merits. In his "struggles first to emulate then to disassociate himself from Brooke," Roulston contends, Amory "finds himself striving, usually without success, to reconcile vestiges of nineteenth century romanticism with the twentieth century, middle class and Catholic sexual morality with amoral eroticism, traditional culture with newer modes of thought and expression, and a yearning for a patrician manner with a left-of-center egalitarianism." Although not altogether successful, this is an admirable attempt to bring cohesion to what is usually considered to be Fitzgerald's most chaotic novel. The only other item we have on a Fitzgerald novel this year is

Gabrielle Winkel's "Fitzgerald's Agge of Denmark" (*FHA 1975*:131–32), another specious speculation on the real-life sources of a Fitzgerald character, this time in *The Last Tycoon.*

Regrettably, we have but two essays and a note on Fitzgerald's short stories. In a pedestrian and wooden piece of research, "Fitzgerald's 'May Day': A Prelude to Triumph" (*ELUD* 2,i[1973]:20–35), Michael P. Gruber does a workmanlike job of tracing the themes which are common to the story and Fitzgerald's other great works—"the mystique of wealth, the pedestal under the woman, the relentlessness of Time." John O. Rees is on a more original track, but his article on "Fitzgerald's Pat Hobby Stories" (*ColQ* 23:553–62) does little more than provide summaries and point out that the series deserves more attention. In " 'The Camel's Back' and *Conductor 1492*" (*FHA 1974*:87–88), Alan Margolies shows that the 1924 silent movie bears almost no similarity to Fitzgerald's short story, despite the notation in his *Ledger* that he had sold the film rights to Warner Brothers and that they had made it into *Conductor 1492.*

***e.* Essays on Specific Works: Hemingway.** Taken as a group, the 30 essays on Hemingway's specific works are much less substantial than those on Fitzgerald, an unusual circumstance.

Of the four articles on *The Sun Also Rises*, only one, Manuel Schonhorn's "*The Sun Also Rises*: I: The Jacob Allusion; II: Parody as Meaning" (*BSUF* 16,ii:49–55), is much more than a note; but it is really two notes with no linkage supplied. In the first, Schonhorn rejects previous assertions of major divergences between Jake and his Biblical counterpart, contending that Jake, like Jacob, attains "those idiosyncratic Hemingway virtues of courage, endurance, and resolution, and a pragmatic truth which enables him . . . to survive, endure, and prevail." In the second, he sketches the parodic nature of the various relationships in the novel. The Cohn-Francis relationship, "with its sexual and psychological hang-ups, is a mocking, fragmented parody of the Jake-Brett relationship"; and the Jake-Brett-Cohn arrangement is mirrored in the later Jake-Brett-Count setup. None of this seems very startling or original; and Schonhorn has difficulty pulling together the various threads of his argument.

Two seemingly innocuous allusions in *Sun* provide subjects for Donald A. Daiker and Ronald Lajoie and Sally Lentz. Daiker's "The Pied Piper in *The Sun Also Rises*" (*FHA 1975*:235–37) centers on a reference in book 2, chapter 15, and equates the Pied Piper to Jake in that the children's loss of control to the Piper foreshadows Jake's "loss of control, his behaving in childish ways, and, consequently, his at least temporary failure to learn how to live." Daiker's efforts to link Jake with Cohn seem questionable as does his basically negative interpretation of Jake. Lajoie's and Lentz's "Is Jake Barnes Waiting?" (*FHA 1975*:229–33) is far more plausible. Lajoie and Lentz use A. E. W. Mason's story, "The Crystal Trench," which Jake reads but never finishes, as lending insight into Jake's "stoic dimension." The parallels they cite between his situation and those in the story no doubt account for its use by Hemingway. Donald M. Murray, in "*The Day of the Locust* and *The Sun Also Rises*: Congruence and Caricature" (*FHA 1975*:239–45), also makes a small but suggestive point when he notes numerous general resemblances between the two novels and finds "definite caricature" in the characterization of Abe Kusich (compared to Cohn) and in the cockfight episode (compared to the bullfight and festival).

Two of the three essays on *The Old Man and the Sea* deal with the role baseball plays in the novel. James Barbour and Robert Sattelmeyer, in "Baseball and Baseball Talk in *The Old Man and the Sea*" (*FHA 1975*:281–87), see the conversations between Santiago and Manolin about baseball as "similar to rites of passage ceremonies: they serve as initiation talks in which Santiago is the teacher, Manolin the pupil, and baseball a topic through which desirable attitudes and behavior are taught." They then consider Joe DiMaggio as a figure who demonstrates "what is great in man: his skill, his endurance, and, most of all, his courage." George Monteiro's "Santiago, DiMaggio, and Hemingway: The Ageing Professionals of *The Old Man and the Sea*" (*FHA 1975*:273–80) begins where Barbour and Sattelmeyer conclude, with a detailed recounting of DiMaggio's remarkable comeback in 1949 as the factual background to Santiago's references. Monteiro observes that Santiago's identification with DiMaggio fades as he loses his battle with the fish. Both of these essays are informative and intelligent, and they are further indications of the burgeoning interest in Hemingway's use of sport alluded to above. The other essay on *Old Man*, Sam S. Baskett's "Toward a 'Fifth Dimension' in *The Old Man and the Sea*" (*CentR* 19:269–86), is concerned with how Hemingway invests the story of Santiago with an added dimension through poetic similes and allusions, through

Biblical allusions, and through other references which augment the dimensions of his struggle. If some of Baskett's claims are overstated, he does do a good job of adding to our understanding of the overtones of this novel.

Frederick von Ende's "The Corrida Pattern in *For Whom the Bell Tolls*" (*ReAL* 3,ii[1970]:63–70) is a fascinating study of "the use of the form and features of the *corrida de toros* as an underlying structural pattern" in *Bell*. Von Ende shows how "each of the major elements of the novel—the setting, characters, action, even the mood—has a more or less direct counterpart in the drama of the bullfight," until it "becomes a kind of large-scale version of the bullfight enacted in the arena of the Spanish Civil War." His examples are carefully selected and clearly articulated, with the result that this is a very convincing essay. Lee Steinberg's major point, in "The Subjective Idealist's 'Quest for True Men' in Hemingway's *For Whom the Bell Tolls*" (*L&I* 13,iii[1972]:51–58), appears to be that, despite the fact that the novel includes in its cast of characters many peasants and workers, it does not celebrate the struggle of the Spanish peasants against Fascism. This is because, on closer examination, we can see that, while "Hemingway pays close attention to the external details of peasant behavior, . . . the souls which he gives them are those of the capitalists and landlords." Steinberg's tone is often petulant and his judgments seem subjective rather than securely based in the text. David McClellan's answer to the question "Is Custer a Model For the Fascist Captain in *For Whom the Bell Tolls*?" (*FHA* 1974:239–41) is highly speculative: "The captain looks and acts a lot like Custer. And Hemingway was a student of the final fight of Custer's life."

We have two essays apiece on *A Farewell to Arms* and *To Have and Have Not*. William Adair's "*A Farewell to Arms*: A Dream Book" (*JNT* 5:40–56) begins with Cowley's observations that Hemingway's fiction has a "waking-dreamlike quality," presenting "nightmares at noon," and then applies this to *Arms*. Adair sees the novel as "a fictional re-dreaming" in that the "nightmare of the wounding—the book's prototypical action—is presented three times (spring, fall, spring), three instances that are *structurally* identical"; the action is re-dreamed until "the fear of death is exorcised in the death of Frederic's other self, in the death of Catherine." This is a complex but intriguing study. John Unrue's note, "The Valley of Baca and *A Farewell to Arms*" (*FHA* 1974:229–34), uses Psalm 84 as a subtext for the irony and pathos of Frederic and Catherine's passage to Switzerland; but the relationship between the psalm and the novel is not always convincing nor is it clearly stated.

Richard Astro's "Phlebas Sails the Caribbean: Steinbeck, Hemingway, and the American Waste Land," in *The Twenties*, ed. Warren French, pp. 215–33, is an effective comparison of *Cup of Gold* and *To Have and Have Not* as novels which employ the "central premises" of *The Waste Land*, "a world of broken images, a chaos of life destroyed and meaning shattered." Astro pursues this specifically through the two protagonists, Henry and Harry Morgan, whom he calls "American Phoenicians who reach the extremities of their conquests and are unable to respond to the demand to 'give, control and sympathize.'" His conclusion is that Steinbeck's vision of the wasteland is "the grimmer of the two." In "Echoes From the Sea: A Hemingway Rubric" (*FHA 1974*:201–05), Richard E. Braun considers the meaning of the title, *To Have and Have Not.* He examines two possible senses: "some have what others lack" and "the same people both have and have not—either the losses of some become others or no one's gain, or people lack what they appear to have." He then cites a passage from Flavius Philostratus' *Life of Apollonius of Tyana*, in which the phrase "each in having hath not" occurs, as a possible source of the title, a far-fetched claim.

In "Metempsychosis in the Stream, or What Happens in 'Bimini'?" (*FHA 1974*:137–43), Francis E. Skipp offers an interesting examination of the episode in which young David Hudson hooks, fights, and eventually heroically loses a large broadbill. Skipp views David as a Christ-like figure and points out the Christian symbolism present in the text. He also shows how Roger Davis, through this episode, comes to identify David Hudson with David Davis, Roger's brother for whose drowning at age eleven he feels responsible. Skipp contends that David Hudson's symbolic crucifixion in the novel redeems Roger's guilt and frees his creative powers. We need not accept all of Skipp's analysis to find it provocative and illuminating.

We have relatively few essays this year on individual Hemingway stories; but we do have a number on several stories considered together. Foremost among these is Jackson J. Benson's "Ernest Hemingway as Short Story Writer," in his *Short Stories* (see section i). Benson ranges widely, beginning with a discussion of Hemingway's apprenticeship as a newspaperman, tracing the influences of Anderson and Stein, citing the autobiographical bases of many of the stories, indicating the stylistic devices used, pursuing a comparison of Hemingway's short fiction with certain "basic themes" in Kafka's work, and closely studying several specific stories. If Benson tries to cover too much, his piece is nonetheless extremely suggestive.

In "Hemingway's Four Dramatic Short Stories" (*FHA 1975*:247–57), J. F. Kobler links "The Killers," "Hills Like White Elephants," "The Sea Change," and "A Clean, Well-Lighted Place" through the dramatic characteristics of each: most of each story is dialogue; most of the narrative sentences in each "are devoted exclusively to descriptions of visual or auditory elements; "the action in each story is immediately rendered in the present, in a time span no longer than required for the action to occur"; "restricted settings are the rule"; and "characters are developed almost completely by what they say and do with little authorial explanation or character introspection." Kobler is as worthwhile, however, when he examines the moments in each story where the dramatic mode is violated, finding that such interruptions in "A Clean, Well-Lighted Place" constitute a "consistent pattern" of choric statements; while they "mar" the other three stories. Larry Grimes's attempt to link two other stories, in "Night Terror and Morning Calm: A Reading of Hemingway's 'Indian Camp' as a Sequel to 'Three Shots' " (*SSF* 12:413–15), rests on the questionable assumption that Uncle George is the father of the child in "Indian Camp." Grimes contends that, while in "Three Shots" he had scoffed at Nick, at the end of the later story "one wonders why Uncle George has disappeared and whether he will sleep without a light that night."

In "*In Our Time*: The Interchapters as Structural Guides to a Psychological Pattern" (*SSF* 12:1–8), David J. Leigh, S.J., sees the interchapters functioning in a variety of contrasting ways with the stories. In the first part, the interchapters reveal the stark violence of war in contrast to the less obvious violence of human life found in the early stages of Nick's education. A second group of interchapters portray the world of the bullring, where ritual achieves some control over violence and preserves "a minimum of purpose and achievement"; this contrasts with the lost world of the expatriate, "where the smoke of dead ideals blinds all to any hope for achievement or self-realization." The final two interchapters, which focus on the deaths of two men—one in glory and the other in shame and terror—contrast with Nick's start on a "new life" in returning to the simplicity of basic sensations, a return that is partly a relief and partly a terror. This is a perceptive and closely reasoned essay on a critically neglected area. Bernard F. Rodgers, Jr., also argues convincingly, in "*The Nick Adams Stories*: Fiction or Fact?" (*FHA 1974*:155–62), for a reordering of the stories based on the chronology of Nick's life, not Hemingway's. Rodgers focuses his attention on "The End of Something" and "The Three-Day Blow," which Young places after the war because some of the events portrayed happened to Hemingway after the war. Through close readings of the texts Rodgers shows how this confuses the meanings of the stories and quite rightly urges that they be approached as fiction rather than fact.

We have one substantial essay and one note on "The Short Happy Life," the only story to be the subject of more than one article. James Gray Watson's " 'A Sound Basis of Union': Structural and Thematic Balance in 'The Short Happy Life of Francis Macomber' " (*FHA 1974*:215–28) sees the story as centered on the Macomber marriage, asserting that Margot is not shooting at her husband but "is quite literally bidding to rejoin the society of her hunter-lovers by shooting well, and her primary motive is neither to murder her husband nor to save him but to save herself." Watson supports this thesis by detailed examination of the two-part structure of the story—in the first half, Francis is isolated; at the end of the second half, Margot is alone—and his study is a surprisingly original approach to what would seem to be a much overworked subject. That subject is worked some more, this time from a ballistic viewpoint, in Jerry A. Herndon's note, "No 'Maggie's Drawers' for Margot Macomber" (*FHA 1975*:289–91). Herndon disputes G. B. Harrison's contention that the 6.5 Mannlicher rifle with which Margot shoots Francis would have recoiled, thus spoiling her aim. Through elaborate data about guns Herndon proves that "the lightest rifle, one quite appropriate for a woman, was left with Margot Macomber."

In a gracefully written close study, "Some Comments on 'The Snows of Kilimanjaro' " (*ELUD* 2,i[1973]:49–58), Ekaterini Georgoudaki discusses the story's language as a key to its structure, meaning, and excellence. Georgoudaki uses this approach to read the ending as optimistic, seeing Harry's death as parallel to "the moment of truth" in bullfighting: "Like the artist-matador, Harry experiences and conveys true emotion through the purity of his style and his honesty and proves that he has regained his integrity as an artist."

In " 'The Killers' as Experience" (*JNT* 5:128–35), W. J. Stuckey argues against Brooks's and Warren's view of the story as one of "a boy's initiation into evil." Stuckley calls it "a story about the refusal of initiation; for Ole Andreson's behavior suggests to Nick . . . not moral victory in the face of defeat, but an almost unbearable failure." Ole is thus not a "code hero" (Brooks and Warren feel he is), but a failed code hero whom Nick rejects; and the story is about "the sudden appearance in the rational world of the terrifyingly irrational" and about "having to face the fact that man is helpless in the presence of that final and greatest danger, death." Because Stuckey puts forward his interpretation carefully and modestly, his essay is reasonable and challenging.

Wayne Kvam's extensive investigation of the background of "Hemingway's 'Banal Story' " (*FHA 1974*:181–91) begins where Phillip R. Yannella (see above) leaves off. Kvam does a thorough job of pointing to specific material in 1925 issues of *The Forum* as the objects of Hemingway's satire in the middle section of the story. He feels that the story can be divided into two contrasting parts, one recording the responses to life offered by *The Forum* and its editor Henry G. Leach, and the other presenting those of the writer. This article weds effective scholarship with an insightful reading of the story.

The remaining pieces on the stories are short notes. In "Two Types of Tension: Art vs. Campcraft in Hemingway's 'Big Two-Hearted River' " (*SSF* 11[1974]:433–34), Lewis E. Weeks, Jr., points to Nick's pulling the sides of the tent tight as a "clear hint as to Nick's abnormal condition" and a symbol of his need for security. The tautness of the canvas "represents Nick's tense mental and emotional state." Lawrence Broer's "Soldier's Home" (*LGJ* 3,ii:11, 32) is a good, brief, close reading of the story which emphasizes Hemingway's artistry in showing how the war has affected Krebs "without ever mentioning the scenes of dying and mutilation and emotional confusion that have worn indelibly" on his mind. In the latest contribution to what he admits "has become a promising light industry in Hemingway studies," George Monteiro offers the views of "Hemingway on Dialogue in 'A Clean, Well-Lighted Place' " (*FHA 1974*:243): in a letter to Judson Jerome, Hemingway commented that the story as published continued to make perfectly good sense to him. And in "Stan Ketchel and Steve Ketchel: A Further Note on 'The Light of the World' "

(*FHA 1975*:325–26), Matthew J. Bruccoli reveals that there was a real fighter named Steve Ketchel, an obscure lightweight who fought in the Chicago area and probably would have been known to Hemingway; but Bruccoli concedes that the story probably does refer to the great Stan Ketchel, who preferred to be called Steve.

Finally, in "Hemingway's 'Defense of Dirty Words': A Reconsideration" (*FHA 1975*:217–27), Carroll Grimes resurrects a September 1934 Hemingway column in *Esquire* for three reasons: "it illuminates the moralistic spirit of the 1930's"; "it focuses more sharply on Hemingway's interaction with his contemporaries during the period in which he was a regular contributor to *Esquire*"; and because "the voice that complained about the comstockery of the 1930's seldom received a fair hearing at the time." Grimes summarizes the column which chastized Ring Lardner and columnists Heywood Broun, Westbrook Pegler, and Alexander Woollcott for their avoidance of four-letter words and for "manifesting a sense of moral superiority" and reprints the angry response to Hemingway's views. This is an interesting account of a somewhat minor literary episode.

***f.* Dissertations.** Doctoral research on both Fitzgerald and Hemingway increased in 1975. We had four dissertations on Fitzgerald and three on Hemingway, with several more studying one or both of them as well as other writers. Interestingly enough, among the Fitzgerald dissertations is William R. Anderson, Jr.'s, on "The Fitzgerald Revival, 1940–1975: A Study in Literary Reputation" (*DAI* 36:883A–84A), while one of the three on Hemingway is Frank L. Ryan's "Ernest Hemingway's Literary Reputation in America, 1924–1966" (*DAI* 36:893A–94A).

University of Maryland[1]

1. This essay could not have been completed without the support of a grant from the General Research Board of the University of Maryland and the research assistance of Nancy Prothro.

Part II

11. Literature to 1800

Robert D. Arner

As might have been expected, scholarly activity devoted to early American authors showed no signs of abating as the Bicentennial approached. There were several solid books—William J. Scheick on Jonathan Edwards, Ann Stanford on Anne Bradstreet, Lewis P. Simpson on the southern revolt against modernity, and the redoubtable Lewis Leary on just about everybody—as well as one splendid one, Sacvan Bercovitch's *The Puritan Origins of the American Self*. Edward Taylor was the subject of Karl Keller's occasionally stimulating but uneven full-length study and a number of interesting articles as well, while Charles Brockden Brown continued to emerge as a major controversial American romancer about whom, despite and partly because of the critical energies expended on his works this past year, the last word has assuredly not been said. Also provocative were articles on William Bradford (Kenneth Alan Hovey), John Josselyn (Philip Gura), Anne Bradstreet (Jennifer R. Waller and William J. Irvin), and Jonathan Edwards (Emily Stipes Watts). And so on. This by no means exhausts the list of commendable publications—there were also more worthless ones than usual—but to keep the preamble from growing longer than the tale, it is perhaps best to cut things off right here and forge ahead into the individual categories.

i. Edward Taylor

For openers, another book on Edward Taylor to complement the one by William J. Scheick last year, this offering by Karl Keller: *The Example of Edward Taylor* (Amherst: Univ. of Massachusetts Press). The book disturbs me on several counts, not the least of which is that it starts very slowly indeed, repeating and embellishing with lines from the poetry the few facts that we know about Taylor's life in

England and in Westfield, as if the poems belonged to Taylor's biography rather than to his creative life. Then there are brief and unsatisfactory chapters on "Gods Determinations" and the "Metrical History," followed by good discussions of Taylor's imagery and of his place in a fundamentalist Connecticut Valley tradition of introspection. Then more trouble: it will not do to call Taylor the "Grandma Moses of American literature," first because the label is far more cute than convincing and, second, because the analogy will not hold up. Primitivism in painting implies something far different from what it might suggest about poetry, in which the true primitive is far harder to come by because of the poet's ready access (even in frontier Westfield) to literary models; Taylor's library may have held few books of poems, but the evidence of his own verses makes it plain that he was familiar with numerous poets, including classical ones, whereas a primitive painter has only nature and a vague memory of painterly traditions (if he has even that) to consult. No need, of course, to spin this objection out at length, but if I had to place Taylor in any artistic tradition, I would be inclined to associate him with late medieval realists like van Eyck. In any case, Keller's main problem, I believe, is that he attempts to offer something for nearly everybody's taste and, having made one or two points about many things, drops his subject almost before he gets going, as he does, for example, with his treatment of the polyrhythmic patterns of Taylor's poems. Precisely for this reason, however, the book is valuable, for surely Keller is right to call for more imaginative and broader perspectives from which to approach Taylor than most readers have been willing to risk in the past.

Far less comprehensive than Keller's study is Albert Gelpi's chapter on "Edward Taylor: Types and Tropes" in *The Tenth Muse*, pp. 15–54. Apart from repeating the fiction that Taylor proscribed publication of his works, this is a knowledgeable discussion, one that adequately handles Taylor's themes, images, and poetic preoccupations (especially his sexual imagery) and helps to rescue him from the charge of archaic irrelevance. Gelpi places Taylor at the head of one main tradition in American poetry, a typological tradition (as opposed to tropological—Gelpi admits that the distinction proves unworkable at times and almost always needs qualification) that includes Emerson, Whitman, Pound, and Williams. Like Keller, Gelpi views the "Preparatory Meditations" as one long, open-ended poem, the forerunner of *Leaves of Grass* or *Paterson*, but unlike Keller—and I believe with better judgment on his side—he argues that, as far as "stanza, meter, and rhyme" are concerned, the Puritan must also be placed with the tropological poets of form and product.

Two of Taylor's youthful exercises were discussed in David Sowd's "Edward Taylor's Answer to a 'Popish Pamphlet'" (*EAL* 9:307–14) and Muktar Ali Isani's "Edward Taylor and Ovid's *Art of Love*" (*EAL* 10:67–74). Sowd outlines the historical background of the London fire of 1666, which inspired both the pamphlet in question and Taylor's poem, traces Taylor's indebtedness to another rhymed response, and argues that Taylor extended the sexual imagery of his poetical predecessor (probably Robert Wild) in anticipation of his later technique of "extended imagery." (This, incidentally, tends to support Keller's thesis that Taylor was perhaps abnormally preoccupied with imagery of filth, defilement, and sexuality.) As for the connection between Taylor and Ovid, Isani has established that by editing the poet's translation of the story of Daedulus and Icarus, an important note because it provides additional evidence of the range of Taylor's intellectual curiosity and because it suggests that, despite the scarcity of direct allusions to classical myth in his poetry, classical authors may have exerted a greater influence on his formative years than meets the eye. Though Isani is uncertain whether the manuscript belongs to Taylor's youth or his maturity, to me the first seems a far more likely conjecture.

Two analyses of individual poems by Taylor also appeared this past year. In "Physiology and Metaphor in Edward Taylor's 'Meditation. Can. 1.3'" (*EAL* 9:315–20), Joel R. Kehler advances physiological definitions for two perplexing terms, "spirits" and "Mammalary Catch," and uncovers a complex of interrelated meanings which unify the poem at a level of theme and imagery; "spirits," he says, refers to Galenic physiology, and "Mammalary" suggests in context not only smell, as Thomas H. Johnson long ago conjectured, but also the breasts and the lungs. And in "The Comic Design of *Gods Determinations touching his Elect*" (*EAL* 10:121–43), John Gatta, Jr., begins commendably enough by pointing out that no single formal analogue of those usually invoked to explain the overall structure of this cluster of shorter poems is finally satisfactory and then proposes that the work is essentially comic in its "generic affiliations" as well as "fairly humorous in its telling." On that last point I remain unconvinced in spite of a comic scene or two, in part because Gatta rather too loosely uses terms such as *witty* and *humorous* without distinguishing between them or without addressing himself to the question of metaphysical wit. Also, the generic designation of the poem as comedy, which I do accept, could and should have led to a consideration of the rich imagery of the poem and how it is related to the dramatic movement but leads only to a paraphrase of the action. The legalistic imagery, for instance, provides a crucial transition between the fallen world of the fathers (who have transgressed the law of the Father) and the redeemed world of the sons (whose redemption, as in comedy, is accomplished by the Son only after the old laws have been revised). Gatta's is an interesting thesis gone slightly awry, in other words, but even so it helps to establish a broad literary framework within which to read Taylor's long poem.

Taylor the preacher was also the subject of one study in 1975, Dean Hall's and Thomas M. Davis's "The Two Versions of Edward Taylor's Foundation Day Sermon" (*RALS* 5:199–216), which corrects Norman Grabo's misleading remarks about the contents of the sermon as preached in 1679; as Hall and Davis show, it was not until October 1690 that Taylor included in his sermon an argument that he hoped would constitute a point-by-point refutation of the Stoddardean heresy that the Lord's Supper was a converting ordinance. In 1679 Stoddard had not yet advanced this notion, contenting himself with urging only the Half-Way Convenant. Hall and Davis then print outlines of both versions of the sermon.

One final note, this one addressed to Taylor's reputation in our own time, is Karl Keller's "A Modern Version of Edward Taylor" (*EAL* 9:321–24), which points out that Taylor has recently joined other colonial authors whose works have inspired other writings, in this case Joyce Carol Oates's collection of short stories entitled *Upon the Sweeping Flood*; but I am at a loss to understand why *EAL* thought this point was worth making in print, since anyone who glances at Oates's title and knows Taylor would surely have understood the allusion and seen the connections anyway.

ii. Puritanism

Easily the outstanding book of the year in early American studies was Sacvan Bercovitch's *The Puritan Origins of the American Self*, discussion of which I defer until later. In the meantime there is Emory Elliott's *Power and the Pulpit in Puritan New England* (Princeton, N.J.: Princeton Univ. Press), which could have been a valuable study if there were not so many problems with it. To begin with, it is not clear why Elliott should find Puritan poetry too self-consciously rhetorical for his purposes while insisting that in the sermon, which is of course as rhetorical in its own way as any Puritan poem, images of generational conflict well up more or less spontaneously from a minister's unconscious and make their appeal directly to the subconscious of the congregation. Elliott takes as psychologically revealing a good many images and even entire passages which are direct allusions to the Bible, though he neither notes this fact nor attempts to deal with it in any way; he is far off base, for example, to refer Cotton Mather's medical imagery only to Mather's personal knowledge of medicine when the evidence he quotes is a scriptural verse. Nor is he always precise in his definitions of which ministers belonged to which generations, though he is probably correct in viewing both Increase and Cotton Mather as ministers who attempted to adapt their rhetoric to the altered social and psychological need of their congregations. But overall both the method and the argument of the book strike me as confused. That there was a generational conflict between the first generation fathers and the second generation sons and that this struggle had both spiritual and economic ramifications are commonplaces of Puritan history, but I am afraid we do not understand the nature of the controversy any better—and may even understand it a little worse—for all the effort that appears to have gone into Elliott's book.

Another study that tries to deal with a broad aspect of Puritan culture is Philip L. Berg's "Racism and the Puritan Mind" (*Phylon* 36:1–7), but this one fares even worse than Elliott's. Not once in the entire six pages (think of that! six pages about this subject) does Berg so much as cite a primary source or mention, for instance, Samuel Sewall's *The Selling of Joseph*, though it is hard to see why anyone would set himself up as an authority on Puritan racial attitudes who did not know that this tract existed. It is Berg's wonderfully inspired thesis that the Puritans preached one thing and practiced another; that will serve as a sample of the originality of his thought, but it is his command of history that is really bedazzling: for example, his citing of Virginia documents (quoted from a secondary source) to confirm what Puritans thought about Indians or, better yet, his neat assertion that the *early* Puritans viewed George III as their "Pharaoh." As a puzzled Mark Twain once asked in another context, "Isn't it a daisy?"

Fortunately, some writers knew a little bit about the subject they proposed to discuss. One of the best essays of the year was Kenneth Alan Hovey's "The Theology of History in *Of Plymouth Plantation* and Its Predecessors" (*EAL* 10:47–66), a sound article which argues that Bradford's history is "not just the product of a single man, but of a school of thought." What Hovey sets out to do is to explore "the relationship between God and man in history" in four Pilgrim narratives and to bring together the two styles of *Of Plymouth Plantation,* the "rhetoric . . . used to exalt God's majesty" and the simple "realistic detail." He finds that in "A Brief Relation of the Discovery and Plantation of New England" emphasis falls upon the theme of God's inscrutable will as opposed to the uncertainty of human existence; in *Mourt's Relation,* on the other hand, the concept of divine providence—the notion that God's power is directly exerted for the sake of the faithful—replaces divine inscrutability, while man's role shifts to a proper maintaining of the rituals of faith; in "Good News from New England" man is seen as the human agent of divine intention, a view which Bradford also favors in *Of Plymouth Plantation* even as he makes use of the other two concepts and weaves all three together to create "a single impression of God and man."

Two other Puritan chronicles which received attention this past year were Edward Johnson's *Wonder-Working Providence* and Benjamin Church's record of King Philip's War. In "*The Wonder-Working Providence* as Spiritual Autobiography" (*EAL* 10:75–87), Edward J. Gallagher follows a lead established by Cecelia Tichi and Sacvan Bercovitch, among others, to pronounce Johnson's history an attempt to "fuse the colonist with the colony," though he fails to distinguish between Johnson's historiographical vision and that of, say, Cotton Mather. Benjamin Church, the Puritan hero of King Philip's War, had no such overriding purpose as Johnson's in mind but turned out a rattling good narrative of that struggle anyway in his *Diary of King Philip's War, 1675–1676,* now re-edited by Alan and Mary Simpson (Chester, Conn.: The Pequot Press). Church, who led the assault on Mount Hope, possessed considerable expertise as an Indian fighter; his editors, alas, cannot make the same claim about their editorial abilities and have left unannotated in this admittedly "popular edition" a number of names and events with which even the professional student can occasionally use help. They also manage to confuse Nathaniel Morton with (of all people) Thomas Morton. Further, their decision to exclude the second part of Church's story, the excursions into Maine, undercuts the value of the edition for historians and literary scholars alike (the only likely audience, after all), for it is in this second part, for example, that Church unfolds his version of the Hannah Duston story. Nonetheless Church's narrative is good to have in print even in a problematical edition that is, for all its shortcomings, at least textually sound because the Simpsons have had the good sense to follow Henry Martyn Dexter's careful 19th-century text.

A nice article on an early visitor to New England is Philip F. Gura's "Thoreau and John Josselyn" (*NEQ* 48:505–18), which raises the question of Thoreau's indebtedness to 17th-century writers. Gura cites a handful of Thoreau's references to Josselyn (and to other early New Englanders, for that matter) before speculating on what the Concord author may have found attractive in Josselyn's writings. The connections include a shared sense of wonder before the limitless possibilities of New World nature, a fascination with the language of the Indians and of the hearty folk, and above all a similar ability to see in nature "*transcendentia* significant and characteristic of God."

This year as last, Leo M. Kaiser continued his task of providing reliable annotated texts of John Leverett's academic addresses. In "The Unpublished *Oratio* of John Leverett, Harvard, 1689" (*Humanistica Lovaniensa* 24:327–45), Kaiser adds a persuasive headnote attributing the *Oratio* to Leverett rather than to William Brattle, the other possible author; his reasoning depends entirely upon a comparison of the style of this address with others Leverett is known to have written. And in "*Apta et Concinna Oratio*: The 1703 Commencement Address of John Leverett" (*Manuscripta* 19:159–70), Kaiser provides substantial and illuminating notes on yet another of Leverett's official addresses.

Another writer adept at Latin, though scarcely Leverett's equal, was Judge Samuel Sewall, whose Diary was the subject of Lyman H. Butterfield's review essay "Re-editing an American Classic" (*NEQ* 48:277–83). Butterfield rehearses the shortcomings, familiar to anyone who has ever tried to work with the Diary, of the Massachusetts Historical Society edition and then commends M. Halsey Thomas's recent *The Diary of Samuel Sewall, 1674–1729* (New York: Farrar, Straus and Giroux, [1973]). Literary students will find most interesting Butterfield's attempt to answer the vexing question of what makes a great diary, even though not everyone is likely to agree with his fourth criterion, that great diaries are always unselfconscious and lack historical awareness.

Puritan poets also fared well in the journals during 1975, with Anne Bradstreet claiming most of the attention. Ann Stanford's *Anne Bradstreet: The Worldly Puritan* (New York: Burt Franklin) now provides the best critical overview of America's first significant poet, superseding both Josephine Piercy's *Anne Bradstreet* (New Haven: Twayne, [1965] and Elizabeth Wade White's *Anne Bradstreet: 'The Tenth Muse'* (New York: Oxford Univ. Press, [1971]), though White's book is still far better on (occasionally conjectural) biography and other critics offer more thoughtful readings of certain poems. To the standard tensions long recognized as central to Bradstreet's poetry, Stanford adds another, the cosmopolitan (Ipswich) poetry versus the frontier (Andover) poetry. A variation of this theme is explored in more detail by Jennifer R. Waller in " 'My Hand a Needle Better Fits': Anne Bradstreet and Women Poets in the Renaissance" (*DR* 54[1974]:436–50). Waller argues that Bradstreet's residence in America benefited her poetry by compounding temporal with spatial distance from English male models, by encouraging self-examination as practically the only inspiration available for her poetry, and by fostering the discovery of a domestic idiom which, says Waller, "the courtly bluestockings in England" were never motivated to discover because their social circumstances were different. This idiom, amplified by a Protestant stress upon the vocation of wife and mother and upon putting "the trivial incidents of domestic life into a stern theological perspective" which bestowed some sort of universal significance upon even the most commonplace household experience, ultimately aided Anne in the struggle to throw off both her self-deprecatory attitude and the derivative vocabulary of Du Bartas and Sidney.

Another good treatment of Bradstreet is William J. Irvin's "Allegory and Typology 'Imbrace and Greet': Anne Bradstreet's 'Contemplations' " (*EAL* 10:30–46), which identifies the underlying dramatic movement of the poem as a shift from allegorical (objective and authorized) to typological (more nearly subjective and personal) perceptions of nature (stanzas 1–17) to an essentially symbolic vision of the "white stone" of the final stanzas; this image "by its very conventionality becomes part of the security of the promise [of permanence amid the flux and change of nature] it offers." Overall, says Irvin, the work moves from the illusory stasis invoked by the opening autumnal images through an awareness of death derived from scriptural archetypes to the discovery of a "fearful joy" inspired by the ongoing processes of nature—the flowing rivers, the caroling birds. It ends with man's awareness of himself as a creature trapped in time but also able to imagine an eternal goal toward which all life's motion flows.

In a general sense Lewis Turco's "The Pro-Am Tournament" (*MQR* 14:84–91) is also about Anne Bradstreet, the "professional" poet whom Turco contrasts with Edward Taylor (the "amateur": these distinctions are based upon each writer's general sensitivity to audience and sense of craft); but the essay overlooks the important private elements of Bradstreet's work, the public ones of Taylor's, and is, besides, so general as to be almost useless. Much better is William J. Scheick's discussion of another Puritan poet in "Standing in the Gap: Urian Oakes' Elegy on Thomas Shepard" (*EAL* 9:301–06), the main thrust of which is directed toward an explication of the key image that Shepard's death will set "eyes abroach, dissolve a stone." I cannot entirely agree with Scheick's equating "eyes" with the eye of reason, stones with those hardened hearts which must be thawed "when conversion genuinely occurs," but his conclusion that Oakes is really talking about his own inadequacy to fill the vacuum left by Shepard and that his self-professed humility has important implications for the style of the poem, which Scheick defines as a restrained poetic midway between the extremes of hyperbole and pedantry, seems both sound and sane.

And so we come to Cotton Mather, whose Life of John Winthrop is ostensibly the subject of Bercovitch's *Origins*. Of course, Bercovitch has really tackled a far bigger problem, as his full title indicates, and though he will have to finish his book on Emerson to make some of what he says about the American character fall into place, he is surely off to an impressive beginning. First of all, it must be said that even as a study of a single life in Mather's *Magnalia*, Bercovitch's book is a careful examination of the various hagiographical, biographical, and hermeneutical traditions which Catholic and Protestant, Lutheran and Calvinist, Englishman and American practiced differently in different eras and ages. But Bercovitch's point is that in spite of all the local and indisputable differences within America itself there exists in this country an essential continuity of what he calls "auto-American-biography," that is, the kind of autobiography which celebrates the individual hero as a representative American. From Mather's Winthrop to Franklin's self-portrait to Emerson's scholar to Whitman's "Self" (and Bercovitch might have added the narrator-Columbus fusion of Barlow's *Columbiad*), he sees a similar rhetorical strategy at work, a strategy which may privately take account of the failures of the present moment but which publicly, and persuasively enough to offset whatever private despair over the American dream may exist, takes refuge in an "intermediate American self." "Refuge" is perhaps the wrong word, since the effort results in a reaffirmation of American possibilities rather than in mere escape; in turning the jeremiad into a myth of the fathers and in emphasizing the notion that the divinely appointed mission of the sons is to serve as an antitype of the fathers, the intermediate self sees its potential prophesied in the heroes of the American past, its fulfillment in those of the future; in the same way, Bercovitch argues, Mather came to imagine Winthrop's identity as his own. As one of the controlling myths of America, this enlarged sense of selfhood represents an extension of and triumph over the rhetorical dangers inherent in Protestant *imatatio Christi*, where the ritualistic stress upon humility and ritualistic denial of the self inevitably led to a proliferation of personal pronouns and a covert exaltation of the self; it helps to resolve the central "paradox of a literature devoted at once to the exaltation of the individual and the search for the perfect community."

For those who might wish to sample Bercovitch's thesis in a smaller dose—actually, of course, there is more than one thesis; I have only touched upon the one I consider most important—there is his essay on "Colonial Puritan Rhetoric and the Discovery of America" (*CRevAS* 6:131–50), which is also part of his book and which tells more briefly of the Puritan effort to unite "*allegoria* and *historia*" on the sacred soil of New England, again focusing upon the Life of Winthrop as the first such successful fusion. Another article on Mather, this time on the Life of Phips, is Jane Donahue Eberwein's " 'In a Book, as in a Glass': Literary Sorcery in Mather's Life of Phips" (*EAL* 10:289–300); Eberwein indicates Mather's failure "to contain Phips within the conventions of his biographical method" but says, finally, that his greatest success lay in his failure, for the demands of dealing with this prototype of Benjamin Franklin (the rags-to-riches theme) who clearly did not fit into the category of a Puritan saint forced Mather to break "beyond his historical literary conventions into the area of romance" and so to invent, accidentally and almost single-handedly, the myth-making American biography and autobiography. On the contrary, argues Gustaaf Van Cromphout in "Cotton Mather as Plutarchan Biographer" (*AL* 46:465–81), most of the lives in *Magnalia*, including the Life of Phips, are formally structured according to the Plutarchan model, foregrounding character against the backdrop of only such history as is necessary to explain a given life; Mather's frequent digressions (of which Eberwein makes so much) are justified by Plutarch's example of introducing historically relevant material. Cromphout seems to have the better of it in this accidental debate, if only because he grounds his analysis more firmly in biographical traditions than does Eberwein, but these are both good articles which nicely complement each other and do not force the reader to choose absolutely between them.

Several other pieces on Mather round out the offerings in Puritan scholarship for the year, the first of them a brief but useful note by Leo M. Kaiser. "On the Latin Verse in Cotton Mather's *Magnalia Christi Americana*" (*EAL* 10:301–06) identifies the sources of many of Mather's allusions and, for those Kaiser cannot identify, names the Latin meter. Carol Gay's "The Fettered Tongue: A Study of the Speech Defect of Cotton Mather" (*AL* 46:451–64) employs modern speech therapy and psychological insights to explain the excessive guilt dramatized in Mather's *Diary* and elsewhere as the result of his youthful self-consciousness about a speech impediment, which he considered an illness visited upon him by God; for literary students the most important parts of the essay are Gay's conjectures that Mather was never cured but simply learned how to select synonyms for words he could not easily pronounce and that, therefore, his speech defect, which affected his ear for language, is reflected in the sound patterns of his prose. And finally, in "Cotton Mather's Unpublished Singing Sermon" (*NEQ* 48:410–22), David P.

McKay prints a hitherto unpublished sermon to go with the others Mather preached on the great psalm-singing controversy (by rote or note?) that troubled the faithful in New England during the early 18th century, noting the conciliatory approach Mather took toward both positions in this heated argument.

iii. The South

Alden T. Vaughan's *American Genesis: Captain John Smith and the Founding of Virginia* (Boston and Toronto: Little, Brown), an important addition to the Little, Brown Library of American Biography series, is a nice, tight summary of Smith's role as leader of the infant colony and, later, as Virginia's preeminent propagandist, though it does not offer much of direct interest to the student of literature. Neither, for that matter, does Philip L. Barbour's "Captain John Smith and the London Theatre" (*VMHB* 83:277–79), which traces a reference in the dedication of Smith's *True Travels* and hypothesizes that the play mentioned there as featuring episodes in Smith's eventful life was probably Richard Gunnell's lost *The Hungarian Lion*, licensed for performance on December 4, 1623. Yet another early Virginia author is the subject of Joan St. C. Crane's "*Good Newes from Virginia*" (*Serif* 11,iv:3–11), a reprinting of the first published work known to have been written by a resident American; Crane also provides a short account of the Virginia massacre of 1622 which prompted the poem, includes a bibliographical overview of the work, and conjectures, quite plausibly, that it was written by Maurice Berkeley.

In the first chapter of *The Dispossessed Garden* Lewis P. Simpson sets himself the task of tracing the continuity of the southern imagination in terms of a reaction against modernism which was firmly established in the South, Simpson believes, even before the Revolution; bedazzled by his powerful prose, I am also convinced by his argument, centered mainly on Robert Beverley, William Byrd of Westover, and Thomas Jefferson, that 18th-century southerners early recognized the incompatibility between their slaveholding system and the ideal literary image, symbolized mostly by the plantation, which they wished to project. Beverley and Byrd were capable of ignoring the "sinister shadow in the foliage" or of referring it through literary allusion to another culture and country, perhaps because in their writings the patriarchal plantation was merely beginning to take literary shape, but by the end of the century Jefferson's greater awareness of the ideal as merely an ideal and his own ambivalence toward the subject of slavery forced him, in the famous Query XIX, to shift the southern imaginative focus from large estates such as his own Monticello (symbol of an elegant and rational society sustained, however, by oppression and force) to the small farm and the yeoman farmer.

Another essay which follows the same general lines, charting the drift from the prose of the "Secret History," in which history and poetry exist in a reciprocal relationship of fact and imaginative definition, to the "History of the Dividing Line," where figurative language has largely displaced historical fact, is Robert D. Arner's "Westover and the Wilderness: William Byrd's Images of Virginia" (*SLJ* 7,ii:105–23). Arner argues that Byrd's psychological needs led him to attempt "civilizing" the wilderness in both versions of the "Histories" but that in the latter version "the wilderness has grown too tame to supply the epic metaphors with historical validity."

One of Byrd's near contemporaries, the satirist Ebenezer Cooke, came in for a good deal of attention in 1975, beginning with Edward H. Cohen's *Ebenezer Cooke: The Sot-Weed Canon* (Athens: Univ. of Ga. Press). The strength of this, the first full-length study of Cooke's poetry, is that it consolidates most of what has previously been known about Maryland's outstanding colonial satirist; its main weakness, as Robert D. Arner has pointed out in a review essay ("Ebenezer Cooke: Satire in the Colonial South," *SLJ* 8,i:153–64), is that it merely consolidates: no speculations on Cooke's place in southern comic tradition are ventured, for instance, very little is done with the poet's language and style, and previously printed scholarship is followed so closely (almost *verbatim* at times) as to come "perilously close to plagiarism." In the same review essay Arner also takes some guesses at the politics which lay behind Cooke's "ELOGY" on Thomas Bordley and at the identity of the "Maid" referred to in the elegy on William Locke. The last word on Cooke (and on the colonial South for this past year) also belongs to Arner in "Ebenezer Cooke's *Sotweed Redivivus*: Satire in the Horatian Mode" (*MissQ* 28:489–96), in which it is argued that, despite the obvious Hudibrastic surface of the poem, Cooke had temporarily abandoned Butler for Horace, whose Epistle I, ii ("To Lollius Maximus") is quoted at the end of the poem, whose narrative strategy seems to underlie its discursive structure, whose deliberately muted and commonplace figures of speech are imitated at many points during the debate between the speaker and the Cockerouse, and whose ideal of the *via media* sustains the verses throughout.

iv. Franklin and the Enlightenment

The topic of considerable speculation in 1975, Benjamin Franklin was not especially blessed with informed commentators. Frances M. Barbour's *A Concordance to the Sayings in Franklin's 'Poor Richard'* (Detroit: Gale Research, [1974]) will undoubtedly prove to be a useful tool, though Barbour's system of cross-referencing key words is perhaps more confusing than it needs to be; the concordance covers the *Almanack* during the years of Franklin's direct association with it (1733–58) and relies, possibly not always wisely, on four leading proverb dictionaries—Appleton, Oxford, Stevenson, and Tilley—to identify original vs. borrowed folk wisdom.

But if Barbour's *Concordance* is worthwhile, what can be said of Melvin H. Buxbaum's *Franklin and the Zealous Presbyterians* (University Park and London: The Penn. State Univ. Press)? Buxbaum is probably the last person in the world to get the news that there are some discrepancies between the self-portrait of the *Autobiography* and the historical Franklin, and, taking this scoop as his point of departure, he starts out on what can only be characterized as a subtle smear campaign. Not, of course, that I have any special love for Franklin myself or expect to make money by trying to keep his mythic image intact for schoolchildren to emulate, but facts used to dispel that myth should probably aim for scrupulous accuracy and interpretations should not unfailingly impute the worst possible motives to Franklin's conduct. I object, in other words, to the tone of the book, a tone that makes me want to attempt vainly to disprove even Buxbaum's valid findings, and I find the "Epilogue" altogether too brief and truncated, as if Buxbaum himself were aware that so one-sided a story really can lead nowhere—certainly not to a greater understanding of the Franklin who actually existed. It is not at all clear, in any case, that Franklin's career from the early 1720s through 1765 (when, in the interests of American unity, he is supposed by Buxbaum to have performed a miraculous about-face) can be entirely comprehended by referring it to his attacks on Presbyterianism. It is easy to guess, for example, what that leads Buxbaum to conclude about Franklin's outrage at the Paxton massacre. Nor are Buxbaum's statistics on Franklin's publication of George Whitefield's sermons open only to the interpretation he chooses to give them: that Franklin wished to promote Whitefield's popularity as a way of undercutting Presbyterian power. Generally speaking, Buxbaum has tailored all the evidence to make his own special kind of coat, a coat so strangely cut that only he could be comfortable wearing it.

While I'm on the subject of troublesome, not to say nearly worthless, scholarship, I should not forget to mention two other pieces, Arthur Bernon Tourtellot's "The Early Reading of Benjamin Franklin" (*HLB* 23:5–41), which tells us nothing we did not already know, and Marc Egnal's "The Politics of Ambition: A New Look at Benjamin Franklin" (*CRevAS* 6:151–64), though Egnal at least has the wisdom to warn us that his portrait of the self-seeking Franklin who wished above all else to be governor of Pennsylvania "relies on deduction" to fill in some of the gaps in the *Autobiography*. Indeed it does: what else is there to go on, unless it is Cecil Currey's *Code Number 72: Benjamin Franklin, Patriot or Spy?* (Englewood Cliffs, N.J.: Prentice-Hall, [1972]), a work which no one else that I know of would feel comfortable quoting.

More considered contributions to Franklin scholarship, while not exactly plentiful, were nevertheless at least to be found occasionally. Marcello Maestro's "Benjamin Franklin and the Penal Laws" (*JHI* 36:551–62) examines "The Speech of Polly Baker" as an early statement of Franklin's interest in legal reform, then discusses his reading of Voltaire's *Treatise on Tolerance* and especially his familiarity with Gaetano Filangieri's *The Science of Legislation*, a work which eventually helped to shape the thought of his famous letter to Benjamin Rush ("On the Criminal Laws and the Practice of Privateering"); during Franklin's tenure as president of Pennsylvania, Maestro reminds us, a law was passed making only rape, murder, arson, and treason punishable by death.

David M. Larson's "Franklin on the Nature of Man and the Possibility of Virtue" (*EAL* 10:111–20) stresses once again Franklin's pragmatic approach to the question of virtuous behavior, arriving at the conclusion that Franklin "embraces man as he finds him and searches for ways to make him better"; according to Larson, Franklin's mature philosophy had room both for vestiges of the early necessitarianism of *A Dissertation on Liberty and Necessity, Pleasure and Pain* and for the apparently pessimistic thoughts he expresses in his letter "To Joseph Priestley."

Also worth reading are three brief notes on Franklin's reputation and continuing influence on American and European letters. In a "Letter to the Editor" (*EAL* 10:220–21), Paul M. Zall wittily responds to Betty Kushen's "Three Earliest Published Lives of Benjamin Franklin, 1790–93: The *Autobiography* and Its Continuations" (*EAL* 9[1974]:39–52) and conjectures that Andrew Allen, not James Jones Wilmer, was responsible for the most unrestrained attack on Franklin's character in Wilmer's *Memoirs of the Late Dr. Benjamin Franklin*; the evidence is admittedly circumstantial but nonetheless persuasive. Quite different is M. E. Grenander's "Benjamin Franklin's Glass Armonica and Henry James's 'Jolly Corner'" (*PLL* 11: 415–17), which briefly discusses an instrument of Franklin's modification as a central symbol in James's story, and Jayme A. Sokolow's "'Arriving at Moral Perfection': Benjamin Franklin and Leo Tolstoy" (*AL* 47:427–32), a nice account of the impact of Franklin's idea that "happiness could only be based on virtue" on Tolstoy's writing. Finally, one of Franklin's contemporaries, Pierre Eugène du Simitière, was the subject of Mary F. Pusey and Anne Stauffenbarg's "The Cipher Book of Pierre Eugène du Simitière" (*Serif* 11,iv:33–41), a bibliographical description of that handsome volume.

v. Edwards and the Great Awakening

The best shall be first: William J. Scheick's *The Writings of Jonathan Edwards: Theme, Motif, and Style* (College Station: Texas A & M Univ. Press). This is the kind of book on Edwards that literary students especially will appreciate, since it combines sound knowledge of Puritan origins with sensitive analysis of selected sermons; it aims to give us not only Edwards the theologian but also Edwards the artist, and in that it is largely successful. Incorporating two shorter pieces into its argument, "Family, Conversion, and the Self in Jonathan Edwards' *A Faithful Narrative of the Surprising Work of God*" (*TSL* 19[1974]:79–89) and "The Grand Design: Jonathan Edwards' *History of the Work of Redemption*" (*ECS* 8:300–314),

Scheick's study focuses on Edwards's imagery and rhetoric as the best way of coming to terms with the minister's commitment to Puritan traditions, the Puritan family, and Puritan society at large ("the expanding context of [spiritual] identity") and with Edwards's solution to the problem of man's postlapsarian estrangement from God. Edwards, says Scheick, gradually moved away from a youthful preoccupation with nature as distant equally from God and man toward a rhetorical strategy which internalized nature as part of the psychic landscape and defined man's spiritual identity in terms of the inner drama of conversion; "the pertinent implication of Edwards's use of nature in this fashion is the elimination of the saint's external being as any definitive basis for identity."

Another and more slender book on Edwards, one which really contains only two essays of interest, is *Jonathan Edwards: His Life and Influence*, ed. Charles Angoff (Rutherford, N.J.: Fairleigh Dickinson Univ. Press). Conrad Cherry's "Imagery and Analysis: Jonathan Edwards on the Revival of Religion," pp. 19–28, makes use of the old distinction between Edwards's emotional and analytical prose in attempting to separate Edwards's brand of revivalism from many of its fundamentalist and antiintellectual successors; for Edwards, Cherry contends, religious emotion did not obviate analytical religion, but rather awakened the heart and mind to a fuller understanding of points of theology. Such dissatisfaction as I felt reading Cherry's article stemmed not from the thesis—that, after all, is almost a self-evident truth about Edwards by now—but from the sense that Cherry had not space enough to work the idea down toward a fresh discussion of the sermons themselves. But that deficiency was largely remedied by Wilson H. Kimnach's "The Brazen Trumpet: Jonathan Edwards' Conception of the Sermon," pp. 29–44, which promises a closer inspection of the rhetorical structure of the sermon than we in fact get but which does plausibly argue that, during his first decade as a preacher, Edwards viewed the sermon both within its traditional context and as a vehicle for the expression of his own philosophical explorations; eventually, Kimnach claims, Edwards found himself caught in the "peculiarly modern trap of overspecialization" and had to sacrifice the traditional sermon form "in his efforts to fulfill the role assigned to him by his father and grandfather, on the one hand, and his need to exercise his philosophic creativity on the other." Kimnach also, in "Jonathan Edwards' Sermon Mill" (*EAL* 10:167–78), reports on the annotations and substantive changes Edwards made in his sermons as he adapted them for varied audiences. Thus, says Kimnach, "the immediate occasion of each sermon is indelibly stamped upon it by shadings in diction, choice of metaphors, and allusions, even when prepared by the author for the press."

One other good article on Edwards is Emily Stipes Watts's "The Neoplatonic Basis of Jonathan Edwards' 'True Virtue' " (*EAL* 10:197–89). This essay traces a number of key ideas and definitions central to Edwards's ethical system, both in the early "Notes on the Mind" and the mature *Nature of True Virtue*, to the Latin text of Henry More's *Enchiridion Ethicum*. Common to both writers are similar definitions of *excellency*, an emphasis upon *complacency* (in More a distinction of human passion, in Edwards "God's love to His beautiful creatures"), an attack upon Hobbesian materialism and mechanism, comparable stress upon *justice* as one of the "primary subdivisions of complacence," and a reversal of the Platonic movement from "love of man to love of God" to an order of "virtuous love from love of God to love of the world."

Edwards's contemporary, Samuel Johnson, was also the subject of a short article, Don R. Gerlach and George De Mille's "Samuel Johnson and the Founding of King's College, 1751–55" (*HMPEC* 44:335–52), a discussion of Johnson's apostasy from Presbyterianism and his role in the development of King's College in the areas of curricular reform and administration.

vi. Revolutionary and Early National Periods

Surprisingly little work was done this past year on major figures of the American Revolution. A minor writer and minister, Samuel Sherwood, was treated in Stephen J. Stein's "An Apocalyptic Rationale for the American Revolution" (*EAL* 9:211–25), which studied Sherwood's *The Church's Flight into the Wilderness* (1776) as a potentially major contribution to the rhetoric of the Revolution in its identification of England as the seat of papal conspiracy; Sherwood, Stein believes, was one of the first to turn loose "upon the English the vast reservoirs of anti-Catholic hostility built up among Protestants for generations," but in this, of course, he is mistaken, since Puritan ministers had been indulging themselves in similar tropes for a good long while before the Revolution came to a head. What can be said is not that Sherwood initiated anything worth remembering, but that his tract reflects an American habit of mind and an American convention of pulpit rhetoric, both of which had drawn on those vast reservoirs of anti-Catholic feeling at least since the days of Nathaniel Ward's *Simple Cobler*.

Among individual authors of the federal period, Joel Barlow fared best, with no less than three articles devoted exclusively or in part to his career. There was, first of all, Victor E. Gimmestad's "Joel Barlow's Editing of John Trumbull's *M'Fingal*" (*AL* 47:97–102). Gimmestad has unearthed a letter (August 2, 1792) from Barlow to the New York merchant James Watson which for the first time proves what many have suspected for a good number of years, that Barlow was indeed the editor of the London edition of *M'Fingal* printed by J. S. Jordan in 1792; for his part, as Gimmestad writes, Trumbull was understandably less than delighted by Barlow's republican footnotes and in response authorized a 1795 American edition, striking out the most offensive of Barlow's notes.

Several other Barlow letters, directed to the poet's wife, Ruth, found their way into print this past year. In "On the Fringes of the Napoleonic Catastrophe: Joel Barlow's Letters from Central and Eastern Europe, 1812" (*EAL* 10:251–72), Clifford L. Egan has made public some correspondence originally intended for a private audience; filled with domestic detail and tender protestations of regard, the letters also paint a vivid picture of "the suffering experienced by millions of humans" in the wake of Napoleon's Russian campaign. A more substantial contribution to Barlow scholarship is John Griffith's "*The Columbiad* and *Greenfield Hill*: History, Poetry, and Ideology in the Late Eighteenth Century" (*EAL* 10:235–50), in which Griffith suggests that Barlow's poem was deliberately built upon a progressive theory of history while Dwight's reflected his notions of history as cyclical and recurrent. I think, though, that Griffith does not give sufficient attention to the cyclical implications of Barlow's epic, especially as these are generated by his historical overview of solar heroes, but nonetheless the article is a good one as far as it goes; particularly interesting are Griffith's comments about the different poetic vocabularies each poet felt it appropriate to employ in presenting his vision of American destiny to the American public.

Another Connecticut Wit who shared the spotlight with Barlow is John Trumbull, the subject of Victor E. Gimmestad's "John Trumbull's Original Epithalamion" (*EAL* 10:158–66). Through a comparison of four printed editions and two manuscripts, Gimmestad establishes the authority of the Detroit Public Library's holograph of the "Epithalamion," an early burlesque which "marked its author's coming of age in the octosyllabic couplet"; Gimmestad also reproduces this version of the poem. And in "John Trumbull, Essayist" (*EAL* 10:273–88) Bruce Granger surveys Trumbull's early *Meddler* and *Correspondent* essays and finds that both serials, while predictably imitative of the English *Spectator*, "not only illuminate the meaning of poems like *The Progress of Dulness*" but also leave "the serial essay tradition in America permanently enriched."

Yet another poet of the same period, Phillis Wheatley, is discussed by Terence Collins in "Phillis Wheatley: The Dark Side of the Poetry" (*Phylon* 36:78–88). Collins contends that Wheatley's black consciousness is to be found not in covert appeals for liberty disguised as pro-American propaganda but in the self-deprecatory tone of her poems, a tone which, he says, is characteristic of black writers in a white society which they both attack and yet wish to find acceptance within.

As for prose writers of the Revolutionary period, Marcus Cunliffe has written a sound article on "Crèvecoeur Revisited" (*JAmS* 9:129–44), arguing that Crèvecoeur's works reflect a tension between his identity as an immigrant (the optative mood of the *Letters*) and his identity as an exile (the nostalgic, reflective mood of the *Sketches*). There were in Crèvecoeur, Cunliffe thinks, "two different men inside one physiognomy—at least two, if not more"; one of them predicated his dreams of the future on an Anglo-American persona, the other tried to reshape his identity as a Franco-American during the years of his consulship in New York (1783–90). Neither a loyalist nor a patriot but a bewildered visitor whose perplexity was somehow symbolized by his residence in the "neutral ground" of New York, Crèvecoeur was a "romantic rather than a political ideologue."

One exception to the drought of articles on major nonliterary Revolutionary War personalities was (as usual) Thomas Jefferson, who of course cannot really be deemed nonliterary even if his main importance to us is not always thought of in terms of his literary artistry. But Merrill D. Peterson lets us judge for ourselves in his handy Viking Portable edition of Jefferson's major works, including the *Summary View*, *Notes*, and the *Declaration*, as well as 79 judiciously selected and significant letters; both historians and teachers of literature will be happy to have this convenient and thoughtful edition. Jefferson's *Declaration* also came in for some criticism in Howard Mumford Jones's "The Declaration of Independence: A Critique" (*PAAS* 85:55–72). In this bicentennial year during which we may be tempted to admire uncritically all things American, Jones has written an essay well worth reading, even if he has nothing strikingly original to charge against Jefferson's document; sometimes humorously, sometimes acidly, he points out the logical flaws of the *Declaration*, notes the wide range of confusing and often contradictory interpretations that have judicially been put upon the "pursuit of happiness" phrase, dispels a variety of familiar myths about the signing, and in general calls into question the relevance of this 18th-century document to a world which no longer operates on the assumption of rationality. Our forefathers, he suggests, knew exactly how to discount Jefferson's political rhetoric "just as we today know how to discount advertising language," but our undue reverence toward this major statement of American ideals has kept us from acknowledging the extent to which it was designed mainly as propaganda.

Two of Jefferson's close political friends and allies, James Madison and Philip Freneau, were discussed briefly in Julian Mason's "Madison's August 1791 Letter Praising Freneau" (*EAL* 9:325–27); Mason reports on a series of almost identical letters Madison circulated among his friends in support of Freneau as editor of the *National Gazette*. Finally, and unconnected with Jefferson or Madison in any way, there is Diane B. Malone's "A Survey of Early Military Theatre in America" (*ThS* 16:56–64), a piece that would be useful only to those who previously knew nothing about the subject; it repeats precisely the kind of information any good introduction to American theater history would supply and neglects to mention, for instance, even so well known an extravaganza as Major John André's *Mischianza*.

vii. Brown and Contemporaries

Lewis Leary's *Soundings: Some Early American Writers* (Athens: Univ. of Ga. Press) brings together 14 selected essays, all of them characterized by that sound judgment and lucid prose in which Leary has few rivals among active early Americanists. All but the chapters on Joseph Dennie and William Dunlap have been printed before, some as long ago as 1942 and some as recently as 1973; there is perhaps nothing especially striking in the treatments of Franklin, Cooper, Irving, or Dunlap, but the essay on Freneau, revised from *Major Writers of Early American Literature*, ed. Everett H. Emerson (Madison: Univ. of Wisc. Press, [1972]), is probably the single best essay on that underrated poet's career, and for writers like Thomas Branagan, Nathaniel Tucker, Samuel Low, Charles Crawford, and Joseph Brown Ladd, Leary's chapters are rich sources of biographical information and models of critical sanity. Taken together, the pieces in *Soundings* represent a selective literary history of the post-Revolutionary decades, a period which by and large continues to be overlooked despite the renewed interest in early American writers in general.

Other more or less comprehensive approaches to the fiction of the federal period include Robert B. Winans's "The Growth of a Novel Reading Public in Late Eighteenth-Century America" (*EAL* 9:267–75) and Patricia Jewell McAlexander's "The Creation of the American Eve: The Cultural Dialogue on the Nature and Role of Women in Late Eighteenth-Century America" (*EAL* 9:252–66). Winans finds it somewhat paradoxical that the reading public was steadily increasing during the very years that Charles Brockden Brown and others were having trouble attracting an audience; he reports on the records of booksellers, social libraries, and, so far as they are available, circulating libraries to demonstrate that, despite severe strictures against novel reading as damaging to morality, Americans between 1770 and 1800 took an increasing fancy to works of fancy; some of his statistical comparisons seem of doubtful validity, but on balance his article is convincing.

Also convincing is McAlexander's examination of women in early fiction. Taking off from Hawthorne's familiar portraits of unbearably pure female characters, McAlexander discusses four basic attitudes toward women which emerged as a result of the "intense cultural dialogue on the subject occurring throughout the western world." Her coherent synthesis presents conservatives as champions of the passivity and moral integrity of women, liberals like Benjamin Rush on the side of female education but trapped in the paradox that education supposedly unfit women to perform their traditional roles, and radicals like Mary Wollstonecraft and the early William Godwin as advocates for the abolition of marriage as an obstacle to the fullest development of an individual's reason. Nominally supporting the conservative position while in fact dramatizing the allure of passion and romance were a host of early American novels, while Godwin's *Memoirs of Mary Wollstonecraft*, intended as a defense of liberated women, became "Exhibit A" in the conservatives' attack.

A similar discrepancy between intention and effect, argues Cathy N. Davidson in "*The Power of Sympathy* Reconsidered: William Hill Brown as Literary Craftsman" (*EAL* 10:14–29), underlies the achievement of Brown's best-known novel, but in this instance she has, I think, unwisely rushed in where angels fear to tread. Brown's novel does indeed fail to communicate its stated theme, but not, contrary to what Davidson tries to establish, because the author cleverly and deliberately enlarges the moral issues of the book; rather, these issues get out of hand because he does not fully understand and therefore cannot control the mix of literary and intellectual traditions, both local and European, he attempts to manipulate in his story.

Among several good pieces on that other and far more talented Brown, Charles Brockden, probably the best is Sydney J. Krause's "Romanticism in *Wieland*: Brown and the Reconciliation of Opposites," pp. 13–24, in *Artful Thunder*. Krause touches once again upon the vexing critical question of Brown's romanticism and decides that the most pronounced romantic tendencies in *Wieland* manifest themselves chiefly in the dialectal tensions of the novel, polarities which are projected from Brown's own divided personality, are reflected in the vocabulary of his characters, and are resolved in the final scene when Wieland, temporarily shaken by Carwin's testimony but then convinced anew of heavenly prompting, attempts through an act of murder to bring heaven and earth into moral balance; Clara's closing warning to frame "juster notions . . . [of] divine attributes" speaks to the same urge for moral balance, linking her imagination with Wieland's and both of theirs, says Krause, with all of ours in the continuing romantic quest "for a *more lasting* reconciliation of the worlds of man and God than life allows." But Joseph V. Ridgely, in "The Empty World of *Wieland*," pp. 3–16, in *Individual and Community* sees the balance for which Brown strives in other terms; the world of *Wieland*, Ridgely says, is both nocturnal and empty. Its nocturnal qualities, established largely through light and shadow imagery, are to be understood as external manifestations of American emptiness, of the chaotic and inevitably ambiguous results of human judgments which "grant ultimate authority to the last recorded sensory data" without attempting to "verify sense impressions in the context of a world which is broader" than individual perceptions and experiences; it is in this sense that the novel most clearly reflects the recent "sundering of America from the parent country" and the consequent "deprivation of a fostering social order, of those traditional institutions by which the individual self attempts to gauge its proper role" and response.

Another good essay on *Wieland* is Wayne Franklin's "Tragedy and Comedy in Brown's *Wieland*" (*Novel* 8:147–63), which explores a number of general parallels among that romance and Shakespeare's *Much Ado* and *Hamlet*. Despite Clara's nearly obsessional fear of inner darkness, he argues, her story resolves itself in an essentially comic manner—marriage and at least a form of happiness—whereas Wieland's madness belongs to a larger world tainted by evil, a tragic world which Clara fails to acknowledge by insisting that Carwin is the sole author of all the ills that have befallen the Wieland family. Clara's concept of herself as a tragic victim of someone else's manipulation, Franklin claims, "is a projection born of her fears: if she can remain a mere innocent victim . . . then she need not face the fact that she fears most, which is her incipient madness." But in "Voices of Carwin and Other Mysteries in Charles Brockden Brown's *Wieland*" (*EAL* 10:307–09), Robert W. Hobson insists with Clara that Carwin is indeed the villain Clara takes him for, that his ventriloquism and not Wieland's madness is responsible for the command to kill both wife and children; "in transposing the actual crime" from the pages of the *New York Weekly Magazine*, "Brown [may have] inadvertently retained the concept of multiple voices without perceiving that this retention places Carwin in a much more incriminating position than he was ever meant to occupy."

Like its title, John Clemans's "Ambiguous Evil: A Study of Villains and Heroes in Charles Brockden Brown's Major Novels" (*EAL* 10:190–219) is perhaps too long for what it tells us, but in arriving at the conclusion that "Brown's purpose [in all four major romances] seems to be thoroughly and purposefully reductionist, to create final situations of moral blandness or paralysis," Clemans offers probably the most detailed treatment to date of the difference between Brown's characters' motives and their deeds, of the contradictions inherent in a single personality, and of some of the complexities which a novelistic point of view produces. Far more modest in scope is the final article on Brown, S. W. Reid's "Charles Brockden Brown's Copy of Johnson's Dictionary" (*Serif* 11,iv:12–20), which discusses the edition of the book which Brown took as his authority on the English language.

Then there is Hugh Henry Brackenridge, subject of Charles E. Modlin's "The Folly of Ambition in *Modern Chivalry*" (*PAAS* 85: 310–13). This brief discussion centers on Brackenridge's allusive comparison between Aaron Burr and Scipio, classical prototype of the unscrupulous politician; the novelist had come to hold this view of Burr during the "protracted presidential election of 1801." Democracy turns into demagoguery so frequently in the novel that, at least according to Modlin, "the vote . . . becomes the ultimate meaning of the book's title. It is modern chivalry itself, the best defense against 'the folly of ambition.'" As one ramification of the theme of folly, Lynn Haines, in "Of Indians and Irishmen: A Note on Brackenridge's Use of Sources for Satire in *Modern Chivalry*" (*EAL* 10:88–92), calls attention to Teague's impersonation of an Indian chief and suggests that Brackenridge may have taken his details for a "typical" Indian speech from Cadwallader Colden's *History of the Five Indian Nations* (1772). Last and easily least, in "The Rarity of *Modern Chivalry*" (*PAAS* 85:309), Marcus A. McCorison discourses on the scarcity of complete sets of Brackenridge's novel before announcing the American Antiquarian Society's acquisition of one such set.

Less important than Brackenridge is Royall Tyler, one of whose lost plays is outlined in Katherine Schall Jarvis's "Royall Tyler's Lyrics for *May Day in Town*" (*HLB* 23:186–98). The essay recovers and reprints from a pamphlet recently located in the Houghton Library 11 songs from which at least a rough synopsis of the action of the play can be surmised. The eight-page pamphlet qualifies as Tyler's earliest printed work and, since the play was performed only a month or so after Tyler arrived in New York, also provides additional (if indirect) testimony to the legendary speed with which he is supposed to have written. Finally, Lawrence J. Friedman and Arthur H. Schaffer study "Mercy Otis Warren and the Politics of

Historical Nationalism" (*NEQ* 48:194–215) and conclude that Warren's wish to provide a national history which would unite all Americans in a shared historical consciousness toned down her pro-Jeffersonian sentiments when she penned her *History . . . of the American Revolution* (1805).

viii. General and Miscellaneous Studies

Perhaps the most important general study of this past year was Rose Marie Cutting's "America Discovers Its Literary Past: Early American Literature in Nineteenth-Century Anthologies" (*EAL* 9:226–51). Cutting discusses this discovery within the context of the rivalry between Rufus A. Griswold and the Duyckincks. Among her more interesting conclusions is that, thanks to Griswold's *Poets and Poetry of America* and the Duyckincks' *Cyclopedia,* Moses Coit Tyler had far more substantial criticism on which to draw for his histories than he admits to be the case.

The first two chapters of Annette Kolodny's *The Lay of the Land* deal with 17th- and 18th-century American authors and so merit some mention here as well. Though the book clearly improves as it goes on, it is far from the study I would have hoped for, and the early chapters, I am tempted to say, are something approaching a disaster. In particular, the narrow range of quotations would not convince anyone that he is in the presence of a scholar who thoroughly knows her subject, and even the few quotations offered are not fully explained or fit into the work from which they are taken. Kolodny's thesis approximates that of Leo Marx in *The Machine in the Garden* (though she claims it does not), but anyone who has read his book—and who has not?—need not bother with hers.

A good collection of early broadsides is John Duffy's and Mason I. Lowance, Jr.'s *Early Vermont Broadsides* (Hanover, N.H.: Univ. Press of New England), though the introduction seems designed more for the novice than for the professional. Two other minor early American genres treated in 1975 were the promotional tract and the almanac. In "Humor in the Colonial Promotional Tract: Topics and Techniques" (*EAL* 9:286–300), Leslie A. Wardenaar examines writings by William Wood, John Josselyn, George Alsop, and John Lawson and isolates four themes that both New England and Southern promotional literature shared: "America's social and economic prospects, vegetation and natural life, animal life, and Indians." Of these, the last two provided the most material for comedy; through far-fetched analogies promotional writers developed an exaggerated style that both defined the unfamiliar in terms of the familiar and spoofed the narrowness of the English experience. And in "American Almanacs and Feuds" (*EAL* 9:276–85), Marion Barber Stowell reminds us that Franklin's famous feud with Titan Leeds had ample precedent in early American almanac publication.

Several useful bibliographies were also published this past year, including Samuel J. Rogal's "A Bibliographical Survey of American Hymnody, 1640–1800" (*BNYPL* 78:231–52), which contends, somewhat questionably, that the "distinctively *American* hymn did not come into existence until the nineteenth century" but which is, of course, chiefly valuable not for its historical comments but for its handy compilation of titles. Herbert Leventhal and James E. Mooney contributed "A Bibliography of Loyalist Source Material in the United States: Part I" (*PAAS* 85:73–308), listing manuscript repositories in Maine, New Hampshire, Vermont, Massachusetts, Rhode Island, Connecticut, New York, New Jersey, Pennsylvania, Delaware, and Maryland. And Lawrence D. Geller and Peter J. Gomes round out this year's work with *The Books of the Pilgrims* (New York and London: Garland), a work that features a solid historical introduction aimed at putting the considerable intellectual life of the Pilgrims into perspective. The bibliography itself lists those books in possession of the Pilgrim Society which are known to have been written or read by the Pilgrims.

University of Cincinnati

12. 19th-Century Literature

Warren French

"A conscious and determined struggle to formulate for themselves the meaning of the landscape characterizes the writing of nineteenth-century Americans," observes Annette Kolodny in one of the year's most perceptive and powerful critical books, *The Lay of the Land*. Perhaps because our national bicentennial celebration has especially fostered introspection about the nature and meaning of our national tradition, most worthwhile scholarship about 19th-century American literature concerned itself during 1975 in some fashion with an analysis and evaluation of efforts to formulate material or mystical connections between the landscape and our national destiny.

i. General Studies

Few recent books provide comprehensive surveys of 19th-century American writing; they either cover a longer span of time or concentrate on some more limited one. Annette Kolodny's survey moves across three centuries in its pursuit of her perception that "the continued repetition of the land-as-woman symbolization in American life and letters . . . suggested a pervasive and dynamic psychohistorical import" (p. ix); but its longest chapter on the early 19th-century forms an autonomous essay. Beginning with the observation that "unable to resolve what is still a central concern within the American psyche—the sense of guilt aroused by the conflict between the impulse to see nature as bountiful and the desire to domesticate it and make it bountiful," John James Audubon "attempted to stop time altogether" (p. 88). Kolodny documents in detail Cooper's previously noted inability to let Natty Bumppo achieve sexual maturity and the less familiar but equally consequential attitude reflected by William Gilmore Simms's novels that behind everything else that troubled the antebellum South, "the response to a landscape whose maternal embrace, once fixed and stylized on the plantations, was so all-enclosing, and apparently all-sufficing, that it defeated any possibility of progress or alteration, aesthetic or cultural" (p. 132). Cautiously understating the significance of her thesis that the 19th-century Americans' destruction and pollution of the land was in large measure the expression of infantile anger at the frustration of the land's promise to prove an unfailing mother and mistress, Kolodny persuades this reader of the urgency of her conclusion that "twentieth century pastoral *must* offer us some means of understanding and altering the disastrous attitudes toward the physical setting that we have inherited from our national past" (p. 137).

Looking also at the South of Simms, Lewis Simpson in his equally impressive and readable *The Dispossessed Garden* treats John Pendleton Kennedy's novel *Swallow Barn* (1831), "usually considered to be the prototypical novel of the literary plantation" rendered in "the nostalgic mode of pastoral," as instead "an uncertain attempt at a pastoral ratification of slavery," exemplifying "a second stage of the displacement of pastoral in the Southern mind." This stage, Simpson believes, follows one characterized by "conflict between an agrarianism which is a metaphor of intellectual and spiritual independence and a recognition of the Southern plantation as symbol of the tyranny of slavery of the mind" (p. 40). As an example of a succeeding third stage, during which slavery "as a unique reaction against modernity" has "dispossessed the garden of the Western pastoral imagination," Simpson singles out Simms, "whose consciousness of himself as a man of letters is entangled with his identification of himself as the representative of an entire social order existing in alienation from modern history" (pp. 51–52)—a conclusion that closely parallels Annette Kolodny's about both Audubon and Simms.

After reading Kolodny's and Simpson's books, I find Edward Halsey Foster's *The Civilized Wilderness: Backgrounds to American Romantic Literature 1817–1860* (New York: Free Press) disappointing. It fails to live up to the promise to sketch out "various backgrounds against which we can profitably view American literature of the years 1817–1860" (p. xi), because the impossibly broad topic is explored in terms of a few scattered examples hardly sufficiently representative of the trends of the times. The already familiar theories of architect Andrew Jackson Downing dominate more than half of Foster's preoccupation with Romantic America's attempt "to provide landscapes which combined civilization with wilderness" (p. 55), and the final account of "the literati at home and abroad" is limited to reports on Hawthorne and Bayard Taylor. Foster's animus is most clearly suggested by his introductory statement that "it is in general fair to say that American Romanticism existed as long as someone profited from it financially—and it was increasingly and substantially less profitable after the Civil War taught Americans to be more concerned with actualities than with the idealities of Romanticism" (p. xix). To reduce the deep-seated psychological tensions that warrant Foster's later statement that there is "a great difference between, for example, Downing's concept of the civilized wilderness and Thoreau's" (p. 123) to mere matters of the marketplace economics of popular taste is to miss the very point that fundamentally concerns Annette Kolodny in *The Lay of the Land*—the point that even as we manipulate our metaphors, we are manipulated by them, so that, far from disappearing, the kind of ambiguous Romanticism that Foster explores superficially still exercises a powerful and possibly disastrous influence on our thought and language. The deplorable effect of books like Foster's is that, like any inadequate exploitations of new prospects, they may discourage the continued intensive exploration that an involved and important subject still requires.

One example of such an important aspect of American artists' struggles to come to terms with the native landscape is explored in Thomas H. Pauly's "The Literary Sketch in Nineteenth-Century America" (*TSLL* 17:489–503). Examining these often slighted works of Irving, Hawthorne, and Henry James, Pauly argues that "for them no less than for the painter, the sketch served as a tentative mode of perception" recording "their own journeys to literary consciousness." The sketches, he concludes, are all grounded in the same problem—"to be a serious writer was to be an alien"—so that these by-products of interest in the picturesque, accommodated "the author's uncertainties while offering a valuable opportunity for testing them."

Two other general articles summarize for wider audiences material already adequately familiar to literary scholars. Daniel Marder's "Exiles at Home in American Literature" (*Mosaic* 3,iii:49–75) reviews the writings of Americans attracted to Europe from Washington Irving to Ernest Hemingway to argue that "of the literary Americans who lived abroad extensively before the era of the lost generation," only Henry James "suffered the sense of exile." Louise

K. Barnett's "Nineteenth-Century Indian Hater Fiction: A Paradigm of Racism" (*SAQ* 74:224–36) supports the thesis that "the ritualistic behavior of the Indian hater constitutes a paradigm for racism . . . which contains a curious set of ambivalences and ironies." This figure thus becomes "the logical embodiment of those dark feelings of race hatred inherent in the white conquest of North America."

By far the most provocative article to appear during 1975 about 19th-century American literature is in *The Sociological Review*. Based on the writings of "astute foreign critics," especially Asian, Harold Kaplan's "Beyond Society: The Idea of Community in Classic American Writing" (*SocR* 42:204–29) sees the opposition between "community" and "society" not as a conflict between two kinds of establishments, "one idealized and good, and the other historically real and corrupt," but rather as an effort "to distinguish between the moral ground of community and the formal structure, the nature in being, or society." "If one looks back on the American writing of the nineteenth century from [the] defeated view of individualism in the present century," Kaplan continues, "the result can be a serious distortion in the literary tradition of democratic culture," because "there is no continuity in this tradition but a break." The "outsider communities" created by Cooper, Melville, and Mark Twain, Kaplan maintains, are not "simply defensive arrangements against an oppressive society," but rather "acts of primary community-making" that take place "beyond society where one is free for an imaginative experience beyond its restrictions of category, caste, class, and function." What looks like social dissolution in the 1970s, he concludes, cannot be imposed upon the 1830s in the imaginations of Cooper and Emerson. Whether or not one accepts Kaplan's challenging analysis of break rather than continuity in our two centuries' "outsider stances," one would be ill-advised to reopen the touchy question of the individual's relationship to American society without weighing his arguments.

Support for Kaplan's theories comes from an unexpected source. Anne Scott MacLeod's *A Moral Tale: Children's Fiction and American Culture, 1820–1860* (Hamden, Conn.: Archon) is a wise and illuminating book. Possibly because of the thinness of the material or the librarian's penchant for cataloging, the study becomes repetitious; but the strongly emphasized main points merit careful consideration. "Every work of fiction written for children before 1860 was dedicated to the moral education of its readers," MacLeod asserts (p. 24). Despite this common impetus, however, the works changed significantly over the four decades considered. "Many of the later stories," MacLeod reports crisply, "revealed their authors' shift from the conservative tradition of middle-class Protestant values which emphasized piety and diligence in a wordly calling to that other strain in the American ideal of success which involved getting ahead through such qualities as aggressiveness, competitiveness, and enterprise in economic endeavor" (p. 140). All of these writings, MacLeod points out further, deal surprisingly with "a number of realities since banished from children's literature"—especially death and poverty and such idealistic reform movements as temperance, abolitionism, and pacifism (p. 55). Of most direct relation to Harold Kaplan's thesis, however, and to the general American effort to comprehend the meaning of the landscape are MacLeod's observations that "whenever they contrasted city life with country life, these authors invariably endorsed country living" (p. 45) and yet that the stories avoided specific settings and took place in highly generalized locales in which "the institutions of society were all but invisible" (p. 55).

Related to the nature of literature for children is the portrayal of "The Saintly Child in Nineteenth-Century American Fiction" by Anne Tropp Trensky (*Prospects* 1:389–413). Trensky finds that many tales about this favorite figure "express a nearly mystical communion between the child and nature . . . but very few are about pure children in a natural setting." The stories "portray the child not as a primitive, natural creature but as some unearthly, almost mystical being." She concludes, therefore, that the figure was not intended to be realistic, but "of divine origin, fresh from heaven, destined soon to return" and meanwhile exerting "a holy influence on people around him."

A larger-scale survey reported by J. Gerald Kennedy in "The Magazine Tales of the 1830s" (*ATQ* 24[1974], supp., pt. 2:23–28) finds that sentimental tales dominated these publications, although sensational tales—especially about madmen—were also numerous. "Humor did not flourish," Kennedy speculates, "for successful comedy has always required a studied detachment from the world of human events" rather than a tearful addiction to melodrama and violence.

A useful volume is Edward E. Chielens's *The Literary Journal in America to 1900* (Detroit: Gale Research), which is not a list of the journals that welcomed the tales that Trensky and Kennedy summarize, but rather a heavily annotated survey of historical and critical books and articles about the individual journals. Although there will be quibbles about inclusions and omissions, we are all in Chielens's debt for summarizing these hundreds of widely scattered accounts. A book like this immediately invites glossing, and I have already added to page 68 the title of Neal Frank Doubleday's "Doctrine for Fiction in *North American Review*" (*Literature and Ideas*, pp. 20–39), which observes that while today the discussion of native American materials may seem repetitious, the repetition seems to indicate a strong need "to convince the public and polemical writers that an American literature was not only feasible but emerging" (p. 22).

Even more awesome in scope than the Chielens's book is "Guide to Dissertations on American Literary Figures, 1870–1910," ed. Noel Polk (*ALR* 8:177–280, 291–348). The greater part of two issues of *ALR* is devoted to lengthy descriptions and criticisms of studies of 59 writers, running alphabetically from Henry Adams to Owen Wister (but excluding Howells, Mark Twain, and Henry James). More than 40 contributors provide reports noteworthy for their thoroughness and candor. The editor's overall conclusion is indeed "distressing": "With only a few notable exceptions, dissertations do not represent high-level doctoral work, either bibliographically or critically, and most in fact fall far short of even minimal scholarly standards" (p. 178).

ii. The Age of Elegance—Irving, Cooper, and Their Contemporaries

"Peripheral" rather than "minimal" seems the word for recent Washington Irving scholarship after the trenchant analyses of several years' past of the writer's significance as a symbol of the Knickerbocker culture so centrally important to the development of the American economy. The most provocative of the short studies is G. Thomas Couser's "The Ruined Garden of Wolfert Webber" (*SSF* 12:23–28), which reads the final piece in *Tales of a Traveler* as emblematic of Irving's transformation of the myth of the destruction of the garden that influenced "The Legend of Sleepy Hollow" into the "myth of the Dutch Burgher" of the type of Diedrich Knickerbocker. Couser's observation suggests that continuing rewarding insights may await a comprehensive study of Irving's seemingly unconnected tales as building-blocks in the construction of an overarching myth.

From the publisher who has recently done most to promote Irving's reputation with striking new editions of his works and books about him and his society comes this year an abridgement of *The Life of George Washington.* ed. Jess Stein (Tarrytown, N.Y.: Sleepy Hollow Restorations) that may rekindle interest in Irving's now infrequently read romantic histories. Another work of this group is examined in James W. Tuttleton's "The Romance of History: Irving's *Companions of Columbus*" (*ATQ* 24[1974]:18–24). Tuttleton characterizes this book, which has usually been overshadowed by that about Columbus himself, as "a romance illuminating history as a conflict between national and racial character" as well as a tract "on the attributes of human nature, brought under the moral scrutiny of the author."

Irving's shift from fictionist to historian is scrutinized in John C. Kemp's "Historians Manqués: Irving's Apologetic Personae" (*ATQ* 24[1974], sup., pt. 2:15–19), which argues that in developing narrators like Diedrich Knickerbocker and Geoffrey Crayon, Irving anticipated the confessions of failure, incapacity, and waywardness by personae in American writers from Hawthorne and Mark Twain to Fitzgerald and J. D. Salinger. After Irving turned to serious history, however, Kemp adds, he abandoned such experimentation, and his rare late efforts in fiction were condescending and lacking in imaginative commitment.

The sources of the *Knickerbocker History* continue to fascinate scholars. James E. Evans, in "The English Lineage of Diedrich Knickerbocker" (*EAL* 10:3–13), illustrates Irving's use of a tradition deriving from Jonathan Swift, Fielding, and especially Laurence Sterne. Closer to home, Robert C. Wess, in "The Use of Hudson-Valley Folk Tradition in Washington Irving's *Knickerbocker History of New York* (*NYFQ* 30:212–25), presents many examples of Irving's drawing upon local traditions, especially of the old Dutch settlers. Finally, Mary Weatherspoon Bowden, in "Knickerbocker's *History* and the 'Enlightened' Men of New York City" (*AL* 47:159–72), identifies in the work a multitude of satirical shafts directed at well-known individuals and institutions, especially those associated with Mayor (later Governor) Dewitt Clinton, who found Irving's book "perfectly disgusting to good taste." Wayne R. Kime's "An Actor among the Albanians: Two Rediscovered Sketches of Albany by Washington Irving" (*NYH* 56:409–25) reprints two satirical letters from the New York *Morning Chronicle* (December 1803) to demonstrate that Irving applied the same needling tactics to the upstate capital. Joanne F. Diderich's "Washington Irving as Lyricist" (*PBSA* 69:91–94) provides still further evidence of the writer's versatility through full details from the June 1840 issue of *Graham's Magazine* about "The Moorish Drum," a pot-boiling song attributed to Irving.

In contrast to these rather petty Irving studies, two essays about Irving's now obscure contemporary James Kirke Paulding make sweeping claims for the importance of his theories while acquiescing in the general consensus that his creative works failed to demonstrate them successfully. Louis D. Owens's "James K. Paulding and the Foundations of American Realism" (*BNYPL* 79:40–50) documents Paulding's desire to establish a uniquely American literature and argues that—William Dean Howells and Alfred Kazin to the contrary—"Paulding is proof that realism did not just happen in America," because his "rational fiction," early in the 19th century, formulated "the basic tenets of realism: truth, simplicity, fidelity to nature and American materials." Thomas F. O'Donnell's "*Koningsmarke*: Paulding vs. Scott in 1823" (*ATQ* 24[1974]:10–17) makes much the same points about Paulding's first attempt to write a novel, adding that "the critical principles developed in Augustan England," especially by Fielding in *Tom Jones*, "when modified and adopted to the American situation," seemed to Paulding, "safer to follow than those stemming from an overimaginative and undisciplined romanticism."

Cooper and Simms, as already mentioned, receive so much attention in books by Kolodny, Simpson, and Foster that the trio might well be discussed in this subsection along with Bette S. Weidman's "White Men's Red Men: A Penitential Reading of Four American Novels" (*MLS* 4[1974],ii:14–26), which discusses not only *The Last of the Mohicans* and Simms's *The Yemassee*, but also Charles Brockden Brown's *Edgar Huntly* and Robert Montgomery Bird's *Nick of the Woods.* Weidman finds these four novels "help us to comprehend the cost of transferring European culture to the new world," if we read Simms and Bird "to understand the pathology of racism," Brown to understand how "interior events shape perception and behavior," and Cooper "to remind ourselves that Americans are at least capable of imagining, if not constructing, a new society."

Other writings about Cooper reinforce with significant details points advanced in these broader studies. Morton L. Ross's "Cooper's *The Pioneers* and the Ethnographic Impulse" (*AmerS* 15,ii:29–40) is a rambling essay not easily summarized; but its most noteworthy point is perhaps a comparison between persons described in the factual *Chronicles of Cooperstown* (1838) and parallel figures in the novel in order to show how Cooper deliberately suppressed colorful eccentricities in his fiction in order to convey a sense of "the characters in their classes." Subsequent American novelists, Ross feels, have subordinated this ethnographic impulse by paying more attention to the individual than to the "typal."

A poignant specific evidence of Cooper's portrayal of the reduction of the individual to the type is described in Lester H. Cohen's "What's in a Name? The Presence of the Victim in *The Pioneers*" (*MR* 16:688–98), which sees the white settlers' changing of the Indian Chingachgook's name to "John Mohegan" as "a symbolic act of annihilation that creates a smooth transition from the Indian past to the American future by absorbing into their culture only that aspect of the Indian which is congenial to their ongoing society." Another reference to the Leatherstocking tales that continue to dominate writing about Cooper, James E. Tanner's "A Possible Source for *The Prairie*" (AL 47:102–04), suggests that "the source of more than one incidental item enhancing the verisimilitude" of the novel may have been Samuel Woodworth's popular song "The Hunters of Kentucky," published in 1822. In one excursion into Cooper's other writings, "Cooper's *Lionel Lincoln*: The Problem of Genre" (*ATQ* 24[1974]:24–30), Donald A. Ringe strains to resolve the hitherto unsuspected problem that he insists the novel poses because, while Cooper described it as his "only historical tale," it is also his most Gothic romance. It is best seen, however, Ringe concludes, as an only partially successful psychological novel in which Lincoln becomes "what we recognize in the works of later writers as a center of consciousness." Perhaps the most intriguing speculations about Cooper, however, are in Allan M. Axelrad's "History and Utopia: A Study of the World View of James Fenimore Cooper" (*DAI* 36:296–97A), a University of Pennsylvania dissertation that is one of the most promising contributions to the study of this period reported in 1975. Axelrad argues that Cooper, influenced by Volney's *The Ruins,* expressed a life-long ideological conservatism based on the classical idea of history as a repeating cycle. Axelrad sees this vision most completely delineated in *The Crater* (1847), a novel built around the five stages of history illustrated in Thomas Cole's allegorical painting, "The Course of Empire." Also of interest to literary scholars in connection with this thesis is Joy S. Kasson's "*The Voyage of Life*: Thomas Cole and Romantic Disillusionment" (*AQ* 27:42–56), which points out how the series of allegorical paintings "sheds light on a dilemma of the romantic imagination which Cole shares with his American contemporaries Hawthorne, Poe and Melville"—and, we may add, Cooper.

Should there be a flowering of William Cullen Bryant studies, critics will find a wealth of new resources at their disposal. William Cullen Bryant III and Thomas G. Voss have edited *The Letters of William Cullen Bryant: Volume I: 1809–1836* (New York: Fordham Univ. Press), which carries the poet-editor through years of hardship and obscurity to his triumphal tour of Europe; and Judith Turner Phair has provided *A Bibliography of William Cullen Bryant and His Critics: 1808–1972* (Troy, N.Y.: Whitston), especially noteworthy for its useful annotations of material not everywhere available. Finally, in "The Patriarchal Mr. Bryant: Some New Letters" (*N&Q* 22:440–41), George Monteiro reproduces a correspondence in 1876 about a lithographic reproduction of a photograph that does indeed, as the editor suggests, manifest an unexpected "ego-involvement" for one celebrating his 81st birthday.

The only recent critical piece about Bryant, however, besides Judith Phair's introductory argument in her bibliography that he is "a far more interesting, complex, and controversial man than his chroniclers have made him" (p. 22), is Douglas A. Niven's "Bryant and Cole in the Catskills" (*BYNPL* 78:270–73), which supplies allegorical and iconographical interpretations to argue that the significance of Asher B. Durand's famous painting of the two friends, "Kindred Spirits," as "a commemoration of Cole's untimely death" has been unduly neglected.

Except in the general books already mentioned, Simms receives less attention than his northern counterparts. David Tomlinson's "Simms's Monthly Magazine: *The Southern and Western Monthly*

Magazine and Review" (*SLJ* 8,i:95–125) simply describes this 1845 periodical as a southern voice of the Young America movement, which supported native literature and international copyright. Simms gave up the effort after 12 issues because "it takes too greatly from the time which we should find more profitably bestowed upon individual labors." Paul Hamilton Hayne seems to have followed the same policies and reached the same conclusions during his attempts to edit literary journals in Charleston. Rayburn Moore supplements his TUSAS book on Hayne (1972) with "Paul Hamilton Hayne as Editor, 1852–1860" in *South Carolina Journals and Journalists*, ed. James B. Meriwether (Columbia: Univ. of S.C. Press), pp. 91–108, a detailed account that had to be omitted from the earlier book.

One grotesque individual labor is brought to light in Hans-Joachim Lang and Benjamin Lease's "The Authorship of *Symzonia*: The Case for Nathaniel Ames" (*NEQ* 48:241–52). Although written to argue for Ames's authorship of satire on the basis of similarities to his known works, the fascinating part is the matter satirized, the theories of Captain John Cleves Symmes that "the earth is hollow, habitable within" and open at the poles—one of our early Republic's most curious "landscape" theories.

iii. Popular Writers of the American Renaissance

The growing concern with the meaning of the landscape to the American experience surely accounts in part for resurgent interest in the frontier humorists. A competent guide to the study of them is at hand: M. Thomas Inge's editing of *The Frontier Humorists: Critical Views* (Hamden, Conn.: Archon). A conservative assemblage of noted overviews by pioneer scholars Franklin J. Meine, Donald Wade, and Walter Blair, with 17 more essays about individual figures and their influence on American literature, completed with a 20-page bibliography, Inge's anthology is not intended to serve as a fresh interpretation of the subject but to bring together the scattered materials that must provide the bases for further informed studies.

Inge's book is ideally complemented by J. A. Leo Lemay's "The Text, Tradition, and Themes of 'The Big Bear of Arkansas'" (*AL* 47:321–42), a model for bringing together information about a key work that exists in variant forms. Lemay explains his reasons for preferring the text in *The Spirit of the Times* (1845) to that of *The Hive of the Bee Hunter* (1854) that others have chosen as containing Thomas Bangs Thorpe's last revisions. Lemay thinks that Thorpe pedantically revised his colloquial prose to reach a more genteel audience. Lemay also argues that although the tale "is solidly within the traditions of American humor, its tone is elegiac and tragic," because "the death of the bear symbolizes the death of the wilderness" and of the "gamecock" man that inhabits it.

Richard H. Cracroft, in "'Half Froze for Mountain Doins': The Influence and Significance of George F. Ruxton's *Life in the Far West*" (*WAL* 10:29–43), continues the effort that Neal Lambert began last year to place the young Englishman's account of his travels beside such tales as Thorpe's as classic chronicles of vanished ways of life. Citing details from the many writers from Mayne Reid to Vardis Fisher who have drawn on Ruxton in their later fiction, Cracroft argues that *Life in the Far West* provided both "much of the matter, many of the characters, and most of the speech patterns" for subsequent depictions of the Mountain Man as well as "an initial exploration of the tensions inherent" in his lonely, reckless life.

To the general overviews collected in Inge's anthology might well be added James M. Cox's "Humor and America: The Southwestern Bear Hunt, Mrs. Stowe, and Mark Twain" (*SR* 83:573–601). In this general consideration of the rise of post-Renaissance "humor" out of the Medieval "humors," Cox claims that the works of the southwestern humorists, "more than any other antebellum literature, show the capacity of American writers to create as well as capture a strong determined dialect" by throwing "a frame of overrefined language around a wild dialect [that] released a remarkable humorous energy from the contrast." These humorists, Cox then argues, were put down by Harriet Beecher Stowe in *Uncle Tom's Cabin* and out of the ensuing conflict (both national and literary) Mark Twain emerged.

One of the southwestern humorists whose work is attracting increasing attention because of its modern relevance is saluted in Charles Israel's "Henry Clay Lewis's *Odd Leaves*: Studies in the Surreal and Grotesque" (*MissQ* 28:61–69). Israel points out Lewis's "conscious artistic use of violence, grotesque episodes and images, and surreal humor" to create a consistent world view of "chaos, alienation, injustice, and imminent despair."

A more startling effort to assert the "modernism" of a popular 19th-century writer is Frank D. McConnell's "Uncle Tom and the Avant

Garde" (*MR* 16:732–45). McConnell finds the "'unique' nature of a small but important number of American books"—including works of Gertrude Stein and Norman Mailer, as well as Harriet Beecher Stowe's *Uncle Tom's Cabin*—in their taking as "their *theme*, as well as their method," the establishment of that "world elsewhere," which Richard Poirier has identified as a key motif in American writing. This world, McConnell continues, is "a visionary republic which demands a new rhetoric, a stylistic 'tradition' of the unique and inimitable." He then goes even further and argues that such a book "insists upon itself as a quasi-legal, quasi-magical institutionalization of its own metaphor." John R. Adams, in "Structure and Theme in the Novels of Harriet Beecher Stowe" (*ATQ* 24[1974]:50–55), takes a less ecstatic view of the uniqueness of Stowe's work. While he does not come right out and say so, he builds a case that forces the reader to draw the conclusion that perhaps because the author had no respect for the novel as a literary type, except for *Uncle Tom's Cabin* her nine novels are "damaged by thin plots, eccentric change of emphasis, digressions, and other structural weaknesses."

Women writers of the period besides Mrs. Stowe continue to receive growing attention. John T. Frederick's "Hawthorne's 'Scribbling Women'" (*NEQ* 48:231–40) covers much the same ground as Henry Nash Smith's "The Scribbling Women and the Cosmic Success Story" (*ALS 1974*, p. 202); but Frederick's superficial account of Maria Susanna Cummins's *The Lamplighter* and other best-sellers of the 1850s provides by no means the useful and provocative introduction that Smith does.

A quite different body of the popular literature of the time is explored in Adrienne Siegel's "When Cities Were Fun: The Image of the American City in Popular Books, 1840–1870" (*JPC* 9:573–82), which takes a hurried tour of a host of forgotten works in order to illustrate the proposition that "in contrast to the sombre images of urban life projected by writers of *belles lettres*, the pop-book of the mid-19th century quite frequently pictured the city as an enticing haven, a refuge from the drudgery and monotony of an isolated rural existence."

Few would expect country-loving Louisa May Alcott to produce such works; but *Behind a Mask: The Unknown Thrillers of Louisa May Alcott*, ed. Madeleine Stern (New York: Morrow) proves that she could on occasion work in the vein of George Lippard's *The*

Quaker City to help meet her impractical family's constant need for money. Miss Stern reprints four Gothic pot-boilers that the young woman contributed—usually using the pseudonym of A. M. Barnard—to Boston penny-dreadfuls like *Flag of Our Union* during the 1860s. Thomas Pauly makes other surprising suggestions about Miss Alcott. Turning to Alcott's best-reputed novel, in "*Ragged Dick* and *Little Women*: Idealized Homes and Unwanted Marriages" (*JPC* 9:583–92), Pauly champions it as possibly "signalling her departure from the prevailing literary standard of her audience" by creating in Jo a character unique in being "a passionate supporter of the Victorian home who rejects the debilitating role it imposed on the women who maintained it." Both Alcott and Alger, Pauly concludes in this iconoclastic piece, entertain in their novels "the same vision of the altar and the happy home," yet "both commit their characters to positions which render such a future either highly improbable or of dubious success."

An equally grim view of the debilitating effects of Victorian mythology emerges from a new study of long-neglected works that are finally receiving the consideration that they deserve. John Stephen Martin dedicates "The Novels of Oliver Wendell Holmes" (*Literature and Ideas*, pp. 111–27) to pointing out how in his three novels Holmes "addressed his talents to a complex problem of his generation not properly noticed in existing commentaries." Martin feels that those who persist in believing that Holmes was building a case for deterministic influences shaping man's moral decisions have failed to read the novels "as literature." Martin argues that Holmes rather persisted in producing parables "of the threat of secular experience to Brahmins of even the best hereditary qualities," not because their Calvinism was illogical but because it "simply had not evidenced in the everyday world that condition of moral freedom necessary for choosing in the face of naturalistic forces" (pp. 125–26). Kathleen Gallagher's "The Art of Snake Handling: *Lamia*, *Elsie Venner*, and 'Rappacini's Daughter' " (*SAF* 3:51–64) also recalls one of Holmes's novels in order to make a strong case for the point that Keats's "Lamia" was a source for Hawthorne's fable and that both Keats and Hawthorne influenced Holmes's conception of *Elsie Venner*.

Some of Holmes's fellow "fireside poets" are receiving the most editorial attention that they have had for many years, although fresh critical discussions of their works remain infrequent. A new edition of James Russell Lowell's works is launched with Thomas Wortham's editing of *The Biglow Papers: A Critical Edition* (DeKalb: Northern Ill. Univ. Press); and one of the most ambitious efforts to reacquaint us with one of this group has come to fruition in John B. Pickard's three-volume edition of *The Letters of John Greenleaf Whittier* (Cambridge, Mass.: Harvard Univ. Press). (For a longer, more detailed review of this massive work than can be attempted here, see Roland Woodwell's essay in *Whittier Newsletter*, No. 14 [1976].) Pickard's work is supplemented by John C. Hepler's "A Letter from Charles Fenno Hoffman to Whittier" (*BNYPL* 79:96–98), which establishes a hitherto unnoted familiar relationship between the writers, and by Robert D. Arner's "Milton's Belial and Whittier's 'Ichabod'" (*ATQ* 24[1974], supp., pt. 1: 17–18), which argues that Whittier portrays Daniel Webster as analogous not to Milton's Satan but Satan's oratorically gifted henchman, Belial. Those seeking further information about Whittier should know that the *Whittier Newsletter* No. 13 describes Elizabeth Gray Vining's *Mr. Whittier* (New York: Viking, 1974) as a children's book, "a convenient and elementary summary of well known facts."

Longfellow, once by far the most prominent of Brahmin writers, is recalled only in Rayburn S. Moore's "'Merlin and Vivien'?: Some Notes on Sherwood Bonner and Longfellow" (*MissQ* 28:181–84), which suggests the influence of the innocently affectionate relationship between Katharine S. B. McDowell and the aging poet on a popular novel, *The Story of Margaret Kent* (1886) by Helen Hayes (pseudonym of Ellen Olney Kirke). Invoking a justifiably nostalgic note in "Oak Hall in American Literature" (*AL* 46:545–49), Steven Allaback reprints some parodies of Longfellow poems by a prosperous clothing-store operator to make the point that while some might find the parodies exploitative, today their like "could not happen because no poet is well known enough for parody . . . to work" (Not even the Beatles?).

While the once mighty thus languish, some obscure figures are being disinterred. Curtis Dahl must have blown away years of accumulated dust to get into "New England Unitarianism in Fictional Antiquity: The Romances of William Ware" (*NEQ* 48:104–15). Dahl points out that in *Zenobia*, *Aurelion*, and *Julian*, the clergyman-novelist followed a European tradition in blending "accurate historical description of the ancient world with vigorous expression of the new social and religious ideas of the Boston Unitarians." Elizabeth Evans, in "William Joseph Snelling: Still a Forgotten Critic" (*MarkhamR* 5:15–20), also revives the case that John T. Flanagan made in 1937 for this New Englander who in 1831 published *Truth: A Gift for Scribblers,* "a serious attempt to chastize bad writers and to encourage good ones," which has a tone "more akin to the acid of Byron than to the impish flaunting of Lowell in the more famous "A Fable for Critics."

iv. Henry Adams and the "Romantic Historians"

The work that has been done over the past five years of intensifying interest in Henry Adams is reviewed in more detail than it is possible to discuss here in Charles Vandersee's "Henry Adams (1838–1918)" (*ALR* 8:13–34), a follow-up to an account of earlier scholarship (*ALR* 2[1969]:89–120). Published just too late to receive Vandersee's attention in the new survey was James G. Murray's *Henry Adams* (New York: Twayne, 1974). This book is not part of the extensive United States Authors' Series, but one of a group of books about "great thinkers" in a "World Leaders Series." The inclusion of Adams in such a series poses problems, for, as Murray admits, "Adams did not conceive of himself as a philosopher" and rarely mentioned philosophy in his works (p. 115). Murray's book is thus not a description of a formal philosophical system, but a portrayal of a man whose personal philosophy gradually moved from a 19-century transcendentalism to a 20th-century existentialism.

Many people besides Adams have made exactly this kind of move during the past century, and Murray treats Adams not primarily as the unique individual most biographers have considered him but rather as an exemplar of man's modern condition. Murray stresses initially Adams's much discussed conception of himself as a "failure" and ends with a meditation on an aging Adams's increasing immersion in the silence that has engulfed many artists and thinkers who have found language no longer an adequate expression of phenomena.

The book cannot be recommended as an introduction to Adams. To get the most out of it, the reader needs already to know a good deal about Adams's life and works, and especially his conception of himself. The study may prove an inspiration, however, to readers who may be led to think through some of their own problems or to be consoled about the impossibility of reaching solutions by identifying their own concerns with those that are so brilliantly typified by Adams's.

The relationship of Adam's "failure" to the enigmatic relationship of Americans to the landscape so central to recent critical speculation is placed in thoughtful perspective in Jeanne Schinto's "The Autobiographies of Mark Twain and Henry Adams: Life Studies in Despair" (*MTJ* 17,iv:5–7), which connects the two writers by finding that "nostalgia for the lost era of the frontier and the corruption of the wilderness" are themes basic to both their memoirs. Adams's "Modernism" is pressed further, however, than in these new works or any older ones that I have seen in one of the most promising dissertations to be completed recently, Joseph Putnam Sperry's "Henry Adams and Thomas Pynchon: The Entropic Movements of Self, Society, and Truth" (*DAI* 35:5428A), which examines the thesis that "the further men move away from instinct and toward rationality in Adams and Pynchon, the more diffuse society becomes." These writers, Sperry concludes, then "turn to art as a means of coping with diffuse reality" by creating "order in an orderless world."

Still another facet of Adams's complex personality is illuminated in William A. Smith's "Henry Adams, Alexander Hamilton, and the American People as a 'Great Beast' " (*NEQ* 48:216–30), which tracks this famous metaphor that Adams attributed to Alexander Hamilton without documentation to a fourth-hand report of Theophilus Parsons, Jr., in his *Memoir of Theophilus Parsons* (1859). Smith perceives that, despite the shakiness of the source, the usually scrupulous Adams could not resist quoting this description of the common people as "a great beast" because the phrase so characterized his distasteful concept of Hamilton. Also revelatory of the Boston mind is a reprinting in Philip B. Eppard's "Frances Snow Compton Exposed: William Roscoe Thayer on Henry Adams as a Novelist" (*RALS* 5:81–94) of one of the earliest reviews of Adams's artistry once he was revealed as the author of his pseudonymous novels. Thayer's general approbation is highlighted by his comment that he doubts whether "any other American novelist has understood women's character more surely than Mr. Adams."

Adams's friend John Hay is also receiving increased attention. Last year's reprinting of his once anonymous novel *The Bread-Winners* is followed up by Kenton J. Clymer's *John Hay: The Gentleman as Dip-*

lomat (Ann Arbor: Univ. of Mich. Press), the first full-scale biography in more than 40 years of the poet-historian who rose to be Theodore Roosevelt's secretary of state. Concerned mostly with Hay's political activities, Clymer mentions the creative works only in passing; yet a valuable clue to understanding the dogged persistence of the genteel culture that Hay personified is Clymer's comment that his subject never rejected the antilabor philosophy of *The Bread-Winners*: "He resisted the social changes that resulted from changing technology and defended nineteenth-century capitalism as a moral system" (p. 209).

A model for a "literary" introduction to a slightly earlier Boston Brahmin turned historian is Donald G. Darnell's *William Hickling Prescott* (TUSAS 251). In a swift-moving, splendidly organized account, Darnell places Prescott against the background of his proud culture, illuminates his personal struggles with physical handicaps, and explains the qualities of his Spanish and Spanish-American histories that made him one of the most popular American historians. Darnell finds Prescott's work "symptomatic perhaps of a nostalgia for a point of view that saw patterns in history and a providence directing the destinies of men and nations." Darnell attributes Prescott's modern appeal, in part, to "our American longing for moral certitude" (p. 121).

Harold Beaver's "Parkman's Crack-Up: A Bostonian on the Oregon Trail" (*NEQ* 48:84–103) makes an important contribution to a controversy over Francis Parkman's *The Oregon Trail.* Although other critics have deplored the dilution of the Brahmin historian's original journals in the book, Beaver claims that Parkman's class and racial snobbism and beliefs in prudency, property, industry, and the sacred innocence of Victorian womanhood are alone responsible for the changes.

Since Frederick Jackson Turner, formulator of the famous and controversial "frontier thesis," warned against the subjectivism of "romantic historians," it may seem surprising to group him with them. Yet, as James D. Bennett recognizes in *Frederick Jackson Turner* (TUSAS 254), the "profound impact" that Turner has exerted upon the writing and teaching of American history is primarily inspirational rather than statistical. This determinedly quantitative historian has become renowned for the unique quality of his thought. Bennett correctly sums matters up when he writes that although "few historians today either accept the thesis in its totality or reject it completely," "rarely has a historian exerted as much influence on the course of American historiography" (pp. 100, 106). Since Turner—unlike the prolific Bostonians—found writing much more difficult than research or teaching, he left a remarkably small printed legacy. Bennett soundly, therefore, concentrates on the relationship of Turner's Wisconsin childhood and early training to his famous thesis and to the waves of attacks upon it and defenses of it. More than perhaps any other American historian, Turner, the man, has disappeared into the dramatic insight that has colored thinking about the United States and the meaning of its landscape for more than 80 years since he announced it in 1893. Bennett's well-focused study enables us to understand how this phenomeon could occur; it deserves to be widely read by those interested in a well-balanced account of one of those uncommon ideas that has taken on a life of its own and of the surprisingly unpontifical man behind it.

v. The Local Color Movement

A year marked by such a preoccupation with American attempts to formulate the historical role of the landscape would seem lacking in something essential if it brought no new comprehensive study of local color fiction—the most self-conscious effort of American writers to feature that landscape in their art. Robert D. Rhode provides the seemingly required piece in *Setting in the American Short Story of Local Color*, SAmL 30 (The Hague: Mouton). Rhode's "different way of asserting the significance of local color writing" is precisely by approaching it "from the standpoint, not of its regional content, but of its literary method of utilizing this content" (p. 38). Beginning with the obvious use of setting as background and ornament (which Rhode feels many writers relied upon to excess), he moves on to the subtler and—he judges—more successful efforts "to integrate setting with character" (p. 87) and finally to create settings which assume or even usurp "the function of character" (p. 136). Limiting himself to ten writers representing four regions (Jewett, Freeman, Page, Murfree, Allen, Cable, Eggleston, Garland, Harte, and Mark Twain), he concludes by calling attention to these principal local colorists' generally unnoticed preoccupation "with philosophical ideas in the rationale of their literary innovations in the use of landscapes or nature in general" (p. 169). Unfortunately, Rhode's construction of his account is often as awkward as his title; and the book remains too much a pedestrian transcript of note cards to become the imaginative fusion of subject and form that this tracing of the movement from physical to metaphysical use of regional landscape in literature deserves.

Rhode considers Sarah Orne Jewett (along with James Lane Allen) the most successful of the writers he examines in integrating setting and character. Bert Bender reinforces this judgment in "To Calm and Uplift 'Against the Dark': Sarah Orne Jewett's Lyric Narratives" (*CLQ* 11:219–29). Bender argues that Jewett's characters speak "with more realistic simplicity" than Wordsworth's, "but with a similar, confident, low-key quality that suggests the underlying unity with the landscape." As a result, he concludes, Jewett produces a lyric prose that goes beyond the logical and chronological conventions of normal prose fiction. Catharine Barnes Stevenson's "The Double Consciousness of the Narrator in Sarah Orne Jewett's Fiction" (*CLQ* 11:1–12) also presents the Maine writer's effects as often more subtle than has been realized. "Jewett in her more successful works," Stevenson maintains, "creates a narrator whose perceptions and emotions are far more complex than has been recognized." "Despite the attractiveness of the past" to such narrators, their desire to stop time (as Annette Kolodny points out Audubon would have), "is undercut by the recognition—conveyed through the imagery—that change is often both necessary and salubrious."

Finally, on the eve of his retirement, one of Miss Jewett's most persistent champions, Richard Cary, edits under the title of "Jewett to Dresel: 33 Letters" (*CLQ* 11:13–19) a new sheaf of letters written between 1886 and 1907 to genteel Bostonian Louisa Dresel that further illuminates our knowledge of Jewett's discerning taste in literary and artistic matters.

Again, as in 1974, Cary's meticulously edited *CLQ* is the only "regional" journal with an unflagging devotion to eastern local fiction. The writers of the South and West continue to be better served —perhaps because of the overwhelming preoccupation with the "frontiers" still fresh in the memory of these regions.

Two complex and convincing essays show great respect for the novel that is probably the local color movement's nearest approach to the epic, George Washington Cable's *The Grandissimes*. Both John

Cleman's "The Art of Local Color in George W. Cable's *The Grandissimes*" (*AL* 47:396–410) and Richard Bozman Eaton's "George W. Cable and the Historical Romance" (*SLJ* 8,i:82–94) agree—as Cleman puts it—that to read the novel "as an example of early realism in which most of [it] is ignored or only tolerated, is to miss a good deal of its artistry and perhaps much of its central concern." Both stress also the importance of Joseph Frowenfeld as the narrator. "In a way that strikingly foreshadows Faulkner," Cleman argues, "the progress of the book in its early stages is a gradual journey into the heart of a civilization, a careful unraveling process by which Frowenfeld and the reader come to know not only the core but also how the ball was wound." Eaton maintains that Cable attempted to assimilate the novel not only to the realistic novel of his own time, but also to the historical romance. Both writers finally find *The Grandissimes* another voicing of the general American concern with the landscape focused upon in so much of this year's criticism. Cleman sums up the matter in the statement that "rather than simply atavism the novel deals in a conflict of feelings about nature, a tension generated by the powerful but qualified admiration . . . for both the wilderness and the civilization that tries to pull away from it."

While Cable's "local color" is increasingly being perceived as romance with universal application, Joel Chandler Harris's is being scrutinized principally as imported folklore. D. J. M. Moffet's "Uncle Remus Was a Hausaman?" (*SFQ* 39:151–66) is a highly technical account of analogous linguistic patterns that suggest that the Uncle Remus tales may have had a specific African origin among the Sudanese Hausa tribes. A danger of treating artistically contrived stories as folklore, however, is suggested by Kathleen Light's "Uncle Remus and the Folklorists" (*SLJ* 7,ii:88–104), which points out that when John Wesley Powell of the Smithsonian Institution Bureau of Ethnology sparked Harris's interest in folklore, the writer could scarcely have foreseen that "ethnological considerations" would prove "a source of aggravation to him in *Nights with Uncle Remus* [1883] and would eventually lead him to the decision to retire Uncle Remus and to write "no more Negro tales." Light maintains that the trouble arose from a clash between the scientific theory that American Negro folklore represented a primitivistic stage of culture and Harris's original interpretation of the tales as "a type of compensatory fantasy which portrayed the triumph of the black man over the white society that had enslaved him." Michael Flusche enters the discussion in "Joel Chandler Harris and the Folklore of Slavery" (*JAmS* 9:347–63) to assert that in Harris's version of the folk stories the humor that was always present became predominant and that after his first two collections Harris "began to take greater liberties with his material." This analysis of Harris, however, is incidental to Flusche's general concern that as a result of selective reporting and of tailoring the material to white expectations, "the collections of folk material that have come down to us concerning slavery all suffuse a false atmosphere of Victorian propriety and sombre piety."

Turning to the Wild West, we find Sanford E. Marovitz looking at "Romance or Realism? Western Periodical Literature: 1893–1902" (*WAL* 10:45–58) and finding virtually what Flusche did. After scrutinizing four popular magazines of the period—*Harper's*, *Overland Monthly*, *The Cosmopolitan*, and *McClure's*—Marovitz reports that "most of the 'Western' writers for the monthlies were Easterners who had little or no genuine sense of the West," but who served proper Victorian Eastern editors and readers who "wanted to read of a romanticized and often sentimentalized West only vaguely based on truth."

Modern tastes are better served by the unsentimental, such as *Bill Nye's Western Humor*, selected and introduced by T. A. Larson (Lincoln: Univ. of Nebr. Press), and the writings of a genuine migrant to the West whose works are catalogued by Richard Etulain in "Mary Halleck Foote: A Checklist" (*WAL* 10:59–65). The most important article about Western writing this year, however, is Frederick W. Turner, III's "The Century after *A Century of Dishonor*: American Conscience and Consciousness" (*MR* 16:715–31), a contribution to a bicentennial gathering on American culture which reviews the book published in 1881 that author Helen Hunt Jackson looked upon as an analogue to *Uncle Tom's Cabin* in the struggle for Indian rights. Turner regretfully observes, however, that this powerful plea for justice "made impossible, not to say lunatic, demands on a still-expanding republic."

More to the taste of those expansive times were the works of the western illustrator whose also successful career as a writer is reviewed in Fred Erisman's *Frederic Remington* (WWS 16). Although "as a participant in the mythologizing of the American West," Remington has—Erisman acknowledges—principally been honored as painter and sculptor, he published eight books and many articles. Interest in these may be expected to rise in response to growing interest in Americans' attempts to articulate their relationship to the landscape, because—as Erisman points out—Remington spoke to Americans "in an era when they were rediscovering the natural world and looking to it as a cure for the ills of city life" and "articulates a highly personal system of values, embracing a respect for individualism, professional competence, the natural world, and the primitive" (p. 35).

vi. William Dean Howells and Genteel Realism

Slowly "A Selected Edition of W. D. Howells" (Bloomington: Ind. Univ. Press) takes shape. Last year's *April Hopes* (a novel originally published in 1887), edited by Kermit Vanderbilt, is followed by a most interesting autobiographical volume that includes the titular *Years of My Youth*, along with three shorter pieces, "Overland to Venice," "An Old Venetian Friend," and "A Young Venetian Friend," along with two sketchy outlines for other autobiographical works never executed, all edited by David J. Nordloh. More material of autobiographical value is summarized by Robert Rowlette in "Addenda to Halfmann: Six New Howells Interviews" (*ALR* 8:101–06). All the interviews described were given during a tour of the Midwest in 1899.

Criticism is beginning to shift from *A Modern Instance* and *The Rise of Silas Lapham* to Howells's less celebrated works. Susan Allen Toth's "Character and Focus in *The Landlord at Lion's Head*" (*CLQ* 11:116–28) reinforces and enlarges upon Paul A. Eschholz's recent argument (*ALS 1974*, p. 215) that Howells uses the novel to expose Bostonian artist Westover's incompetence in dealing with human nature. Toth argues that if Westover is seen as limited by "his self-inflicted isolation from any emotional contact or communication," the novel can no longer be regarded only as a study of landlord Jeff Durgin's amorality, but must be seen also as "a severe and often agonized examination of the kind of society Westover espouses and therefore represents."

Charles L. Crow, in "Howells and William James: 'A Case of Metaphantasmia' Solved" (*AQ* 27:169–77), advances the surprising claim that such "psychic romances" as *Questionable Shapes* "contain some of Howells' finest writing and anticipate . . . key issues and concerns of twentieth-century fiction." He then demonstrates his point by "solving" the story mentioned in his title and crediting Howells with inventing in it "a form of stream-of-consciousness narrative years before the writers who gave it literary currency."

John W. Crowley's "Howells' *Questionable Shapes*: From Psychologism to Psychic Romance" (*ESQ* 21:169–78) contradicts Crow on several points. Crowley first finds that the psychic romances "do not measure up to [Howells'] best work" and then observes that they offer no final answers to the problems raised. Crowley thinks that the importance of these works lies in Howells's "struggle to treat realistically material seemingly immune to realistic treatment," which he did solve by presenting psychic case histories within the ancient device of a fictional frame, so that "he could at once leave the psychic phenomenon inviolate and establish the aesthetic distance which his agnosticism demanded between himself and it."

Crowley turns also to one of Howells's psychological problems in "Howells's Obscure Hurt" (*JAmS* 9:199–211), to argue that in *A Fearful Responsibility* (1881) Howells exorcises the guilt he felt about not participating in the Civil War that he had struggled with in *A Foregone Conclusion* (1875), "by employing the opportunity of non-participation—the challenge of interpreting not the war itself . . . but rather its profound effects on American culture." Howells then, Crowley continues, was able to abandon international themes to begin a critical exploration of the postwar United States. Yet even so late a work as "Editha" (1907) suggests that he may have borne the "obscure hurt" of guilt to the end.

Fiction *about* the Civil War has also been resurrected. Cruce Stark's "The Man of Letters as a Man of War: James K. Hosmer's *The Thinking Bayonet*" (*NEQ* 48:47–64) describes an inept novel published in 1865 by a young minister who enlisted as a Union private after graduating in 1862 from Harvard Divinity School. Stark outlines Hosmer's inspirational story of a fighting scholar who rises through the ranks of the army to document the uplifting thesis that the intellectual must demonstrate both "masculine equality with the common man" and "superior leadership." In "A Boy's Own War" (*NEQ* 48:362–77) Sam Pickering finds much the same moralizing optimism characterizing New England attitudes toward the war in novels for boys by Horatio Alger, Harry Castlemon [Charles Fosdick], and Oliver Optic [William T. Adams].

Howells's utopian writings received no special attention this year; but Tom H. Towers's "The Insomnia of Julian West" (*AL* 47:52–63) puts forward the arresting argument that Edward Bellamy's *Looking Backward* is "at heart . . . not a document of social reform so much as a romance of the loss and restoration of individual selfhood," which is "informed by Bellamy's acute awareness that a traditionally unified consciousness is impossible in a society mortally divided by the class warfare of modern industrialism." Towers finds the leading character's insomnia symbolic of his "nineteenth-century agony," but contends also that the sleep Julian West finds in the 21st-century is connotative of "passive oblivion," suggesting "the failure of both the futurism and the nostalgia" of Bellamy's views.

Last year I gathered writings about Charles W. Chesnutt among studies of local colorists, but I think this was a mistake. I also think that Chesnutt's work should be treated not just with that of other black writers but also with the productions of the genteel traditionalists because of his unique importance among both groups of writers.

Writing in 1975 concentrated on how well we really know Chesnutt. William L. Andrews's "A Reconsideration of *Charles Waddell Chesnutt: Pioneer of the Color Line*" (*CLAJ* 19:136–51) argues that "the fullness of Chesnutt's opinions, feelings and thoughts as reflected in the Fisk [University] Chesnutt Collection does not appear" in his daughter's 1952 biography, because of editorial practices that tended to oversimplify, to delete the unpleasant or controversial, and to lionize the man rather than look at him objectively. Robert O. Sedlack's "The Evolution of Charles Chesnutt's *The House Behind the Cedars*" (*CLAJ* 19:125–35) identifies three stages in the composition of this work that the author "cared about more deeply than any other," during which it evolved from "a sketchy short story that attacks racial prejudice obliquely" to a novel "that placed the blame for the tragic unhappiness of both black and white characters squarely on white racism." (See also Black Literature, ii. Fiction.)

Philip B. Eppard's "Rebecca Harding Davis: A Misattribution" (*PBSA* 69:265–67) corrects a curious but quite serious mistake about another realistic writer who was much concerned with social and racial issues. Eppard explains that the novel *Pro Aris et Focis* sometimes attributed to Mrs. Davis (for reasons too complicated to go into here) is actually the work of an ultraconservative British writer, Fanny Aikin Kortright. The error has had regrettable consequences because the views expressed in the novel about woman's place in society have confounded those who have taken them for Mrs. Davis's definitive statement on the matter, despite the utter inconsistency of these views with her usual positions.

In "Shifting Interpretation of Protestantism" (*JPC* 9:593–603) David S. Reynolds examines the evolving position of those committed to the Social Gospel of the late 19th-century as embodied in the two best-selling novels of these genteel militants: Edward P. Roe's *Barriers Burned Away* (1873) and Charles M. Sheldon's *In His Steps* (1897). In the earlier novel, Reynolds explains, we see "a farm boy rise to respectability by being a good Christian"; but the latter "portrays a group of socially established Protestants relinquishing prosperity and eagerly accepting the burdens of poverty in the interest of society." This change in direction is indicative of the Social Gospel's redefinition of philanthropy.

vii. The Ironic Vision of Stephen Crane

Surprisingly, the only critical book in 1975 to be devoted exclusively to a single one of the many creative writers considered in this chapter is Frank Bergon's *Stephen Crane's Artistry* (New York: Columbia Univ. Press), but it more than compensates for the paucity of others. I wish that everyone had something as new to say as Bergon does before venturing into print. His effort is not entirely successful, but it surely suggests a rewarding new way of looking not only at Crane, but at other artists as well.

Bergon begins forthrightly: "This book is concerned with Stephen Crane's habit of imagination as it declares itself throughout his work—that personal quality of awareness which informs his work and makes it uniquely his own" (p. vii). He ends portentously proclaiming that Crane "went beyond the rim of normal perception and transformed the truly significant into the color and form of certain apparitional moments, which by their nature are inevitably intense, fleeting, radiant, sometimes dreadful, sometimes splendid, always awesome" (pp. 148–49). The key words in the passages just quoted—*awareness* and *perception*—have both physical and metaphysical senses; the flutteriness of the book comes from Bergon's hovering between the two like an uncertain bee who because he cannot settle on one exhausts neither. Bergon employs another word that also turns up at the end

—*apparitional*—so doggedly throughout the book that he seems always about to call Crane a visionary, but he never quite does. Is he frightened at the possible temerity or does he seek to create a montage that will force the reader to draw the conclusion for himself? Perhaps the stopping short must be blamed on the critical decorum instilled by our graduate schools and academic presses to tame the wildeyed.

I intend no disparagement of a book full enough of discerning fragmentary insights to crowd this chapter with quotations; but Bergon opens rather than closes doors, so that those pursuing the truth with magic-marking pencils may become perturbed. Bergon's statement of Crane's aims seems to express his own: "The ultimate purpose of his art seems to be a creation of a similar artistic sensibility in the reader himself" (p. 58). This follows upon a brief consideration of the opening section of the first and final drafts of "Moonlight on the Snow," a discussion which best illustrates Bergon's theories about Crane's transformation of the "realistic" into the apparitional. It is these theories that have made me see Crane's relationship to the persistent theme of recent criticism—the American struggle to discover the meaning of the landscape, especially the wilderness frontier: Crane found the Old West particularly congenial for his storytelling because its landscape was literally disappearing before his eyes—the authentic being superseded by the artificial, the hallucinatory.

Bergon draws about as extensively upon Crane's gnomic poetry as on his fiction. Access to the verses that have grown increasingly appealing to critics over the years will be greatly facilitated by two new reference works: Herman Baron's *A Concordance to the Poems of Stephen Crane* (Boston: G. K. Hall, [1974]), ed. Joseph Katz and keyed to Katz's *The Poems of Stephen Crane: A Critical Edition*; and Andrew T. Crosland's *A Concordance to the Complete Poetry of Stephen Crane* (Detroit: Gale Research), which may be more in demand—though it costs more than twice as much—because it is keyed to *Poems and Literary Remains*, volume 10 of the CEAA edition of Crane's works, ed. Fredson Bowers (Charlottesville: Univ. Press of Va.).

This uniquely useful volume last mentioned contains not only texts of Crane's collected and uncollected poems, with Bowers's history and analysis of them, but also transcriptions of all the "known independent unfinished manuscripts," notes by Cora Crane for a proposed biography of Stephen, two newly discovered publications —a fable and a New York City sketch—eleven pages of corrections and revisions to previous volumes, and an index of assigned and variant titles in the whole 10-volume set. The long-awaited volume 2, containing *The Red Badge of Courage*, also edited by Fredson Bowers, has also appeared; and the edition becomes complete in 1976 with volume 3, containing Bowers's editing of the two late novels, *The Third Violet* and *Active Service.*

We are thus supplied with the kind of exhaustive, meticulously edited materials for the study of Crane that we as yet lack for any other American novelist. Let us hope that the University of Virginia's exemplary production of this magisterial edition establishes a precedent to be followed soon and often again.

The text of the newly discovered fable mentioned above—the earliest known by Crane—is also reprinted from *Puck* (Feb. 7, 1894) in William L. Andrews's "A New Stephen Crane Fable" (*AL* 47:113–14). Another discovery is reported in Robert A. Morace's "A 'New' Review of *The Red Badge of Courage*" (*ALR* 8:163–65), which reprints John O'Hara Cosgrave's comments from San Francisco's *The Wave* (Oct. 19, 1895), only the third known contemporary review from the West Coast.

Bergon's comprehensive critique of Crane's artistry is complemented by several recent considerations of individual works. In the most ambitious of these, "Impressionism in 'The Open Boat' and 'A Man and Some Others'" (*RS* 43:27–37), James Nagel tries to work out what Joseph Conrad meant when he called Crane "an impressionist." Nagel's argument reinforces Bergon's by pointing out that the insight in both stories named in the title "is related to both literal and figurative developments in perception." These insights involved "the recognition of a distinction between reality and what man perceives as reality" and "the development of a new level of perception, the revision of thought to perceive nature now as indifferent"; and these two insights Nagel considers "the most explicit impressionistic themes" in Crane's work.

Less sympathetically, John R. Cooley in "'The Monster'—Stephen Crane's 'Invisible Man'" (*MarkhamR* 5:10–14) contradicts earlier criticism by arguing that the story reflects both "an artistic maladroitness or a loss of nerve in handling a character who demanded utmost care" and "a sadly limited racial consciousness." According to Stanley

Wertheim's "Stephen Crane's 'A Detail'" (*MarkhamR* 5:14–15), one can discover the "dramatic irony" in this New York city sketch only by realizing that the two girls are actually streetwalkers mistaken for gentlewomen by a naive old lady. Finally, Clarence O. Johnson in "Crane's 'I Was in the Darkness'" (*Expl* 34:item 6) suggests that this poem based on Crane's rejection of his parents' religion is more likely to have been based on Matthew IV:16 than on Psalm 18, as has been assumed.

viii. Frank Norris and the 1890s: Naturalism and Decadence

Frank Bergon's *Stephen Crane's Artistry* suggests also a vivid rationale for describing much of the "naturalistic" fiction of the last decade of the 19th century as decadent. By then the effort to "stop time" that Annette Kolodny attributes to John James Audubon has deteriorated into a complete schism between physical and psychic that leads either to utter escape from the landscape through annihilation (in Kate Chopin's *The Awakening* or later in Jack London's *Martin Eden*) or complete capitulation of an untrustworthy consciousness to a natural order embodied in the landscape (in Frank Norris's *McTeague* and *The Octopus*).

A great aid to a probable expansion of the already increasingly intense study of one these authors will be *Frank Norris: A Reference Guide*, ed. Jesse E. Crisler and Joseph R. McElrath, Jr. (Boston: G. K. Hall, 1974), which provides a chronological list of Norris studies through 1972. Many of these disagreeing criticisms are scanned in Richard A. Davison's "Frank Norris's *The Octopus*: Some Observations on Vanamee, Shelgrim, and St. Paul" (*Literature and Ideas*, pp. 182–203) in order to provide a background for stressing once again that "Vanamee is a much more reliable philosophical frame of reference for the author than is usually granted," "a barometer of the moral implications of the novel" (p. 193). Davison sees Norris as closer to Hawthorne and Melville than to his contemporary muckrakers, because "in *The Octopus* when man lives for goodness or dies tragically aware, he does so in the matrix of a well-ordered universe. . . . In this real world Norris creates it is possible for a mystic to vibrate with the fecund rhythm of nature—Emerson's or Whitman's vast continuum" (p. 198).

Something of Norris's concern with a natural order is indicated also in D. B. Graham's "Art in *McTeague*" (*SAF* 3:143–55). Graham defends Norris's own defense of the ending of the novel against many detractors: "Thematically and structurally the ending of *McTeague* is justified; far from being anticlimactic, it climaxes the evaluation of landscapes, of interior and exterior space, that forms a central and controlling tension in the novel." Graham then shows how a chromo of Millet's "The Angelus" gauges "the extent of McTeague's estrangement from tradition and tranquility" and how "if McTeague's cardinal aesthetic principle is space, Trina's is constriction." McTeague at last escapes "Trina's rat-hole world," but only to enter Death Valley, "the ultimate Darwinian landscape . . . the furtherest possible remove from Millet's ploughed ground." Graham also suggests, in "Aesthetic Experience in Realism" (*ALR* 8:289–90), the attention that Norris lavished on "interior decoration and the problem of perception."

Although Louis J. Budd's "Objectivity and Low Seriousness in American Naturalism" (*Prospects* 1:41–61) is broadly concerned with literary Naturalism as a "new plane" that can be described negatively "as a swearing off from comedy, satire, and irony," Budd's analysis focuses on *McTeague*. He considers that "the controlling purpose" of the novel is "to shift away from satire and resume the portrait of a blundering, simple-minded, burly, and inarticulate man." "Though naturalism as a rallying cry is passé," Budd concludes, "the options it established will stay vital so long as the insensitive or self-centered or the privileged or the ironically minded deny others a literary hearing on their own terms." "Passé" may not, however, be the judgment that is to the point here; rather, while many of the quarrels over a definition of Naturalism now seem banal, those works that have been grouped as Naturalistic may take on a new significance when viewed not as bold new formal experiments, but as the forms that the American dream took when—bereft of its genteel pretensions —it decayed into nightmare.

Study of the *Damnation of Theron Ware*, the novel that is winning increasing attention as a key fictional embodiment of American pastoral decadence, will be greatly facilitated by a companion volume to the Norris reference guide mentioned above, *A Bibliography of Writing by and About Harold Frederic*, comp. Thomas F. O'Donnell, Stanton Garner, and Robert H. Woodward (Boston: G. K. Hall).

Other work on Frederic in 1975 includes two similar essays in

Nineteenth-Century Fiction. Scott Donaldson's "The Seduction of Theron Ware" (29:441–52) attributes the title character's downfall to "the unholy gospel of expediency which Sister Soulsby preaches"—a gospel based on the pragmatic planks that "good and evil co-exist in all of us" and that one must manipulatively attempt to be all things to all men. Donaldson's rather sketchy analysis is much broadened in Luther S. Luedtke's "Harold Frederic's Satanic Soulsby: Interpretation and Sources" (30:82–104), which also sees Sister Candace as "the agent of a *damnation* that has moral as well as social reality," because her teachings doom Theron Ware "to a future of venery without love and opportunism without hope." Luedtke thus reads the novel not as a story "of reconciliation to the community but of a driving out and a rejection of the moral affirmation on which true community rests." He also finds models for Frederic's work in Dickens's *Bleak House* and perhaps British women's leader Lucy Helen Muriel Soulsby.

More perceptive and important than either of these carefully documented arguments, however, is Thomas LeClair's "The Ascendant Eye: A Reading of *The Damnation of Theron Ware*" (*SAF* 3:95–102). While agreeing that Ware becomes "the makeshift creation of Sister Soulsby," LeClair is principally concerned with the novel as a forerunner of the intensive Modernist concern with identity problems. "At the center of the book," he begins, "is a conception of identity as extrinsic and provisional . . . awarded to the individual by the looks and comments of others." Since all of the other characters "are wrong about Theron's superiority and potential for transformation" and because he himself "lacks a sense of himself independent of others' characterization," "he comes to have an over-blown sense of his capacities for expanding the self." Thus he "does not simply avoid the truth by turning his eyes away from it; he also invents a replacement for reality by projecting his own wishes into the eyes of others." Fascinated with this self-created apparition, Theron Ware is self-damned.

Interested in anchoring the novel not in such debates about its contemporary significance but rather in the classical literary tradition, Thomas F. O'Donnell, in "Theron Ware, the Irish Picnic, and *Comus*" (*AL* 46:528–37), explores a possible source in Milton's masque, itself a variation on the ancient myth of Circe. O'Donnell points out in detail ways in which the Irish picnic episode, by far the longest in the novel, "unfolds as a version of [*Comus*] so revised as to reflect moral ambiguities and ironies characteristic of Gilded Age America."

Last year Kate Chopin was discussed among the local colorists; but the emphases in recent criticism make me feel that the regional elements in her fiction (distractingly exotic as Louisiana settings are) are incidental to her contribution to the artistic portrayal of dissociated sensibilities that culminates in T. S. Eliot's "Waste Land" writings and other central documents of Modernism.

My thesis is strongly supported by Robert D. Arner's "Kate Chopin" (*LaS* 14:5–139). Although presented as a "Special Kate Chopin Issue" of a Southern interdisciplinary journal, with a foreword by Lewis P. Simpson, Arner's book-by-book analysis of all of Chopin's works is actually a substantial book in itself, designed to illustrate his perception that in her later work, Chopin shifts her attention from local color "to motivation" and "usually attempts to integrate setting and ethnic background into plot and characterization" (p. 16). Arner stresses especially something that I believe relates Chopin's conception of motivation to that of the Naturalist/Decadents. He argues that the short story "A Lady of Bayou St. John" is centrally important to Chopin's work because "Madame Delisle's decision to remain true to the memory of her husband is not made in response to the promptings of morality," but is "instead the result of a quirk in her character" (p. 60). Since such characters lack either the stability fostered by adherence to an imposed morality or adequate self-awareness, they suffer frequent identity problems and, for others besides Edna in *The Awakening*, "freedom is possible only in death" (p. 88). "In Kate Chopin's view," Arner continues in his analysis of the story "Vagabonds," that character who "lives close to the primitive and uninhibited . . . is [the] closer to the genuine" (p. 129).

What is especially valuable about Arner's monograph is his unprecedented concern with Chopin's self-conscious artistry and structural skill, which leads him in discussing "Désirée's Baby," for example, to observe that those who pay attention to the clues woven into the story will have "little reason to object that the ending . . . is contrived to satisfy the reader's sense of justice" (p. 54). Since this study can be extraordinarily useful in suggesting the value of stories that have often been overlooked in the concentration on *The Awakening*—especially their use in all kinds of introductory thematic and structural literary studies—I hope that a publisher will prevail upon Arner to revise his work and reinforce it with an annotated bibliography and an index in order to encourage the wider circulation it deserves. Some revision is desirable, since the excellent summaries and analyses provided are not as fully linked together as they might be. Missing is some overarching thesis about the development and fictional embodiment of Kate Chopin's vision that would link it more closely with Norris's and Frederic's.

The identity problem that Arner discerns in many of the stories is also treated in two essays by Peggy Skaggs. "Three Tragic Figures in Kate Chopin's *The Awakening*" (*LaS*[1974]:345–64) finds each of three principal female figures in this best-known work "tragic in her inability to achieve her full identity." Edna, Skaggs continues, is different from the others, however, in that she refuses to accept a partial identity as "mother-woman" or "artist-woman," so that "unable in her milieu to have a full human identity," she "chooses to have none at all." In " 'The Man-Instinct of Possession': A Persistent Theme in Kate Chopin's Stories" (*LaS* 14:277–85), Skaggs examines how the women in other stories often "find their sense of identity" through relationships "made painful and unrewarding by male possessiveness." The critic then persuasively traces "a remarkable maturing" of Chopin's handling of this theme during the few years separating the sentimental "A No-Account Creole" from the shocking "The Story of an Hour."

The most comprehensive and convincing of the many analyses that have so far appeared of *The Awakening* is Otis B. Wheeler's "The Five Awakenings of Edna Pontellier" (*SoR* 11:118–28). Wheeler observes that the novel enraged Victorian reviewers not because of Edna's adultery and suicide, but rather "because she so totally rejected the pervasive Victorian notion that sexual love is, or should be, a variety of religious experience." Although in the bulk of her fiction, Wheeler continues, Chopin embodies "changing or ambiguous views" of the sexual roles of the female as "angel in the house" or "scarlet woman" assigned by the Victorian mind, in *The Awakening* she "coolly rejects both mythic roles," as does her heroine. But whereas Edna Pontellier is reduced to existential despair, the novelist's "rejection is a balanced act of the imagination . . . discovering to the reader the inauthenticity of the myths."

Bernard J. Koloski, author of one of the most perceptive earlier readings of *The Awakening* (*ALS 1974*, p. 211), turns his attention to Chopin's earlier novel to argue in "The Structure of Kate Chopin's *At Fault*" (*SAF* 3:89–95) that although this work displays "a keenness of insight and a sureness of structure characteristic of Kate Chopin at her best," its concluding episode, in which the heroine "largely through chance, manages to unify her two realms and achieve a sense of peace," is not, "like the closing scene of *The Awakening*, the inevitable result of the heroine's actions throughout the novel." Elsewhere in the same journal Donald A. Ringe in "Cane River World: Kate Chopin's *At Fault* and Related Stories" (*SAF* 3:157–66) maintains, much as Robert Arner does in his long study, that while *At Fault* "exhibits some of the thinness and lack of control of a first novel," its happy ending serves "an important thematic function." Certain characters are destroyed, Ringe argues, because they are incapable of change; but with the marriage of Thérèse and David, "the potential for change in the Cane River world at last can be fulfilled." "To a very great extent," he concludes, the novel is "about the changing social world of the post-Reconstruction South."

Other work on Chopin includes Thomas Bonner, Jr.'s "Kate Chopin's European Consciousness" (*ALR* 8:281–84), which reminds us that although Chopin's reputation during her lifetime rested upon her regional writings, 34 of the 51 stories uncollected then are set elsewhere and that the stories with European settings are her "laboratory experiments with unorthodox themes and subjects." Emily Toth's "The Independent Woman and 'Free' Love" (*MR* 16:647–64) also relates *The Awakening* to concerns that European women writers displayed at the end of the 19th century. Toth has begun editing a *Kate Chopin Newsletter* at the University of North Dakota, and Bonner, in "Kate Chopin: An Annotated Bibliography" (*BB* 33:101–05), describes the abundant criticism of her work since 1970.

Another neglected woman writer of the 1890s is claiming a place beside Kate Chopin. Both Beate Schöpp-Schilling's " 'The Yellow Wallpaper': A Rediscovered 'Realistic' Story" (*ALR* 8:824–86) and Loralee MacPike's "Environment as Psychopathological Symbolism in 'The Yellow Wallpaper' " (*ALR* 8:286–88) deal with this fictional history of a wife's "psychic disintegration" that Charlotte Perkins Gilman published in 1892.

Scholars continue to find Ambrose Bierce's personality as intriguing as his bizarre tales. Joseph W. Slade's " 'Putting You in the

Papers': Ambrose Bierce's Letters to Edwin Markham" (*Prospects* 1:335–68) prints correspondence between 1896 and 1899, illustrating how Bierce's initial "paternal, even proprietary interest" in Markham turned to hostility when Bierce was upset by the poet's extreme political stance in his sensationally successful "The Man with the Hoe." Bierce regarded the protest against the degradation of the farm worker as "a cry of unjustified rage." In "Some New Ambrose Bierce Fables" (*ALR* 8:349–52) William L. Andrews reprints from *Fantastic Fables* (1898) six negligible "Fables of the Deep Blue Sea" that Bierce understandably omitted from his *Collected Works.*

A more ambitious essay in rediscovery gives us a book about a kind of subject infrequently studied—a superseded literary historian. Robert T. Self's *Barrett Wendell* (TUSAS 261) recalls one of the last of the Boston Brahmins, whose pioneering *A Literary History of America* (1900) "probably helped to solidify the professional attitude against American literature in the universities" (Preface). Self labors valiantly to refute the negative picture usually offered of Wendell by exploring the ways in which his innovations in the teaching of composition and literature during his years at Harvard (1880–1917) lightened the path for later artists and critics; but Self constantly labors under the handicap of Wendell's inability to decide what he believed in. While this book illuminates the way in which Wendell's concern over his country's "national inexperience" and his despair about the future made him an easy target for positive thinkers, the principal result of this revival is to show how Wendell—like many transitional figures—seems inconsequential to a later age, because the issues that he found impossible to resolve simply no longer seem worth bothering about. In the light of the growing interest in Frank Norris, Harold Frederic, and Kate Chopin, Barrett Wendell is most intriguing as the last decayed stump of the once-flourishing genteel Brahmin tradition; Self has missed the note that would give his subject a particular interest today.

Ross C. Murfin's "The Poetry of Trumbull Stickney: A Centennial Rediscovery" (*NEQ* 48:540–55) provides a fitting conclusion for this essay that deals with 19th-century Americans' "conscious and determined struggle to formulate for themselves the meaning of this landscape." Gilded-Age versifier Stickney exhibited the ultimate reaction to his native landscape by rejecting it altogether. Murfin examines the productions of this scion of a wealthy, expatriate Hartford family, which restlessly sought a peaceful place to study classical literature, and centers upon the poem "In Ampezzo" to illustrate "the conflict between the desired and the possible in life" that drove Stickney "to escape from the autumn landscape's reality into various visions," which nourish him in "memory, childhood, ecstasy, power, and death."

After reading the material discussed in this review, I feel more confidence about the future of American literary scholarship than at any time during the decade that I have worked on this project. Although the coincidence of the publication of Annett Kolodny's, Lewis Simpson's, James Bennett's, Anne Scott MacLeod's, and Frank Bergon's books was unplanned, they are closely related to each other in that all deal with significant contributions to understanding how over the course of the 19th-century the land of promise that had been the United States was transformed into an apparition of despair. The books are effectively complemented by perceptive articles—to cite only a few indispensable to future studies—by Thomas Pauly, Harold Kaplan, James Nagel, Frank McConnell, Catharine Barnes Stevenson, and Otis Wheeler, all of which deal with some aspect of the American's relationship to his once unexploited landscape, turning from loving but perhaps careless embrace to disenchanted rejection. Almost nothing that I perused this year has proved to be the waste of time or space that so many American academic exercises have been in the recent past. And there are at least 60 new doctoral dissertations —to which I cannot do detailed justice—that deal with individual writers or general subjects from this period. Many of these apprentice works parallel, in some measure, the studies discussed here; but, although these parallels may prove frustrating when the new scholars seek publication, I think that they are evidence not of stagnation, but rather of the excitement that attends the opening of any new territory when many perceptive explorers are making complementary discoveries faster than news of them can be disseminated.

Indiana University–Purdue University at Indianapolis

13. Fiction: 1900 to the 1930s

David Stouck

In 1975 the women writers covered in this chapter received by far the greatest amount of critical attention. Interest in Cather, Wharton and Stein produced seven new volumes of literary criticism and a bibliography for library shelves, while criticism of novelists like Anderson and Dos Passos, on the other hand, resulted in only a handful of unimportant articles. Books of criticism often originate in doctoral theses; perhaps the future trend is reflected in the dissertations completed in 1975, which were more or less evenly distributed among the different authors and were frequently comparative in approach.

No books or articles addressed themselves specifically to this period of American literature, but of some interest is "Eden, Oedipus, and Rebirth in American Fiction" (*ArQ* 31:353–65) by William L. Nance, who argues that the 19th-century quest for Eden in the wilderness is transformed by the 20th century to a tale of Oedipal conflict, where a young man pursuing Eden in the form of a beautiful woman is stopped by an older, stronger man. Nance cites Anderson's Winesburg story, "An Awakening," Cather's *A Lost Lady*, and Dreiser's *An American Tragedy* as classic examples.

A potentially useful tool for the graduate student is Noel Polk's "Guide to Dissertations on American Literary Figures, 1870–1910" (*ALR* 8:177–279, 291–348). Authors represented in this essay include Mary Austin, Willa Cather, Robert Herrick, Booth Tarkington, Edith Wharton, and Owen Wister. Dissertations on each author are described in separate essays; the essayist outlines briefly the theses, comments on the various patterns and trends in scholarship, and indicates where parts of dissertations have been published. A more specialized kind of bibliography can be found in Frances King's "Treatment of the Mentally Retarded Character in Modern American Fiction" (*BB* 32:106–14).

i. Willa Cather

Again Willa Cather received the largest amount of attention with the appearance in 1975 of three book-length studies, a bibliography, and 15 critical articles of some interest. Cather is now represented in the Twayne series with Philip L. Gerber's *Willa Cather* (TUSAS, 258), a substantial introduction to this author, but one which diverges somewhat from the Twayne format. Instead of focusing squarely on Cather's major works, Gerber has shaped his study around a thesis. He sees Cather's novels turning on two major themes: youth's struggle toward accomplishment and America's fall to materialism. Gerber examines these themes carefully, draws examples from Cather's early short fiction and criticism as well as the novels, and effectively demonstrates a thematic unity in the author's work. But the thesis is presented at the expense of a close examination of the major works. As the most detailed study of youth's climb toward a significant goal, *The Song of the Lark* is given extensive consideration, while *My Ántonia*, a finer novel, serves largely as an anti-thesis for, as Gerber argues, the heroine of that novel serves life rather than a transcendent ambition. Similarly *One of Ours* is treated comprehensively as Gerber shows how "in the late 1920s the spectacle of her 'geliebtest' land at the mercy of moneygrubbers became [Cather's] major lament"; *Death Comes for the Archbishop* examined in this same light is discussed briefly as an elegy for a way of life betrayed by materialism.

Probably more valuable are Gerber's chapters on the author's life and on her artistic principles. In recounting the biographical findings of other scholars, Gerber places emphasis on the long apprenticeship that Cather served and on the internal struggles and doubts she must have experienced before finding her true vocation as novelist. This is a healthy emphasis, for in retrospect it is too easy to see the young artist moving without hesitation toward her remarkable destiny. Gerber also gives an interesting review of Cather's growing reputation as her novels were published and assesses her position in the pantheon of American letters.

The chief purpose of David Stouck's *Willa Cather's Imagination* (Lincoln: Univ. of Nebr. Press) is to illuminate the timeless and universal dimensions of Cather's art. Stouck examines the Cather canon from three critical vantage points: mode, form, and theme.

The study is not biographical, but follows roughly the chronological development of the author's career and brings her life and art into some conjunction.

Part 1 of Stouck's book illustrates the breadth of Cather's imagination by considering the various modes through which her fiction moves. Such early stories as "Eric Hermannson's Soul" and two novels, *Alexander's Bridge* and *O Pioneers!*, are viewed in the light of the epic imagination, while *My Ántonia*, *A Lost Lady*, and numerous stories and poems are considered as pastorals. *One of Ours* and *The Professor's House* are discussed as works of the critical or satirical imagination. Part 2 explores the depth of Cather's moral vision and the literary forms she found to express it. Stouck sees three of Cather's major works as comprising a "mortal comedy": he looks at *My Mortal Enemy*, a novella, as incisively dramatizing an "inferno" of self-hatred; *Death Comes for the Archbishop*, a saint's legend, as presenting a paradisal vision; and *Shadows on the Rock*, a historical novel, as giving a glimpse of man's purgatorial suffering in a world burdened with time.

Part 3 looks at art's relation to life, a theme running throughout Cather's fiction. *The Song of the Lark* and those writings in which art is viewed most positively are contrasted with Cather's last four books (*Obscure Destinies*, *Lucy Gayheart*, *Sapphira and the Slave Girl*, and *The Old Beauty and Others*) in which the author appears to doubt art's redemptive power and gives supremacy to life values.[1]

Mona Pers's doctoral dissertation, published as *Willa Cather's Children*, Studia Anglistica Upsaliensia, 22 (Uppsala: University of Uppsala) takes up a subject central to Cather's art. Part 1 describes the different children Cather knew and tries, unwisely I think, to account for her emotional life in terms of her childlessness. More usefully Pers shows how in Cather's fiction characters who like children are invariably sympathetic and how children are unfailing sources of love and hope. In Part 2 Pers describes how Cather recreated her own childhood in the lives of many fictional characters,

1. Your editor, who reviewed this book for *JML*, wrote as follows: "David Stouck's book is an illuminating study . . . the product of a fine critical intelligence, a work full of insights and good judgment. Stouck . . . brings a fresh perspective to . . . Cather scholarship, and there are things to be learned even by one who thought he knew all there was to know about Willa Cather. It is felicitously written . . . full of perceptive observations and a valuable vade mecum . . . . It is based on a thorough assimilation of the biographical and bibliographical discoveries of the last decade, and I recommend it highly."

pointing out that Cather believed childhood to be the fully imaginative period of one's life. She also shows how some of the central absorptions of childhood such as play-acting, hero worship, and storytelling remain central to Cather's imaginative world. In part 3 Pers considers the fictional implications of Cather's rejection of maturity—the few happy marriages in her fiction, the disillusioned adults, the artistic weakness of the novels themselves when they describe an artist's adult life. In a brief "afterthought" Pers shrewdly concludes that readers who cherish their own memories of childhood will always value Cather's fiction highly, while those who reject their past and childhood will find little appeal in her art.

There is no definitive Cather bibliography nor any immediate prospect of one, but in the meantime the University of Nebraska Press has published *Willa Cather: A Checklist of Her Published Writings*, comp. JoAnna Lathrop. This volume lists all the identified pieces of Cather's writing (776 items to date), plus reprints and editions, and is indispensable to scholars and students working closely on Cather.

The range and complexity of Cather's writings is reflected in the variety of approaches taken in critical articles about her work. Evelyn Thomas Helmick's fine essay, "The Broken World: Medievalism in *A Lost Lady*" (*Renascence* 28:39–46) is part of a longer study of myth and archetype in the works of Willa Cather. Here Helmick shows how Cather's treatment of the Midwest in the late 19th century has parallels with the decline of feudal society in medieval Europe and how *A Lost Lady* has the characteristics of a courtly romance, a popular genre of the late medieval period. The details Helmick chooses to substantiate her thesis are suggestive and convincing, and the thesis itself underscores the universal and timeless dimensions of Cather's art. In "Willa Cather and Hawthorne: Significant Resemblances" (*Renascence* 27:161–75) John J. Murphy looks at Cather in the context of American literature and compares the way Cather and Hawthorne handle perennial American themes such as the Edenic myth, alienation, and the quest for a world of one's own making. Murphy also comments on the two authors' interest in Catholicism and their feeling for southern European civilization. His concern is not to document an influence of Hawthorne on Cather, but to place Cather in the mainstream of American writers whose concerns and attitudes she inherited.

Two essays are concerned with the religious elements in Cather's writing. In "Willa Cather and *The Varieties of Religious Experience*" (*Renascence* 27:115–23) William M. Curtin speculates on the possible influence of William James on Cather. Curtin points out that both James and Cather were interested in religious experience rather than religious beliefs and institutions. He relates James's idea that we can find the greatest peace in a union with something larger than ourselves to Cather's description of Thea in *The Song of the Lark*, finding her own artistic drive continuous with the artistic desire of the ancient Indians in Panther Canyon. In "The Ecstasy of Alexandra Bergson" (*CLQ* 11:139–49) L. Brent Bohlke draws an analogy between the erotic dream of the heroine of *O Pioneers!* and the vision of St. Teresa of Avila. Bohlke does not argue a direct influence of the Spanish nun's writings on Cather's, but rather he shows how they share a universal mystical experience, whether it is directed toward Christ or a god of the soil and harvests. Two other essays are concerned with structure in Cather's fiction. In "The Problem of Point of View in *A Lost Lady*" (*Renascence* 28:47–52) Dalma H. Brunauer argues that, like James's John Marcher, Cather's Niel Herbert is blind to love and that Marian Forrester is only "lost" or guilty in the eyes of the prudish and evasive hero. And in "The Function of Structure in Cather's *The Professor's House*" (*CLQ* 11: 169–78), Marilyn Arnold examines the three parts of the novel as dramatizing a conflict between society and solitude.

Willa Cather for the most part resists feminist critics, but she is the subject nonetheless of a chapter in Jane Rule's *Lesbian Images* (Garden City, N.Y.: Doubleday). Rule denounces Cather's critics for misreading the texts in order to prove, in the absence of biographical evidence, her emotional and erotic preferences for women. In this thoughtful essay Rule argues that what distinguishes Cather is not a masculine sensibility but a capacity to transcend the sexuality of her characters to see their more complex humanity, and an ability to create characters through a sympathetic immersion which renders them beyond judgment. She also sees Cather as "nearly alone among female writers" in her preoccupation with the role and nature of the artist. Cather's contemporaneity is the subject of Bernice Slote's "An Appointment with the Future: Willa Cather" (*The Twenties*, pp. 39–49). Slote shows how Cather's novels in the twenties were informed by a wasteland vision not unlike T. S. Eliot's, although the two writers, Slote points out, did not influence each other. She also shows how Cather's countervision was not really nostalgic, but rather anticipated many of our concerns in the seventies—rejection of material values, concern for the environment, faith in individuality.

Inevitably there were essays of limited value. "Myra Henshawe's Mortal Enemy" (*C&L* 25:7–40) is a rambling study by Dalma Hunyadi Brunauer and June Davis Klamecki of Cather's shortest novel. These critics look at the novel in terms of style, imagery, point of view, and characterization, and come to the rather strained conclusion that Myra's enemy is her own mortal body. Larry Rubin's "The Homosexual Motif in Willa Cather's 'Paul's Case'" (*SSF* 12:127–31) looks at the fairly obvious homosexual innuendos surrounding Paul's physical description, his dress, his relationships with others. Rubin thoughtfully concludes, however, that such a portrait is another measure of Cather's craftsmanship in that she conveyed "her protagonist's inner being without violating any of the literary taboos of her time." A glaring example of poor scholarship can be found in a lengthy essay by Catherine M. McLay entitled "Religion in the Novels of Willa Cather" (*Renascence* 27:125–44). McLay writes that Cather was attracted to the Catholic church by its aestheticism and its provision of a sanctuary or refuge. Her thesis has long been a commonplace in Cather criticism and the essay does not merit the space it is given in the journal. But more disturbing are the errors of various kinds which riddle the essay: although McLay discusses *Shadows on the Rock*, she says Cather is not concerned with guilt and suffering or the need for redemption in her novels; she writes "Ann Kronberg," referring to Anna Kronborg, sets the Virginia novel, *Sapphira and the Slave Girl*, in the Southwest, etc. More original and careful, though still limited, is "The Dialectic of Willa Cather's Moral Vision" (*Renascence* 27:145–59), in which Paul Borgman applies to Cather's fiction a schema of hope and faith, derived from Unamuno and equated with the Dionysian and Apollonian principles. Borgman sees the dialectic culminating in the perfect marriage of Sapphira Colbert, a woman of willful vitality, and Henry Colbert, a gentle, thoughtful man of good faith.

Finally, three overviews of Cather appear in somewhat unlikely places. They are Mildred R. Bennett's "Willa Cather and the Prairie" (*Nebraska History* 56:231–35), Bernice Slote's "Willa Cather and the West" (*Persimmon Hill* 4,iv[1974]:48–59), and James Woodress's "The World and the Parish: Willa Cather" (*Architectural Association Quarterly* [London] 7,ii:51–59). These essays contain little new material but are worth noting because they present summary views by veteran Cather scholars.

ii. Edith Wharton

Surely the outstanding event of American scholarship in 1975 was the publication of R. W. B. Lewis's *Edith Wharton: A Biography* (New York: Harper & Row). Edith Wharton, with her tremendous energy, left behind her not only a massive *oeuvre*, but a wide circle of literary friends and a vast correspondence; Lewis has gone carefully through this formidable collection of materials and produced an immensely readable and elegant literary biography. The book's most striking contribution is to change our picture of Edith Wharton from a cold, aloof grande dame to a woman who knew intimately the joys and treacheries of physical passion. She had virtually a sexless marriage with Teddy Wharton, but Lewis documents a passionate affair with a journalist, Morton Fullerton, during her middle years; as further witness to her lively sexuality Lewis reproduces a highly artistic fragment of poronography entitled "Beatrice Palmato," apparently written when Edith Wharton was over 70. The latter describes the physical culmination of an incestuous passion between father and daughter, and Lewis wonders how much this tells us about the set of the author's imagination. Lewis has tremendous admiration for his subject, but he is always scrupulously objective and does not conceal an unattractive side to Wharton's character. Edith Wharton's energy as a writer and hostess was dazzling, but it seems to have covered a lack of intimacy in her relations with others. Her ambition, moreover, seems to have been destructive to her husband and to other members of her family from whom she grew increasingly alienated. In her wide circle of friendships there was something impersonal and calculated.

Lewis does not really interpret Edith Wharton's fiction—this is a life—but he does see her best work as turning on two major preoccupations: the theme of entrapment and the drama of the generations. The former theme particularly interests Lewis. He sees a fundamental tension in Edith Wharton between her roles as a wealthy *femme du monde* and a serious artist. He believes that as a young woman she often felt trapped by the society role and that eventually her work as an artist provided her with an escape, but that at the same time she could never quite shake the conviction of her class that her money and position were more important than her achievements as a writer. Lewis sees these tensions fundamental to many of the women characters in her fiction. Like other critics, Lewis gives highest ranking to *The House of Mirth*, *The Custom of the Country*, and *The Age of Innocence*, but he feels *The Reef* and *Summer* also stand with the best of her novels.

There is only one problem with Lewis's book and that is a matter of footnotes. At the end of the book Lewis lists alphabetically his major sources and acknowledgments, but he does not relate the information chapter by chapter to specific sources. Lewis's biography has assimilated an enormous amount of factual materials and while one scarcely doubts the authenticity or integrity of Lewis's account, one feels the need of fuller notes. Future scholars must either quote Lewis as the final authority or go back to the original papers.

Edith Wharton's novels are subjected to careful scrutiny in Gary H. Lindberg's *Edith Wharton and the Novel of Manners* (Charlottesville: Univ. Press of Va.). This study focuses almost entirely on *The House of Mirth*, *The Custom of the Country*, and *The Age of Innocence*. Lindberg is particularly interested in the novel of manners as a genre and makes his most valuable points when showing how Wharton develops the genre in her own unique way. The major purpose of her fiction, he points out, is to show precisely "how social convention limits the life of the spirit," but unlike most other novelists her focus rests not on the romantic yearnings of the protagonist in conflict with society, but rather on the social forms that contain the individual. Wharton's affiliations, he suggests, are not primarily American but European, for her characters are never, like Isabel Archer, innocent of class distinctions and codes of manners; yet Wharton is American, he argues, in that her protagonists are thoroughly frustrated or destroyed by society where the European protagonists would find a means of compromise. In this same vein Lindberg examines the tragic sense in Edith Wharton's philosophy of the individual in relation to society. He points out that Wharton believed in the necessary connection between the individual and his society to give coherence to human activity, yet found social structures invariably unsatisfactory and destructive to the inner life.

In individual chapters which provide careful readings of the three novels, Lindberg considers Wharton's handling of the essential elements of fiction. Her plots, he argues, have two dimensions: the overt plot dramatizes movements of the social order and the protagonist's relation to it, while a "buried fable" in each novel tells the story of an inward or spiritual rescue that is rarely completed. Wharton's settings, he shows, are an elegant surface of descriptive detail beneath which various kinds of power (reputation, sexuality, family, money) are in conflict. Most of her characters, he argues, are conceived as representatives of a social system at work, and he shows how genuine individuals like Lily Bart and Newland Archer are shaped by the psychological impact of their societies. Finally he shows how Wharton's style, frequently abstract and epigrammatic, conveys the subtleties and complexities of the social order but seldom the imaginative range of the individual mind. Lindberg's study is sometimes tedious in its theorizing and close scrutiny of detail; nonetheless its thesis is sound and its numerous insights are of considerable value.

Articles on Edith Wharton focus largely on the same novels. In "Edith Wharton: The Nostalgia for Innocence" (*The Twenties*, pp. 27–38), Eleanor Widmer suggests that while the author satirized the New York society of her youth for equating conformity with personal fulfillment, she could never really make a break with that era and its conventions. Widmer contends that Wharton accordingly could not come to terms with the innovative twenties in her novels because duty before love remained the fixed moral code for her heroines. (Are other readings now more likely since Lewis's discovery of the Fullerton affair?) Irving Jacobson, in "Perception, Communication, and Growth as Correlative Themes in Edith Wharton's *The Age of Innocence*" (*Agora* 2[1973]:68–82), similarly sees Newland Archer dissatisfied with the past but unable to face a new future. Jacobson describes the forms of evasion, ignorance, and hypocrisy in the novel that are necessary if the characters are to remain within the framework of the old society.

More interesting are two brief pieces on literary patterns in Wharton's fiction. In a valuable note entitled "Edith Wharton's *The*

House of Mirth: Sermon on a Text" (*MFS* 21:572–76), Curtis Dahl shows how the first 12 verses of Ecclesiastes, where Edith Wharton found the title of her book, are resonant throughout the novel. These verses, Dahl points out, advise that a good name is better than precious ointment, that it is better to go to the house of mourning than the house of mirth, that the patient spirit is better than the proud; these are all moral lessons, says Dahl, that Lily Bart must learn. And in "The Dance of Death: A Study of Edith Wharton's Short Stories" (*SELit* 51[1974]:67–90). Miyoko Sasaki, obtaining a cue from the title, "After Holbein," shrewdly delineates a *danse macabre* pattern operating in several of Wharton's best stories.

iii. Gertrude Stein

Criticism of Gertrude Stein divides sharply between serious interest in her experiments with language and fascination with her role as "Mother Superior of a Parisian art salon." Interest of both kinds is growing, as is reflected in two new books and nine articles on this difficult author. The question of Gertrude Stein's real value is raised by William Wasserstrom, who, at the outset of his essay "The Sursymamericubealism of Gertrude Stein" (*TCL* 21:90–106), asks whether Stein's current réclame serves the fashionable taste for nostalgia, memoirs, anomalous chic, or whether she is in fact a genius. Wasserstrom is clearly of the latter persuasion, and in this multifaceted study he argues that several mainstreams in modern art, from symbolism to surrealism and cubism, merge in Stein's work. She gives them a special American stamp, he argues, through her genius for creating movement in art. Wasserstrom singles out the preoccupation in modern art with the sensations that objects provoke, and in this light he sees Stein's *Autobiography of Alice B. Toklas* as a particular work of genius, for by making Alice the narrator, he says, Stein has created at once both the object (Gertrude) and the effect it produces (Alice); or, in other words, by transforming herself into an object, Stein, like the Cubist painters, has created a figure perceived by two perspectives simultaneously (Gertrude's and Alice's), thus uniting object and viewer.

Carolyn Faunce Copeland's *Language and Time and Gertrude Stein* (Iowa City: Univ. of Iowa Press) is also a serious study which traces, through Stein's long career, her use of the fictional narrator.

Copeland divides her study and Stein's career into three parts. The discussion of Stein's first period, 1903–12, I found the most interesting, for here Copeland describes with great care the development of Stein's narrator from the obtrusive third person narrator typical of 19th-century fiction to the narrator creating a work in nonrepresentational language. *Q.E.D.*, says Copeland, fluctuates between the obtrusive third person narrator and the narrator, who, like James, presents the interior of a single, central intelligence. In *Three Lives*, says Copeland, Stein used Flaubert's short, impassive sentences with a narrator who blends imperceptibly into the speech patterns and rhythms of the characters. "Melanctha" she cites as the first instance of Stein's use of deliberate narrative repetition—what Stein preferred to call "emphasis" or "insistence." In *The Making of Americans* and "Ada" Copeland finds the narrator creating a continuous progression by using the present participle, while in "Two: Gertrude Stein and Her Brother" she can point to the first instances of autotelic or nonrepresentational language. The narrator in "Two," writes Copeland, is a *histor*, searching for the reality and truth of the characters and their relationship by sifting through much contradictory evidence.

In the discussion of the "middle years," 1913–32, Copeland uses the Cubist's ideas to explain what Stein was doing in her art. Just as the painters were trying to create a world rather than reflect it, says Copeland, so Stein in a book like *Tender Buttons* was using language to create something with physical properties of sight and sound rather than meaning. Looking at *Lucy Church Amiably*, Copeland focuses on Stein's use of color, alliteration, and rhyme. In these works, says Copeland, we witness the narrator in the process of creating the work. Considering the later period, 1932–44, Copeland shows how in the *Autobiography of Alice B. Toklas* Stein made Alice a fictional character in order to effect her own lionization, and how in *Ida* she uses an unreliable narrator to convey the elusive nature of one's personal identity. Copeland's study does not have the allusive sophistication of Sutherland's or Bridgman's, but it has the virtue of being a clear, straightforward analysis of a difficult writer's work and as such is a valuable addition to Stein scholarship.

Such clarity is lacking in Neil Schmitz's "Gertrude Stein as Post-Modernist: The Rhetoric of *Tender Buttons*" (*JML* 3[1974]:1203–18), where a kind of critical rhetoric frequently becomes deliberately obscure jargon. Schmitz's argument is that Stein challenges the epistemological categories of narrative and gives us instead a world in process where "everything is contingent, changing as it moves and the mind moves." To write in this mode of perception, states Schmitz, "Stein constantly presses against the order of language those elements of syntax and signification that provide philosophical and scientific discourse with its stability." With a similar interest in Stein's fictional world of process, Sharon Shaw, in "Gertrude Stein and Henry James: The Difference Between Accidence and Coincidence" (*Pembroke Magazine* 5[1974]:95–101), asks whether Stein's concept of the continuous present differs from James's conviction that all the minutiae of experience have to be included if the re-creation of an experience is to be authentic. Shaw's opinion is that James and Stein had very similar intentions, but where James was able to relate the minutiae of the suspended moment back to a larger whole (the "coincidental" or intended purpose achieved), Stein failed to do so and her writing remains accidental, fragmentary. Schmitz would say that her failure was intentional. In "The Steinian Portrait" (*YULG* 50:30–40) Wendy Steiner looks at Stein's relation to the other James and discusses how, under William James's influence, Stein rejected the prevailing idea of "the individual as a static configuration of physical or spiritual traits" and how through her style of repetition with variation she was able to create character as an ever-changing dynamic process. Steiner describes succinctly three distinguishable phases in Stein's portraiture from 1908 to 1946 and *YULG* reproduces three hitherto unpublished portraits following Steiner's article.

Three other essays are concerned more with Stein's moral vision than her technical experimentation. In her essay on Gertrude Stein in *Lesbian Images* Jane Rule sees *Q.E.D.*, a novel of love between women, as embodying the struggle between morality and forbidden desire, and the story "Melanctha" as an extension of the same struggle except cast in heterosexual terms. Rule finds the psychological tension in "Melanctha" more arbitrary since heterosexual marriage is an obvious possible solution, but she also finds the story powerful, for it "embodies the basic separateness of human beings, which was to remain Gertrude Stein's view of the nature and limitation of human relationships." In "The Becoming of Gertrude Stein's *The Making of Americans*" (*The Twenties*, pp. 157–70), Kenneth Frieling sees Stein eliminating the basic separateness of human beings by ceasing to create individual characters in her long novel. Through repetition, Frieling argues, Stein created a character's " 'bottom nature,' " making him indistinguishable from all other characters. He concludes that *The Making of Americans* is in essence a wasteland novel about dislocated, rootless people in a country that is too young to give men a distinct sense of self or tradition. In the opposite vein Benjamin T. Spencer, in "Gertrude Stein: Non-Expatriate" (*Literature and Ideas*, pp. 204–27), insists that Stein was a proud American, preoccupied with her national identity, and, like Wasserstrom, he urges that her concept of America as primarily movement in space is at the basis of her abstract, repetitive style.

I will just mention briefly those pieces on Stein which turn on the fashionable cult of personality and the avant-garde. Richard Kostelanetz's "Gertrude Stein: The New Literature" (*HC* 16,iii:2–15) is a general overview of Stein with a prevailing emphasis on the contemporary nature of her work. Paul K. Alkon's "Visual Rhetoric in *The Autobiography of Alice B. Toklas* (*CritI* 1:849–81) is a highly speculative discussion that assumes some complex strategies in the author's use of illustrations for the *Autobiography*. Janet Hobhouse's *Everybody Who Was Anybody: A Biography of Gertrude Stein* (New York: G. P. Putnam's) is a coffee-table version of Mellow's *Charmed Circle* (see *ALS 1974*, pp. 238–39). Like Mellow, Hobhouse is interested in describing an artistic milieu and does not really concern herself with Stein's experimental prose. Her biographical material is by now familiar reading, although Hobhouse does interpret her subject somewhat by emphasizing the idea that Stein was childlike in personality. Describing Gertrude's reaction to her own work, she writes: "It was like a baby's delight in its own physical processes, and Alice, like a mother, would be there to congratulate Gertrude on what had been produced." Hobhouse's book does not embody new material, but it is very readable, lavishly illustrated, and makes a good introduction to the popular, colorful aspects of this author.

iv. Jack London

Interest in Jack London remains high, with the appearance of another book-length study, two editions of London's short stories, and several new articles about the author. James I. McClintock's *White*

Logic (Grand Rapids, Mich.: Wolf House Books) is a careful study of the aesthetic and philosophical attitudes in Jack London's short fiction. In part 1 of his book McClintock describes London's attempts to master the formula of writing commercially viable stories and shows how he was influenced by the practice of Kipling and the literary theory of Herbert Spencer's *Philosophy of Style*. In the first part he also shows how London combines the much-debated elements of realism and romance. London's protagonists, he says, are made to confront the disturbing realities of nature while undertaking a romantic quest for identity. The consequences of this dual approach are examined in the Alaskan stories in the second part of the book. There McClintock argues that the explicit theme of the stories is that a rational man can achieve mastery over a hostile environment, but that the implicit theme is that rationality ultimately fails to sustain men when they venture into the unknown. This, says McClintock, is the grim truth, the "white logic" of the wasteland demonstrated in such stories as "To Build a Fire." In London's best tales, says McClintock, we come up against "the tragedy that man's most highly prized attributes are merely self-sustaining illusions which cannot protect him from the terrifying suspicion that life is empty of significance." In a final section McClintock traces the decline of London's story writing in the socialist stories and its renewed vitality in the psychological Hawaiian stories written shortly before London's death. McClintock's book lacks an index, but otherwise it is a sound scholarly study which advances our appreciation of London as an artist.

There appeared in 1975 two overlapping collections of London's science-fiction stories: *Curious Fragments: Jack London's Tales of Fantasy Fiction*, ed. Dale L. Walker (Port Washington, N.Y.: Kennikat Press), and *The Science Fiction of Jack London*, ed., new intro. Richard Gid Powers (Boston: Gregg Press). Powers argues that in London's science-fiction fantasies there lies a deeply imbedded hatred of traditional civilization which in America wholly alienated the proletariat from its goals. He points out that the two theories informing London's science fiction were on the one hand revolutionary socialism, as in *The Iron Heel* or "A Curious Fragment," and on the other evolutionary racism, as in "The Unparalleled Invasion," with a preponderance of fiction informed by the latter. He suggests that London is probably at his best as a science-fiction writer because he had little understanding of himself or human nature, and therefore fiction that turned on ideas was more congenial to his talents than the realistic novel, which demands complex, believable characters.

Two articles deal effectively with similar issues. In "Jack London and the Tradition of Superman Socialism" (*AmerS* 16:23–33) Geoffrey Harpham relates the contradictory impulses in London toward rugged individualism on the one hand and socialism on the other to a form of literary socialism at the turn of the century which tried to merge the vision of a just society with the idea of the romantic hero. Harpham also shows how in *The Iron Heel* the hero, Everhard, is the antagonist of the wealthy and privileged classes, but at the same time has contempt for the masses and sees himself as a Christ-like savior, a man set apart. In "Male and Female in London's *The Sea-Wolf*" (*L&P* 24[1974]:135–43), Robert Forrey takes up the question of characterization. Forrey suggests that the effeminate Van Weyden is a homosexual who represses his instincts and gradually becomes a he-man modeled on Wolf Larsen because he recognizes that otherwise he is not likely to survive in a brutal world where "the strong eat the weak." Forrey's reading accounts for the sensual and romantic portrait of Larsen and the bloodless nature of the heroine Maud Brewster.

Generally, the essays in the 1975 *Jack London Newsletter* were not of a very high calibre. Some are too narrow in scope to mention here, while others, such as James Glennon Cooper's "The Womb of Time: Archetypal Patterns in the Novels of Jack London" (*JLN* 8:1–5), excerpted from a doctoral dissertation, involve too cursory a treatment of an important subject to be of real value. Some pieces seem to have little purpose: "Jack London's Humanism" by Chandra Mohan (*JLN* 8:40–49) makes the obvious statement that London's humanism "arises out of his deep interest in the study of human nature and his keen desire to work for the betterment of mankind," while David B. Haire and Dennis E. Hensley have set up a rather pointless comparison of London with W. S. Maugham (*JLN* 8:114–18).

Of more substance and interest is Francis Lacassin's "Jack London Between the Challenge of the Supernatural and the Last Judgment" (*JLN* 8:59–65), which describes the apocalyptic vision of violence, war, and ruin in works like *The Iron Heel* that London believed necessary before an egalitarian society could be born. Lacassin is particularly interested in London's pessimism as revealed in a story like "The Scarlet Plague," where the new society owes nothing to the socialist struggle but is the result of a natural catastrophe—a terrifying epidemic. Interesting too is Dennis E. Hensley's "A Note on Jack London's Use of Black Humor" (*JLN* 8:110–13), in which Hensley observes that London's humor consisted of yoking together a brutal act with naive reporting, or a narrator given to understatement. The most interesting article in exploring London's lasting literary value is Lawrence Clayton's "*The Sea-Wolf*: London's *Commedia*" (*JLN* 8:50–54), which draws structural parallels between London's novel and Dante's epic poem. Clayton's point is not to suggest that London was imitating Dante but rather to point to an archetypal, universal structure in *The Sea Wolf*, one which, for example, illuminates the role of Maud Brewster as a redemptive Beatrice figure and explains the Platonic relationship between Humphrey and Maud.

v. Theodore Dreiser

There were two Drieser books from 1974 which were overlooked in last year's essay and which I will first mention here briefly. R. N. Mookerjee's *Theodore Drieser: His Thought and Social Criticism* (Delhi, India: National Publishing House) is a biography which attempts "to analyze and evaluate Drieser's role as a social critic during the last twenty years of his life." Mookerjee's study traces the development of Dreiser's thinking through social Darwinism and philosophies of determinism to the question of socialism and communism. The ideas discussed here are not new, but the scholarship is thorough and it is useful to have it organized so well in one place. Mookerjee's book, however, is only of limited interest to students of literature because the focus is almost exclusively on Dreiser's books of social commentary (*Dreiser Looks at Russia*, 1928; *Tragic America*, 1931; and *America is Worth Saving*, 1941) and not on the major imaginative works.

James Lundquist's *Theodore Dreiser* (New York: Frederick Ungar) is largely an introduction for nonspecialists, but in the chapter on *An American Tragedy* Lundquist makes the original and valuable suggestion that Dreiser's masterpiece can be viewed as a folk-epic, weaving together a number of popular but specious American myths such as the Horatio Alger rags-to-riches dream, the appearance of the rich uncle, the story of the seduced country girl, the story of the poor boy in love with a rich girl, the fighting D.A., conversion on death row. This reading coincides with Dreiser's statement that "it was a story common to every boy raised in the smaller towns of America." There also appeared in 1974 an interesting article by Robert Roulston entitled "The Libidinous Lobster: The Semi-Flaw in Dreiser's Superman" (*Rendezvous* 9:35–40). Roulston argues that in the trilogy Cowperwood should not be seen as either a tragic or a realistic hero but rather as a foil against which the pruderies and hypocrisies of American society can be measured. Cowperwood, says Roulston, is a type of Nietzschean superman whose only flaw is that he is too brilliant and energetic to escape the notice of his puritanical rivals who try to defeat him.

The most important event in Dreiser scholarship for 1975 was the publication of *Theodore Dreiser: A Primary and Secondary Bibliography* (Boston: G. K. Hall), comp. Donald Pizer, Richard W. Dowell, and Frederic E. Rusch. This is the first full-scale bibliography of Dreiser's works and the writings about him, containing more than 4,100 entries. In addition to information about Dreiser's publications there is information on interviews and speeches, adaptations of works for stage and screen, and library holdings of Dreiser materials.

None of the articles published in 1975 will figure very significantly in future bibliographies of Dreiser criticism. Three pieces focus on *An American Tragedy*, marking its 50th year since publication. In the best of these, "Theodore Dreiser and the Tragedy of the Twenties" (*Prospects* 1:9–16), Robert H. Elias urges that the real tragedy for Clyde Griffiths is that he cannot realize his dreams in terms of human relations, that social involvement is incompatible in a world where individualism is sovereign. "In such a world the commitment to the humanity of another is a subtraction from self," writes Elias, and consequently the tragedy of Clyde and Roberta is the pain of loneliness. Novelist James T. Farrell, in "Dreiser's Tragedy: The Distortion of American Values" (*Prospects* 1:19–27), writes that the book is tragic not because the central characters die, but because Clyde has been raised to follow the false materialistic values of his society. Farrell sees the book as a wholesale indictment of America. Carol Clancy Harter, in "Strange Bedfellows: *The*

Waste Land and *An American Tragedy*" (*The Twenties*, pp. 51–64), looks at Eliot's and Dreiser's dissimilar works and shows that they nevertheless reflect in imagery and themes a common preoccupation with loss of values in the 20th century. Wasteland imagery also figures in "*Sister Carrie*: Dreiser's Wasteland" (*AmerS* 16:41–47), in which Clark Griffith compares the genuine passion and tenderness between Hurstwood and Carrie when they meet in the park in chapter 15 with the rationalized desires of the urban world in which they live during the rest of the novel. For Griffith the narrative voice in *Sister Carrie* is like that of Tiresias in Eliot's *The Waste Land*—detached, yet infinitely pitying, telling what happens but powerless to prevent it.

Three other articles are concerned with sources and revisions. In "Hyde's Tabbs and Dreiser's Butlers" (*DN* 6:9–11) Philip L. Gerber suggests that Dreiser's characterization of the Butlers in *The Financier* probably owes more to his reading of Henry M. Hyde's *The Buccaneers* than it does to the Yerkes family prototypes around which the novel was built. In "Thomas Edison and *Sister Carrie*: A Source for Character and Theme" (*ALR* 8:155–58), Lawrence E. Hussman, Jr., explores the possibility of Thomas Edison and his philosophy of work as the only happiness as informing the portrait of Bob Ames in *Sister Carrie.* And in " 'The Cruise of the "Idlewild" ': Dreiser's Revisions of a 'Rather Light' Story" (*ALR* 8:1–11), D. B. Graham shows how the anthologized version transforms the sketch into a story and develops the latent social commentary in the sketch, particularly the deterministic environment and man's need to dream. The same issue of *ALR* prints three hitherto unpublished letters from Dreiser to a young friend while Dreiser was still in his teens. Finally, in "Dreiser and the Prophetic Tradition" (*AmerS* 15:21–35), Robert Forrey demonstrates that the religious spirit in Dreiser's novels is prophetic rather than ritualistic or mystical, and suggests that it would be more accurate to see Dreiser as coming out of a prophetic religious tradition than the literary tradition of naturalism.

vi. Sinclair Lewis

Although Sinclair Lewis no longer figures as prominently in American literature as he did during his lifetime, he nonetheless continues to draw some critical attention. During 1975 he was the subject of a book-length study as well as of a few articles. In *The Quixotic Vision of Sinclair Lewis* (West Lafayette, Ind.: Purdue Univ. Press), Martin Light examines the conflict of romance and realism in Lewis's fiction as an expression of quixotism. He finds numerous examples of protagonists like Carol Kennicott who, schooled on sentimental novels and romantic ideals, ride forth in the modern world to conquer, but are brought up short by the reality of the Gopher Prairies and find that the world is more than the projection of their illusions. Quixotism, according to Light, is one of Lewis's major vehicles for satire. Light focuses on *Main Street*, *Babbitt*, *Arrowsmith*, and *Dodsworth*, but *Main Street* probably best exemplifies the pattern. Light has selected his materials judiciously and writes well, but this is nonetheless a slight book, spun out on too limited a thesis to contribute substantially to Lewis scholarship. As Light himself acknowledges in a preface, critics such as Mark Schorer and Sheldon Grebstein have already examined the conflict between romance and realism in Lewis; his own book is only a variation on the same theme.

Articles on Lewis were also rather lightweight. David G. Pugh's "Baedekers, Babbitry, and Baudelaire" (*The Twenties*, pp. 87–99) plays with the problem of Lewis's continuing relevance over the years ("does Lewis show us How We Live Today?"), but does not venture any firm opinions on the question. Pugh is intrigued rather by shifts in tone and meaning in works of literature over the years, and points out that our reading of Lewis in 1975 will inevitably "adulterate" the original experience, whether through nostalgia, disinterest, or contempt for the period. In "The Short Stories and Sinclair Lewis's Literary Development" (*SSF* 12:99–107), Clara Lee Moodie tells us that in the 76 stories Lewis wrote before publishing *Main Street* one can find themes and techniques which anticipate his major books. The brevity of Moodie's article almost precludes the demonstration of her thesis, but her bibliographical list of Lewis's stories, not undertaken by James Lundquist's Merrill checklist, is of considerable value to the serious scholar.

vii. Sherwood Anderson

The most important addition to Anderson scholarship in 1975 was Martha Mulroy Curry's publication of *The "Writer's Book" by Sher-*

wood Anderson: A Critical Edition (Metuchen, N.J.: Scarecrow Press). The "Writer's Book," never published before, is one of the projects Anderson left unfinished at his death and consists of seven essays and stories addressed to fellow writers. Anderson takes up such topics as "How to Write to a Writer" and the difference between a short story and a novel, but probably most interesting to Anderson scholars is the first and longest section of the book titled "Prelude to a Story" wherein Anderson both tells a story and describes the processes by which a story takes shape in an author's mind. Martha Curry's edition includes an introduction describing in detail the manuscript of the "Writer's Book" and its relation to Anderson's other works; there is also a massive "commentary," which represents a thorough explication of the text in the light of Anderson scholarship to date. Curry's edition is an impeccable work of scholarship, a model for those undertaking a similar task. The year 1975 also saw the publication of the first number of *The Winesburg Eagle*, a newsletter put out by the Sherwood Anderson Society, University of Richmond, Richmond, Virginia. So far the newsletter has published brief memoirs of Anderson by men and women who knew him, but it is also committed to keeping a bibliographical checklist on writings about Anderson up to date and thus is of special value to scholars currently working on Anderson.

As mentioned previously, none of the recent articles on Anderson is of major significance. The best of these is William V. Miller's "Earth-Mothers, Succubi, and other Ectoplasmic Spirits: The Women in Sherwood Anderson's Short Stories" (*MidAmerica* 1[1974]: 64–81), a disjointed but sometimes perceptive essay on an important aspect of Anderson's fiction. Miller begins with the familiar thesis that Anderson's characterizations of women reflect "the doubts and frustrations of his own relationships with women, especially with his mother, Emma Anderson, and his four wives." But then Miller goes on in a more original vein to show how the four types of women in Anderson's fiction ("managers, defenders of the home, feeders of men, and frustrated gropers after a higher life") are not created as fully rounded characters but in accordance with Anderson's idea of a story being the result of a sudden passion illuminating the essential quality of a character or relationship. Miller also points out that Anderson did not believe the feminine sensibility capable of creative imagination, yet in his stories he created women like Kate Swift and

Elizabeth Willard, who suggest an imaginative capacity he would not have granted real women.

The other articles are of minimal value. Eberhard Alsen's "The Futile Pursuit of Truth in Twain's 'What is Man?' and Anderson's 'The Book of the Grotesque'" (*MTJ* 17,iii[1974]:12–14) suggests that Anderson's ironic view of truth in *Winesburg, Ohio* was likely influenced by Twain, but, like so many source studies, this "discovery" does not lead to a greater understanding or appreciation of Anderson's book. Mark Helbling's "Sherwood Anderson and Jean Toomer" (*NALF* 9:35–39) reviews the contradictory attitudes Anderson expressed toward black Americans and Primitivism in art, while in a diffuse essay entitled "Sherwood Anderson and the Lyric Story" (*The Twenties*, pp. 65–74) Eileen Baldeshwiler examines some of the ways Anderson handles the narrative element in his Winesburg stories so that they achieve a highly poetic effect. One hopes that critically Anderson will fare better in 1976, his centennial year.

viii. Glasgow, Cabell

As a woman writer Ellen Glasgow also attracted more than the usual amount of critical attention in 1975; there were three critical studies of her fiction as compared to one in 1974. In "Ellen Glasgow: The Great Tradition and the New Morality" (*CLQ* 11:98–115), N. E. Dunn looks at Glasgow's examination of both the old code for living and its modern replacement. According to Dunn, Glasgow did not idealize one code in favor of the other but was critical of both: pride, evasive idealism, the masculine subjugation of women, and the tyranny of family all characterized the old order "while materialism was the first cause in the new morality." In "Glasgow's Psychology of Deception and *The Sheltered Life*" (*SLJ* 8,i:27–38), J. R. Raper argues that *The Sheltered Life* is Glasgow's "finest achievement" because it is the most intense study of evasive idealism, her major theme. Raper discusses the characters of the novel, showing how they each manoeuvre to evade reality. And in "History in *Barren Ground* and *Vein of Iron*: Theory, Structure, and Symbol" (*SLJ* 8,i: 39–54), Judy Smith Murr shows how the conflicts of history are paralleled in the conflict of desire and will within the individual.

Devotees of Cabell will welcome the publication of *The Letters of James Branch Cabell*, ed. Edward Wagenknecht (Norman: Univ. of Okla. Press). The editor, in collaboration with Cabell's widow, has chosen not to compile a "complete" letters, feeling "the time is not yet," and some of the letters have been reproduced only in part. In the brief introduction Wagenknecht states that "what we aimed at was to print the materials which would be of the greatest interest to Cabell's readers covering the years of his literary fame and shedding the most light upon his mind and work." Included are letters to Mencken, Sinclair Lewis, Carl Van Vechten. Of particular interest are those to Ellen Glasgow for they give a glimpse into the formal nature of the "Glasgow-Cabell Entente." The book is handsomely produced with numerous illustrations and an index.

Some articles on Cabell were also of interest. In "The Illusion of Diabolism in the Cabellian Hero" (*Novel* 8:241–45), Richard Warner argues that the rebelliousness of Cabell's hero is not diabolical in nature but romantic. Cabell's hero, he argues, does not rebel against an ideal but against the *spiritus mundi* or "things as they are." The Cabellian rebel, says Warner, belongs to the rebellious tradition not of Satan but of Martin Luther and Thomas Jefferson. In "Cabell as Precursor: Reflections on Cabell and Vonnegut" (*Kalki* 6:113–37), Joseph M. Flora draws parallels between the 1920s and the 1960s, then juxtaposes readings of Cabell's *The High Place* and Vonnegut's *Cat's Cradle*, showing how both authors repudiate scientific truth and create unreal worlds in which religion and beauty give dramatic if illusory shape to reality. And in "La Belle Dame and the Sestina" (*Kalki* 7:19–22) Stanley K. Freiberg shows how Cabell in the novel *Chivalry* takes up the story of Keats's lovers 30 years after the time period of "La Belle Dame Sans Merci" and how he follows through the Keatsian preoccupation with mutability and the powerful mistress by making the loved woman an aging, despotic ruler.

ix. Proletarian Writers

There was a remarkable amount of critical material published on Upton Sinclair, a minor author whose place in American literature is tenuous at best. Three new books about this author appeared in 1975, which may argue that he has been unjustly neglected in the past or may reflect the narrowing field of new subjects for scholarship. Jon A. Yoder's *Upton Sinclair* (New York: Frederick Ungar) is a critical introduction which argues Sinclair's importance to many disciplines but does not demonstrate his significance to literature. Yoder's discussion of Sinclair's most famous book, *The Jungle*, focuses on the author's hope that his novel would awaken Americans to the social and political ills of capitalism, not simply to malpractices in the meat-packing industry. Yoder discusses at length Sinclair's optimistic faith in American democracy and his undying belief that right would finally prevail. His book is not very literary in its emphasis, but at present it fills the need for a brief introduction to this author.

Yoder's monograph is overshadowed by Leon Harris's critical biography, *Upton Sinclair: American Rebel* (New York: Thomas Y. Crowell). Working through a colossal amount of manuscript materials, Harris has produced what seems a balanced account of the famous muckraker's life. His sympathy for Sinclair's political idealism is held in check by dismay at Sinclair's boyish naïveté and self-delusion. Leaning heavily on autobiography, Harris first recounts Sinclair's failed attempts at lyrical fiction inspired by his idol, Shelley, then describes his conversion to socialism and the messianic desire to redeem mankind. Like Yoder, Harris does not evaluate Sinclair's vast output (87 books) in literary terms, although he does suggest that Sinclair's failure as an artist stemmed from "too much concern with ideas, too little with people and plot." Harris believes that of Sinclair's books *The Jungle*, *Oil!*, and *Boston* will continue to be read. The fight for social justice, writes Harris, was the chief preoccupation of Sinclair's life and novels were only a means to that end. Harris's book is very much a life, and it is vividly there: Sinclair's tremendous energy, his Puritanism, his preoccupation with fad diets, with spiritualism, his disastrous collaboration on a film with Eisenstein, his candidacy for governor of California. The focus and the assumptions of this substantial biography are summed up in the concluding chapter where Harris writes: "Whether or not Sinclair's place in American literature will finally be deemed to have been significant, the importance of his role in his country's history seems secure." The task of evaluating Sinclair's books as literature still remains. Harris's book is well documented, although its index, I found, is not reliable.

The remaining volume, *Critics on Upton Sinclair* (Coral Gables: Univ. of Miami Press), brings together a wide selection of critical responses to Sinclair's work (from Mencken, D. H. Lawrence through to Walter Rideout) and provides a historical perspective on Sinclair's shifting fortune with the critics.

There were also a couple of articles about Sinclair. In "Upton Sinclair, Lanny, and the Liberals" (*MFS* 20:483–504) Jon A. Yoder focuses on the Lanny Budd series and shows how Lanny's behavior during World War II and the Cold War reflects the American liberal's failure to believe in his own idealism. Yoder's article, like his book, is more about politics and history than literature. And in a short piece entitled "Searching for a Theatre in France: Upton Sinclair vs. Albert Camus, André Malraux and Jean Vilar" (*BSUF* 15,ii [1974]:77–79), André Muraire documents the correspondence between Sinclair and the French writers surrounding Sinclair's attempt to get his 1959 play, *Cicero*, produced in France. We learn that Camus's premature death in 1960 cut short a promised staging, while the nondramatic nature of the play itself discouraged Malraux and Vilar from proceeding with a production; but all three Frenchmen we find exhibited admiration and filial respect for the then 80-year-old crusader.

B. Traven also received more than usual attention in 1975. Donald O. Chankin's *Anonymity and Death: the Fiction of B. Traven* (University Park: Penn. State Univ. Press) makes an important contribution to the small body of English criticism accumulating around this elusive author. Chankin begins with the inevitable question of Traven's identity and, taking a psychological approach, suggests that Traven's numerous disguises can be related to a fear of losing his sense of self, of being betrayed and swallowed up in an anonymous death. In the major works, *The Death Ship*, *The Treasure of the Sierra Madre*, and *The Bridge in the Jungle*, Chankin finds a repeated pattern wherein the protagonist, in flight from society, descends into an underworld tomb, variously represented by a death ship, the bowels of the mountain, a jungle river. Chankin interprets society as the threatening father figure and the underworld tomb as a mother's womb (almost literally so in the Sierra Madre, which translates Mountain of the Mother) from which rebirth and a new identity are possible. In *The Treasure of the Sierra Madre*, Chankin points out, Dobbs does not find a new life; rather he meets an anonymous death through greed, but Howard, the old prospector, becomes a medicine man among the Indians and thereby gains a certain control over death. Chankin believes the most significant of Traven's later works is the novella "Macario," in which a poor Mexican woodchopper shares a turkey dinner with Death and in return is made by Death a medicine man among his people with power to restore the sick and dying to life. Chankin interprets this tale as Traven's final coming to terms with his fear of death and loss of identity.

Although Chankin's study is heavily psychological, it is literary in its emphasis as well. Chankin explores, for instance, the possible influence of Dante, Melville, and Conrad on *The Death Ship*, and he shows how *The Treasure of the Sierra Madre* is a modern version of Chaucer's *The Pardoner's Tale*, where three companions also search for gold and instead find death. This is a fine study and should certainly be given a place in university libraries.

With more of an eye for the proletariat cause, Philip Melling, in "*The Death Ship*: B. Traven's Cradle" (*The Twenties*, pp. 139–56), describes in some detail the progress of the novel's hero from despair to hope and the capacity for love via the hard labor, physical pain, and filth in the boiler room of a maverick ship. The grim realities of the boiler room, says Melling, give the hero a genuine foundation for a life of humility and sympathy. Melling points out that Traven saw big business and bureaucracy crippling mankind and that *The Death Ship* (1926) was one of the first novels about social overturning, dispossession, and violence, themes that would dominate American literature in the 1930s.

Because there were only two articles on Dos Passos in 1975 I will include him here with other writers of liberal sympathies rather than in a separate section. Both articles focus primarily on *Manhattan Transfer*. In "The Newspaper and Other Sources of *Manhattan Transfer*" (*SAF* 3:167–79) Craig Carver discusses how Dos Passos's verbatim use of newspaper accounts creates a chronology for his novel as well as giving it historical authenticity, a technique which became the "Newsreel" in *U.S.A.* Carver also demonstrates briefly how popular songs, advertisement jingles, and slogans function as thematic allusions in *Manhattan Transfer*. In "Dos Passos in the Twenties" (*The Twenties*, pp. 123–37) A. S. Knowles, Jr., describes the affinities of Dos Passos's early works with the other writings and art forms current in the period. He sees the sensibility of the Harvard aesthete just as evident in Dos Passos's *Streets of Night* as in T. S. Eliot's *Prufrock and Other Observations*; he also sees Dos

Passos absorbing the imagery of Cezanne and Monet into the texture of *Three Soldiers*, and compares the imagery and moral framework of *Manhattan Transfer* to Eliot's *The Waste Land.*

x. Western Writers

Papers presented at the Rølvaag Symposium held at St. Olaf College, October 1974, have been published as *Ole Rølvaag: Artist and Cultural Leader* (Northfield, Minn.; St. Olaf College Press). Generally, the most interesting essay in the collection is Robert Scholes's "The Fictional Heart of the Country: From Rølvaag to Gass," (pp. 1–13), which sees Rølvaag's major novel, *Giants in the Earth,* in relation to other novels from the Midwest. Scholes's thesis is that the story of America is the story of a second fall from paradise, and that the pioneer vision celebrated by Rølvaag's Per Hansa (the vision of boundless space and endless resources) was "deeply and tragically wrong." Scholes traces the erosion of this flawed pioneer ideal through Cather's *My Ántonia* where it has become a beautiful memory, through Lewis's *Main Street* where the focus of prairie life has shrunk to the petty affairs of the small town, to William Gass's *In the Heart of the Heart of the Country* where that heart is revealed to consist of asphalt and plastic. Scholes laments the failure of contemporary man to live in harmony with the rest of the biosphere and sees Beret Hansa's fears and madness as darkly prophetic. In a similar vein Kristoffer Paulson, in "Rølvaag as Prophet: The Tragedy of Americanization" (pp. 57–64), examines the author's concern with the immigrant's loss of cultural identity, focusing particularly on *Peder Victorious* and *Their Father's God,* where Per and Beret Hansa's son rebels against the family and Norwegian culture by marrying an Irish Catholic girl and pursuing a career in American politics. Paulson sees Peder as living in a spiritual desert and argues that the tragedy of the American dream rests in its demand "that the immigrant relinquish his language, his culture, his soul." Neil Eckstein in "O. E. Rølvaag: The Marginality of the Bi-Cultural Writer" (pp. 65–68) also takes up this issue of cultural identity in relation to Rølvaag.

Other papers focus more specifically on *Giants in the Earth.* Einer Haugen, in "O. E. Rølvaag: The Man in His Work" (pp. 15–24), sees Rølvaag torn between Per Hansa's optimistic belief in the future and Beret's sensitivity to the past and to human suffering. Haugen also urges that we see Rølvaag's pioneer more universally as "man himself, pressing onward from east to west, from birth to sunset land," and notes that we are invited from the book's title, drawn from Genesis, to see the immigrants as part of the heroic pageant of history. Paul Reigstad, in "Rølvaag as Myth-Maker" (pp. 51–55), considers *Giants in the Earth* briefly in light of the Norwegian myth of the Ash Lad's fatal encounter with the trolls and, unlike Haugen, interprets the giants of the title as referring not to the early settlers remembered for their strength and heroism, but to "the hostile powers accosting the settlers: storm, drought, prairie fire . . . loneliness." Barbara Meldrum, in "Fate, Sex, and Naturalism in Rølvaag's Trilogy" (pp. 41–49), believes that the conflict in the novel can best be understood in terms of sexual tensions in the characters, that sex is a powerful determinant force in Rølvaag's work. The rest of the papers in the collection are readings of less significant works by Rølvaag.

Two additions to the Western Writers Series (Boise, Idaho: Boise State University) are of only marginal interest. Ann Ronald's *Zane Gray* (*WWS*, 17) describes the formula that made Zane Gray's fiction so popular—a failure from the East comes West, meets the challenge of the elements and becomes a man who can defend those he loves—but shows too how Gray failed to raise the pattern to a mythic and artistic level. Ronald also discusses how Gray's fiction, with its conservative ideals, filled a need for many people in a period of rapidly changing values. Judy Alter's *Stewart Edward White* (WWS, 18) gives no similar sense of why this author might be of historical interest today. Alter tells us that White believed fiction should embody the strenuous life, and she describes the plots of several novels, but otherwise one gets a very limited picture of this author's life and achievements. In a general article entitled "Tales and Legends in Western American Literature" (*WAL* 9:239–54), Hector H. Lee distinguishes tales from legends on the ground that the latter have historical origins, and then discusses how legends grow by absorbing materials from a variety of sources, frequently inauthentic but faithful to the spirit of the original story.

Finally there were a few articles about minor midwestern authors that will be included here rather than grouped in a separate section. Jonas Spatz's "Ring Lardner: Not an Escape, But a Reflection" (*The Twenties*, pp. 101–10) is a perceptive and useful overview of Lardner's work, arguing that the author moves in his career from detached amusement through anger to despair. The gentle humor, says Spatz, of the rube in the big town (the Busher in *You Know Me Al*) gives way to satire in stories like "Champion," where Lardner reveals that "only those willing to violate every rule of decency and live completely without feeling can become champions in the ring and, by extension, in the American marketplace." The later stories, says Spatz, are no longer about competition and the drive for success, but about boredom, frustration, and loneliness, with Lardner at the very last turning to forms of humor where the unintentional pun and the non sequitur reveal "the absurdity and impotence of language itself." Also interested in Lardner is Forrest L. Ingram, whose "Ring Lardner's Wry Wasteland" (*The Twenties*, pp. 111–22) focuses on the stories published during the 1920s, when Lardner's humor grew blacker, and is particularly concerned with the author's technique of self-deprecation and the gullibility of the reader. There were also a couple of articles on Floyd Dell, whose feminism has made him a subject of some interest again. In "Floyd Dell: Freedom or Marriage" (*MidAmerica* 2:63–79) Gerald L. Marriner describes how Dell, who had been best known for his advocacy of free love, eventually found the conventional marital state more suitable to his nature. In "Community and Self in the Midwest Town: Floyd Dell's *Moon-Calf*" (*MidAmerica* 2:88–92), Park Dixon Goist argues that the small town gives the hero, Felix Fay, a sense of community and that his departure is not a "revolt from the village" but the next stage in a quest for self. To conclude, there was an article on Glenway Wescott which deals with the failure of the westering experience, a theme which preoccupied the imagination of so many writers in the early part of the century. In "Glenway Wescott's Variations on The Waste Land Image" (*The Twenties*, pp. 171–79), Sy Kahn discusses Wescott's rendering of modern Wisconsin as a cultural wasteland and barren ground for artists. Kahn points out that in *Good-bye, Wisconsin* Wescott describes the material prosperity that has displaced the imagination of the pioneers and the standardized thinking rather than self-awareness that underlies the actions of the people.

Simon Fraser University

14. Fiction: The 1930s to the 1950s

Margaret Anne O'Connor

Publication of the letters of John Steinbeck, the correspondence of Wallace Fowlie and Henry Miller, Andrew Lytle's family history, and the recent lectures of Anaïs Nin makes 1975 an important year for scholars interested in writers who grew to prominence between 1930 and 1950. The appearance of major biographies of Robert McAlmon, James Thurber, John O'Hara, and Carson McCullers highlight the criticism appearing in 1975. Many biographers and critics chose to approach literary figures through the journals, magazines, and publishers that brought their work to the attention of the contemporary reading public. Dougald McMillan's excellent study of *transition* and Hugh Ford's study of English-language publishers in Paris provide new perspectives on the expatriate community between the wars. A special number of the *Journal of Modern Literature* offers the memoirs of Frances Steloff, owner of the Gotham Book Mart, and the index to these memoirs could well serve as a *Who's Who* in the literary world of the entire period covered by this review essay. In her introduction to the memoirs, "Frances Steloff and the Gotham Book Mart" (4:737–48), Kathleen Morgan stresses the importance of this New York bookstore as a center of literary life to writers in America and abroad. While no critics attempted an overview of this period as a whole, William Targ's *Indecent Pleasures* (New York: Macmillan) captures the tenor of the times through anecdotes, brief portraits, and reminiscences of an editor-publisher-bookseller. Targ's memoirs have an 18th-century quality about them as he displays an affinity for digressions and free associations flavored with "excremental vision." At one point early in the volume Targ jumps from giving an account of his recent proctosigmoidoscopic examination to a tribute to Henry Miller, his "mentor-hero." In his introductory comments his bookseller instincts lead him to make the following offer: "So if you're interested in writing, reading, the process of bookmaking, book design, book collecting, publishing, one publisher's way of living, the gossip of the trade and some of the curious or bizarre fauna, then I have a few things to disclose" (p. 2). His brief portraits of Miller, Carl Sandburg, Simone de Beauvoir, Sylvia Beach, Richard Wright, and many others are quite flattering to his subjects and while he seldom gives strikingly new information or precise analysis, his memoirs make for lively reading.

i. "Art for Humanity's Sake"—The Proletarian Writers

As writers and critics seek more encompassing descriptions of the work of authors usually thought of in this group, the label of "proletarian writer" has become anathema. It still serves to identify writers who began their careers from the 1930s to the early 1950s with the purpose of focusing attention on current social problems, however. Three dissertations on John Steinbeck and one on Josephine Herbst continue the investigation into works of writers often associated with this school of fiction. Frances F. Kleederman's "A Study of Language in Henry Roth's *Call It Sleep*: Bilingual Markers of a Culture in Transition" (*DAI* 35:4434A) appends an interview with Roth in which he discusses his use of language and general purposes. Terry Long's "Interview with Granville Hicks" (*AR* 33,ii:93–102) concerns the critic's involvement with *The New Masses*, his own fiction, such as his novel *Small Town* (1946), as well as his opinions of contemporary writers. While Hicks would prefer to shake off the labels of the 1930s, he feels this is impossible, given the current interest in the period. His literary tastes remain consistent, judging from his appraisal of Nabokov, whose works "annoy" him since "nothing really matters to him except technique." Hicks considers Edmund Wilson America's best literary critic and "has reservations" about Lionel Trilling, who took himself too seriously in Hicks's view.

Henry Hatfield presents a brief comparison of Trilling's *The Middle of the Journey* (1947) and Thomas Mann's *Magic Mountain* (1924) in "The Journey and the Mountain" (*MLN* 90:363–70), finding that both novels argue for a middle course between political extremes. In a perceptive survey of "The Liberal Novelist in the McCarthy Era" (*TCL* 21:253–64), Ruth Prigozy discusses the same Trilling novel with four other works of this period—Mary McCarthy's *The Groves of Academe* (1952), Irwin Shaw's *The Troubled Air*

(1951), Merle Miller's *The Sure Thing* (1949), and Norman Mailer's *Barbary Shore* (1951). Prigozy sees each of the novels as failures and is particularly hard on McCarthy's work: "Her contempt for her characters is so pervasive that the reader is forced to conclude that liberals are far more reprehensible than the witch-hunters who never appear in the novel." She concludes that Mary McCarthy's "brand of McCarthyism is no more attractive than the Senator's." Noting the absence in all five novels of characters strong enough to meet the demands of the times, Prigozy suggests that "the old liberalism was dead, and all the liberal novelists were able to do in the end was to brood over the corpse."

S. Jay Walker's "Zora Neale Hurston's *Their Eyes Were Watching God*: Black Novel of Sexism" (*MFS* 20:519–27) finds "an active awareness of the stifling effects of sexism" in the 1937 novel. Chronicling the three marriages of Janie Killicks Starks Woods, Hurston shows that only in the third marriage contracted between equals is the couple able to overcome the racism of their society. Walker notes that Hurston is not a radical feminist in her treatment of her heroine, however; Janie still seeks and finds happiness through the men in her life, not through personal growth or a sense of her own individuality.

Steinbeck: A Life in Letters (New York: Viking), ed. Elaine Steinbeck and Robert Wallsten, offers more biographical information on the author than any previous work and goes a long way in explaining Steinbeck's darkened view of himself and society in his later years. Despite the close personal relationships between Steinbeck and the editors, his widow and his friend, the 861 letters included were selected for their interest value, not in an attempt to project a single favorable image of the man. The editors explain the context of individual letters with informative connecting passages which create the effect of a biography in letters. Steinbeck's wit shines through the vast majority of the letters, as does his great capacity for friendship. Though he writes often of his own work and the practical concerns of authorship, he says little about the craft of fiction or contemporary writers whose work might have bearing on his own. *A Life in Letters* presents Steinbeck as a personality and ultimately as a national figure, not as a self-conscious artist. Perhaps this view of the man can only emerge from the studies which will undoubtedly be prompted by the appearance of these letters.

Nelson Valjean, one of Steinbeck's classmates at Stanford, writes "an intimate biography of his California years" in *John Steinbeck: The Errant Knight* (San Francisco: Chronicle Books). Despite his acquaintance with Steinbeck, Valjean's work is not a memoir. His familiarity with the California setting and the many friends they had in common gives a personal touch to Valjean's discussion of Steinbeck from his birth to his marriage to Elaine Scott in 1950. A major source for information are Steinbeck's letters to his close friend from his Stanford days, Carlton A. Sheffield. Since the most valuable of these letters are included in their entirety in *A Life in Letters*, Valjean's extensive quotations from them offer no information that isn't available in the more usable source. Valjean avoids discussion of Steinbeck's works and offers little of biographical interest. A much more valuable contribution to Steinbeck scholarship is made in Warren French's radical revision of his 1961 critical study. The 1975 *John Steinbeck* (TUSAS 2) does more than simply update the earlier volume. French suggests in his Preface that the revision could be subtitled "Steinbeck and the Drama of Consciousness." Excising material from the original study which concerned "Steinbeck's allegorizing, nonteleological thinking, and transcendentalist tendencies" because these observations have become critical commonplaces in work on Steinbeck, French approaches his subject from a different angle: "What is needed is analysis that relates this work to emerging concerns of literary and social criticism in the 1970's, especially the growing interest in heightening of the consciousness." Using a definition of "the drama of consciousness" posed in Jerry H. Bryant's study of Post-World War II authors, *The Open Decision* (See *ALS 1971*, p. 246), French considers Steinbeck's entire career and the shifts in his world view which account for the uneven quality of his work. French's expanded study includes condensed versions of his earlier treatment of *The Red Pony*, *The Grapes of Wrath*, and *Cannery Row* set in a different context.

Steinbeck and the Arthurian Theme, Steinbeck Monograph Series, 5 (Muncie, Ind.: Ball State Univ.), ed. Tetsumaro Hayashi, contains four new essays on the significance of the Arthurian legends in Steinbeck's work, as well as introductory comments by Joseph Fontenrose and "A Selected Bibliography" of critical treatment of the theme in published books and articles. Essays by Warren French and Roy S. Simmonds are the most far-reaching. In "Steinbeck's Use of Malory" (pp. 4–11) French notes the revival of interest in Arthurian legends in American popular culture prompted by the works of E. A. Robinson. Steinbeck's own fascination with the theme began when he was nine and it appears clearly in works such as *Cup of Gold* (1929) and *Tortilla Flat* (1935): "What interests Steinbeck is not the grail quest itself, but its ultimate frustration and the dissolution of the Round Table. He saw the modern 'civilized' world as one in which the knightly bond of the Round Table could not survive." Roy S. Simmonds pictures Steinbeck himself as a frustrated Arthurian "quester" in "The Unrealized Dream: Steinbeck's Modern Version of Malory" (pp. 30–43). Simmonds discusses Steinbeck's work on a modern version of the legends in "A Note on Steinbeck's Unpublished Arthurian Stories" (pp. 25–29) by reviewing the manuscript of this unfinished work at the Humanities Research Center of the University of Texas at Austin. Arthur F. Kinney's "*Tortilla Flat* Re-Visited" (pp. 12–24) traces the Arthurian strain in the work most influenced by Malory and suggests structural as well as thematic parallels. Kinney defends the episodic novel against critics who have demanded social realism from this essentially romantic work.

The *Steinbeck Quarterly* carried some of the best scholarship on Steinbeck in 1975, but inevitably some of the weakest as well. In "A Study of Female Characterization in Steinbeck's Fiction" (8:50–55), Sandra Falkenberg states that the topic of her essay has been overlooked by other critics. Yet her basic premises—that "male characters and male relationships dominate Steinbeck's novels" and that women are seen primarily in their relationships to men—are established views of his work. Darlene Eddy's "To Go A-Buccaneering and Take a Spanish Town: Some Seventeenth-Century Aspects of *Cup of Gold*" (8:3–12) suggests John Esquemeling's *The Buccaneers of America* (London, 1684) as Steinbeck's primary source of information on the life of Sir Henry Morgan, his hero in *Cup of Gold.* In comparing passages from the two works, Eddy presents convincing evidence of several striking parallels in the style and wording. Unfortunately she does not discuss the availability of Esquemeling's work to Steinbeck and settles for asserting "Steinbeck's obvious familiarity with Esquemeling" as her conclusion.

Several useful bibliographic articles also appeared in *StQ* this year. In "The First Publication of Steinbeck's 'The Leader of the People'" (8:13–18), Roy S. Simmonds elaborates on a point he first made in *StQ* in 1971 ("John Steinbeck: Works Published in the British Magazine *Argosy*" 4:101–05) when he noted that the August 1936 appearance of "The Leader of the People" in *Argosy* predates what has been considered its first publication in Viking's *The Long Valley* (1938). In his current article Simmonds collates the two versions and finds only minor changes. Simmonds also collaborates with Tetsumaro Hayashi to compile "John Steinbeck's British Publications" (8:79–89), an "annotated chronological checklist of the materials Steinbeck published in Great Britain." In a brief note Hidekazu Hirose reviews "Japanese Steinbeck Criticism in 1972–73" (8: 56–59). The major fault Hirose sees in many of the 18 articles he discusses is a problem in the United States as well: "Several of these articles were published with little reference to the [critical] books and articles already available."

In "Steinbeck's Blakean Vision in *The Grapes of Wrath*" (8:67–73), Duane R. Carr valiantly attempts to summarize Blake's world view—"the innocence to experience and to higher innocence theme"—in four sweeping paragraphs. Carr agrees with those critics who see Steinbeck as a Romantic rather than a Naturalist but notes that those novels most closely linked with the Romantic poet William Blake, *Cup of Gold* and *Burning Bright*, are among Steinbeck's least popular works. He finds the Blakean vision in Steinbeck's most acclaimed novel as well. He cites several convincing textual parallels, noting for instance, that Casy's message for Tom that "all that lives is holy" echoes Blake's *The Marriage of Heaven and Hell*, which states "Everything that lives is holy." *StQ* also reprints a portion of Warren French's revised Twayne text in "After *The Grapes of Wrath*" (8:73–78), which considers three often overlooked works—*The Forgotten Village* (1941), *The Moon Is Down* (1942), and *Bombs Away* (1942)—as "a verbal triptych."

Three of the best articles in *StQ* deal with Steinbeck's late travelogues. Richard Astro's "Travels with Steinbeck: The Laws of Thought and the Laws of Things" (8:35–44) shows that in Steinbeck's work travel becomes the test of preconceived ideas. Working primarily with *Travels with Charley* (1962), Astro also considers *A Russian Journal* (1948) and *Sea of Cortez* (1951) and finds each flawed in its own way. He feels that *Travels* ends in showing Steinbeck's "profound sense of loss" during this period in his life. John Ditsky concurs with this view in "Steinbeck's *Travels with Charley*:

The Quest that Failed" (8:45–50). He grants the book "considerable charm" but reads it primarily as "a record of what seems to have gone on in Steinbeck's spirit as he drove, gradually losing force and purpose like a river entering a desert place." Roy S. Simmonds assumes the stance of a "non-American" in "'Our Land . . . incredibly dear and beautiful': Steinbeck's *America and Americans*" (8:89–95) as he reviews work done in the years following Steinbeck's receipt of the Nobel Prize in 1962. On the whole, Simmonds sees this work as journalistic, hurried, and occasionally bordering "dangerously on the edge of mere diatribe." *America and Americans*, the only book-length work written during this period, Simmonds views as an exception. Despite the book's pessimistic elements, Simmonds sees the work leaving "a legacy of affirmation."

Two additional articles on Steinbeck appeared in other journals in 1975. Max L. Autrey, in "Men, Mice and Moths: Gradation in Steinbeck's 'The Leader of the People'" (*WAL* 10:195–204), suggests that an index to protagonist Jody's maturation is his recognition of "the *little* chain of being" (patterned after A. O. Lovejoy's *The Great Chain of Being*, 1936) established in the story. It is "the gradations within creation" and the immutability of man's position in the universe that lead to answers in Jody's search for identity. Linda Ray Pratt compares two writers who share a concern for the rural white poor in "Imagining Existence: Form and History in Steinbeck and Agee" (*SoR* 11:84–98). While Steinbeck's works of social realism such as *The Grapes of Wrath* "illustrate the distortion of social history into literary myth," Agee demands that art give way to "actuality" in his best work, *Let Us Now Praise Famous Men*. The major contrast Pratt delineates is that Steinbeck essentially accepts American values, while Agee opposes them; Steinbeck's stance leads to New Deal politics while Agee demands revolution to resolve the economic and social problems he presents.

Martha Heasley Cox and Wayne Chatterton collaborate in *Nelson Algren* (TUSAS 249), the first book-length critical study of the author. Working with published materials as well as taped interviews and correspondence with Algren initiated by the authors, Cox and Chatterton trace Algren's literary career, treating his journalism, stories, novels, and poetry. The most impressive chapter in the volume considers *The Man with a Golden Arm* (1949) from several perspectives—its themes, characterizations, imagery, humor, and, most importantly, its structure. The authors find the novel to be "Algren's most comprehensive expression of his conviction that America's great middle class should be made to recognize the personal worth and dignity of the socially disinherited" (p. 132). Agreeing with Maxwell Geismar that Algren's social protest literature is out of fashion with today's writers, Cox and Chatterton still argue convincingly that Algren's work was an important influence in the shaping of contemporary fiction.

Matthew Josephson presents a valuable overview of the radical writers of the 1930s and their fall from popularity and public esteem in the McCarthy era in "Leane Zugsmith: The Social Novel of the Thirties" (*SoR* 11:530–52). Admittedly a minor figure despite her eight well-received volumes of fiction published in the 1930s, Zugsmith is Josephson's subject because she "seems to epitomize the spirit of the left literary movement of her epoch; her experience, her case history, so to speak, is symptomatic." Josephson, whose interest is essentially biographical, refers to Zugsmith's works primarily as sources for insight into her life. Josephson met Zugsmith at one of the frequent gatherings she and her husband Carl Randau gave in their Manhattan apartment, gatherings attended by "New York's liberal and left intelligentsia" such as Heywood Broun, Lillian Hellman, and Dashiell Hammett. Like many of the writers of this group, Zugsmith and her husband were forced into "internal exile" during the McCarthy Era. Josephson compares the Randaus' response to the political pressures of the times with those of William Carlos Williams, Dalton Trumbo, and Ring Lardner, Jr.: "During those years the inflexible ones, such as Carl, and the sensitive plants, such as Leane, were crushed." When Zugsmith died in 1969, her accomplishments 30 years earlier were all but forgotten; yet Josephson suggests the current "vigorous revival of popularity" of the work of proletarian writers such as Agee, Algren, Michael Gold, Edward Dahlberg, Robert Cantwell, and Henry Roth might spread to Zugsmith's work as well. Josephson's fine article puts this group of writers in perspective.

ii. Expatriates and Emigrés

The expatriate community existing in Paris between the wars provided the background for three excellent book-length studies in 1975. Each emphasizes the role of the publisher in sustaining the climate for creativity so apparent in the work growing out of this place and era. In *Published in Paris* Hugh Ford gives the histories of the small publishing concerns begun by Americans Sylvia Beach, Robert McAlmon, Bill Bird, Gertrude Stein, and Harry and Caresse Crosby, as well as British figures Jack Kahane and Nancy Cunard, and the truly international Edward Titus. Ford shares a wealth of information in extremely readable fashion and includes as an appendix a "List of Press Publications, Periodicals, and Newspapers" (pp. 404–17) which were printed in English not only in Paris but in Berlin, Vienna, Majorca, and Rome. Ford's well-documented study stresses the importance of the often-amateur publishers to the careers of the writers they championed.

In *Adrift Among Geniuses: Robert McAlmon, Writer and Publisher of the Twenties* (University Park: Penn. State Univ. Press), Sanford J. Smoller traces McAlmon's career through published memoirs and McAlmon's correspondence with William Carlos Williams, Norman Holmes Pearson, John C. Thirlwall, Gertrude Stein, and William Bird. Unpublished remembrances of the McAlmon family also enhance the list of Smoller's sources. While Smoller's prose style is rather dry, the materials researched substantially add to the biographical information on McAlmon available in earlier studies. Smoller lauds McAlmon's achievement as a publisher of Hemingway, Williams, H. D., Stein, Djuna Barnes, and Nathanael West, but agrees with other critics that McAlmon never realized his potential as a writer.

Dougald McMillan's admirable study *transition, 1927–38: The History of a Literary Era* (London: Calder and Boyars; New York: George Braziller) relies greatly on Eugene Jolas's unpublished autobiography, "Man From Babel," in reconstructing the history of the small literary magazine Jolas founded and edited for 11 years. Never seriously threatened by the chance to make *transition* a money-making venture, Jolas and his Kentucky-born wife Maria published the magazine as a labor of love, often making up the financial deficits from their own pockets. The magazine was indeed revolutionary as many contemporary critics noted, but not in the political terms many detractors such as Wyndham Lewis proclaimed. According to McMillan, "Jolas and many of his contributors were concerned with the problem of reshaping the post–World War I world and 'discovering a new notion of man,' but they chose to concentrate their attention on aesthetics rather than politics" (p. 35). McMillan appends the impressive tables of contents from the 27 numbers of *transition* as his best evidence of the importance of this small journal. In separate chapters he considers some of the best-known contributors to the magazine—Joyce, Stein, Hart Crane, Samuel Beckett, and Dylan Thomas—and compares their aesthetic orientations with Jolas's publishing policy. McMillan's *transition* is a valuable source of information on the magazine and the period as a whole.

Djuna Barnes's *Nightwood* (1936) was the subject of a dissertation and two articles in 1975. In "*Nightwood* and the Freudian Unconscious" (*IFR* 2:159–63) Robert L. Nadeau suggests that the novel has been undervalued by a reading public that demands the realism of "human interaction on the level of conscious, waking existence." Nadeau reads the novel as "a dream world in which the embattled forces of the human personality take the form of characters representing aspects of that personality at different levels of its functioning." Though Nadeau documents his approach very well, his interpretation of the novel seems unduly restrictive, for he identifies Dr. O'Connor as the ego, Robin the id, and Nora the superego of the composite mind that he feels the novel encompasses. Donald J. Greiner's "Djuna Barnes' *Nightwood* and the Origins of Black Humor" (*Crit* 17,i:41–54) considers the novel in relation to West's *Miss Lonelyhearts* (1933) and sees both as early successful exponents of Black Humor. Characteristics of black humor exhibited in *Nightwood* include "the extreme detachment of the author," the "comic treatment of ugliness and violence," and the "disruption of conventional forms of the novel."

Henry Miller's canon of published works expands with the addition of two new volumes in 1975. *The Nightmare Notebook* (New York: New Directions) gives Miller's reactions to his trip across America in the early 1940s in prose and drawings. The $150 pricetag on this facsimile, signed, limited edition will exclude it from the personal libraries of all but the most fortunate of Miller's readers, but it is worth a visit to a rare book room to use it. In *Letters of Henry Miller and Wallace Fowlie* (New York: Grove Press) readers are treated to a record of the growing friendship between the writer and the critic from its inception in the early 1940s when Miller wrote a fan letter to francophile Fowlie and began a correspondence of ten years duration. Not surprisingly, letters often concern the French writers both men knew well. In a fine concluding essay Fowlie writes of "Henry Miller and French Writers," noting those writers who most influenced Miller's work. Jonathan Cott's "Reflections of a Cosmic Tourist: An Afternoon with Henry Miller" (*Rolling Stone*, Feb. 27, 1975, pp. 38–41, 43, 45–46, 57) casually interviews Miller in his home near Los Angeles. Cott elicits some delightful responses to a wide variety of questions covering Miller's friendship with Anaïs Nin, his reaction to criticism of his work by feminists, and his interest in mysticism while he was in the Villa Seurat. Lawrence Durrell contributed to the last portion of this valuable interview. Alex Bolckmans investigates Miller's interest in the work of a Norwegian Nobel Prize winner in "Henry Miller's *Tropic of Cancer* and Knut Hamsun's *Sult* (*Scan* 14:115–26). Miller claimed a familiarity with Hamsun's work in general in his 1952 list of "The Books in My Life" and Bolckmans notes that he must have read most of the older writer's works in German translations, though his first novel *Sult* was available in English. The major portion of Bolckmans's article compares the first novels of each man, attempting to prove direct influence. The parallels drawn, however, are weak, particularly in the areas of style. Bolckmans compares an untranslated paragraph of Norwegian with Miller's English, despite his earlier statement that Miller knew Hamsun through English or German translations.

Anaïs Nin also adds new work to her canon in 1975, but as with her five volumes of diaries she gives others the task of organizing her material for publication. *A Woman Speaks: The Lectures, Seminars, and Interviews of Anaïs Nin* (New York: Swallow) is very ably edited and introduced by Evelyn J. Hinz. Hinz combines transcripts of 38 taped lectures Nin has given since 1966, excises the redundancies, and reshapes them to produce "a characteristic lecture" on eight different topics. While none of the 38 lectures or interviews appears in its entirety, paragraphs drawn from them are unobtrusively keyed to the original source, making the text useful to scholars needing precise documentation. The book is enhanced by its unusual format. With the recent burst of enthusiasm for Nin, particularly the popularity of her diaries, several weak anthologies and collections of her work have appeared; Hinz's volume is a happy exception to this trend.

Vladimir Nabokov remains the most illustrious emigré in American literature, judging by the great interest in his work in 1974 and

1975. While the six dissertations completed last year are not matched by the two appearing in *DAI* in 1975, it would be foolhardy to suggest that interest in his work is waning. To the four critical volumes devoted to Nabokov's work reviewed in these pages last year must be added Alfred Appel's *Nabokov's Dark Cinema* (New York: Oxford Univ. Press [1974]), which escaped this reviewer's attention. In this fascinating volume Appel looks at the popular culture of America, primarily the cinema of the 1940s and early 1950s, as a source for many seemingly obscure references in Nabokov's work. Terming Nabokov "the most learned and mandarin of living writers," Appel places special emphasis on *Lolita* (1955), "a vision of the 1947–52 period" which Appel feels "succeeds better than any other postwar American novel in its rendering of the ways in which songs, ads, magazines, and movies create and control their consumers" (p. 15). Virtually one-third of the volume consists of illustrations—stills from movies, comic strips and cartoons, and photographs of popular ad campaigns such as the men's underwear ads which so captivated John Shade's Aunt Maud in *Pale Fire*. Appel justifies this nostalgic trip down memory lane in the best scholarly fashion: "Employing a Flaubertian shorthand of characterization, Nabokov continually uses movies, as well as novels, paintings, and magazines, to define the minds and souls of his creations, the total nature of their existence" (p. 34). While using such materials, however, Nabokov withholds approval of the popular culture which so involves his characters; he manages to "mock 'popular trash' more often and more consistently than any other modern author" in Appel's view. The meaty sections of this study concern the years Nabokov wrote *Lolita* and the transformation of the novel into a movie in 1962. A portion of Appel's treatment of the pre-*Lolita* years appears as "The Road to *Lolita*, or the Americanization of an Émigré" (*JML* 4[1974]:3–31).

Four critical articles in 1975 also focus on *Lolita*. In "*Lolita*: Nabokov's Critique of Aloofness" (*PLL* 11:71–82), Harold Brent argues that most critics emphasize Nabokov's "playfulness," rather than his equally apparent "passion." Brent finds *Lolita* to be a critique of the quality of "artistic aloofness" which most critics associate with Nabokov. Fashioning his own story in *Lolita*, Humbert Humbert is an artist, and at the novel's end he is able "to take reality out of the quotation marks in which it is so often found these days." In Brent's view "*Lolita* shows that a book cannot be about truly valuable art unless it is also about real life." Mathew Winston suggests that readers become Humbert Humbert's jury in "*Lolita* and the Dangers of Fiction" (*TCL* 21:421–27). Humbert Humbert's bid for immortality can only succeed if the reader heeds his closing plea: "Please, reader, imagine me; I shall not exist if you do not imagine me." Elizabeth Proileau investigates the parallels between *Lolita* and Lewis Carroll's novel in "Humbert Humbert *Through the Looking Glass*" (*TCL* 21:428–37). In both works man is trapped in a world of mirrors "which seal man in his solipsistic and temporal cell." Phyllis A. Roth also recognizes the parallels between *Lolita* and *Through the Looking Glass* in her essay "In Search of Aesthetic Bliss: A Rereading of *Lolita*" (*CollL* 2:28–49). Roth's major interest, however, is in demonstrating that Quilty functions as Humbert Humbert's *doppelgänger* in the novel. One minor confusion occurs in the introductory comments to the article which identify "Sirlin," rather than "Sirin," as Nabokov's pseudonym in several early works. This and other typographical errors suggest that this new journal could improve its proofreading.

While *Lolita* received more critical attention than any other single work by Nabokov this year, his novel *Pale Fire*, his autobiography *Speak, Memory*, and the short stories written between 1930 and 1950 were not neglected. Phyllis A. Roth contributes a second article on Nabokov's use of the double in "The Psychology of the Double in Nabokov's *Pale Fire*" (*EIL* 2:209–29). Noting that Nabokov parodies psychoanalytic principles in many of his works, Roth gives a Freudian analysis of *Pale Fire*. In her view "Kinbote's self-portrayal requires a psychoanalytic reading which reveals in his situation at New Wye—the situation of the alienated and ridiculed homosexual seeking approval from a paradigmatic Oedipal dilemma—a forced adjustment which leads from self-preoccupation, narcissism, and homoeroticism, to hatred of women and heterosexuality." Roth seems to fall victim to the dangers of Freudian reductionism, which Nabokov warns against, in this humorless reading of the novel. In "The Scientific Art of Nabokov's *Pale Fire*" (*Criticism* 17:223–33), Timothy F. Flower delineates the requirements Nabokov's "scientific style" places on his reader. Nabokov's ideal reader must share the author's own interests; he must be a scholar, expert in languages and literature, as well as a natural scientist, expert in taxonomy, geography, ornithology, entomology, and lepidopterology.

Dabney Stuart reclassifies Nabokov's 1966 autobiography in "The Novelist's Composure: *Speak, Memory* as Fiction" (*MLQ* 36:177–92). Suggesting that any good autobiographer is in "the act of making one's self up" as a novelist makes up his characters, Stuart notes the "thematic designs" in *Speak, Memory* which make the work "imaginative narration in which events, actions, and details of landscape (both indoor and out), in themselves neutral, are formed, shaped, and rendered significant by a single, ordering consciousness. It is, in short, fiction." In his treatment of *Speak, Memory* Stuart ignores recent criticism on autobiography as a genre such as James Olney's excellent study *Metaphors of Self* (1972), which grants all of the qualities Stuart associates with fiction to the autobiography but still recognizes autobiography as a distinct genre. In "Nabokov's Dozen Short Stories: His World in Microcosm" (*SSF* 12:213–22), Carol T. Williams suggests that the 13 stories written from the 1930s to the 1950s collected in *Nabokov's Dozen* (1958) offer a convenient entry into the entire world of Nabokov's fiction. Williams treats the stories individually and occasionally points out parallels and contrasts between these short works and Nabokov's novels.

iii. The Southerners

The uniqueness of a southern orientation was defined, confirmed, and questioned in many of the 16 dissertations on southern writers abstracted in *DAI* in 1975. The work of Robert Penn Warren was the subject of four dissertations; Eudora Welty and Carson McCullers prompted two dissertations each and a third considered the authors together; James Agee, Katherine Anne Porter, Thomas Wolfe, and Caroline Gordon were also the subjects of individual dissertations. Certainly one of the most important contributions to the study of southern writers in the period covered by this review essay is Virginia J. Rock's "They Took Their Stand: The Emergence of the Southern Agrarians" in *Prospects* (1:205–95). Rock's 1961 doctoral dissertation, "The Making and Meaning of *I'll Take My Stand*: A Study in Utopian Conservatism 1925–39," has been required reading for anyone interested in the Agrarian and Fugitive groups at Vanderbilt. This new study does far more than merely update a substantial portion of the dissertation, however. Rock shows that this manifesto of a small group of southern "reactionaries" published in 1930 takes on new meaning in the 1970s for the generation (described by Charles Reich in *The Greening of America* [1970]) that is in sympathy with the 12 essayists in the collection who see the advantages of the "Agrarian versus the Industrial" way of life. Rock does a superb job of relating the men and ideas of 1930 in the American South to America in 1975. Many of the informational notes appended could have been published as complete essays themselves. This study adds significantly to previous books on this subject by John Bradbury, Louise Cowan, and John L. Stewart.

Virginia Rock notes that Donald Davidson termed Andrew Lytle "a Fugitive *de facto*," and Lytle's *A Wake for the Living: A Family Chronicle* (New York: Crown) confirms his attachment to the poetic and philosophic tenets of this group. *A Wake for the Living* presents the virtues of "a country society" by reproducing the rich family existence Lytle enjoyed in his youth in central Tennessee. The book grows from the premise that "if you don't know who you are or where you come from, you will find yourself at a disadvantage" (p. 3), a hindrance to personal development Lytle sees as endemic in urban environments. Lytle's tone is nostalgic and his mood lyric as he proclaims the loss of the world of his youth. Stories and anecdotes of the Civil War seem as alive and pertinent to daily family activities of the 1940s as vignettes of World War II. The book is autobiography but impressionistically presented; it does not hold out the chronology of the author's life as a convenient thread to tie the vignettes and reminiscences together. It is a lyrical presentation of a lost way of life and only incidentally one man's story.

Barnett Guttenberg concentrates on the protagonists of Robert Penn Warren's nine novels in *Web of Being: The Novels of Robert Penn Warren* (Nashville, Tenn.: Vanderbilt Univ. Press) and finds that the search for selfhood and eventual acceptance of personal responsibility are keys to these characterizations. A revision of Guttenberg's 1972 Cornell dissertation (*DAI* 33:1169A), *Web of Being* treats Warren's novels chronologically with a chapter devoted to each work. An important consideration in each discussion is Guttenberg's concept of Warren's "fully conceived world view": "In Warren's mythology . . . derived largely from Coleridge and with distinct affinity to Heidegger, one falls from the harmony of childhood into the chaos of the world. His redemption begins with the realization that the chaos is an extension of himself. From that realization comes a sense of involvement and responsibility, of freedom and direction, all of which define the reintegrated will and make possible a new world, an Eden which has been earned" (pp. 162–63). While Guttenberg's general thesis is not new, his careful readings of the novels, particularly of *All the King's Men,* confirm the importance of the progression toward selfhood in Warren's work.

John T. Hiers compares Madison Jones's little-known novel of 1963 with Robert Penn Warren's *Flood* in "Buried Graveyards: Warren's *Flood* and Jones' *A Buried Land*" (*EIL* 2:97–104), noting that in both works the flooding of graveyards by the TVA threatens "the obliteration of a relatively homogeneous way of life." The flooding serves as the central image in both works for the struggle between urban and agrarian values. Warren's protagonist, Brad Tolliver, succeeds in understanding himself and his changing world but Jones's hero, Percy Youngblood, does not. Hiers considers Warren's successful resolution of Tolliver's dilemma a reason for the favorable critical acceptance of Warren's novel while Jones's inflexible idealism overwhelms the dramatic promise of his protagonist.

Wilton Eckley returns to the subject of his 1965 dissertation in his critical biography *T. S. Stribling* (TUSAS 255). Despite the admittedly dated quality of all Stribling's novels, even his Pulitzer Prize winning *The Store* (1931), Eckley argues that Stribling made a positive contribution to the Southern Renaissance in the 1920s and 1930s. Emphasizing the novels set in the South, Eckley treats Stribling's exotic fiction growing from his travels in Latin America in only a cursory fashion. In *Bright Metal* (1928) Eckley finds a picture of small-town Tennessee life presented in the vein of Sinclair Lewis's *Main Street.* A satirist, Stribling obliquely makes a case for change in the social order of the South, a stance which Eckley argues might be responsible for the neglect he has suffered from critics of southern literature more interested in the conservative stance of the Fugitives and Agrarians. Eckley's taped interviews with Stribling made in 1964 augment the biographical information to be gleaned from the sparse list of published criticism appended to the study. While Eckley argues persuasively for the importance of Stribling's work historically, no case is presented for the literary merit of the work.

R. J. Gray writes of a figure he sees as "one of the most, if not *the* most popular of all modern Southern writers" in "Southwestern Humor, Erskine Caldwell, and the Comedy of Frustration" (*SLJ* 8,i:3–

26). Gray traces the history of southwestern humor and finds that "Caldwell owes a profound debt to the southwestern humorists and to George Washington Harris in particular." *God's Little Acre* and *Tobacco Road* are the two novels most directly influenced by Harris's Sut Lovingood, but Gray sees the same comic tradition pervading all of Caldwell's fiction.

Three volumes on Thomas Wolfe—a juvenile biography, a critical study, and a collection of contemporary reviews of his novels—appeared recently, and each serves its intended audience well. Leo Gurko's *Thomas Wolfe: Beyond the Romantic Ego* (New York: Crowell) is aimed at a teenage audience and presents Wolfe as a personality with whom many young people might identify. The book serves as an excellent, though demanding, introduction to Wolfe's works for this level of reader and encourages young readers to go beyond *Look Homeward, Angel* to works less often taught in high-school English classes in order to understand Thomas Wolfe the man. C. Hugh Holman's *The Loneliness at the Core: Studies in Thomas Wolfe* (Baton Rouge: La. State Univ. Press) presents eight essays revised and reworked from scholarship Holman has published in journals and festschriften over the last 20 years. The new volume not only makes these valuable studies more accessible; the format enhances the individual essays and gives a clear picture of Wolfe as a southerner and an American. In *Thomas Wolfe: The Critical Reception* (New York: David Lewis, 1974), Pascal Reeves collects reviews of Wolfe's book-length works to illustrate the varied responses they received in the contemporary press. Reviews which distinguish themselves through style, perspective, or insight are reprinted in their entirety, with only unnecessary plot summary or familiar biographical sketches deleted; reviews not reprinted are listed at the end of each chapter devoted to a specific work. While he concentrates on the critical responses made in national magazines and New York newspapers, Reeves also includes a good sampling of the British response to Wolfe's work and that appearing in small-town southern newspapers. Reeves's volume is part of The American Critical Tradition Series under the general editorship of M. Thomas Inge. Future works in this useful series will be published by Burt Franklin Company.

The lively debate over Thomas Wolfe's manuscripts continues. In "Thomas Wolfe's Last Manuscript" (*HLB* 23:203–11) Richard S. Kennedy presents a minute investigation of the rough outline for

Wolfe's unfinished novel in support of his assertion that the outline (appended to Kennedy's *The Window of Memory: The Literary Career of Thomas Wolfe* [1962]) was composed by Wolfe and typed by his secretary, not written by Edward Aswell, his editor, as was alleged by Patrick Miehe in a brief note in *HLB* (21 [1973]:400–401). Kennedy cites biographical evidence, comparisons of typewriter keyboards, interviews and correspondence with figures who handled the manuscript to substantiate his view of authorship. Kennedy recommends the re-editing of these manuscripts to answer other questions scholars have concerning these works.

John Idol discusses a 16-page excerpt from Wolfe's manuscripts selected for separate publication by Maxwell Perkins in 1939 in "Thomas Wolfe's 'A Note on Experts'" (*SSF* 11[1974]:395–98). Idol concentrates on the satiric elements in the piece, noting particularly the Lardnerian humor in Wolfe's treatment of the sportswriter Vila. Idol continues his discussion of Wolfe as a satirist in "Thomas Wolfe and Jonathan Swift" (*SCR* 8,i:43–54). Recognizing that Wolfe's belief that "all serious work in fiction is autobiographical" argues against the existence in his work of the detached perspective necessary to a satirist, Idol still finds satire prominent in many of Wolfe's works. A substantial portion of the article delineates affinities between *Look Homeward, Angel* and *Gulliver's Travels* and makes a case for the direct influence of Swift in Wolfe's first novel.

The 13 essays collected in David Madden's *Remembering James Agee* (Baton Rouge: La. State Univ. Press [1974]) are written by friends and associates of Agee who attended a commemorative gathering held in his honor at his prep school, St. Andrew's Episcopal, near Sewannee, Tennessee, in October 1972. Nine of the essays are reprinted from other sources and of the new essays, that contributed by the author's widow is the most illuminating. "Faint Lines in a Drawing of Jim" (pp. 153–62), which Mia Agee wrote with the help of Gerald Locklin, answers the charge made by several critics that Agee "wasted his time and diffused his talent" with journalistic writing and work in Hollywood done to fit formulas dictated by editors and movie producers. Mia Agee asserts that he was not restricted by these boundaries: "Incapable of doing a hack job" at any assigned task, Agee "felt challenged by the idea of having to write within a set format but working at all times against that format, creating a kind of tension and seeing just how far he could go" (p. 154).

Victor Kramer's familiarity with the Agee manuscripts in the Humanities Research Center at the University of Texas at Austin is a great strength in his extremely readable study *James Agee* (TUSAS 252). Kramer uses the format of the series well, giving a thorough, well-documented account of Agee's life but not permitting biographical information to overshadow the individual treatments of his works. He devotes a chapter each to Agee's recognized masterpieces, *Let Us Now Praise Famous Men* and *A Death in the Family*, but also considers his poetry, short stories, and screenplays in detail. It is Agee's "moral vision" that assures the "enduring value" of his best work. His major theme is "a celebration of immediacy bounded by death." In "'Religion at its Deepest Intensity': The Stasis of Agee's *The Morning Watch*" (*Renascence* 27:221–29), Victor Kramer elaborates on the reading of Agee's posthumously published novella presented in his Twayne volume. Rejecting a common interpretation of the work which sees it primarily as an initiation story, Kramer finds the protagonist's desire to achieve stasis to be the central focus of the story. The novella celebrates "the immediacy of what is experienced," not change, which is the domain of the initiation story.

Katherine Anne Porter's "Noon Wine" received two very different readings this year and both were convincing. In "Strangers in a Strange Land: A Reading of 'Noon Wine'" (*AL* 47:230–46), M. Wynn Thomas approaches the story through stylistic analysis, emphasizing recurring key words and their subtle change in meaning by the story's end. Mr. Thompson, Porter's protagonist, becomes a stranger to his own language, an estrangement which underscores his reasons for suicide. Thomas F. Walsh fits the story into Otto Rank's "literature of the double" in "Deep Similarities in 'Noon Wine'" (*Mosaic* 9,i:83–92). Walsh draws his title—and the major support for his thesis—from Porter's 1956 article "'Noon Wine': The Sources" (*YR* 46:34–35), in which she comments on the "deep similarities" existing among the three main characters in the story. Following Porter's lead, Walsh reads the story as an internal struggle within Mr. Thompson. Helton and Mrs. Thompson serve as his psychological "doubles" in the story.

While Porter's controversial *Ship of Fools* was not a direct subject of critical debate this year, its nature and merit were discussed in relation to Porter's short fiction in two new journals. In his reading of "Katherine Anne Porter's 'Holiday'" appearing in a short-lived revival of the *Southern Literary Messenger* (1:1–5), John Edward Hardy views the story as essentially comic, though its central concerns, "the themes of bestiality and human recognition," are also part of the "satiric tragedy" of *Ship of Fools*. Hardy's brief article supports the interpretation of the novel given in his *Katherine Anne Porter* (see *ALS 1973*, p. 242). *SLM* has apparently folded after issuing only two numbers of its first volume. *International Fiction Review*, however, seems to have a brighter future. Joan Givner's "Katherine Anne Porter, Eudora Welty and 'Ethan Brand'" (*IFR* 1[1974]:32–37) suggests that Hawthorne's concept of "the Unpardonable Sin" determines the character of Welty's "Petrified Man" and Porter's protagonist in "Theft." Both contemporary writers show the inhuman nature of their antiheroes, turning them into grotesque characters resembling Ethan Brand. Givner prefers Porter's use of "subtlety and understatement" in "Theft" as opposed to Welty's emphasis on the "sensational nature" of the main character in her story. In a later number of *IFR* Orlene Murad contributes a note "On Joan Givner's Article . . ." (1:162–63), which laments the very quality of Porter's work that Givner seems to admire. Murad finds Porter's tendency to treat evil as a physical entity to be "her major weakness." Viewing this tendency to allegorize as "a narrow, simplistic, melodramatic view which undermines her work," Murad sees that it "greatly mars an ambitious novel like *Ship of Fools* and to a lesser degree a modest short story like 'Theft.'"

Mildred K. Travis also recognizes ties between Welty and Hawthorne in "A Note on 'Wakefield' and 'Old Mr. Marblehall'" (*NConL* 4,iii[1974]:9–10). Travis briefly compares the title characters in the story and suggests that the Hawthorne story is a direct influence on Welty's work. Travis's point is well taken and deserves a more thoroughly developed discussion. Several other brief notes on Welty's fiction offer snacks, if not food for thought. In "Is Sister Really Insane?: Another Look at 'Why I Live at the P.O.'" (*NConL* 5,i:5–7), Walter Herrscher argues for the "strength and stability" of the narrator of Welty's story, who, in his view, has been unjustly maligned by other critics. Accepting the narrator as a reliable commentator on the action, Herrscher loses the ironic level of humor which has made the story one of Welty's most popular works. Except for defending the honor of a lady, he accomplishes little else in his reading of the story. In another brief note, Franklin D. Carson rehashes an old issue in "Recurring Metaphors: An Aspect of Unity in *The Golden Apples*" (*NConL* 5,iv:4–7). Noting the repetition of several metaphors throughout the seven stories in the collection, Carson sees them as evidence of the essential unity of the book. He has the same general purpose in mind in his "The Passage of Time in Eudora Welty's 'Sir Rabbit'" (*SSF* 12:284–86), as he calls attention to the time change in the third story included in *The Golden Apples.* Overlooking this shift in time has caused other critics to distort the meaning of the story in relation to the collection as a whole. In a final brief note on Welty's work Margaret Bolsterli discusses "The Wide Net" in "A Fertility Rite in Mississippi" (*NMW* 8:69–71). A rigorous comparison of the characters, images, and events of the story with the specific fertility myths Bolsterli has in mind would have been very informative, but Bolsterli deals instead with vague generalities in a casual and offhand manner.

Although his conclusions are arguable, A. R. Coulthard makes a strong case for the "amateurish inconsistency" of "Point of View in Eudora Welty's 'Old Mr. Marblehead'" (*NMW* 8:22–27). Two narrators control the story, one a first-person voice whose imagination invents a double life for Mr. Marblehead but whose own limited intelligence cannot present the complexities of the situation and must be augmented by comments from a second omniscient narrative voice. The nature of the narrative leads Coulthard to the conclusion that "from a technical standpoint, then, 'Old Marblehall' is one of Miss Welty's weaker stories." Robert J. Kloss's "The Symbolic Structure of Eudora Welty's 'Livvie'" (*NMW* 7[1974–75]:70–82) goes overboard in the search for phallic symbols and tangible signs of Livvie's thwarted desire for motherhood. Since Kloss is merely giving further support for Alfred Appel's interpretation of the story from *A Season of Dreams: The Fiction of Eudora Welty* (see *ALS 1965*, pp. 196–99), his cataloguing of sexual symbols offers no new approach to the story. Susan L. Myers lacks the linguistic vocabulary for the close stylistic analysis she attempts in "Dialogues in Eudora Welty's Short Stories" (*NMW* 8:51–57). Noting that in Welty's fiction "one is judged by the way he speaks," Myers makes reference to "The Wide Net" and "A Worn Path" to show that Welty's characters display their social backgrounds through their dialects. Again, this is hardly a new insight into Welty's work.

Charles E. Davis proposes to break new ground in "The South in

Eudora Welty's Fiction: A Changing World" (*SAF* 3:199–209). Treating her major works chronologically, Davis finds "the persistent theme of the disappearance of the Old South and the resultant rise of the New South." In Davis's view critics such as Vande Kieft, Appel, and John Hardy have been "faintly apologetic" about Welty as a southern writer, "virtually ignoring the significance of her southern setting" in order to stress her accomplishment in "transcending locale." Davis inexplicably excludes Welty's most recent novel, *The Optimist's Daughter* (1972) from his discussion, though it fits well into his thesis. In "The Use of Marriage in Welty's *The Optimist's Daughter*" (*Crit* 17,ii:36–46), William J. Stucky fits the work into the tradition of the novel of manners. He finds, too, that Welty's southernness plays an important part in the novel, not merely in the setting but in the distinctive treatment of the past: "Eudora Welty is a Southern writer who writes of the past—not the past of Faulkner's South, but a personal past that can be carried away . . . and through the operation of memory can be brought in touch with the present."

Virginia Spencer Carr spent seven years researching and writing *The Lonely Hunter: A Biography of Carson McCullers* (New York: Doubleday) and her product makes fascinating reading for the literary scholar and general reader alike. Carr devotes only 40 pages of her 537-page text to McCuller's "Georgia Girlhood," memories of which prompted McCullers's best work. This early period of her life is overshadowed in the biography of her communal life in the Brooklyn house she shared with George Davis and W. H. Auden, which must have been the Grand Hotel of the literary elite in the 1940s. McCullers sought the support of other artists in her sojourns at Breadloaf and, much more frequently, Yaddo. Her stormy marriage and emotional attachments to both men and women make spicy reading but also give further insight into the author's longing for acceptance and union with others. Carr's sources, for the most part, are unpublished letters and dozens of taped interviews with McCullers's friends and acquaintances. While Carr's prose is marred by occasional sentimental passages and repetitious identifications of the many figures who move in and out of McCullers's life, *The Lonely Hunter* is, on the whole, quite well written. Attempting no critical readings of McCullers's works themselves, Carr only occasionally refers to their contents as she seeks to explain McCullers's inner feelings. In his introductory comments to the volume, Tennessee Williams objects to the biographical treatments McCullers has received in the past, which see McCullers as a physical and emotional invalid. Carr successfully puts McCullers's medical history in perspective and paints a detailed, sympathetic portrait of an often misunderstood figure.

Carr's excellent biography is destined to overshadow Richard Cook's more modest study *Carson McCullers* (New York: Frederick Unger). Yet biography consumes only a small portion of the 150-page study and Cook's critical readings of individual works, particularly of *The Member of the Wedding*, are thorough and revealing. His assumption that a major theme in McCullers's works is her antipathy toward the South, challenged as this view is in Carr's biography, weakens Cook's general conclusions. Francis B. Dedmond considers biographical information in "Doing Her Own Thing: Carson McCullers' Dramatization of *The Member of the Wedding*" (*SAB* 40,ii:47–52). Dedmond reviews the history of McCullers's decision to dramatize her novel and attributes her interest in the project to the influence of Tennessee Williams, a view supported by Carr's account of the genesis of the play (*Lonely Hunter*, pp. 274–75). Dedmond compares the two treatments of this story of spiritual isolation and shows the differing requirements of each art form. He terms the conversion a success, despite earlier critical disparagement, which saw the play as only a weak reflection of the novel. Charlene Kerne Clark contributes two articles on McCullers's novels in 1975. In "Selfhood and the Southern Past: A Reading of McCullers's *Clock Without Hands*" (*SLM* 1,ii:16–23), Clark takes issue with critics who feel the novel is of limited value to serious students of southern literature. She sees the work in contrast, as "by far Mrs. McCullers' most 'Southern' novel," not in the mere parochial sense that it deals with political and racial issues that are peculiar to the region, but in its embodiment of a tragic sense of history that is seen as distinctly southern. In "Pathos with a Chuckle: The Tragicomic Vision in the Novels of Carson McCullers" (*SAmH* 1:161–66), Clark finds "a saving humor in the grimmest situations" in McCullers's work. It is "the juxtaposition of the immense with the trivial" which accounts for the humor in McCullers's work, a quality McCullers herself saw as common to the work of the Russian realists and many writers of the American South.

Lee Zacharias discusses Truman Capote's story in "Living the American Dream: 'Children on Their Birthdays'" (*SSF* 12:343–50).

She reads it as a story of initiation and finds affinities to Nabokov's *Lolita* and other novels of the 1940s that she groups together under the heading "the adolescent novel."

In an article that ranges far more broadly over southern literature than the chronological confines of this review essay, James H. Justus questions some of the generalizations which are used to distinguish southern from national literature. "On the Restlessness of Southerners" (*SoR* 11:65–83) attacks the often-cited contrast between national "mobility" and the southern regional impulse toward "containment." Justus supports C. Hugh Holman and C. Vann Woodward, who recognize a broader base of writers as defining the southern spirit than the conservative contributors to *I'll Take My Stand* or more recent commentators who assume "that the South *should* stand for containment, rootedness, familial and regional loyalty, and easiness of living, even laziness." To Justus "those images—compounded of history, myth, ancestor worship, wish fulfillment—are true, too, if a trifle simple-minded." Justus considers the national trait of "restlessness" first delineated by de Tocqueville as it appears in the works of Mark Twain, Thomas Wolfe, Erskine Caldwell, Eudora Welty, and the "most southern of southern writers," William Faulkner. Justus's thought-provoking overview of southern literature seeks to discover where "the distinctive metaphors of national and regional consciousness intersect," not where they differ, as has been the purpose of most critical treatments of southern writers.

iv. Popular Fiction

Opening the pages of three biographical works published in 1975, a reader finds the same photograph of Harold Ross, founder and long-time editor of *The New Yorker.* Hair pasted down and chin resting on the palm of his hand, Ross waits to give testimony to a state agency in favor of banning the playing of Musak in Grand Central Station. As Brendan Gill explains in his memoirs, *Here at the New Yorker* (New York: Random House), this small victory for peace was only one of the many services Ross performed for his town. Ross is a comparatively minor figure in Burton Bernstein's *Thurber: A Biography* (New York: Dodd, Mead) and Matthew Joseph Bruccoli's *The O'Hara Concern: A Biography of John O'Hara* (New York: Random House). The subjects of these two biographies do not fare as well as

Ross in Gill's account of his almost 40 years with *The New Yorker.* James Thurber's cruel pranks are not dismissed lightheartedly in the chapter Gill devotes to the humorist. Picturing Thurber's relationship with E. B. White, for instance, Gill remarks: "It was in Thurber's nature to wish to inflict pain, and I suppose it was in White's nature to wish to accept it" (p. 290). Beginning his discussion of "not only our best short-story writer" but also "our most prolific" (225 stories appearing in *The New Yorker*), Gill cries "Oh, but John O'Hara was a difficult man!" (p. 264). By way of summary he grudgingly adds that "O'Hara was a truculent and often mean-spirited man, but he had standards" (p. 279). Lesser lights gleaming from the pages of *The New Yorker* receive more praise and Gill even seems to send a line of encouragement to one of the magazine's "lost sheep": "Though Salinger's absence from the pages of the magazine is from week to week and from year to year an obscurely felt deprivation, the fact is that he goes on writing, and surely some day he will be willing to let us observe the consequences" (p. 228). Gill loves *The New Yorker,* warts and all, but he certainly finds a lot of warts.

While James Thurber's widow Helen might be disappointed that Burton Bernstein "treated her husband's life in too negative a fashion," as the author notes in his Foreword, *Thurber: A Biography* seems the model of fairness. Thurber's early disappointments, primarily his childhood eye injury which led to his virtual blindness in the 1930s, tempers the picture of the often-bitter Thurber of his late years. With the cooperation of Thurber's family and access to their records and correspondence, Bernstein has a wealth of information to share. He has done an admirable job of researching his subject in published materials as well, though his method for documenting this research leaves much to be desired. Partial entries in the notes and bibliography as well as Bernstein's failure to repeat the date or year of activities described at reasonable intervals, make the volume difficult to use as a quick source of information. Bernstein also avoids discussing Thurber's works, though this would have enhanced his study. Still, Bernstein writes with humor, candor, and understanding of Thurber's life.

Many of the weaknesses of Bernstein's volume are the strengths of Matthew Joseph Bruccoli's *The O'Hara Concern.* Bruccoli has done a good job of scholarship and presented his material with clarity and enthusiasm. The egotistical snob Brendan Gill pictures is still present in Bruccoli's study but, perhaps with the advantage of having had no personal contact with O'Hara, Bruccoli is able to look beyond his difficult personality to the man and his work in conjunction. Bruccoli discusses all of O'Hara's novels and many of his best pieces of short fiction in detail and justifies this attention in the extravagant concluding paragraph of the biography: "For forty years he wrote truthfully and exactly about life and people, scorning fashion, to produce a body of work unsurpassed in American literature in scope and fidelity to American life. He was one of our best novelists, our best novella-ist, and our greatest writer of short stories" (p. 345). It is a pity that Bruccoli has to weaken a good piece of scholarship by making such exaggerated claims for a writer who no doubt will remain a figure of second-magnitude importance.

Richard H. Goldstone points out in his Foreword to *Thornton Wilder: An Intimate Portrait* (New York: Saturday Review Press of E. P. Dutton) that his study is not "a formal biography." Instead, it is "an intimate portrait" drawn from the impressions "of persons who have stood close to Thornton Wilder," including Wilder's sister Isabel. Goldstone also includes himself on the basis of his 30-year acquaintance and correspondence with Wilder. In his individual treatments of works and general assessment of Wilder, he is far from being uncritically adulatory of his friend. In fact, Goldstone treats Wilder's life and career as if he were a failure personally and professionally and the discussions of individual works contribute to this effect. He ends his study by weakly defending Wilder against critics who believe "Wilder's artistic deficiencies stem from a weakness of nerve" or who find "that the failure of his life comes from too little commitment." Rejecting these explanations but not the basic premises, Goldstone suggests that "Wilder was shaped and straitjacketed by the traditions that bred him, and to the extent that was possible he fought loose from some of them" (p. 268). This negative appraisal of Wilder's accomplishment will no doubt prompt as much critical response as Bruccoli's praise of O'Hara.

Roy S. Simmonds writes two articles on the author of *The Bad Seed* which may in themselves raise interest in this neglected figure. Simmonds modestly describes "A William March Checklist" (*MissQ* 28:461–88) as "a fairly comprehensive, though by no means definitive, survey of the William March canon." The detailed, annotated list of primary and secondary sources which follows includes reviews and unpublished doctoral dissertations and provides the necessary information for a thorough evaluation of March's work and critical reputation. In "An Unending Circle of Pain: William March's *Company K*" (*BSUF* 16,ii:33–46), Simmonds contrasts William March Campbell, businessman, and William March the writer. He also emphasizes the biographical ties between March and his episodic novel *Company K* (1945). Simmonds remains objective as he notes the flaws in the work while he lauds its experimental structure. Overall he finds it "one of the most considerable works of art to have emerged from the holocaust of World War I."

In "Toward New Archetypal Forms: Jean Stafford's *The Catherine Wheel*" (*Crit* 17,ii:77–92), Jeanette W. Mann finds the 1952 novel a "New England Gothic tale" in the tradition of Hawthorne. The work differs from Stafford's earlier works primarily in its "incremental narrative method" which achieves order through "repetition and juxtaposition rather than logical progression." Mann gives a lucid reading of the work in terms of its relationship to the legend of St. Catherine of Alexandria.

Gerald C. Nemanic's "Ross Lockridge, *Raintree County*, and the Epic of Irony" (*MidAmerica* 2:35–46) sees the work as "a valiant failure" which attempted "to dramatize the essential experience of America." Nemanic gives a convincing reading of the novel as a *bildungsroman* flawed by "a perplexing doubleness" in the treatment of the main character's "quest." Nemanic is not sure if this tendency to "rhapsodize and satirize" the quest is a product of conscious irony on Lockridge's part or a "sign of a perilous personal dilemma" which may have led to the author's suicide only months after the novel appeared in 1948.

Conrad Aiken is the subject of two articles this year, both of which lament the neglect the writer-poet is currently suffering. Carolyn Handa's "'Impulse': Calculated Artistry in Conrad Aiken" (*SSF* 12:375–80) argues that most critics still find themselves defending their interest in Aiken's work in general, rather than focusing their attention on explications of particular works. Handa considers the structure and imagery of "Impulse" as an example of the type of precise criticism possible on the works of this author who "uses poetic methods in his fiction." Malcolm Cowley's "Conrad Aiken: From Savannah to Emerson" (*SoR* 11:245–59) is primarily a biographical sketch of Aiken which concentrates on an important shift in attitude in his works presented in geographical terms in Cowley's title. Dealing specifically with Aiken's poetry, Cowley suggests that "in Aiken's beginnings, he had been poles apart from Emerson. He had been atheistic and pessimistic, not optimistic and unitarian" as he became in his late years.

Thomas D. Clareson reviews criticism on H. P. Lovecraft and science fiction in general in "Studies of Lovecraft and Asimov" (*Extrapolation* 16:125–29). His brief annotated bibliography is very useful. Barton Levi St. Armand contributes a needed biographical essay in "H. P. Lovecraft: New England Decadent" (*Caliban* 12:127–56). Noting parallels in both life and work between Lovecraft and Poe, St. Armand gives several readings of Lovecraft's late works which show his affinities with Poe's followers of the Decadent school of the 1890s.

Holden Caulfield is only one of many literary characters treated by Peter L. Hays in "Runaways on a One-Way Ticket, or Dropouts in Literature" (*ArQ* 31:301–10). Hays traces a strain of American literature depicting characters who seek escape from their responsibilities. Holden Caulfield's American predecessors include Rip Van Winkle, Natty Bumppo, Bartleby, Huck Finn, and 20th-century figures such as Nick Adams and Ike McCaslin. The tradition seems far from dead, judging from the contemporary figures of Yossarian in Heller's *Catch-22* and Kesey's McMurphy. L. Moody Simms, Jr., looks at another Salinger hero in "Seymour Glass: The Salingerian Hero as Vulgarian" (*NConL* 5,v:6–8). Simms finds Seymour Glass a unique being who attempts to overcome his revulsion at the vulgar society around him by becoming part of it himself. His inability to become assimilated into his contemporary culture leads to his suicide.

Detective-fiction buffs will be interested in a brief survey of the genre written from a British perspective by Melvin Barnes. *Best Detective Fiction: A Guide from Godwin to the Present* (Hamden, Conn.: Linnet Books) treats American writers primarily in chapters dealing with "Detection in the Thirties, Forties and Fifties" and "The Hard Boiled School." Barnes has great praise for Dashiell Hammett and Raymond Chandler and identifies Ross MacDonald as the most eminent contemporary writer in their tradition. While this survey is far too brief to be useful for readings of particular works, it does evaluate the current attitudes toward major American writers of detective fiction.

Howard Kaye defends *The Long Goodbye* (1954) against detractors in "Raymond Chandler's Sentimental Novel" (*WAL* 10:135–54). Kaye proclaims Chandler's control of his materials when he concludes that "*The Long Goodbye* is not a sentimental book but a book about sentimentality." An intriguing feature of his article is his comparison of the archetypal heroes of detective fiction and those of Western novels. George N. Dove treats all seven of Chandler's novels in his attempt to assess the quality of his literary achievement in "The Complex Art of Raymond Chandler" (*ArmD* 8:271–74). Dove looks for "evidences of a consistent, conscientious craftsmanship" in Chandler's works and finds it particularly in Chandler's adroit handling of complex plotting. In his conclusion he is content to term Chandler simply "a master in the craft of construction." Despite the personal opinion implicit in his title, Dove leaves the question of whether or not Chandler's skill makes these novels "works of art" up to his readers's own definitions of "art." Two bibliographical articles in *ArmD* are particularly noteworthy. In "Shadowing the Continental Op" (8:121–24) William F. Nolan lists the 36 Hammett stories featuring the Continental Op, noting the collections and anthologies in which they have appeared. Continuing a very useful service *ArmD* annually offers, Walter Albert lists and occasionally annotates books and articles on the detective genre in "A Bibliography of Secondary Sources for 1974" (8:290–93, 274).

Life imitated art according to Richard Gid Power's "J. Edgar Hoover and the Detective Story" (*JPC* 9:257–78). Hoover emerges as a very effective PR man who created positive images for his bureau through skillfully conforming to and then manipulating the tastes of the popular crime-novel reader of the 1930s and 1940s: "What Hoover did was to infiltrate the action detective story. To do this he demonstrated the parallels between the actual cases of the F.B.I. and the plots of the action story. Then he persuaded writers, artists, filmmakers, and other mass entertainment producers that they would do well to make F.B.I. agents the heroes of their fictional dramas."

Dissertations on individual western authors such as Oliver La Farge, John G. Neihardt, Walter Van Tilburg Clark, Mari Sandoz, and Wilbur Daniel Steele, as well as a general study of several writers including Steinbeck and Rølvaag in "Migration Epics of the Trans-Mississippi West" (James Earl Fitzmaurice, *DAI* 35:5399–5400A) confirm that the regional identity of western writers is as strong as that claimed by critics of southern literature. Hector H. Lee looks at folklore's influence in "Tales and Legends in Western American Literature" (*WAL* 9:239–54) and sees the timeless themes of these myths and legends continuing in television Westerns as well as in literature. The careers of two minor western writers are reviewed in Maurice Legris's "The Western World of Forrester Blake" (*SDR* 13,v:64–77) and Barbara Meldrum's "Duality and the Dream in S. K. Winther's Grimsen Trilogy" (*PrS* 49:311–19). Meldrum offers the more informative assessment of her subject's work. While Legris limply concludes that "Blake's principal interest is the land and its people," Meldrum delineates the epic themes of Winther's three novels concerning Danish immigrants in Nebraska, tying them into the traditions of western literature.

A better-recognized figure is the subject of William T. Pilkington's *Harvey Fergusson* (TUSAS 257). Though his careers as journalist and screenwriter carried Fergusson to Washington, D.C., New York, and Hollywood and he wrote fiction set in these locales, Pilkington sees Fergusson's best novels and nonfiction growing from Fergusson's early life in New Mexico. In his best work dealing with the Southwest, Fergusson was a realist rather than a romanticizer of the American West. Pilkington accounts for Fergusson's comparative neglect by critics of western literature in noting that "while much Western writing is notoriously committed to a simplified and attractive view of history, Fergusson approached the past gingerly and warned of its dangers when an individual uses it as a retreat from the chaotic present." Thus he remains outside the romantic tradition associated with other recognized western writers. Pilkington argues that the intrinsic merit of works such as *Grant of Kingdom* (1950) and *The Conquest of Don Pedro* (1954) makes them "easily the equal" of writers such as Walter Van Tilburg Clark, Vardis Fisher, Frederick Manfred, or Frank Waters, and he suggests the need for a redefinition of western literature broad enough to include Fergusson's contribution.

Frances King's useful article, "Treatment of the Mentally Retarded Character in Modern American Fiction" (*BB* 32:106–14), lists and annotates fiction published between 1903 and 1970 which has retardates as important characters. As useful as this "preliminary bibliography" is, King draws some weak conclusions from her study in her single-page introduction. In one confused paragraph she notes:

"It is possible that William Faulkner's *The Sound and the Fury* is the great 20th century American novel. If it is, and if Benjamin Compson is its chief protagonist, then the hero of the great American novel of the 20th century is a 33-year-old idiot. A curious anomaly."

The three dissertations on Hollywood novelist Nathanael West in the 1975 *DAI* discuss in turn his religious convictions, use of technical devices, and affinities with the work of Djuna Barnes and Malcolm Lowry. In published criticism I. Lloyd Michaels notes West's use of popular forms of entertainment in "A Particular Kind of Joking: Burlesque, Vaudeville, and Nathanael West" (*SAmH* 1:149–60). Michaels refers to the stars and favorite routines of burlesque and vaudeville circuits of the first quarter of the 20th century and finds similarities to, if not direct influences on, the "ritualized mayhem" in West's work. He also cites biographical evidence of West's interest in these forms of popular entertainment and associates West's major characters with stock vaudeville characters. Shrike resembles "the deadpan monologist," Lem a "stooge," Gilson an impersonator, and Abe a freak who could have been drawn from a carnival sideshow. James F. Light also sees signs of burlesque in his "Varieties of Satire in the Art of Nathanael West" (*SAmH* 2:46–60), but presents it as only one of several differing traditions of humor to be found in West's work, each of which Light associates with a specific novel or story. Treating West's fiction chronologically, Light sees "A Boldfaced Lie" (1929) dominated by folk humor from the American tall-tale tradition; *The Dream of Balso Snell* shows "the comic distortion of surrealism," while black humor dominates *Miss Lonelyhearts*. Light associates parody and burlesque primarily with *A Cool Million* and fits *The Day of the Locust* into a category he terms "apocalyptic humor." Light's rigid categories detract from his observations since many of the types of humor he discusses occur simultaneously in individual works. The overall treatment is excellent, however.

In "West's *Miss Lonelyhearts*" (*Expl* 34:item 11) David R. Mayer suggests that Shrike's sacrilegious parody of the Anima Christi sets the tone for the novel, which he views as "an instance of religious quest gone awry." Herb Russell's "West's *The Day of the Locust*" (*Expl* 33:item 36) points out West's use of Emily Dickinson's "discoverer" Mabel Loomis [Todd] as the model for the personality of Maybelle Loomis in the novel. Both are manipulators, "guilty of the same kind of selfish advancement" at the expense of others. Stanley

Trachtenberg's intriguing article, "West's Locusts: Laughing at the Laugh" (*MQR* 14:187–98), compares *Locust* with Steinbeck's *Grapes of Wrath* as two novels appearing in 1939 dealing with the issue of social progress. In Trachtenberg's view, while Steinbeck affirms the possibility of social progress, West makes fun of the entire concept. Finding no comic redemption in *The Day of the Locust*, Trachtenberg terms it "a comedy which makes the assertion of existence at the expense of life."

University of North Carolina, Chapel Hill

15. Fiction: The 1950s to the Present

James H. Justus

The most substantial scholarship in contemporary fiction in 1975 centers on Saul Bellow (with two special collections of essays, many of them reevaluations) and Thomas Pynchon, whose three novels are the occasion for superior work. Interest remains high in Norman Mailer and Flannery O'Connor, but the secondary bibliographies for them are showing signs of repetitiveness. The Wretched Excess Award for the year goes to the interview; though this is a form which rarely turns out as well as the idea behind it, its popularity rages unchecked.

The number of dissertations reported in 1975 is about the same as for the previous year. O'Connor is still a favorite subject for dissertation writers: five in all, three of them exclusively on her works. Other favorites continue to be Mailer, Bellow, and Oates (three each) and Vonnegut, Barth, and Hawkes (two each). Other dissertation subjects were Kerouac, Pynchon, Updike, Styron, Coover, and Momaday (one each). More thematic topics are listed in 1975 than in any recent year, ranging from studies of myth and the Jewish-American family to the American academic novel and Vietnam War fiction of the late 1960s; the list also includes subjects on the new journalism, adolescent girlhood, the baseball metaphor, popular westerns, Chicano fiction, "Adam and Eden" in the western, "secular apocalypse," and the "theology of play."

i. General Studies

***a.* Overviews and Special Topics.** Borrowing terms from Ihab Hassan (who in turn borrowed them from Elizabeth Sewell), Jean E. Kennard distinguishes between two kinds of responses to a "Post-existentialist world view" in *Number and Nightmare: Forms of Fantasy in Contemporary Fiction* (Hamden, Conn.: Archon). The fictional language of "number" is antimyth and antiform, and that of "nightmare" uses conventions of myth and realism in its "rearrangements" of truth; the first is seemingly all-American (represented by Heller, Barth, Purdy, and Vonnegut), the second all-British (represented by Burgess, Murdoch, and Golding). What holds all these writers together are the philosophical premises of Sartre and Camus, which the British writers refute and the Americans reflect and reinforce through reliance upon the theater of the absurd, authorial self-consciousness, shifting identities, and other techniques which suggest that even art is self-destructive. Noted previously are Kennard's segments on Barth (*ALS 1970*, p. 275) and on Heller (*ALS 1971*, p. 258).

In *The Story-Shaped World: Fiction and Metaphysics, Some Variations on a Theme* (Notre Dame, Ind.: Univ. of Notre Dame Press), Brian Wicker argues for a parallel between "the current literary debate about the vocabulary appropriate to fiction and a corresponding debate about the appropriate language for describing religious experience." After contrasting Robbe-Grillet and Mailer in their attitudes toward metaphor and the search for "freedom," Wicker devotes part 1 of his study, theological and linguistic as well as critical, to a theoretical exploration of metaphor, the analogical way of rendering a world view; part 2 is essentially a series of "applications" in the work of modern (mostly British) fictionists.

Harold Bloom's desultory observations on "The Dialectics of Literary Tradition" (*Boundary* 2[1974]:528–38) are unnecessarily crabbed. The portentous question, "Do the dialectics of literary tradition condemn us, at this time, either to an affirmation of belatedness, via Kabbalistic inversion, or to a mock-vitalistic lie-against-time, via an emphasis upon the self-as-performer?" cannot of course be answered simply, but the reference is to the agony of having to prefer Pynchon's voluntary parody to Mailer's involuntary one.

In "The Literary Essay and the Modern Temper" (*PLL* 11:317–35), Mary E. Rucker discusses the cultural contexts of a genre seemingly more attuned to a pre-1950 literary climate, but she finds the new journalism of Tom Wolfe, Mailer, and Dan Wakefield notable exceptions. In "The Apocalyptic Fact and the Eclipse of Fiction in Recent American Prose Narratives" (*JAmS* 9:69–83), Mas'ud Zavarzadeh explores an indisputably post-1950 subject. Since ordinary linear fiction based on causal relations is "almost escapist," contemporary fictive realities "demand radical responses," which means scrapping "antiquated notions of aesthetic order." Zavarzadeh finds proper responses in those fictionists who approach "zero degree of interpretation" (Barth, Barthelme, Pynchon) and in the nonfiction novelists who insist on "neutral registration" of today's fantastic actualities (Warhol, Mailer, Wolfe).

Frederick Busch's "The Friction of Fiction: A *Ulysses* Omnirandum" (*ChR* 26,iv:5–17) is a perceptive and subtle account of how Joyce has influenced later admirers, with the introduction of his shift away "*from where* the narrative eyes see, *to where* they squint, *to whom* they" communicate. Those writers who both recognize and use Joyce's discovery are Paul West, Barthelme, Barth, Pynchon, and Coover. Edward Marcotte isolates for praise "The Space of the Novel" (*PR* 41[1974]:263–72), the ambiguous ingredient in the novelist's art which attests to the writer's "unquenchable yearning to seize and incorporate landscape, to achieve the ideal fusion of the spatial and the schematic."

Versions of the Past: The Historical Imagination in American Fiction (New York: Oxford Univ. Press [1974]) by the late Harry B. Henderson III will remain more important for its treatment of 19th-century writers (*ALS 1974, passim*) than for its thinner segments on 20th-century ones; other critics have more thoroughly analyzed the ideological split between fictionists of the "liberal conscience" (Warren, Malamud, Styron) and those of "apocalyptic parody" (Barth, Pynchon). Despite its title, Malcolm Bradbury's "Leaving the Fifties: The Change of Style in American Writing" (*Encounter* 45,i:40–51) is *about* the 1950s, in which the pivotal tension was between moral need and "social determinants," particularly in the work of Bellow and Malamud. The theme itself created a stylistic balance between absurdity and realism; and just as Lionel Trilling's *The Middle of the Journey* encapsulates that spirit at the time, so Philip Roth's *My Life as a Man* captures it in a kind of after-gaze. Ruth Prigozy's "The Liberal Novelist in the McCarthy Era" (*TCL* 21:253–64) is a fairly predictable piece on how five novelists (Trilling, Mary McCarthy, Mailer, Irwin Shaw, and Merle Miller) all raised key issues (but resolved nothing) concerning the liberal's quandary about political direction.

W. T. Lhamon, Jr., defines cultural and stylistic departures in the writers of the 1960s in terms resonant with social aspiration. In "Break and Enter to Breakaway: Scotching Modernism in the Social Novel of the American Sixties" (*Boundary 2* 3:289–306), Lhamon convincingly suggests that the Alger pattern of "breaking in, a push toward power, acceptance, or marriage" disintegrates in the fiction of Heller, Pynchon, Mailer, and Brautigan, who formulate alternate patterns (lighting out, hiding, evading) focused against the entire "endemic system of felt value."

Blanche Gelfant discusses the "subterranean city novel" as a spatial metaphor for transformation in her fine and suggestive "Residence Underground: Recent Fictions of the Subterranean City" (*SR* 83:406–38); Gelfant's main purpose is definitional, though there are frequent illustrations from Pynchon, Ishamel Reed, and Kerouac, and her analysis shows that an excremental vision informs such fiction, usually in satiric, surreal, and scatalogical modes. In both modern and contemporary texts William L. Nance relates the classic thematic pattern of "flight into a wilderness that conceals death" and what he calls the pattern of "Oedipal rebuff," a later manifestation. "Eden, Oedipus, and Rebirth in American Fiction" (*ArQ* 31:353–65) touches on Mailer's *An American Dream*, Bellow's *Herzog*, and Barth's first two novels.

Both Louis Hasley and Bruce Janoff find a certain inadequacy in the Black Humor fiction of such writers as Donleavy, Barth, and Vonnegut. In "Black Humor and Gray" (*ArQ* 30[1974]:317–28) Hasley detects so little playfulness and so much preaching about the theme of meaninglessness that the theme amounts to a theological message. In "Black Humor, Existentialism, and Absurdity: A Generic Confusion" (*ArQ* 30[1974]:293–304), Janoff frankly states his preference for the existentialist's position and style because of the hope for possible renewal. Thomas LeClair emphasizes the "funereal" implications of this mode in "Death and Black Humor" (*Crit* 17,i:5–40); a concern with death gives both a "philosophical ultimacy" and an aesthetic to the work of Donleavy, Heller, Barth, Percy, Vonnegut, and Pynchon, in which black comedy simultaneously endangers and protects our consciousness by fusing death and comedy. LeClair admits that this funereal stance seems not to apply to Terry Southern, Bruce Jay Friedman, and Barthelme.

While his thesis in "American Jewish Fiction: Local Color Movement of the Fifties" (*CLAJ* 18:404–11) is self-explanatory, Sidney Poger also traces the reasons behind its rise (the writers celebrated a self-conscious Jewish identity) and its decline (other "local color" models, notably black ones, provided metaphors more engaging to the popular imagination). That decline is the subject of Stanley Schatt's "The Torah and the Time Bomb: The Teaching of Jewish-American Literature Today" (*CLAJ* 18:434–41), which, among other things, notes the distortion of real-life Jews in modern fiction and the ignorance among Jewish students of the *shtetl* culture out of which Jewish literature of the 1950s came.

As he properly warns, Peter Aichinger is not writing literary criticism in *The American Soldier in Fiction,* but even as cultural history, it is too often perfunctory and thin. The contention that the war novel began to appear about the time the frontier was disappearing has a certain instinctive validity, but it needs more elaboration and evidence to make credible history. Aichinger breaks down his subject into such categories as "The Civilian Soldier" and "The Professional Officer" and into such chronological segments as "1939–1952" and "1953–1963." A number of authors and works are cited, almost none of them in any detail, but Aichinger concludes that James Jones is the only American writer who can be "regarded solely as a war novelist." What is now needed is a comprehensive treatment of the American experience of that war akin to Paul Fussell's *The Great War and Modern Memory,* a haunting study of the English experience in what Fussell calls "The Matter of Flanders and Picardy."

***b.* The New Fiction: Theories and Modes.** It is easy to be annoyed by Jerome Klinkowitz's *Literary Disruptions: The Making of a Post-Contemporary American Fiction* (Urbana: Univ. of Ill. Press), because in order to celebrate the achievements of "Vonnegut and company," Klinkowitz finds it necessary to dismiss most of the writers whose reputations have been made in the last two decades (Heller, Kesey, Updike, Roth, Bellow, Malamud), with his particular contempt reserved for those who pose as innovators but are really "regressive parodists" (Barth, Pynchon). His fictionists are those who set a "clear trend" in the 1967–68 publishing season; besides Vonnegut—the old man of this group—Klinkowitz includes Barthelme, Kosinski, LeRoi Jones, James Park Sloan, Ronald Sukenick, Raymond Federman, and Gilbert Sorrentino in what he describes as a "definite style and school" whose common traits are formal experimentation, a thematic interest in the "imaginative transformation of reality," and a self-conscious artistry.

Klinkowitz's tack is to treat that breakthrough season in the same authoritative way that most of us describe cycles and make judgments on authors who came into their own during the 1850–51, 1885–86, and 1925–26 seasons. Never mind that all this may be premature; Klinkowitz has mapped out the *now* as his territory, and he is in fact to be commended not only for his clear judgments, which we may or may not accept, but also for the clarity of his prose—nothing here of the mimetic nightmare of meta-, sur-, or para-criticism. A first chapter admirably stakes out the issues of fictional theories, the false starts, the boxed-in endings, and the full-fledged commitments to render a new imaginative mode. In an epilogue Klinkowitz returns to the attack on the "funereal taste" of the entrenched critics of American fiction who still prefer the densities of Bellow to the "celebrants of unreason, chaos, and inexorable decay." In 20 years Klinkowitz may flinch at the easy way he is having his judgment day now, but his *Literary Disruptions* is an important book for the moment and must be considered a reliable index to the doctrinal persuasions of the critical Church of What's Happening Now.

Klinkowitz is one of the contributors to Raymond Federman's anthology of mostly theoretical pieces, *Surfiction: Fiction Now and Tomorrow* (Chicago: Swallow Press), which consists, besides Federman's own introduction, of 17 essays of varying authority and originality, some reprinted from earlier publications. Some of the important pieces are Ronald Sukenick's "The New Tradition in Fiction," Phillipe Sollers's "The Novel and the Experience of Limits," and Richard Kostelanetz's "Towards a Language of Doing."

Morris Dickstein's "Fiction Hot and Kool: Dilemmas of the Experimental Writer" (*TriQ* 33:257–72) is a sensible survey of an influential body of fictional theory of the 1960s which helped to codify modernist attitudes and in effect ignored current practice in writing. While Alain Robbe-Grillet, Richard Gilman, and William H. Gass were stressing the aesthetic autonomy of the work of art and its nonreferential status as artifact, we were getting novels by Barth, Pynchon, and Vonnegut which subsumed rather than junked realistic conventions. Only in the late 1960s did newer writers press toward a mode that would make the novel "a body of words *and no more*: its own devices would become its only subject." Barthelme's *Snow White* is the clear winner here. Like Dickstein, Gerald Graff explores the relationship between Modernism and its successor in "Babbitt at the

Abyss: The Social Context of Postmodern American Fiction" (*TriQ* 33:305–37). Modernist fiction (an expression of "inward 'consciousness' set over against the rational discourse of the public, objective world") never fully scrapped the "privatization" of human experience; and, tending to carry the logic of its theories to their limits, it has often been weakened by an "inability or refusal to retain any moorings in social reality."

Edward Marcotte concentrates on the intentional fragment in "Intersticed Prose" (*ChR* 26,iv:31–36)—paragraph-like segments separated by space, notes, meditations, diary entries and the like; what is important here is the visual potential, the shape of words on the printed page, and it is a form which Marcotte believes is destined to further the split between serious and popular fiction. William A. Johnsen chides all those who attempt to divorce themselves from Modernism without first understanding the intricate relationships between that movement and those who manifest its latest characteristics. "Toward a Redefinition of Modernism" (*Boundary 2* 2[1974]: 539–56) is a useful corrective to those who too single-mindedly want to "merchandize the newest sensibilities." Johnsen sees the struggle as a classical Oedipal one—a new sensibility defines itself by defining the works immediately preceding its own as old, repressive, totalitarian, neurotic; it calls for "releasing" works that make possible what earlier writers repressed.

"The Corpse of the Dragon: Notes on Postromantic Fiction" (*TriQ* 33:273–303) is Frank McConnell's provocative argument that much of contemporary fiction is a reworking of the "dragon myth," the dramatization of the "oldest *other*" as an opponent of the hero. *Gravity's Rainbow*, for example, rediscovers at an elemental level "the uncertainty of the struggle between the civilizing, human hero and his Great Adversary," a theme which is revitalized in other works by Barth and John Gardner. R. E. Johnson's "Structuralism and the Reading of Contemporary Fiction" (*Soundings* 58:281–306) is a good introduction to a complicated subject; along with examples of Gass, Barthelme, and Coover, Johnson also appends a useful bibliography. Bruce Morrissette's "Post-Modern Generative Fiction: Novel and Film" (*Crit I* 2:253–62) is a synchronic analysis of generative theory and practice, mostly using Robbe-Grillet and other French writers, but the essay will be of interest to theorists of contemporary fiction in general.

ii. Norman Mailer

Jean Radford's *Norman Mailer: A Critical Study* (New York: Barnes and Noble) is a solid, unflashy book which seems especially designed to avoid the hip, mimetic criticism which frequently plagues commentary on Mailer. Like others, Radford traces the development of Mailer's view of human nature (from determinism to existentialism), but, unlike most of the other critics, carefully stresses the continuities rather than the breaks between *The Naked and the Dead* and the later work. The best insights now available into the political matrix of *Barbary Shore* and *The Deer Park* can be found here; and in establishing the influence of Farrell and Dos Passos (on the first novel) and Kafka, Dostoevsky, West, and Faulkner (on the second and third novels) Radford provides a rationale for the breakthrough of Mailer's own "muscular" style in *Advertisements for Myself*. Better than earlier critics, Radford pinpoints the stylistic innovations both large and small, with the implication that the "problem of voice" was not finally resolved until *Why Are We in Vietnam?* A concluding chapter argues that in *Of a Fire on the Moon* and *The Prisoner of Sex* a "desperate and unquestioning loyalty" to a vision of "anachronistic and utopian radicalism" threatens Mailer with a dead end; in an epilogue on the work of 1972–73, Radford sees considerable evidence of Hemingwayesque self-parody.

In "Mailer and the Big Plot Being Hatched by Nature" (*Story-Shaped World*, pp. 195–207), an analysis of Mailer's rhetoric generally and metaphor specifically, Brian Wicker asserts that the conclusion of *The Armies of the Night* is disappointing because Mailer relies compulsively on mixed metaphors (mechanical and biological) to evoke a sense of metaphysical power inherent in the system of the nation; and that *Of a Fire on the Moon* posits Mailer's faith that the mysteries spawned by science and technology can be understood only by using a language of "primitive metaphorical richness."

Testing *An American Dream* against the prospectus which Mailer announced in *Advertisements*, Timothy Evans ("Boiling the Archetypal Pot: Norman Mailer's American Dream" [*SwR* 60:159–70]) finds that the stereotype of struggle-and-success is actually an inverted Oedipal compulsion in disguise; the novel's insufficiency lies in the hero's defeat in terms of a carelessly improvised subplot, the romance between Rojack and Cherry. James J. Sheridan finds the

Inferno a probable source for Kelly's coat of arms ("Mailer's *An American Dream*," *Expl* 34:item 8).

Two very different writers who were aroused but not overwhelmed in the 1960s with its "politics of immediate demand" are the subject of "Armies of the Planet: A Comparative Analysis of Norman Mailer's and Saul Bellow's Political Visions" (*Soundings* 58:69–83), in which Jeffrey Klein contends that despite the different thematic and ideational thrusts, *The Armies of the Night* and *Mr. Sammler's Planet* both attack the present in "quintessentially Jewish ways"—i.e., both authors are obsessed by the moral meaning of events. In Laura Adams's "Existential Aesthetics: An Interview with Norman Mailer" (*PR* 42:197–214), the novelist speaks frankly about cosmology, technology, human "electrical intensity," his belief in both an all-powerful God and existentialism, and his contract for his next novel ("that big book I've been braying about to America for the last fifteen years").

iii. Flannery O'Connor

The debate over the religious primacy of O'Connor's fiction is not over. John R. May, in "Flannery O'Connor: Critical Consensus and the 'Objective' Interpretation" (*Renascence* 27:179–92), argues that "objectivity" is relative to historical periods and that within the community of literary critics and theologians the need for consensus must include evaluation of critical methods as well as the interpretation itself. "Critical consensus," says May, "seeks not only to harmonize all of the concrete details of a work (the horizontal dimension), but also to explore in open dialogue the depth of meaning in the work's images (the vertical dimension)." In "The Sacramental Irony of Flannery O'Connor" (*SLJ* 7,ii:33–49), however, Judith F. Wynne believes that literary critics must resist theology-minded readers who want to reduce the author's "grace-bearing" figures to "allegorical formal signs" without recognizing their ironic reality. The fiction is apocalyptic in Northrop Frye's sense—i.e., it "reveals" only on its own terms, which are aesthetic, not religious. Above all, cautions Wynne, the sacramental in O'Connor's works should not be construed as illustrations of her own theology.

Despite her own worried disclaimer that her work was different from Faulkner's, O'Connor shared some obvious points of contact with the Mississippian, and "Comedy and Humor in Flannery O'Connor's Fiction" (*FOB* 4:1–12) is Carter Martin's somewhat desultory attempt to cite some similarities. The essay veers off into speculations about comic fiction in light of Jonsonian and Bergsonian theories, which, if properly done, would require considerably more than 12 pages.

Donald Gregory's "Enoch Emery: Ironic Doubling in *Wise Blood*" (*FOB* 4:52–64) covers some of the same ground worked by previous critics, but it is sensible and acute: Emery is said to provide a comic counterpoint which heightens the tragic aspect of Haze's quest; and though the isolation which moves both characters to violence is not unique, their responses are. In "The Shifting of Mr. Shiftlet: Flannery O'Connor's 'The Life You Save May Be Your Own'" (*MissQ* 28:55–59), John F. Desmond properly distinguishes the focal Tom T. Shiftlet from that other mysterious stranger, the peripheral Manley Pointer of "Good Country People." Through Mrs. Crater's attempt to dehumanize him, Shiftlet, who begins as a partially redemptive agent, becomes a satanic figure, refusing to "fall into the ambiguous human community."

In a disappointing formalistic study of plot based on R. S. Crane's methods, "The World of Guilt and Sorrow: Flannery O'Connor's 'Everything That Rises Must Converge'" (*FOB* 4:42–51), Robert D. Denham comes to the same conclusion that most readers have been coming to all along: that it is Julian's story, and the mother's death "becomes the terrible means by which he can grow toward maturity." John V. McDermott, however, sees no optimism in Julian's fate. "Julian's Journey into Hell: Flannery O'Connor's Allegory of Pride" (*MissQ* 28:171–79) is a stringent reading which begins by escalating the import of O'Connor's phrase—"his entry into the world of guilt and sorrow"—into "nothing less than his entrance into the world of hell," proceeds by emphasizing the author's "sustained symbolism," and concludes with an object lesson on how excessive pride is self-destructive.

Two essays give delightful insights into O'Connor's keen and watchful eye on the world about her. "The Uses of Banality" (*FOB* 4:13–24) is J. O. Tate's argument for O'Connor as a "banality-collector," taking her place alongside Gogol, Flaubert, and Joyce. The banal comprises objects, situations, ideas, even characters, ranging from Haze's peeler and Sally Poker Sash's Girl Scout shoes to

Rayber's lectures to young Tarwater. Banality, argues Tate, is not simply an index of tastelessness but the "falsehoods perpetrated in attempts to ignore or deny the condition of temporality, the human condition itself." In "Image and Imagination: Flannery O'Connor's Front Page Fictions" (*JML* 4:121–32), Harvey Klevar reports on his examination of the Milledgeville *Union Recorder* files. Especially enlightening is the way in which O'Connor transformed the stories and press photographs into "metaphors for understanding" in the stories "A Late Encounter with the Enemy" and "The Displaced Person."

There is not much new in Mark G. Edelstein's "Flannery O'Connor and the Problem of Modern Satire" (*SSF* 12:139–44): "A Circle in the Fire," "Good Country People," and "The Life You Save May Be Your Own" are discussed in terms of human complacency and O'Connor's technique (shock). Stuart L. Burns, in "How Wide Did 'The Heathen' Range?" (*FOB* 4:25–41), reporting on the manuscript fragments of O'Connor's unfinished work (*Why Do the Heathen Rage?*), concludes that O'Connor's talents were indeed for the short story, not the novel. Of the last ten stories O'Connor wrote, one was extracted almost verbatim from this "unmalleable novel-material"; another had its genesis there; still another contains a big chunk from it; and "most of the rest manifest some relationship to that work."

"No Vague Believer: Flannery O'Connor and Protestantism" (*SwR* 60:256–63) is a sampling of Thomas F. Gossett's collection of O'Connor letters, in which the author comments on Protestants—most of her insights are amusing, all of them knowledgeable. In "The Protestantism of Flannery O'Connor" (*SoR* 11:802–19) Robert Milder, after exploring at some length the "heresies" of Jansenism—the insistence on the corruption of natural man and the exaltation of private religious experience at the expense of the sacraments and the institutional church—convincingly demonstrates that the Catholic Christianity revealed in the works is "virtually indistinguishable from the Fundamentalist Protestantism of the South."

James E. Dorsey's "Carson McCullers and Flannery O'Connor: A Checklist of Graduate Research" (*BB* 32:162–67) supplements earlier bibliographies by listing M.A. theses and Ph.D. dissertations. The text accompanying Barbara McKenzie's "Flannery O'Connor Country: A Photo Essay" (*GaR* 29:329–62) will be of no help to specialists, but the photographs are superb.

iv. Saul Bellow, Bernard Malamud, and Philip Roth

In *Saul Bellow: A Collection of Critical Essays* (Englewood Cliffs, N.J.: Prentice-Hall), Earl Rovit has assembled Gordon L. Harper's 1967 *Paris Review* interview and 11 essays, six of which are new. Rovit himself contributes an exciting comparison-contrast with his "Saul Bellow and Norman Mailer: The Secret Sharers" (pp. 161–70); what they share is a naturalistic vision of man against which they nevertheless battle. M. Gilbert Porter's "The Scene as Image: A Reading of *Seize the Day*" (pp. 52–71), an explicitly old-fashioned piece whose methodology stems from I. A. Richards, makes considerable sense out of the transactions between images of human failure and images of drowning.

In "The Ambiguous Assault of Henderson and Herzog" (pp. 72–80), Richard Pearce discusses these very different but "heroic" figures in terms of Whitman's "embrace" of and Melville's "assault" on reality; in each case Bellow reflects his concern not only with character but also with the form of the modern novel. Richard Poirier updates, but not by much, his 1965 review of *Herzog*, here appearing as "Herzog, or, Bellow in Trouble" (pp. 81–89), an attack on Bellow's disaffection from the subcultural fashionableness of the late 1960s, the same kind which Poirier was then courting.

Victoria Sullivan, in "The Battle of the Sexes in Three Bellow Novels" (pp. 101–14), finds that Bellow's women are like his men, sad and mixed-up. Destructive ones tend to victimize the heroes, and the "nurturing" ones tend to be vicitimized by them, but each kind has a full range of idiosyncrasies. "Saul Bellow and Mr. Sammler: Absurd Seekers of High Qualities" (pp. 122–34), Ben Siegel's review of the misreadings of *Mr. Sammler's Planet*, judiciously elucidates both the similarities and distinctions between author and protagonist. Irving Malin gives a curiously inconclusive interpretation of Bellow's "powerful, shrewd, and funny" play, *The Last Analysis*, in "Bummy's Analysis" (pp. 115–21).

Salmagundi 30, a first-rate Bellow number, is the result of a Skidmore College symposium, to which Tony Tanner here contributes an introduction and Stanley Kauffman a conclusion. In separate essays John Bayley and Robert Boyers discuss Bellow's most controversial novel. In "By Way of Mr. Sammler" (pp. 24–33) Bayley sees the creation of Sammler and Gruner as a rebuke to a contemporary consciousness enslaved by "authenticity" and self-indulgence characteristic of the new fiction. In "Nature and Social Reality in Bellow's *Sammler*" (pp. 34–56) Boyers explores the diverse philosophical concepts of nature and their effects on the "idea of character conceived both in its moral and aesthetic dimensions."

Ben Belitt believes that the stance in all the work can be seen in Joseph of *Dangling Man*; in "Saul Bellow: The Depth Factor" (pp. 57–65) he says that the entire corpus demands to be seen not singly but as a "vast system of cancellations, reversals, repetitions, pulsars, contradictions"—a fictive phenomenon inseparable from the romantic premise that the imagination tends to dissolve or dissipate whatever seems given or gratuitous, to hold off obvious reality until it can be created anew. Working with *Herzog* as his chief text, Harold Kaplan suggests in "The Second Fall of Man" (pp. 66–89) that "an ambiguous and dialectical humanism" lies at the center of Bellow's imagination, a perception of humanity which marches between mystical intuition and scientific demonstration.

Finally, in what is clearly the most profound and intensive engagement with Bellow ever attempted, symposium participants collaborate in "Literature and Culture: An Interview with Saul Bellow" (pp. 6–23). Bellow speaks modestly but firmly of the moral function of writers, his own feelings about *Herzog* and *Mr. Sammler's Planet* and his ambivalence to the counterculture, and the process by which the combined forces of the universities and the media destroyed an independent literary culture in America (*The Partisan Review*, for example, became "corrupt and doddery" when acquired by Rutgers). (Less successful is "An Interview with Myself" [*NewRev* 2,xviii:53–56] in which Bellow is curiously snappish with himself as well as the universities, where the teaching of literature has been a "disaster.")

Though not new, the discovery of the effects of Wilheim Reich on Bellow is nowhere so detailed and comprehensive as in Mark Shechner's sprightly "Down in the Mouth with Saul Bellow" (*AmerR* 23:40–77). Unlike the influence on Paul Goodman, Allen Ginsberg, Mailer, and Kerouac, Reich's political dimensions (the "bioenergetic program") are resisted by Bellow, who refuses to ascribe public virtue to therapeutic radicalism.

In "Saul Bellow's Idea of Self: A Reading of *Seize the Day*" (*Renascence* 27:193–205), Richard Giannone discusses Bellow's "canonical revision" of romantic ideology concerning the uniqueness of the self. Manifesting itself largely through characterization and tone, Bellovian "humanness" is not a process of acquiring but of losing, so that at the end Wilhelm understands the real antagonist to be time and the self. Carol M. Sicherman's "Bellow's *Seize the Day*: Reverberations and Hollow Sounds" (*STC* 15:1–31) is a firm essay which argues for the debasement of language as the principal theme of the novel.

Instead of discovering the universal within a Jewish character, the usual symbolizing process in Jewish authors, Bellow discovers the Jewish within an American Everyman: this is the argument in Steven Gould Axelrod's "The Jewishness of Bellow's Henderson" (*AL* 47: 439–43). Carol Pearson, in "Bellow's *Henderson the Rain King* and the Myth of the King, the Fool, and the Hero (*NConL* 5,v:8–11), keys this novel to the myth found in William Willeford's *The Fool and His Sceptor* (1969).

"Mr. Bellow's *Sammler*: The Evolution of a Contemporary Text" (*SNNTS* 7:425–44) is Keith Cushman's account of the "making" of the novel through a careful examination of the holographs, typescripts, and galleys in the University of Chicago library. Noriko M. Lippit contributes a brief reading of "Leaving the Yellow House" in "A Perennial Survivor: Saul Bellow's Heroine in the Desert" (*SSF* 12:281–83).

Robert Ducharme's twin purpose in *Art and Idea in the Novels of Bernard Malamud: Toward "The Fixer"* (The Hague: Mouton [1974]) is to trace shifts in authorial attitudes toward the familiar themes, especially that of suffering, and to demonstrate Malamud's use of the mythic method; only occasionally do these two enterprises seem to merge, but the treatment of each one is brisk and convincing, if somewhat predictable. Ducharme finds that the theme of responsibility, an idea that often conflicts with that of suffering, climaxes in *The Fixer*, where Yakov Bok repudiates suffering; and borrowing patterns out of Jessie Weston, Maud Bodkin, and Joseph Campbell, Ducharme sees wasteland myths structuring Malamud's four major novels, with the most "natural and sustained expression" of the technique coming in *The Fixer.*

In "Malamud's Fixer—Jew, Christian, or Modern?" (*Renascence* 27:101–10), John F. Desmond is less happy with *The Fixer*, an "extremely polemical" novel whose thematic burden is ethically questionable. He believes that Malamud approves of Bok's willingness to commit political murder and that the symbolic identification of Bok with Christ warps Christian history by introducing existentialist principles.

In "A Reading of Bernard Malamud's *The Tenants*" (*JAmS* 9:85–102) Brita Lindberg-Seyersted discusses this novel's circular structure, which dramatizes the need to continue to understand "the other" (here, the black writer and double) with whom the protagonist struggles. Especially perceptive is her discovery of the function of Malamud's shifting tenses and narrative focus. In "Malamud's Allusive Design in *A New Life*" (*WAL* 10:115–23) Paul Witherington stresses the importance of literary allusions (Thoreau, Hawthorne, Melville) in Levin's progress from idealism and its testing to a state of moral freedom with all its ambiguities.

David R. Mesher finds that the first story of the Fidelman sequence is pivotal both to Malamud's early and late fiction. "The Remembrance of Things Unknown: Malamud's 'The Last Mohican'" (*SSF* 12:397–404) is a careful reading which places great importance upon Susskind's intervention. The way in which Malamud ironically counterpoints Cooper's noble savage in the search-and-chase episodes is the subject of H. Harbour Winn, III's "Malamud's Uncas: 'Last Mohican'" (*NConL* 5,ii:13–14); and Charles A. Sweet, Jr., finds a parallel and source in *The Waste Land* for another short story in "Unlocking the Door: Malamud's 'Behold the Key'" (*NConL* 5,v:11–12). "The Art of Fiction: Bernard Malamud" (*ParisR* 61–64:40–64) is an interview taped on the novelist's 60th birthday in which Malamud discusses the importance of revision in the creative process, muses on the question of whether teaching careers interfere with a writer's talent, and downplays his identification as a Jewish writer.

Despite an annoyingly colloquial style and a clutch of misspellings and neologisms, Sanford Pinsker's *The Comedy That "Hoits": An Essay on the Fiction of Philip Roth* (Columbia: Univ. of Mo. Press) is both perceptive and useful. Seeking a correspondence between "the public dimensions of Roth's scathing satire and the private realm of his self-abasement," Pinsker concludes persuasively that, like D. H. Lawrence, Roth is a writer out to " 'shed his sickness' in the discipline or pattern-making of art." The separate intrepretations are firm and discriminating for a writer whose talent in *Goodbye, Columbus* "has not yet quite managed to fulfill itself."

The other work on Roth is minor. Arnold E. Davidson's "Kafka,

Rilke, and Philip Roth's *The Breast*" (*NConL* 5,i:9–11) is self-explanatory; and Robert F. Willson, Jr., wonders why Roth failed to cite an obvious source for his baseball novel—Ira and H. Allen Smith's anecdotal *Low and Inside* (1949)—in "An Indisputable Source for the Spirited Account of a Baseball Contest Between the Port Ruppert Mundys and the Asylum Lunatics in *The Great American Novel* by Mr. Philip Roth" (*NConL* 5,iii:12–14). "Philip Roth in Conversation with Joyce Carol Oates" (*NewRev* 2,xiv:3–7) is a garrulous piece in which Oates invites Roth's musings on the joys of solitude and the burdens of being reviewed by unsympathetic critics.

v. John Barth, Thomas Pynchon, and John Hawkes

In "The Drama of Digression: Narrative Technique in John Barth's *The Floating Opera*" (*CimR* 29[1974]:34–44), Joseph C. Voelker sees a consonantal appropriateness in a Sisyphean narrator, who generates a disgressive tale touching on all his past adventures with absurdity, which casts doubt on the accuracy of all rational apprehension of reality.

In the process of investigating Barth's investigations in "Ebenezer Cooke, Sot-Weed Factor Redividus: The Genesis of John Barth's *The Sot-Weed Factor*" (*BMWMLA* 8:32–47), David Morrell focuses on the novelist's transition from the two realistic novels to his third one, a dramatization of how men distort the world about them. Although armed with a thesis suggested by others before him, James F. Walter, in "A Psychronology of Lust in the Menippean Tradition: *Giles Goat-Boy*" (*TCL* 21:394–410), fully demonstrates that the "extravagant spirit of parody which holds nothing sacred finally except the integrity of its hero's vision" places this work with *Don Quixote*, *Gulliver's Travels*, and *The Satyricon*, Menippean satires which attempt to embrace simultaneously extreme limits of human experience.

The structure of *Lost in the Funhouse* is the subject of very different essays by Gerald Gillespie and Christopher D. Morris. In "Barth's 'Lost in the Funhouse': Short Story Text in Its Cyclic Context" (*SSF* 12:223–30), Gillespie sees a "seven-step dialectic" (involving cabbalistic and theosophic patterns) in the story cycle, which provides the reader with a movement "between planes of consciousness." In "Barth and Lacan: The World of the Moebius Strip" (*Crit* 17,i:69–77), Morris uses the French poststructuralist Jacques Lacan as a conceptual model for the "meaningless, autonomous phonemes" constituting the book; selfhood there is a "metaphor of a metaphor rather than the presence of anything real."

In "'It's a Chimera': An Introduction to John Barth's Latest Fiction" (*Rendezvous* 10,ii:17–30), Dante Cantrill proposes the use of a "binocular method of explication" (i.e., using complementary perspectives offered by metaphors, puns, etymologies, folklore, philosophy) on *Chimera*, a "highly structured, self-reflecting triad of novelle that at least resembles a carnival funhouse, complete with tumbling barrel and mirror maze." Campbell Tatham's "Message [Concerning the *Felt* Ultimacies of One John Barth]" (*Boundary 2* 3:259–87) is a cute, parodic exploration (in the form of a Mad Hatter symposium) of Barth's implications, evasions, premises, and negations. In "A Spectatorial Skeptic: An Interview with John Barth" (*Caliban* 12:93–110), the novelist confides to Annie le Rebeller his discomfort with all academic labels used to classify him: existentialist (in the 1950s), black humorist (in the 1960s), and fabulator (in the 1970s).

Joseph W. Slade's *Thomas Pynchon* (New York: Warner [1974]) is an enthusiastic introduction to the writer whose scope "is matched in this century only by Joyce's." Not only is the critic's excitement contagious; his skillful plot summaries—as well as his insights—are actually useful. There are two chapters each on *V.* and *Gravity's Rainbow*, one on *The Crying of Lot 49*, and a conclusion; but especially fresh is a chapter on the short stories, in which Slade argues that from his first published fiction, "Mortality and Mercy in Vienna" in 1959, to *Gravity's Rainbow*, Pynchon has made technology and its relationship to human activity his most persistent concern. Slade is also careful to locate the influence of Machiavelli, Sir James Frazer, and Max Weber, as well as the more familiar traces of Whitehead, Einstein, and Henry Adams.

In "Describing the Demon: The Appeal of Thomas Pynchon" (*PR* 42:112–25), Neil Schmitz sees "Melvillean masquerades" played out in a Manichean world in which the author himself is the con man. In his latest novel, by trying to reinvent evil with the ethic of the "desperado" and a style of "self-indulgence," Pynchon insists upon his "otherness, his anarchic criminality."

In a special Pynchon number—*TCL*,ii—George Levine and David Leverenz guest-edit a gathering of important pieces. Thin but elegant, Richard Poirier's "The Importance of Thomas Pynchon" (pp. 151–62) manages to relate the younger novelist to American classic authors of the last century. William Vesterman's "Pynchon's Poetry" (pp. 211–20) is a messy but interesting essay which finally makes too much of the author's fondness for interpolated songs and poems. Only the most dedicated buff will be able to follow Lance W. Ozier's fiercely technical "The Calculus of Transformation: More Mathematical Imagery in *Gravity's Rainbow*" (pp. 193–210), an addendum to an earlier essay (*ALS 1974*, pp. 304–05).

In his provocative, dense, and brilliant "Pentecost, Promiscuity, and Pynchon's *V.*: From the Scaffold to the Impulsive" (pp. 163–76), W. T. Lhamon, Jr., claims that the novelist's effort is nothing less than a reimagining of the Apocalyptic as a literary genre, which he then parodies. Pentecost ("an ultimate ascent into the spiritual") is as formless as entropy (the ultimate collapse into "material"); and "Pentecostal entropy" is a lively death which maintains expressiveness "in tongues." Those interested in Pynchon's first novel may not want to begin with Lhamon, but they may well end with him.

Scott Sanders's "Pynchon's Paranoid History" (pp. 177–92), a clearly formulated statement of modified admiration, is an analysis of the conspiratorial view of history which haunts Pynchon. After persuasively tracing the way in which implicit mental structures delineated in the fiction reproduce dominant features of Calvinist doctrine, Sanders ends with four cogent "objections" to Pynchon, the most signal being the relative ease with which he leaps from "historical observation" to a "metaphysical assertion" that closes out all possibilities for historical impulses toward renewal or recovery.

Despite the specific title, "The Sacred, the Profane, and *The Crying of Lot 49*" (*Individual and Community*, pp. 182–222) is an ambitious and admirable overview of Pynchon by Edward Mendelson. *Lot 49* "finds the intrusive energy that is needed to reverse the process that *V.* describes"—the onslaught of inanition and decline. If the processes of *V.* "isolate," those of the second novel enact "the response made by men and women to their recognition of the connectedness of the world." This rich essay compares *Lot 49* to Goethe's *Elective Affinities* (in the transformation of the impersonal language of science into one of great emotional power); argues that *V.* is really a gloss on Henry Adams's chapter on the "Dynamo and the Virgin" in *The Education* (Pynchon's V. is the virgin who *becomes* the dynamo);

and finds that *Lot 49* has a Borges story from *Ficciones* as its concealed and unacknowledged source.

John Stark advises us to learn more science in order to appreciate Pynchon. In "The Arts and Sciences of Thomas Pynchon" (*HC* 12,iv:1–13), an introduction in the best sense, Stark agrees with those Pynchon admirers who see entropy and cybernetics as increasingly functional, but he also shows how Pynchon's strong humanistic strain puts his books in an honorable tradition of classic "informational" books in American culture (*Walden, Moby-Dick, The Confidence-Man*). André Le Vot, in "The Rocket and the Pig: Thomas Pynchon and Science Fiction" (*Caliban* 12:111–18), concentrates on those features which *Gravity's Rainbow* shares with science fiction, the most notable of which is the awareness of a dichotomy between living nature and the technological urge "to use it, degrade it, kill it." In "Anarcho-Romanticism and the Metaphysics of Counterforce: Alex Comfort and Thomas Pynchon" (*Paunch* 40/41:78–107), John M. Krafft uses "The Ideology of Romanticism," Comfort's 1946 essay, to clarify Pynchon's vision of Western civilization.

In "Hawkes in Love" (*Caliban* 12:65–79), an excellent general essay on Hawkes's art, Marcus Klein makes pertinent comments on the idea and practice of form and on the prominence of the ruthlessly comic satire. He points out that though his landscapes are not created out of experience and his details do not always square with observation, Hawkes writes stories about characters "who as a matter of primacy are defined culturally and socially"—out of a vision that is both historical and apocalyptic.

John Kuehl describes his *John Hawkes and the Craft of Conflict* (New Brunswick, N.J.: Rutgers Univ. Press) as the first systematic exploration of "the connection between form and content" in Hawkes's work; but his most important contribution is in elucidating the functional tension between Thanatos and Eros. Only after *The Lime Twig* are these opposing forces sufficiently defined to create sustained conflict; the increasing power of Eros in the later work transforms static landscapes into dynamic ones, negative myths into ambiguous ones, and flat characters into round ones. Unfortunately, Kuehl tends to be satisfied with merely listing examples (of physical cruelty to children, of sexual aberrations, of historical and literary names) when analysis is needed. After a brief postscript linking *Death, Sleep & the Traveler* to *The Blood Oranges*, Kuehl appends an interview with

Hawkes, who emphasizes the positive thrust of his fiction and professes ignorance of such religious and literary classics as the Bible and *The Golden Bough*.

Hawkes's insistence on *The Blood Oranges* as a pastoral novel in that interview finds confirmation in Lois A. Cuddy's "Functional Pastoralism in *The Blood Oranges*" (*SAF* 3:15–25), which describes the tension between two conceptually antagonistic strands of the pastoral tradition: the longing for a pure rural world of enduring marriage and sexual fidelity (represented by Hugh), and the pastoral of self-contained happiness (represented by Cyril). John V. Knapp, however, emphasizes the ethical use of sexuality in "Hawkes' *The Blood Oranges*: A Sensual New Jerusalem" (*Crit* 17,iii:5–25). To support his belief that Hawkes's intent here is nothing less than the creation of a new morality "to supplant the outworn asexuality of a moribund Christianity," Knapp examines several key scenes for modulations of Christian imagery.

Two critics speculate on the kind of "departure" represented by Hawkes's most recent fiction. Donald J. Greiner, in "*Death, Sleep & the Traveler*: John Hawkes' Return to Terror" (*Crit* 17,iii:26–38), sees not a completed divorce from the previous work but argues that Allert's fantasies "veer toward derangement" of the kind seen in *The Beetle Leg* and *The Owl*. In "Psychic Sores in Search of Compassion: Hawkes' *Death, Sleep & the Traveler*" (*Crit* 17,iii:39–52), Elisabeth Kraus insists that the underlying theme is the same one that Hawkes has been dramatizing for 25 years: "the conflict between the rational, judgmental ego and the irrational, imaginative id of our culture-repressed unconscious." Daniel Plung's "John Hawkes: A Selected Bibliography, 1943–1975" (*Crit* 17,iii:53–63) includes reviews and previous bibliographies.

vi. Kurt Vonnegut, Ken Kesey, and Richard Brautigan

Most of this year's work on Vonnegut concerns values and vision. Lynn Buck's "Vonnegut's World of Comic Futility" (*SAF* 3:181–98), about half of which treats the recurring theme of fathers and sons, is a meandering essay which makes no distinctions among the works. Vonnegut has three weapons to combat futility, says Buck: illusion, love, and laughter.

"Hemingway and Vonnegut: Diminishing Vision in a Dying Age"

(*MFS* 21:173–91) is Clinton S. Burhans, Jr.'s extended comparison-contrast of these two writers (in moral vision and as spokesmen for their respective ages). Though trapped in the void of nada, Hemingway still maintained his sturdy 19th-century belief in man's ability to find and create order for himself; for Vonnegut the empty universe is "both source and measure" of an utterly futile state of man. Jean E. Kennard uses a similar reading to argue against Vonnegut's wide reputation as a satirist in "Kurt Vonnegut, Jr.: The Sirens of Satire" (*Number and Nightmare*, pp. 101–28); since Vonnegut denies the possibility of absolute values, he can only imitate the true satirist, using the genre and method to attack satire itself. *Cat's Cradle* most successfully fits Kennard's thesis; *God Bless You, Mr. Rosewater*, because it hints at some "consistent ethical scheme," seems to contradict it.

Though it is short on critical analysis that would demonstrate how Vonnegut is a disruptive fictionist, Jerome Klinkowitz's chapter on Vonnegut in *Literary Disruptions* (pp. 33–61) is a useful disentangling of the complex publishing history and an account of the author's reputation. In "The Dramatization of Kurt Vonnegut, Jr." (*Players* 50:62–64), Klinkowitz succinctly traces the origins and contexts of *Happy Birthday, Wanda June*, which, like the fiction, is concerned with pacifism and the transforming possibilities of a world where time is relative and catastrophe can be avoided; unlike the fiction, however, the world in this play has already been transformed, leaving its protagonist behind.

Wayne D. McGinnis discusses how the use of cultural junk is chosen to give the effect of chaos, but that "epiphanies of reduction" demonstrate the American penchant for the "grotesquely asinine." But in "Vonnegut's *Breakfast of Champions*: A Reductive Success" (*NConL* 5,iii:6–9), McGinnis never quite defines his key term. A more significant essay by McGinnis, "The Arbitrary Cycle of *Slaughterhouse-Five*: A Relation of Form to Theme" (*Crit* 17,i:55–67), traces the movement away from framing and linear narration to a more unresolved circular structure, which suggests a cyclical "return" embodied in the Tralfamadorian concept of time. McGinnis also discusses cinematic and stream of consciousness techniques without overstressing their importance. In "Vonnegut's *Sirens of Titan*" (*Expl* 34:item 27) Donald M. Fiene comments on the relationship of the title and color symbolism.

Although in *Ken Kesey* (WWS 12) he discusses the diverse influences (mythic implications of the title, apocalyptic and millenarian sources, the Beats, classic American romance writers), Bruce Carnes mostly concentrates on the relationship of form to Kesey's recurring theme, the American Dream and the possibilities of heroism. The tightly organized plot of *One Flew Over the Cuckoo's Nest* he sees as analogous to Kesey's moral certainties about experience; the looseness of *Sometimes a Great Notion* parallels his loss of assurance that experience is "readily comprehensible and malleable." In the only substantial discussion of Kesey's *Garage Sale* Carnes describes that curious grab-bag as a transitional work.

In "The Post-Modernist Art of Protest: Kesey and Mailer as American Expressions of Rebellion" (*CentR* 19:121–35), Kingsley Widmer perceptively compares *One Flew Over the Cuckoo's Nest* and *The Armies of the Night* as social-aesthetic responses of the artist-as-activist. Both works are essential elaborations of the same metaphors; both are "half-protests" which dramatize the "American 'he-man' playing at religion"; and both betray the contradictions in the decade's sensibilities.

Don R. Kunz argues that the seemingly contradictory symbols of Kesey's first novel derive from two mutually exclusive "visions"—American behaviorism and a revitalization of one existentialist stance, totemism. In "Mechanistic and Totemistic Symbolization in Kesey's *One Flew Over the Cuckoo's Nest*" (*SAF* 3:65–82), Kunz shows that both kinds of symbols emerge from Bromden's vision of McMurphy—one involving images of wheels, carnivals, and mobility; the second, centering on McMurphy's search for a salvational totem (animals and birds) to serve as a countertherapy to the "therapy" of Big Nurse.

In "Big Mama, Big Papa, and Little Sons in Ken Kesey's *One Flew Over the Cuckoo's Nest*" (*L&P* 25:34–44), Ruth Sullivan contends that even though the novel disparages psychoanalytic therapy, Kesey structures his fictive human relationships according to his own understanding of the Oedipus complex. The crucial emotional issue for the sons (the patients) is "how to define their manliness in relation to the mother figure" (Big Nurse) and with the help of the father (McMurphy).

Andrew S. Horton's "Ken Kesey, John Updike and the Lone Ranger" (*JPC* 8[1974]:570–78) is considerably weaker on *One Flew Over the Cuckoo's Nest* than on Updike's *Rabbit Redux*; the modest point here is that Kesey reverses the traditional story—Tonto saved by the Lone Ranger. "Ken Kesey's Psychopathic Savior: A Rejoinder" (*MFS* 21:222–30) is Robert Forrey's impassioned response to Terence Martin's essay (*ALS 1973*, p. 283), which Forrey sees as the culmination of a trend among male critics to overpraise a novel which is conservative, sexist, and lowbrow "in terms of the level of sensibility it reflects"—i.e., one shaped by comic books. Joseph Weixlmann's "Ken Kesey: A Bibliography" (*WAL* 10:219–31) is a nine-part listing, including "published letters written to Kesey," poetry "written about him," and previous bibliographies.

The only substantial piece on Brautigan this year is the casual and pleasant "Fishing the Ambivalence, or, A Reading of *Trout Fishing in America*" (*WHR* 29:29–42), Kent Bales's exploration of the welter of associated myths and cross-purposed motifs from the national consciousness pervading that work (Trout Fishing, Making It, Conquering the Continent, Making Myself Anew, etc.). Brautigan, says Bales, deftly weighs beginnings against the conclusion, chapters against chapters, motifs against motifs, "not so much to shore fragments against ruins in order to survive as to remind us that, while the play is in earnest, it is still play."

vii. Joyce Carol Oates, John Updike, and James Purdy

Robert H. Fossum, in "Only Control: The Novels of Joyce Carol Oates" (*SNNTS* 7:285–97), concludes that Oates is sometimes weak in capturing "the peculiar social texture of a given time and place" but strong in illuminating the emotional lives of her characters, most of whom are their own worst enemies.

Despite her title, Eileen T. Bender's "Autonomy and Influence: Joyce Carol Oates' *Marriages and Infidelities*" (*Soundings* 58:390–406) is also a general survey of the work (described as linear and "realistic"), which recounts the "grim romance of the ego"—the insecurity born of the simultaneous dream for the autonomous self and the dread that one's self-expression has been predetermined by external forces. That her characters usually embrace rather than resist the patterned and structured life is seen as a reflection of Oates's distaste for contemporary "fabulators" who champion romantic, "corrupt" notions of autonomy. Bender chooses three stories which are "reimaginings" of stories by Kafka, James, and Joyce, a process which dramatizes the "inexhaustible energies and resources" of a patterned artistic tradition.

Rose Marie Burwell attempts a Jungian reading in "The Process of Individuation as Narrative Structure: Joyce Carol Oates' *Do with Me What You Will*" (*Crit* 17,ii:93–106), but her conclusion is simply commonsensical: that this novel is not simply the story of a woman raised to a higher level of consciousness through love and sexuality, but one in which a "complex and nearly perfect tension exists between personal individuation and the societal forces resistant to it."

Oates herself delineates "Updike's American Comedies" (*MFS* 21:459–72) with a cheerful disregard for the integrity of genres: Updike's "genius is best excited by the lyric possibilities of tragic events that, failing to justify themselves as tragedy, turn unaccountably into comedies." Although this provocative, many-directioned piece is affectionately admiring, Oates manages to give important insights into Updike's Calvinism, the religious aura of transformation involved in the very act of writing, and what she calls the recurring "nuclear fable" in his fiction (the mother who wears down female rivals and even the son).

Albert E. Wilhelm, in "The Clothing Motif in Updike's 'Rabbit, Run'" (*SAB* 40,iv:87–89), observes that the changes in clothing and the gradual stripping away of all attire suggest the symbolic stages of Rabbit's uncertain social definition. In "Rabbit Brought Nowhere: John Updike's *Rabbit Redux*" (*SCR* 8,i:35–42) Kermit Turner argues that the passivity, egoism, and the tendency to live by impulse so prominent in *Rabbit, Run* continue into the sequel. Robert W. Cochran attempts to distinguish the little epiphany in one Updike story from the Joycean kind, but "The Narrator Then and Now in Updike's 'Flight'" (*Rendezvous* 10,i:29–32) finally fails in clarifying that difference.

Henry Chupack declares that James Purdy is a fundamentally honest craftsman, whose power and style are rare in contemporary writing, but in *James Purdy* (TUSAS 248), he also points out deficiencies (an unbalanced world in which there are no happy characters, no Jews, and few "good" people; an exceptionally dour vision of man and society; an obsessiveness about rape and orphans). Purdy goes beyond the Black Humorists of the 1960s, says Chupack, who rightly assesses his achievement as not the sensational exploitation of the "merely odd and freakish" but the "dark underside and interiors of the human soul," a concern which extends back to Poe. While claiming that Purdy's style—spare, lean, icy—is uninfluenced by any of his contemporaries, or even by his mentor, Dame Edith Sitwell, Chupack perceptively suggests links to other midwestern writers. This critic is to be commended, incidentally, for quoting from hardback editions of Purdy's works, though he gives information on available paperbacks as well.

If Chupack finds only perceptible traces of Black Humor in Purdy, Jean E. Kennard, in "James Purdy: Fidelity to Failure" (*Number and Nightmare*, pp. 82–100), sees him differing from Heller and Barth as well: the "Post-existentialist dilemma" in Purdy is cause for further despair, not ironic laughter. That his works illustrate the failure of all love relationships and the failure of communication is an observation made before, but Kennard shrewdly links Malcolm to the non-identity of Sartrean "being-for-itself" and notes the process by which the action of *Malcolm* progressively "unmakes itself."

viii. William Styron, Walker Percy, James Dickey, and Reynolds Price

In "The Graveyard Epiphany in Modern Southern Fiction: Transcendence of Selfhood" (*SHR* 9:389–403), John T. Hiers focuses on those moments in the fiction of Agee, O'Connor, Wolfe, Welty, and Styron when the place of death becomes also "a sacred place of spiritual or imaginative rebirth," exhibiting the human capacity "to transcend time by transcending self." Styron's use of such moments is more bleakly pessimistic than that of his other fellow southerners, Hiers finds.

Robert K. Morris and Irving Malin have edited a fine collection of essays in *The Achievement of William Styron* (Athens: Univ. of Ga. Press). In an intelligent and elegantly written overview they describe the arc of Styron's career, make a good case for calling this novelist a "visionary," and are particularly acute in their discussion of *The Confessions of Nat Turner*, which they see as a culmination of the "transfiguration patterns" in the earlier fiction. In addition to reprints of excellent essays by Louis D. Rubin, George Core, and Seymour L. Gross and Eileen Bender, the editors present six new essays.

John O. Lyons ("On *Lie Down in Darkness*," pp. 88–99) reassesses Styron's first novel downward, citing its generally derivative nature and concentrating especially on its melange of styles. While noting similar defects in an essay which tries to do too much, "Permutations of Death: A Reading of *Lie Down in Darkness*" (pp. 100–21), Jan B. Gordon tries to go beyond the derivativeness, finding geographical analogues for the eddying narrative action; explores the relationship between death-in-life and life-in-death "in a civilization which is itself trapped between the two"; differentiates Styron from other southern writers by claiming that his emphasis is upon nostalgia rather than memory; and traces some of the relationships based on the intersecting of the human imperatives (*love, need, want*).

Robert Phillips, in "Mask and Symbol in *Set This House on Fire*" (pp. 134–49), investigates symbolic resonances of the characters' names and a variety of myths and literary sources, the interfusing of which produces the characteristic dreamlike effect. Phillips sees that the theme of all the fiction is "the individual's revolt and outrage against the system." Norman Kelvin, however, in "The Divided Self: William Styron's Fiction from *Lie Down in Darkness* to *The Confessions of Nat Turner*" (pp. 208–26), finds that the common theme is "the meaning and action of evil." Though Kelvin feels that Styron is often at his best in creating "the pain of being a divided person," he too often resolves narrative dilemmas sentimentally. The editors contribute their own essays: Morris on Styron's play, *In the Clap Shack* (pp. 227–41), and Malin in an extensive exploration of symbolic relationships between Culver and Mannix in *The Long March* (pp. 122–33). Morris also conducts "An Interview with William Styron" (pp. 24–50), in which the author reassesses his own position as a "southern" writer, expresses delight in the novel form, and talks about his work in progress. This handsome, well-made book is made more useful by Jackson R. Bryer's "William Styron: A Bibliography" (pp. 242–77), now the most complete bibliography available on Styron.

Two other Styron items should be noted. In "Transcendence and Failure: William Styron's *Lie Down in Darkness*" (*Caliban* 12:157–66), Anthony Suter discusses Peyton's suicide as "the only act of hope" in the novel, contrasting it to the inability of all the other characters to break out of their own prison-like existence. And James L. W. West, III, has edited "William Styron's Afterword to *The Long March*" (*MissQ* 28:185–89); these four paragraphs, appearing for the first time in English, West declares to be important because they establish the autobiographical basis of the novel.

Ambitious, scholarly, and often severe, "Walker Percy and Gabriel Marcel: The Castaway and the Wayfarer" (*MissQ* 28:21–53) by John F. Zeugner extends earlier studies of existentialists who influenced the novelist by exploring key concepts (*transcendence, intersubjectivity*) in Percy's nonfictional writings as well as in his novels. Zeugner finds that the "muted celebration" of *The Moviegoer* darkens in *The Last Gentleman,* which accentuates a peevish satiric bent, and in *Love in the Ruins,* which allows condescension and abstractionism to flower unchecked.

Paul G. Italia's "Love and Lust in James Dickey's *Deliverance*" (*MFS* 21:203–13) is a first-rate, sensitive reading which explores the relationship of sodomy to the larger issue of love. Sex is not merely a metaphor here, says Italia, but the "energy that shapes all life." David L. Arnett conducts "An Interview with James Dickey" (*ConL* 16:286–300), in which the immodest author talks again about the gestation of *Deliverance,* its relationships to certain of his poems, and his philosophical affinities.

Drawing with commendable restraint on such theorists as Bachelard and Poulet, Simone Vauthier gives the most impressive reading yet of Price's most famous novel with "'The Circle in the Forest': Fictional Space in Reynolds Price's *A Long and Happy Life*" (*MissQ* 28:123–46). Norfolk, a synecdoche of urban America and a "metonomy connating the way of life in cities," sets the country mores of Afton in perspective so that the total meaning of the fictional space created by the novel depends on "the correlation of the character's perception of a given place and the reader's."

ix. Donald Barthelme, Robert Coover, and Other Innovators

In his chapter on Barthelme (*Literary Disruptions,* pp. 62–81), Jerome Klinkowitz links the author's concern over the debasement of language to Orwell's a generation ago. One function of Barthelme's technique is to shatter expectations; the stories become "radical stopgap measures to sane experiences which might otherwise be eroded with our loss of traditional standards."

Among the clutch of pieces on Barthelme in *Crit* (16,iii) are Klinkowitz's "Donald Barthelme's SuperFiction" (pp. 5–18), a juxtaposition of "fragments," graphics, and a mini-anthology of the author's work, and "Donald Barthelme: A Checklist, 1957–1974" (pp.

49–58), which not only gathers the expected items but also lists "Publicly Disavowed Forgeries" and items by Barthelme's publicly avowed pseudonym, "Lily McNeil." This special number also includes a note which stresses the author's "additive" technique—Tom Whalen's "Wonderful Elegance: Barthelme's 'The Party' " (pp. 44–48), and two essays on *Snow White*. Larry McCaffery's "Barthelme's *Snow White*: The Aesthetics of Trash" (pp. 19–32) is a clear introduction to the rationale behind the famous techniques, Barthelme's desire to incorporate the decayed elements of his world into an idiom mocking the languages of other disciplines and professions. Betty Flowers stresses the absence of any central vocabulary and point of view in her "Barthelme's *Snow White*: The Reader-Patient Relationship" (pp. 33–43) with some fine close readings of characteristic passages to illustrate "pseudo-symbolic saturation of meaning."

In "Donald Barthelme and the Death of Fiction" (*Prospects* 1:369–86) William Stott examines several stories and *Snow White* as illustrations of "what happens to private values when all facts are treated as public." Paradoxically, Stott believes that Barthelme discovers a curiously reserved privacy, a "selfhood," in publicity. Using a study of Pierre Marivaux—described as a being without past or future and whose present is based only on accidental, not causal, principles—James R. Giles analyzes Barthelme's Robert Kennedy in "The 'Marivaudian Being' Drowns His Children: Dehumanization in Donald Barthelme's 'Robert Kennedy Saved from Drowning' and Joyce Carol Oates' *Wonderland*" (*SHR* 9:63–75); the author's "K" is not just Kennedy but also Kafka's alienated Everyman. In Oates's novel Jesse fits such a definition.

" 'With Ingenuity and Hard Work, Distracted': The Narrative Style of Donald Barthelme" (*Style* 9:388–400) is an important essay by John M. Ditsky, who uses "Daumier" to demonstrate his contention that brevity—which results in a "concentration of movement and effect," even "busyness" of texture—is Barthelme's most important technique.

Frank W. Shelton, in "Humor and Balance in Coover's *The Universal Baseball Association, Inc.*" (*Crit* 17,i:78–90), argues that the two perspectives on reality—the folk view of most of the ballplayers and the urban one of Henry Waugh—provide a balance which posits not despair but purpose and hope. In "Robert Coover—'The Babysitter': An Observation on Experimental Writing" (*Style* 9:378–87), E. B. Weinstock first defines experimental writing (a serious attempt "to utilize the data of traditional experience in order to produce new forms"); then enumerates and discusses such specific Coover techniques as the "blocking" of text and the teasing richness of texture which challenges reader participation; and concludes that Coover's "highly ordered chaos" is a traditional aim of art.

Jerome Klinkowitz contends that the survival of the self is the central theme in all of Jerzy Kosinski's writings (*Literary Disruptions*, pp. 82–101); this is a valuable essay because Klinkowitz pays attention to Kosinski's masters thesis and his two works of political and social commentary, as well as drawing substantially from the fiction. David H. Richter's bibliographical study of Kosinski's *The Painted Bird* (*ALS 1974*, p. 308) should be supplemented with a clarification by Richter and Klinkowitz, "Two Bibliographical Questions in Kosinski's *The Painted Bird*" (*ConL* 16:126–29).

Klinkowitz's "Michael Stephens' Superfiction" (*TriQ* 34:219–32) is not so much an essay on this writer as an introduction to his work by Stephens himself; the critical device is so involuted and self-conscious that the talent in question is still in need of some neutral presentation. Klinkowitz's chapters on Gilbert Sorrentino in *Literary Disruptions* (pp. 154–67) and Ronald Sukenick and Raymond Federman (pp. 119–53) are descriptive and useful. Of all contemporary fictionists Sorrentino is the most insistent that the old notion of suspension-of-disbelief is a fraud and that fictive truths lie not in novelistic imitation of life but in authorially executed patterns. The most important figure behind Sukenick, Klinkowitz points out, is Wallace Stevens, on whom Sukenick has written a critical book; an important parallel figure behind Federman is Samuel Beckett, on whom Federman has written a critical study.

Douglass Bolling's "The Waking Nightmare: American Society in Rudolph Wurlitzer's *Quake*" (*Crit* 16,iii:70–80) explores the relationship of entropic metaphors, images of disorder and anarchy, and this novelist's belief in the inadequacy of language to deal with stresses beneath the surface of American society. Albert Howard Carter, III, provides an overview of *The Sporting Club* and two other novels in "Thomas McGuane's First Three Novels: Games, Fun, Nemesis" (*Crit* 17,i:91–104). Joseph McElroy's "Neural Neighborhoods and

Other Concrete Abstracts" (*TriQ* 34:201–17) is an impressionistic romp through the genesis of *A Smuggler's Bible* with some disquieted side-glances at some celebrated rivals.

x. Others

***a.* Bruce Jay Friedman, Stanley Elkin, and Thomas Berger.** To place his author in *Bruce Jay Friedman* (TUSAS 219 [1974]), Max F. Schulz tends heavily toward the spirit of the times, as if the last decade of big Hollywood culture and World War II did not help to shape a wide variety of writers. In the first chapter Friedman gets stuck with what Schulz himself calls a "beguilingly vague" term, Black Humor; "realism forced to the extreme of a metaphysical truth" might apply to American naturalists or Dickens as well as Friedman. Schulz, while being reasonably acute in his reading of the separate novels (especially *A Mother's Kisses*), betrays the essentially banal sensibility of his subject while overestimating the importance of Black Humor. Except for his own book on Black Humor (*ALS 1973*, pp. 262–63), Schulz makes no use of any secondary commentary since the 1960s, and his prose style too often lapses into a banality of its own. I do not believe, for example, that Friedman (or anybody else) writes a prose that is "nervously responsive to both the stereophonic-stroboscopic scene and to the dark totemic surges of our blood and the dark satanic mills of the mind."

In a minor little piece, "Rootlessness and Alienation in the Novels of Bruce Jay Friedman" (*CLAJ* 18:422–33), Stuart A. Lewis argues that the protagonists of all three novels experience a physical displacement and that a recurring theme is relocation, seen in images of fragmentation, voyeurism, and broken communication.

In his survey of the entire work, "The Obsessional Fiction of Stanley Elkin" (*ConL* 16:146–62), Thomas LeClair finds that the protagonists are ordinary men suddenly possessed with "improbable possibilities of the self's expansion," and who derive their obsessions from "natural authorities, common needs, or the promises of a popular culture rather than from some social, psychological, or religious ideology" (as in Mailer, Hawkes, or O'Connor). Some of the qualities which make Elkin's work important are his imaginative inconclusiveness, a psychology registering multiplicity and contradiction, and a concern for the detailed "transactions of an individual and the popular culture." Scott Sanders's "An Interview with Stanley Elkin" (*ConL* 16:131–45), which projects an author both interesting and believable, reveals Elkin's passionate interest in the use of language through those writers he admires (Faulkner, Gass, the early Barth).

In "The Schlemiel as Humorist: Thomas Berger's Carlo Reinhart" (*Cithara* 15,i:3–21) Douglas A. Hughes strikes another writer from the ranks of Black Humor, since the laughter which Berger evokes is "bright, humane, and never bitter." In this discussion of the Reinhart trilogy, Hughes shows that the failures of the Candide-like hero are actually moral successes.

***b.* Detective and Science Fictionists.** Popular culture, says William Ruehlmann, is "history in caricature, an exaggerated portrait of a nation's psychic nature," and the private detective he sees at the center of the urban murder story, the quintessential narrative of our time. Except for only an occasional injection of Vietnam-inspired moralism about violence, *Saint With a Gun: The Unlawful American Private Eye* (New York: New York Univ. Press [1974]) is an admirable example of how the stuff of popular culture can be rendered seriously. Disputing the popular conception of the "innocent" private eye, Ruehlmann declares, "the typical tough-guy private eye does not merely interact with social corruption, he collaborates in it." This study traces the origin of the figure in real-life, Allen Pinkerton, to its fictional versions in Black Mask fiction and all the way to the most recent development: a final chapter concentrates on the "crypto-soldier" with a grudge who shows up sporting such anonymous *nommes de guerre as* "Executioner," "Revenger," and "Destroyer," all demonstrating the "national sense of impotence" in dealing with organized crime. This is a must book, like John G. Cawelti's *The Six-Gun Mystique* (1971), for those interested in the "evangelism of violence."

Glossing *The Godfather*, Cawelti himself sees a significant change in our myths of American crime in "The New Mythology of Crime" (*Boundary 2* 3:325–57). With contemporary stories of "capers which involve either a Don or an Enforcer as the protagonist," the new criminal image mirrors our sense of the decline of "security, significance, and order in the corporate society." Another tack is taken by Wilson Carey McWilliams in "Natty Bumppo and the Godfather" (*ColQ* 24:133–44), an essay in cultural history focusing on concepts of natural aristocracy and barbarism; McWilliams believes that Puzo documents our transition from the Natty Bumppos, "who go to meet the barbarians," to new heroes, barbarians "who can *survive* and *succeed* within civilization itself."

In a feminist study, "Beauty As the Beast: Fantasy and Fear in *I, the Jury*" (*JPC* 8:775–82), Judith Fetterley demonstrates convincingly how the Spillane novel develops two primary images (the sadistic killer and the ultrafeminine blonde) which turn out to be the same; the book itself, says Fetterley, "fails to fulfill the logic of its tension" because of the "unconscious necessities of the mind of the male protagonist whose story it is." Connections are again drawn between the cowboy and the private detective in Fred Erisman's "Western Motifs in the Thrillers of Donald Hamilton" (*WAL* 10:283–92), the purveyor of both kinds of fiction in the 1950s.

The only significant scholarship in science fiction this year is on Ursula K. Le Guin in *SFS*, ii. Jeff Levin provides "Ursula K. Le Guin: A Select [*sic*] Bibliography," and the author herself contributes a brief note on the significance of the figural Alien. There are nine pieces in all, including essays and fragmentary musings by Rafail Nudelman, Frederic Jameson, Ian Watson, and John Huntington. In "Philip Jose Farmer's Fiction" (*Caliban* 12:61–64) Leslie Fiedler praises the only major writer of science fiction in the 1950s to deal explicitly with sex.

c. **Popular Fictionists.** Lenemaja Friedman, in *Shirley Jackson* (TUSAS 253), cannot quite decide whether her subject is "more the entertainer than the conveyor of serious messages"; noting that stories with unexpected endings are the most popular, she regrets that the domestic autobiographical stories written for the women's magazines are not taken more seriously. Friedman tries to downplay Jackson's reputation for dealing mainly with witches and witchcraft in favor of those superior works which she classifies under "Novels of Setting," i.e., *The Sundial, The Haunting of Hill House*, and *We Have Always Lived in the Castle*. For an overview Friedman is content to explain Jackson in negative terms, as a writer uninterested in love or sexual relationships or "broad social problems"; akin to Hawthorne and Poe, her specialty is in the little enactments of evil in the world.

In his close reading of several key passages in William Peter Blatty's *The Exorcist*, "The Exorcist Dies So We Can All Enjoy the

Sunset Again" (*UWR* 11,i:5–24), Bruce Merry demonstrates how the novel plays on a "fantasy of disruption and novelty" centered on the strongest source of the conspiracy against order, the Devil. Of stylistic interest is "Conversion of America's Consciousness: The Rhetoric of *The Exorcist*" (*QJS* 61:40–47) by Thomas S. Frentz and Thomas B. Farrell. Edward T. Silva's "From *Candide* to *Candy*: Love's Labor Lost" (*JPC* 8:783–91) is a forgettable piece on the use of the incest taboo in the film version of *Candy*—along with an unintegrated segment on the publishing history of *Candide*.

In *Edwin O'Connor* (TUSAS 242 [1974]) Hugh Rank clarifies the general impression that O'Connor was an overnight success when *The Last Hurrah* appeared in 1956. In fact, he was 38, the author of a previous novel (*The Oracle*), dozens of short stories, and a clutch of unfinished long fictions; and he had already achieved a modest reputation as a broadcasting satirist. Rank is adept, in a pleasantly old-fashioned way, at providing plot summary, detailed structural and thematic analysis, and compositional and chronological contexts.

***d.* Miscellaneous.** A gathering of essays in *Crit* (17,iii) on an underrated novelist, Vance Bourjaily, is welcomed. In "The Motif of Names in Bourjaily's *The Hound of Earth*" (pp. 64–72), William A. Francis believes that the use of connotative Indian and Christian place names says much about the author's assessment of the spiritual state of America. John M. Muste explores the realistic impulse in Bourjaily's best work through a study of the narrative voice of Quincy in "The Fractional Man as Hero: Bourjaily's *Confessions of a Spent Youth*" (pp. 73–85). The novelist is described as a writer of "reaction and re-evaluation" by William McMillen in "The Public Man and the Private Novel: Bourjaily's *The Man Who Knew Kennedy*" (pp. 86–95), which presents the impact on an "ordinary man of his generation" of a cataclysmic public event. Daniel Towner traces parallels between Bourjaily's *Brill Among the Ruins* and Bellow's *Henderson the Rain King* in "Brill's Ruins and Henderson's Rain" (pp. 96–104), and although both protagonists share important traits, their significance is never made quite conclusive. This number is completed by William McMillen and John M. Muste's "A Vance Bourjaily Checklist" (pp. 105–10).

Despite the 1972 pamphlet by Merrill and Lorene Lewis (*Wallace Stegner*, WWS 4), there is still no adequate treatment of another underrated novelist. Kerry Ahearn, in "*The Big Rock Candy Mountain* and *Angle of Repose*: Trial and Culmination" (*WAL* 10:11–27), argues that Stegner's most distinguished works have "temporal and spatial scope," a reflection of his belief that life reveals itself by accretion. Ahearn analyzes the themes of both novels (western history and its influence on identity), but finds the more recent novel superior because of its technical accomplishment in point of view. Audrey C. Peterson's "Narrative Voice in Wallace Stegner's *Angle of Repose*" (*WAL* 10:125–33) counters a frequent complaint by arguing that the "intruding" authorial voice actually enriches the fiction without loss of credibility. Both Ahearn and Peterson insist on a separation between narrating characters and Stegner.

J. C. Wilson discusses five works in "Wright Morris and the Search for the 'Still Point'" (*PrS* 49:154–63), seeing them as explorations of the dichotomy between the material physical world and the timeless and eternal world; in *The Field of Vision*, Boyd's growth "from stasis to lucidity" is seen as partially resolving the problem. Ruth Laney conducts "An Interview with David Madden" (*SoR* 11:167–80), a younger fictionist who has done much to keep attention focused on Morris. Madden discusses at some length the role of nostalgia in *Bijou*, the technical possibilities which make the revision process so important, and his work in progress.

Judith K. Gardiner's "'A Sorrowful Woman': Gail Godwin's Feminist Parable" (*SSF* 12:286–90) fails to make this 1971 story very significant or very different from any number of other "feminist parables." The most interesting part of Jerome Klinkowitz's "Ideology or Art: Women Novelists in the 1970s" (*NAR* 260,ii:88–90) is not on Erica Jong, Grace Paley, and Susan Quist, but the observation that the feminine portrayals in Roth and Mailer to which feminist critics object have been succeeded by a far different kind of characterization in such innovative novelists as Michael Stephens, Ronald Sukenick, and Walter Abish.

George Dardess contends that Jack Kerouac's famous "method" was not the mindless babbling which hostile critics charged but a method of a writer who knew his business, who was able to dramatize that understanding, and who played the role of teacher and student "with his own experience as the main text." "The Logic of Spontaneity: A Reconsideration of Kerouac's 'Spontaneous Prose Method'"

(*Boundary 2* 3:729–45) includes two short lists of pedagogical instructions by Kerouac himself.

Peter William Koenig has examined the manuscripts of *The Recognitions*, the 1955 novel of underground success, and concludes in "Recognizing Gaddis' *Recognitions*" (*ConL* 16:61–72) that one impetus behind the work was a satire on literary reviewers of the 1950s. This is a disjointed essay, but it is valuable for what it reveals about Gaddis's structure, whose techniques may anticipate Pynchon's. In "Shirley Ann Grau: Nature Is the Vision" (*Crit* 17,ii:47–58), Ann Pearson argues that nature, which is at the focal point of this writer's best fiction, is always chilly and impersonal; her surroundings are a "donnée without significance."

There is no great point to Sam Bluefarb's "Pictures of the Anti-Stereotype: Leslie Fiedler's Triptych, *The Last Jew in America*" (*CLAJ* 18:412–21) except that the protagonists all represent the breakup of stereotypes; a plot summary is provided. In "Alienation and Analysis in Doctorow's *The Book of Daniel*" (*Crit* 16,iii:101–10), John Stark examines the parallels in E. L. Doctorow's novel to Biblical allusions which describe the Jews enduring as aliens in Babylon.

In "Native Americans and the American Mix: N. Scott Momaday's *House Made of Dawn*" (*ISSQ* 28:75–91), Joseph F. Trimmer considers the appropriateness of the 1969 Pulitzer Prize novel; he finds that though it scarcely upholds the committee's traditional requirement (to depict the "wholesome atmosphere of American life"), it also reminds us that the majority culture is no longer indifferent to the complexities of Indian culture and its "alien version" of the American experience. "The Enigma of Amado Jesus Muro" (*WAL* 10:3–9) is Gerald Haslam's brief appreciation for the late Chester Seltzer (1915–71), who adopted the name of Muro in writing his stories of southwestern Chicanos.

Indiana University

16. Poetry: 1900 to the 1930s

Richard Crowder

i. General

Encore un change! Whereas last year we bade farewell to Pound and Eliot and welcomed the rest of the Fugitives to join Ransom, this year chapter 17 has yielded Wallace Stevens to this one in an effort to make that chapter more manageable.

In 1975 *Expl* includes only four items about our poets, even fewer than last year. There are two on Stevens and two on Hart Crane. "Peter Quince at the Clavier" is the subject of 33:item 43, and "Thirteen Ways of Looking at a Blackbird" of 34:item 2. Crane's poems that are considered are "At Melville's Tomb" (33:item 73) and "*The Bridge*: 'The Tunnel'" (34:item 16).

If my count is accurate, *DAI* for 1975 (vol. 35, nos. 7–12, and vol. 36, nos. 1–6) lists 13 topics of relevant interest. George Sterling, Jeffers, and H. D. each are the subject of one dissertation. Crane (alone) is the subject of two studies and of one more with other authors. Frost is the sole subject of three and shares the honor with others in a fourth. Stevens enters the field with eleven dissertations, six alone, three shared with several others, and one each shared with Eliot, Valéry, and Wordsworth. Frost and Stevens have been leaders for several years. They seem to be emerging—with Eliot and Pound—as the generally conceded most challenging poets of this century up to post–World War II, at least in the opinion of graduate students and their mentors.

There are fewer books this year on the major figures. Last year the Frost centenary was marked by no less than seven volumes, some more useful than others. This year we have only one full-length contribution on Frost. No books devoted solely to Stevens have surfaced. There is a book on Cummings, one on Millay, one on Trumbull Stickney (actually from 1973), and two on Amy Lowell. A book on the novels of Warren is only of marginal interest here.

As suggested in this chapter last year, studies of the period as a whole might well begin to appear now. Surely the problem of finding synthesizing trends in subject matter, theme, mood, and technique is not beyond solving. Are we telling each other that the mine has been overworked? The poems themselves are certainly as demanding and exciting as ever. Comparative and contrastive studies might be a next step, not just of two or three poets together (there is one such essay this year, on Frost and Stevens) but of many of the poets who flourished in the 1920s and 1930s.

ii. Frost

Frank Lentricchia gives us a book this year which has, despite certain negative criticisms, a degree of excitement in showing Frost in relation to "modernist" thinking. In *Robert Frost: Modern Poetics and the Landscape of Self* (Durham, N.C.: Duke Univ. Press) Lentricchia frequently summons the names and ideas of Immanuel Kant, Friedrich Nietzsche, Friedrich von Schiller, Hans Vaihenger, George Santayana, William James, and Wallace Stevens. In the first long part he studies poems centered on the metaphors of brook, house, and woods, emphasizing again and again the poet's faithfulness to the observed object, "redeemed," however, by the imagination in the Poundian process of making it new. Frost, says Lentricchia, welcomes a chaotic world as the raw material for the creative talent to work on as he builds for himself, at least for the moment, a means of protection from the world "out there."

The shorter second part of the book (including an epilogue) shows Frost's power of using language to catch the direct existential presence of a human act. Frost uses his own consciousness to give shape to his vision of an object. As readers we learn something about that consciousness but nothing of the thing observed, though through delicate irony Frost constantly reminds us that we must always start with the things of this world. Lentricchia borrows from Stevens the phrase "supreme fictions" to show what Frost creates. This book is a scholarly, readable exploration of an original idea.

John F. Sears complements Lentricchia's thesis of the influence of James on Frost (as in the necessity of making choices). "William

James, Henri Bergson, and the Poetics of Robert Frost" (*NEQ* 48: 341–61) adds parallels between Bergson's belief that "the creative imagination is . . . indivisible" and Frost's own certitude that the making of a poem consists of searching through experience and discovering relationships heretofore unrecognized. Where Bergson speaks of "sprouting and flowering," Frost's term is "unfolded." A poem for Frost is the result of both assertion and surrender (i.e., discipline and "recapitulation of a magical process of thought and feeling").

On Frost's 100th birthday, March 26, 1974, four authorities read essays at the Library of Congress discussing various aspects of the poet's life and work. The studies are now collected in a pamphlet, *Robert Frost: Lectures on the Centennial of His Birth* (Washington, D.C.: Library of Congress). Helen Bacon, chairman of the Department of Greek and Latin at Barnard College, discusses " 'In- and Outdoor Schooling': Robert Frost and the Classics" (pp. 3–25). Among other points Bacon makes the distinction that "Frost is more a georgic than a pastoral poet." She details the influences of and parallels with the poets of Greece and Rome. Peter Davison, poetry editor of the *Atlantic Monthly*, uses the biographical approach in " 'Toward the Source': The Self-Realization of Robert Frost, 1911–1912" (pp. 27–40). We all know these were crucial years in the growth of the poet's career and reputation. Davison declares that in England, at the age of 39, Frost discovered that he was a top-drawer genius "two years before the world would get around to finding out."

Robert Pack of Middlebury College points up Frost's agnosticism, which the poet turned to his own uses: if he were to be true to the God he believed in but did not know, he had to emulate his enigmatical creator by continuing to create poems with "proper enigmatical reserve." Pack's lecture is titled, in fact, "Robert Frost's 'Enigmatical Reserve': The Poet as Teacher and Preacher" (pp. 43–55). It is not surprising that the last speaker, Allen Tate, chooses as his title " 'Inner Weather': Robert Frost as Metaphysical Poet" (pp. 57–68). He takes an interesting hard look at several poems, such as "The Witch of Coös," "Birches," "Mending Wall," and "Stopping by Woods on a Snowy Evening," the last of which he says is as great as Tennyson's "Tears, Idle Tears." In spite of Frost's not being his "kind of poet," Tate admits willingly that some of Frost's poems rank with the best of all time.

In an incredible essay in *ModR* (137:267–69) Ramachandran Nair says that Frost led a "long life of spiritual calm and serenity." Has Nair ever read Lawrance Thompson's biography? Calling the poet "a great drifter," Nair says the child drifted from California to New Hampshire. (Actually, he had little to do with his mother's decision to move east.) As a teacher Frost "drifted away from the syllabus." His "next decisive drift [oxymoron?] was his going to England in 1914." (The fact is he went to England in October 1912 and returned in 1915—Nair says 1916.) From that point on Nair drops the "drifter" theme. He claims that Frost is "one of the least understood of modern poets" but does nothing to clarify the enigma. Frost "coexisted" with nature, was leary of a departmentalizing society, tempered with bantering tone his limited cynical view of man, was even playful with his own God, with whom he was "very thick." This essay, entitled "From Delight to Wisdom: A Tribute to Robert Frost in His Centenary Year," is an oddity, to say the least.

"A most difficult poet" is Hayden Carruth's judgment in "Robert Frost" (*Parnassus* 3,ii:35–41). Though on rereading, Carruth finds a few top-notch poems, many are flawed—"talky, insistent, too literal" before they are finished. For him Frost is generally at his best in the long poems, for the short ones, such as "Stopping by Woods on a Snowy Evening" (here he differs with Tate), are too often contrived and consciously controlled. In the conclusion of "Two Tramps in Mudtime" both the tramps and the mudtime are lost in the poet's insistence and in his vanity. In discussing the successes, Carruth includes "Mending Wall," "The Black Cottage," "A Servant to Servants," "The Hill Wife," and "Acquainted with the Night."

In *Rendezvous* 10:11–14 John J. L. Mood's interpretation of "The Road Not Taken" corrects the frequently encountered "moral cotton candy" reading. "Frost's Dark Road Taken—A Pedagogical Inquiry" finds the poem subversive, "shatteringly honest." It strikes out in many directions at once: at "old men, moralists . . . the myth of experience, the lust for experience, 'road' itself as symbol . . . symbol-hunters, critics, admirers of poets, those who distrust poets, making decisions . . . young men . . . thus the generation gap itself . . . ." If it does all this and more, "The Road Not Taken" is indeed iconoclastic without discrimination. In this connection readers might be interested in "Reading Frost: 'The Road Not Taken' " (*EngR* 26:91–93) to discover how Roberts French reacts to the same poem. Another study that shows the poet's "doctrine" to be "disturbing" draws on *A Masque of Reason* and *A Masque of Mercy* to support the argument that Frost is in fact "not warm, nostalgic, friendly, harmless" as some early reviewers and critics would have him. Roberta F. Sarfatt Borkat demonstrates how courageous and unflinching the poet was in facing up to the 20th century. Her essay is entitled "The Bleak Landscape of Robert Frost" (*MQ* 16:453–67). As noted, Lentricchia uses the same metaphor.

Saying nothing really new, Richard Eberhart's "Robert Frost in the Clearing" (*SoR* 11:260–68) uses poems chiefly from *In the Clearing* to analyze Frost's feelings about eschatology, the mystery of the universe, and his preference for earthly experiences. William A. Sutton examines eight documents—letters, recommendations, a commencement program, etc.—recently made available by Leslie Frost Ballantine, that give evidence of the personal traits, ambitions, and family relationships of the poet's parents. "Robert Frost's Parents" (*BSUF* 16,ii:4–8) helps unravel the poet's own embroideries on the "facts" of his background. *Shenandoah* 26,ii:52–68 carries Stewart L. Udall's "Robert Frost, Kennedy, and Khrushchev: A Memoir of Poetry and Power," in which the former cabinet member recalls the poet as his "closest friend in Washington." He traces the vicissitudes of both the Frost-Kennedy and the Frost-Udall relationships and describes Frost's meeting with Khrushchev in Moscow. In spite of an earlier embarrassment, Udall reminds us, a few weeks before his assassination Kennedy dedicated the Robert Frost Library at Amherst, saying, "When power corrupts, poetry cleanses." Laurence Perrine has contributed another of his intelligent close readings in "The Tone of Frost's 'The Literate Farmer and the Planet Venus'" (*NConL* 5:10–13).

"Robert Frost and Wallace Stevens: 'What to Make of a Diminished Thing'" (*AL* 47:64–83) ingeniously compares the attitudes of two New England poets. Both Frost and Stevens think of their poems as inquiries; many of their poems actually try to show how they build a poem ("Birches" and "The Idea of Order at Key West," for example); both poets associate love and belief with their work. Admitting the terror of the universe, they both work at restoring their fellow human beings "to the world and to ourselves." Todd M. Lieber is the author of the article.

The final Frost item this year is by no means the least significant:

the facsimile reprinting of Frost's first book, *Twilight* (1894), which exists in a unique copy in the Barrett Collection at the University of Virginia Library. How Frost had this volume privately printed in an effort to induce Elinor White to marry him is summarized in a brief introduction by Clifton Waller Barrett, *Proof* 4:3–5, followed by the facsimile, pp. [6–22]. Joan St. C. Crane discusses "The Printing History of *Twilight*," pp. 23–30.

iii. Stevens

Referring specifically to Stevens are essays on where a poem comes from and on the necessity of replacing religious faith with a "supreme fiction." Frank Doggett remarks that for Stevens the difference between will and chance (what is "made" and what is "given") is often hard to distinguish. In "Stevens on the Genesis of a Poem" (*ConL* 16:463–77) Doggett traces the poet's search for a theory of creative imagination through numerous poems, lectures, and essays and defends the point that Stevens's faith in poetry was so intense as to be a positive driving force. Robert Pack, too, sees Stevens's belief in the efficacy of poetry as a replacement for rejected religious faith. "Wallace Stevens' Sufficient Muse" (*SoR* 11:766–78) focuses on the necessity of faith in a fiction with the knowledge that it is indeed a fiction so that ideas become as real as anything material. The "Muse" of the essay's title is the poet's power to remake himself in fictionalizing the world, though in all honesty Stevens acknowledges nostalgia for lost religious belief. Readings of "Autumn Refrain," "The Plain Sense of Things," "The Woman in Sunshine," and "Note on Moonlight" show how the poet's "fictive music" in the long run gives him the capacity for bearing himself "with realized nobility."

In a book on Hemingway, Eliot, Pound, and others—*A Homemade World*—Hugh Kenner considers Wallace Stevens *passim.* (There is a good index.) In one of two extended passages Kenner develops the thesis that, in spite of Stevens's involvement with unusual diction and syntax, his poems can be paraphrased as "discursive variations on the familiar theme of a first-generation agnostic." In the other passage Kenner's thesis is that the world Stevens creates has no people (rather, highly stylized inventions; cf. Matisse and Picasso). Chief evidence here is "Sunday Morning" and "Thirteen Ways of Looking at a Blackbird." Like Marianne Moore and Williams, Stevens sees a wordless world that needs to be described.

Using the by-now hackneyed critical principle that "imagination and reality" are Stevens's basic materials, Bhupendranath Seal, in "Winter as Seen by Wallace Stevens" (*ModR* 138:172–73), says that winter often holds promise for the poet, for winter passes. Also, as the winter landscape is stripped barren, so the mind must strip away illusion and recognize abstract reality. This rather slight article dutifully quotes from several poems about winter. *Modern Review*, published in Calcutta, often carries a few articles relevant to this chapter, but they do not contribute much to scholarship.

Chapter 5 of Daniel J. Schneider's *Symbolism: the Manichean Vision* is entitled " 'The War That Never Ends': Patterns of Proliferation in Wallace Stevens's Poetry" (pp. 154–203). There is also an "Appendix: Some Observations on Wallace Stevens's Symbolism" (pp. 219–23). Of more substance than Seal's brief sally, Schneider's chapter says the struggle will never end between imagination and reality because "fictions change, as the self, as feelings, change." Schneider examines recurring symbols—Negro, serpent, dove, etc.—and codifies them in a search for clarification of the poet's thinking. The catalogue includes such headings as "Reality's Crudity," "Imagination's Refinement," "Reality's Physical Abundance," "Imagination's . . . Nothingness," and so on. (These classifications are akin to the more statistical evidence in the author's 1956 dissertation at Northwestern.) By the end of his career Stevens had demonstrated that reality and imagination are "balanced in every line." The Appendix lists sample passages in which characteristic symbols appear, such as *floor, round, day, wood, rise and fall,* and *pierce.* If not challenging, Schneider's work nevertheless lends solid support to every Stevens scholar's awareness of the constant conflict between imagination and reality.

Like Kenner, Susan Brown Weston, drawing on her 1974 Columbia dissertation, sees a relationship between Stevens and Picasso. Her essay, "The Artist and Guitarist: Stevens and Picasso" (*Criticism* 17: 111–20), zeroes in on the 1935 issue of *Cahiers d'Art,* containing comments by and about Picasso which absorbed Stevens so much that he created one of his favorite images, the guitarist, and discovered a new spareness in tone and diction as well as "nobility for oneself in an ignoble time." Relying on Freud and Nietzsche for a phenomenological interpretation of several Stevens poems, Kathleen A. Dale, in "Extensions: Beyond Resemblance and the Pleasure Principle in Wallace Stevens' Supreme Fiction" (*Boundary 2* 4:255–73), finds a Freudian parallel in Stevens's penchant for identifying *resemblance* as an inborn human process, but, she says, the poet goes along with Nietzsche in supporting the necessity of breaking up resemblances—"ordered connections"—to satisfy the poet's need for "joy and power." Among other poems she cites "The Pleasures of Merely Circulating" and "Analysis of a Theme."

Other articles, for the most part, are explications of single poems. Richard P. Adams sees the influence of Monet and of the various Symbolistes in "Pure Poetry: Wallace Stevens' 'Sea Surface Full of Clouds'" (*TSE* 21[1974]:91–122). James E. Mulqueen gives us "A Reading of Wallace Stevens' 'An Ordinary Evening in New Haven'" (*Perspective* 17:268–77), in which he finds the poet meditating on the polar desires of the imagination, "comforting illusions," and the apprehension of reality. In poetry man may sing out against a reality he cannot get at.

Robert J. Bertholf, in "Parables and Wallace Stevens' 'Esthetique du Mal'" (*ELH* 42:669–89), is of the opinion that the voice here is that of a lecturer who, through a series of fictions, introduces a reluctant student to the inevitability of pain, indigenous to the world after the Fall. Bertholf reminds the student, however, that the imagination—and its fictions—can nevertheless be a source of delight. "In the end, the free pragmatic function of the mind is the ultimate good." "Structures of Sound in Wallace Stevens's 'Farewell to Florida'"(*TSLL* 16:755–64) considers various kinds of syllables (those in end position, those preceding pauses, those receiving primary accent, and so on). The author, Adelyn Dougherty, comes to the somewhat banal conclusion that beneath the surface the poet creates sounds pleasing in themselves. Two other essays on single poems are Nageswara Rao's "Crispin's Passage to Yucatan" (*LHY* 16:125–30) and Richard F. Patteson's "The Failure of Consolation in *The Auroras of Autumn*" (*CP* 8,ii:37–46).

iv. Crane, Cummings, Robinson

Robert L. Perry has made some small contributions to Crane scholarship from two parts of his 1975 dissertation at the University of Colorado ("Hart Crane and the Critics: Problems in the First Twenty Poems of *White Buildings*"). "Critical Problems in Hart Crane's 'Chaplinesque' " appears in *CP* 8,ii:23–27. Perry uses the well-worked point of view here that the poem is about the artist's plight in the modern world. "Critical Problems in Hart Crane's 'Sunday Morning Apples' " (*Rendezvous* 10:15–22) discusses the opinions of Sherman Paul and R. W. B. Lewis. Perry sides with Paul in concluding that the third stanza "probably" describes a painting by William Sommer, to whom the poem is dedicated. George S. Lensing shows (once again?) Crane's escape from Eliot's *weltanschauung* in "Hart Crane's Tunnel from *The Waste Land*" (*ArielE* 6,iii:20–35).

Two essays seize upon Crane's phrase "the logic of metaphor" to explain the poet's disposing of the conventional views of the external world in trying to bring unity to all experience. John T. Irwin examines ellipses and shocking juxtapositions in *The Bridge* and "Voyages" in "Naming Names: Hart Crane's 'Logic of Metaphor' " (*SoR* 11:284–99). Gregory R. Zeck's "The Logic of Metaphor: 'At Melville's Tomb" (*TSLL* 17:673–86) concludes that "The logic of metaphor . . . is alogical, and the poet cannot paraphrase it, the critic doubt it out of existence."

Dickran Tashjian devotes chapter 7 (pp. 143–64) to "Hart Crane and the Machine" in *Skyscraper Primitives: Dada and the American Avant-Garde, 1910–1925* (Middletown, Conn.: Wesleyan Univ. Press). In a highly readable essay, part biography, part criticism, the author traces through the poet's letters and poems the developing urge for Crane to face technology as his dominant theme. Tashjian provides a careful reading of *The Bridge* to demonstrate Crane's power of synthesis. (The poet had rejected the techniques and attitudes of Dada after Gorham Munson had explained it to him.)

In *Artful Thunder* Vivian Pemberton contributes a biographical essay, "Hart Crane's Heritage" (pp. 221–40). Pemberton has acquired many heretofore unrecorded details pertinent to the artistic interests of Crane's family and their influence on the poet. She has been diligent (through interviews, telephone conversations, and correspondence) in discovering Crane's father's passion for reading, his Uncle Frederic's gift for verse-writing, his Aunt Alice's creative devotion to music and poetry, his mother's interest in singing and acting, and his cousin Helen Hart Hurlbert's ability as organist, writer, and painter.

As a follow-up to "The Hart Crane–Yvor Winters Correspondence" (see *ALS 1974*, p. 337), Thomas Parkinson, in "Hart Crane and Yvor Winters: A Meeting of Minds" (*SoR* 11:491–512), explains that he is making an extended study of the literary relationship of the two men. Here he presents in narrative context more letters of Crane to Winters and examines the role of Allen Tate in the relationship. *Bancroftiana* 60:6–7 catalogs the "Hart Crane Letters" in the Bancroft Library at the University of California at Berkeley.

In addition to the chapter on Crane, in chapter 8 (pp. 165–87) Dickran Tashjian writes on "E. E. Cummings and Dada Formalism." In spite of high awareness of Dada, Cummings was not out to shock his readers with peculiar typography but used Dada techniques as models for his genuine interest in changing form and even content in poetry. Tashjian cites various poems, especially from those submitted to *Broom* in 1922 and 1923, to illustrate Cummings's experiments. He points out the similarity between Cummings and Crane in their satirical use of advertising slogans and discusses the play *Him* (1927) at length in the context of Dada and as representative of the background of the poems of the 1930s, 1940s, and 1950s. Like the Crane chapter, this essay is a combination of biographical fact and imaginative commentary and offers some new notions for the reading of the poems.

In "E. E. Cummings, Painter" (*HLB* 33:117–38) Rushworth M. Kidder shows the poet to have been an analytical and intellectual craftsman, though art critics were never very enthusiastic. Cummings's idea was that both paintings and poems should be "like a pile of jackstraws" (intricately unified): if one part were dislocated or subtracted, the entire structure would fall (fail). Also related to Cummings as graphic artist is Robert Tucker's "E. E. Cummings as an Artist: The Dial Drawings" (*MR* 16:329–53). Tucker explicates some of the poems from the point of view of their individuality, innovations, intricate verbiage, and indignation at popular culture. Following a collection of reproductions of drawings is a discussion comparing their economy and abstract mode with the poems. Incidentally, in the same issue (*MR* 16:253–56) Dagmar Reutlinger, in "E. E. Cummings and the Dial Collection," gives an art critic's description of the drawings, using such phrases as "playful diagrammatic simplifications and distortions" and "fluent, precise and disciplined."

Cummings is a sitting duck for linguists and their excesses. Irene R. Fairley's book is a case in point. *E. E. Cummings and Ungrammar: A Study of Syntactic Deviance in His Poems* (Searington, N.Y.:

Watermill Publishers) employs the elaborate methods of linguistic analysis to arrive at conclusions conceivably possible by more traditional methods. To clarify the "ungrammar" and provide new interpretations is a worthy goal, but this book is often little but an intricate mystery with a modicum of usable insight. The author is sometimes quite off base, as in an eight-page performance built on "quick i the death of thing."

It is probably only coincidence, but interesting nevertheless, that since Richard Cary's retirement the number of articles on Robinson in *CLQ* has been decidedly reduced. This year there are only three items to report. Celia Morris writes on "E. A. Robinson and 'The Golden Horoscope of Imperfection' " (*CLQ* 11:88–97). She demonstrates how, in *Lancelot* and *Merlin*, the poet delineates the principal characters as simultaneously recognizing their personal needs and their societal obligations. Robinson seems to be saying, however, that man's fate is inexorable once he takes the determining step.

The other two articles deal with "Richard Cory." Jerome Kavka, in "Richard Cory's Suicide: A Psychoanalyst's View" (*CLQ* 11:150–59), sees Cory as a narcissist who, when he fails to achieve overt approval from the people on the street, descends into despair and commits the ultimate "exquisitely narcissistic" act. Kavka is of the opinion that Robinson himself found salvation in being "enormously useful to others" through his poetry. Lawrence Kart's response to Kavka follows immediately (160–61). In "Richard Cory: Artist without an Art" Kart says Cory is artistically sensitive: he knows the effect he creates whenever he goes downtown. The problem is that he is himself the only product of his art and apparently has no way of gauging audience reaction. The poet appears to be saying that unless an artist can produce works outside himself and sense their effect on others, he must be a failure.

v. Women and Fugitives

Two books about Amy Lowell in any one year seem excessive at best. Jean Gould, with almost blind partisanship toward her subject, as usual (see *ALS 1969*, p. 276, on her Millay book), makes extravagant claims for Lowell's influence on Frost, D. H. Lawrence, MacLeish, H. D., and others of her time as well as for her pioneering efforts for Stevens, Williams, and Cummings, and women like Plath and Sexton.

Amy: The World of Amy Lowell and the Imagist Movement (New York: Dodd, Mead) makes substantial (though unsubstantiated) hints at a Lesbian relationship between Lowell and her nurse-companion, Ada Dwyer Russell. On the other hand, there are lively passages from Lowell's enormous correspondence and some excellent photographs from the Harvard collection. In spite of a questionable degree of dependability, the book does entertain the reader.

The other book, by Glenn Richard Ruihley, is called *The Thorn of a Rose: Amy Lowell Reconsidered* (Hamden, Conn.: Shoe String Press). Like Gould, Ruihley goes to excess in defending his subject. He labors too hard at explicating Lowell's verse, in an effort to place her among the major poets. He overworks her rather murky debt to Zen Buddhism. He frequently indulges in the risky business of equating poem and autobiography. True, many events and situations in the poet's flamboyant life were deeply touching, and there can be no doubt that the cause of poetry was strengthened by her support. But Ruihley's perfervid partisanship makes him overly laudatory.

Walter S. Minot thinks Edna St. Vincent Millay was burdened with patricidal inclinations, perhaps unconscious. He has found, in "Sonnets from an Ungrafted Tree" in *The Harp-Weaver* (1923), manifestations of unresolved psychological conflicts that produced unfortunate neuroses and possibly impaired Millay's capacities as a poet and even as a person. Millay is, Minot says, representative of the plight of the woman who would be poet in America. His essay is titled "Millay's 'Ungrafted Tree': The Problem of the Artist as Woman" (*NEQ* 48:260–69).

Anne Cheney's *Millay in Greenwich Village* (University: Univ. of Ala. Press) grew out of her dissertation (e.g., she thanks her "committee"). After an opening chapter on Millay's early years, from Maine through Vassar, Cheney turns her attention to Greenwich Village, which she describes in some detail—its organizations, bars, habitués, and generally Bohemian attitudes. (There are some interesting pictures.) The chapters that follow are devoted to the men in her life: Floyd Dell, Edmund Wilson, and Arthur Davison Ficke. A chapter on "Millay's Other Men" sketches the poet's relationships (more transient) with Witter Bynner, Allan Ross Macdougall, W. Adolphe Roberts, Frank Crowninshield, and Harrison Dowd. Her husband, Eugen Boissevain, is pictured at length in still another chapter. What the author has tried to do is to analyze the influence of these men—"a psychological portrait." A six-page Summary is somewhat gratuitous, a graduate-school requirement presenting a brief restatement of the disclosures and surmises of the preceding chapters. Cheney's conclusion is that Millay's Village years developed in her "the quality of courage—the courage to live spontaneously, to love deeply, to feel grief and loneliness unashamedly, to defy death." I am not sure but that we have known this about the poet for some time.

Some of the Fugitives were given brief attention in 1975. Ronald Berman, in "Confederates in the Backfield: Mr. Ransom and the Cleveland Browns" (*NewRep* 173,xiv:21–22), refers to Ransom's penchant for technique as accounting for his delight in the football games of the Cleveland Browns. Berman says Ransom's literary criticism reflected this interest in the technically complex. Withal sanity was his mark. For all his dazzle (metaphors and rich allusions), his feet were on solid ground. Writing in *SoR* 11:243–44, Robert Penn Warren pays tribute to "John Crowe Ransom (1888–1974)." In Ransom, he says, there resided the polarities of "rigor and tenderness, hardheadedness and love," all joined "in a sense of grave joy."

Richard Howard reviews Warren's 1975 book, *Or Else—Poem/Poems, 1968–1974* in *GaR* 29:37–41. He opines that the poet's voice is prose mostly, with occasional breaks in the lines. Of tangential interest here is Barnett Guttenberg's *Web of Being: The Novels of Robert Penn Warren* (Nashville, Tenn.: Vanderbilt Univ. Press). Allen Tate offers his *Memoirs and Opinions, 1926–1974* (Chicago: Swallow Press), consisting of previously published essays conveniently gathered together. The book includes, among other subjects, Tate's views on Frost and Hart Crane and his recollection of the days of *The Fugitive* (1922–25). The author pays his profound respects to Ransom and to Donald Davidson.

vi. Jeffers, Sandburg, Stickney, and Others

The *Robinson Jeffers Newsletter* nos. 41, 42, and 43 are filled with "News and Notes," letters, unpublished poems, reports of collections of Jeffers-related material, and interpretive and scholarly articles. No. 41 publishes some letters of Mrs. Jeffers and three hitherto unpublished poems of Jeffers himself. No. 42 contains a detailed description of Tor House by Jeffers's son Donnan, an account of the poet's father, the Rev. William Hamilton Jeffers, by James Karman, and a descriptive bibliography of the Jeffers holdings at Stanford. No. 43 presents more materials on Jeffers's father, including the eulogy delivered at his funeral and a summary of his writings. Also in this issue an essay on "The Interactive Voice of Jeffers' 'Hungerfield,' " by Tim Hunt, stresses the poet's interest less in philosophy than in meditation and ritual as a means of achieving "moments of vision." *RJN* continues to be an indispensable tool for readers interested in Jeffers. Edward Nickerson's "Robinson Jeffers and the Paeon" appears in *WAL* 10:189–93, and Stephen Bluestone contributes "Robinson Jeffers and the Prophets: On *The Book of Jeremiah* and 'The Inhumanist' " to *NConL* (5:2–3). Covington Rodgers and John M. Meader, Jr., have compiled the 32-page *Robinson Jeffers Collection at the University of Houston: A Bibliographical Catalogue* (Houston, Tex.: Univ. of Houston Libraries).

Sandburg as a tyro writer, before he became plain Carl, is the subject of two items. His early poetry and prose contributions to the *Fra*, an Elbert Hubbard magazine, and to *To-morrow* (a "freethinker, socialist-oriented magazine") interest George Knox in "Idealism, Vagabondage, Socialism: Charles A. Sandburg in *To-morrow* and the *Fra*" (*HLQ* 38:161–88). Knox passes judgment on 13 poems written between 1901 and 1910 and quotes them copiously (except when, as in the case of "A Fling at the Riddle," a poem is too "painfully bad" to print in full). He also evaluates Sandburg's prose contributions, such as "Jack London: A Common Man" and "Explaining God," and quotes from the young man's letters about Hubbard and the Roycrofters. Knox decides that in the first decade of this century Sandburg was a mere "poetaster."

The industrious Joan St. C. Crane (*ALS 1974*, pp. 322–23, reviews her *Robert Frost*) has compiled *Carl Sandburg, Philip Green Wright, and the Asgard Press, 1900–1910* (Charlottesville: Univ. Press of Va.), to which Sandburg's daughter Margaret has written a foreword. This is a "descriptive catalogue of early books, manuscripts, and letters in the Clifton Waller Barrett Library." Several unpublished Sandburg manuscripts are discussed and transcribed, including what is probably the poet's first piece on Lincoln, dating from 1906–07. Of the 84 letters from Sandburg to Wright here printed, 62 appear for the first time. This is a very useful volume for students interested in Sandburg's emergence.

Marc Chénetier, in "Knights in Disguise: Lindsay and Maiakovski as Poets of the People" (*MidAmerica* 2:47–62), compares the midwesterner and the Russian (Vladimir Maiakovski) in their view of poetry as a means of reaching the masses, though he says both men were finally estranged from the very people they were trying to reach. Malcolm Cowley considers Conrad Aiken in terms of New England and relates his thinking to Transcendentalism in "Conrad Aiken: From Savannah to Emerson" (*SoR* 11:245–59). At the same time he points out Aiken's differences from Emerson, e.g., his atheism and pessimism. Cowley attempts to explain the public and critical neglect of Aiken, who himself felt at the end of his life that his work had been good and would "some day" achieve considerable recognition. Harold Aspen's article "'The Menagerie' Revisited" (*MarkhamR* 4:97–100) is a close reading of William Vaughn Moody's well-known poem and reaches the unsurprising conclusion "that the little man's optimistic and marvelous revelation is accessible to open-minded and sensitive human beings and that his faith in nature's grand evolutionary scheme is unshaken."

Moody's Harvard friend Trumbull Stickney has been receiving modest attention lately. Ross C. Murfin was prompted to write an article after the publication in 1972 of Ambreys R. Whittle's definitive edition of Stickney's poems. "The Poetry of Trumbull Stickney: A Centennial Rediscovery" (*NEQ* 48:540–55) reviews the poet's life and comments on several poems ("Lakeward," "In the Past," "Mnemosyne"). Murfin pronounces "In Ampezzo" Stickney's "finest poetic effort." Though admitting sometimes clumsy syntax, Murfin sees Stickney as nevertheless expressing effectively, even if only in fragments, a *carpe diem* urgency. At his best the poet combines "conversational abruptness . . . and absolutely precise imagery."

Inadvertently Ambreys R. Whittle's biography, *Trumbull Stickney* (Lewisburg, Pa.: Bucknell Univ. Press, 1973) was not reviewed in this chapter of *ALS* for the year it was published. The book provides some details of the life otherwise difficult to find. Whittle summarizes the poet's present-day critical status and discusses his work in all genres—fiction, essays, and criticism as well as dramatic and lyric poetry. The problem is that the biographer is often superficially sketchy. For example, there is only the barest mention of Stickney's two doctoral dissertations written in French. In the critical chapters more analysis and less detailing of content would have helped. Stickney is pictured at the center of the literary scene in his undergraduate days at Harvard. There is still a need for a more thoroughgoing book-length examination of this brilliant man's life and work.

In "A Puritan's Satanic Flight: Don Marquis, Archy, and Anarchy" (*SR* 83:623–42), Edward A. Martin devotes a few pages (635–42) to the verses about Archy and Mehitabel. In disclosing "man's inadequacy before the terrors of" the universe and in emphasizing how foolish man is in his "claim to superiority," Marquis, in irony, glorifies both irrationality and anarchy.

Purdue University

17. Poetry: The 1930s to the Present

Linda Welshimer Wagner

i. General

In 1975 the increasing emphasis on comparative subjects in dissertations continued, evident in titles like "Poetry and Anti-Poetry in the United States and Chile: Robert Lowell—William Carlos Williams; Enrique Lihn—Nicanor Parra"; as did that on studies of definition (two dissertations on "confessional" poetry, one on "objectivism," another on "open field" poetics, etc.). Almost half of the 35 dissertations listed as completed in 1975 studied more than one poet. Poets appearing most frequently were William Carlos Williams (five dissertations and parts of four others), Sylvia Plath (three and parts of four others), and Theodore Roethke (two). The work of the following poets was the subject of at least one complete study: John Ashbery, John Berryman, Elizabeth Bishop, Robert Bly, Robert Creeley, Randall Jarrell, Denise Levertov, Robert Lowell, Charles Olson, Gary Snyder, Richard Wilbur, James Wright, and Louis Zukofsky.

Critical attention in essays and books also indicates a need to define movements in contemporary poetry. Ann Stanford's essay, "The Elegy of Mourning in Modern American and English Poetry," *SR* 11:357–72, describes the extensive use of the elegy among writers today, noting that the qualities of the modern elegy are "the use of contemporary idiom, free manipulation of line and of rhythm, a tendency to emphasize the reaction of the mourner, and a broad spectrum of possible ways of working through the inescapable dilemma of death." Most of the criticism devoted to definition and location of trends, however, is less technically oriented; and attempts to chart thematic and philosophical directions. The best of it is helpful; the less successful, quibbling.

Several poets went on record in 1975 as disapproving what seemed to be weaknesses in contemporary poetry. Wendell Berry ("The Specialization of Poetry," *HudR* 28:11–27) bemoaned "a grievous division between life and work." Not that modern writers have created a separation between the two areas, but that they are using their lives to feed their work, living for the purpose of having something to write about. In Berry's view this practice "makes of the most humane of disciplines an exploitive industry." John Haines's objections ("The Hole in the Bucket," *NWR* 15:5–13) are that poetry today lacks ideas, that poets have "no unifying outlook on life." What Haines finds as a "lack of resonance" in poetry is not only a language problem; it also stems from the notion that personal experience is enough to make poems from. He laments the absence of historical continuity, or any knowledge of myth. Howard Nemerov, too, finds the most contemporary poetry burdened with the weight of a reverence for the Imagist movement that can only be limiting ("Poetry and History," *VQR* 51:309–28). He traces the poets' interest in the concrete as a defense against their discomfort with the changing patterns of history—history that, complicated by World War I, defied being written into "meaningful" poems—but concludes that poetry must return to its traditional business, and must speak to the concerns of history and human life in a large sense. "Imagism seems to me a crippled and crippling response, though it has its rare triumphs" (p. 312), Nemerov concludes. (Other interesting views of the Imagists, with attention to H. D. and Marianne Moore as well as the other central figures, can be found this year in "From Imagists to the Black Mountain," pp. 221–29, in Geoffrey Grigson's *The Contrary View: Glimpses of Fudge and Gold,* London: MacMillan, 1974; Daniel Hoffman's "Others: Shock Troops of Stylistic Change," *The President's Lectures,* Philadelphia: Univ. of Pa.; and J. B. Harmer's *Victory in Limbo: Imagism 1908–1917,* New York: St. Martin's Press.)

Essays that serve to answer these complaints in their views of present-day poetry are Stuart Peterfreund's "American Poetry: Beyond the Minimal" (*New* 25–26: 117–21), which compares poetry with painting in which the minimal approach forces the artist, and the reader, to make "fresh assumptions" about that art; John Judson's "Regionalism and Contemporary Poetry" (*New* 25–26:96–99), which opts for the poet who recognizes the sources of his individual strengths (a "sense of place") in contrast to those who write formula poems with an eye to commercial success; and John Woods's "Brief: In William Duffy's Hammock" (*NWR* 15:15–20), in which Woods refutes the concept that poetry must express philosophy: "Except in the mnemonic sense, poetry is not a very good vehicle for ideas" (p. 18). One of the most interesting of these defense essays is Alan Williamson's "Silence, Surrealism, and Allegory" (*Kayak* 40:57–67), in which Williamson defines surrealism as "a turning inward toward intangible mental atmospheres." He admires the tendency in recent poetry, but feels that the direction has limited itself, has become formulaic: "inhuman imagery of stones, light, wounds, mingled with the too easily religious or chthonic; its detached parts of the body and animated articles of clothing; its bald but quietly breathless syntax; its endless stress on silence, absence, ignorance." Williamson suggests that the poems that result are allegories about the irrational rather than explorations of it. He sees Robert Bly, James Wright, and W. S. Merwin as important originators, and discusses the work of Mark Strand, Charles Simic, and Gregory Orr to illustrate the trends of more recent books.

Another view of the most recent poetry appears in *Chicago Review* 27, i. Three critics, Robert von Hallberg, Michael Davidson, and Robert Pinsky, find in the poems of 1975 a reaction against "screaming," poems that reveal "a mind in movement along a middle way," a mode Pinsky labels "discursive" ("primarily neither ironic nor ecstatic . . . . The idea is to have all the virtues of prose, in addition to those qualities and degrees of precision which can be called poetic," p. 133). Davidson points to some helpful analogies with painting and pop art in his "Languages of Post-Modernism" (pp. 11–22) as he comments particularly on Frank O'Hara's poetry as an extension of Charles Olson's "field" poetics. Looking to the future, von Hallberg predicts poetry that will be "quiet, mundane, modest in its demands, and sincere about its conclusions" (p. 10).

One of the harshest criticisms of present-day poetry occurs in Marjorie Perloff's review essay, "The Corn-Porn Lyric: Poetry 1972–73" (*ConL* 16:84–125). Lamenting the "sexual revolution" in these collections, Perloff excepts Adrienne Rich and John Wieners from her censure, but finds both younger and established poets subject to the infection of either oversentimentality or a reliance on private, often sexual experience to center the poetry. She chooses Diane Wakoski,

Clayton Eshleman, and Erica Jong to illustrate her thesis that much contemporary poetry is based on the notion that re-creating experience is adequate for any poem; and her real argument seems to lie with the voice and the diction of the poets criticized.

Wakoski, both in her review of Eshleman's *Coils* ("Birthing the Myth of Himself," *IR* 6:132–38) and in the pamphlet *Creating a Personal Mythology* (Los Angeles: Black Sparrow), explains the use of personal experience as a means to personal mythology: "It is not autobiography you are writing, but your life you are using in order to write about life as other people experience it too . . . the poet either invents his autobiography by selecting what is most important or interesting about his life to write about, or he in fact is smart enough to know that his life is dull but his mind isn't and he then gives his reader a fantasy self which *is* interesting." Wakoski continues to explain that details, used repeatedly, come to convey an emblematic sense, just as do images, and, in her poetry, experiences—whole narratives, complete with characters. But her purpose in writing what may seem to be a "personal" poetry is to reach readers in the reality of their own lives, and her vehicle is the mythology of her personal narratives.

Ralph J. Mills, Jr., has focused the essays in *Cry of the Human: Essays on Contemporary American Poetry* (Urbana: Univ: of Ill. Press) on the "personal element" in poetry, and explains that this personal voice, in one mode or another, dominates the contemporary scene as a reaction against society's dehumanization: "The poet invites us to share in his pursuit of identity." In addition to a summary chapter, "Creation's Very Self," the collection includes Mills's studies of Roethke, Ignatow, Kinnell, Hall, and Levine, essays reviewed in previous *ALS* chapters.

Other collections of essays by poets are W. D. Snodgrass's *In Radical Pursuit: Critical Essays and Lectures* (New York: Harper & Row) and Stanley Kunitz's *A Kind of Order, A Kind of Folly, Essays and Conversations* (Boston: Little, Brown). Each collection gives some idea of the wide range of interest in the lives of both Snodgrass and Kunitz, with the classics occupying as much a part of their enthusiasm as does poetry or the process of writing it. Individual essays not previously mentioned in *ALS* will appear in appropriate sections of this essay.

ii. William Carlos Williams

Three books of critical interest and Reed Whittemore's biography of Williams appeared this year. Rod Townley's *The Early Poetry of William Carlos Williams* (Ithaca, N.Y.: Cornell Univ. Press) presents the early poems as "somatic," fragments of a "fluidic, imaginative world" rather than a series of separate masterpieces. Just as Williams found his identity through sensual relationships with his environment, so his poems grew from the same supraconscious life rhythms. Townley, accordingly, takes a critical view that includes the poet's life as well as his art, with attention to both his "emotional and spiritual crises." The only limitation of the book is that it is surprisingly lacking in new material; Townley treats work only through 1923. For all the novelty of his approach, the author gives very little innovative insight into the poetry.

The same observation might be made of the Williams section of Louis Simpson's *Three on the Tower*. While Simpson's readings and biographical comments are interesting, and should appeal particularly to the more general reader, there is very little new material to be found by the Williams specialist.

Robert Coles's *William Carlos Williams, The Knack of Survival in America* (New Brunswick, N.J.: Rutgers Univ. Press) takes a much broader approach. Coles reads Williams's work, especially the stories and fiction, as a parable for America, "its contradictions and ambiguities, its quite apparent wealth and power, its episodic idealism, its strong appetites—and its mean, self-centered, exploitative side." Given Cole's own interests, his description of Williams's fiction is reasonable and of broad humanistic interest. Coles also couples Williams with John Dos Passos, as writers whose fascination with the meaning of their country probably did them as much damage as writers as it did good.

Paul L. Mariani surveys the critical scene in his *William Carlos Williams: The Poet and His Critics* (Chicago: American Library Association). As the second book in this series which will list and evaluate all criticism written on selected modern poets, Mariani's book is thorough and perceptive. After two chapters describing the criticism written from 1910 to 1930 and from 1930 to 1945, Mariani devotes his third chapter to a discussion of *Paterson* as both the turning point in Williams's critical fortune and as his best poem. Chapter 4 continues the emphasis on *Paterson* by surveying the criticism from 1946 to 1963; and the last chapter includes work through 1973. One might wish for a less imperious tone in this supposedly objective survey, but Mariani makes clear his own critical views as he comments on other critics, so his point of view is clearly available.

Reed Whittemore's *William Carlos Williams, Poet from Jersey* (Boston: Houghton Mifflin) is a strange mixture of easy writing and what seems to be personal spleen. The paucity of new information in the biography is disappointing, as is Whittemore's tendency to trust Williams's own autobiography (a book which was admittedly inaccurate in places). When facts are used, Whittemore tends to handle them impressionistically, a method which places Whittemore at center stage instead of Williams. Repeatedly we are given Whittemore's summation of very complicated matters. He speaks about the character of the nurse in Williams's *The Cure*, his last play, for example: "What the young poet in the play did with her—that is, struggle steadily to bring her down into bed with him—must have been WCW's own aged dream" (p. 340). Or about Williams's ambition as writer: "There was modesty in WCW's manner but not in his literary ambitions, not in his designs upon the future. . . . That sort of determination has been the source of great sadness in American letters, since there is more to literature than the doing it" (p. 349).

It must eventually be the task of the good biographer to make these summations, but what is disconcerting about Whittemore's study is his giving so few facts and then making pronouncements with such ease. His views of poetry and the literary life in general are also less than objective, or even balanced.

An interesting exchange took place between J. Hillis Miller and Joseph Riddel concerning Riddel's 1974 study of Williams (*ALS 1974*, pp. 353–54) in *Diacritics* 5. Miller, in "Deconstructing the Deconstructors" (ii:24–31), regarded the study as "self-contradictory." Riddel's response was "A Miller's Tale" (iii:56–65).

Essays concerning Williams's work were also plentiful. John Vernon describes Williams's open methods in all his poems in "Naked Poetry" (*APR* 4,ii:16–18); James C. Neely champions the whole body of Williams's work, taking a biographical perspective, in "One Man's Dr. Williams" (*YR* 65:314–20); Frances Steloff reminisces about him in *JML* 4:822–23. The studies concerning *Paterson* are wide-ranging:

Margaret Lloyd Bollard discusses "The Interlace Element in *Paterson* (*TCL* 21:288–304), tracing the use of various recurring elements, logically continuous materials (newspapers, letters, historical excerpts) and cross-reference patterns of narrative sequences, events, or images; she also studies "The 'Newspaper Landscape of Williams' *Paterson*" (*ConL* 16:317–27) and concludes that Williams saw a harmony between art and the newspaper in the former's use of "facts," in the role of newsmaker as well as recorder, and in the mosaic method of composition of heterogeneous items. Thomas Pison's argument in "*Paterson*: The Discontinuous Universe of the Present" (*CentR* 19:325–37) is that Williams's rationale in the long poem is to refute the linear concept of narrative: "All the habitual expressions within linearity—sequence, succession, continuity, duration—would have to be supplanted by a new 'plan for action,' . . . and *Paterson* was to be the proving ground for this new aesthetic" (p. 327).

Christine Rabin also attempts to put Williams's late work in contemporary perspective in "Williams' Autobiographeme: The Inscriptional *I* in *Asphodel*" (*MPS* 6:157–74). Her approach is to read the later work as a graphic construct, with reference to the French structuralists; and to emphasize his use of the pronoun *I* (used 120 times in the poem) as the index of the poet. Less technically, Paul Mariani also praises the late poems ("The Eighth Day of Creation: William Carlos Williams' Late Poems," *TCL* 21:305–18), admiring them for Williams's "more relaxed way of saying and with it a more explicit way of seeing the all-pervasive radiating pattern at the core of so much that Williams wrote."

The comparative interest in Williams is evident in Henry Wells's "William Carlos Williams and Traditions in Chinese Poetry" (*LHY* 16,i:3–24) and in Robert Kern's "Williams, Brautigan, and the Poetics of Primitivism" (*ChR* 27,i:47–57). As Kern relates Williams's aesthetic to the need to be beyond history, or perhaps before it, and thus to create nonliterary or primitive poems, Cary Nelson relates it to "verbal space" in his provocative study *The Incarnate Word: Literature as Verbal Space* (Urbana: Univ. of Ill. Press, 1973). Nelson sees the metaphor of flower and of space as central to Williams's poetry and poetics, and traces its use through his poetry and prose chronologically. So too does Hugh Kenner insist on Williams's poetry as arranged shape, made object rather than poem emphasizing content. While Kenner pairs Williams with Stevens in much of his discussion, his points might well have been made about Williams alone (*A Homemade World*).

The first issue of the *William Carlos Williams Newsletter* appeared in the fall of 1975. Including commentary by Emily Wallace, Robert Creeley, Norman Holmes Pearson, and editor Theodora Graham, the newsletter also contains reviews, unpublished materials of Williams, and facsimiles of manuscript materials. Also of bibliographical interest is Charles Doyle's "Addenda and Amendments to Wallace: *William Carlos Williams*" (*PBSA* 69:407–09).

iii. Charles Olson, Robert Creeley, Allen Ginsberg, Robert Duncan, Gary Snyder, Lawrence Ferlinghetti

Two books and the publication of *The Maximus Poems*, III, make 1975 an important year for Olson criticism. *Charles Olson and Ezra Pound: An Encounter at St. Elizabeths* (New York: Grossman) is a touching, informative memoir, carefully edited by Catherine Seelye from the Olson journals and papers of the mid-1940s. Staying within the context of Olson's writings, however fragmentary, proves much more useful in capturing the Olson color than does Charles Boer's approach in *Charles Olson in Connecticut* (Chicago: Swallow Press). Because Boer intends to describe Olson as he knew him—a frequent visitor to his home, friend, master poet—there is a duality in the presentation: at times the reader knows more about Boer than about Olson. At times moving, Boer's intensely personal reactions to Olson's life, and death, are generally more obtrusive than they are helpful.

Olson, The Journal of the Charles Olson Archives, includes sections L–N of the poet's reading, excerpts from four journals kept during Olson's teaching at the University of British Columbia in 1963 (by Clark Coolidge, Pauline Wah, Daphne Marlatt, and George Bowering), unpublished poems, and a taped discussion from Vancouver (Olson, Creeley, Duncan, and Ginsberg).

Of the essays Don Byrd's "The Open Form of Charles Olson's *Maximus*" (*Athanor* 6:1–22) proposes that Olson's thought is nearer that of Whitehead than Descartes. Sherman Paul, in a major two-part essay, discusses many of the influences on *Maximus*, both philosophically and geographically. Paul points to the unusual force of Olson's oppositions (in-out, love-kill) and finds the many moral statements prepared for by the use of history ("In and About the *Maximus* Poems," *IR* 6,i:118–30 and 6,iii–iv:74–96). Also of interest is Olson's "Encounter with Ezra Pound" (*Antaeus* 17:73–92).

Several essays focus on the later poems of Robert Creeley: Sherman Paul's "A Letter on Rosenthal's 'Problems of Robert Creeley'" defends the poet's work in *A Day Book* and *Pieces*, as does Linda Wagner's "The Latest Creeley" (*APR* 4,v:43–45). To see the poet's shift from word phrases to single words, and even pieces of words, as a logical progression in his linguistically oriented poetics gives credence to the idea of development in his work.

A. K. Weatherhead gives an important perspective to the criticism of Robert Duncan in his "Robert Duncan and the Lyric" (*ConL* 16: 163–74). Viewing Duncan as a traditional poet, influenced by modern emphases on discontinuity, fragmentation, and speed, Weatherhead finds that the poet "must corrupt the linear melody for the strategy of the collage, break up thematic unity with elements recalcitrant and untamed, and bring in contemporary horrors." Duncan's "strong sense of music" may be his chief poetic strength, but his poems are also contrived visual objects, attempting to graphically encompass "primordial reality."

Dolores Elise Brien relates Duncan to Emerson ("Robert Duncan: A Poet in the Emerson-Whitman Tradition," *CentR* 19:308–16) as poet-priest, aligned in their views of poetic process and the role of the poet. She traces Duncan's attitudes through his prose and poetry, and finds affinities to Whitman as well, bringing evidence to label Duncan "a nineteenth century American romantic *redivivus*."

Discussion of the importance of Gary Snyder's vision occur in Alan Williamson's "Gary Snyder: An Appreciation" (*NewRep* 173, xviii:28–30) and in Robert Kern's "Toward a New Nature Poetry" (*CentR* 19:198–216). Kern traces the evolution of modern nature poetry, ending with Snyder's "Mid-August at Sourdough Mountain Lookout," a statement of "the radical unity of man and nature that lies beyond apparent differences." One of the most affirmative views of Snyder's recent work is that of Sherman Paul ("Noble and Simple," *Parnassus* 3,ii:217–25), who sees "I Went into the Maverick Bar" as Gary Snyder's "The Desert Music," a portion of his "spiritual autobiography." Paul finds Snyder's strengths to be "his secure sense of happiness in being at home in the world" and "his militancy, his fear" that the best of the world will be extinguished.

Crale D. Hopkins surveys the range of poetry of one of the most important San Francisco poets in "The Poetry of Lawrence Ferlinghetti: A Reconsideration" (*Ital Am* 1[1974]:59–76). With important biographical information, Hopkins traces some points of origin for Ferlinghetti's early poems; the essay is enlivened with the poet's own annotations and corrections throughout.

iv. Theodore Roethke

Rosemary Sullivan's *Theodore Roethke, The Garden Master* (Seattle: Univ. of Wash. Press) is a lucid chronological reading of the major poems, the sequences. A thoughtful compilation of biography and critical readings, the study stresses the continuity in the themes of Roethke's poems, described by Sullivan as being "his sensitivity to the subliminal, irrational world of nature; his relationship to his dead father, who occupies the center of his work, adding to it an urgent dimension which often impels it through a persistent pattern of guilt and expiation; his attempts to explore other modes of consciousness which carried him to the edge of psychic disaster; his interest in mysticism; his debts, so well repaid, to the poetic ancestors from whom he learned his craft; and the calm joyousness which rests at the core of his work" (xi).

Among single essays of interest are Jenijoy LaBelle's "Theodore Roethke's Dancing Masters in 'Four for Sir John Davies'" (*CP* 8,ii: 29–35), in which LaBelle traces the poetic influences of Raleigh, Davies, and Yeats on Roethke, and "Martyr to a Motion Not His Own: Theodore Roethke's Love Poems" (*BSUF* 16,ii:71–75), where the kinds of literary references included in the poems indicate the poet's response to the woman in question. William V. Davis provides a sensitive reading of a villanelle in "The Escape into Time: Theodore Roethke's 'The Waking'" (*NConL* 5,ii:2–10); Penelope S. Cambly Schott does some perceptive correlating in "'I Am!' Says Theodore Roethke: A Reading of the Nonsense Poems" (*RS* 43:103–12); and Donald Parker treats "The Lost Son" (*ContP* 2,i:13–16).

Among reprinted essays on Roethke are the University of Minnesota pamphlets (in *Seven American Poets From MacLeish to Nemerov: An Introduction* (MacLeish, Eberhart, Roethke, Jarrell, Berryman, R. Lowell, and Nemerov), ed. Denis Donoghue (Minneapolis: Univ. of Minn. Press); W. D. Snodgrass's two earlier essays, revised as "That Anguish of Concreteness—Theodore Roethke's Career" *In Radical Pursuit* (New York: Harper and Rowe), pp. 101–16; and Stanley Kunitz's four earlier essays in *A Kind of Order* (Boston: Little Brown), pp. 77–109. Snodgrass sees Roethke's contributions as great, yet perhaps limited: leading in the war against formal shapes (for no reason except tradition), Roethke yet came to take refuge from censure in his own metaphysics. In the early poems "Roethke had opened out before himself an incredible landscape . . . areas of the psyche where the powerful thoughts and feelings of the child—the raw materials and driving power of our later lives—remain under the layers of rationale and of civilized purpose. The explorations made possible by this book alone could have engaged a lifetime. Yet Roethke never seriously entered the area again" (p. 104). Kunitz, in contrast, finds Roethke's best poems throughout his career marked by the archetypal knowledge that Snodgrass also admires: "Roethke belongs to that superior order of poets who will not let us rest in any one of their poems, who keep driving us back through the whole body of their work to that live cluster of images, ideas, memories, and obsessions that constitutes the individuating source of the creative personality" (p. 88).

v. Sylvia Plath, John Berryman, Robert Lowell

Letters Home by Sylvia Plath: Correspondence, 1950–1963, ed. with an intro. by Aurelia Schober Plath (New York: Harper & Row) has provoked much controversy about the persona of the poet. Unfortunately, no reader can ever tell what role Sylvia Plath's mother assumed as editor; but the evidence presented seems to indicate rather clearly that Plath's letters home were the expression of one of her natural roles, that of daughter, of competent young wife and mother, whose concern for her own mother probably kept her from expressing the doubts and anxieties evident in her poems. Like any collection of letters to a single reader, these must be viewed in combination with other papers, letters, and the work itself. There are some marvelously touching pieces of writing here, and any reader of Plath's poetry can benefit from reading this collection.

Paunch (42–43: 65–122) has devoted half of its double winter issue to a "festival" gathering of essays on Plath's poem "Tulips." Arthur Efron opens the discussion, and closes it, by stating some of the problems in this particular poem, different as it is from many of Plath's late poems: Efron reads it as her statement against the demands of her, or any person's, society (pp. 69–75, pp. 110–22). Brian Caraher extends this discussion ("The Problematic of Body and Language," pp. 76–89) by using Plath's "thick language" to trace "the tension between sets of values and assumptions," the poem's chief strength. M. D. Uroff (pp. 90–96) sees the poem as a journey to health, with an affirmative ending, implicit from the outset of the poem, while Marjorie Perloff finds the tone of the poem much more mixed, its theme a "depiction of the basic, timeless tension between death and life" (and would argue with Efron's reading of the poem, claiming that Plath's private tragedy was a wanting to belong, to excel, in all society's testing grounds). Robin Reed Davis writes with reference to the first published version of "Tulips" in the *New Yorker* (pp. 97–104), concluding that the speaker has acknowledged that she is still far from health.

R. J. Spendal reads "Sylvia Plath's 'Cut'" (*MPS* 6:128–34) as an analogy to her own "disunity," a further step to her suicide. Other close readings of single poems are Jon Rosenblatt's "Plath's 'The Couriers'" (*Expl* 34:item 28); Vincent Balitas's "A Note on Sylvia Plath's 'The Hanging Man'" (*N&Q* 220:208); and Gary Lane's comment on the same (*ContP* 2,i:40–43).

John Berryman Studies continues its practice of including the supplemental checklist of both primary and secondary items, compiled by Richard J. Kelly and Ernest C. Stefanik, Jr. Among the essays included in the 1975 numbers of this periodical are Peter Stitt's essay on *Homage to Mistress Bradstreet* (*JBS* 1,ii:2–11) in which he aligns Bradstreet and Berryman, the latter's struggles given identity through the description of the former's, and proves that this poem is perhaps the best-unified of all the Berryman poems; Toshikazu Niikura's appreciation of Berryman (pp. 14–17); and Shozo Tokunaga's comparison of Berryman and Robert Lowell (pp. 18–23). Other essays include Gary Arpin's "Mistress Bradstreet's Discontents" (*JBS* 1,iii: 2–7), Laurence Lieberman's memoir (pp. 8–11), and Ann Hayes's "The Voices of John Berryman," in which Hayes discusses Berryman's critical writing as well as his poetry (pp. 17–20). The most comprehensive discussion of Berryman's work is found in J. D. McClatchy's *MPS* essay, "John Berryman: The Impediments to Salvation" (4:246–77), in which Berryman's use of his attitudes in the

Crane study is transferred to his poetry. McClatchy sees part of the poet's fascination with Crane to be his search for a father figure, not in the sense of replacement, but in order to become his own father. A close reading of the poems to the end of Berryman's life supports some of the suggested parallels.

Another provocative essay is Charles W. Thornbury's "The Significance of Dreams in *The Dream Songs*" (*L&P* 25:93–107). Shorter notes focus on specific poems, as Margaret M. McBride's "Berryman's 'World's Fair!'" (*Expl* 34:item 22) and R. Patrick Wilson's "The Ironic Title of Berryman's *Love and Fame*" (*NConL* 5,iv:10–12).

A major study of the poetry of Robert Lowell appeared in 1975. Stephen Yenser's *Circle to Circle: The Poetry of Robert Lowell* (Berkeley: Univ. of Calif. Press) is a well-conceived, well-argued book. Taking as his thesis the concept that Lowell has been writing "one poem," Yenser traces themes, images, and particularly a circular structure in the most mature collections: "each new work labors directly under the burden of the past. . . . He has used virtually all the available material in weaving the net in which he is enmeshed; and yet he is convinced, this unlikely Penelope of the littoral, that it is his obligation to go on knotting and undoing the tarred rope" (p. 323). Because Yenser has included all the Lowell volumes through 1975, this is an especially valuable study.

Vivian Smith's *The Poetry of Robert Lowell* (Sydney, Australia: Sydney Univ. Press [1974]) is a clear-headed treatment of the poems through the 1970 *Notebook*. Intended to be a "reader's guide," the study focuses on single poems, and Smith wisely spends the most time with the obviously difficult and the early poems. She finds Lowell a major poet, and does a competent job of relating the early work to the later.

Helen Vendler ("The Difficult Grandeur of Robert Lowell," *AtM* 235:68–73) answers the poet's recent critics with a committed defense of his poetry (not "comfortable," she admits, but lasting). She finds that Lowell's appeal lies in his philosophy ("behind cruelty, malice, and deadly observation lies a covert idealism, sometimes self-indulgent and knowingly sentimental, sometimes pure"), and explains that the difficulty in his latest poems stems partly from the fact that his free association there makes his wide learning evident: "Like some crowded Tiergarten, Lowell's poetry exhausts all species."

George McFadden's "'Life Studies'—Robert Lowell's Comic

Breakthrough" (*PMLA* 90:96–106) treats the 15 poems in part 4 of *Life Studies* as a unit, the important result of Lowell's experiences in San Francisco around 1957, mainly his impatience with his own early work as he gave readings there. McFadden emphasizes the comic strategies at work in these poems, as well as the mythic structures.

vi. Denise Levertov, Adrienne Rich, Anne Sexton, Diane Wakoski, Maxine Kumin, Elizabeth Bishop, H. D.

Ronald Wallace points out in his "Alone with Poems" (*ColQ* 23:341–53) that women's poetry has always been more frequently about the themes of home and family; but that thematic concern is perhaps more visible in today's emphasis on the personal. He treats the poems of Mona Van Duyn, Denise Levertov, and Diane Wakoski in particular. Cary Nelson gives reasonable comment on the various poet's war poems, Levertov's among them, in his "Whitman in Vietnam: Poetry and History in Contemporary America" (*MR* 16:55–71). David Ignatow praises Levertov's most recent collection, *The Freeing of the Dust,* because it contains poems reminiscent of her earlier work, while yet showing that she has moved—powerfully—into new areas. Most impressive for Ignatow is the tone of "sweetness, a tenderness toward life" (*NYTBR* 30 Nov.:55). Julian Gitzen, in "From Reverence to Attention: The Poetry of Denise Levertov" (*MQ* 16:328–41), traces Levertov's development from the early collections.

The issue of feminist poetry was the subject of one of Levertov's own essays, "Poems by Women," *Trellis* (Spring:57–60), in which she championed the asexual quality of good women's poetry. In her essay, "Anne Sexton: Light Up the Cave" (*Ramparts* 13,v:61–63), Levertov again refused to give Sexton any special accolades because of her feminine themes. Instead she viewed Sexton as a member of the twentieth century, "caught in history's crossfire . . . . To recognize that for a few years of her life Anne Sexton was an artist *even though* she had so hard a struggle against her desire for death is to fittingly honor her memory."

Several other essays in memoriam offer important critical insights into Sexton's poetry. *APR* supplement (May/June:15–20) contains poems and essays by Maxine Kumin (on *Awful Rowing* and Sexton's need for positive religion), Susan Fromberg Schaeffer, Kathleen

Spivack (on imagery and Sexton's persistent work), Lucien Stryk, and C. K. Williams. J. D. McClatchy's essay in *CentR* 19:1–36, "Anne Sexton: Somehow To Endure," is the most comprehensive yet published. Following her work chronologically, McClatchy points to recurring themes and modulations of technique and form; his "postscript" adds a memoir to his criticism. Also of interest is Joyce Carol Oates's *"The Awful Rowing Toward God"* (*NYTBR* 23 Mar.:3–4), a discussion of Sexton's concept of God as expressed in this collection. Sexton is also mentioned in several interviews with Maxine Kumin (*Crazy Horse* 16, Summer:20–25 and *MR* 16:317–27).

Barbara Charlesworth Gelpi and Albert Gelpi have edited and selected *Adrienne Rich's Poetry* (New York: W. W. Norton) a collection which includes selections from the poetry, statements by Rich about her work (some taped informally with the Gelpis, others reprinted from published interviews); and a selection of secondary criticism. Among the essays reprinted are those by W. H. Auden, Randall Jarrell, Robert Boyers, Helen Vendler, Erica Jong, Wendy Martin, Nancy Milford, and Albert Gelpi. The edition includes a chronology and bibliography. New essays on Rich's poems appeared in *SWR* 60:370–88 (Willard Spiegelman, "Voice of the Survivor: The Poetry of Adrienne Rich"); in *SoR* 11,iii:668–80 (James K. Robinson, "Sailing Close-hauled and Diving into the Wreck: From Nemerov to Rich"), in *APR* 4,ii:4–7 (Eleanor Wilner, " 'This Accurate Dreamer': An Appreciation"); and in *Parnassus* 4,i:50–67 (Rosellen Brown, "The Notes for the Poem Are the Only Poem"). Each of the four critics sees Rich's strength as poet in her ability to change, both in life-style and in art; and each connects her, readily, with the women's movement.

Two comprehensive essays on the poetry of H. D. appeared in 1975. Susan Friedman's "Who Buried H. D.? A Poet, Her Critics, and Her Place in 'The Literary Tradition' " (*CE* 36:801–14) is an overview of both the work and the criticism, calling attention to the fact that H. D. is largely ignored. Less polemically, but with an equal understanding of H. D.'s excellence as a poet, John Peck traces her poetics from her reliance on single images to her use of "the neoplatonic image or eidolon," the greater image that could express her own knowledge of psychoanalytic thought and various other interests ("Perpetuae H. D.," *Parnassus* 3,ii:42–74).

Jerome Mazzaro sees Elizabeth Bishop as a "post-modernist" because of "the consciousness of her control, the conjectural nature of her vision, and her intellectual clarity" in "Elizabeth Bishop and The Poetics of Impediment" (*Salmagundi* 27, Fall[1974]:118–44). Willard Spiegelman's "Landscape and Knowledge, The Poetry of Elizabeth Bishop" (*MPS* 4:203–24) gives a close reading of many of the poems, placing Bishop's control of the poem in her visual sense but viewing her as an "epistemological poet in the tradition of William Wordsworth and S. T. Coleridge."

vii. William Stafford, Robert Bly, Galway Kinnell, James Wright, W. S. Merwin

The Stafford issue of *MPS* (6,i) included essays by George Lensing, Linda Wagner, and Roger Dickinson-Brown. Lensing pictures Stafford as "mythmaker" (pp. 1–16), his myth being his feeling for the earth and his use of the imagery of living—caught, ritualized through language and its repetition. Wagner's "William Stafford's 'Plain-style'" (pp. 19–30) locates characteristic tone and rhythm linguistically, and Dickinson-Brown's study is of Stafford's narrative methods and structures ("The Wise, The Dull, The Bewildered: What Happens in William Stafford," pp. 30–38). Robert Coles discusses the poet's concept of America in "William Stafford's Long Walk" (*APR* 4,iv:27–28). History intrigues the poet, in his view of the country as "a land of compelling opposites." Sanford Pinsker's "conversation" with Stafford appears in the same issue (pp. 28–29), and William Childress's interview is published in *PN* 2,ii:1–2, 37. Alberta T. Turner also gives Stafford's language attention in "William Stafford and the Surprise Cliché" (*SCR* 1,ii:28–33).

Only a few essays appeared this year on the work of Robert Bly and James Wright. Charles Molesworth contributed a major study of the former ("Thrashing in the Depths: The Poetry of Robert Bly," *BRMMLA* 29:95–117), while Howard Nelson surveyed Bly's newest work ("Welcoming Shadows: Robert Bly's Recent Poetry," *HC* 16,ii:1–15). James Wright's interview with Peter Stitt for the *Paris Review* includes much information about himself and his friends (62:34–61).

Two items on Galway Kinnell were substantial readings of single poems: J. T. Ledbetter's "Kinnell's 'The Bear'" (*Expl* 33:item 63) and Linda Wagner's "'Spindrift': The World in a Seashell" (*CP* 8,i:5–9).

More interest than usual was evinced in the poetry of W. S. Merwin this year. Richard E. Messer discussed "W. S. Merwin's Use of Myth" in *PAPA* (Fayetteville) 1,iii:41–48; somewhat the same approach was used by Cheri Colby Davis in "Time and Timelessness in the Poetry of W. S. Merwin" (*MPS* 6:224–36). Davis sees an important motif to be "time's passage," with all its loss. Relating Merwin's outlook to Hofmannsthal's rather than to Vico's, she finds one primary theme to be "the interpenetration of death and language." Natural objects—starlight, star sounds—become Merwin's symbols.

Anthony Libby finds Merwin's strength in describing "human emptiness with the chill accuracy it deserves." Monothematic, the voice developing to better express the single theme, Merwin's poems have turned increasingly to the surreal (his use of myth is a means toward his genuine belief in the mystic). Libby finds Merwin one of the most important contemporary poets ("W. S. Merwin and the Nothing That Is," *ConL* 16,i:19–40).

Reed Sanderlin comments on "Merwin's 'The Drunk in the Furnace,'" (*ContP* 2,i:24–27), seeing the poem as characteristic because a social outcast shows the poet a means to joy.

Evan Watkins's "W. S. Merwin: A Critical Accompaniment" (*Boundary 2*, 4:187–99) compares the poet with Robert Coover. Coover's writing is marked by artifice and the absence of personality; Merwin's writing allows personality but moves beyond it. Watkins convincingly discusses *The Lice*, *The Carrier of Ladders*, and *Writings to an Unfinished Accompaniment*.

viii. Randall Jarrell, Howard Nemerov, Stanley Kunitz, W. D. Snodgrass, and James Dickey

A book-length study appeared this year on Jarrell: Helen Hagenbuchle's *The Black Goddess: A Study of the Archetypal Feminine in the Poetry of Randall Jarrell* (Zurich: Francke Verlag). Although Ms. Hagenbuchle forces her thesis at moments, the work will probably be helpful for any reader of Jarrell's poems.

James Atlas discusses the career ("Randall Jarrell," *APR* 4,i:26–28) as motivated by political awareness. Jarrell's strengths from the beginning of his writing life were his use of the colloquial voice, coupled with an audacity where language was concerned (informality did not preclude rich diction); the variable in his life was his political stance, whether or not he felt himself in harmony with his culture.

Howard Nemrov finds Jarrell the poet most easily identified with change (both artistic and personal) in his essay "What Will Suffice" (*Salmagundi* 28:90–103). See also Robert Boyers's "An Interview with Howard Nemerov" (*Salmagundi* 31–32:109–19). Boyers also discusses Nemerov's poems in *APR* 4,iii:4–9 ("Howard Nemerov's True Voice of Feeling"), finding that his most impressive quality is the "sharp sense of troubled waters" beneath the cool facade of modern diction.

William Mills's *The Stillness in Moving Things: The World of Howard Nemerov* (Memphis, Tenn.: Memphis State Univ. Press) provides a phenomenological reading, justified because Mills sees that Nemerov shares many of the concerns of Husserl and Heidegger, both in the use of language and in philosophy. Mills contends that there is a unity both in serious (contemplative) and lighter (satiric) poetry because language gives being to things, the act of expressing is affirmative. Even though not all the readings stay as close to the announced method as they might, Mills's study is useful. One might wish for a more substantial conclusion, however.

Included in *Artful Thunder* is Gloria L. Young's essay, "'The Fountainhead of All Forms': Poetry and the Unconscious in Emerson and Howard Nemerov," pp. 241–67. Using both poets' theory and poetry, Young proves their correspondences, at least in some respects.

Cynthia Davis's "Stanley Kunitz's 'The Testing Tree'" (*CP* 8,i:43–50) offers helpful information concerning this key poem, while Robert Weisberg's "Stanley Kunitz: The Stubborn Middle Way" (*MPS* 6:49–73) defends the poet's somewhat unfashionable position—an accurate and sane poet, producing solid, even impressive poetry—with attention to his moderation in all areas.

Somewhat the same argument is J. D. McClatchy's about Snodgrass in "W. D. Snodgrass: The Mild, Reflective Art" (*MR* 16:281–314). See also David Dillon's "Toward Passionate Utterance: An Interview with W. D. Snodgrass," *SwR* 60:278–90.

Thomas Landess surveys the position of James Dickey in regard to academic stances toward art in "Traditionalist Criticism and the Poetry of James Dickey" (*OR* 3:5–26), and Wayne D. McGinnis covers slightly worn ground in "Mysticism in the Poetry of James Dickey" (*NLauR* 5,i–ii:5–10). Also of interest is David L. Arnett's interview with Dickey in *ConL* 16:286–300.

ix. A. R. Ammons, John Ashbery, and Frank O'Hara

With supporting critics like Harold Bloom and William Harmon, Ammons will probably emerge from the 1970s one of the major poets of the decade. Bloom's "A. R. Ammons: The Breaking of the Vessels" (*Salmagundi* 31–32:185–203) places his work in the continuum of the romantic, change-oriented, innovative poets of the past hundred years. Harmon's *SLJ* essay, "'How Does One Come Home': A. R. Ammons' *Tape for the Turn of the Year*" (7,ii:3–32), focuses attention on that single collection, but views it progressively, as a culmination of certain strengths within the earlier work. Denis Donoghue, in his "Ammons and the Lesser Celandine" (*Parnassus* 3,ii:19–26) faults the long poem (*Sphere*) for its paucity of both feeling and craft, finding Ammons a better poet with the short, well-defined attempts.

Alfred Corn ("A Magma of Interiors," *Parnassus* 4,i:223–33) finds John Ashbery's strength in his recognition of ambiguity (and more than seven kinds of it). The Ashbery poem can best be read as "a sort of *auberge espagnole.*" Both John Malcolm Brinnin (*NYTBR* 10 Aug:7–8) and Fred Moramarco find *Self Portrait in A Convex Mirror* (*APR* 4,vi:43–44) a convincing work; in fact Moramarco claims it "a masterpiece, a classic of its genre, as elegant and erudite a poem as has appeared in this country in very many years."

Criticism of both Ashbery and Frank O'Hara has begun, properly, to stress the affinity between these men's poetry and their interest in graphic art. Frank O'Hara's two collections of essays, many about painting and painters, were published this year: *Art Chronicles, 1954–1966* (New York: George Braziller) and *Standing Still and Walking in New York*, ed. Donald Allen (Bolinas, Calif.: Grey Fox Press). The latter is more useful to people interested in O'Hara as poet because Allen has taken all the essays not particularly related to painting, combined them with the full text of Edward Lucie-Smith's interview with O'Hara in 1965 (which opens with O'Hara's explanation of his affinity with painters in New York), and created a vivid portrait of the poet.

Charles Molesworth assesses the poetry in an *IR* (6,i:61–74) essay, " 'The Clear Architecture of the Nerves': The Poetry of Frank O'Hara," in which he sets up criteria for judging the place of O'Hara's *Collected Poems*. He finds that they are contradictory because they operate "with a high degree of consciousness about themselves as literature" and yet flout "notions of decorum." Molesworth finds that O'Hara is best at improvisation, his reliance on nostalgia and autobiography, and his ability to compose in phrases rather than in lines. He sees three basic modes within the poems, and finds their significance in their combination of "the exaltation of sensibility and the celebration of the world of things."

The quantity of criticism on contemporary poetry—only, unfortunately, hinted at in this essay—and its increasing attempt to find perspectives, critical vantage points, from which readers can view the process of active writing can only be cheering to observers of the literary scene. As long as interested readers are willing to share their enthusiasms and perceptions, growth—in both art and the criticism of it—seems likely. As Howard Nemerov reminded us this year, "poetry is a place where contradictions do not destroy one another." And, further, "Poetry perceives the world as a miracle transcending its doctrine, or any doctrine" ("Thirteen Ways of Looking at a Skylark," *Poetry* 126:294–305). In "The Question of Poetic Form" (*HudR* 28:491–501). Hayden Carruth also emphasizes the relationship between the sometimes inexplicable processes of art and the role of the critic, in what may serve as gentle warning for all of us engaged in the writing of criticism: "A real theory of art begins with process and accepts the inevitability of mystery; it rests content with its own incompleteness. A spurious theory of art begins somewhere else and tries to explain everything."

Michigan State University

18. Drama

Jordan Y. Miller

The sheer volume of scholarly output in the study of drama continues to challenge one's ability to give everything fair treatment in a volume such as this. The following choices have therefore been made in the hope of establishing a reasonable balance:

1. All items from foreign publications, whether published in English or not, have, with the exception of a few Canadian references, been omitted.

2. Unless there is some clear justification for inclusion, items dealing mainly with the theatre, such as details of historical structures, actors and acting troupes, and frontier and early regional companies, have been omitted.

3. Dissertations have been restricted to a subdivision of each main subject heading. In view of the almost geometric proliferation of these graduate efforts, notations have been sharply limited.

i. From the Beginning to the Early 20th Century

Diane B. Malone explores a subject that generally gets short shrift in drama and theatre histories except as a matter of passing curiosity. In "A Survey of Early Military Theatre in America" (*ThS* 16:56–64) Malone provides a good general summary of the military theatre, mainly British but some American, in colonial times, during the French and Indian wars, and under the British garrisons in Massachusetts, New Jersey, and Philadelphia. A comparatively unknown sidelight of Royall Tyler's career is revealed in "Royall Tyler's Lyrics for *May Day in Town*" by Katherine S. Jarvis (*HLB* 23:186–98), which reproduces and discusses briefly Tyler's jogging verses for this 1787 light opera that did not survive its opening performance. "Historical interest" is about the best one can say of Tyler's efforts. "The Prejudice Against Native American Drama from 1778–1830" by

Harold J. Nichols (*QJS* 60:279–88), while showing that numerous American works beyond the familiar *Contrast* were staged during that period, confirms the existence of underlying prejudices against native works. The patriotic attitudes of the War of 1812 and Edwin Forrest's prizes helped to break down unfavorable audience attitudes.

The record is set straight regarding one of the more famous plantation plays in John A. Degen's highly interesting "How to End the Octoroon" (*ETJ* 27:170–78). The general assumption that American audiences would not accept a final union between Zoe, the Octoroon, and George, her white sweetheart, but that British audiences, less racially prejudiced, could, is disproved in this account of Boucicault's struggles on both sides of the Atlantic to provide a satisfactory ending acceptable to all. A theme that even Dante found appealing concerns Claude R. Flory in "Boker, Barrett, and the Francesca Theme in Drama" (*Players* 50:58–61). Flory takes a surprisingly strong positive attitude toward Boker's play, viewing it as among the finest dramas anywhere using the Francesca theme and even regarding the Lawrence Barrett acting version as one of the best English-language plays between the times of Sheridan and Shaw.

The origins of American musicals are discussed in W. L. Slout's "The Black Crook: First of the Nudies" (*Players* 50:16–19) and Roger A. Hall's "*The Brook*: America's Germinal Musical?" (*ETJ* 27:323–29). Slout writes a popular account, including some doggerel verses of amusing criticism from the New York *Clipper*, of the sensational success of what has nearly always been regarded as the first American musical, presented in 1866. Hall, while acknowledging that *The Brook*, produced in Galveston a decade later, using current popular tunes, *Beggar's Opera* fashion, is not exactly the "germinal cell" of modern musicals, as some would have it, nonetheless maintains that it was the first to employ the more traditional musical comedy form and that its subsequent influence was considerable. Patti P. Gillespie's "James A. Herne: A Reassessment" (*Players* 51:66–71) adds to the slowly growing body of criticism on this 19th-century innovator about whom we still know relatively little. Gillespie's view that Herne's weakness lay in his lack of "artistry of execution," thus denying him a secure position as a substantial American playwright, is a valid assessment. A final item is a report on an American Pepys called "Michael Valentine Ball—Faithful Diarist, Passionate Playgoer," by

John L. Marsh (*Players* 50:38–43). Of strictly historical rather than literary interest, this article presents an account of the observations of this playgoing doctor of Warren, Pennsylvania, who witnessed over 90 productions from *East Lynne* to Shakespeare between 1884 and 1886.

***a.* Dissertations.**[1] In a dissertation of special interest in the area of regional theatre, which should be acknowledged here, Patrick S. Gilvary (Ohio State) writes "The Floating Theatre: An Analysis of the Major Factors of Showboat Theatre in the United States" (36:3223), in which he makes a strong plea for more recognition of this unique form of theatre that was such a vital force on the frontier. In frontier subject matter Marilyn J. Anderson (Minn.) surveys the noble and not so noble savage in "The Image of the American Indian in American Drama from 1766 to 1845" (35:4494–95), concluding that the characterization of the Indian was manipulated in order to define the white man's own confusing role in his attempt to bring "civilization" to this child of nature.

John B. Lynaugh (Wisc.–Madison), in "The Forgotten Contributions and Comedies of Dion Boucicault" (35:5569), holds that the farces and melodramas of the time, including the more sophisticated and "elevated" comedies of Boucicault, who wished to be taken as a serious artist, helped pave the way for later realism. Leonard Korf (UCLA), in "An Examination of Some Obscurities in the Life of Dion Boucicault" (35:1905), reinforces Lynaugh's approach by pointing out that Boucicault was a more important figure than is generally recognized through his lectures and teaching efforts in later life. Thomas J. Lyttle (Bowling Green), in "An Examination of Poetic Justice in Three Selected Types of Nineteenth-Century Melodrama: The Indian Play, the Temperance Play, and the Civil War Play" (35:7438–39), finds that poetic justice moved from the primitive and uncomplicated to the more "Christian" and "sophisticated." The growing body of critical study of 19th-century playwrights includes "Bartley Campbell: Playwright of the Gilded Age" (36:1901) by Wayne H. Claeren (Pittsburgh) and "Denman Thompson and His

1. Numbers in parentheses here and in the following sections on dissertations indicate volume and page in the "A" or Humanities sequence of *Dissertation Abstracts International.*

Production of The Old Homestead: Their Place in the Evolution of New England Rural Drama" (35:6849) by Shelton B. Leach, II (NYU).

ii. The Modern Period: General

A major contribution to the scholarly study of theatre figures of the late 19th and early 20th centuries has been made by Lise-Lone Marker in *David Belasco: Naturalism in the American Theatre* (Princeton, N.J.: Princeton Univ. Press). This is an important volume because of its full exploration of Belasco's artistic philosophy, which, in addition to demanding absolute personal control of every aspect of the production, completely eschewed the serious, literary nature of drama by devoting its full energies to theatricality and the sense of absolute reality, or, as Belasco put it, the "reality of experience." A bibliography, a chronology, and several illustrations including ground plans for key Belasco productions contribute to the usefulness of this excellent study. In *The Three Masks of American Tragedy* (Baton Rouge: La. State Univ. Press, [1974]) Dan Vogel writes a stimulating study of contemporary American tragedy. The "masks" (Oedipus, Christ, and Satan, with the shadow of Aristotle in the background) are treated under such attention-getting titles as "Ephraim Rex" and "Willy Tyrannos." Vogel develops his discussions of O'Neill, Williams, Miller, and Anderson in terms of the classic nature of their tragic protagonists and very nearly persuades this reader, at any rate, that some of his own pet ideas about American tragic characters may not be entirely justified. A valuable contribution.

John Simon's sharp tongue provides a lot of good reading in his two volumes brought out by Random House in 1975. *Uneasy Stages: A Chronicle of the New York Theatre, 1963–1973* discusses New York productions season by season during the decade, and finds that the theatre is in "desperate shape" and may have outlived its usefulness. *Singularities: Essays on the Theatre 1964–1974* contains reviews and other articles on a wide variety of plays and playwrights, audiences and critics.

Ethnic drama and women's movements form the subject of five generally good items. Neil L. Shumsky's "Zangwill's *The Melting Pot*: Ethnic Tensions on Stage" (AQ 27:29–41) devotes a moderately long discussion to this English writer's "radically different" play of

1908 presented in Washington, D.C. Donald Schwartz's "The Yiddish Art Theatre" (*Players* 50:138–41) briefly reviews the history of this important group which brought to New York some early productions of Chekhov, Ibsen and Shaw under the hand of Jacob Ben-Ami. Lois C. Gottlieb writes two essays on the status of women, both of pertinence in this era of ERA. In "The Perils of Freedom: The New Woman in Three American Plays of the 1900s" (*CRevAS* 6:84–98) Gottlieb effectively maintains that Walter's *The Easiest Way*, Fitch's *The City*, and Moody's *The Faith Healer* do not come to grips with the truth of women's existence. In "The Double Standard Debate in Early 20th Century American Drama" (*MichA* 7:441–52) she dwells essentially on the same subject, but turns to the ideas of Crothers's *The Three of Us*, Moody's *The Great Divide*, and Mitchell's *The New York Idea*. Gottlieb convincingly demonstrates that in the end the double standard in these plays is regarded by the playwrights as a "necessary foundation" for successful male-female relationships. Deborah S. Kolb, in "The Rise and Fall of the New Woman in American Drama" (*ETJ* 27:149–60), finds that the rise and fall of the "New Woman" on stage follows closely the simultaneous rise and fall of the "professional feminist" or "New Woman" movement of the early part of the century. The cycle begins with Herne's *Margaret Fleming* in 1890, which still regards woman as a domestic figure, and ends with Rachel Crothers's *When Ladies Meet* in 1932.

A discussion, with pictures and ground plan, of one of the lesser-known productions by Orson Welles in his early heyday is in "The Shoemaker's Holiday at the Mercury Theatre" (*ThS* 16:150–64) by Richard France. William W. Lannon, in "The Rise and Rationale of Post World War II American Confessional Theatre" (*ConnR* 8,ii:73–81), finds that plays such as Kopit's *Indians*, Miller's *Salesman*, and Albee's *American Dream* have enjoyed the "act of confession with a curious relish" in apologia for the American dream, the American South, and so on. Donald A. Borchardt's "The Audience as Jury" (*Players* 50:10–15) discusses trial plays as "factual theatre." Borchardt makes clear that all stage trials, even as literal as *The Trial of the Catonsville Nine* or *In the Matter of J. Robert Oppenheimer*, can succeed only when the "facts" are selective and the play "artistically cohesive." *The Twenties* focuses its attention on T. S. Eliot's *The Waste Land* as a theme for the literature of the decade. Jordan Y. Miller, writing on the drama in "Expressionism: The Waste Land Enacted," pp. 439–54, explores the views of expressionistic dramatists who see the society of the time in terms of Eliot's unreal city, "almost purely a human creation from which faith and the gods had fled in terror." The same subject, limited to one American playwright, is treated in "Two Expressionistic Interpretations of Dehumanization: Rice's *The Adding Machine* and Mũniz's *El Tintero*" (*EIL* 2:245–55), by Loren L. Zeller.

a. **Dissertations.** Joanne M. Loudin (Univ. of Wash.), continuing in the vein of Gottlieb and Kolb above and discussing some of the same writers in addition to more modern dramatists such as Barry, Howard, Kelly, and Behrman, explores changing audience attitudes toward marriage, divorce, and careers in "The Changing Role of the Comic Heroine in American Drama from 1900 to 1940" (36:3224). Gabrielle Rowe (Mich.), in writing on "Structural and Thematic Functions of the Face Mask in the Development of Modern Drama" (35:7325–26), necessarily limits treatment of American writers to Eugene O'Neill. "Modern American War Plays" (36:4498) by Joseph E. Sanders (UCLA) is a thematic and generic study of everything from *What Price Glory?* through *Bury the Dead* to *Sticks and Bones*, showing that since World War II America has become a warrior nation coincidental with the development of American drama as a mature art. Sylvia V. Zastrow (Northwestern), in "The Structure of Selected Plays by American Women Playwrights: 1920–1970" (36:4117), examines past criticism and analyses of comments on the creative activity of women dramatists from Crothers to Megan Terry. Jack D. Starr, Jr. (Minn.) studies "Manifestations of 'Sexuality' on the American Stage as Illustrated by Selected Plays from 1960–1969" (35:8065), treating the social phenomena which now permit overt sexual activity to be displayed on stage. Robert R. Miller (Middle Tenn. State) pursues the tragic theme in "Tragedy in Modern American Drama: The Psychological, Social, and Absurdist Conditions in Historical Perspective" (36:3717). O'Neill, Williams, and Miller receive the emphasis in their concern for the threatening "mechanicalism" of the modern age. This might well be a good companion volume to Vogel's study (see above).

Several other dissertations emphasize the American theatre and those who perform within it more than dramatic literature, but at least three should be noted here. They are: "The Dramaturgy of the Playwrights' Company" (36:1172) by Alice M. French (Mo.); "The History of the Actors' Studio 1947–1975" (36:3222–23) by David Garfield (NYU); and "Rosamond Gilder and the Theatre" (35:8062) by Caroline J. Dodge (Ill.).

iii. Modern Dramatists

***a.* Edward Albee.** Christopher W. E. Bigsby, the brilliant British scholar whose outstanding study of Albee (Edinburgh: Oliver and Boyd, [1969]) has unfortunately never appeared in this country, has edited *Twentieth Century Views of Edward Albee* (Englewood Cliffs: Prentice-Hall), in which he has included two of his own important articles, one on *Tiny Alice* from his original book, and a new one on *Box-Mao-Box*. Bigsby consistently maintains one of the sanest and most perceptive critical approaches to Albee, and his excellent choices for this volume include pieces by Martin Esslin, Diana Trilling, and Henry Hewes. Richard M. Coe, in "Beyond Absurdity: Albee's Awareness of Audience in *Tiny Alice*" (*MD* 18:371–83), regards Albee rightly, I think, as an absurdist, but, unlike others who treat absurdity as "virtually a ritual for initiates only," Albee, in Coe's view, attempts to make it clear and accessible to his audiences. "Albee in Wonderland" by C. N. Stavrou (*SWR* 60:46–61) reviews the major plays from *The Sandbox* through *Tiny Alice*, characterizing Albee as one whose forte is "baneful banalities and bizarre juxtapositions" in an "absurdist world where sense is nonsense" and where man is balanced on the edge of the abyss from which he must dive in, or build anew on the edge of the precipice. Robbie Moses, having pursued Albee in a dissertation (see below), contributes "Edward Albee: A Voice in the Wasteland" (*ForumH* 12,iii:35–40), and Philip C. Kolin in "Two Early Poems by Edward Albee" (*RALS* 5:95–97) briefly discusses Albee's early poetic bent and reprints two poems, "Eighteen" and "Chopin," from 1945 and 1946.

***a-1.* Dissertations.** Albee increasingly attracts graduate scholarship approaching the level of the attention given O'Neill. Robbie Moses (Houston) shows death to be a unifying factor in 13 of Albee's plays from his earliest Choate works through *All Over* in "The Theme of Death in the Plays of Edward Albee" (35:4443–44). Burton Baker (Wisc.), in "Edward Albee's Nihilistic Plays" (35:5387), takes exception to the view that Albee writes "reformist" protest and attempts to prove that he takes the "deepest nihilistic point of view" in exploring "man's inescapable propensity for victimization and defeat." Along the same line Patricia A. Brand (NYU), in "Decline and Decay in the Plays of Edward Albee" (36:3708), takes each play through *Seascape* to illustrate Albee's questioning of free will, in the order of Spengler's *Decline of the West*, witnessing the decline as "inevitable and irreversible." Still in the same area is Sarah H. McCants (Southern Miss.), whose "The Shade and the Mask: Death and Illusion in the Works of Edward Albee" (36:6722) covers *The Zoo Story* to *Tiny Alice* and finds Albee to be more traditional than most of the absurdists but still writing about dead tradition, alienation, futility. Departing from the rather heavy emphasis on the dark side of Albee, Elizabeth Hull (Loyola–Chicago), in "A Transactional Analysis of the Plays of Edward Albee" (36:313–14), examines the plays from *The Zoo Story* to *All Over* in terms of the relatively new ideas of TA, which are found to account for much of the psychology of Albee's realism. Albee is the only American playwright considered by Linda M. Hill (Yale) in "Language as Aggression: Studies in the Postwar Drama" (35:4524), who uses *The American Dream* to demonstrate that language is pernicious rather than inadequate.

***b.* Arthur Miller and Tennessee Williams.** While Miller continues to hold his own in scholarly interest, Williams seems to have fallen off abruptly, both in general items (only one to be reported here) and in graduate research.

Three articles on Miller appear in the March 1975 issue of *Modern Drama*. The lead essay is "The Action and Its Significance: Arthur Miller's Struggle with Dramatic Form" (*MD* 18:1–14) by Orm Overland. From *Sons* to *Creation* Miller is seen to have a continuing problem of proper dramatic form, with a consistent distrust of the theatre as a means of communication, leading to a relatively unsuccessful use of narrators, direct address, and intrascene explanations as in the published version of *The Crucible*. "*All My Sons* and the Larger Context" by Barry Gross (*MD* 18:15–27) continues the discussion of certain of Miller's artistic failings by showing that Miller's plays are not understood as he conceived them. For instance, *All My Sons*, says Gross, is not about war profiteering but about Keller's family relationship, in which the rest of the world has little meaning. The third item is by Lawrence D. Lowenthal, who writes "Arthur Miller's *Incident at Vichy*: A Sartrean Interpretation" (*MD* 18:29–41). The play is found to be an "explicitly dramatic rendition of Sartre's treatise on Jews," providing a clear structural example of Sartre's definition of existential 'theatre of situation.'" In *AL* (47:247–58) Irving Jacobson writes "Family Dreams in *Death of a Salesman*" to demonstrate how Willy seeks desperately for the security of a "home" which he finds with those who supposedly admire him outside his own family. The old salesman Dave Singleman, whom Willy would emulate in his declining years, thus becomes the ideal. Singleman's importance in the play is further developed by Larry W. Cash in "The Function of Ben and Dave Singleman in *Death of a Salesman*" (*NConL* 5,i:7–9).

There is only one major item on Williams to report this year. Thomas P. Adler's "The Dialogue of Incompletion: Language in Tennessee Williams' Later Plays" (*QJS* 61:48–58) focuses on *Small Craft Warnings, Out Cry*, and *In the Bar of a Tokyo Hotel* in its discussion of Williams's syntactical devices of uncompleted dialogue, inner monologues, and similar devices which are found to impart distinctive tone and quality to the plays.

***b-1.* Dissertations.** Miller's themes of family drama, the tragedy of the common man, and historical and political drama are subjects of comparison in "Major Themes in the Plays of Antonio Buero Vallejo and Arthur Miller: A Comparative Study" (36:3221–22) by Dorothy S. Cummings (Ark.). "The Plays of Arthur Miller: Theory and Practice" (36:1172) by Jack Feldman, (Wisc.–Madison) contributes comparatively little new material in its application of "Miller's own standards" instead of Aristotle's in deciding the value of everything in plays from *The Man Who Had All the Luck* to *Creation of the World.* John M. Roderick III (Brown) writes "Arthur Miller and American Mythology: The Dream as Life Force in Twentieth-Century American Drama" (35:7324). Miller's characters are seen as 20th-century Everymen who struggle with the dream and its influence. The crisis of identity and "generativity" of Miller's lead characters from *Sons* through *Price* is explored by Dutta Ramesh Thippavajjala, (Kan.) in "The Heroes of Arthur Miller" (36:894).

Only two dissertations on Williams concern us here. The first is by Glenn T. Embrey (UCLS), "Sexual Confusion in the Major Plays of Tennessee Williams" (36:309), which finds that Williams's plays except *Menagerie* have been weakened by a confusion concerning how to regard human sexuality. David C. Williams (Columbia) in "The Ritual of Self-Assassination in the Drama of Tennessee Williams" (35:6147) puts Williams in the tradition of Strindberg, Artaud, and Cocteau instead of being merely a regionalist in Gothic horror.

***c.* Eugene O'Neill.** Despite the fact that *Lazarus Laughed* has never received a commercial production, nor did O'Neill ever really intend it to, it continues to offer attraction as one of O'Neill's most intriguing and mystifying plays. In *STC* (15:51–76) Frank R. Cunningham writes a substantial study in "*Lazarus Laughed*: A Study in O'Neill's Romanticism." Through the use of frequent quotations from the dialogue and backed by references to a wide variety of critics, Cunningham develops very well his thesis that "it is difficult to imagine in dramatic literature, save Goethe's *Faust II*, such an attempt to create the Transcendental ideal."

Lowell A. Fiet's "O'Neill's Modification of Traditional American Themes in *A Touch of the Poet*" (*ETJ* 27:508–15) goes back to MacKaye's *Hazel Kirke* and Herne's *Shore Acres* to point out that O'Neill is still linked to 19th-century concepts, particularly with regard to the nuclear family, which is shown to be both the protector and defiler of personal integrity. Arthur H. Nethercote discusses a favorite O'Neill theme in "Madness in the Plays of Eugene O'Neill" (MD 18:259–279). He touches very little that is new in pointing out that virtually every O'Neill play in one way or another involves madness. Some of the points are badly stretched by his citing such passages in the dialogue as "Are you crazy?" and "He acts crazy" as examples of O'Neill's treatment of the subject. In another article Nethercote looks at O'Neill's final effort in "O'Neill's *More Stately Mansions*" (*ETJ* 27:161–69), showing how O'Neill's theme of "preoccupation and obsession" involving madness, loneliness, and mysticism is well developed in this last rough-hewn play.

Jordan Y. Miller contributes two items, the first a brief negative review of the television performance of *A Moon for the Misbegotten* in "Murky Moon" (*KanQ* 7:103–05) and the second, "The Other O'Neill," a longer item in *The Twenties*, pp. 455–73, placing O'Neill's stylization and expressionism into the book's "Waste Land" theme. Birk Sproxton, in "Eugene O'Neill, Masks and Demons" (*Sphinx* [Univ. of Saskatchewan] 3:57–62), is an extended review of Louis

Sheaffer's two-volume biography, which is given high praise for its new look toward the understanding of O'Neill the man and artist. Carole and Brian McDonough explore two more of O'Neill's perennial themes in "*Mourning Becomes Electra*: A Study of the Conflict be-between Puritanism and Paganism," (*EngRev* 3:6–19).

c-1. **Dissertations.** Susan R. Brown's "'Mothers' and 'Sons': The Development of Autobiographical Themes in the Plays of Eugene O'Neill" (Conn., 36:4481) treats an almost too-familiar O'Neill subject. In somewhat the same vein, William A. Nash (Utah), in "The Homecoming Motif in Selected Works by Eugene O'Neill" (36:4116), finds that "nobody has dramatized (this motif) more searchingly" than O'Neill. Gerald L. Ratliff (Bowling Green) looks at still another well-known O'Neill theme in "An Examination of the Parabolic Nature of 'Suffering' in Selected Plays of Eugene O'Neill, 1913–1923" (36:1900), restricted to earlier plays and centering on an examination of the dimensions of O'Neill's religious thought in an attempt to better understand his tragic vision. In a much lighter vein Gwendolyn D. Ross (Tulsa) writes on "Comic Elements in the Late Plays of Eugene O'Neill" (36:1511), showing O'Neill's subtle yet discerning sense of humor which exposes the reality of man's condition as comic rather than tragic, using plays from *Ah, Wilderness!* to *Misbegotten*. Paul D. Voelker (Wisc.) partakes in a growing interest in O'Neill's apprenticeship in "The Early Plays of Eugene O'Neill: 1913–1915" (35:5433), a survey of the earliest surviving works as precursors of later themes and techniques.

d. **Other Dramatists.** Four TUSAS volumes this year are pertinent to the drama, two of them important contributions, two less so. Kenneth T. Reed's study, *S. N. Behrman*, is the better of the first two and comes highly recommended. It develops an excellent picture of Behrman's position as an artist in American letters, providing clear perspectives on his prose as well as his drama, with emphasis on the development of his sophisticated drawing-room comedy in the manner of Maugham and Barry. Foster Hirsch's *George Kelly* is not as well written as Reed's volume, but it is a much-needed study of a recently neglected American playwright whose limited successes left some permanent impressions on the American theatre. This is the only substantial study of Kelly with which I am acquainted, and I regret that it contains too much detailed plot review and too little genuine critical insight. Max F. Schulz's *Bruce Jay Friedman* and Joan Brittain's *Laurence Stallings* complete the quartet; the dramatic works of these two are distinctly minor in volume and importance. Then there is the monster 700-page volume by Scott Meredith, *George S. Kaufmann and His Friends* (Garden City, N.Y.: Doubleday, [1974]). Don't be misled by the size. It provides a delightfully fascinating trip through the lives and loves of one of American drama's best writers of original comedy, a highly effective play doctor, and one of the American theatre's most successful directors. There are many illustrations of both Kaufmann and friends. Brendan Gill of *The New Yorker* has edited a collection of note, *States of Grace: Eight Plays by Philip Barry* (New York: Harcourt Brace Jovanovich), with Gill's own introductory biographical essay and a series of 12 leaves of illustrative plates. A welcome edition to any drama library.

"Robert Anderson: Playwright of Middle-Aged Loneliness" by Thomas P. Adler (*BSUF* 16,ii:58–64) sees the theme of loneliness as Anderson's metier ever since *Tea and Sympathy*. David M. Knauf's "Notes on Mystery, Suspense, and Complicity: Lowell's Theatricalization of Melville's *Benito Cereno*" (*ETJ* 27:40–55) is an interesting analysis of Lowell's success in fashioning a dramatic "psychological tale of intrigue" with relative fidelity to the original. F. B. Dedmond, in "Doing Her Own Thing: Carson McCullers' Dramatization of *A Member of the Wedding*" (*SAB* 40,ii:47–52), discusses the novelist/playwright's adaptation of the successful book into the highly successful play. "A Rhetoric of American Popular Drama: The Comedies of Neil Simon" by Helen McMahon (*Players* 51:11–15) consists mostly of a discussion of Simon's critical reception with some comment on the faults of his "buffo comedies," which are not and probably ought to be, according to McMahon, satires. Jerome Klinkowitz briefly looks at a figure more popular in fiction than on stage in "The Dramatizations of Kurt Vonnegut, Jr." (*Players* 50:62–64), centering, of course, on *Happy Birthday, Wanda June*. Martin Blank takes *Hello, Dolly*'s forbear and offers a good explanation of its original failure in "When Farce Isn't Funny: The Original Production of *The Merchant of Yonkers*" (*Players* 50:90–93), citing inept production, miscasting, and other assorted disasters. In volume 8 of *ALR* the list of dissertations on American literary figures includes Glaspell, Fitch, Boker, Gale, and Herne.

***d-1.* Dissertations.** Two studies of Paul Green are pursued by Lois J. Faucette (Howard) in "Paul Green and the American Drama" (36: 4486–87) and Fred A. Eady (Mich. State) in "Paul Green: Folk Dramatist, Social Critic" (36:32–33). The first considers Green's philosophy and concept of the American dream and American democracy; the second concentrates on the extent and significance of the playwright's concern for the plight of the American black. Frank J. Rinaldi (Univ. of Mass.), in "Philip Barry: The Matter of Marriage" (36:3718), finds that this dramatist must be regarded as the most eminent American writer of comedy during his lifetime. Joseph M. Epolito (Ohio State) investigates an important secondary dramatist in "A Study of Character in Selected Plays of William Inge" (35: 7437) and finds Inge to be an excellent writer with consistency of character in Aristotelian terms.

Suzanne F. Norton (Wisc.—Madison) returns to the early century in "William Vaughn Moody: Conflict and Character in the New World" (35:6850). She contends that Moody's dramatic vision formed the basis of the theatre of O'Neill. "Clifford Odets: Playwright-Poet" (36:1499) by Harold Cantor (SUNY—Binghamton) attempts to eliminate Odets as an agit-prop writer by defining him as an Emersonian neoromantic. Susan H. Dietz (Penn.), in "The Work of Ronald Ribman: The Poet as Playwright" (35:5396), discusses this contemporary writer of legitimate and television drama. Richard C. Graves (Denver) offers an important survey that probably could become a useful publication in "The Critical Response to the Produced Full-length Plays of Elmer Rice" (36:4115). The "regional" writer, generally regarded as a mere dilettante in the theatre, receives serious study in, appropriately enough, an Indiana dissertation, "Booth Tarkington: A Man of the Theatre" (35:6851–52) by John E. Torrents.

iv. Black Drama and Theatre

In the past items pertaining to minstrelsy, black or blackface, have been included in sections dealing with early American drama. However, the whole area of the minstrelsy and its Afro-American stereotypes is frequently the subject of discussion in articles primarily devoted to contemporary black drama and theatre as well as in those found in important black journals. This section, therefore, includes all references to black and blackface theatre and drama under this common heading. (See also pp. 437–38.)

Robert C. Toll's book, *Blacking Up: The Minstrel Show in 19th Century America* (New York: Oxford Univ. Press, [1974]), is one of the best on the subject I have recently encountered, a truly scholarly work. The emergence of the minstrel show as an outgrowth of demand for a "common man's culture," its romantic image, the consistent portrayal of the black as inferior and subordinate, and the ultimate late-century appearance of blacks themselves in the minstrelsy are all discussed. This is not only interesting to read but a handy reference as well.

The entire issue of *Black World* of April 1975 is devoted to black theatre. The two lead articles deal with the important black director, Woodie King, Jr., who has been responsible for the introduction to New York of such luminaries as Ed Bullins and Lonne Elder. Peter Bailey, in "Woodie King, Jr.: Renaissance Man of Black Theater" (24:4–10), outlines King's accomplishments as an actor (*The Great White Hope*) and head man in the New Federal Theatre in the Henry Street Settlement House. "Stage, Screen, and Black Hegemony: Interview with Woodie King" (24:12–17) by Hoyt W. Fuller presents King's conclusion that there is not much of a future for commercial black theatre in New York as long as blacks continue to play before white audiences. The first black writer to have had significant production in this country is the subject of "Willis Richardson: Pioneer Playwright" (24:41–48) by Barnard L. Peterson, Jr. Larry Thompson, in "Stereotypes, 1760–1930: The Black Image in Early American Drama" (24:54–69), chooses five basic images of the black—lazy Sambo, devoted slave, lustful beast, carefree child, tragic mulatto—from earliest times through the minstrel shows to the present. Thompson attributes the image of Flip Wilson, along with the Amos and Andy syndrome, to the popularity of the minstrelsy. Thomas D. Pawley, in "Dunbar as Playwright" (24:70–79), discusses Paul Laurence Dunbar, known mostly for nondramatic works, as a playwright of limited reputation. Also contained in this special *Black World* issue is the "Annual Round-Up of Black Theatre in America" (24:18–38), containing a rundown of productions in New York, Chicago, and Washington.

Floyd Gaffney investigates the importance of a leading black writer in "Black Theatre: The Moral Function of Imamu Amiri Baraka" in *Players* (50:123–131). He finds that no other black artist has done more "to articulate the relationship between art and politics." John L. Tedesco, in "*Blues for Mister Charlie*: The Rhetorical Dimension" (*Players* 50:20–23), sees the play as one of suasion, with its rhetorical aspect basically "agitational," and deserving of much more serious attention than it has yet received. In "Lorraine Hansberry as Ironist: A Reappraisal of *A Raisin in the Sun*" by Lloyd W. Brown (*JBlS* 4:237–47), three separate critics of Hansberry, who view her in three distinctly different manners—Duprez, Bigsby, and Miller—are taken to task, with Brown presenting a very good case indeed for the playwright as a controversial writer in the tradition of Baldwin, Ellison, and Jones (Baraka).

The black in the theatre and the position of the minstrelsy are treated in three pertinent articles. Randolph Edmonds covers the entire field in "The Negro in the American Theatre, 1700–1969," a two-part article in *PanA* 7:13–28 and 297–322. This long discussion is mainly concerned with significant plays about the Negro by whites and covers some of the same ground explored by Thompson, above, using plays from *Othello* to *The Hot Mikado* and others to make the point. More on the black image is contained in "Harlequin Jim Crow: Continuity and Convergence in Blackface Clowning" (*JPC* 9:682–701) by George F. Rehin, who finds that the narrow focus of scholarly examination into the subject gives a distorted picture so that the cultural importance of the blackface theatre must be restudied. The possible connection between the *zanni* characters of the *commedia dell'arte* such as Harlequin and certain black stereotypes may be tenuous, but Rehin argues well. Minstrelsy as an important element in the American experience is the subject of "Blackface Minstrelsy and Jacksonian Ideology" by Alexander Saxton (*AQ* 27:3–28). Saxton notes that the rise of this most popular of entertainments also coincided with the rise of mass political parties and mass circulation newspapers in this country, as well as with Jacksonian aspects of suppression such as the Indian removal, and the establishment of white supremacy philosophies.

An item of great usefulness is Helene Keyssar-Franke's "Afro-American Drama and Its Criticism, 1960–1972: An Annotated Check List with Appendices" (*BNYPL* 78:276–346). This is a detailed listing of 1,350 entries including anthologies containing black plays, general histories and criticism, books, theses, essays and articles of all kinds on Afro-American writers and their plays.

a. **Dissertations.** "The Black Theatre Movement" (36:34) by Gerald T. Goodman (Penn.) examines the movement up to 1939. Biodun Jeyifous (NYU), in "Theatre and Drama and the Black Physical and Cultural Presence in America: Essays in Interpretation" (36:1905), discusses minstrelsy and its denigration of blacks, 19th-century stereotypes, and black artists in the early decades of this century. Helene Keyssar-Franke (Iowa) in "Strategies in Black Drama" (35:7909–10) investigates plays such as *Raisin* and *Dutchman* among others, concluding that much more needs to be done in the study of reactions to black plays by a variety of audiences. Henry C. Lacey (SUNY–Binghamton), in "A Study of the Poetry, Drama, and Fiction of Imamu Amiri Baraka" (36:1505), considers three phases of the playwright from "schwartz Bohemian" through rebel to committed black writer. Carole W. Singleton (Maryland), in "Black Theatre as Cultural Communication: An Educative Process" (36:3217–18), treats the impact of black theatre in American culture in three eras, 1920–40, 1954–64, and 1965–70.

v. The Experimental-Innovative-Radical Theatre

Although most of the emphasis of the following items is on theatricality rather than the literary and dramatic, so much serious study is currently being devoted to the wide variety of experimental and radical theatre movements that they cannot be entirely ignored, particularly in view of the fact that several of the most active and well-known groups continue to offer original interpretations of classic and other "conventional" plays. Notations will be kept very brief.

Lunatics, Lovers, and Poets: The Contemporary Experimental Theatre by Margaret Croyden (New York: McGraw-Hill, [1974]) is a general exploration of the whole field. *The Drama of Social Reality* by Stanford Lyman and Marvin B. Scott (New York: Oxford Univ. Press) looks into the whole concept of life as drama—"reality is drama, life is theatre, and the social world inherently dramatic." *The Radical Theatre Notebook* by Arthur Sainer (New York: Avon) discusses Street Theatre, Open Theatre, Participatory Theatre, and ensembles such as Bread and Puppet Theatre and The Performance Group. Jay Williams's *Stage Left* (New York: Scribners, [1974]) calls attention to the lack of serious consideration heretofore given the theatre of the left, which he feels had considerable influence on the big-name writers to come.

Three issues of TDR are devoted to the whole general area of experimental-innovative theatre. The June 1975 issue bears the title "Political Theatre." Of pertinence here: Carlos Morton's "Sugar-coated Socialism" (19:61–68), treating the Off Center Theatre (off Lincoln Center, that is) and its free street shows; Paul R. Ryan's "The Performance Group in Brecht's *Mother Courage*" (19:79–93), including a description and photographs of the February 1975 production at the Performing Garage; Mel Gordon's "San Francisco Mime Troupe's 'The Mother'" (19:94–101); and Michael Kirby's "On Political Theatre" (19:129–134), a general discussion of political theatre from the Greeks to Joseph Papp. The September 1975 issue, entitled "Expressionism" does not treat the expressionistic movement of the 1920s and 1930s but relates entirely to contemporary theatre. This is particularly interesting, I think, because "expressionism" as a stylistic term in the theatre relative to present-day productions is not often used, being generally relegated to the historical Expressionism of World War I and the Depression years. Included in this issue are the full script of "Turning the Earth," a short play by Julian Beck and Judith Malina (19:94–105); "The Iowa Theater Lab's *Moby Dick*" by Harris Levy (19:63–67) containing the scenario and highly subjective description of the writer's feelings; and a large section on the University of Michigan Invitational Festival of Experimental Theatre in May 1975 (19:68–93). The final item, "Theatre Report" by Arnold Aronson (19:106–10), discusses Robert Wilson's and Christopher Knowles's "The $ Value of Man," complete with diagrams and illustrations. The December 1975 issue is "New Performance and Manifestos." Mostly about writers and performers other than American, it does include two items for notice here: *Sakonnet Point*, by Arnold Aronson (19:27–35), concerning the Performance Group production of the Gray-LeCompte work in June 1975; and "Third Manifesto" by Richard Foreman (19:71–81), a free verse, not always comprehensible expression of concern for the special kind of understanding needed for the theatrical experience.

a. **Dissertations.** After reading the various manifestos of Richard Foreman one should probably study Florence A. Falk's "The Aperspective Theatre of Richard Foreman" (Rutgers, 36:2489), which discusses this operator of the "Ontological-Hysteric Theatre Co." who wrote 30 plays since 1968, 16 of which have been produced. Other dissertations, fairly self-explanatory in their titles, are "A Critical Study of the Origins and Characteristics of Documentary Theatre of Dissent in the United States" (36:1173) by Paul D. Lion (USC), "Social Reform and the American Theater: 1880–1920" (35:6036–37) by Thomas E. Dennery (Mich. State), and "Melodrama, 1870–1904: The Dramatic Reflection of Social Development in America" (36: 3664–65) by Carol O. Sweedler (Calif.–San Diego).

vi. Miscellaneous

Of considerable interest to scholars of American literature, certainly including the drama, is the large two-volume *Stark Young: A Life in the Arts—Letters, 1900–1962*, ed. John Pilkington (Baton Rouge: La. State Univ. Press). John Elsom's *Erotic Theatre* (New York: Taplinger, [1974]) doesn't do too much with straight drama, but reflects attitudes of two periods, 1890–1910 and 1950–72, in a discussion of pornography and eroticism from *A Doll's House* to *Oh, Calcutta!* Routledge and Keegan Paul of Boston published two books in 1975 with more than passing relevance to American drama. In *Families Under Stress: A Psychological Interpretation* by Tony Manocchio and William Petitt and *The Psychology of Tragic Drama* by Patrick Roberts, Miller and, of course, O'Neill receive rather extended discussion. The first volume, from the Centre for Therapeutic Communications, London, discusses "conjoint family therapy" using *Salesman* and *Long Day's Journey* as American examples. The second devotes a full chapter to *Mourning Becomes Electra.* O'Neill also gains emphasis in "All Irish Here: The 'Irishman' in Modern Drama" (*DR* 54:94–102). Roger E. Stoddard attempts to collect, locate, collate, and describe all the dramatic imprints of an early 19th-century publisher in "A Catalogue of the Dramatic Imprints of David and Thomas Longworth, 1802–1921" (*PAAS* 84:317–406) listing 429 editions of 347 plays.

University of Rhode Island

19. Black Literature

Charles Nilon

Black and white critics who write about black literature continue to be concerned about the images of black persons in literature and in the media. Many of the critics are engaged in making evaluations and reevaluations of writers and works whose value and quality have been questioned. A good deal of stress is being placed on giving an author or a work an adequate reading. Several critics try to determine what black experience is and how it is used by the black writer. Often these critics discuss the Black Aesthetic or the use of black music and black folklore in the work of black authors. The articles that appear in journals this year indicate a strong interest in the critical process, in literary history, and in sources. The largest number of essays are about fiction and fiction writers. Fewer books were published on black literature than were published in 1974.

Although they are not listed here, more than 50 dissertations on topics in Afro-American literature were accepted by American universities during the year.

i. General Bibliography

James de T. Abajian's bibliography, *Blacks and Their Contribution to the American West: a Bibliography and a Union List of Library Holdings through 1970* (Boston: G. K. Hall [1974]), is an excellent tool for scholars who are interested in the black experience in the West, and of some value to the scholar who is interested in black literature. Leonard Pack Bailey's illustrated biographical directory, *Broadside Authors and Artists* (Detroit: Broadside Press, [1974]), is not only a good reference tool but an introduction to the excellent achievement of publisher-poet Dudley Randall. The two-volume *Black American Writers Past and Present: A Biographical and Bibliographical Dictionary* (Metuchen, N.J.: Scarecrow) by Theresa

Gunnels Rush, Carol Fairbanks Meyers, and Esther Spring Arata is particularly useful for identifying young, not-well-known writers and contains, in addition to lists of publications, brief biographies. Newbold Miles Puckett's collection of names, *Black Names in America: Origin and Usage*, ed. Murray Heller (Boston: G. K. Hall), is a contribution to onomastics, has a good bibliography, and points out interestingly that some of the names that may have been thought to be Anglo-Saxon are African. "The 54th Massachusetts Volunteer Black Infantry as a Subject for American Artists" by Chadwick Hansen (*MR* 16:745–59) contains a list of the poems and other literary results of the attention given to that regiment. Reference is made in the essay to Paul Laurence Dunbar's Robert Gould Shaw poem and to Booker T. Washington's memorial address. Boris Gilenson's "Afro-American Literature in the Soviet Union" (*NALF* 9:25, 28–29) is a short bibliographical essay. "Forgotten Pages: Black Literary Magazines in the 1920s" (*JAmS* 8:363–82) is a description of five black journals that were published during the twenties: *Stylus, Fire, Harlem, Black Opus*, and *Saturday Evening Quill.* George Kent's "Notes on the 1974 Black Literary Scene" (*Phylon* 36:182–203) is a short bibliographical and critical essay on books by and about black persons. Geraldine Matthews's *Black American Writers, 1773–1949* (Boston: G. K. Hall) is a classified guide to the work of more than 1,600 authors of books. Its basic purpose is to identify black writers in various fields. Matthews was aided in completing this work by the African-American Materials Project staff at North Carolina Central University. Carole A. Parks's "An Annotated Directory: The Black Book Publishers" (*BlackW* 24,v:72–79) contains a brief critical survey of the black publishing industry and an annotated list of 21 publishers.

In that same issue of *Black World* there is an exchange between novelist John A. Williams and Dudley Randall of the Broadside Press. Williams is critical of black publishers in "Black Publisher, Black Writer: An Impasse" (*BlackW* 24,v:28–31). Dudley Randall responds to the charges in "Black Publisher, Black Writer: An Answer" (*BlackW* 24,v:32–37).

ii. Fiction

***a.* Dunbar, Chesnutt, Johnson.** Critics are looking very carefully at these early black novelists in an effort to determine their merit. It is generally agreed that Paul Laurence Dunbar is a good poet and that his poetry is better than his fiction. "Literature as Catharsis: The Novels of Paul Laurence Dunbar" by Addison Gayle, Jr., "The Masking of the Novelist" by Kenny J. Williams, "The Lyrical Short Fiction of Dunbar and Chesnutt" by Bert Bender, three essays in the volume of essays, *A Singer in the Dawn*, ed. Jay Martin (New York: Dodd, Mead), present a careful survey and judgment of Dunbar's fiction. Gayle believes that Dunbar's "predecessors, who had wavered between formulating a theory of literature which would redefine the old definitions and one which would serve as an instrument to assault the conscience of white men, had failed him." They had not, he says, constructed new images and symbols, and Dunbar, because they "failed to till the ground" for him, was forced to deal with the images and stereotypes of black people "laid down in the literature of Southern and Northern propagandists." Kenny Williams looks at Dunbar after having called her reader's attention to the work of the black novelists who wrote before him (William Wells Brown, Frank Webb, Martin Delany, James H. Howard, Frances E. W. Harper, Walter Stowers, and J. McHenry Jones) and to certain white novelists (among whom were Francis Marion Crawford, Archibald Clavering, S. Weir Mitchell, and Winston Churchill) who were writing at the time that James wrote, compares Dunbar's general purposes with those of Charles W. Chesnutt and Sutton E. Griggs, and points out that "in a period when the Negro novelist overtly concerned himself with race and by virtue of this wrote a protest fiction . . . Dunbar veiled what he had to say." Williams argues that Dunbar fulfilled his own theory of literary art and at the same time gave voice to those concerns, including racial concerns, that troubled him. He "looked upon race," she says, "not as the controlling force of his artistic life but only as an incidental fact." Williams thinks that Dunbar and his black contemporaries were victimized by literary hostility, stereotypes, and racial propagandists. Perhaps her strongest assertion and show of positive respect for Dunbar are her recognition of his "growing awareness and use of racial subjects" and the fact that he at no point substituted "his pride and dignity for the mess of pottage which was to be his reward for critical acclaim." Both Williams and Bender find Dunbar, given his circumstances and in a general sense, a more effective writer than Gayle does. Writing about his short fiction, Bender argues that in his best fiction Dunbar approaches his material with a lyrical attitude, as Sarah Orne Jewett does, and that he published stories—"The Ingrate," "The Lynching of Jube Benson," "The Scapegoat," "Jamsella," and others—which were "directly expressive of the emotional discontent in black America" and that these stories are informed by Dunbar's "dream of freedom and equality for his people." In *Down Home* (New York: G. P. Putnam), a history of Afro-American short fiction, Robert Bone says some of the same things about Dunbar that Gayle does—that he was in the plantation tradition, etc.—but in spite of Dunbar's limitations, he believes, "Dunbar played an important role in the evolution of the Afro-American short story" and that "he established a pastoral tradition that would come to fruition in the era of the Harlem Renaissance." He sees Dunbar as the founder of a populist, antiintellectual tradition which runs from Langston Hughes to the revolutionary writers of the Black Power movement.

Charles Waddell Chesnutt, whose short fiction is compared with Dunbar's in Burt Bender's essay, is written about in six essays. In tone and generally in purpose, each of these essays is an attempt at evaluation or reconsideration, an effort to determine value and to provide an accurate record. Three of the essays are examinations of Chesnutt's use of folk materials in the development of his fiction. Charles L. Andrews, in "The Significance of Charles Waddell Chesnutt's Conjure Stories" (*SLJ* 7,i:78–99), finds that Chesnutt maintains a balance between the demands of popular, local-color realism and the obligation of the artist to reveal truth to nature. Melvin Dixon, writing about "The Teller as Folk Trickster in Chesnutt's 'The Conjure Woman'" (CLAJ 18[1974]:186–97), identifies the narrator as a folk trickster who is doing what the tricksters do in the tales that he tells in order to gain the ends that he had set for himself. "Gothic Sociology: Charles Chesnutt in the Gothic Mode" (*SLitI* 7:101–19) is an essay in which Robert Hemenway examines the conjure stories and shows that they are Gothic in their detail—that they are filled with tales of magic, ghosts, and much of the lore of the occult. Because of Chesnutt's purpose and use of these details, Hemenway says that the conjure stories are not part of the Gothic tradition.

William L. Andrews's "A Reconsideration of Charles W. Chesnutt: A Pioneer of the Colorline" (*CLAJ* 19:136–51) is an attempt to judge the effect of the editing out of certain essential sentences and paragraphs from letters and other documents in Helen Chesnutt's biography of her father. The essay attempts to reveal as much of Chesnutt as a man as is possible and shows that the portrait in the biography is less exact than it might be because of things of significance that are edited out of the documents that are in the text. Robert Hemenway's "'Baxter's Procrustes': Irony and Protest" (*CLAJ* 18[1974]:172–85), in another effort to look at Chesnutt as a man, provides a careful analysis of a story that uses irony to show Chesnutt's response to being refused membership in the Cleveland Book Club. The analysis of the story enlarges the details of Chesnutt's response to being refused membership in the prestigious club and provides an analysis of a story that illustrates perfectly Chesnutt's effective use of irony.

Joel Faxel studies some of the Chesnutt stories that are analyzed by Andrews and Hemenway in "Charles Waddell Chesnutt's Sambo: Myth and Reality" (*NALF* 9:105–08). Faxel shows that Chesnutt uses Sambo characteristics, exploits a stereotype, in order to show how his characters survive. He concludes that Chesnutt's use of the Sambo myth does not support Stanley Elkin's thesis. This essay is further support of Burt Bender's observation that Chesnutt combines irony and protest in his short fiction. "The Evolution of Charles Chesnutt's *The House Behind the Cedars*" by Robert P. Sedlock (*CLAJ* 19:125–35) traces the development of one of Chesnutt's best novels from its beginning as a fairly awkward short story to its present form —a ten-year task in which Chesnutt's control of content and structure mature considerably. (See also 19th-Century Literature, vi., William Dean Howells and Genteel Realism.)

Saunders Redding's "James Weldon Johnson and the Pastoral Tradition" (*MissQ* 28:417–21) is not primarily a study of Johnson's *The Autobiography of an Ex-Coloured Man*, but a section of this novel; the section which describes the narrator's return to the South after his mother's death and his life there for several years is identified as an example of the pastoral. Redding thinks that Johnson, in that section of his novel, satisfies Empson's definition in *Some Versions of the Pastoral*. Most of this essay is devoted to a discussion of Johnson's poetry, and some of it is devoted to his critical opinions. Stephen M. Ross's "Audience and Irony in Johnson's *The Autobiography of an Ex-Coloured Man*" (*CLAJ* 18[1974]:198–210) is a treatment of Johnson's use of irony and the purpose of that use. The novel, Ross says, was written, in a sense, for a white audience and it was necessary for Johnson to find a way to say what this novel says to that audience. The result of this effort, Ross claims, is that the novel is more artfully created than a mere sociological survey of Negro life. "The *Autobiography* solves the problem of audience, in a sense, by turning the tables on literary convention; by employing stereotyped portrayals of the white world Johnson elicits the otherwise unwilling sympathy of his white reader by creating his protagonist's story out of conventional fictional situations; then, through careful irony, he demonstrates that the psychological impulses and moral values underlying those conventions are themselves the cause of the hero's tragedy."

***b.* Harlem Renaissance Writers: Toomer, Larson, Fauset, Hurston, McKay, and Schuyler.** The writers of fiction in this group wrote during the years of the Harlem Renaissance, but most of the criticism of their work that is mentioned here does not contribute in a general sense to an understanding of that period and its significance. Most of this criticism is of particular works, some of which were written after the years of the Harlem Renaissance. Because George Schuyler's novel *Black No More* is a satire on the writers and events of the period, Michael Peplow's essay may contribute to an understanding of the period. George Kent points out in his essay that Claude McKay's *Banana Bottom* is not a genuine Harlem Renaissance novel.

Jean Toomer and his novel *Cane* are attracting a good deal of attention from a variety of critics. The novel is looked at often as a novel; sometimes it is looked at for the purpose of understanding Toomer's life. Charles Davis's essay, "Jean Toomer and the South: Region and Race within a Literary Imagination (*SLitI* 7:23–37), argues that the South that Toomer made reversed DuBois's conviction that the South oppressed black people, that Booker T. Washington's prediction about economic progress was false, and that the Talented Tenth must provide an improved life for black people. Toomer's reversal was not, Davis says, achieved through the use of facts, but through Toomer's emotional response. It was "a young man's impression of the black heritage he had returned to discover" in the South. Davis claims that Toomer's southern exposure produced a wholly new way of looking at southern life, "one that is clearly related to the position of the Nashville Fugitives . . . ," but that, because it was black, was different from it. Following this assertion, given the continuing lack of agreement about the structure of *Cane*, Davis's contribution in this article is his discussion of the novel's structure. He regards the poem "Song of Son" as a preface to *Cane* and says that it "presents the consciousness that stands behind the varied verbal structures in *Cane*" and that "preoccupation with the problems of consciousness" is responsible for the design of *Cane*. Two other essays that deal with the structure of *Cane* are Michael Krasny's "The Aesthetic Structure of Jean Toomer's *Cane*" (*NALF* 9:42–43) and Bernard W. Bell's "Jean Toomer's *Cane*" (*BlackW* 23,ix:4–19, 92–97). Krasny thinks that *Cane* moves from the simple forms of life in the South to the more complex forms in the North and back to the South. Bernard Bell says that when analyzed as a poetic novel the disparate elements and illusive meanings of the book "coalesce into an integral whole." In " 'Spirit-Torsos of Exquisite Strength': The Theme of Individual Weakness vs. Collective Strength in Two of Toomer's Poems" (*CLAJ* 19:261–67), Udo Jung argues that people in *Cane* are unable to come together. Jung says that the two poems, "Cotton Song" and "Prayer," which are part of the text of *Cane*, achieve the end of bringing characters together.

Toomer's identifying or not identifying himself as a black person has presented problems of interest to a good number of his critics. Charles Scruggs offers some evidence that dates the beginning of a period in Toomer's life during which he did not consider himself a black person. In "Jean Toomer: Fugitive" (*AL* 47:84–96) Scruggs states, "I agree that there was in fact neither a sudden apostasy in 1923 nor a significant change in outlook thereafter. Whatever happened to Jean Toomer happened in two or three years before March of that year. Specifically he developed a self-image which precluded the possibility of defining himself as a Negro or Negro writer." Scruggs says that the two critical events in this development were Toomer's reading of Romain Rolland's *Jean-Christophe* (1903–12) and his encounter with Waldo Frank. The essay includes some discussion of familiar episodes from Cane: "Mr. Costyve Duditch" (a story by Toomer published in *The Dial*, 1928); an unpublished Toomer play, "Natalie Man"; and the unpublished novel *Caromb*. Scruggs suggests that *Jean-Christophe* becomes a kind of artistic model for Toomer and that Frank's *insistence* (my word, and perhaps too strong) that he be a black writer led him to choose not to identify himself as a black writer.

Mark Helbing's article "Sherwood Anderson and Jean Toomer" (*NALF* 9:35–39) contains evidence of some importance on the question of Toomer's attitude on racial identification and on his relationship with Anderson. Anderson insisted that Toomer should be known as a black person. This article includes paragraphs from letters by Anderson and Toomer and references to Alain Locke and Jessie Fauset. In addition, it offers a brief statement about Anderson's attitude toward black people. John M. Reilly's "Jean Toomer: An Annotated Checklist of Criticism" (*RALS* 4:27–56) lists Toomer criticism written from 1923 to 1973.

Jessie Fauset and Nella Larson gave a good deal of attention in their novels to the subject of miscegenation and to persons with black blood who passed as white. Mary Mabel Youman studies Nella Larson's treatment of these subjects in "Nella Larson's *Passing*: A Study in Irony" (*CLAJ* 18[1974]:235–41). Generally she believes that this novel is inferior to Larson's *Quicksand*. Its values are in the author's perception of her subject. It shows that black persons can and do lose the spiritual values of blackness, although they remain in the black world. The protagonist, Irene, although she does not pass into the white community, as she could, has more truly lost her heritage than Clare, who moves into the white world, marries, and lives as a white person. The consequences of Irene's loss are tragic.

In his essay "Greek Patterns in a Black Novel: Jessie Fauset's *The China Berry Tree*" (*CLAJ* 18[1974]:211–15), Joseph T. Feeney, S.J., says that the use of Greek patterns adds a dimension of universality and bloodless horror to a story of love and domestic life among middle-class black persons.

S. Jay Walker's "Zora Neale Hurston's *Their Eyes Were Watching God*: Black Novel of Sexism" (*MFS* 20:519–27) begins with the idea that black, women's, and gay liberation each demand a definition of self, an ending of oppression, and an acceptance of the group's own goals regarding itself. In his discussion of Hurston's novel Walker shows that Janie achieves each of these and that the novel deals more with sexism than with racism. He thinks that Hurston shows an awareness of the stifling effects of sexism and indicates why the feminist movement has failed to grasp the imagination of the black woman. Through a presentation of Janie Wood's three marriages, two of which bring her wealth and safety, Hurston explores the class implications of women's liberation. Ann L. Rayson looks in a general way at all four of Hurston's novels in "The Novels of Zora Neale Hurston" (*SBL* 5,iii[1974]:1–9): *Jonah's Gourd Vine* (1934), *Their Eyes Were Watching God* (1937), *Moses: Man of the Mountain* (1939), and *Seraph on the Suwanee* (1948). Despite their surface differences, Rayson finds that the four novels, in their structure, exhibit a similar pattern. The characters, men or women, speak a southern folk idiom, espouse a transcendent philosophy of harmony with their own sexual roles and cosmoses, and demonstrate that the individual must go beyond bourgeois life to a comprehension of what is ultimately meaningful. In each of Miss Hurston's plots a protagonist finds the way to understanding and love. Rayson agrees that *Their Eyes Were Watching God* is the best of the four novels.

Two essays make appraisals of Claude McKay's fiction: George E. Kent, in "Claude McKay's *Banana Bottom* Reappraised" (*CLAJ* 18[1974]:222–34), an excellent discussion of the novel, distinguishes it from the genuine Harlem Renaissance novels. He concludes that the book is not a searching analysis of the problem of identity and that it does not resolve (as some critics say it does) the identity problems that are raised in McKay's earlier novels. Part of his questioning the novel's success grows from the way in which Bita is portrayed. Helen Pyne-Timothy discusses McKay's women in "Perceptions of the Black Woman in the Works of Claude McKay" (*CLAJ* 19:152–64). She says the black woman is her best self when she demonstrates near-perfect understanding of her environment and recognizes that her personality may fully flower if she both develops her intellectual capacities and achieves physical union with the black man. She must provide psychological help and other support for him when he needs these.

George Schuyler is a Harlem Renaissance writer who perhaps has not received as much attention as he should have. Michael W. Peplow, in "George Schuyler, Satirist: Rhetorical Devices in *Black No More*" (*CLAJ* 18[1974]:242–57), claims that Schuyler has been misunderstood because critics have misunderstood the purpose of satire and the rhetorical devices used by satirists. Peplow shows the historical relation of Schuyler's novel to the Harlem Renaissance by a careful presentation of its themes, analysis of its plot, and identification of persons and ideas that are the materials of Schuyler's satire. Schuyler wrote near the end of the Harlem Renaissance and, because he was able to observe the movement largely retrospectively, seems to have been struck by certain basic inconsistencies in it.

***c.* Baldwin, Ellison, Wright.** It is probably true that James Baldwin, Ralph Ellison, and Richard Wright have received more critical attention during and since the 1950s than other black writers, and it is generally admitted that they are among the significant American authors. The criticism given them this year and during the past several years supports this idea. Critics, it appears, still are trying to determine precisely how to value them—how to talk about them appropriately. More white critics are reading them. Some qualities of these authors that were viewed as artistic limitations in the past appear to some critics now not to be limitations.

Shirley S. Allen compares Ellison and Wright briefly with Baldwin in "Religious Symbolism and Psychic Reality in Baldwin's *Go Tell It on the Mountain*" (*CLAJ* 19:173–99). She says that the major conflict in this novel, unlike that in *Invisible Man* and *Native Son*, is not black against white, but the more universal problem of youth achieving maturity, and that Baldwin's novel has a literary parallel in Dickens's *David Copperfield* and *Great Expectations*. Although a reader may compare this novel with the Dickens novels profitably, the central action of the novel, which Allen probably identifies correctly, is determined by the conflict between black and white. John's movement from dependence to a sense of self includes, I think, the acceptance of his blackness. The need to accept it and the manner in which he realizes this need and accepts is determined by the conflict between black and white.

Alvin Starr's reading of Richard Wright, in "The Concept of Fear in the Works of Stephen Crane and Richard Wright" (*SBL* 6,ii:6–10), is informative in the parallels that it brings to the reader's attention. Starr says that the depiction of paranoiac fear in *Native Son* is similar to Crane's depiction of it. He notices metaphysical qualities in the fear depicted by both authors and presents an effective comparison of the use of fear in Crane's "The Blue Hotel" and Wright's "Big Black Good Man." The comparisons that are made in this essay, however, do not justify Starr's claim that "this similar use of fear by both authors certainly suggests some influence, whether conscious or unconscious, of Crane on Wright." A psychological study of the novel, "The Role of Paranoia in Richard Wright's *Native Son*" (*KanQ* 7:111–24) by H. Philip Bolton, suggests that Bigger's fear is classical paranoia and identifies in Bigger the delusions of grandeur that are characteristic of the paranoid person. Bolton identifies this in Bigger's fantasy play with his friends. He says that Bigger is never catatonic as in the Freudian model of the disease, "but his behavior and perceptions have the logic of the disease."

Bigger's fear contributes to the horror that is produced in the novel. Phyllis R. Klotman, in "Moral Distancing as a Rhetorical Technique in *Native Son*: A Note on Fate" (*CLAJ* 18[1974]:284–91), argues that the third section of the novel provides relief from the horror of the first two parts. This section, in which Boris Max is the spokesman, is an example of what Wayne Booth, in *The Rhetoric of Fiction*, calls moral distancing. Klotman discusses the function of the device and suggests that, by reducing the close proximity to Bigger's life and act, Wright is able to make a more successful shift of the burden of Bigger's guilt to society.

A survey of the criticism of the third section of *Native Son* and a discussion of that portion of the novel is given in Paul N. Siegel's "The Conclusion of Richard Wright's *Native Son*" (*PMLA* 89[1974]:517–22). Siegel charges that Howe, Kazin, Bone, McCall, Margolies, and Brignano (I believe no black critics are mentioned in this group) are some of the critics who make the error of responding to Max's speech with a conditioned reflex. He argues that the conclusion of *Native Son* has caused many critics to go astray—that these straying critics read into the conclusion "their own preconceptions instead of perceiving the author's purpose." Max's long speech in the courtroom and his final scene with Bigger, he says, are often misunderstood. Siegel offers evidence that Max, who is not a Communist, does not offer a party-line defense of Bigger. He further indicates that with reasoned choice, Max places the case in the hands of a judge and rejects a trial by an all-white jury. Siegel argues convincingly that Max does understand Bigger.

His arguments, however, are questioned in a letter to the *PMLA* editor (90:122–23) by David G. Lank. Lank suggests that Siegel's argument for Max is novel and that it glosses over several important points. Lank uses the position of Donald Gibson (*AQ* 21:729) and Wright's disenchantment with Communist literary dogma (as Wright describes this disenchantment in *The God that Failed*) as part of the support for his objection to Siegel's analysis. In his response to Lank (*PMLA* 90:294–95) Siegel contends that Lank does not take issue with his two main points. Klotman's essay does not resolve this argument; it does, however, suggest that this section of the novel may be less flawed rhetorically than it is sometimes said to be.

Mary Ellen Doyle's "The Alienated Protagonist of Ralph Ellison's Short Fiction" (*CLAJ* 19:165–72) gives an example of Ellison's claim that folklore preserves and projects the Negro's wisdom, his sustaining values, and his effort to humanize the world. Doyle concludes, "It makes sense then that [Wright's] protagonists find human connection with the world primarily and inevitably through the folk." Isaac Sequeira's "The Uncompleted Initiation of the Invisible Man" (*SBL* 6,i:9–13) traces the quest of the narrator of Ellison's novel, defines its stages as stages in the initiation process, and concludes that his initiation is incomplete at the story's end. Although the article is interesting, it does not add much to the reader's knowledge of the significance of the ritual.

In a note, "Ellison's Invisible West" (*WAL* 10:237–38), a comment on the Westward-Ho interlude near the end of chapter 8 of *Invisible Man*, Martin Bucco says that the novel presents a cinematic vision of western myths and that the novel treats the West as a state of mind.

***d.* Attaway, Motley, Petry, Yerby.** Some of the early criticism of William Attaway's two novels presented them as examples of proletarian literature. In his essay "From Pastoralism to Industrial Antipathy in William Attaway's *Blood on the Forge*" (*Phylon* 36:422–25), Philip H. Vaughn thinks this novel represents a literary achievement and at the same time the portrayal of the transition of a people from a structured, authoritarian, rural existence to an industrial, urban frontier.

At the beginning of "The Short Fiction of Willard Motley" (*NALF* 9:3–10) James R. Giles and N. Jill Weyant say that their essay is an effort to appraise and perhaps to value more accurately an author whose first novel, *Knock on Any Door* (1948), was a popular success and won some critical acclaim. Motley did not write about the black experience, and his focus was integrationist. Most of his fiction that is discussed in this essay was written during the early years of his career and was never published. The stories are important because they give a fuller and positive view of the author's talent, because they show the development of the central character in *Knock on Any Door,* because some of them do treat the black experience, and because they do show that Motley had a capacity for depicting injustice.

David Madden's analysis, in "Ann Petry: 'The Witness'" (*SBL* 6,iii:24–26), comments on Petry's technical skills and the acuteness of her ideological perception. Through the protagonist of this story, he says, Petry shows that the assimilated black middle class can never put behind them their blackness and the danger of the potential violence of the bright, upper-middle-class white youth. The story ends with the humiliated black protagonist in ignominious flight from the children of the upper-middle-class whites of a small New England town. Thelma J. Shinn's "Women in the Novels of Ann Petry" (*Crit* 16,i:110–20) has provided a survey of the treatment of women in Petry's three novels, *The Street, Country Place,* and *The Narrows.* Shinn's comment on the woman characters is, in most instances, equally applicable to Petry's men. Shinn holds that Petry's characters, black and white, show that the individual with the most integrity is often destroyed, often forced "to become an expression of the very society against which he is rebelling," and that the novels show that the weak, regardless of race, are "misled by illusions and stifled by poverty."

Although they differ in quality, productivity, and aesthetic and social goals, Motley, Petry, and Yerby have been regarded by some black critics, particularly since the sixties, as being not appropriately sensitive to their responsibilities as black authors. Yerby has, until recently, received little serious criticism. Two essays published this year look at his work and his ideas and find in qualified ways social responsibility and a mastery of craft that is commendable. Jack B. Moore, in "The Guilt of the Victim: Racial Themes in Some Frank Yerby Novels" (*JPC* 8:746–56), examines racial attitudes in a select number of Yerby's novels for the purpose of making Yerby's role in the history of black literature better understood. Moore reviews the qualified but generally positive criticism that has been done on Yerby by Darwin Turner and Saunders Redding and calls attention to the several "serious" stories that Yerby wrote before he began writing popular novels. From a study of *Griffen's Way* (1962), *A Woman Called Fancy* (1951), *Speak Now* (1969), and *Fairoaks* (1957),

Moore concludes that Yerby has written constantly about racial horrors in America and their historic beginning in Africa, and that some of his writing suggests the guilt of the victim. Moore thinks that Yerby tells of the danger to blacks of assimilation by the white world and of the corruption of the white world. Margemma Graham discusses questions of this kind with Yerby in "Frank Yerby, King of the Costume Novel" (*Essence* 6,Oct.:70–71, 88–89, 91–92) and finds that Yerby feels that he has done essentially what Moore says he has. Graham feels that Yerby and many black writers from the South have been unable to have the advantage of roots as Faulkner and Eudora Welty, for example, have roots in Mississippi. This she feels affects the work of the black writer. She says that Yerby is a careful researcher and that he has admirable technical skills. Her interview shows Yerby's respect for his audience. Some biographical details are contained in her essay.

***e.* Baraka (Jones), Gaines, Kelley, Reed, Williams.** A considerable group of black writers came to the attention of the public in the 1960s and 1970s or began writing during those years. For some of them, critical estimates are still tentative, but Imamu Baraka (LeRoi Jones), Ernest Gaines, William Melvin Kelley, Ishmael Reed, and John A. Williams, who have received a good deal of critical attention, appear now to have stable literary reputations as novelists of high quality.

Lloyd W. Brown's article, "Jones (Baraka) and His Literary Heritage in *The System of Dante's Hell*" (*Obsidian* 1,i:5–17), argues that LeRoi Jones's achievements as a writer cannot be fully measured in isolation from that western heritage "which is so evident in his allusory structures and which requires rather careful examination at this time because so many of Jones's own statements in his criticism and in his political essays seem to repudiate that heritage in its entirety." Brown observes that Dante, Eliot, and Joyce are used extensively in this novel and that it is the eschatological system of Dante's nine circles that provides Baraka with a symbolic structure for his ethnic themes. The effect of Baraka's identifying Roy with Stephen Dedalus is to link the ethnic development of his protagonist with James Joyce's insights into the growth of the artistic imagination.

W. T. Shannon looks at another side, perhaps the side that is thought to be more typical of Baraka, in "Baraka and the Bourgeois Figure" (*SBL* 6,iv:18–21). This article is an examination of "The

Death of Horatio Alger," what Shannon calls the pivotal story in Baraka's *Tales.* In this story western culture is, in a sense, rejected, and a black man learns that he and his culture are different from mainstream America and evaluates the revolutionary possibilities that are in him and in his culture. Shannon compares Mickey, Baraka's character, with Ellison's invisible man and William Faulkner's Flem Snopes. He says that the way in which the invisible man "climbs back into American responsibility" is little different from the way Flem climbed in Faulkner's trilogy. Mickey does not climb back. In making his analysis Shannon finds that Baraka "participates in and qualifies the analysis that Herbert Marcuse makes in *One-Dimensional Man.*"

The process of becoming a man is part of what is shown in Mickey's development in Baraka's story. Two other articles discuss the quality of manhood as it is portrayed in Ernest Gaines's fiction. The five stories in *Bloodline* are discussed in Walter R. McDonald's "You Not a Bum, You a Man" (*NALF* 9:47–49). McDonald shows that Gaines defines manhood and shows certain of its consequences and responsibilities as they are presented in each story. In "Ambiguous Manhood in Ernest J. Gaines' *Bloodline*" (*CLAJ* 19:200–209, Frank W. Shelton notices the aesthetic virtues of Gaines's work in these stories and points out his large concern with the achieving and maintaining of manhood in his novels. In Gaines's fiction he finds the quest a laudable goal deftly shown, which sometimes results in a loss of heart. Tom Carter's "Ernest Gaines" (*Essence* 6, July:52–53, 71–72) is essentially biographical.

William Melvin Kelley portrays a process of developing manhood in the central character of *A Different Drummer* in "Strategic Withdrawal or Retreat: Deliverance from Racial Oppression in Kelley's *A Different Drummer* and Faulkner's *Go Down, Moses*" (*SBL* 6,iii:1–6). Hugh J. Ingrasci compares Faulkner's Sam Fathers and Kelley's Tucker Caliban, their motives and their ways of achieving liberation and manhood. He points out the significance of Kelley's reiterating in a 1962 interview that "each Negro must realize that his worth as a human being comes from his being unique" and shows that this contrasts sharply with Faulkner's portrayal of Sam. Sam relies upon things outside himself. Tucker does not. In an overall comparison of Faulkner and Kelley, "Paradox as Tribute: William Melvin Kelley's *A Different Drummer* and Faulkner" (*SBL* 5,iii:25–28), Richard Beards points out certain similarities in technique in Faulkner and Kelley. Despite the Faulknerian echoes and resources in Kelley's work, he finds that *A Different Drummer* embodies a vision that is distinctly Kelley's. Beards includes a Kelley checklist at the end of his essay. In her article, "Technique as Evaluation of Subject in *A Different Drummer*" (*CLAJ* 19:221–37), Gladys M. Williams says that there is an integration of romance, realism, and naturalism in the novel's structure. The essay is an explication of the use of its several modes. Williams concerns herself in some detail to show how Tucker Caliban is developed. Jill Weyant, in "The Kelley Saga: Violence in America" (*CLAJ* 19:210–20), discusses *A Different Drummer*, Kelley's three other novels, and his collection of stories—the whole of his saga. She believes that in the saga Kelley attempts to "redefine the complete man and to overturn inaccurate stereotypes." She says that he portrays the white man's loss of the ability to feel, to empathize, to express himself uninhibitedly, and that his unexpressed emotions are released in aggressions. The black characters in the saga are in touch with their emotions and are for this reason nonviolent. She feels that the weakness in the saga is that "the steadfast division of races into two camps tends toward deck-stacking dogma." Again in this essay there is an analysis that is useful in defining the quality of black manhood.

Grace Eckley's "The Awakening of Mr. Afrinnegan: Kelley's *Dunfords Travels Everywheres* and Joyce's *Finnegans Wake*" (*Obsidian* 1:27–41) is a consideration of the novelist's method and technique. Eckley argues that the novel reveals Kelley's extension of the concepts of Joyce's *Finnegans Wake* and his application of them to black culture. She feels that this novel is superior in its control of technique to Kelley's earlier novels and that it clarifies Kelley's position on racial identity. She finds the novel similar to Joyce in setting, language, and use of mythology. "Just as Joyce envisioned Earwicker as a mountain and Anna Plurabelle as river, so Kelley projects his alma mater theme through describing the mother continent, Africa, in the shape of a buxom woman."

Umum Newsletter (4,iii and iv, unnumbered pages), which is published by the Philadelphia Black History Museum, is devoted to Ishmael Reed. It includes "Neo Hoodooism: A Perspective" by Leandre Jackson, a review of *The Last Days of Louisiana Red* by Houston A. Baker, and "Hoodoo Manifesto #2 on Criticism: The

Baker-Gayle Fallacy" by Ishmael Reed. Jackson defines neohoodooism and discusses Reed's syntax and symbolism. Reed uses, he says, the same syntax and symbolic form in both his novels and poems. He stresses the complexity of Reed's language and points out that Reed has used his studies in Egyptology and the religion of voodoo as a means of distinguishing neohoodooism from traditional forms of American literature.

Houston Baker argues that *The Last Days of Louisiana Red* is too formulaic, that it relies too heavily on the protagonist and patterns of mumbojumbo; and he questions the seriousness of Reed's purpose. In his response to the Baker review, Reed says that the Afro-American tradition is the source for his satire, and he attacks the black critics who theorize about a "Black Aesthetic."

Jerry H. Bryant, in "John A. Williams: The Political Use of the Novel" (*Crit* 16,iii:81–100), says that Williams stands close to the center of the fiction of the 1960s, that he is concerned with revolution, and that all of his work has a distinctly political focus. "He has picked up the baton from Richard Wright and set out to use art to help his people" by embodying the sociological concerns of black America in fictional form. Bryant believes that *The Man Who Cried I Am* is the best of Williams's novels. He demonstrates the particularity of Williams's technique by comparing *Sissie* and James Baldwin's *Go Tell It on the Mountain.*

iii. Poetry

I wish to mention three valuable books on poetry. Dorothy H. Chapman's *Index to Black Poetry* (Boston: G. K. Hall [1974]), which contains a foreword by Samuel W. Allen, may be the most useful of these. The book's subject index affords a broad perspective of the themes which have absorbed black poets for over three centuries. The book indexes the work of poets, black and white, who write on black subjects. Bernard W. Bell's *The Folk Roots of Afro-American Poetry* (Detroit: Broadside Press [1974]) examines the use of folk art in the poetry of the Harlem Renaissance, in the black arts movement, and in contemporary Afro-American poetry, and determines that the use of folk material in this poetry is generally consistent with the Herderian folk ideology. Bell's generalizations are reached soundly and suggest the continuing importance of folk materials in black poetry. His study is evaluative and is a significant demonstration of how black experience is used by black poets. Gwendolyn Brooks with Keorapetse Kgositle, Haki R. Madhubuti, and Dudley Randall have published *A Capsule Course in Black Poetry Writing* (Detroit: Broadside Press). This handbook contains four essays of general technical advice for beginning poets. Its focus is nationalist.

***a.* Wheatley, Horton, Whitman, Dunbar.** William H. Robinson's *Phillis Wheatley in Black American Beginnings* (Detroit: Broadside Press) is probably the most sympathetic study that has been done of Wheatley's work. It adds, I think, substantially to what is told about her in earlier biographical and critical works. Robinson supports his charge that "neither those who praised" Wheatley nor "those who found her poetry bad have found the time to read all of her poetry and to consider it against the pressure of her times." His review of Wheatley criticism is useful. As far as he can, he corrects the details of her biography and makes the public aware of the recent additions to her known work.

Uniformly the attention given to Phillis Wheatley in 1974 and this year provides evidence of her merit and her social awareness in a sense that the content of her published book of poems may not suggest. Ann Applegate points out, in "Phillis Wheatley: Her Critics and Her Contribution" (*NALF* 9:123–26), that few of Wheatley's critics attempt to provide the proper literary perspective to establish her position in American literature. Her own appraisal of Wheatley is close to that given by William Robinson. Gregory Rigsby's essay, "Form and Content in Phillis Wheatley's Elegies" (*CLAJ* 19:248–57), represents a kind of serious appraisal that Wheatley has not often been given. He finds that 14 of her 17 elegies appeared in her collected poems, that they were written in a fixed threnodic convention, and that they have the triple purpose—to praise, lament the subject, and comfort the bereaved. He finds that their spirit is medieval and that Wheatley was influenced by the Puritan funeral elegy. Charles W. Aker's essay, "Our Modern Egyptian: Phillis Wheatley and the Whig Campaign against Slavery in Revolutionary Boston" (*JNH* 60:397–410), does not add to our knowledge of Wheatley's skill as a poet. It does, however, provide evidence that she did protest against slavery. Evidence of this is found in a letter addressed to the Indian preacher Samson Occom in which Wheatley emerges as a black woman who is fully conscious of her origins and power. Terence Collins in "Phillis Wheatley: The Dark Side of the Poetry" (*Phylon* 36:77–88), attempts, as many Wheatley critics have, to discover whether Wheatley was affected by and responded to slavery and being a slave. He says "that she lived in a neutral zone, neither black nor white," but "the slave mentality went deeper than the surface of her life." His analysis of her writing records a self-hatred that is identified as characteristic of slave mentality. Collins's judgment that Wheatley's husband was weak, a generally held notion, is refuted convincingly in William Robinson's book.

Richard Walser announced the discovery of another acrostic, "Newly Discovered Acrostic by George Moses Horton" (*CLAJ* 19:258–60), which brings the total that have been found to five. This acrostic was found among the Biddle-Carraway papers in the North Carolina archives at Raleigh.

Carl L. Marshall, after examining two long poems, "Not a Man and Yet a Man" and "The Rape of Florida," in "Two Protest Poems by Alberry A. Whitman" (*CLAJ* 19:50–56), concludes that Whitman is the best black American poet before Dunbar.

A Singer in the Dawn (see section ii, Fiction) contains four essays that judge Dunbar's poems: "Paul Laurence Dunbar: The Poet and the Myths" by Darwin T. Turner, "Racial Fire in the Poetry of Paul Laurence Dunbar" by James A. Emanuel, "On Dunbar's 'Jingles in a Broken Tongue': Dunbar's Dialect Poetry and the Afro-American Folk Tradition" by Dickson D. Bruce, Jr., and "Dunbar and Dialect Poetry" by Myron Simon. Darwin T. Turner, in a reexamination of Dunbar, identifies the myths that have blurred the author's reputation, judges them, and makes a general evaluation of Dunbar as a poet. He looks carefully at Dunbar's versification, tone, subjects, diction, attitudes towards black characters, and talent and concludes that Dunbar "was an artist for the folk—not just for black people, but for all common people. . . ." James A. Emanuel reviews the critical estimates of Dunbar from James Brawley in the 1920s to Darwin T. Turner in the 1960s and concludes that a judgment favorable to Dunbar today must reveal in his work "racial fire." After a general but careful survey of Dunbar's poems, Emanuel concludes that "Dunbar, as a sensitive black man who felt no inherent inferiority to other people, had to feel racial fire in resistance to prejudice." The fact that "the fire glows in only one poem out of every twenty that he wrote is not dispraise of him as a man or as a poet. . . ." One of the myths about Dunbar is that his dialect poetry did not rise above the level of the plantation tradition. Dickson D. Bruce, Jr., agrees that the dialect poems were not far removed from that tradition. He argues, however, that Dunbar's treatment of the material of the tradition was different; "Dunbar's plantation preacher may have been given to flights of Biblical oratory, but he was ignorant of neither the real meanings of his words nor of the moral force behind them. . . ." Bruce says at the end of his essay that "the key difference" between Dunbar's dialect poetry and that of the plantation writers was "that Dunbar knew what he was talking about. . . . Dunbar was capable of going beyond the level of the superficialities of black folk tradition to a deeper understanding of the world view that lay at the base of the tradition." Myron Simon places Dunbar in the tradition of American poets who wrote dialect poetry before Whitman and before James Weldon Johnson discovered the possibilities of the vernacular that he explores in *God's Trombones*. Further, he says that Dunbar, whose relation to the local-color tradition extended beyond the conception of literary dialect, was fated "to achieve recognition as a dialect writer at the very time when a revolutionary change in the character of poetic language was occurring which would obliterate the distinction between the two voices he had cultivated and make his conception of dialect speech obsolete."

***b.* Hughes, Brown, Tolson, Brooks.** Cary D. Wintz, in "Langston Hughes: A Kansas Poet in the Harlem Renaissance" (*KanQ* 7:58–71), says that Hughes continued, during the Harlem Renaissance and after it, to be influenced by his Kansas experience. R. Baxter Miller uses Maude Bodkin's explanation of the function of the female image in literature in an attempt to show that different transformations of this image are essential to the thematic image and structure of many of Hughes's poems in "'No Crystal Stair': Unity, Archetype, and Symbol in Langston Hughes's Poems on Women" (*NALF* 9:109–14). Peter Mandelik and Stanley Schatt have published *A Concordance to the Poetry of Langston Hughes* (Detroit: Gale Research).

Robert G. O'Meally's "An Annotated Bibliography of the Works of Sterling A. Brown" (*CLAJ* 19:268–79) covers the 50 years during which that poet has been publishing. In addition to Brown's poetry and critical works, the bibliography includes a list of his speeches that are on records and tapes. A special edition of the Philadelphia Black History Museum's *Umum Newsletter* (4,v and vi, unnumbered pages) is devoted to Sterling Brown. The issue contains a selected bibliography by Gregory Day and James Less (17 pp.) and brief statements about the author, his work, and his influence by Cynthia Taylor, Stephen E. Henderson, Isaac J. Foy, Leopold Sidar Senghor, Lofton Mitchell, Alan Lomax, Dudley Randall, Michael Harper, Darwin T. Turner, and others.

Two brief essays on poetry are printed from Melvin B. Tolson's *Journal*, "Quotes and Unquotes on Poetry" (*KanQ* 7:36–38) and "The Foreground of Negro Poetry" (*KanQ* 7:30–35). The comments from the *Journal* in the first article are important because they make clear Tolson's sense of Eliot's influence on his poetry. It appears from these journal entries that there was less influence than critics have suggested. The second essay from the *Journal* is a laudatory summary of the effort of black American poets, a speech that Tolson had planned to deliver on the 100th anniversary of the Emancipation Proclamation.

Gloria T. Hall, in "A Note on the Poetic Technique of Gwendolyn Brooks" (*CLAJ* 19:280–85), says that Brooks has idiosyncrasies of manner—quaint and unusual diction, an imperative tone, personification, economical language, and sly satiric humor—which in combination make her poetry unique and define her to the poetic ear.

iv. Drama (See also pp. 411–14)

Larry Thompson's "The Black Image in Early American Drama" (*BlackW* 24,vi:54–69) provides a brief survey of the use of the black person in the early American theatre, in plays and on the stage. Thompson's account of black actors and playwrights is a good introduction to black theatre. Contemporary black theater activity in New York, Chicago, Washington, a general report on theatre activity, is presented in "Black Theater in America" (*BlackW* 24,vi:18–38). The essay contains regional reports by Peter A. Bailey, Dierdra Dyson, and Jeanne-Marie A. Miller.

Abiodun Jeyifous's "Black Critics on Black Theatre in America" (*TDR* 18[1974]:34–45) has identified three critical approaches to black drama by black critics: critics who write about black sensitivity and theatre participation, Alain Locke and those who confronted the observations of blacks and their culture, and the critics who reject commercial theatre (Baraka, Bullins, Neal). There is also classifying in Darwin Turner's essay "Visions of Love and Manliness in a Blackening World: Dramas of Black Life from 1953–1970" (*IowaR* 6:82–99). Turner questions dividing the black drama written during the three decades into two kinds—black arts drama and traditional drama. He finds universality in all of the plays written during these years and that the plays may be better classified according to which of three questions they attempt to answer: What is a good life? What is love? What is manhood? Plays by Louis Peterson, Lorraine Hansberry, James Baldwin, Imamu Baraka, Ed Bullins, Lonnie Elder, Charles Gordone, and Melvin Van Peebles are mentioned in the articles.

Helene Keyssar-Franke's "Afro-American Drama and Its Criticism, 1960–1972: An Annotated Checklist with Appendices (*BNYPL*, 78:276–346) is a useful reference tool.

The April issue of *Black World*, the anual theatre issue, also contains several articles on individual black dramatists. One of the most important of these articles, "Dunbar as a Playwright" (24,vi:70–79), which is written by Thomas D. Pawley, gives further evidence of the kind of attention that has been given Dunbar this year and, as the other essays and books do, offers further evidence of the quality of his talent. Pawley says that Dunbar's play about Robert Herrick shows talent and that his dialogue for musical comedy accommodates itself to white taste. Bernard L. Patterson's essay, "Willis Richardson: Pioneer Playwright" (24,vi:40–48, 86–88) is useful because it places Richardson in a historical context, provides a chronology of his life and work, identifies certain of his unpublished plays, and suggests which of these are in the Schomburg Collection.

Robert L. Tener analyzes Adrienne Kennedy's *The Owl Answers* in "Theatre of Identity: Adrienne Kennedy's Portrait of the Black Woman" (*SBL* 6,ii:1–5). James V. Hatch identifies the playwright Theodore Ward and gives the production history of two of his plays—*Big White Fog* (1940) and *Our Love* (1947)—in "Theodore Ward: Black American Playwright" (*Freedomways* 15:37–41). John L. Tedesco points out the rhetorical structure and strength of James Baldwin's play in "'*Blues for Mr. Charlie*': The Rhetorical Dimension" (*Players* 50:20–23). He classifies the play as platform drama, says that it is agitational and is intended to serve as an instrument of suasion.

v. Criticism

Addison Gayle, Jr.'s *The Way of the New World: The Black Novel in America* (New York: Anchor Press) is a study of the black novel from its beginnings to the present. Among black novelists, Gayle believes, "Wright and his followers, Chester Himes, William Gardner Smith, and Ann Petry were the first black literary iconoclasts," who by 1960 had succeeded in changing, as they developed certain ideas that were present in the work of some of the younger Harlem Renaissance writers, the course of the African-American novel. He says the romantic assimilationist novel did not appeal to black audiences after Richard Wright because, "acknowledging the existence of the Bigger Thomas living constantly in his skull, the black writer was capable of seeing newer visions. . . ." His analysis suggests that that black writers who followed Wright in time are "outside the realm of hate and fear" and "that they posit a world far different from that vouchsafed by the Americans." Gayle's perspective is historical and consistent with the theoretical assumptions of the Black Aesthetic, which stimulates much of the current discussion among black and white writers about black literature.

In Robert Bone's *Down Home*, a history of Afro-American short fiction from its beginnings to the end of the Harlem Renaissance, particularly in his introduction, a rather different way of looking at black fiction is proposed theoretically in opposition to the assumptions that are made in Gayle's introduction. Bone attempts to show in this book that "the alternating rhythms of the Afro-American short story are derived from the employment of two traditional literary modes: pastoral and antipastoral," and he employs this thesis to investigate the development of the black short story through the Harlem Renaissance. The soundness of his thesis is questionable. It works better in the first part of the book than it does in the second, where its application sometimes seems forced, and some of his assertions of literary influence in both sections need, to be convincing, more support than he provides.

***a.* The Black Aesthetic.** A comparison of Bone's and Gayle's treatment of black-fiction writers through the Harlem Renaissance, which is where Bone's study stops, is useful for what it reveals in contrast of critical methods and in the contrast of social and political assumptions. Bone states his attitude toward the Black Aesthetic without specific reference to it in the introduction to his book. In "Reclaiming the Southern Experience" (*BlackW* 23, xi[1974]:20–29), which has the subtitle "The Black Aesthetic 10 Years Later," Gayle does several things. He says that the southern experience is important because the South is where black people are closest to their roots; he gives a summary of the Black Aesthetic; and he provides a critical statement about two recent books (Houston Baker's *Long Black Song* [1972] and Askia Muhammad Toure's *Songhai* [1972]), whose content is supportive of his theory and of his concern about the South. The essay is valuable because the reader can observe in it the theory of the Black Aesthetic put into practice. In the essay (*BlackW* 24, ii[1974]:30–48), in which Gayle and Martin Kilson debate under the common title "The Black Aesthetic," both men discuss the nature and validity of the Aesthetic. Kilson argues that it is part of the Black Power movement and that it is not universal in its norms. He argues that Gayle believes "that no meaningful aesthetic exists outside of human or political needs." Whether Kilson's argument is sound or not, a good summary of the Aesthetic is given in it. Generally Gayle's defense makes clearer the meanings that he gives to the content of the Aesthetic.

John Lindberg, in "Minority or Mainstream" (*NAR* 260:48–52), finds Black Aesthetic to be a confusing term. He says that it defines itself in practice both by what it rejects and by what it accepts and that it is, in a sense, derived from white culture. He does not believe that there is the unity in the stance and values of white critics that black critics suggest. Although he is not certain that his understanding of the Black Aesthetic is adequate, and he finds himself in disagreement with some of its assertions, he feels that American criticism has benefited in certain ways from it. Specifically, he finds value in the critical assumptions of Imamu Baraka, James Emanuel, Julian Mayfield, Ron Karenga (Karenga's ideology is part of Gayle's support of the Aesthetic), and Ralph Ellison's *Shadow and Act.*

The tensions and differences of opinion among black critics over the theory of the Black Aesthetic are large. Stephen Henderson, who accepts the Black Aesthetic (or who is attempting to formulate an acceptable Black Aesthetic), has given an excellent description of it in two of his earlier works (*Militant Black Writers* with Mercer Cook and the introduction to *Understanding the New Black Poetry*). Some descriptions of the Black Aesthetic suggest that it urges the black artist not to consider form. In his essay "Saturation: Progress on a Theory of Black Poetry" (*BlackW* 24,viii:4–17), Henderson makes it clear that form is important. He says that saturation, theme, and structure are basic in the valuing of a poem. By saturation he means "the communication of Blackness in a given situation and a sense of fidelity to the observed and intuited truth of the Black Experience." Henderson says there are two traditions in black poetry—folk and formal and that they must be seen as a totality. "The overriding theme of Black Poetry," he says, "is the idea of Freedom and/or Liberation." He says that saturation is a category for describing and for evaluating black poetry.

I do not remember that Ezekiel Mphahlele mentions the Black Aesthetic in his discussion in "The Function of Literature at the Present Time" (*UDQ* 9:16–45), but he addresses effectively certain of the issues raised by it. He holds that literature functions at the personal level and at the social level, and that there is generally agreement about what literature does at the personal level. He recognizes what he calls ethnic imperatives and says that they help validate the cultural revolt of a group. For him the Black Aesthetic may be an ethnic imperative. If literature is going to be written, he says, "a group has the right to determine what language it is going to restore and exercise a propriety over, seeing that the dominant culture fashioned a language that is meant to maintain its supremacy." Further, he adds, "Poetry conceived by the dominant culture will not do for ethnic aspirations."

The issues that are raised in a general way under the subject of the Black Aesthetic are given some exploration in C. L. Innes's "Language in Black and Irish Nationalist Literature" (*MR* 16:77–91) and in Geneva Smitherman's "The Black Idiom and the New Black Poetry" (*New Creation* 6:81–86). Innes thinks that "an artist who uses language . . . is using a medium which is itself meaningful, and if he chooses the language of his colonizer, he is working with a vocabulary and syntax which express the perception and characteristic modes of thinking of a culture which has scorned his own." "In the United States," he says, "the choice between a native language and the metropolitan one is not possible. The choice of nationalist writers is limited to various forms." Commenting on the questions that are raised about the language choices that are open to black writers, Robert Filgar argues, in "Black Content, White Form" (*SBL* 4,iv[1974]:28–31), that "as long as formal units from Western literary tradition are used—words, sentences, paragraph, essay, short story, novel, play, poem—the subject matter will be undermined by the framework."

Smitherman discusses generally the function of the new black poetry. She recognizes the problem of finding an appropriate language to satisfy the purposes of the new black poet. She points out that "there is a quest among black arts writers for a style rooted in Afro-American cultural sensibility, a style that is emerging as an identifiable black aesthetic." Such a style, she thinks, is "revealed in the language of the new black poetry."

H. Bruce Franklin, in " 'A' is for Afro-American: A Primer on the Study of American Literature" (*MinnR* NS,v:53–64), argues that "if we wish to continue to use the term 'American Literature' we must either admit that we mean white American literature or construe it to include the literature of several peoples, including the Afro-American nation. This latter course leads to a fundamental redefinition." The novelist John A. Williams's concern about American literature is related to Franklin's. In "The Crisis in American Letters" (*Blacks* 6:67–72) he says "that most white writers in the United States can no longer speak generally or truthfully for all Americans" and that many white writers refuse to recognize the right and ability of nonwhites to speak for themselves.

***b.* African Influence.** A significant number of critical articles that attempt to show a relationship between African and Afro-American thought and literature have appeared during the year. These articles contribute to an understanding of some of the content of the Black Aesthetic.

Wilson J. Moses's "The Poetics of Ethiopianism: W. E. B. DuBois and Literary Black Nationalism" (*AL* 47:411–26) suggests that DuBois's early works struggle to merge two complementary but different mythological traditions. The first of these is "Ethiopianism," a literary-religious tradition common to English-speaking Africans regardless of nationality. The other is the European tradition of interpretative mythology, transplanted to America by its European colonizers. Ethiopianism was based on an interpretation of the Biblical passage (Psalms 68:31), "Princes shall come out of Egypt; Ethiopia shall soon stretch out her hand unto God," and was an interpretation of that passage to mean that Africa would rise and the West would decline. Ethiopianism was, in fact, the effort of the English-speaking black person to view his past enslavement and present cultural dependency in terms of the broader history of civilization. There are echoes of Ethiopianism in the Black Aesthetic.

George W. Shepperson, in "The Afro-American Contribution to African Studies" (*JAAS* 8:281–301), is not primarily interested in literary matters, but his essay suggests the extent and the development of Ethiopianism and some beginning concerns with African aesthetic and linguistic questions. His essay traces Afro-American interests and contributions to the study of Africa to the present. Shepperson points to the use of the Bible as a source of knowledge of Africa and to the development and use of African history by Afro-Americans. Consistent with the influences that may be drawn from Shepperson's essay, Thomas H. Henriksen says, in "African Intellectual Influence on Black Americans: The Role of Edward W. Blyden" (*Phylon* 36:279–90), that Blyden and other African intellectuals through their aggressive achievement are a significant source of present-day black pride. Michael Fabre describes the response of black Americans to René Maran after the publication of his novel *Batouala* (1921) and during the early years of the negritude movement. He points out in "René Maran, The New Negro and Negritude" (*Phylon* 36:340–45) that Alain Locke, Langston Hughes, W. E. B. DuBois, Jessie Fauset, and John F. Matheus were influenced in some way by the novel's appearance or through contact with its author. Maran and his novel were written about in *The Crisis* and *Opportunity* magazines.

vi. Autobiography, Biography, Interviews

The conscious awareness of a need for fidelity to the black experience that both the critic and the writer are expressing now in their several ways makes the importance of biography and autobiography large. Some critics whose essays are listed here give a good deal of attention to both of these when dealing with the problems of the texts about which they write. There is a tradition of black biography, beginning with the slave narratives, continuing and becoming very important in the last two decades. Two books published in 1974 provide in their different ways a sense of the scope of this genre—Russell Brignano's *Black Americans in Autobiography*, an annotated bibliography of autobiographies and autobiographical books written since the Civil

War (Durham, N.C.: Duke Univ. Press), and Stephen Butterfield's *Black Autobiography in America* (Amherst: Univ. of Mass. Press).

Houston A. Baker, in "The Problem of Being: Some Reflections on Black Autobiography" (*Obsidian* i:18–29), says that the nature of the black autobiographer's situation forces him to move to a public version of the self that is moulded by the values of white America. In support of this opinion, he compares Frederick Douglass's 1893 version of his biography with the 1845 version and says that the later work is "public—rooted in the language of its time" and considerably less existential than the earlier version. Baker comments on Booker T. Washington's *Up from Slavery* and on *The Autobiography of Malcolm X.*

Elizabeth Schultz, in "To Be Black and Blue: The Blues Genre in Black American Autobiography" (*KanQ* 7:81–96), says that there are two modes for this genre—the slave narrative and the oral account. "The emotional drive of the written narrative, as with traditional church testimonial, is toward the reader or listener, whereas the impact of the oral narrative, as with traditional blues, is first upon the individual writer or singer himself. . . ." The required public nature of black autobiography is referred to as the impulse to express "the unchanging needs of Black people" in Mary W. Berger's "I, Too, Sing America: The Black Autobiographer's Response to Life in the Midwest and Mid-Plains" (*KanQ*, 7:43–57). In the article Berger compares the autobiographies of William Wells Brown, who was born in Missouri, and Gordon Parks and Langston Hughes, who were born in Kansas.

Several essays provide interesting useful biographical information about authors. Michael Krasny, in "Jean Toomer's Life Prior to *Cane*: A Brief Sketch of the Emergence of a Black Writer" (*NALF* 9:30–31), traces Toomer's life from his high school graduation through 1921 to his going south with Waldo Frank. He tells what Toomer read after he left the City College of New York and shows some of his racial ambivalence. Jack Conroy, in "Memories of Arna Bontemps: Friend and Collaborator" (*American Libraries* 5[1974]:602–06), writes about his friendship with Arna Bontemps during the time that they worked on the Chicago Federal Writer's Project in the 1930s. Some facts are given about Bontemps's writing. An address that Gordon Parks gave before a student audience in 1973, "A Look Back" (*KanQ* 7:5–10), is partially autobiographical. Ann Allen Shockley's

"Joseph S. Cotter, Sr.: Biographical Sketch of a Black Louisville Bard" (*CLAJ* 18[1974]:327–40) provides little information about Cotter's poetry but is a good chronicle of his life. Cotter was a friend of Paul Laurence Dunbar and the father of Joseph S. Cotter, Jr.

Several interviews with black writers provide some biographical material, although most of them provide an understanding of the author's taste, critical values, and attitudes toward his craft. Barry Beckham tells Sanford Pinkster, in "A Conversation with Barry Beckham" (*SBL* 5,iii[1974]:17–20), that he thinks the Black Aesthetic is a term that means "an artistic way of living and writing that's peculiarly black. He says he thinks that Ralph Ellison's *Invisible Man* is grounded in the Black Aesthetic. Alice Childress and Toni Morrison, in "Conversation with Alice Childress and Toni Morrison" (*Creative Movement* 6:90–92), talk about the relation of art and politics, the difference between the function of the artist and the function of the critic, and the artistic consciousness of black women. In his talk with Abraham Chapman, "An Interview with Michael S. Harper" (*ASoc* 2:462–71), Michael Harper explains his concept of poetry and the influence of black music and musical forms on poetry.

The New Fiction: Interviews with Innovative American Writers (Urbana: Univ. of Ill. Press [1974]), edited by Joe David Bellamy, contains an interview with Ishmael Reed. John O'Brien and Raman K. Singh have published an "Interview with Robert Dean Pharr" (*NALF* 8[1974]:244–46), the author of *The Book of Numbers*.

Interviews with Ernest Gaines and Frank Yerby are mentioned above (see ii. Fiction, d,e).

University of Colorado, Boulder

20. Themes, Topics, Criticism

Michael J. Hoffman

It is difficult to explain why one year should see the publication of many books of high quality, after the previous year had produced merely works of competence. Readers will recall my lamentation in *ALS 1974*. However, so many stimulating and exciting books were published in 1975 that it will be impossible to do all of them justice in this essay. There are, for instance, two to three times the number of overviews of American literature as there were last year.

In order to deal with this pleasant problem, I have adopted the following scheme. Rather than simply omit books that in other years would have received detailed attention, I shall speak at length about those works that seem likely to be read a few years from now or that raise important literary questions; the other books I shall discuss only briefly.

i. Overviews of American Literature

***a.* Traditional, Historical Studies.** I shall open with a brief mention of Sacvan Bercovitch's excellent *The Puritan Origins of the American Self*. Well written and deeply learned, this is not merely a book about the Puritans but a demonstration of how the Puritan concept of the individual self and the federal mission ultimately became the basis of the American sense of selfhood and nationhood. While Bercovitch opens with a discussion of Cotton Mather's biography of John Winthrop, *Nehemias Americanus*, his real point is to demonstrate how the Puritan qualities in Mather's conception of Winthrop finally manifest themselves in Emerson. It has often been generalized that Emerson is a Puritan *manqué*, but Bercovitch's treatise is the fullest and most convincing proof of this generalization I have read. This book is a major work in American literary study.

Hugh Honour's *The New Golden Land: European Images of*

America from the Discoveries to the Present Time (New York: Pantheon) is a beautifully produced and scholarly art book that documents the reaction of European artists throughout history to the experience, reality, and myth of America. As one might imagine, the myth quite often dominates the vision. Honour's approach is both historical and categorical, with chapters on such matters as natives, Indians, images of liberty, American art work, and images of the growth of big business. The paintings are well reproduced, with 30 of them in color. Honour is able to show how the traditional responses to America have remained fairly constant and how the symbolic interpretation of America—whether that of the obsessive images of cannibalism in early responses or of Goethe's *Amerika, du hast es besser*—has been crucial in the European understanding of the American experience.

Two encyclopedic works deal broadly with American culture in the republican period in the 19th century: J. Meredith Neil's *Toward a National Taste: America's Quest for Aesthetic Independence* (Honolulu: Univ. Press of Hawaii) and Henry Blumenthal's *American and French Culture, 1800–1900: Interchanges in Art, Science, Literature, and Society* (Baton Rouge: La. State Univ. Press). Neil's book is an encyclopedic history of the development of American standards of taste in a number of categorical areas relating to the arts during the early republic, 1783–1815. It is Neil's thesis that American taste had become largely formed by 1815 in all the arts except literature, where the transition from the Classic to the Romantic took much longer. If Neil is right, the book is a good corrective to those of us who tend to assume that all elements of the culture were at that time moving at primarily the same speed. Neil's approach is conventional, and on reading the book through from beginning to end, I found the documentation occasionally tedious. This is probably a work that is best when dipped into.

The Blumenthal book, also highly encyclopedic, is the first on the subject since Howard Mumford Jones's shorter work of the late 1920s. Blumenthal explores the cultural interactions between the two countries during the 19th century, working by categories such as theatre, literature, music and dance, painting, and sculpture. His book is an enormous compilation of data, competently written but even harder to read as a continuous narrative than Neil's. I am disappointed, too, that there is so little evidence here of a well-thought-out theory of culture other than the most traditional notion of highbrow taste and artifactual evidence.

Annette Kolodny's *The Lay of the Land* is another cultural study, though more heavily based in literature, which traces fairly well a key pattern in American experience, that of the land as a metaphor—and particularly as a metaphor of women. Kolodny's treatment extends from the early survey reports of New England and the South through Faulkner's *Go Down, Moses.*

A more explicit treatment of women in American literature is Ernest Earnest's *The American Eve in Fact and Fiction, 1775–1914* (Urbana: Univ. of Ill. Press, [1974]). This book attempts to present contrastive views of American women by presenting historical and biographical documentation, on the one hand, against fiction on the other. Earnest's theme is that American fiction promoted ideal stereotypes that are not supported by historical documentation. Earnest tries to show, for instance, that American women were more sexually oriented and experienced than contemporary novels would lead one to believe. He proceeds historically by using such categories as education, sex, and feminism. While the writing is functional but graceless and the author's tone is often annoyingly patronizing, both the thesis and the documentation are convincing.

Warwick Wadlington's *The Confidence Game* begins with a promising thesis but disappoints quite quickly. The thesis is that all literature is some form of a confidence game and the author the quintessential con artist. Wadlington does not follow through his metaphor as well as he might in relation to some of the individual authors—Melville, Twain, Nathanael West—that seem perfect setups for his thesis. Another problem is that, aside from the book's often opaque writing, it is not always easy to locate the thesis. The author often seems to do his analyses for their own sakes. The Susan Kuhlman book, *Knave, Fool, and Genius*, which I reviewed in these pages two years ago, was better.

In *The Tenth Muse* Albert Gelpi has produced the best general overview of American poetry since Roy Harvey Pearce's *The Continuity of American Poetry.* More an essay than a literary history, *The Tenth Muse* is nonetheless historically solid. The author's psychological orientation is heavily Jungian, but his application of it is not reductive. While the book focuses on the 19th century, Gelpi refers constantly to modern poets to show the continuous relevance of his hypothesized tradition. Like others, it has Emerson and Whitman at its center. Gelpi can speak with authority about both poetic technique and literary theme, and he has fresh insights into a number of major American poets.

A slender but provocative work is Lewis Simpson's *The Dispossessed Garden*, an essay that distills his important book of 1973, *The Man of Letters in New England and the South.* For Simpson, the major myth that American literature has derived from the 17th-century settlers of both New England and the South is the myth of the garden—in New England the "garden of the covenant," in the South the "garden of the chattel." Simpson develops his thesis out of a study of Election Day Sermons from early New England and suggests that southern culture transmuted the myth of the garden because of the presence of slaves. In this unique historical situation the slaves became the gardeners, thus enabling the pastoral community to become, as it did traditionally, the "homeland of the life of the mind" (p. 23). The failure to justify this situation both politically and intellectually led to the condition of southern alienation that helped the South rise to a position of literary importance in the 20th century. Simpson's discussion ranges from John Pendleton Kennedy and William Gilmore Simms through William Faulkner and Allen Tate to Robert Penn Warren and William Styron, to show not only the inescapability of the southern past but how the South's history inexorably inculcates loneliness. This is a literate, thoughtful book.

Another work that traces a historical theme through American literature from the 19th century to the present is Peter Aichinger's *The American Soldier in Fiction.* It has had the misfortune to be published in the same year as Paul Fussell's *The Great War and Modern Memory.* Although it is not as good as that fine book, this one does cover different ground and it provides insights into the way war has been portrayed in American literature in the last 150 years. The author's military background gives him a sympathy with the material that he maintains without partisanship, even though his theses are not terribly new. American war literature, Aichinger claims, is largely about enlisted men except for most books about the First World War. Because Americans are always outraged by war, says Aichinger, they see it as an aberration in human behavior rather than, as in the European view, a recurring human phenomenon. The book is a short one, but it does cover a lot of ground, albeit in a skeletal fashion, and it provides the framework for further studies that can approach the subject in greater depth.

Paul Fussell's marvelous *The Great War and Modern Memory* develops one aspect of Aichinger's subject into a sensitive treatment of the literature of World War I. Not simply a history of the relevant literature in England, it is rather a study of the ways the First World War affected modern literary consciousness. It has won the National Book Award.

Fussell's basic research is impressive. He has read diaries and memoirs, histories and newspapers, and has gone to the archives. While his primary focus is on writers like Siegfried Sassoon, Robert Graves, and Edmund Blunden, he also shows in what ways various terms and habits of mind have carried over from that period into the work of Norman Mailer and Thomas Pynchon. This beautifully written book, while mostly about British authors, is still indispensable to students of modern American literature.

On a different subject altogether is Hugh Ford's *Published in Paris.* This book focuses in separate chapters on the little publishing companies that flourished in Paris between the two world wars, including many that helped shape advanced literature at the time. Among the many publishers discussed are Sylvia Beach, Alice Toklas, Jack Kahane, Robert McAlmon, and Harry Crosby. It is an interesting idea and one that has needed the right person to do it. Hugh Ford is that person. He has done his homework, knows Paris, and writes well. He also understands the strange nature of the little press.

This is in many ways an excellent literary history. Almost all the characters who played a role in literary Paris between the wars appear in this book. The main characters who reappear throughout are, not surprisingly, James Joyce and Gertrude Stein. The particular angle on the material provides the book with a flavor one cannot often get in more conventional literary histories. In some of the chapters there is good basic scholarship, particularly where the story is not well known. In others, such as in the story of Sylvia Beach and the publication of *Ulysses*, where the material is well known already, Ford retells the tale well from the publisher's point of view. There are enough anecdotes to fill a month of lectures.

A very different kind of work is *A Homemade World*, the latest from the prolific Hugh Kenner. This alternately fascinating and disappointing book contains essays on many American writers who stayed home—Wallace Stevens, Marianne Moore, Faulkner, William Carlos Williams, the Objectivist poets—or on those who drew their themes, as he puts it, directly from American life, such as Hemingway and Faulkner. The reader will look in vain, however, for a discussion of what constituted Modernism or of the peculiar nature of the American variety. Certain insights emerge as the book unfolds, but they do not add up to a thesis.

Kenner's impressionistic technique reminds one of a sophisticated Van Wyck Brooks. But the main problem is that although many of its insights are witty and provocative, the book is not original enough to satisfy specialists in the field; and it is too sophisticated for non-specialists. Still, there is a fine chapter on *The Great Gatsby* and the Horatio Alger myth. This is a far cry from *The Pound Era*, but Kenner is always an intelligent raconteur.

***b.* Recent American Literature.** This section will be concerned with books written about American writers active since the Second World War. The productive Robert Scholes has, in *Structural Fabulation: An Essay on Fiction of the Future* (South Bend, Ind.: Univ. of Notre Dame Press), produced a logical sequel to his earlier volume, *The Fabulators.* Originally given as lectures, the chapters of this book constitute some of the best work Scholes has done. He describes the death of realism: "It is because reality cannot be recorded that realism is dead. All writing, all composition, is construction. We do not imitate the world, we construct versions of it. There is no mimesis, only poiesis. No recording. Only constructing" (p. 7). The new forms of postrealist fiction are works of structural fabulation, which the author defines as follows: "In works of structural fabulation the tradition of speculative fiction is modified by an awareness of the nature of the universe as a system of systems, a structure of a [sic] structures, and the insights of the past century of science are accepted as fictional points of departure" (p. 41).

The early sections of this short book are the most convincing, because Scholes's Structuralist machinery overwhelms the slight works about which he writes. Also, Scholes is too apologetic about treating such traditionally "pop" material and pumps a bit hard for some of his science-fiction enthusiasms, such as Olaf Stapledon (*Star Maker*) and Ursula Leguin (*The Left Hand of Darkness*). There is a short bibliography for science-fiction beginners at the end of the book.

Lawrence Langer's *The Holocaust and the Literary Imagination* (New Haven, Conn.: Yale Univ. Press), although not about American authors, is about a topic that has profoundly influenced recent American thought and writing. A thoughtful, well-written, and carefully researched book, it studies the way a number of writers in various genres, from all over Europe, have attempted to come to terms with the systematic destruction of European Jews. Most but not all of the writers are Jewish; many were themselves in concentration camps.

Langer argues against the theory that after Auschwitz literature is impossible, claiming that a number of important works have emerged from such writers as André Schwarz-Bart, Jakov Lind, Jerzy Kosinski, Elie Wiesel, and Nellie Sachs. Langer's approach is thematic rather than historical, and he concentrates on certain modes of response to the Holocaust experience rather than simply on genres. He is not fanatically partisan, but he is eloquent, with just the right personal distance from his material to deal with it adequately. This bracing book, in spite of its subject, leaves one feeling positive about humanity.

Josephine Zadovsky Knopp's *The Trial of Judaism in Contemporary Jewish Writing* (Urbana, Ill.: Univ. of Ill. Press) deals with one of the major literary subcultures in contemporary American writing and is a good companion to Langer. Knopp tries to define the distinctively "Jewish" qualities of American Jewish writers, claiming that these derive from the *stetl* concept of *mentshlekhkayt*, a kind of moral concept of adult community. The early pages of her book define this concept. Her claim is that within the context of *mentshlekhkayt* contemporary Jewish writers are putting Judaism itself on trial in their works, and that it is this trial that characterizes them as "Jewish" writers. The authors she discusses are mostly American, and all of them establish the trial of Judaism quite differently. Among them are I. B. Singer, Nelly Sachs, André Schwarz-Bart, Elie Wiesel, Bernard Malamud, and Saul Bellow. Knopp's chapters on the Holocaust are competent but not as good as those in Langer.

Jerome Klinkowitz, in *Literary Disruptions: The Making of a Post-Contemporary American Fiction* (Urbana: Univ. of Ill. Press), claims that 1968 was an *annus mirabilis* in the history of the novel because it saw the "discovery" of Kurt Vonnegut, Jr., and the winning of the National Book Award by Jerzy Kosinski for *Steps*. Klinkowitz uses a long introduction and conclusion to surround his chapters on

Donald Barthelme, Jerzy Kosinski, Imamu Baraka (LeRoi Jones), Ronald Sukenick, Raymond Federman, and Gilbert Sorrentino, including at the end of the book a "complete" bibliography of each writer. The problem is that the author so intently sells his thesis that he overestimates his favorite writers. Kurt Vonnegut, for instance, is for him the best writer of the period, and the most profound. It is difficult to take such judgments seriously.

Many of Klinkowitz's writers have been interviewed in Joe David Bellamy's *The New Fiction: Interviews with Innovative American Writers* (Urbana: Univ. of Ill. Press, [1974]). If interviews with writers are your cup of tea, this is not a bad way to become acquainted with the producers of our current literary disruptions. The interviews are competently done and compare favorably with those that have been appearing for years in the *Paris Review*. You might in particular wish to look at the ones with Barthelme and Jerzy Kosinski.

Another companion volume is Raymond Federman's *Surfiction: Fiction Now and Tomorrow* (Chicago: Swallow), a collection of essays. Federman's thesis is similar to that of Klinkowitz, although more moderately stated, and his partisanship is understandable since he himself contributes to the literature of disruption. Most contributors to this volume are themselves fictionists. The best essays are by John Barth ("The Literature of Exhaustion"—still a stimulating essay), Ronald Sukenick, Richard Kostelanetz, Jean Ricardou, Jerome Klinkowitz (the opening chapter of *Literary Disruptions*, in fact), and Jacques Ehrmann. This is a well-produced book, physically readable but of mixed quality. One does not have to read all the essays to get the general message.

The chief polemicist among the recent fictionists is Richard Kostelanetz, whose *The End of Intelligent Writing: Literary Politics in America* (New York: Sheed and Ward [1974]) is the angriest, shrillest book in quite a while. Kostelanetz's bête noire is the "literary establishment," primarily that of New York. Kostelanetz quite convincingly documents how difficult it is to get published for someone who has anything "new" to say. He emphasizes the fact that literature is a big business, that certain reviewers and journals have undue authority in making and breaking authors, that powermongers control literature just as much as they control politics, crime, and finance. All this could be made a lot more acceptable were it not for Kostelanetz's perpetual tone of outrage. He is an extremely well-read, intelligent writer, but he has gone to his typewriter so much that his tone has become slick, his attitude a posture.

***c.* Elder Statesmen.** Books by three of America's established "men of letters" appeared during 1975, one of them posthumously. The latter, edited by Leon Edel, is Edmund Wilson's *The Twenties: From Notebooks and Diaries of the Period* (New York: Farrar, Straus, and Giroux). The book contains an excellent introduction by the editor, which is a good, nonadulatory overview of Wilson and his work. The diaries definitely convey the flavor of stateside literary life in the 1920s. Wilson was preparing the book for publication before he died and had supplied some explanatory material [within brackets] to update the diary entries. Edel has written capsule introductions to each section of the book to explain unfamiliar names and places. Footnoting would, however, have been a welcome addition.

A number of reviewers have commented on Wilson's sexually explicit descriptions of his encounters with women. These are in keeping with what we remember from *The Memoirs of Hecate County*, but they seem a bit dated. There are disappointingly sparse accounts of many of Wilson's literary friendships, although we do read a few juicy anecdotes about the Fitzgeralds. The overall impression one gets of the author is that of a cold, somewhat analytical man whose emotions lie well below the surface. But he is an extraordinary social observer who gives one a feeling for the life and times of the 1920s and who provides us with memorable observations of his friendships with Edna St. Vincent Millay and Eleanor Wylie. Any student of the period should read this book.

Allen Tate's *Memoirs and Opinions, 1926–1974* (Chicago: Swallow) is a mixed package. The memoirs are only mildly interesting. While we learn a few things about his early friendships in the Fugitive group, Tate is too much a gentleman to say anything either controversial or even speculative about another person. Even when annoyed he is only mildly ironic. The memoirs could use Edmund Wilson's precise acerbity.

The "opinions" are most interesting, the essays being often lively and intense, with the energy and strong opinion that the book's first section lacks. There are both very recent and very early essays here. The fascinating piece on "Humanism and Naturalism" (1929) whets the reader's appetite for more about that old controversy. There is also a fine essay on "Faulkner's *Sanctuary* and the Southern Myth." The best of Tate's criticism remains, however, in his *Essays of Four Decades.*

Robert Penn Warren's *Democracy & Poetry* (Cambridge, Mass.: Harvard Univ. Press) was first given as the 1974 Jefferson Lecture in the Humanities. The informality of the tone manifests itself in (1) a kind of populist spirit with which Warren wishes to engage his audience; and (2) his highly personal, nonsystematic style of dealing with the material, which places a burden on the way we respond to the author's sensibility. For this reader that response was negative.

The first essay, "America and the Diminished Self," suggests that American literary history reflects a growingly diminished self—hardly an original idea. Warren takes us on a superficial, speedy trip through history, ending with quotations from the Nixon tapes, a touch that, in the context, seems more "relevant" than profound. The second essay, "Poetry and Selfhood," is a bit better. Less historical and more personal, it is a poet's testament. Warren's statement about the modern sensibility is worth quoting: "Fluidity of selves replaces the integrity of self as the source of effectiveness, and identity is conceived in terms of mere action, with action determined completely by the fluctuating contingencies of the environment" (pp. 58–59). Warren also has a lot to say about the relation between selfhood and technology. Here he speaks as a poet and is more interesting than as either a critic or literary historian.

***d.* Language.** Three interesting books on the American language are worth the attention of *ALS* readers. J. L. Dillard's *All-American English: A History of the English Language in America* (New York: Random House) examines the history of those elements of English that developed on the American continent and came to constitute the American language. Stressing the differences between British and American English, Dillard seeks their sources in two major areas: (1) "contact languages" such as Pidgin and Creole; and (2) the *Koine*, or those peculiar linguistic amalgams developed by the many American immigrant groups. Dillard is a descriptive linguist who stresses vocabulary and diction more than such matters as syntax, which is the focus of most contemporary linguists. His ear for language is superb, his examples often amusing.

A good reference text is the *Harper Dictionary of Contemporary*

Usage, ed. William and Mary Morris (New York: Harper and Row). This up-to-date work is more practical than those by Partridge, Fowler, or Follett. A collaborative effort, it was put together by 136 writers and editors but very few professors. One wonders why. The editors use their experts as a panel by submitting to them certain key words for whose use there is no immediately available standard of judgment. On words such as "hassle" and "skyjack," as well as on the use of a preposition at the end of a sentence, the editors list many interesting comments on usage made by the panelists. Most of the book's opinions are quite sensible and contemporary, although some, such as the suggestion on where to place "only," might offend purists. The dictionary format is easy to use.

Very entertaining to read is Jacques Barzun's latest work, *Simple & Direct: A Rhetoric for Writers* (New York: Harper and Row). This lively, informal, and witty book discusses writing from a common-sense point of view. Although Barzun uses a lot of quotations, prescriptions, and exercises, he does not make his work seem like a textbook. His discussions are both enjoyable and intellectually stimulating, particularly his witty and merciless dissection of some marvelous examples of bad writing. *Simple & Direct* will not replace Strunk and White, but it ought to go on the shelf beside it.

***e.* Cinema.** Three very interesting books that treat American moving pictures as literary and cultural artifacts demonstrate a rising interest in the film among critics of literary competence. The most entertaining of them is *America in the Movies: or, "Santa Maria, It Had Slipped My Mind!"* (New York: Basic Books), by Michael Wood, a critic at Columbia who has published a book on Stendhal. Wood, a transplanted Englishman who has a great but critical love of American popular culture, develops the following thesis about the films of Hollywood's great era of the 1930s, 1940s, and 1950s: "The movies did not describe or explore America, they invented it, dreamed up an America all their own, and persuaded us to share the dream" (p. 23). This book is basically a cultural study, as one would imagine from the above quotation, but Wood has no particular theory of culture to peddle. He presents us with films, retells their stories, draws out their cultural and literary implications, and asks the questions he thinks they imply about both the historical and literary consciousness of the period. Wood does not downgrade what is popular and escapist. Rather he asks why a particular kind of escapism thrived at a particular time. The tone is light, but the book is serious. As for the subtitle, the only clue I shall give the reader is that the remark is made in one of his films by Tyrone Power.

Frank McConnell's *The Spoken Seen: Film & the Romantic Imagination* (Baltimore: The Johns Hopkins Univ. Press) adopts a more serious tone of high criticism. McConnell says that because film continues the Romantic tradition in poetry and fiction, it is therefore our age's most important literary form. (McConnell has previously published a book on *The Prelude.*) His thesis is that "film seems to make the most sense to us and the most sense of our condition as an especially powerful, iconic version of the epistemological and imaginative problems which also beset our poetry, fiction, and indeed, our attempts to lead fully conscious, fully human lives" (p. 11). McConnell uses correspondingly serious diction when writing about such imperishable masterpieces as *Warlock, Creature from the Black Lagoon,* and *Pickup on South Street.* One wonders occasionally about going mouse-hunting with an elephant gun. Still, this is a well-written, though overly enthusiastic book, and it shows how techniques of literary analysis can be used to understand a great narrative form.

Another book that levels heavy critical guns on moving pictures is Will Wright's *Six Guns and Society: A Structural Study of the Western* (Berkeley and Los Angeles: Univ. of Calif. Press). Wright is a sociologist as well as literary critic who draws on both Lévi-Strauss and Vladimir Propp. The theory of myth he develops in his opening chapters, along with a few Structuralist charts, derives from Lévi-Strauss's *Mythologiques.* In "The Structure of the Western Film" Wright, through discussing a few key films, isolates some of the Western's central generic characteristics. His main thesis is that films narrate and reflect themes of social action. The history of the Western evolves from the story of lonely heroes and villains to the story of men in groups and in communities. *Shane* is a late example of the first category; *High Noon,* of almost the same year, a classic of the second.

Like McConnell, Wright takes films with great seriousness. While each author has an occasional tendency to overwhelm his material, both agree with Roland Barthes that nothing is too trivial for serious analysis. We must change our orientation toward films and begin to treat them as a major narrative genre.

ii. Literary Criticism and Theory

a. **Theory of Fiction.** Three interesting works of 1975 add to our knowledge of the theory of fiction. Brian Wicker, in *The Story-Shaped World; Fiction and Metaphysics: Some Variations on a Theme* (South Bend, Ind.: Univ. of Notre Dame Press), uses a linguistically based structuralist analysis to suggest that metaphor always reveals an underlying metaphysical system. He focuses on certain key terms, such as analogy, fiction, nature, God.

The book is divided into two parts. The first deals with the theory outlined above, and its chapters develop Wicker's key terms. The second part analyzes a few novelists in relation to the theory: D. H. Lawrence, James Joyce, Evelyn Waugh, Samuel Beckett, Alain Robbe-Grillet, and Norman Mailer. Wicker's major critical technique is the use of binary oppositions. While its ideas are stimulating, the book is not always an easy one to get through.

David Richter's *Fable's End: Completeness and Closure in Rhetorical Fiction* (Chicago: Univ. of Chicago Press) attempts to define a genre of fiction. The author distinguishes the "rhetorical" from the "philosophical" novel by suggesting that the former operates "paratactically" rather than with narrative continuity. It is the sense of an ending that gives a work its sense of closure, as both Frank Kermode and Barbara Hernsteinn Smith have claimed. For Richter novels have rhetorical as well as dramatic closure: "Any quest," he says, in relation to *Rasselas*, "has three possible conclusions: either the desired object is found, or the quest is abandoned unfulfilled, or we must be made to feel that the search will go on forever" (p. 26). These are the minimal conditions for formal closure. Richter disputes the contention that there is any such possibility as an open form.

Although he sets up his critical categories historically, Richter has described a modern fictional mode. He writes interesting essays on *Lord of the Flies*, *L'Etranger*, *V.*, and *Catch-22*, a series of works that indicate the kind of "rhetorically" constructed work Richter finds dominant in contemporary fiction. He provides a list of more such works in his Appendix. I think this book constitutes an important statement about a new fictional mode and will be referred to frequently by critics of fiction.

Another fine work, this one from an established critic, is Robert

Alter's *Partial Magic: The Novel as a Self-Conscious Genre* (Berkeley and Los Angeles: Univ. of Calif. Press). Alter's theory is that two major streams dominate the history of the novel: the realistic, and the self-conscious or fabulistic. The realistic stems from the movement of 19th-century realism, the self-conscious from Cervantes and from 18th-century English novelists like Fielding and Sterne. Alter suggests that the origins of the novel lie in the tradition of self-consciousness rather than in realism. "A fully self-conscious novel," he says, "is one in which from beginning to end, through the style, the handling of narrative viewpoint, the names and words imposed on the characters and what befalls them, there is a consistent effort to convey to us a sense of the fictional world as an authorial construct set up against a background of literary tradition and convention" (p. xi).

There are long readings of *Don Quixote* (as paradigm), Diderot's *Jacques le fataliste*, Balzac and Stendhal (as realists), and Nabokov (*Pale Fire* as the quintessential self-conscious novel). The last chapter, "The Inexhaustible Genre," tries to hold out hope for the future of the novel, but this is more a wishful than a logical argument. Alter uses Jorge Luis Borges as an ambivalent example of both the failure and future of narrative fiction.

***b.* Poetry and Poetics.** I shall begin this section by briefly mentioning two works. The first is a new collection of essays by I. A. Richards, *Poetries: Their Media and Ends* (The Hague: Mouton [1974]), published to mark Richards's 80th birthday. Many of these are fugitive pieces, and they are mixed in quality. Still, this is a better volume than the valedictory one put out by Harvard in 1973 and reviewed in these pages (*ALS 1973*, pp. 421–22).

The other book is the enlarged edition of a basic reference work, the *Princeton Encyclopedia of Poetry and Poetics*, ed. Alex Preminger, Frank J. Warnke, and O. B. Hardison, Jr. (Princeton, N.J.: Princeton Univ. Press). It remains the best book of its kind. No changes have been made in the original body of the text. Rather, at the end the editors have added an 84-page supplement, 75,000 words in all, with many new items of emerging relevance, among them historicism, interpretation, poetic closure, projective verse, Phenomenology, semiotics, and Structuralism. The additions maintain the high standard established by the original edition.

An exciting work I was unable to treat last year is Octavio Paz,

Children of the Mire: Modern Poetry from Romanticism to the Avant-Garde, trans. Rachel Phillips from the Spanish (Cambridge, Mass.: Harvard Univ. Press [1974]). A penetrating study of Modernism, it is written in a polemical style that is erudite and philosophical. Paz, himself a major poet, talks at length about modern poetry's attitude toward time. Modernism makes a cult of change and the future, but it also denies the future. "Modernity," says Paz, "is never itself; it is always *the other*" (p. 1). The end of Modernism means the end of the future.

For Paz, a critical attitude laced with irony is central to Modernism. Duchamp is a central figure in his theory, particularly in his "ready-mades" that act as tacit criticisms of "*art as object*." The tone of the book is argumentative throughout, but the reader interested in the topic must nonetheless confront its ideas.

A more polite, academic work is John Hollander's *Vision and Resonance: Two Senses of Poetic Form* (New York: Oxford Univ. Press), a collection of essays about poetic techniques. Hollander, also a practicing poet, is concerned primarily with the prosodic and aural, although one of his chapters, "The Poem in the Eye," is about the visual aspects of poetry. The first chapter points out that verse and music have been considered separable poetic elements for only 300 or 400 years. Hollander speaks with great ease about the musical qualities of verse and makes even the subtlest technicalities of prosody accessible. Although the book is not formally organized as a text on prosody, it is nonetheless the best book I know on the subject, and it does discuss many important aspects of poetic technique. The last two chapters have much to say about a number of American poets.

Geoffrey H. Hartman's first collection of essays since *Beyond Formalism* is entitled *The Fate of Reading and Other Essays* (Chicago: Univ. of Chicago Press). The quality of this collection is consistently high. There is no question that Hartman has a first-rate critical intelligence and sensibility and that he is thoroughly aware of all the recent developments in literary criticism. I wonder, then, why reading the book all the way through was unsatisfying. It may be that Hartman is more an essayist than a systematic critic. Although his range and erudition are impressive, he nonetheless comes across as hermetic, self-indulgent, and gnomic. Is it that the new Yale School of Criticism talks primarily to itself? Hartman refers continuously to his friends and colleagues; he even reviews their books. I find this troubling. I also find troubling what I detect as a fixed point of view. For instance, in a short essay, "On the Theory of Romanticism," there is no mention of Morse Peckham anywhere in a well-footnoted piece. Ever since René Wellek unfairly lambasted Peckham more than a decade ago, no one from Yale has mentioned his work. Whatever one may think of Peckham, to omit him altogether from a discussion of Romantic theory is tantamount to discussing Wordsworth without once mentioning Geoffrey Hartman.

The psychoanalytic interpretation of literature has a number of eloquent American practitioners, but perhaps none so radical or intelligent as Harold Bloom. To the series begun in 1973 by *The Anxiety of Influence*, Bloom has added two more books in 1975 and will add yet another two in 1976. The two 1975 books are *A Map of Misreading* (New York: Oxford Univ. Press) and *Kabbalah and Criticism* (New York: Seabury). (Any discussion of either book must, by the way, presuppose a reading of *The Anxiety of Influence*.) By "misprision" Bloom means misreading. His revision of Freud leans heavily on two French thinkers, Jacques Derrida and Jacques Lacan, both of whom claim that language is basic to being. Bloom employs Derrida's technique of "deconstruction" as an analytical tool.

Bloom maintains the "revisionary ratios" he established in *The Anxiety of Influence*, including their Greek names: clinamen, tessera, kenosis, daemonization, askesis, apophrades. He finds his correspondences for these in the following categories: images in the poem, rhetorical tropes, psychic defenses. The dialectic within which these operate as categories is limitation-substitution-representation. To accept Bloom's critical technique as valid, one must also accept his view of human psychology, which claims that strong poets deal directly with their Oedipal precursor-poets. The poems of strong poets allude to these precursors in two different ways: (1) by specific allusions such as recognizable quotations and similar details; (2) by structural allusion, a kind of allusiveness that is much more difficult to detect.

A Map of Misreading contains practical applications of Bloom's theory. The problem in using his techniques is that in addition to understanding them, what is also required is an encyclopedic memory and a total control of at least the poetic tradition in English. Bloom gives extended readings of Wordsworth (whose precursor was Milton), Shelley (whose precursor was Wordsworth), Keats (Milton, Shelley, and Wordsworth), and Stevens (Shelley, Whitman, Emerson). Bloom talks at length about Emerson who seems to have had the greatest possible influence on American writers (which one might know without recourse to Bloom's categories), and certainly on Professor Bloom himself. In fact, as Bloom points out, Emerson himself had a great deal to say on the subject of influence.

Bloom's own writing is heavily allusive, so much so that it would be helped by some footnoting or similar documentation. (The book does not even contain an index.) One is often not told the work of a given author from which a quotation is taken. Also, Bloom is more hortatory than logically convincing. He tries to carry the reader by the sweep of his argument rather than by its rationality. This is not, however, to dismiss his very real power.

In *Kabbalah and Criticism* Bloom indulges his bent for exhortation and mystical reading to the point of prophecy. This book uses Kabbalistic materials ingeniously to point out the similarity in structure between medieval Jewish mysticism and the theory of poetic misprision developed in *The Anxiety of Influence* and *A Map of Misreading*. Bloom leans heavily on the scholarship of Gershom Scholem and shows himself to have a genuine understanding of these difficult materials. The first two chapters are excellent demonstrations of the relevance to Bloom's theory of the Kabbalistic notions of *sefirot* and *behinot*, concepts that are similar to the Greek-named categories Bloom developed in *The Anxiety of Influence*. One is curious as to whether Bloom studied the Kabbalah before or after developing his theory.

The last chapter is much less good because there Bloom is most unrestrainedly prophetic. He reminds the reader of W. B. Yeats (a precursor) at his windiest. Bloom becomes suddenly large; he contains multitudes; but he is really only being self-indulgent. Still, with all the bemusement with which one must read some of Bloom's work, I look forward eagerly to writing about his two forthcoming books in these pages next year.

c. Language and Stylistics. Much important work in literary thought is now derived from the study of language and the various forms of linguistics. In our time the major name in linguistics is Noam Chomsky, whose new book, *Reflections on Language* (New York: Pantheon), attempts to make his highly technical theories accessible to the general reader. The first section, "The Whidden Lectures," presents Chomsky's theory of Universal Grammar. Briefly, this theory suggests that an innate human mental structure creates the capacity to learn languages. This structure is not physical, but is rather a mental capacity. It is difficult either to prove or disprove this theory, and many of Chomsky's critics seem to think he is talking about a physical structure or physiological process rather than a kind of effective ordering procedure. This theory has had a tremendous impact on modern semiological thought, and Chomsky's exposition of his own ideas is as good a description as one can find.

The second part of the book, which is Chomsky's extended answer to many of his critics, is not nearly as effective. Master dialectician that he is, he is nonetheless long-winded and too full of special pleading.

A quite extraordinary book about language is George Steiner's *After Babel: Aspects of Language and Translation* (New York: Oxford Univ. Press). More than a book about translation, it presents an entire theory of language. For Steiner, all linguistic communication involves acts of translation. The historical basis of language is not its communication of direct "meanings" but the gnostic, ritualistic way it excludes outsiders from the privileged circle of those who understand.

Steiner reviews not only theories of language; he exhaustively reviews theories of translation from the Romans to the present time, making it clear that there has never been an adequate theoretical statement about the ideal translation. Steiner sees translation as a form of epistemology, and he refers to Quine and Wittgenstein as often as Chomsky and Jakobson. Steiner is also eloquent on the communicative difficulties posed by Modernist authors for whom language is inadequate to express meaning. Difficult modern texts are unexplainable by footnotes in the way, for instance, a difficult passage can be explained in a modern edition of Shakespeare.

The tone of this learned book is surprisingly personal. Steiner is himself a linguistic resource, being utterly fluent in English, French, German, and Italian. In spite of the fact that the book goes on too long, it is erudite and instructive on every page. *After Babel* is the definitive statement on translation and an important addition to the theory of language.

The extension of theories of language into literary criticism is well represented in *Style and Structure in Literature: Essays in the*

New Stylistics, ed. Roger Fowler (Ithaca, N.Y.: Cornell Univ. Press), an excellent volume. This collection of essays is a "progress report" and an overview of "the work being done in the linguistic and structural analysis of literature." The theories underlying the collection are primarily Structuralism and transformational-generative linguistics. The book's assumptions are laid out clearly in the introduction: "(a) poetics (in the relevant sense) yields a specific and sufficient technique of literary analysis; (b) it is validated, both for theory and results, by the science of linguistics; (c) exhaustive analysis is possible; (d) all linguistic facts are poetically relevant; (e) there is no hierarchy of value among these facts" (p. 3). While all the essays are good, those especially recommended are pieces by E. L. Epstein, Jonathan Culler, and Seymour Chatman.

***d.* Literary Theory and the Study of English.** There were a great many books published in this general category during 1975, and I shall not be able to discuss them all at sufficient length. Brief mention goes first to the new edition of Richard D. Altick's *The Art of Literary Research* (New York: Norton) which continues in its new avatar to be the best book of its kind. Its lucid, sensible prose makes literary scholarship seem an important and rewarding vocation. The book is best on problems in literary history, such as attribution, reliability of evidence, and dating. It must be supplemented for beginning graduate students by texts on literary criticism and bibliography.

A new and burgeoning area of literary study, feminist criticism, is represented in a collection of essays, *Feminist Literary Criticism: Explorations in Theory*, ed. Josephine Donovan (Lexington, Ky.: The Univ. Press of Ky.). The quality is mixed, not only because of competence but also because of varying levels of ideological distortion. The first esasy, by Cheri Register, "American Feminist Literary Criticism: A Bibliographical Introduction," is an excellent introduction to the field, because it explains a lot of terms that have special meanings in feminist circles, including ideology, realism, consciousness-raising, her/his, s/he, authenticity, humanism. All the critics in the book stress "humaneness" and "reality" as virtues. The problem with the field as with the book is that it still has not worked out the uneasy balance between aesthetic response and ideological demands.

A very disappointing book is F. R. Leavis's *The Living Principle: 'English' as a Discipline of Thought* (New York: Oxford Univ. Press).

Leavis, now largely concerned with justifying previous critical stances, refers continuously to his critics and his own writings. His tone is cantankerous, the sentences crabbed and vague. Leavis has never been much of a prose stylist, but this book is the worst-written one of his I have read.

More than ever the prophet of doom, Leavis refers constantly to the impending disaster confronting civilization, but he never says what it is. It is always difficult to follow Leavis's thesis. Especially in section 1, "Thought, Language and Objectivity," he never lays out specifically what he is railing against. His thesis seems to be that literature ("English") is a discipline in training the moral sensibility. The "educated" person is highly moral, has objective standards (whatever that means), and makes value judgments. Confirmed Leavisites may not be troubled by any of the problems I have raised; other readers will be. The book seems very dated.

Another major British critic, Frank Kermode, has published a more stimulating book in *The Classic: Literary Images of Permanence and Change* (New York: Viking), adapted from the T. S. Eliot Memorial Lectures (delivered at Eliot College, Univ. of Kent, 1973). Kermode is responding to Eliot's 1944 essay "What Is a Classic?" in which the latter posited Vergil as the archetypal classical poet. Kermode describes Classicism as being "imperial," defining his terms specially in relation to the permanence of polity and governance, and directing a discussion of church history into a presentation of Dante as a classicist in the vernacular. In tracing Classicism through British and American literature, Kermode discusses such matters as Augustanism, Darwinism, and Hawthorne as a typologist. In regard to the latter Kermode suggests that Hawthorne uses typology as a way of fixing permanence while dealing with change. For Kermode Hawthorne is a "modern" author because he presents ambiguities resolvable only by individual readers in particular ages. This leads Kermode to define the modern classic as that work that can sustain such interactions with readers throughout the ages even if different meanings always emerge.

Frederick Crews's first book in a few years, *Out of My System: Psychoanalysis, Ideology, and Critical Method* (New York: Oxford Univ. Press), contains a series of essays written since 1966 on a variety of subjects, most of them either psychoanalytic or political. It is clear from reading these essays how strongly Crews was touched by the events of the 1960s. He tries to argue a balanced left-academic position, but he is basically conservative and rationalistic. Each essay is preceded by a short note that places it within the context of its composition.

Crews does not normally present a positive model for his arguments. Rather, he proceeds negatively and even somewhat defensively, telling us what the psychoanalytic critic is *not* in essays like "Can Literature Be Psychoanalyzed?" and "Do Literary Studies Have an Ideology?" His only positive reading occurs in "Conrad's Uneasiness—And Ours," which proceeds much like the analyses Crews essayed in his book on Hawthorne. This is a well-written, intelligent, and limited book—a disappointment.

Norman Holland has, to my taste, been writing the most interesting American psychoanalytic criticism for a number of years. In what is probably his major work to date, *5 Readers Reading* (New Haven, Conn.: Yale Univ. Press), Holland puts forth a full-scale study of readers' responses to works of literature. Using short stories such as Faulkner's "A Rose for Emily," Hemingway's "The Battler," and Fitzgerald's "Winter Dreams," he sets five student subjects to work interpreting their responses to these tales.

Holland's model is Freud's *Jokes and Their Relation to the Unconscious.* If, he claims, psychoanalysis worked so well in Freud's analysis of jokes, then it should work just as well in analyzing literary works and readers' responses to them. Holland develops an elaborate theory of literary forms as psychic defenses and of how we must use Freudian tools to decode readers' responses in relation to these defenses. To demonstrate his theory, Holland analyzes the analyses of his readers. The result is a sophisticated modern version of I. A. Richard's *Practical Criticism.* Holland is a committed Freudian who treats psychoanalytic theory as an established way of looking at the world. The noncommitted reader may have problems in making the necessary adjustment to those assumptions.

Perhaps the most fascinating speculative critical work of 1975 is Ihab Hassan's *Paracriticisms: Seven Speculations of the Times* (Urbana: Univ. of Ill. Press), essays written since the 1960s but unified by a common theme and tone. Hassan is frankly seeking a new form and subject for literary criticism. He is a futurist who has been influenced by and has absorbed most of the important speculative thinkers in both American and European criticism. Many of his essays are gnomic in form and tone. The hand of Norman O. Brown and Marshall McLuhan can be felt, but Hassan is not blindly imitative.

For him the critical task today is to define the shape of the future, and to do this he attempts to draw distinctions between Modernism and Post-Modernism. In this search for a definition the important text for Hassan, as for McLuhan, is *Finnegans Wake.* But he also discusses science fiction and is willing to study any text that can serve as a focal point for what is actually a form of cultural criticism and an attempt to see literature as a steadily changing key to human consciousness. Hassan's writing has a creative intensity not unlike Harold Bloom's, although it is a bit more tempered. He is not an analytical critic; ideas sweep him along and he is a master quoter. This is an uneven but brilliant book by a major critic.

In the next paragraphs, because of limitations of space, I shall give capsule descriptions of a number of books to which in a less vintage year I might have devoted more pages. All of them are worth a look. The first work is Göran Hermerén's *Influence in Art and Literature* (Princeton, N.J.: Princeton Univ. Press), an attempt to systematize and quantify the ways of discussing such matters as how one artist influences another. Scholarship and rigor abound but the work is unimaginative next to Bloom's. Bennison Gray's *The Phenomenon of Literature* (The Hague: Mouton) is an ambitious, large-scale attempt to develop a theory that literature is basically fictional, and to come to a definition of literary modes. It is not, as the title might lead one to believe, a Phenomenological study, but is rather an attempt to be systematic and precise in defining genres. Daniel Schneider's *Symbolism: The Manichean Vision* is a literate attempt to define symbol systems in terms of sets of opposites. The theory is well developed and the readings of individual authors are as good as the theory.

In theatre three books deserve attention. Morton Gurewitch, in *Comedy: The Irrational Vision* (Ithaca, N.Y.: Cornell Univ. Press), looks at comedy as an attitude or general mode rather than as a distinct literary genre. He leans heavily on Freudian theory and his main comic interest is in farce. A good overview of the field. In *Achilles' Choice: Examples of Modern Tragedy* (Princeton, N.J.: Princeton Univ. Press), David Lenson attempts to show that tragedy, and particularly the tragic spirit, is not dead in modern literature. The book is a well-written, thoughtful search for an instrumental definition. Michael Goldman's *The Actor's Freedom: Toward a Theory of Drama*

(New York: Viking) comes at drama from another point of view, that of the actor. It is one of the most literary and imaginative studies that I have read of the role of the actor in drama, ranging throughout all of dramatic literature for its references.

Using theater as a metaphor, two sociologists, Stanford A. Lyman and Marvin B. Scott, in *The Drama of Social Reality* (New York: Oxford Univ. Press) attempt to prove that a "theory of human affairs is . . . a theory of action" (p. 2). They work outward from such plays of Shakespeare as *Macbeth, Hamlet, Troilus and Cressida*, and *Antony and Cleopatra* to develop their theory of a "sociology of the absurd." Another work that moves from literature to social theory is Eleanor Wilner's *Gathering the Winds: Visionary Imagination and Radical Transformation of Self and Society* (Baltimore: Johns Hopkins Univ. Press). The book develops a theory of the imagination as an apocalyptic, prophetic agent in transforming society, drawing on Jung, Lévi-Strauss, and especially Mircea Eliade. Wilner's texts are taken from Beddoes, Blake, Yeats, and Marx. The theory tends accasionally to overwhelm the text.

***e*. Structuralism and Semiology.** A number of first-rate works were published in 1975 on these subjects. William Righter, in *Myth and Literature* (London and Boston: Routledge & Kegan Paul), has written an excellent brief introduction to contemporary literary thought on the subject of myth. Although he is impressed with Northrop Frye's categories in *Anatomy of Criticism*, he finds them too rigid to be valid. In fact, he makes greater use of Frank Kermode's general theories of fictions. Much taken with Lévi-Strauss and Structuralist theories of myth, Righter nonetheless feels that as a vital movement myth criticism is coming to a close. Frye's work is the monument at the end of a tradition. In place of traditional myth criticism Righter accepts Roland Barthes's metaphoric concept of myth as a general set of cultural beliefs, assumptions, and communication systems.

Philip Pettit's *The Concept of Structuralism: A Critical Analysis* (Berkeley and Los Angeles: Univ. of Calif. Press) analyzes Structuralism as a philosophical movement and an analytical methodology. Pettit cautions that the traditional linguistic metaphor of Structuralism cannot be applied systematically and without modification outside of linguistics. Semiology, in fact, applies linguistic concepts as a model for studies of human "sign" systems in the plastic arts, music, and "customary arts" such as fashion. Pettit discusses both the Lévi-Strauss and the Barthes use of such models.

For readers with some (though not necessarily great) knowledge of Structuralist texts, this is the best systematic overview of the philosophical basis of the movement. Pettit, by the way, does not think Structuralism will be considered a major movement in the history of philosophy because of the limitations inherent in the linguistic model.

If Pettit's book is the best study of Structuralism as a philosophical movement, the best short study of it as a literary movement is by Jonathan Culler: *Structuralist Poetics: Structuralism, Linguistics, and the Study of Literature* (Ithaca, N.Y.: Cornell Univ. Press), winner of the MLA's James Russell Lowell Prize. Culler begins, as does Pettit, by examining the linguistic model through a discussion of such linguists as Jakobson, Greimas, Saussure, and Chomsky. He explains that linguistics and Structuralism share an assumption that all aspects of the world interrelate in a massive communication system. Most attempts at a Structuralist synthesis have foundered, however, on their attempts to develop too close an analogy to linguistics.

When Culler talks about literary competence he means somewhat the same thing as Chomsky does when he talks about linguistic competence: a person's knowledge of the conventions. Culler uses literary conventions to develop the beginnings of a Structuralist poetics and theory of fiction. He talks at length about the tasks remaining to Structuralism, being more positive about its literary future than Pettit is about its philosophical one. If Lévi-Strauss has been the most commanding intellect of the movement, Barthes is for Culler the most important literary figure and the one who is designing the movement's future program.

Pierre Guiraud's *Semiology*, trans. George Gross (London and Boston: Routledge & Kegan Paul) is an excellent intoduction to "the science which studies sign systems" (p.1), and is a good preparation for reading a critic like Roland Barthes. Semiology—called semiotics in American theory—includes all aspects of communication and incorporates many disciplines, including linguistics, anthropology, information theory, literary criticism, and myth studies. Guiraud bases his version of semiology on Saussure's distinction between the "signifier" and the "signified." With Barthes, he takes as semiology's province all oral, written, and nonlinguistic communication. Fashion, advertising, myth, science, everything is in some way part of a communication system. Readers whose appetites have been whetted by this slender book should turn next to Barthes's *Elements of Semiology* and his *Mythologies*.

A number of Roland Barthes's books have been rendered into English during the past few years; in 1975 it was *The Pleasure of the Text*, trans. Richard Miller (New York: Hill and Wang). Barthes's books are difficult to translate well because he relies heavily on puns and on French words that have special, nontransmissible overtones. The form of this book is a series of statements, ranging from a few lines to a few pages, about various aspects of reading. They are organized in French alphabetical order. Just as *S/Z*, Barthes's extended reading of a Balzac tale, was a poetics of reading fiction, so *The Pleasure of the Text*, suggests Richard Howard in his introduction, is an "erotics" of the text. The erotics Barthes discusses, however, is more easily communicated in French than in English.

Barthes distinguishes between pleasure and bliss, the latter being a deeper (more basic) experience than the former. It is not always clear what Barthes means by the two terms, although bliss has to do in one sense with orgasmic pleasure (*jouir*—to come—is a ready-made pun on *jouer*—to play). Pleasure without *jouir* is a more controlled experience than bliss. Writing can be merely an act of pleasure because of the nature of verbalizing. Reading, however, can be an act of bliss because of the various rhythms possible during reading. It is the text (whose author has disappeared) that provides the occasion for the experience of bliss, but the text is not bliss itself.

It is difficult to capture the book's essence easily because of the author's playful, poetic sensibility. Barthes is a man of marvelous intelligence and the book offers genuine pleasure, if not bliss.

I am pleased to close this chapter with the year's most exciting literary book, Edward W. Said's *Beginnings: Intention and Method* (New York: Basic Books). This is the most original work composed in English that I have read on Structuralism and its related methodologies. It is neither a popularization nor a summary, but an original work of scholarship, criticism, and thought. Because the style, while elegant, is sinewy and dense, however, the book does read slowly.

Said begins by distinguishing between origins and beginnings, using Saussure's doctrine of "difference" as refined by Jacques Derrida. Beginning is a step of action; origins have to do with metaphysics. The subtlety of Said's argument in developing the notion of a beginning is impossible to summarize, but it rests on the Structuralist notion of binary opposites, in this case the difference between the existence and nonexistence of an action and therefore—since beginning a text is an action—of the text itself. Like many Structuralists, Said is excellent in discussing the nature and ontology of the text.

But *Beginnings* is not merely a theoretical work. It contains brilliant analytical discussions of a number of writers as diverse as Freud, T. E. Lawrence, Conrad, Vico, and especially Michel Foucault. There is an excellent discussion of how Modernist literature is difficult because its authors face a perpetual dilemma of how to "begin." There is also a fascinating consideration of the following paradox: Structuralist theorists consider language the almost exclusive province of being, but they are unable to discuss at all well the language of individual literary instances, since, for them, all texts are but examples of and part of a universal linguistic being. This is a book I shall read many times.

As should now be clear, 1975 was a fine year for both literary theory and overviews of American literature. With the announcement and publication of new books by Harold Bloom (two of them), E. D. Hirsch, Claude Lévi-Strauss, Murray Krieger, Roland Barthes (at least two), and the first volume of David Perkins's study of modern British and American poetry, to name but a few, one may fondly hope we are in a major period of literary study.

University of California, Davis

21. Foreign Scholarship

i. French Contributions

Jean Rivière

Two aspects of French scholarship in the field of American literature for 1975, the second perhaps a consequence of the first, must be explained in some detail. First, the year 1975 did not see the publication in book form of any doctoral dissertation in France. The chief reason for this deficiency is probably due to the fact that since 1968 publication no longer has been mandatory previous to the defense of the dissertation. Also, subsidies for publication are often awarded years after the thesis has been defended and in the best of cases do not cover more than 20 percent of the actual expenses. At the same time, during the last ten years, paper and printing costs have suffered a yearly double-digit inflation and, strangely enough, so has the size of the dissertations. The 600-page typescript of the late sixties has grown into 1200 pages in the midseventies, with some recent works even totaling over 1500 pages). The cost of publication is therefore equivalent to the yearly salary of an assistant professor. Some candidates, of course, trim their theses for publication, but it often takes years before their books are published. The problem will remain acute as long as subsidies are so meager and as long as candidates don't want to reduce their work drastically, i.e., to something like a 300-page book. Two dissertations on American literature are due for publication in 1976, however, and will be reviewed in due course.

Second, as a consequence of this situation many frustrated authors and their colleagues have, in the last half dozen years, decided to establish periodicals specializing in American literature in order to mine their theses for articles or, as is the usual case, to publish original articles, rather than to perish in the wilderness of nonpublication. The most important of these periodicals are *Delta*, Université Paul Valéry, 34032 Montpellier; *Annales du Centre de Recherches sur l' Amérique Anglophone*, Université de Bordeaux III, 33405 Talence; *Recherches Anglaises et Américaines*, 22 rue Descartes, 67000

Strasbourg: and *Revue Française d'Etudes Américaines*, 1 Place de l'Odeon, 75006 Paris.

For the second quarter of 1975 *Sud* published an issue (nos. 14–15) entirely devoted to Faulkner and more particularly to the quality of vision in his fiction. Jacques-Pierre Amette opens the series with a description of Faulkner as the first novelist of the unconscious (with James Joyce) who turned the linear and realistic narrative of 19th-century fiction into the obsessional recreation of sexual conflicts and pulses expressed in an appropriately distorted language. "Le regard et le désir chez Faulkner" by Michel Gresset is the best study I have read of the relationship between Popeye and Horace Benbow in *Sanctuary*. "Quentin Compson ou de regard du poète" by François Pitavy describes Quentin as the artist trying to reconcile dream and reality in his own life and expressing Faulkner's doubts and anxieties as a literary creator. "La terreur et la nausée ou le langage des corps dans *Sanctuaire*" by André Bleikasten shows through illuminating and dense analyses (as only Bleikasten knows how to express in the most pregnant language) that bodies reveal themselves not as sanctuaries but as cesspools exhaling their "shameful and sticky secrets." "Pourquoi ris-tu, Darl?—ou le temps d'un regard" by G. Morell traces the genesis of Darl's madness in *As I Lay Dying* and shows that the thin edge between genius and lunacy gives Darl, as the author suggested in *Faulkner in the University*, a "superception," similar to that of the writer who is "a liar that tells the truth." Finally, "Inceste et mélange des sangs dans l'oeuvre de William Faulkner" by Jean-Marie Magnan studies the theme of incest through the ambiguous relationships between Benjy, Quentin, Jason, and their sister Caddy in *The Sound and the Fury*, and miscegenation through the characters of Joe Christmas, Charles Bon, and Nancy Mannigoe.

The 1975 issue of *Caliban* (tome 12) is devoted to contemporary American fiction without any particular emphasis on any theme or any novelist. The volume opens with a study of William Gaddis's *The Recognitions*, a book wavering between chaos and an underlying sense of the sacred and describing a world unwittingly bearing Christ's stigmata. Monique Bouchouk explains how art to Gaddis is finally an unveiling, a "recognition" of the hidden meaning of a bewildering universe, just like a picture by Picasso. "Richard Brautigan, écriveur: notes d'un ouvre-boîtes critique" by Marc Chénetier is a thorough study of Brautigan's narrative technique, an autonomous and free speculation on the possibilities of all forms of fictitious expression outside traditional forms. In Brautigan's works, Stendhal's mirror has broken into a thousand pieces reflecting the fascination of the world. "The Science-Fiction of William Burroughs" by Gérard Cordesse reviews all of Burroughs's major works, showing that "science-fiction adds excellent tools to his literary panoply." In Burroughs's writing science fiction is lifted out of the world of pulp magazines to become "a legitimate literary device among others." "La fabrique de la fiction: lecture du roman de Marguerita Young, *Miss Macintosh, My Darling*" by Régis Durand is typical of the new school of French criticism inspired by Ricardou and the *nouveau roman.* Instead of cataloging themes, symbols, myths, and allusions, the purpose of the critic is to tell "the avatars of fiction-writing," not to give "a sort of lifeless inventory of appearances." Any literary text therefore contains indications concerning its own working and hints on how not to fall into illusory interpretations. "*Visions of Cody* ou Jack Kerouac, Voyeur de l'Amérique" by Yves Le Pellec shows how the book puts an end to the Neal Cassidy trilogy and expresses the author's joy to see and be seen. "Kerouac invites us to become voyeurs of ourselves." "The Rocket and the Pig: Thomas Pynchon and Science-Fiction" by André Le Vot is a study of *Gravity's Rainbow* and the impact of science-fiction: "Science-Fiction has a preeminently cohering function . . . as a centripetal force that prevents the book from falling apart, from being fragmented into a multitude of unrelated pieces as in the fiction of Robert Coover or Donald Barthelme for instance."

Delta's first issue (no. 1) deals with Edgar Allan Poe. The new magazine will be entirely devoted to the study of the American literature of the South in the light of the new textual criticism of cross-readings of literary works. Its motto might be: "the text, the whole text and nothing but the text." The issue starts with a new translation of "The Tell-Tale Heart" ("Le Dit du Coeur," instead of "Le Coeur Révélateur") giving more muscle and pungency to Baudelaire's version. "La double voix dans 'The Tell-Tale Heart' " describes the short story as the confession of a megalomaniac trying to destroy, by killing the old man, his own obsession with Evil. "Discours et contre-discours dans 'The Tell-Tale Heart' " by Claude Fleurdorge is a very intricate study of speech and counterspeech in Poe's narrative in which the predicament of the hero is even more that of the damned narrator. The many references to the most recent discoveries in linguistics make the reading particularly difficult to the layman. "Le grand singe fauve" by Mireille Vincent tells us how "the large tawny ape" stands for a petrification of speech and the deity which can be elucidated only by the mystery solver, C. Auguste Dupin: he is a permanent recreator of a cliché-ridden speech. C. Lecompte's "The Homeo-Cameleopard ou la mort de Dieu" shows the perversion of religion in the narrative and denounces a false spirituality, that of the worship of man by man. The issue closes with "L'écriture d'Arthur Gordon Pym" by Claude Richard: Pym's adventures outside the American and Christian universe prove that human writing is nothing but a forgery, "a degraded imitation of the writing of a Poet-God."

The 1975 harvest is so diverse as to defy any generalization; through much critical acuteness (sometimes mired in obscurity and jargon), it displays a vigorous and original approach, more perhaps to Literature with a capital *L* than to American literature as such.

Université Paris IX, Dauphine

ii. German Contributions

Hans Galinsky

In 1975 German scholars' responses to American literature have changed in five respects: (1) editorial work, though still small in scope, has progressed, while bibliographies and state-of-research reports have held their ground; (2) teams of collaborators contributing to volumes of collected essays on comprehensive topics have limited themselves to 19th- and 20th-century subjects or even to shorter period themes instead of covering the whole history of American writing; (3) the comparative approach, never rare before, has grown so remarkably that it represents a major part of a special subsection of this report; (4) the predominance of literary history has somewhat weakened in favor of literary criticism and theory; (5) scholarly productivity has remained high, once again yielding more than a hundred published items.

Among the publications for 1975 book-length studies show a gratifying increase. Obviously, foreign publications in book form will receive wider attention from most reviewers than articles. Because this is detrimental to up-to-date international information and distorts the actual scholarly reception of American literature abroad, this survey includes a fair number of articles selected on the strength of new results obtained and/or new methods applied.

***a.* Literary History—General.** Multiperiod coverage is achieved by two encyclopedias, a bibliography, and a genre-oriented research report. Gottfried Krieger, Klaus-Jürgen Popp, and Manfred Pütz have contributed more than three hundred thumbnail sketches to the second edition of *Lexikon der Weltliteratur,* ed. Gero v. Wilpert (Stuttgart: Kröner). Because of these authors an important German reference book now offers updated information about and sound evaluation of American literature. Similarly, *Kindlers Literatur-Lexikon* has rendered a special service by republishing separately *Hauptwerke der amerikanischen Literatur: Einzeldarstellungen und Interpretationen*, ed. Gertrud Baruch (Munich: Kindler), with an introductory essay by Edgar Lohner which provides a historical frame and a modern perspective. Berlin's John F. Kennedy Institute of North American Studies has augmented its useful series of bibliographies with *Studies on the Interaction of Society and Culture in American Past and Present: A Bibliography of Dissertations, 1938–1973*, ed. Dirk Hoerder (Berlin: John F. Kennedy Institute). Manfred Pütz's "The American Short Story: A Survey of Recent Publications in Germany" (*Kritikon Litterarum* 4:177–87) affords critical information about what is still the most popular genre in German high school and university teaching. Two festschriften, one dedicated to Teut A. Riese, a Heidelberg Americanist, another occasioned by the anniversary of an institution, have also drawn on the works of many periods. *Geschichte und Gesellschaft in der amerikanischen Literatur*, ed. Karl Schubert and Ursula Müller-Richter (Heidelberg: Quelle and Meyer) includes 13 German contributions among its total of 20. All are restricted to the 19th and 20th centuries, the German essays reaching from John Neal's historical novel *Rachel Dyer* to Terrence McNally's play *Botticelli.* Coherence is established by the social or historical themes treated by the American authors who figure in this volume as targets of exploration. *Interculture: A Collection of Essays and Creative Writing Commemorating the Twentieth Anniversary of the Fulbright Program at the Institute of Translation and Inter-*

pretation, University of Vienna (1955–1974) (Wien and Stuttgart: Braumüller) spans a still wider area as it adds linguistic to literary studies of America and even finds room for American poetic responses to Austria. A third collective effort, *Zur Aktualität T. S. Eliots*, ed. Helmut Viebrock and Armin Paul Frank (Frankfurt: Suhrkamp), combining six reprints of American and British essays (in translation), one abridged and revised chapter from a German monograph, and three original German contributions, includes 19th-century poets like Byron and Poe.

***a–1.* Colonial, Revolutionary and 19th Century.** With Winfried Herget among the four editors and introducers of *Thomas Hooker: Writings in England and Holland* (Cambridge, Mass.: Harvard Univ. Press), a young German scholar has taken an active hand in the editing of the pre-exodus corpus of a Puritan divine of prime importance to New England literature in its infancy. Since Herget has been in charge of editing "Spiritual Munition," "The Church's Deliverances," and "The Carnal Hypocrite," his report, "The Transcription and Transmission of the Hooker Corpus" (ibid., pp. 253–70), yields insight into the basis for his editorial practice.

From the European roots of colonial American literature scholarly interest takes a jump to its Edwards, Franklin, and Paine. The 17th-century founding fathers and their children proved to be of little intrinsic attraction this year, but they are not entirely bypassed. Karl Dieterich Pfisterer's *The Prism of Scripture: Studies on History and Historicity in the Work of Jonathan Edwards*, Anglo-American Forum, 1 (Bern and Frankfurt: Lang) does include Thomas Shepard's *The Parable of the Ten Virgins*, Edward Johnson's *The Wonder-Working Providence of Sions Saviour in New England*, and William Hubbard's *A General History of New England.* For the first time in post-1945 German-American Studies, colonial historiography, less as a fine, literary art than as a complex of ideas, has received a penetrating book-length study. Its thesis, that "Scripture is, as it were, a prism, for Scripture as a literary document and that the prism as a technological apparatus displays a structure which makes possible a substantial coexistence of simplicity and variety," has been amply proved.

American history, too, although of social and political interest rather than theological and literary, is the domain explored by Horst Dippel in three essays on Franklin and one on Paine. Yet none of them overlooks the literary achievements of these two founding fathers of the republic. "Die Theorie der bürgerlichen Gesellschaft bei Benjamin Franklin" (*Historische Zeitschrift* 220:568–618), and "Bürgerlichkeit als Lebensprinzip: Kritische Bemerkungen zu neuer Franklin-Literatur" (*AmS* 20:155–63) test the applicability to Franklin of such a complex concept as "middle-class mentality." Less keen to encapsulate him in a concept than to turn international research results into the portrait of a many-faceted character, Dippel has written "Benjamin Franklin" and, in a similar vein, "Thomas Paine" for Vol. 6 of the encyclopedia *Die Großen der Weltgeschichte* (Munich: Kindler), pp. 467–81, 745–59.

The earlier 19th century as reflected in German scholarship reveals the traditional concentration of interest on fiction, with the customary preference for Hawthorne and lesser attention to Irving and Melville. Rewardingly atypical are studies on John Neal and Nathaniel Ames. An awareness of the multiethnic composition of the period's literature has persisted and supports the continuing republication of Charles Sealsfield's complete works. In 1975 Vol. 10, *Morton oder die große Tour* (first published in 1835), came from the press (Hildesheim and New York: Olms).

Helmbrecht Breinig's "'The sober page of history': Irvings kürzere historisch-biographische Schriften zwischen Faktographie und Dichtung" (*AmS* 20:7–28) approaches Irving in terms of an esthetic opposition that has but recently emerged in the criticism of post-1945 prose, yet its cautious application to Irving's shorter historical and biographical pieces throws new light on his recurrent experiments in blending fact and imagination. A decisive step forward in the disentanglement of an authorship problem is due to the joint, German-American, effort of Hans-Joachim Lang and Benjamin Lease. Their article "The Authorship of *Symzonia*: The Case for Nathaniel Ames" (*NEQ* 48:241–51) is a model of cool reasoning for Ames as author of a spirited satire and precursor of Poe's *Arthur Gordon Pym* and Melville's *Mardi*. A common zest for historical fiction links Lang's "Drei Wurzeln der Wahrheit im historischen Roman: John Neal's *Rachel Dyer*" (*Riese Festschrift*, pp. 9–32) with Ursula Brumm's "Hawthorne's 'The Custom-House' and the Problem of Point of View in Historical Fiction" (*Anglia* 93:391–412). Lang's article results in a more precise definition of Neal's dual place of practitioner and theorist in the evolution of the American historical novel, with "historical truth," "rational truth," and "the truth of the human heart" presenting the "three roots." Ursula Brumm's inquiry, by placing a much discussed Hawthorne problem in the larger, though special, context of a structural device such as point of view, proposes a satisfying solution. Questions of genre also crop up in Alfred Weber's "Hawthornes 'Ethan Brand' als Fragment eines Romans" (*Riese Festschrift*, pp. 33–48), while a problem of style underlies Manfred Markus's "Hawthornes 'Alice Doane's Appeal': Eine Absage an den 'Gotischen' Erzählstil" (*Germanisch-Romanische Monatsschrift* 25:338–49). Weber's probing into the generic origin of "Ethan Brand" and Markus's case for the author's "rejection of the Gothic narrative style" put forward valid arguments, but the debate will surely continue. Both reception and criticism of *The Scarlet Letter* and *The Blithedale Romance* are likely to benefit from Ruth and Hans-Joachim Lang's revision of Franz Blei's translation into German, and from Lang's thoughtful afterword (Munich: Winkler). Narrative form is also discussed in Klaus P. Hansen's article "Herman Melvilles *Moby-Dick*: Intendierte Inkonsistenz der Erzählform" (*AmS* 20:29–43). Unperturbed by the specter of the "intentional fallacy," it asserts the intentionality of often-observed inconsistencies in the narrative form of *Moby-Dick*. The relativization of objective truth by "different world views" implied in the narrative device of "different points-of-view" is asserted to run parallel to the relativization of "the novel itself by juggling" with these "points-of-view, thereby exposing its purely fictional nature."

While there are no books on literature of the earlier part of the 19th century to review this year, the late 1800s provide two studies. Siegfried Neuweiler's *Das "Internationale Thema" in Reiseberichten und Essays: Eine Untersuchung amerikanischer Zeitschriftenliteratur im späteren 19. Jahrhundert*, Studien und Texte zur Amerikanistik, 1 (Frankfurt: Lang) delineates an adequate background against which to project and assess the uses of the same theme by Henry James. Hans Borchers's *Hamlin Garland (1860–1940): Die Entwicklung eines amerikanischen Realisten* (ibid., vol. 3)testifies to a similar recent attractiveness of literary realism as discernible in Ulrich Halfmann's "Dreiser and Howells: New Light on Their Relationship" (*AmS* 20:73–85). Dreiser's first word on Howells, an interview printed in the April 1898 issue of *Success* magazine, is revealed to be "largely a fake." It shows "perhaps not really interest in Howells at all, but one more manifestation of Dreiser's obsessive interest in himself." At the Howells end of the relationship "deep-rooted mental and temperamental reservations," due to "his first contact with Dreiser," are adduced to explain why he "virtually ignore[d] Dreiser's future work." Revived attention to literary realism has also led to the republication of, and critical commentary on, realistic fiction by Jack London. Walter Pache has published his translation of, and an afterword to, Jack London's "To Build a Fire" and "Told in the Drooling Ward" as part of a new bilingual edition (Stuttgart: Reclam).

Autobiographical prose of the period meets its only critic in Herwig Friedl. His essay, "*The Education of Henry Adams* oder ein interesseloses Mißfallen" (*Riese Festschrift*, pp. 86–101), draws meaningful comparisons between Adams, Charles Sanders Peirce, and William and Henry James, which throw incisive differences into relief.

In poetry German scholars' interest in American realism has not yet advanced beyond the idyllic realism of Whittier's *Snow-Bound*. Placed against the background of English, Scottish, and German 18th-century idyls on the one hand and anti-idyllic tendencies in modern literature on the other, it receives a sympathetic interpretation in Rudolf Haas's "Literatur als Bestätigung des Lebens" (*Literatur als Kritik des Lebens: Festschrift zum 65. Geburtstag von Ludwig Borinski*, ed. Rudolph Haas et al. [Heidelberg: Quelle and Meyer], pp. 185–203).

***a–2.* 20th-Century Poetry.** In striking contrast to the previous year, American poetry does not evoke any broader response except for that of Pound and Eliot. Hans-Joachim Zimmermann's "Die Aphrodite mit dem goldenen Zweig des Argostöters" (*Riese Festschrift*, pp. 166–74) explicates an allusive motif of Pound's "Canto I" by tracing its earlier variations in Homer's *Odyssey*, Vergil's *Aeneid*, and John Heydon's Rosicrucian *Holy Guide* (1662). Barbara Rupp's "Die Textgenese des *Waste Land* als Paradigma moderner literarischer Kommunikation" (*Zur Aktualität T. S. Eliots*, pp. 163–89) is an instructive example of literary communication theory applied to Eliot's classic poem, whereas Rudolf Germer's "T. S. Eliot before *The Waste Land*: 'The Death of Saint Narcissus' " (*Riese Festschrift*, pp. 143–53) obtains equally reliable results with more traditional methods of exegesis. Most significant, however, is Günter Auerbach's "Von Poe zu Eliot" (*Zur Aktualität T. S. Eliots*, pp. 56–91). Awareness of "dis-simultaneity in simultaneity," "depersonalization," and "symbolism" unite the two poets in spite of their distance in time. "T. S. Eliot: Neuerscheinungen seit 1965" (ibid., pp. 272–86) provides a useful checklist of book-length studies. The only pertinent monograph of the year, Joseph C. Schöpp's *Allen Tate: Tradition als Bauprinzip dualistischen Dichtens* (Bonn: Bouvier) is the first detailed contribution of a German Americanist to the study of a pre-1945 leading figure of southern poetry and literary criticism. Although a book with a narrow thesis, it imparts well-informed and balanced criticism to the debate on Tate's stature.

***a*–3. 20th-Century Drama and Fiction.** The pre-1945 part of *Amerikanisches Drama und Theater im 20. Jahrhundert*, ed. Alfred Weber and Siegfried Neuweiler (Göttingen: Vandenhoeck and Ruprecht), originally a series of public lectures given by six American and eight German scholars, combines one essay on general trends with two on specific authors. Of the three Gerhard Hoffmann's "Auffassungsweisen und Gestaltungskategorien der Wirklichkeit im Drama" (ibid., pp. 60–123) deserves special mention because, in addition to the well-known tragic and comic elements, it stresses the less familiar satiric and grotesque ones of O'Neill's plays. With social criticism permeating German life and letters of the 1970s, Susanne Vietta's "Formen der Sozialkritik in Elmer Rice's *The Adding Machine* and Clifford Odet's *Waiting for Lefty*" (*Riese Festschrift*, pp. 188–210) and Herbert Grabes's "Über die Wirkungsstrategie des agitatorischen Dramas: Clifford Odets' *Waiting for Lefty*" (*NS*, pp. 70–79) represent timely discoveries of counterparts on the American stage of the 1920s and 1930s. Continued concentration on these two plays, however, unduly narrows the angle of vision.

Scholarly reactions to pre-1945 20th-century fiction have dwindled remarkably. Only Sherwood Anderson has held his own. Admittedly, Horst Groene's "The American Idea of Success in Sherwood Anderson's 'The Egg' (*Neusprachliche Mitteilungen* 28:162–66) amounts to flogging a dead horse since the theme of success has been treated excessively over the years, yet Helga Koriff's monograph, *Die amerikanische Kleinstadt: Untersuchungen von literarischen und soziologischen Darstellungen der Kleinstadt in den Zwanziger Jahren*, Europäische Hochschulschriften, ser. XIV: Angelsächsische Sprache und

Literatur 35 (Bern: Lang), discovers new aspects of an equally old subject by juxtaposing sociological with literary views of empiric reality. In "William Faulkner and the Rebirth of Dixie" Ursula Brumm contributes a crucial chapter to Vol. 9, *American Literature since 1900*, of *Sphere History of Literature in the English Language*, ed. Marcus Cunliffe (London: Barrie and Jenkins), pp. 214–41. The dual cause-and-effect relationship of Faulkner with the Southern Renaissance has been treated with exemplary clarity.

***a–4.* Fiction since 1945.** Once again the spell of the contemporary has manifested its hold on scholars. Four books, two more than the whole literature of the 19th century could inspire, a collection of essays, and 21 articles serve as witnesses. Symptomatically, three of the book-length studies are devoted to minority authors, although most of them have long transcended ethnic barriers. Peter Bischoff's *Saul Bellows Romane: Entfremdung und Suche* (Bonn: Bouvier), Herbert Grabes's *Erfundene Biographien: Vladimir Nabokovs englische Romane* (Tübingen: Niemeyer), and Fritz Gysin's *The Grotesque in American Negro Fiction: Jean Toomer, Richard Wright, Ralph Ellison*. The Cooper Monographs, 22 (Bern: Francke) represent three typical intellectual interests: alienation and search for identity, fusion of genres such as biography and the novel, and the grotesque as emotional judgment on contemporary reality. The fourth monograph, Brigitte Scheer-Schäzler's *Konstruktion als Gestaltung: Interpretationen zum zeitgenössischen amerikanischen Roman*, Salzburger Studien zur Anglistik und Amerikanistik, 2 (Vienna: Braumüller), has a broader sweep, unfolding as it does a fascinating panorama of modern novel-writing. The critic's assertion of constructivism as a basic characteristic of contemporary fiction is surely justified on the strength of the works selected. Not unity but variety in post-1945 novel-writing is aimed at by the cooperative undertaking *Amerikanische Erzählliteratur: 1950–1970*, eds. Frieder Busch and Renate Schmidt-v. Bardeleben (Munich: Fink). Dedicated to Hans Galinsky on the occasion of his 65th birthday, the volume includes interpretations of 13 novels and 4 short stories by senior and junior Americanists, most of them present, some former members of Mainz University. The novels chosen range from Truman Capote's *The Grass Harp* to Saul Bellow's *Mr. Sammler's Planet*, while the short stories selected extend from Salinger's "De Daumier-Smith's Blue Period" to Barth's "Lost in the Funhouse." What all of these essays have in common is the principle of studying the individual work with reference to its author's whole accomplishment so that the representative value of the single piece may be defined. The principle is flexible enough to invite any method of interpretation from the New Criticism to literary sociology. Doing justice to each contribution is impossible within the limits of this report.

***a*-5. Drama and Poetry since 1945.** On a smaller scale than does *Amerikanische Erzählliteratur: 1950–1970*, the second part of the aforementioned collective enterprise, *Amerikanisches Drama und Theater im 20. Jahrhundert*, mirrors thematic and methodological preferences in its respective, dramatic field. Miller and Albee, represented twice, are well known over here, whereas Siegfried Neuweiler's "Zur Lage der Nation: Robert Lowells *The Old Glory*" (ibid., pp. 223–47) and Herbert Grabes's "Möglichkeiten der Gesellschaftskritik im Drama: Jean-Claude van Itallies *America Hurrah*" (ibid., pp. 328–49) introduce plays or rather dramatic trilogies new to the German public. The latter are discussed as contrastive examples of the appeal to understand the present in the light of the past on the one hand, and of the call to criticism and active reform on the other. Both trends, the concentration on Albee and the attention to unfamiliar dramatists or, as in Lowell's case, to an author less familiar in the capacity of playwright, operate outside of Weber's and Neuweiler's collection as well. Hedwig Bock's and Edda Schütt's "Edward Albee, *The Zoo Story*: Versuch einer formalästhetischen und psychoanalytischen Interpretation" (*Jahrbuch der Psychoanalyse* 8:91–119) and Regine Brede's state-of-research report "Forschungsbericht Edward Albee" (*LWU* 8:30–46) reveal the first tendency; Karl Schubert's above-mentioned study in McNally's *Botticelli* manifests the second.

Post-1945 poetry is this year's undeserving loser. If it were not for Roswith von Freydorf's "James Welch, eine junge Stimme Alt-Amerikas" (*Riese Festschrift*, pp. 252–81), contemporary poetry would have evoked no response. Because of Freydorf, however, the multiethnicity of American literature once again asserts itself, and this time through the work of an American-Indian poet previously unknown to German readers.

***b.* Literary Criticism, Theory, and Comparative Studies.** In striking contrast to post-1945 poetry, literary criticism and theory are well represented this year. Stimulated by the functionalism of the machine age, and by constructivism in modern literature, Ulrich Horstmann's *Ansätze zu einer technomorphen Theorie der Dichtung bei Edgar Allan Poe* (Bern and Frankfurt: Lang) traces beginnings of the functionalist view in Poe's concept of poetry. The results are not completely new but well reasoned and soundly assessed. Of even wider scope, Winfried Fluck's *Ästhetische Theorie und literaturwissenschaftliche Methode: Eine Untersuchung ihres Zusammenhangs am Beispiel der amerikanischen Huck Finn-Kritik*, Amerikastudien; Eine Schriftenreihe, 43 (Metzler: Stuttgart), provides an overview of almost three generations of American literary criticism by refracting it in the prism of Twain's novel. Armin Paul Frank's "Der anhaltende Nutzen von Eliots 'konkreter Kritik' " stresses the continued importance of a method illustrated best by Eliot's essay "Andrew Marvell." In " 'A whole cultural history': Zu einigen neueren Versuchen kulturwissenschaftlicher Synthese" (*AmS* 20:337–57) Fluck advances from literary criticism to interdisciplinary cultural history. With the *American Culture Series* and the *Documents in American Civilization Series* for material, he analyses concepts of culture underlying them and critically examines their appropriateness for integrating into them manifestations of "high" culture such as major works of art. With Michaela Ulich's "Die politische Autobiographie als Gegenstand der Literaturwissenschaft: Probleme der Rezeption von *The Autobiography of Malcolm X*" (*AmS* 20:261–80) interest shifts to the status in literary scholarship of a form-type such as the political autobiography.

Still more startling than the growth of receptivity to literary criticism and theory is the increased use of the comparative method in dealing with works of American literature. Close to 20 articles fall into this category. A representative selection will emphasize (1) studies in international effect, one-way or mutual, i.e. reception, influence, and images of American culture, including literature, in foreign literatures and (2) strictly comparative studies disregarding the "effect" factor.

Reception research is represented by a most useful book, Hartmut Grandel's *Die Aufnahme der Werke von Henry James in der deutschen Literaturkritik: Die zeitgenössische Rezeption von 1875 bis*

1916, Studien und Texte zur Amerikanistik, 2 (Frankfurt: Lang). Influence investigations, too, bear on James but also take in the impact of the American crime story on the European. Hans-Joachim Lang skillfully unravels "the contributions of four literatures," Russian, French, English and American, in "The Making of Henry James's *The American*" (20:55–71), while Jens Peter Becker's "The Mean Streets of Europe" follows "the influence of the American hard-boiled school on European detective fiction" (*Superculture*, ed. C. W. E. Bigsby [London: Elek]). Reaching back to ancient Greek literature, Gerd Schmidt's "T. S. Eliots aristophanisches Melodrama" (*Riese Festschrift*, pp. 154–65) inquires into Aristophanic elements in Eliot's *Sweeney Agonistes*. Germany's literary images of America find a panoramanic presentation by a team of American and German scholars in *Amerika in der deutschen Literature: Neue Welt—Nordamerika—USA*, ed. Sigrid Bauschinger et al. (Stuttgart: Reclam). A less comprehensive survey of 20th-century visions, often conveyed by American ingredients of German literary style, is attempted in Hans Galinsky's "The Uses of American English in Modern German Drama and Poetry: Brecht, Benn, Bachmann," *Teilnahme und Spiegelung: Festschrift für Horst Rüdiger*, ed. Beda Alleman and Erwin Koppen (Berlin and New York: deGruyter), pp. 499–530. The 20th century and Germany's classic age blend their images of America in Rudolf Sühnel's "Amerika aus Goethes Sicht—heute" (*Riese Festschrift*, pp. 175–87), a brilliantly succinct essay ending with a hint of a converse, American concept of Germany and Europe, T. S. Eliot's Hamburg lecture "Goethe as the Sage."

Predominantly comparative lines are followed in two monographs and two articles on literary genres. In *Sherlock Holmes and Co.: Essays zur englischen und amerikanischen Detektivliterature* (Munich: Goldmann) Jens Peter Becker examines differences and similarities in the evolution of two national types of the crime story. In addition to the English and the American variety, the Anglo-Irish one figures in the thorough treatment given the short play in Rudolf Halbritter's *Konzeptionsformen des angloamerikanischen Kurzdramas: Dargestellt an Stücken von W. B. Yeats, Th. Wilder und H. Pinter*, Palaestra, 263 (Göttingen: Vandenhoeck and Ruprecht). The historical novel in a comparative context (Scottish and American) is central to Ursula Brumm's thoughtful essay, "The Historical Novel and Historical Criticism: Notes on the Critical Reception of Scott and Faulkner" (*Riese Festschrift*, pp. 102–13). Comparison, although not mentioned in the title of Erwin Haeberle's "Norman Mailers Reportagen (*The Armies of the Night/Miami and the Siege of Chicago*)" (ibid., pp. 232–51), connects a contemporary author and a seemingly modern narrative genre with Goethe and his *Campagne in Frankreich, 1792*. The juxtaposition yields an unexpected insight into the Western tradition of distinguishing the factual verities of profane life from the "higher" truth of art. For its use of the dual reflection technique Helmut Viebrock's "Eliot and Byron: wechselseitige Enthüllung" (*Zur Aktualität T. S. Eliots*, pp. 92–117) is not only of thematic but also of methodological significance.

It is the continued diversity of themes taken up and of methods applied as well as the abundant harvest of almost 20 monographs, with subjects ranging from Edwards to Bellow, from America's literary image of its small towns to Germany's vision of America, that stand out in retrospect most prominently, proving the persistent range and intensity of German scholarly responses to American literature in 1975.

Johannes Gutenberg Universität, Mainz

iii. Italian Contributions

Rolando Anzilotti

The publication in 1975 of the delayed volume of *Studi Americani* 18 (1972) has given bulk to this year's production, which might have been slimmer than in previous years. In fact very few books appeared in 1975, while the number of articles remained at an average level. The range of Italian contributions was from colonial writing to contemporary poetry, with the usual stress on modern fiction.

Starting with studies on fiction, Giorgio and Barbara Melchiori's *Il gusto di Henry James* (Torino: Einaudi [1974]) deserves belated notice before turning to the 1975 publications. The book has James's constant education of his own taste as a general theme; it is made up of essays that are exemplary fruits of the long devotion to James of the two critics, and are here arranged to produce a cumulative effect. Of these essays only the one on *Princess Casamassima* never had appeared before; it is certainly one of the finest. The authors delineate the formation of the novelist's taste, which they identify with the sense of everything that is proper and the exhibition of such sense, and they ably analyze the influences James received from European culture and art as well as the importance of this influence on his work.

The only essay in 1975 dealing with early American literature, as well as two articles on 20th-century writers, looks at its subject from a Marxian orientation. Rosa Maria Colombo adds another chapter to her work on 18th-century writers with "Hugh Henry Brackenridge e la frontiera americana" (*SA* 18:7–28), a not always consistent discussion of Brackenridge's essays, which emphasize, she finds, the frontier spirit theme and offer many elements for her somewhat Marxian reconstruction of the historical background of *Modern Chivalry.* In his clearly written assessment of London's work, "Il ritorno di Jack London" (*Il Ponte* 10:1172–90), Maurizio Flores d'Arcais attempts an intelligent, even if not wholly convincing, reevaluation of the novelist from a Marxian point of view. He points out London's ambivalence toward bourgeois and proletarian values and shows how, being caught between the two at the time of his success, he felt himself rejected by both worlds that cherished such values, and committed suicide. The third Marxian approach is presented by Mario Corona in his "Un esteta al fronte: John Dos Passos e la prima guerra mondiale" (*SA* 18:269–99). Through a close analysis of two early books (*One Man's Initiation—1917* and *Three Soldiers*) the author strives to demonstrate that Dos Passos has always been a decadent, individualistic aesthete at heart, which, he maintains, is perfectly consistent with the novelist's conscious turn to the conservative right in his later years.

Black literature received its usual plentiful share of attention this year. As an aid to Italian understanding of black American culture, Bruno Armellin's edition of *La condizione dello schiavo: Autobiografie degli schiavi neri degli Stati Uniti* (Torino: Einaudi) aptly fulfills the need. Made up of a wide selection of excerpts from well-known and less well-known autobiographical narratives by former slaves, the book is preceded by a valuable introduction in which the editor draws on an extensive knowledge of the subject to review crucial aspects of slavery and to see a continuity between antebellum proslavery theorizations in the South and later imperialistic and racist ideas in the United States. In "*The Autobiography of an Ex-coloured Man* di James Weldon Johnson" (*SA* 18:241–67) Alessandro Portelli provides an attentive reading of the novel. After showing its thematic links with American and later black fiction, he deals with the novel as a "fascinating" document of the contradictions of an early 20th-century black intellectual. Johnson's allegiance to the "black bourgeoisie's" values and aspirations made him despise black lower classes, although it did not prevent his sympathetic appreciation of the rich forms of art expressed by the latter. "I romanzi di Arna Bontemps" (*SA* 18:345–68) is a well-written essay by Mario Materassi. Bontemps's multiform activity to save the black cultural heritage from oblivion is sympathetically evaluated, his three novels are finely discussed, and recognition as a minor masterpiece of 20th-century American fiction is convincingly claimed for *Black Thunder* on the basis of its formal qualities and psychological depth. Materassi again is the author of "La conciliazione degli opposti in 'Notes of a Native Son' di James Baldwin" (*Paragone* 302:3–18). Resorting to a "hard-core" structuralistic approach, he proves how Baldwin's essay in its sections and as a whole has the same structural organization as its first paragraph in which a complex of opposites (such as father/son, death/life, white/black, man/society, etc.) is distributed according to two paradigms—the first contrasting, the second conciliating the opposites. In its "perfect segnic balance" the essay is a metaphor of the moral and political balance called for by Baldwin. Notwithstanding a certain reductionism due to a ruthless passion for symmetries, Materassi's essay stands out, for rigor and clarity, from the other contributions to the *Paragone* 302 issue, which is devoted to contemporary American fiction.

The other articles in this issue of *Paragone* may be summarized briefly. In "Barth, o della rilettura" (pp. 38–63) Guido Fink seems to be basically concerned with the adjustments required of the reader by Barth's sophisticated narrative strategies. He describes—intelligently, though somewhat too discursively—recurrent themes, ideas, and devices, and suggests that Barth's opus offers itself as an erotic object to the reader's pleasure and also praises it as a hard-won way out of the modern horror of the blank page. In "Le strade dell'Apocalisse: il nuovo romanzo americano" (pp. 19–37) Franco La Polla strides through the regions of the most recent fiction with the haste of an explorer who has time only for naming new-found things. Amid a welter of names, titles, and obscure hints at more names and titles, the authors who receive a little more analytical treatment are Brautigan, Hjortsberg, Hawkes, Berger, and Westlake. In "Dalla fossa dei serpenti al nido di cucù" (pp. 97–104), a note where Kesey's best-known novel is related to Faucault's and Lacan's ideas on sanity/madness, La Polla proves to be victim to a sort of "mimetic fallacy" that compels him to treat obscure things in a an obscure way. "*Gravity's Rainbow* come antientropia" by William S. Di Piero (pp. 105–08) is an enthusiastic appreciation of Pynchon's latest fiction.

The identification that Norman Mailer has made of his destiny as a man and an artist with the destiny of contemporary America is the theme of Caterina Ricciardi's article on "Norman Mailer: metafora dell'America contemporanea" (*SA* 18:369–95). The author examines Mailer's recent autobiographical journalism and finds that the role chosen by the novelist in a decaying world is that of the "noble physician," and the only way to salvation is to go deep into destruction and degeneration in order to transcend them and spring up again. Mailer's discovery is, the critic argues, that neither science nor technology can save us, but only art and imagination: these are the elements that will give birth to the new great novel repeatedly promised by the writer. William Styron's first novel is interestingly studied by Giordano De Biasio in his "*Lie Down in Darkness*: libertà e destino nella *domestic tragedy* styroniana" (*AIULM* [1974]:281–95). Accurately (though not always lucidly) De Biasio shows how *Lie Down in Darkness* develops on the two separate planes of obsessive past and sterile present, and examines its narrative techniques in order to establish its characters' free will and predestination. A very able assessment of James Dickey's work and his transition from poetry to fiction is presented by Maria Stella in her "James Dickey: della poesia alla narrativa" (*Trimestre* 7 [1974]:420–36). Special emphasis is placed by the author on the elements which caused, she thinks, *Deliverance* to fail as a structurally unified work of art. The failure was mainly one of language and was due to the need felt by the writer to stress both symbol and reality while keeping them in opposition.

An intelligent examination of the fiction dealing with the encounter of the American soldiers and the Italian people during World War II is the object of Laura Coltelli's useful essay, "L'Italia nel romanzo di guerra americano" (*RLMC* 28:47–73, 132–45). The novels analyzed are particularly those of John Hersey, Harry Brown, J. H. Burns, and Alfred Hays. In such works Italy is not any more the mythical place of the "passionate pilgrim" but a stark reality made of living and suffering people, who, though defeated and conquered, can often teach their conquerors the spiritual values they have forgotten. Although Guido Almansi's *L'estetica dell'osceno* (Torino: Einaudi [1974]) can hardly be taken exclusively as a serious scholarly endeavor (there is much in it that is parody of critical procedures, pure *divertissement* and sheer will to shock), one of the essays, "Tre versioni di un articolo su Miller" (pp. 111–28), quite sensibly suggests that the words spoken by a character of *Tropic of Cancer*, "The images are real, even if the whole story is false," point out the right way of approaching Henry Miller's controversial work.

This year's interest in poetry has produced a few valuable contributions, among which should be counted a book of translations of W. D. Snodgrass's poems by Francesco Binni: *L'ago del cuore* (Milano: Mondadori). In his perceptive introduction Binni reviews the poet's entire career, focusing on the complex relation between experience and style that characterizes it. The personal and existential quality of Snodgrass's poetry is duly accounted for as well as his keen awareness of the absolute, "Orphic" value of language and craft. Renzo Crivelli's "E. E. Cummings: la poetica del movimento" (*SA* 18:313–43) is a well-reasoned essay that provides an interesting (if not always original) figurative reading of several poems by E. E. Cummings. The poet's concern with experimentation is actually connected, Crivelli maintains, with his effort to capture the dynamic, elusive quality of modern reality; and it is motion itself, the ever-changing experience, that eventually becomes the subject matter of his poems. Elsa Rossi Linguanti has written the first Italian contribution on Sidney Lanier: "La poesia di Sidney Lanier (*SA* 18:151–73). It is a good assessment of Lanier's culture and ideas on art and society as well as an earnest attempt at evaluating the techniques used in his best-known poems. Composed in a lighter vein, "Robinson e la poesia americana" (*NA* 524:239–45) by Tommaso Pisanti appears to be a brief, sensible introduction to E. A. Robinson's poetry. Four letters and a poem by Thomas Merton, together with an introductory essay that discusses the poet's apocalyptic message to the world, are first published by Silvana Ranzoli under the title: "Incontro epistolare con Thomas Merton" (*Humanitas* 1:43–51). Ranzoli corresponded with Merton while writing her thesis on his poetry.

Ezra Pound never showed any critical interest in Italian literary movements, except in Futurism, which he first refused to accept, then later approved as something good only for Italy. The ideological phases of his relations with Futurism and its founder, F. T. Marinetti, are clearly reconstructed in Niccolo Zapponi's "Odi e amori futuristi di Ezra Pound" (*SA* 18:299–311). Zapponi's contribution stands out for its careful research and documentation. Less scholarly and less convincing is Charles Matz's "The Americanness of Ezra Pound (*AIULM* [1974]:379–88). Matz, who knew Pound "as a neighbor in Venice for many years," ramblingly tries to explain the "expatriatism" of the poet, arguing that he, like others, was not seeking to escape being American; on the contrary, he was seeking to remain American.

Robert Bly and Michael Casey were the two poets presented in translation by Riccardo Duranti and Silvano Sabbadini respectively in the annual contemporary poetry selections issued by Mondadori (*Almanacco dello Specchio* 4:115–17, 309–11). Duranti's introduction is a short enlightening essay that sees Bly as a surrealist whose originality consists in a fine fusion of the brightness and warmth of the southern American tradition and that of the mystic, visionary North, filtered through Whitmanian veins.

There were only three articles on drama. Cecilia Pietropolli's "Il teatro di Edward Albee tra avanguardia e tradizione" (*Spicilegio Moderno* 4:169–85) is certainly the most interesting. It is a well done, even if disparaging, assessment of Albee's theatre, using the theatre of the absurd as touchstone. Albee fails in his attempted synthesis of American and European technique for lack of a coherent commitment to one or the other, and also for lack of true social awareness. In her longish essay "Happenings" (*SA* 18:413–43) Maria Carmela Coco Davani investigates the relevant analogy she finds in the "ritualistic" character both of the "happening" theatrical medium and the Beat movement and literature. The creators of these two cultural expressions seem to value as meaningful only the process of artistic creation and not the end product of the artistic creation itself. Laura Caretti in "Jack Gelber a contatto con il *Living Theatre*" (*SA* 18:445–56) tells the story of Gelber's encounter with the "Living Theatre" and analyzes the fruitful contribution that his play *The Connection* gave to a theatre that wanted to effect a deeper relationship between the audience and the stage.

As for literary history, after mentioning Tommaso Pisanti's "Dal puritanesimo all'illuminismo" (*NA* 523:542–58), which is basically an outline of the development of American thought, it is comforting to encounter a well-researched study of the fortune of Mazzini in the

Anglo-American world by Michèle Rivas: "Mazzini et les écrivains anglais et américains de son temps" (*SA* 18:53–110). The author accurately documents the relations between the Italian patriot and the English and American writers of his time, then draws a picture of him as he was described by them, giving at the end an assessment of his influence on their writings. Carlo Pagetti's "La tradizione narrativa inglese in America" (*SA* 18:175–216) belongs more appropriately to literary criticism. Pagetti reminds us how in the last two decades of the 19th century English fiction (especially Scott's romances and works of mid-Victorian authors) came under the attack of Howells and other American writers engaged in the battle for realism and a renewal of the novel form. Along with Howells's, the opinions of James, Twain, Crane, Norris, and Garland on English fiction are clearly reviewed and evaluated. A new reading of Vittorini's American literary criticism is offered by Louise K. Barnett in her article "Elio Vittorini and the criticism of Amercan Literature: A Re-examination" (*SA* 18:395–413). Taking issue with all previous scholars who have dealt with the subject, Barnett demonstrates persuasively that Vittorini's writings on American literature are not to be taken only as documents of the cultural enthusiasm of a young antifascist novelist, but as original, objective criticism that did not need to undergo any major reconsideration on the part of the novelist in his maturity. Ruggero Bianchi's "Il problema dell'arte e dell'artista in Poe, Hawthorne e Melville" (*SA* 18:111–49) would have deserved more than merely being mentioned here, had it not been already included in his *La dimensione narrativa*, a volume that received dutiful notice in *ALS 1974*, pp. 448–49.

One of the very few books that were published this year comes under the category of popular and youth culture. Alessandro Portelli's *La canzone popolare in America: La rivoluzione musicale di Woody Guthrie* (Bari: De Donato) is a work that has sprung from a youthful enthusiasm for American popular songs and for Guthrie. Though based on extensive reading and vast information on folk songs, the book regretfully does not come up to the scholar's expectations: it is uneven, often confused and lacking in logical coherence (which in this case should be of a Marxian type), and prone to journalistic and polemical generalizations. It must be admitted, however, that it succeeds in telling the story of the folk song and of Woody Guthrie within the framework of the struggles of the working class in America.

There is enthusiasm and a certain knowledge of the subject in Stefano Rizzo's "Messaggio poetico e comunicazione di massa in Bob Dylan" (*Paragone* 302:69–85), but a lack of clarity in ideas leads to confusion of expression in writing, so that the article is unfortunately of very little value.

Università di Pisa

iv. Japanese Contributions

Keiko Beppu

Interest in American writers—especially contemporary writers—continues in Japan. The January issue of *The Rising Generation* featured a series of essays on American novels of the 1970s, concluding with Tetsuji Akasofu's article, "The *Raison d'Être* of New Writers" (120: 450–63). Also significant is the fact that there is a tendency on the part of Japanese scholars to see influence *and* confluence between American and Japanese writers; one critic even declares in his article (see below) that contemporary Japanese literature is part of American literature. This interest in the contemporary American scene is also observed in the popular reception of American literature in this country; there has been a steady growth in Japanese translations of American novels—notably of contemporary works. At the same time the phenomeon does not preclude essays and books on 19th- and 20th-century writers.

The year 1975 saw the publication of two literary histories: *America Bungaku Shicho-shi: Shakai to Bungaku* [*Main Currents in American Thought: Society and Literature*] ed. Rikutaro Fukuda et al. (Tokyo: Chukyo Shuppan), and *Sōsetsu America Bungaku* [*The History of American Literature: General Introduction*] comp. Kenzaburo Ōhashi et al. (Tokyo: Kenkyusha). Both books follow the well-trodden pattern of American counterparts, but with discussions on hitherto neglected areas they are valuable student guides. The first mentioned devotes one chapter to black literature (chap. 7) and another to Jewish and new writers (chap. 8). In *The History of American Literature: General Introduction* writings after 1930 are treated under the heading: "Literature of the Absurd" (chap. 5).

Among works on individual writers Tadamasa Shima's *Heming-*

way no Sekai [*The World of Hemingway: General Introduction and Discussion of "In Our Time"*] (Tokyo: Hokuseido) is an unpretentious study of the novelist intended for students. So is Fumi Adachi's book on Fitzgerald: *Scott Fitzgerald Kenkyu* [*F. Scott Fitzgerald: A Critical Study*] (Tokyo: Hokuseido). More ambitious works in this category are Tatsuo Kambara's *Kodoku no Henreki: Herman Melville Ko* [*Herman Melville, Solitary Pilgrim: A Critical Biography*] (Tokyo: Kobian Publishing Company) and Noboru Okaniwa's *Faulkner: Tsurusareta Ningen no Yume* [*Faulkner: The Dream of the Hanged Man*] (Tokyo: Chikuma Shobo).

Kambara's critical biography is strongly personal, which attests to the writer's emotional involvement over a period of "ten years" with Melville's works—both prose and poetry. The book is moving, which, ironically, presents a critical problem. Kambara uses "I" persistently, referring to the narrator in each of the novels and tales he discusses. Whether the "I" is exclusively the persona of the novelist, or Melville himself, or worse still, Kambara himself is seldom clear. Yet on the whole the book is readable and an important addition to Melville scholarship done in this country. In this regard an essay on Melville's *Billy Budd* is also worth mentioning: "Captain Vere's 'Mystery of Iniquity' and the Salvation of Herman Melville"* in *Eibei Bungaku* [*Studies in English and American Literature*] (Kwansei Gakuin University) 20:64–83).[1] Here Taizo Tanimoto, a devoted Melville scholar, shows his profound insight into the central issue of Melville's work by making some corrections to Lawrance Thompson's *Melville's Quarrel with God.* The article reflects Tanimoto's quarrel with Thompson and offers an answer to the question raised in Hawthorne's comment that Melville could not believe but was uncomfortable in his unbelief. Tanimoto's essay may be summarized by saying that Melville found peace of mind before his death and that *Billy Budd* is sufficient testimony to the salvation of the "solitary pilgrim."

Noboru Okaniwa's book on Faulkner (mentioned above) is an interesting anomaly among the works here surveyed. Poet and essayist, Okaniwa is also well versed in Faulkner scholarship. He perceives a governing principle in the conception of the Faulknerean hero—Joe Christmas, Popeye, Thomas Sutpen, Miss Rosa, Emily Grierson, Quentin Compson. He argues that the desire (or the dream) of these

1. Starred titles denote articles written in English.

hero-victims can best be understood as defiance to that facile fiction called "reality" and "nature"; he refutes the critical consensus that a Faulkner character finds salvation in his reconciliation with "nature." Indeed Okaniwa finds Faulkner the best arbiter of the problem of modern man. Through his analysis of Faulknerean heroes Okaniwa develops a literary theory of his own. The book is heavy philosophical reading, yet rewarding and unusual in that Faulkner is not only the object of criticism but becomes a critical tool in expounding the writer's literary theory, which in its turn sheds light on contemporary writings as well as on Faulkner's works.

Analysis of 20th-century literature is given in Yutaka Shimizu's *Gendai America Bungaku to Shakai* [*The Contemporary American Scene: Social Backgrounds for Literature*] (Kyoto: Minerva Shobo) and in Masayuki Sakamoto's *Nijusseiki America Shosetsu Oboegaki: Shimin-Zo no Shoso* [*Notes on the Twentieth Century American Novel: Different Faces of the Commoner*] (Tokyo: Eichosha). The term *contemporary* applied to O. Henry, Erskine Caldwell, and Hemingway in the title of Shimizu's book is misleading, however, unless it is simply applied to Shimizu's own age. The book surveys various social factors which have fostered the aforementioned writers; it is, as the author admits, a simple analysis of its subject.

Sakamoto has published two books on the American Renaissance. In his latest work he deals with some 20th-century writers (1920–50). *Notes on the Twentieth Century American Novel* is a collection of eight essays which explore different modes of the conflict confronting 20th-century man caught between equal desires to conform to the norm of "the average capable American" and to remain intact and whole, to keep his own identity. The three essays on Sinclair Lewis are a valid analysis of the problem and constitute the best part of the book. Sakamoto's choice of Lewis's novels—*Babbitt, Main Street,* and *Dodsworth*—is a happy one and serves his purpose well. Sakamoto contends that Lewis's criticism of philistine values in these novels, however, offers no solution to the problem of conflict between conformity and identity. Sandwiched between the essays on Lewis are discussions of Richard Wright, Malamud, Salinger, Mailer, and Thomas Wolfe. Sakamoto sees variations of the theme in the works of these writers; his analyses of these novels are mostly judicious, but they do not quite coalesce with those on Lewis's works.

Similarly, the search for national identity or one's personal identity persists in the field of poetry, as the subtitle of Shunichi Niikura's book indicates: *America Shi-Ron: Doitsusei no Uta* [*A Century of American Poetry from Whitman to Berryman: the Song of Oneself*] (Tokyo: Shinozaki Shorin). Like Sakamoto's book, *A Century of American Poetry* is a collection of essays which appeared in various periodicals and essay collections. Trained in new criticism, Niikura now seeks a unifying leitmotif in some 20 poets who fall, in his opinion, into two groups: those in the major key—not necessarily great—and those in the minor key—they all sing "the song of oneself." The chapters on Emily Dickinson and on John Berryman are the jewel pieces of the book—a result of Niikura's long research into the works of these poets and his involvement with them. It is difficult to do full justice to this book in limited space, but the chapter entitled "Ashes and Sparks—American Poetry and Contemporary Japanese Poetry" (pp. 332–61) deserves amplification. Niikura's discussion is exhaustive of the subject, demonstrating his intuitive reading of and keen insight into the American poetry of the last century and Japanese poets. The chapter is of special interest to those foreign scholars engaged in comparative literature or interested in Japanese literature. In this respect two articles deserve attention: Shiro Wajima's "T. S. Eliot and Kitaro Nishida" in *The Rising Generation* (121:4–8) and Hisao Kanaseki's study of Kenzaburo Ōhe, "American Literature and contemporary Japanese Literature" (ibid. 122:454–57). Kanaseki contends, with a flair of his own that Ōhe is not merely influenced by American writers or heroes such as Huck and "Rabbit," but Ōhe's work *is* American in its imagination and sensibility.

Articles which deserve consideration in addition to those discussed above are Shunsuke Kamei's "American Literature in Japan"* (ibid., 121:8–13, 56–59); Akiko Miyake's "Ezra Pound's Vorticism"* in *Studies in English Literature* (52:49–66); Kichinosuke Ōhashi's "Sherwood Anderson and Three Japanese Correspondents" in *The Rising Generation* (121:156–57, 199–200, 261–62, 300–02, 361–63, 395–97, 478–80, 525–27, 579–81) in nine installments, and Miyoko Sasaki's "Between Appearance and Substance: A Study of Edith Wharton"* in *Studies in American Literature* (11:30–47).

Kobe College

v. Scandinavian Contributions

Rolf Lundén

In 1974 Scandinavian scholars limited themselves to studying the literature of the 19th century. During 1975 their interest shifted radically and was directed exclusively to American letters of the 20th century, with a certain preference for the decades since the last World War. Like the previous year, however, almost all Scandinavian contributions were devoted to fiction; only one was devoted to poetry and none to drama. But within this limitation there was great variety: studies of stylistic as well as thematic questions, interest in poetic prose as well as nonfiction, focus on the South and Harlem as well as Nebraska.

Nebraska is a fundamental concept in Willa Cather's fiction. So is the state of childhood, as Mona Pers shows in her published dissertation, *Willa Cather's Children*, Studia Anglistica Upsaliensia, 22 (Uppsala: Univ. of Uppsala). Basing her study on a wide selection of material, in several instances hitherto unpublished, Pers demonstrates the significance of childhood in general, and Willa Cather's own childhood in particular, to the author's production. The book has a three-partite structure. The first part deals with the state of childhood and what it stands for in the works of the Nebraska writer. Mona Pers convincingly shows how Willa Cather remained "child-centered" all her life in spite of, or because of, her childlessness; how she saw children as symbols of such redemptive forces as love and hope; how she used children to characterize grown-ups (their treatment of children reveals their character). Part II of the study analyzes Willa's own childhood and how it is reflected in her novels and short stories. Mona Pers argues that Cather, after a time of apprenticeship, found her "quiet center of life" from which she could write to the world. This center was "the child within," the girl she had once been, her "best self." As Pers makes clear, there are numerous parallels in Cather's writings between the author's experience and feelings as a child and those of her protagonists. One may only mention Thea Kronborg in *The Song of the Lark* and Jim Burden in *My Ántonia.* In the final section Pers discusses the fact that in Cather's world it is sad to grow up. She sees little excitement, and little love, in adulthood, a lack of enthusiasm which has had negative effects on a few of her novels, primarily *The Song of the Lark*. In spite of a somewhat loose structure and some confusion in a chapter on the child's imagination, this study draws attention to many of the nuances of Cather's art.

The generation after Cather was represented this year by Eliot and Hemingway. In "The Voices of *The Waste Land*" (*ASS* 7:1–15), Lars Hartveit tries to bring order to the much-debated problem of the various voices in Eliot's masterpiece. Like other critics before him, Hartveit sees one "pervading consciousness" set off from a group of inarticulate "personages." But he elaborates this point, stating that a liturgical pattern is visible in the interplay of the voices. The main speaker is an officiator and a mediator between the audience and the supernatural. He has had an "overwhelming spiritual experience of a mystical kind," which may explain the seemingly paradoxical tones of his voice. Sometimes he uses the confessional tone of the private, mystical experience; sometimes he is the prophet addressing the external world in a condemnatory/rhetorical way. As a contrast to this officiator is set the audience, which consists of the other voices as well as the readers. The alternating voices of main speaker and chorus create a pattern similar to liturgy. Although the main speaker dominates the last two parts of *The Waste Land*, Hartveit maintains that a response pattern is still visible.

Erik Arne Hansen is also concerned with myth and a mystical experience in "On Hemingway's 'Indian Camp'" (*Meddelelser fra Gymnasieskolernes Engelsklaererforening* 73:3–21). Distrusting such terms as "interpretation" and preferring "description," Hansen argues for establishing "some kind of neo-simplism" in criticism. The description of a poem/story should ideally proceed according to a scheme or a set of questions: where? when? who? what? and how? Using "Indian Camp" as a model for such an investigation, Hansen makes it apparent how many things in the story are implied, "making for complication and resisting simplification." The story depicts, for instance, how "the son experiences the father experiencing *him* experiencing the Indian husband's suicide." Hansen sees "Indian Camp" as a romance in Frye's sense of the word, a journey of sacral initiation comparable to that of "Young Goodman Brown." To achieve this effect Hemingway has used a technique of contrast that includes numerous symbols.

Narrative technique and the use of symbolism are also main concerns for Eleanor Wikborg in her dissertation, *Carson McCullers'*

"The Member of the Wedding": Aspects of Structure and Style, Gothenburg Studies in English, 31 (Gothenburg: Univ. of Gothenburg). Wikborg seeks, as she says, "to isolate certain structural and stylistic features . . . and to discuss their role in the expression of the novel's themes." After an introductory chapter on such major themes as the Sense of Isolation, the study shows how objects in the novel's first part develop, in part 2, into implicit and explicit symbols; how certain key scenes and moods are repeated throughout the story; and how these concepts often change in quality from part 1 to part 2 (the sky develops from being a mirror of the inscrutability of life to an image of freshness and promise). Through an investigation of phoneme repetition and rhythm patterns Wikborg shows that there is little foundation for regarding McCullers's prose as more rhythmical or musical than that of other prose writers. Since the result of this investigation is negative, it should have been given considerably less space in the dissertation. The study also suffers occasionally from tediousness and a tendency to explain the self-evident.

The creative process is likewise the object of Inger Aarseth's "Absence of Absolutes: The Reconciled Artist in John Barth's *The Floating Opera*" (*SN* 47:53–68). Aarseth divides Todd Andrews's development into three stages: (1) from birth to 1937, a period in which the protagonist is involved in life in spite of a growing alienation; (2) the day of his suicidal attempt in 1937, which Aarseth considers the antithesis of Stage 1 because of Andrews's total detachment; and (3) from 1937 to 1953, which constitutes a synthesis of the two earlier phases. Aarseth argues that there is a parallel development in Andrews's artistic career: too much involvement is followed by excessive technical brilliance and detachment only to be synthesized in the third phase, the evidence of which is *The Floating Opera* itself. In the end the artist "has reconciled himself to the impossibility of reaching the Absolute in art." It seems, however, as if Aarseth has tried to squeeze the novel into a preconceived formula. The three-stage pattern she discerns is disputable, and so is the evidence she presents. Todd Andrews reveals too little of his life after 1937 for anybody to be able to say whether he finds his identity in a synthesis.

In *The Theme of Identity in the Essays of James Baldwin: An Interpretation*, Gothenburg Studies in English, 32 (Gothenburg: Univ. of Gothenburg) Karin Möller focuses on an essential aspect of Baldwin's view of life. Basing the study on his five collections of essays, she distinguishes between five types of identity—racial, national, sexual, artistic, and human—a division which causes much confusion and overlapping. Möller discusses one collection of essays after another in chronological order, but little consideration is given to the development of the theme of identity, apart from pointing to the increased militancy of *No Name in the Street.* Möller's argument is often impaired by a lack of definitions and a general vagueness. The discussion would furthermore have profited from being put into a larger context. There is no indication of the fact that Baldwin shares the theme of identity with most other contemporary American writers, black or white.

Another piece of criticism on Baldwin shows more awareness of the cultural background so essential to a correct understanding. Sigmund Ro's long, well-written article, "The Black Musician as Literary Hero: Baldwin's 'Sonny's Blues' and Kelley's 'Cry for Me' " (*ASS* 7:17–48), analyzes how these two short stories may be seen as representative of the decades in which they were created. There are numerous similarities between the settings and plots of the stories, but the differences are more revealing. "Sonny's Blues" is a tale in the existentialist tradition of Kirkegaard-Sartre-Camus, a story which in the end is nonracial, stressing the universality of the black man's situation. Ro points to Sam Greenlee's "Sonny's Not Blue" to show that more recent, militant writers look upon Baldwin's vision as "too pessimistic, individualistic, and white-oriented to be acceptable." Conversely, Wallace in Kelley's "Cry for Me" is a representative of the race, a mythic black hero who is the new John Henry. Wallace's soul ethos repudiates the individualism and industrialism of the white man's culture. He has no desire to identify with white America, but, with his art, he wants to "humanize his fellow men irrespective of race, creed, or color."

Uppsala University

Author Index

Subject Index